3 9082 12206 0021

D0660167

917.291
C
2016

ROYAL OAK

SEP 2 0 2016

PUBLIC LIBRARY

Footprint Handbook
Cuba

SARAH CAMERON

This is
Cuba

When I first visited Cuba in the 1990s, the mantra was to see this last bastion of Communism 'before Castro dies'. Two decades later, both Fidel and Raúl are still there, revolutionary slogans still adorn walls and highways, and the island is still a one-party state. However, after years of extreme hardship and state control, tourism has blossomed. Travellers are now free to explore the length and breadth of the country, eschewing the state sector if they wish, staying in family-run bed and breakfast places and eating at private restaurants. Following the recent rapprochement with the USA, negotiations are under way to open up the country still further: now the mantra is to see Cuba 'before the Americans arrive'.

While both visitors and Cubans have new freedoms, much of Cuba remains in a time warp. In city centres, from Havana to Santiago, ramshackle streets are lined with decaying colonial mansions and art deco towers, while brutalist Soviet apartment blocks dominate the suburbs. American Cadillacs from the 1950s chug alongside horse-drawn carriages, arthritic rickshaws, tin-can Ladas and battered Chinese bikes, swiftly overtaken by bright yellow eggshells on motorbike chassis. This is a place with no advertising hoardings, no multinational fast-food takeaways and no identikit shopping malls. In the countryside, fields are ploughed by oxen or rickety old tractors, and horses are still the *vaqueros*' transport of choice. Everywhere, though, you will be immersed in the richness of Cuba's traditional music and dance, the products of a fruitful cultural mixture that has produced extraordinary creativity and exuberance in the arts and entertainment.

Cuba is the largest island in the Caribbean and offers plenty of scope for exploration. You can cycle from one end to the other, dive around offshore cays and coral gardens, hike in mountainous forests to secluded waterfalls or simply laze on a deserted beach. There are miles of sand on the north coast and mangroves and sheltered harbours along the south, so that even though the island receives four million visitors a year, you can still find an idyllic, isolated spot.

Best of
Cuba

❶ La Habana Vieja

Fortresses, palaces, churches and mansions frame the grand plazas of this Spanish colonial city which has barely changed since the 19th century. It's a UNESCO World Heritage Site and is the main focus for tourists to the capital, with buzzing streetlife and iconic sights. Page 42.

❷ Las Terrazas

Part of a Biosphere Reserve in the Sierra del Rosario, Las Terrazas offers birdwatching and hiking amongst tropical forests, old coffee plantations and waterfalls. There's an orchidarium at Soroa nearby. Page 114.

❸ María la Gorda

Very remote and low key, this dive resort offers pristine reefs, caves and tunnels with an abundance of sea life. Part of the Península de Guanahacabibes, a Natural Biosphere Reserve, it is also popular with keen naturalists and beach lovers. Page 129.

❹ Valle de Viñales

Declared a UNESCO World Cultural Landscape, this beautiful valley in Piñar del Río province is characterized by steep-sided limestone *mogotes* that rise out of the red earth, surrounded by tobacco fields ploughed by oxen. Page 131.

❺ Bay of Pigs

The site of the botched CIA-backed counter-revolutionary invasion in 1961 is now a prime dive site, teeming with tropical fish. The surrounding Zapata Peninsula is a national park whose swamps and lagoons are home to crocodiles and migratory water birds. Page 168.

❻ Cienfuegos

A port on the south coast, Cienfuegos' wealth from trading can be seen in the lavish mansions and eclectic architectural styles of its 19th-century buildings. Page 180.

❼ Santa Clara

The decisive battle of the Revolution was fought here under the leadership of Che Guevara. A huge monument, mausoleum and cemetery mark his last resting place and commemorate his fallen comrades from both Cuba and Bolivia. Page 195.

❽ Remedios

A charming old town, known for its Christmas festivities, Remedios is within easy reach of the northern cays and of Santa Clara to the south. It is a pleasant place to stay for a few days in a boutique hotel or a *casa particular*. Page 209.

❾ Trinidad

Frozen in time, with its cobbled streets and tiled roofs, Trinidad has remained unchanged since the sugar barons left in the 19th century. Now a UNESCO World Heritage Site, it is one of the leading tourist attractions on the island. Page 226.

❿ Camagüey

Magnificent 18th-century churches and plazas characterize this colonial city, known for its maze of streets built at odd angles to deter pirate invasion. To the north are several lovely beaches and cays that are home to flocks of flamingos. Page 263.

⓫ Coast of Holguín

The beautiful bays and inlets at Guardalavaca have been developed as a major resort. In contrast, Gibara is a quiet and unassuming fishing town, with caves and unspoilt beaches to explore. There are also several Amerindian sites you can visit. Pages 301 and 304.

⑬ Santiago de Cuba

This is the hottest city on the island, both in terms of temperature and in the vibrancy of its music. Cultural activities reach a crescendo in July for a month of festivals and carnival celebrations. Spruced up for its 500th anniversary in 2015, Santiago is a gem. Page 330.

⑭ Baracoa

The first town founded by the Spanish, but accessible only by sea until the 1960s, Baracoa has an air of self-sufficiency born of isolation. Seafood, coconut and cocoa provide welcome sustenance after a day's hiking in the surrounding hills and forests. Page 367.

⑫ Sierra Maestra

Hike to Castro's secret revolutionary headquarters in the mountains at Comandancia de la Plata, or do a two to three-day trek up Pico Turquino, the highest mountain in Cuba, for tremendous views. Page 318.

Gulf of Mexico

Florida Straits

1 **HAVANA**

2 Las Terrazas ○

Bauta ○

Matanzas ○

VILLA CLARA

8

4

Viñales ○

PINAR DEL RIO

ARTEMISA

MAYABEQUE

MATANZAS

7

Santa Clara ○

Remedios ○

CIENFUEGOS

Pinar del Río ○

Archipiélago de Canarreos los Canarreos

Cienfuegos ○

6

Sancti Spíritus ○

3

María La Gorda ○

Nueva Gerona ○

5

Trinidad ○

SANCTI SPIRITUS

9

ISLA DE LA JUVENTUD

Caribbean Sea

N

50 km
50 miles

1 **La Habana Vieja**

2 **Las Terrazas**

3 **María la Gorda**

4 **Valle de Viñales**

5 **Bay of Pigs**

6 **Cienfuegos**

7 **Santa Clara**

Atlantic Ocean

Archipiélago
Jardín del Rey

CIEGO
DE AVILA

Ciego
de Avila

10

Camagüey

CAMAGÜEY

Archipiélago
Jardines
de la Reina

LAS
TUNAS
Las Tunas

11

Holguín

HOLGUIN

Bayamo

GRANMA

12 **13**

SANTIAGO
DE CUBA

Santiago
de Cuba

GUANTANAMO
Guantánamo

Baracoa

14

Route planner

Cuba is the largest island in the Caribbean, with an area of around 110,000 sq km. If your time is restricted you should decide which end of the island you would prefer to see in detail. If you have got all the time in the world, then start at one end and work your way to the other. An excellent road runs all the way from Havana to Santiago down the centre of the island, passing through many of the important cities, with side roads off to other interesting places.

One week: Havana and around

have a capital time

The colonial city of Havana is unmissable. You need a day to see the old city with its palaces, mansions, museums and plazas and a couple more days to get round some of the major sites in the suburbs as well as take in some of the nightlife in music-mad Vedado. Use the capital as a base for day trips out to the countryside or to the beaches along the coast. Places within striking distance of Havana include the lush green valley of Viñales, with its steep-sided limestone hills, the fields of top-class tobacco around Pinar del Río, or the beaches to the east of the capital: Playas del Este, Jibacoa and the resort of Varadero.

Two weeks: Havana and the Centre West

diving, hiking and revolutionary history

With two weeks you could spend more time in the western province of Pinar del Río. Divers will particularly appreciate a few days at isolated María la Gorda in the far west. You could stay a night at Las Terrazas eco-lodge en route and visit the colourful orchid gardens at Soroa before heading up to the north coast beaches.

Alternatively head east from the capital into the sugar-growing farmlands and forested mountains in the centre of the island. Allow yourself a couple of nights in the charming old town of Remedios, with day trips to Santa Clara, last resting place of Che Guevara, and to the cays off the north coast.

Trinidad, the UNESCO World Heritage Site with its single-storey 18th- and 19th-century houses and cobbled streets, is a must-see on anyone's itinerary. Allow plenty of time to explore the town and surrounding areas, including the Valley of the Sugar Mills, the Escambray mountains and the beach at Ancón, as well as to enjoy the nightlife. If you have your own car, the return trip to Havana could take in Cienfuegos for its colonial architecture and fortress, the Bay of Pigs and the Zapata Peninsula. Otherwise, the route Havana–Santa Clara–Trinidad–Cienfuegos–Havana can be done by bus.

Two weeks: Santiago de Cuba and the east

heat up in the city, cool off in the mountains

You need up to two weeks to do justice to the east of the island. Although you can fly to Santiago, Cuba's second city, many people choose to fly to Holguín and start from there. The main towns can be reached by bus (or unreliable train), but places off the beaten track are difficult to get to by public transport, so it is advisable to rent a car. An easterly round trip from Holguín would take in Bayamo, the jumping-off point for hiking in the Sierra Maestra and for visiting Castro's atmospheric revolutionary headquarters. From Bayamo, head to Manzanillo and then spend a few days in Santiago de Cuba. This lively city is an infectious contrast to the capital: the climate is hotter and drier, and the Afro-Caribbean culture is laced with French influences.

Continuing east, visit Guantánamo (see the US Naval base through binoculars) and Baracoa, currently one of the most popular destinations thanks to its beaches, rivers, hiking and laid-back lifestyle. On your return to Holguín, relax on the beaches of Guardalavaca or hang out in the small fishing town of Gibara: it's unassuming and attractive, with boutique hotels, good food and lovely views.

A month or more: doing it all

undeveloped beaches and little-visited towns

With a month you will have time to get to know both ends of the island and some places in between. The central towns are often missed by travellers keen to concentrate on one end of the island or the other. However, they are often good jumping-off points for the north coast beaches, allowing you to explore without being restricted to an all-inclusive resort. North of Ciego de Avila is Morón, from where you can drive out to Cayo Coco and Cayo Guillermo. Camagüey is well worth a day's exploration, and from here you can take in a day trip to the beach at Playa Santa Lucía. From Las Tunas, divert to Puerto Padre for undeveloped beaches nearby, and from Holguín you have access to the beaches of Guardalavaca or the less visited coastline around Gibara.

Music & dance

Tradition and roots

Cuban music, famously vibrant, is a marriage of African rhythms, expressed in percussion instruments, and the Spanish guitar. It is accompanied by an equally strong tradition of dance. There are four basic elements out of which all the other forms have grown. First of these is the *rumba*, one of the original black dances, which transferred from the plantations to the city slums around the end of the 19th century. Originating in eastern Cuba, *son* is the music out of which salsa was born. Buena Vista Social Club brought *son* to worldwide attention, while Los Van Van have long been the most popular exponents of salsa. *Danzón* was originally ballroom dance music and was the source for the cha-cha-cha, invented in 1948. The fourth tradition is *trova*, the itinerant troubadour singing ballads, which has been transformed post-Revolution into the *nueva trova* and made famous by singers such as Pablo Milanés and Silvio Rodríguez. The new tradition adds politics and everyday concerns to the romantic themes. There are many other styles, such as the *guajira* (the most famous example of which is the song, 'Guantanamera'), *tumba francesa* drumming and dancing, and Afro-Cuban jazz, performed by internationally renowned artists like Irakere and Arturo Sandoval.

Rhythm, ritual and reggaeton

From traditional *son* to Cuban rap via jazz and salsa, drums beat out the rhythm of the island's Afro-Caribbean heritage. The sacred *cueros batá* (the three drums used in Santería rites) have been incorporated into mainstream bands, while performances of Yoruba and Congo devotional and profane song and dance are colourful spectacles, with Cubans fervidly chorusing the Santero chants and swaying to the infectious *guaguancó*. Carnival festivities are exuberant and colourful: the best is in Santiago in July, when rum-fuelled revellers take to the streets to dance the conga to ear-splitting drum music. More recently, reggaeton, a fusion of reggae, rap, Latin and electronic rhythms, has taken dance floors by storm, despite official reservations about its 'neoliberal' influence. It is street music with raunchy lyrics and a sensual beat, hugely popular with young Cubans. Cuban reggaeton can't be found in shops, nor on the radio; it is recorded independently at makeshift studios in people's homes and is distributed via home-made CDs and flash memory sticks. However, it is not a subversive political movement, and one artist, Yoandys 'Baby' Lores, has even composed a song, 'Creo' (I believe), dedicated to Fidel Castro.

Venues

In every town there is a Casa de la Trova, where you can find old-timers crooning the traditional songs, and a club or disco where the local youth party until the small hours. Bars are patrolled by trios, or other small groups, playing all the old favourites and tunes on request while trying to sell their CDs. The Casa de Cultura in any town is always a good place to find out about local concerts and other events, which are often held in the open air, even in the atmospheric shell of a ruined building awaiting funds for restoration.

La Habana Vieja

When to go

Climate

The high season is from mid-December to mid-April, when there are more dry days, more sunshine and less humidity. The season for hurricanes and tropical storms begins in August and can go on until the end of November. A serious hurricane does not come every year by any means, but in the last few years there have been several storms that have caused flooding and damage to houses and crops. There are also variations in climate on the island: it is hotter and drier in Santiago than in Havana, and wetter and cooler in the mountains than in the lowlands.

Northeast trade winds temper the heat, but summer shade temperatures can rise to above 30°C in Havana, and higher elsewhere, particularly in Santiago where it can be unbearably hot in July and August. Fortunately, most offices, hotels and leading restaurants are air-conditioned. In winter, average day temperatures drop to 20°C (68°F) and there may be a few cold days below 10°C (50°F), with a north wind. Average rainfall is noticeably greater in the west of the island; it falls mostly in the summer and autumn, but there can be torrential rains at any time.

Festivals

In contrast with other Latin American countries, Cuba has no national religious festivals, although you will find some patron saints' days (often linked to *Santería*) celebrated in churches, such as Día de la Caridad de Cobre (8 September), Cuba's patron saint's day. Processions are usually limited to the church itself rather than around the streets of the town. Easter is an important time but Christmas Day was only reintroduced as a public holiday in 1997 prior to a visit from the Pope, having been banned after the Revolution. It has become a regular event in the Western tradition, with Christmas trees and tinsel, but a whole generation missed out on celebrating it and there is little awareness of what it signifies.

Public holidays are political and historical events and are marked by speeches, rallies and other gatherings, often in each town's Plaza de la Revolución. New Year is celebrated everywhere as the anniversary of the 1959 Revolution, Liberation Day, when you can expect speeches, parades and parties, with lots of music and dancing, much of it outdoors.

Carnival is making a comeback in several towns, although it is not a pre-Lenten festival as in Trinidad or Rio de Janeiro. Despite limited budgets, carnival events are colourful, energetic and have a raw vibrancy. Parades are accompanied by music, drumming, dancing and competitions requiring lots of stamina. In Havana, carnival was suspended during the Special Period and then became a movable feast, but is now usually held in August. The best carnival, despite the heat, is in Santiago de Cuba in July. It is preceded by the **Festival del Caribe** or **Fiesta del Fuego** in the first week of the month, with theatre, dancing and conferences. Carnival itself is a week-long musical extravaganza taking in the city's patron saint's day on 25 July, although it pauses for a day on 26 July to commemorate the Moncada uprising in 1953 with political celebrations. A variation on carnival is Remedios' *parrandas* in the days leading up to Christmas, where floats from two neighbourhoods compete against each other amid a cacophony of fireworks and music.

Cuba has many cultural and sporting festivals, so there is nearly always something going on at any time of year. One of the most famous is the **Havana International Jazz Festival**, 'Jazz Plaza', in December, sponsored by Chucho Valdés with the Cuban Institute of Music and attracting the world's leading musicians. It is preceded by the **International Festival of the New Latin American Cinema**, when prize-winning films are shown at cinemas around Havana. This is the foremost film festival in Latin America showcasing the best of Cuban and Latin American films along with documentaries and independent world cinema. Another important film festival, the **Festival Internacional de Cine Pobre de Humberto Solás**, takes place in Gibara in April and showcases low-budget movies.

The **International Ballet Festival of Havana** takes place every other year (28 October to 6 November 2016) and brings together dancers and choreographers from around the world in a non-competitive cultural exchange, with performances and workshops in theatres in Havana and other cities.

Among the many sporting events, Havana's marathon, **Marabana**, in November, is increasingly popular with visiting runners. Its route, starting and finishing on the Prado and out along the Malecón, is particularly scenic. Competitive cycling has been huge since the 1960s, with the biggest race being **Vuelta a Cuba**, traditionally going through all the regions of Cuba. Economic hardship sometimes led to the cancellation of the race in years gone by, but it is now being resurrected, with a Camagüey–La Habana race in 2014; a 12-stage, 1344-km Guantánamo–La Habana race in February 2015, and plans for even more events in the future.

What to do

from climbing the heights to diving the depths

Caving

There are huge cave systems in Cuba, some of which are developed tourist attractions. The Santo Tomás and Cueva del Indio caves in Viñales are visited by thousands of people every year, but many others are almost unknown. Amerindian pictographs can be found in some, including Los Generales, Las Mercedes, Indio and Pichardo caves in the Sierra de Cubitas, Camagüey; El Paraíso, Perla de Agua and other caves around Baracoa, and the Cuevas del Punta del Este on the Isla de la Juventud. The largest stalagmite in Cuba can be found in the Cueva Martín Infierno near Trinidad, 67 m high and 40 m at its base. In the Zapata peninsula there are flooded caves, which can be dived, as can Tanques Azules, at Caletones. An adventure park at the Silla de Gibara offers rock climbing, caving, potholing and cave diving, or you can get in touch with the local speleologists to explore underground rivers and caves in the area. In Matanzas province there are some 350 caves, of which about 20 can be visited. The Bellamar caves receive hundreds of visitors daily, while the Saturno caverns have underwater tunnels suitable for trained cave divers.

Climbing

Climbing is still in its infancy in Cuba and has not, so far, been hijacked by state tour companies with organized excursions. However, you can't go off and climb wherever you want, as access to national parks is restricted. Climbing in the Sierra Maestra, for example, is effectively out of bounds. Climbing is also prohibited in the Valle de Viñales, even though this is the best destination in the country, thanks to the mogotes, which are a magnet for climbers. Life can be made very difficult for Cuban climbers who contravene regulations – several have even left the country – but the local authorities often turn a blind eye or issue warnings to foreign climbers; no foreigner has yet been prosecuted. Climbing gear is in short supply in Cuba, so take everything you need and more to donate to local climbers. See www.climbingcuba.com for advice.

Cycling

Bicycles became the only reliable form of transport during the petrol shortages of the Special Period and they remain a common sight in both cities and rural areas. For active visitors, cycling is an increasingly popular way of exploring the country, because you can set off where and when you please. Beyond the cities, quiet roads wind through flat or rolling countryside, where the majestic Royal palm towers over farmers' thatched cottages (*bohíos*) and oxen are still used to work the fields. If you do not have the time to cycle the length and breadth of the island, you can always put your bike on the train (if it is running) or on a domestic flight.

In Havana, you can cruise the cycle lane along the Malecón with the salt spray in your face and a bright yellow cocotaxi at your side. To get out to the beaches east of Havana, ride with your bike on the *ciclobus* through the tunnel under the harbour before picking up the Vía Blanca. For a multi-day trip to the Western Sierras, head out along Salvador Allende and Avenida Rancho Boyeros past the airport to San Antonio de los Baños and the next day to Viñales. Side trips can be made in the Sierra del Rosario, with some demanding hill climbs.

From Santa Clara you can cycle to Trinidad (88 km) via Manicaragua and Condado, head west along the coast road to Guajimico (44 km), Cienfuegos (43 km) and inland to Hanabanilla (51 km) via Cumanajagua. There is a steep 7-km climb to the Hanabanilla lake. Return to Santa Clara (47 km) via La Moza and Manicaragua, giving you some steep hills.

Test yourself and your bike in the mountains of the Sierra Maestra. Leave Santiago, heading west along Avenida las Américas, and cycle to El Saltón (87 km) via El Cobre. Then to Bayamo (67 km), Manzanillo (93 km), Punta Piedra (99 km), Chivirico (100 km) and return to Santiago

(68 km). This takes in the mountains and the outstanding coast road squeezed between the mountains and the Caribbean.

If you don't want to go it alone there are many organized group tours, although you will need to bring your own bike. You may also be able to join a group of Cuban bikers (mostly English-speaking) through the **Club Nacional de Cicloturismo Gran Caribe** (National Bike Club), or one of the regional clubs, such as the **Club de Cicloturismo Comandante Che Guevara** in the west. They run tours of one to 28 days in all parts of the country, some with political themes. Most tours offer a fully supported programme and have a dedicated back-up team including tour leader, mechanic and support vehicle. Even better, luggage is carried for you while you cycle. The **Cuba Solidarity Campaign**, T020-72636452, www.cuba-solidarity.org.uk, runs an annual sponsored bike ride in western Cuba and delivers consignments of medical aid to a Havana Policlínico (local medical centre). See Friendship Associations, page 483, for possible contacts in other countries.

Fishing

Cuba has been a fisherman's mecca for decades, not only for its deep-sea fishing, popularized by Ernest Hemingway, but also for its freshwater fishing in the many lakes and reservoirs spread around the island.

Freshwater fishing Freshwater fishing is mostly for the large-mouth bass (*trucha*), which grows to a great size in the Cuban lakes. The main places are: Maspotón in Pinar del Río, where you can fish in both La Juventud reservoir and in the mouth of the Río Los Palacios or Río Carraguao; Laguna del Tesoro in the Ciénaga de Zapata, where there is a wide variety of fish; Presa Alacranes in Villa Clara province, which is the second-largest reservoir in the country; Presa Zaza, in Sancti Spíritus, the largest artificial lake in Cuba, where the record catch of *trucha* is 16.5 lbs; Lago La Redonda, near Morón in Ciego de Avila province, and in the province of Camagüey on the Porvenir, Muñoz and Mañana de Santa Ana dams. Equipment can be hired, but serious fishermen will prefer to bring their own, plus a large quantity of insect repellent. Freshwater fishing is allowed all year round.

Deep-sea fishing This can be organized at marinas around the island, although most of the tournaments and the best facilities are at the Marina Hemingway, just west of Havana. Marlin, swordfish, tarpon, sawfish, yellowfin tuna, dorado, wahoo, shark and a host of others are all caught here. Varadero is a good point from which to take advantage of the Gulf Stream, which flows between Key West in Florida and Cuba, but records have been broken all along the northern coast in the cays of the Archipiélago de Sabana and the Archipiélago de Camagüey. There is also good fishing off the south coast around the Isla de la Juventud and Cayo Largo.

Bonefishing This is excellent off the south coast in the Archipiélago de los Jardines de la Reina, or off Cayo Largo. It is also increasingly popular at Las Salinas, the salt flats on the Zapata peninsula, previously a protected area, but recently opened to fly fishermen. Still tightly controlled, with only six anglers allowed into the national park at any one time, you have your own personal guide and a flat-bottomed skiff to take you through the many channels to the shallow lagoons, where you can wade or fish from the boat. Flats species include bonefish, permit, jack crevalle and barracuda.

Hiking

The highest peaks are in the Sierra Maestra in the east, where there are also many historical landmarks associated with the Wars of Independence and the Revolution. A three-day walk will take you from Alto del Naranjo up the island's highest peak, Pico Turquino, and down to the Caribbean coast at Las Cuevas, giving you fantastic views of the mountains and the coastline. The Sierra del Escambray in the centre of the island is conveniently located just north of Trinidad, and has some lovely trails in the hills, beside rivers, waterfalls and caves. The mountains of the west of the island, the Sierra del Rosario and the Sierra de los Organos, have some of the most unusual geological features, as well as a wide variety of flora and very rewarding birdwatching.

The first months of the year are the best for walking, as they are drier and cooler. However, temperature varies with altitude: the higher you get in the Sierra Maestra, the cooler it will become, so take appropriate clothing. Also remember that in the rainforest there are few days when it does not rain, so expect to get wet. The months from August to November are the wettest, when the risk of hurricanes

Spectator sports

Baseball Cuba is a baseball-mad nation despite having fallen in the world rankings in recent years. During international matches every television set in the island is tuned to the match. The Serie Nacional baseball season runs from November to May, culminating in the national play-offs, followed a couple of weeks later by the Liga Superior, which lasts a month. In August, 'Que Siempre Brille el Sol' is a popular tournament, with US baseball teams invited for the first time to compete against Cuban teams in June 2016. Baseball games have a fanatical following and can last up to three hours. Later that night and the following day you can see groups of fans in plazas around the country heatedly discussing the recent match with wild gestures and raised voices. See Havana, page 96, for information on matches there.

Basketball Young Cuban men can be seen playing basketball in every town and village. This is the second most popular sport in the country and visitors are welcome to join in. The main stadium is the Ramón Fonst stadium near the Plaza de la Revolución in Havana and the season runs from September to November.

Boxing Cuban boxers are always expected to come out of the Olympic Games with a clutch of medals in all boxing weights and Cubans enthusiastically support their athletes. The best place to catch a tournament or just watch some training matches for international team events is the Sala Kid Chocolate in Havana.

Cycling There is keen interest in cycling as a sport and Cuba is a respected competitor in the Americas. Havana's professional racetrack is at the Velódromo Reinaldo Paseiro, part of the Estadio Panamericano, built in 1991 for the Pan-American Games. It is located on the southern side of the Vía Blanca, next to the swimming facilities. Cuba hosts several international competitions including Vuelta a Cuba, a staged road race.

or tropical storms increases, but you can still encounter days when there is plenty of sunshine. At all times of year, it is best to start early, before it gets too hot. Always carry plenty of drinking water, some food, a hat and suntan lotion. Good footwear is essential and a walking stick is extremely useful on hilly forest trails. Good large-scale maps are non-existent so you are advised to take a guide when embarking on long walks. Not only will this prevent you getting lost, but you will learn a lot more about your surroundings, as many of the guides are professional botanists or ornithologists. If you are walking in national parks a guide is compulsory.

Scuba-diving

The majority of Cuba's coral reefs are alive and healthy and teeming with assorted marine life. There are believed to be some 900 species of fish, 1400 species of mollusc, 60 species of coral, 1100 species of crustacean, 67 species of shark and ray and four types of sea turtle around the island, as well as the manatee. Much of it is protected.

There are three main marine platforms: the Archipiélago del Rey, the Archipiélago de la Reina and the Archipiélago de los Canarreos. The main dive areas are Isla de la Juventud, Varadero, Faro de Luna, María La Gorda, Cayo Levisa, Guardalavaca, Playa Santa Lucía and close to Santiago de Cuba. Most offer a variety of diving, including reefs and walls and an assortment of wrecks, from the remains of ancient Spanish ships to many modern vessels intentionally sunk as dive sites.

All dive shops are government-owned. Most staff speak Spanish, English and often German, Italian or French. Diving is usually done as part of an all-inclusive package, although dives can be booked direct with dive shops for around CUC$35-40, including all equipment. Most companies use European dive gear. Good-quality, basic rental gear is available, but if you use your own you should be prepared to bring all your spares and replacement parts with you (batteries, regulator mouthpiece, photographic equipment, etc), as these are not usually available.

The south of the island suffers from *agua mala*, or 'bad water' in the summer months, when the sea is full of tiny jellyfish which will sting exposed skin so wear a tropical hood to protect the neck and face in jellyfish season. Dives can sometimes be delayed for a variety of reasons, so patience is needed. The authorities are very concerned about security, as boats have been 'borrowed' in the past for a quick getaway to Florida.

Shopping tips

The main souvenirs to take home with you are, of course, **rum** and **cigars**. The street price of a bottle of rum ranges from CUC$2 to CUC$10 depending on its age and quality (see box, page 164). Cigars can cost whatever you are prepared to pay (see box, page 120). Remember that all the best tobacco leaves go into cigar-making rather than cigarettes. Note that there are strict Customs regulations on taking cigars out of the country, see page 470. If you are after a specific cigar brand, go to a specialist shop. Remember to keep the official receipt in case you have to show it at customs on departure.

In recent years Cuban **handicrafts** have been developed for the tourist market. As well as souvenirs, there is a considerable amount of **artwork** of varying degrees of worth, but you may pick up a bargain. If you are a serious collector, skip the markets and go straight to the galleries in Havana. Taking art out of the country requires a special licence.

Improve your travel photography

Taking pictures is a highlight for many travellers, yet too often the results turn out to be disappointing. Steve Davey, author of Footprint's *Travel Photography*, sets out his top rules for coming home with pictures you can be proud of.

Before you go
Don't waste precious travelling time and do your research before you leave. Find out what festivals or events might be happening or which day the weekly market takes place, and search online image sites such as Flickr to see whether places are best shot at the beginning or end of the day, and what vantage points you should consider.

Get up early
The quality of the light will be better in the few hours after sunrise and again before sunset – especially in the tropics when the sun will be harsh and unforgiving in the middle of the day. Sometimes seeing the sunrise is a part of the whole travel experience: sleep in and you will miss more than just photographs.

Stop and think
Don't just click away without any thought. Pause for a few seconds before raising the camera and ask yourself what you are trying to show with your photograph. Think about what things you need to include in the frame to convey this meaning. Be prepared to move around your subject to get the best angle. Knowing the point of your picture is the first step to making sure that the person looking at the picture will know it too.

Compose your picture
Avoid simply dumping your subject in the centre of the frame every time you take a picture. If you compose with it to one side, then your picture can look more balanced. This will also allow you to show a significant background and make the picture more meaningful. A good rule of thumb is to place your subject or any significant detail a third of the way into the frame; facing into the frame not out of it.

This rule also works for landscapes. Compose with the horizon two-thirds of the way up the frame if the foreground is the most interesting part of the picture; one-third of the way up if the sky is more striking.

Don't get hung up with this so-called Rule of Thirds, though. Exaggerate it by pushing your subject out to the edge of the frame if it makes a more interesting picture; or if the sky is dull in a landscape, try cropping with the horizon near the very top of the frame.

Fill the frame
If you are going to focus on a detail or even a person's face in a close-up portrait, then be bold and make sure that you fill the frame. This is often a case of physically getting in close. You can use a telephoto setting on a zoom lens but this can lead to pictures looking quite flat; moving in close is a lot more fun!

Interact with people

If you want to shoot evocative portraits then it is vital to approach people and seek permission in some way, even if it is just by smiling at someone. Spend a little time with them and they are likely to relax and look less stiff and formal. Action portraits where people are doing something, or environmental portraits, where they are set against a significant background, are a good way to achieve relaxed portraits. Interacting is a good way to find out more about people and their lives, creating memories as well as photographs.

Focus carefully

Your camera can focus quicker than you, but it doesn't know which part of the picture you want to be in focus. If your camera is using the centre focus sensor then move the camera so it is over the subject and half press the button, then, holding it down, recompose the picture. This will lock the focus. Take the now correctly focused picture when you are ready.

Another technique for accurate focusing is to move the active sensor over your subject. Some cameras with touch-sensitive screens allow you to do this by simply clicking on the subject.

Leave light in the sky

Most good night photography is actually taken at dusk when there is some light and colour left in the sky; any lit portions of the picture will balance with the sky and any ambient lighting. There is only a very small window when this will happen, so get into position early, be prepared and keep shooting and reviewing the results. You can take pictures after this time, but avoid shots of tall towers in an inky black sky; crop in close on lit areas to fill the frame.

Bring it home safely

Digital images are inherently ephemeral: they can be deleted or corrupted in a heartbeat. The good news though is they can be copied just as easily. Wherever you travel, you should have a backup strategy. Cloud backups are popular, but make sure that you will have access to fast enough Wi-Fi. If you use RAW format, then you will need some sort of physical back-up. If you don't travel with a laptop or tablet, then you can buy a backup drive that will copy directly from memory cards.

Recently updated and available in both digital and print formats, Footprint's Travel Photography by Steve Davey covers everything you need to know about travelling with a camera, including simple post-processing. More information is available at www.footprinttravelguides.com

Where to stay

All hotels are state owned. In the resort areas, the best are those with foreign investment or foreign management contracts. There are hotels to suit most budgets, even if they are basic at the lower end. Peso hotels are reserved for Cubans and are rarely available to foreigners, although Cubans are now permitted to stay in resort hotels if they have sufficient CUC$.

It is legal to stay with a Cuban family and rent a room as long as the family is registered and pays taxes. These places are known as *casas particulares*. There are also *casas particulares* reserved for the Cuban market, identifiable by the different coloured logo above the door. Cubans on holiday stay in campsites (*campismo*), which are cabins, not tents, a few of which accept foreigners.

Hotels

The **Gran Caribe** chain owns the four- and five-star grand old hotels, such as the **Nacional** and the **Riviera** in Havana. **Cubanacán** has upmarket, modern resort hotels, with an international standard of accommodation and facilities, as does **Gaviota**, owned by the military, which has most of the strategic beach areas. The Cubanacán group comprises all the Brisas, Club Amigo, Cubanacán, Horizontes and Hoteles E (Encanto) labels. Hoteles E are renovations of colonial mansions into boutique hotels in provincial towns and are some of the nicest places to stay at very reasonable prices. **Islazul** owns the two- and three-

---

Price codes

Where to stay	Restaurants
$$$$ over CUC$150	$$$ over CUC$12
$$$ CUC$66-150	$$ CUC$6-12
$$ CUC$30-65	$ under CUC$6
$ under CUC$30	

Prices refer to the cost of one night in a double room in high season (15 December-15 March).

Prices refer to the cost of a two-course meal for one person.

star, older hotels, often in the countryside. **Habaguanex** is in charge of the renovation of colonial mansions in La Habana Vieja and their conversion into hotels, restaurants, bars, etc.

Most three-star hotels were built in the 1940s and 1950s and are showing their age, but some have been refurbished and are now considered four star. In remote beach resorts the hotels are usually all-inclusive and classify themselves as four or five star. At the cheaper end of the market you can expect old bed linen, ill-fitting sheets, intermittent water and electricity, peeling paintwork, crumbling tiles and indifferent service.

Accommodation for your first day in a hotel should be booked in advance of travelling. You have to fill in an address (any hotel will do) on your tourist card, and if you leave it blank you will be directed to the reservations desk at the airport, which is time consuming. A voucher from your travel agent to confirm arrangements is usual, and hotels expect it as confirmation of your reservation. This can be done abroad through travel agencies, accredited government agencies, or through **Turismo Buró** desks in main hotels. It's a good idea to book hotel rooms generally before noon. In the peak seasons, December to February and August, it is essential to book in advance. Lack of sufficient rooms has sometimes forced tourists to sleep in their cars in Trinidad in December and in the plaza in Viñales in August.

At other times it is possible to book at the hotel reception. Prices given in the text are for a double room in high season (15 December-15 March); low-season prices are about 20% lower. Shop around for prices; travel agencies can get you a better deal than the hotel, which will usually offer you the rack rate. **Cubaism** offers real-time hotel availability and online reservations for a number of hotel groups, www.cubahotelbookings.com.

Casas particulares/private accommodation
Cuba is geared more to package tourism than to independent visitors, but self-employment has opened up opportunities that can prove rewarding for the visitor. Lodging with a family is possible at CUC$20-40 per room depending on the season, the length of stay and the location, with the highest rates charged in Havana and Trinidad. Cubans are allowed to rent out rooms subject to health and hygiene regulations and incorporation into the tax system. Hustlers on the street will offer accommodation, but it is safer to arrange rooms through our recommendations or other contacts if you can. A guide or hustler (*jinetero*) taking you to a private home will expect CUC$5 commission per night, which goes on your room rate. Less obvious, but still an insidious form of touting is the networking of the *casa particular* owners. Most have an address book full of

owners in other towns. If you ask whether they know someone in the next town you are going to, they will happily ring up a 'friend' and book a room for you. This may be a useful service, but you will be charged CUC$5 extra a night for the favour, a sum

Tip...
Take a torch. There may not be good street lighting in the area, let alone power in your house.

which will be sent to the first owner as his commission. Some owners take this so seriously that they travel around the country in low season, inspecting the properties they recommend and getting to know the families.

Private homes vary considerably. Houses in the town centre can be very noisy if your room is on the street and traffic starts at 0530. Colonial houses have no soundproofing and even a door shutting can be heard all over the house at 0600. Bear in mind that facilities often don't work, and there may be water and power cuts. The sheets don't always fit the bed; the pillows are often old and lumpy. Bathrooms should be exclusively for tourists' use, but towels are usually very small so take your own to complement theirs. Soap will probably be provided, but don't rely on it.

However, over the last few years *casa* owners have invested large amounts of money, time and effort into improving and expanding their visitors' accommodation. The houses we list are in a good state of repair, newly painted and offer a private bathroom with new fixtures and fittings (although the water may still be tepid and the pressure poor), air conditioning and either a ceiling or free-standing fan and usually a fridge. Theft is not a problem, as the licence would be revoked if there was a serious complaint against the owner but you should always be careful with your belongings.

Food is nearly always better at a *casa particular* than in a state restaurant or private *paladar*. The family eats at a different time and the food is prepared in stages, but it will still be fresher and made from better ingredients than in a restaurant. Remember that what Cubans can buy with ration coupons is not enough to feed a visitor and any extra food has to be bought in CUC$.

It is best to check that the *casa particular* you stay in is legally registered and pays taxes. All legal *casas particulares* should have a sticker on their front door showing two blue chevrons on a white background with *Arrendador Inscripto* written across it. Those with red triangles rent in pesos to Cubans only and it is illegal for them to rent to foreigners. If you stay at an illegal residence and it is discovered, the Cuban family will have to pay a huge fine. Illegal homestays are usually reported to the police by neighbours. All clients must sign and complete address and passport details in a Registration Book within 24 hours of arrival. This book must be made available to municipal inspectors.

If you have made a phone booking in advance and are arriving by Viazul, your host may come to the bus station with a taxi to collect you. This is not just for your benefit. A common scam is to steal guests, sometimes from the bus terminal and sometimes from outside the front door. If you are told by someone in the street that the owners no longer rent, or are full, or have asked this person to take you to another *casa*, do not go with them until you have rung the bell and checked the story with someone inside the house. *Jineteros* are very skilled at diverting you from your intended path. Some even change the numbers above the door to take you to another house where they will receive a commission.

Always reconfirm your booking with your *casa* owner the day before your arrival otherwise you may find the room has been let to someone else. If you have booked through an agency, the owner will get their money whether you turn up or not, but if you are arranging things independently and they don't hear from you, they will not want to lose that income. There are numerous booking agencies that reserve rooms in *casas particulares*. You will of course pay a premium on the room rate for the service, but with that you get convenience and peace of mind. Websites worth consulting include www.cubadirect. co.uk, www.airbnb.com, www.casaparticularcuba.org, www.cuba-junky.com, www.casaparticular.com and www.mycasaparticular.com. There are also local businesses, such as www.trinidadrent.com, and Bed and Breakfast in Viñales, www.bbinnvinales.com, now island-wide.

Camping

There are Campismo Popular sites all over the island, although not all are in operation. They are usually in nice surroundings and are good value. They consist of basic cabins rather than tents and are designed for Cubans on holiday rather than

> **Tip...**
> Camping out on the beach or in a field is forbidden.

foreigners. Many of them have been renovated and upgraded with games and sports equipment as well as improved food services. **Campismo Popular**, www. campismopopular.cu, has reservation offices all over the country and bookings should be made in the region where you want to stay.

Food
& drink

rice, beans and a bottle of rum

Food is not Cuba's strong point, although the supply of fresh food has improved in recent years. In Havana the Ministry of Agriculture has set up many *organopónicos* to provide the capital with fresh vegetables grown under organic conditions and to avoid transport costs. However, although the peso food situation is improving, there are still shortages. It is not unusual to be told "*no hay*" ("there isn't any") at restaurants where you would expect the full menu to be available. (An Italian restaurant, for example, may not have any tomatoes, let alone the mozzarella and parma ham that are on the menu.)

Outside Havana shortages are not so bad, but the island is not self-sufficient. Shops sell mostly imported supplies in CUC$, such as tins of food from Spain, packets of biscuits, cookies and crackers. Farmers' markets are good places to buy fruit and vegetables. Tourists do not have access to local stores, or *bodegas*, as these are based on the national ration card system. Bread, rice, beans, sugar and coffee are rationed to Cuban families but they are not given enough to live on and have to purchase the balance at market prices. Milk is rationed only for children up to the age of seven. You can buy almost anything in CUC$.

Food

Beans (frijoles) are a staple of the Cuban creole (*criollo*) diet. The national dish is *congrís* (rice mixed with black beans), roast pork and yuca (*cassava*) or fried plantain. Rice with kidney (red) beans is known as *moros y cristianos*. Pork and chicken are the most common and cheapest meats available. Pork is traditionally eaten for the New Year celebrations, so in late December you'll see all the pigs that have been fattened up on people's balconies or smallholdings on the move in the backs of trucks, cars and bicycles to be sold privately or at the markets. Despite government investment in fisheries, seafood, such as lobster and shrimp, is reserved for the export and tourist markets. There is a story that the government tried to improve the diet of the Cuban people by reducing the price of fish, but all that happened was that the cats got fat; not even price manipulation could wean Cubans off their habitual diet of pork, rice and beans.

The most common side dishes are starchy root vegetables and plantain (*plátano*). The latter is ubiquitous, eaten ripe (*maduro*) or unripe (*verde*), boiled, mashed or fried. Most food is fried and can often be greasy and bland. Spices and herbs are not commonly used and Cubans limit their flavourings to onions and garlic. A marinade called *mojo* may be added to yuca to give it a bit of flavour. Salads in restaurants are mixed vegetables which are slightly pickled and not to everyone's taste. Shredded pickled cabbage and sliced cucumber are a common garnish to the main dish.

Cuba's range of tropical fruit is magnificent, so take advantage of whatever is in season. At the right time of year there will be a glut of avocado, banana (the smallest varieties are the sweetest), custard apple, guava, mango, orange, papaya, pineapple and soursop. The national fruit is the brown-skinned *mamey*, known elsewhere as *zapote*, whose bright pink-orange pulp is best made into juice. Fruit is generally served at breakfast and made into juices, but rarely used as a dessert except in ice cream. It is harvested in season and then disappears until next year, although some *casa particular* owners freeze things in times of plenty so that you can have mango or papaya juice at any time of the year.

Cubans are particularly hooked on ice cream, although it usually only comes in vanilla, strawberry or chocolate flavours. The ice cream parlour, **Coppelia**, can be found in every town of any size and is quite an experience, with long queues because of its popularity. There are other ice cream parlours for a change.

Drink

Rum is the national drink and all cocktails are rum based. There are several brand names and each has a variety of ages, so you have plenty of choice (see box, page 164). Do not buy cheap firewater, or cane spirit, as it is unlikely to agree with you and you may be ill for a while. The good stuff is cheap enough.

Cuban beer is good, and there are regional varieties, which come in bottles or cans. The most widely available **beer** throughout the island is Cristal, made by **Cervecería Mayabe** in Holguín. Found in bottles or cans at 4.9% alcohol content, it costs CUC$1-1.15 in supermarkets and CUC$1.50-2.50 in bars. From the same brewery is Mayabe, with Ordinary at 3.5% and Extra at 5%, both costing the same as Cristal and also popular with more flavour. Sometimes you can find Mayabe beer in pesos cubanos, at 18 pesos. Hatuey, made in Havana, is reckoned by some to be the best of Cuba's many beers, named after an Amerindian chief ruling when the Spanish arrived, but it is very hard to find. Bucanero, from Holguín, is easily bought in the east of the island, 5.4% in bottles or cans. Tínimo (from Camagüey, good with more flavour than Cristal) is also difficult to find. In Havana and in Santiago de Cuba there are now state-

ON THE ROAD
Cuban cocktails

Most bars have their own specialities, but there is a range which is fairly common to all. However, even the standard cocktails will taste different when made by different barmen, so don't expect a mojito in Havana to be the same as a mojito in Varadero. Cocktails come in all colours and flavours, short or long, and some are even striped or multicoloured. All should be presented as a work of art by the barman, who has probably spent years at his training.

Cubanito A cubanito is a Cuban version of a Bloody Mary, with ice, lime juice, salt, Worcester sauce, chilli sauce, light dry rum and tomato juice. Note that tomato juice is not always available everywhere.

Daiquirí See box, page 348.

Ernest Hemingway special An Ernest Hemingway special is light dry rum, grapefruit juice, maraschino liqueur, lime and shaved ice, blended and served like a daiquirí.

Havana Special A Havana Special is pineapple juice, light dry rum, maraschino liqueur and ice, shaken and strained.

Mojito To make a mojito, put half a tablespoon of sugar, the juice of half a lime and some lightly crushed mint leaves in a tall glass. Stir and mix well, then add some soda water, ice cubes, 1½ oz light dry rum and top up with soda water. Serve with a garnish of mint leaves and, of course, a straw.

Mulata A mulata is lime juice, extra aged rum, *crème de cacao* and shaved ice, blended together and served in a champagne glass.

Piña colada The old favourite, piña colada, can be found anywhere: coconut liqueur, pineapple juice, light dry rum and shaved ice, all blended and served with a straw in a glass, a pineapple or a coconut, depending on which tropical paradise you are in.

Saoco Another old recipe best served in a coconut is a saoco, which is just rum, coconut milk and ice.

Zombie One to finish the day off, and maybe even yourself, is a zombie, a mixture of ice, lime juice, grenadine, pineapple juice, light dry rum, old gold rum and extra aged rum, garnished with fruit.

owned micro-breweries which produce a range of beers priced for tourists rather than Cubans.

Cuba now also produces **wines** under the Soroa label, grown and produced in Pinar del Río. Standards are improving thanks to Spanish technology and assistance. There is also a more expensive range sold for about CUC$9-10, including Cabernet Sauvignon, Chardonnay, Tempranillo and other grapes,

A thirst for freedom

The first Cuban resistance fighter we know of was an Amerindian chief called Hatuey, who has become a symbol of rebellion. He lived on the island of Hispaniola at the time of the Spanish invasion by Diego Velázquez. When Hatuey realised the brutal reality of the Spanish occupation, he travelled from Hispaniola to Cuba to warn the Cuban Taínos of the conquistadores' plans. However, his attempts to mobilize the people were no match for the better-armed Spaniards, who chased him into the mountains, captured him and burnt him alive. The story goes that when a priest asked Hatuey before his execution whether he would like to make his peace with God and go to heaven, the chief enquired whether there would be Spanish people in heaven. When he was told that there would be, he declined the offer, saying he certainly didn't want to go there. Nowadays, Hatuey has the dubious honour of having a beer named after him.

produced with the help of a Spanish company in a joint venture. However, if you really want wine, an imported bottle is still your best option.

The locally grown coffee is good, although hotels often manage to make it undrinkable in the mornings. Some of the best coffee comes from back gardens, home grown and home roasted.

Eating out

Cubans eat their main meal at lunch time, but they expect foreigners to eat at night. Generally, although restaurants have improved in the last few years, eating out in Cuba is not very exciting. Restaurants are more innovative in Havana than elsewhere and some of the *paladares* are eccentric in their tastes. While quality and style of cooking naturally varies, as a general rule you will get fresher food in *casas particulares* than you will in state restaurants, which have the reputation of recycling meals and reheating leftovers.

State restaurants/hotels
State-owned 'dollar' restaurants are recognizable by the credit card stickers on the door, where meals are about CUC$10-40, paid only in CUC$. Some can be quite good, and there are some international variations, including Italian, Spanish or French. You get what you pay

Tip...
Be warned that the Cuban idea of Chinese food is unlike anything you might find in your home country or in China and is very sweet.

for, and at the cheap end of the market you can expect poor quality, limited availability of ingredients and disinterested staff. Always check restaurant prices in advance and then scrutinize your bill: discrepancies occur in both the state and private sector.

Resort **hotels** tend to serve buffet meals, which can get tedious after a while, but breakfast here is usually good and plentiful and you can stock up for the day. If you're not eating at a buffet, service can be very slow; this applies regardless of the standard of the restaurant or hotel and even if you are the only customer.

Paladares/casas particulares

Paladares are privately owned restaurants that are licensed and taxed. Some very good family-run businesses have been set up, offering a three-course meal in Havana for CUC$10-20 per person, or less than that outside the capital. Portions are usually generous, but olives, coffee and

> **Tip...**
> Remember that if someone guides you to a *paladar* he will expect a commission, so you end up paying more for your food.

other items are usually charged as extras, so be sure to check what the meal includes. You will always find pork and chicken cooked in a variety of ways and accompanied by several side dishes, including rice, salad, fried plantain, yuca or sweet potato. Some *paladares* also serve lobster (CUC$15-20), shrimp and fish, which are excellent value, fresh and tasty. There are also illegal *paladares*, which will serve meals with meat for CUC$3-5 per person. We do not list them.

The cheapest legal way of getting a decent meal is to eat in your *casa particular* (see Where to stay, above). The food here is generally of excellent quality and served in plentiful, even vast, portions. The hosts can usually cook whatever you want, with advance notice, so they are able to cater for vegetarians and special diets. They spend a lot of time scouring the various food supply outlets every day to make sure they have a wide range of provisions for their guests. A meal is usually CUC$6-10; chicken and pork are cheaper than fish, shrimp and lobster. Many Cubans have no more than a cup of coffee for breakfast but will serve guests with coffee, fruit and/or fruit juice, bread, honey and eggs or a cheese and ham sandwich; at CUC$3-5, this is far better value than in a state hotel.

Fast food and peso stalls

For a cheap meal try one of the Cuban **fast-food** restaurants, such as **El Rápido** or **Burgui**, or a *cafeteria*; these can be found all over the island. As well as chicken and chips or burgers, they offer a range of sandwiches: cheese, ham, or cheese and ham, but they do come in different sizes. A sandwich in Havana

Menu reader

For standard Spanish words and phrases, see page 485.

boniato cream-coloured sweet potato

chicharritas thin slices of fried plantain

chirimoya custard apple

congri black beans with rice

frijoles beans

fruta bomba papaya

guineo banana

malanga starchy root vegetable, known as taro or dasheen in the English-speaking Caribbean.

mamey brown-skinned fruit, sometimes known as *zapote*.

mojo marinade or sauce made of onions, garlic and bitter orange or lime juice.

moros y cristianos kidney beans with rice

plátano plantain, eaten ripe (*maduro*) or unripe (*verde*), boiled, mashed or fried.

piña pineapple

potaje soupy black beans served with white rice

ropa vieja literally 'old clothes', but actually pulled or shredded beef flank, slow cooked with onions, peppers and tomatoes. Beef can often be tough in Cuba so this is a good way of tenderizing it.

tostones thick slices of plantain, fried, then squashed, then fried again.

yuca cassava

costs about CUC$4, a coffee costs CUC$1. In a provincial town you can pay as little as CUC$2 for a sandwich and beer for lunch. All towns and cities have **peso street stalls** for sandwiches, pizza and snacks; you'll need about CUC$10 for a two-week stay if you're planning to avoid restaurants entirely. In out-of-the-way places, you will be able to pay for food in pesos (CUP$), but generally you will be charged in CUC$.

Vegetarians

For vegetarians the choice of food is very limited, normally only cheese sandwiches, spaghetti, pizzas, salads, bananas and omelettes. Even beans (and *congris*) are often cooked with meat or in meat fat. If you are staying at a *casa particular* or eating in a *paladar*, they will usually prepare meatless meals for you with advance warning. Always ask for beans to be cooked in vegetable oil. Some vegetarians even recommend taking your own oil and lending it to the cook so that you can be absolutely sure that lard has not been used. Hotels usually have quite extravagant all-you-can-eat buffet spreads you can choose from.

Havana

an intoxicating blend of hedonism and history

Of all the capital cities in the Caribbean, Havana has the reputation for being the most splendid and sumptuous. Before the Revolution, its casinos and nightlife attracted the megastars of the day. There may be no casinos now, but Havana's bars and clubs with their thriving music scene are still a major draw for foreigners and Cubans alike.

Unlike most cities, Havana has not been subject to tacky 21st-century modernizations, partly because of a consistent lack of finance and materials. Low-level street lighting, relatively few cars (and many of those antiques), no (real) estate agents or Wendyburgers, no neon and very little advertising (except for political slogans), all give the city plenty of scope for nostalgia.

Havana is probably the finest example of a Spanish colonial city in the Americas. Many of its palaces were converted into museums after the Revolution and more restoration work has been carried out since La Habana Vieja (the old city) was declared a UNESCO World Heritage Site in 1982. There is also some stunning architecture from the first half of the 20th century. That said, much of the city is fighting a losing battle against the corrosive effects of the sea air.

Best for
Architecture ▪ Cocktails ▪ Museums ▪ Music

Havana

Footprint
picks

★ Museo Nacional Palacio de Bellas Artes, page 49

A fascinating collection of art, both international and Cuban.

★ Plaza Vieja, page 54

A beautifully restored historic square, packed with museums, galleries, bars and restaurants.

★ Malecón, page 60

Day and night, the city's seafront drive attracts fishermen, school children, athletes, lovers and old cars.

★ Callejón de Hamel, page 61

For Sunday afternoon fun in the sun, with hot and steamy Afro-Cuban music and dance.

★ Cementerio Colón, page 67

A huge cemetery with intriguing tombs and extravagant statues.

Essential Havana

Finding your feet

Havana is situated in the western half of Cuba on the north coast, spreading largely west and south from the Bahía de Habana, which is linked to the Straits of Florida by a narrow inlet. **José Martí international airport**, the largest in the country, is 18 km southwest of central Havana and is the main hub for onward domestic flights to other parts of the island. All flights from abroad use Terminal 3, the newest terminal, with the exception of flights from Cancún which arrive at Terminal 2; domestic flights use Terminal 1. As many transatlantic flights arrive late at night, it can be sensible to arrange a transfer from the airport to your hotel in advance with your travel agent. The long-distance **Viazul bus station** for foreigners is based far away from the old city in Nuevo Vedado (southwest of Vedado) and a taxi will be needed to get to your destination. The central train station at the southern end of the old city was closed for renovation in late 2015, so trains were using **Estación La Coubre**, nearby. Both are within walking distance of hotels in La Habana Vieja or Centro Habana, but a taxi is advised at night. For further details see Transport, page 98.

Footprint picks

1 Museo Nacional Palacio de Bellas Artes, page 49
2 Plaza Vieja, page 54
3 Malecón, page 60
4 Callejón de Hamel, page 61
5 Cementerio Colón, page 67

Weather Havana

January	February	March	April	May	June
25°C 17°C 27mm	26°C 17°C 24mm	27°C 18°C 18mm	28°C 20°C 15mm	31°C 21°C 53mm	31°C 23°C 85mm

July	August	September	October	November	December
31°C 23°C 52mm	31°C 23°C 77mm	31°C 23°C 54mm	29°C 21°C 39mm	27°C 20°C 12mm	26°C 18°C 25mm

Getting around

Havana is very spread out along the coast: it is more than 8 km from La Habana Vieja to Miramar along the Malecón (the seafront boulevard). Much of the city can be covered on foot, but most visitors restrict themselves to one district at a time. Local bus travel is not recommended for the uninitiated, involving complicated queuing procedures and a lot of pushing and shoving. Instead, the **HabanaBus** (see page 98) and taxis are the preferred method of transport for tourists, who pay in CUC$. Alternatives are to hire a classic car with driver, an overpriced, bright yellow *cocotaxi*, or even a *bicitaxi* (bicycle taxi) for short journeys. It is also possible to hire scooters and cars to drive yourself, although you should exercise extreme caution on Havana's dangerous roads. For details of all these options, see Transport, page 98.

Guides

Many Cubans in Havana tout their services in their desperate quest for CUC$: they are a considerable nuisance and nearly all tourists complain of being hassled. If you feel you trust someone as a guide, make sure you state exactly what you want, eg private car, *paladar*, accommodation, and fix a price in advance to avoid shocks when it is too late. *Casas particulares* can often be a good source of information on reputable guides. You may find, however, that the police will assume your guide is a prostitute and prohibit him or her from accompanying you into a hotel.

Orientation

The city of Havana (population 2,204,300) has 200 districts in 15 municipalities, including 14,000 *manzanas* (blocks). These municipalities are: **Playa**, **Marianao** and **La Lisa** in the west; **Boyeros** in the southwest; **Plaza de la Revolución**, **Centro Habana**, **La Habana Vieja**, **Cerro** and **Diez de Octubre** in the centre; south-central **Arroyo Naranjo**; **Regla**, **San Miguel del Padrón** going eastwards; **Cotorro** in the southeast; and in the east, **Playas del Este** and **Guanabacoa**. The centre is divided into five sections, three of which are of most interest to visitors, **La Habana Vieja** (Old Havana), **Centro Habana** (Central Havana) and **Vedado**, linked by the Malecón, a picturesque thoroughfare along the coast.

Addresses

Streets have names in La Habana Vieja and Centro, but numbers or letters in Vedado and numbers in Miramar, although some of the main roads in Vedado are still referred to by names. An address is given as the street (*Calle* or *Avenida*), the building number, followed by the two streets between which it is located, eg **Hotel Inglaterra**, Prado 416 entre San Rafael y San Miguel. However,

Tip...

Don't forget to look up. Habaneros live in the open air and their balconies are as full of life as the streets below.

Tip...
Some museums charge for use of cameras and videos, others don't, but in order to film for professional purposes you must have permission from **Gestión Cultural de Patrimonio**, Oficios 8, T7-8644337

sometimes this is shortened to showing merely which corner it is on, eg **Hotel Florida**, Obispo 252 esquina Cuba. A large building will not bother with the number, eg **Hotel Nacional**, Calle O esquina 21. Cubans usually abbreviate *entre* (between) to e/ while *esquina* (corner) becomes esq.

When to go

The driest and least humid time of the year is between December and March, when you can have completely cloudless days. From July to August is the hottest time but most public buildings have air conditioning and there is usually a breeze along the Malecón. Rain falls mainly in May and June and then from September to October, but there are wet days all year round. In recent years, the worst storms have hit between September and November, destroying many of the decrepit houses in the city, but Havana is exceptionally well prepared for hurricanes and loss of life is rare. Many cultural festivals (jazz, ballet, film, etc) and sporting events (baseball, cycling, boxing, fishing, sailing, etc) take place throughout the year. There are also numerous festive days, for example José Martí's birthday (28 January 1853), which are not national holidays but are very important in Havana. New Year celebrations are a major event, coinciding with the anniversary of the triumph of the Revolution on 1 January 1959. Carnival is in August.

Time required

Two to three days is enough to get an overview of the different areas of the city and enjoy some of the nightlife, spending a day in Old Havana with time left over for visits to other districts. With a week you could do a couple of day trips, to the beaches to the east or even out to Las Terrazas or Viñales in the west.

Best cocktail spots
The pool at the Saratoga hotel, page 72
The garden at the Hotel Nacional, page 75
The rooftop bar at La Guarida, page 81
The bar at La Torre restaurant, page 82
El Delirio Habanero, page 91

Sights

Most of Havana's sights of interest are in La Habana Vieja, the oldest part of the city. Around the Plaza de Armas are the former Palacio de los Capitanes Generales, El Templete and Castillo de La Real Fuerza, the oldest of all the forts. From Plaza de Armas two narrow and picturesque streets, Calles Obispo and O'Reilly, go west to the heart of the city around the Parque Central. To the southwest rises the white dome of the Capitolio (Capitol). From the northwest corner of Parque Central, a wide, tree-shaded avenue with a central walkway, the Paseo del Prado, runs to the fortress of La Punta. The Prado technically divides the old city from the largely residential district of Centro, although architecturally there is little distinction.

West of Centro is lively Vedado, with clubs, bars, theatres and hotels with murky pre-Revolution tales to tell. Vedado can be reached along Havana's beguiling oceanfront highway, the Malecón, which snakes westward from La Punta. Further inland is Plaza de la Revolución, with the impressive monument to José Martí at its centre and the much-photographed, huge outline of Che Guevara on one wall. West of the Río Almendares is Miramar, once an upper-class suburb, where embassies and hotels for businesspeople are located.

Reached by tunnel or ferry from La Habana Vieja, Casablanca is the area on the east bank of the harbour, dominated by the two massive fortresses of El Morro and La Cabaña.

La Habana Vieja (Old Havana) *Colour map 1, A5.*
colonial palaces and mansions now house boutique hotels, museums and galleries

The old city is the area with the greatest concentration of sights and where most work is being done to restore buildings to their former glory. New museums, art galleries, hotels, restaurants and shops are opening all the time in renovated mansions or merchants' houses. Several days can be spent strolling around the narrow streets or along the waterfront, stopping in bars and open air cafés to take in the atmosphere, although the nightlife is better in Vedado.

Plaza de Armas and around

This is Havana's oldest square and has been successfully restored to its original appearance. The statue in the centre is of the 'Father of the Nation', the revolutionary 19th-century landowner

> **Fact...**
> No Spanish king or queen ever visited Cuba in colonial times.

Carlos Manuel de Céspedes. On the north side of the Plaza are the **Palacio del Segundo Cabo, which was** the former private residence of the Captains General, and the former **Supreme Court**, a colonial building with a large patio. It is closed for renovation at

1 Havana orientation

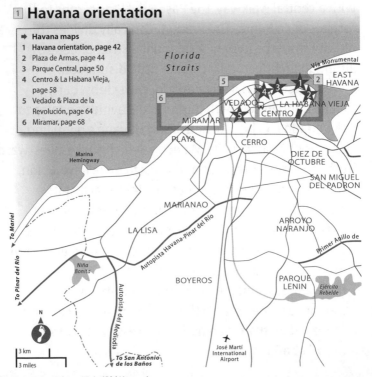

➡ **Havana maps**
1 Havana orientation, page 42
2 Plaza de Armas, page 44
3 Parque Central, page 50
4 Centro & La Habana Vieja, page 58
5 Vedado & Plaza de la Revolución, page 64
6 Miramar, page 68

present, with the support of the EU and UNESCO, and will become a centre for cultural relations between Cuba and Europe.

Castillo de la Real Fuerza ⓘ *O'Reilly entre Av del Puerto y Tacón, T7-8644490, Tue-Sun 0930-1700, CUC$3.* Just north of the plaza, this is Cuba's oldest building and the second oldest fort in the New World. It was first built in 1558 after the city had been sacked by buccaneers and was rebuilt in 1582. It is a low, long building with a picturesque tower from which there is a grand view.

El Templete ⓘ *Baratillo 1 entre O'Reilly y Narciso López.* In the northeast corner of the square is this small neoclassical church finished in 1828 (renovated 1997). A column in front of it marks the spot where the first Mass in Havana was said in 1519 under a ceiba tree. Allegedly, the bones of Columbus reposed in state under its branches before being taken to the Cathedral. A sapling of the same tree, blown down by a hurricane in 1753, was planted on the same spot. This tree was cut down in 1828 to be replaced by the present tree and the Doric temple. Habaneros celebrate the anniversary of the first Mass and the first town council of San Cristóbal de la Habana here every 16 November. It is also the starting point for all guided tours of La Habana Vieja.

Inside El Templete there are paintings by the Frenchman, Juan Bautiste Vermay, a pupil of the Master David and the first director of the Academia Nacional de Bellas Artes, founded in 1818. The paintings in El Templete are his greatest artistic work. They represent the first Mass celebrated on that spot, the first *Cabildo* (local council) and the consecration of the small temple.

South of El Templete on the east side of the Plaza is the small luxury hotel, the **Santa Isabel**.

Museo Nacional de Historia Natural ⓘ *Obispo 61, entre Baratillo y Oficios, Plaza de Armas, T7-863 2687, museo@mnhc.inf. cu, Tue-Sun 0930-1700, also Mon in Jul, Aug, CUC$3, guided visit CUC$4 including children over 5, CUC$1 if they visit the children's hall, camera CUC$2.* In a modern building on the south side of the square you will find lots of stuffed animals, with information (in Spanish) on Cuban bats, butterflies and endemic species. You can find out, for example, that a flock of 50,000 bats eats 200 kg a night, or that there are 87 species of cockroach, two thirds of which are endemic. This is not the most exciting museum, especially if you're Spanish isn't

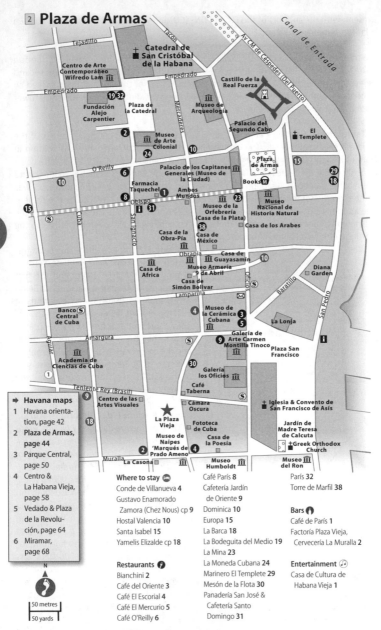

② Plaza de Armas

Catedral de San Cristóbal de la Habana

Centro de Arte Contemporáneo Wifredo Lam

Castillo de la Real Fuerza

Tejadillo

Empedrado

Fundación Alejo Carpentier

Plaza de la Catedral **19 32**

Museo de Arqueología

Palacio del Segundo Cabo

El Templete

Museo de Arte Colonial **2** **24**

O'Reilly **6**

Palacio de los Capitanes Generales (Museo de la Ciudad) **10**

Plaza de Armas

Books

15

29
18

Farmacia Taquechel **1**

Ambos Mundos

Museo de la Orfebrería (Casa de la Plata) **23**

Museo Nacional de Historia Natural

Obispo **8** **i** **31**

Casa de la Obra-Pía

Casa de México **38**

Casa de los Arabes

Casa de Africa

Museo Armería 9 de Abril

Casa de Guayasamín **10**

Diana Garden

Casa de Simón Bolívar

Lamparilla

Banco Central de Cuba

Museo de la Cerámica Cubana **4** **3** **5**

La Lonja

Amargura

Galería de Arte Carmen Montilla Tinoco **9**

Plaza San Francisco

Academia de Ciencias de Cuba **1**

30

Galería los Oficios

Café Taberna

Teniente Rey (Brasil) **9**

Centro de las Artes Visuales **18**

Cámara Oscura

Iglesia & Convento de San Francisco de Asís

★ La Plaza Vieja

Fototeca de Cuba

Jardín de Madre Teresa de Calcuta

Museo de Naipes 'Marqués de Prado Ameno' **2**

Casa de la Poesía **4**

Greek Orthodox Church

Muralla — La Casona

Museo Humboldt

Museo del Ron

N

50 metres
50 yards

Where to stay
Conde de Villanueva **4**
Gustavo Enamorado Zamora (Chez Nous) cp **9**
Hostal Valencia **10**
Santa Isabel **15**
Yamelis Elizalde cp **18**

Restaurants
Bianchini **2**
Café del Oriente **3**
Café El Escorial **4**
Café El Mercurio **5**
Café O'Reilly **6**

Café París **8**
Cafetería Jardín de Oriente **9**
Dominica **10**
Europa **15**
La Barca **18**
La Bodeguita del Medio **19**
La Mina **23**
La Moneda Cubana **24**
Marinero El Templete **29**
Mesón de la Flota **30**
Panadería San José & Cafetería Santo Domingo **31**

París **32**
Torre de Marfil **38**

Bars
Café de París **1**
Factoría Plaza Vieja, Cervecería La Muralla **2**

Entertainment
Casa de Cultura de Habana Vieja **1**

good enough to read the information provided. Outside the museum is a small, second-hand **book market** ⓘ *daily 1000-1700.*

Museo de la Ciudad ⓘ *Tacón 1 entre Obispo y O'Reilly, T7-869 7358, museologia@ patrimonio.ohc.cu, Tue-Sun 0930-1700, CUC$3, guided visit CUC$5.* On the west side of Plaza de Armas is the former **Palacio de los Capitanes Generales**, built in 1780, a charming example of colonial architecture. The Spanish Governors and the Presidents lived here until 1917, when it became the City Hall. It is now the historical museum of the city of Havana. The museum houses a large collection of 19th-century furnishings that illustrate the wealth of the Spanish colonial community, including large 'his and her' shell-shaped baths in marble. There are portraits of patriots, flags, military memorabilia and a grandly laid out dining room. The building was the site of the signing of the 1899 treaty between Spain and the USA. The nation's first flag is here, together with a beautiful sword encrusted with diamonds belonging to Máximo Gómez. There is a curious portrait of Calixto García featuring his unusual wound: he was shot through the neck and the bullet emerged through his forehead. Also on display is the original slave freedom charter signed by Céspedes. The courtyard contains Royal palms, the Cuban national tree. Outside is a statue of the unpopular Ferdinand VII of Spain, with a singularly uncomplimentary plaque. In front of the museum is a collection of church bells.

Plaza de la Catedral and around
La Catedral de San Cristóbal de La Habana ⓘ *Empedrado esq San Ignacio, T7-861 7771. Mon-Fri 0900-1700, Sat, Sun 0900-1200, Mass Mon-Fri 1800 in chapel (entrance on San Ignacio), Sat 1500 in chapel, Sun 1030 in main Cathedral. Cathedral tower CUC$1.* Northwest of the Plaza de Armas is one of Havana's most iconic and beautiful monuments, the Catedral de San Cristóbal de la Habana. Construction of a church on this site was begun by Jesuit missionaries at the beginning of the 18th century. After the Jesuits were expelled in 1767, the church was converted into a cathedral. On either side of the Spanish colonial baroque façade are bell towers: the left one (west) is half as wide as the right (east), which has a grand view.

The church is officially dedicated to the Virgin of the Immaculate Conception, but is better known as the church of Havana's patron saint, San Cristóbal de la Habana or the Columbus cathedral. The bones of Christopher Columbus were sent to this cathedral when Santo Domingo was ceded by Spain to France in 1795; they now lie in Santo Domingo (Dominican Republic). There is much speculation over whether the bones were indeed those of Columbus; they could have been those of his brother or son, but the Dominican Republic is convinced of their authenticity.

Centro de Arte Contemporáneo Wifredo Lam ⓘ *San Ignacio 22, esquina Empedrado, just next to the cathedral, T7-8646282, divulgacion@wlam.cult.cu, free.* The work of Cuba's most famous painter can be seen here, along with changing exhibition programmes that feature mostly Cuban artists but also world masters. Lam directed most of his work to a non-Latin American audience. The building was renovated in 2009 and is a fine exhibition centre.

Opposite is the **Fundación Alejo Carpentier** ⓘ *Empedrado 215 entre Cuba y San Ignacio, T7-8615506, www.fundacioncarpentier.cult.cu, Mon-Fri 0800-1600,* which was the setting for Carpentier's novel *El Siglo de las Luces.* The foundation runs literary courses and there is a small museum of the writer's letters and books. Alejo Carpentier is revered throughout Latin America as the founder of Magical Realism.

BACKGROUND
The development of Havana

Havana was founded in 1519 on its present site at the mouth of a deep bay. In the colonial period, this natural harbour was the assembly point for ships of the annual silver convoy to Spain. Its strategic and commercial importance is reflected in the extensive fortifications, particularly on the east side of the entrance to the bay where there are two large fortresses, El Castillo de los Tres Reyes del Morro, built in 1589-1630, and San Carlos de la Cabaña, built in 1763-1774. On the west side of the canal are the smaller, 16th-century Castillo de la Punta and the Castillo de la Real Fuerza.

The city was prey to pirate attacks as well as being a pawn in European wars. In the 18th century, the British attacked Havana and held it from 1762 to 1763, but exchanged it for Florida. From that point, the city's importance as the gathering place for the silver convoy was superseded by trade. The local planters and merchants had briefly discovered the value of trading their crops with Britain and North America. From the second half of the 18th century to the end of the 19th century, ships came in to Havana carrying slaves, while exports of coffee, tobacco and, most importantly, sugar were the mainstay of the local economy.

From the beginning of the 19th century, the local sugar plantocracy began to move out of the walled city to build neocolonial villas or country estates in what are now the municipalities of Cerro, 10 de Octubre and the high part of Marianao. By the 1850s, the city walls had more or less collapsed and the Prado was absorbed into the old city instead of running outside its walls. The city expanded westwards from the 1870s onwards; the rise of Vedado reached its high point in the 1920s, when neoclassical, romantic and art nouveau villas with internal courtyards vied with each other for luxury and originality. The Colón cemetery reflects this bourgeois competitiveness.

By 1918, Miramar, on the western outskirts across the Río Almendares, now Playa municipality, began to take over as the salon of the city, with beach resorts, exclusive seaside clubs and, of course, casinos. Many wealthy Miramar residences are today occupied by embassies and government buildings, but there are also many abandoned villas. Major developments took place after the two World Wars, including the extension of Nuevo Vedado and the construction of high-rise buildings

Museo de Arte Colonial ① *San Ignacio 61, Plaza de la Catedral, T7-862 6440, colonial@ patrimonio.ohc.cu, Tue-Sun 0930-1700, CUC$3, guide CUC$5 including use of camera and video.* In the former Palacio de los Condes de Casa Bayona is the exquisite colonial art museum, with exhibits of colonial furniture and other items, plus a section on stained glass.

Museo de Arqueología ① *Tacón 12 entre O'Reilly y Empedrado, T7-861 4469, tony@ patrimonio.ohc.cu, Tue-Sat 0900-1700, Sun 0930-1300, CUC$1, CUC$2 with guide, CUC$15 to use video camera.* East of Plaza de la Catedral, the museum has displays on colonial archaeology uncovered during excavation works in La Habana Vieja and the bay. Exhibits feature Cuban and Peruvian aboriginal artefacts. The house was built in the 17th century but redesigned in 1725 by Juana Carvajal, a freed slave who inherited the building from her owner, Lorenza Carvajal. It was further expanded by the Calvo de la Puerta family, who like the Focsa and the Hotel Nacional. The sea was regarded as a threat during most of Havana's history and only became an asset in the 20th century. The Malecón seafront drive was built in 1901, the tunnel to Miramar (replacing a bridge) in 1950, and the tunnel leading to Playas del Este, on the other side of the bay, in 1958.

After the Revolution, construction moved away from Havana to the rest of the country, which had been largely forgotten in preceding decades. However, new neighbourhoods were built in the east of the city in an attempt to improve living conditions. Both the Camilo Cienfuegos barrio, dating from 1961, and Alamar, from 1970, were built by microbrigades, with citizens helping to build their own apartments, schools and clinics. The decades since construction have taken their toll, however, and the tropical climate and sea winds have eaten into the concrete and metal structures, leaving these districts looking run down and depressed.

Contemporary Havana

Before the Revolution, Havana was the largest, the most beautiful and the most sumptuous city in the Caribbean. Today, it is rather run down and the weather has wreaked havoc on both pre- and post-Revolution buildings. Thanks to the government's policy of developing the countryside, it is not ringed with shanty towns like so many other Latin American capitals, although some reappeared in the 1990s. Nevertheless, the city is shabby and visitors are often taken by surprise by living conditions. Half the people live in housing officially regarded as sub-standard, and many buildings are shored up by wooden planks. In fact, thanks to renovation projects, the ancient palaces, colonnades, churches and monasteries are now in considerably better shape than the newer housing developments.

The old city is a United Nations World Heritage Site. Priorities include the restoration of the historic centre, under the auspices of UNESCO and the City Historian's Office, whose brief it is to rebuild communities in the widest sense of the word, with income from cultural tourism and aid from European NGOs. Restoration will encompass the Malecón, starting from the historic centre, where housing has been badly affected by salination and sea damage, and the Bosque de la Habana, crossed by the Río Almendares, now suffering from pollution and contamination, which is a potentially rich green belt, extending over several kilometres.

acquired it in 1748. In 1988 it was restored and converted into a museum. Just outside, on the corner of Tacón and Oficios, is an archaeological excavation site, dug in 2006, with photos of the artefacts discovered there.

Castillo de la Punta and northern Habana Vieja

Castillo de la Punta ① *Av del Puerto y Paseo del Prado*. Built at the end of the 16th century at the northernmost part of the old city to protect the entrance to the harbour, the Castillo del la Punta is a squat building with 2.5-m-thick walls. There are three permanent exhibition rooms covering the history of the castle, naval design and construction and marine archaeology, although the whole building was still closed for repairs in late 2015. On the seafront plaza in front of La Punta are metal floor plans of the local fortresses with numbers and a key. Opposite the fortress, across the Malecón, is the **monument to Máximo Gómez**, the independence leader.

The **Policía Nacional Revolucionario Comandancia General** is in another fortress in the block bounded by Cuba, Chacón, Cuarteles and San Ignacio. It is not open to the public but if you want to visit you can go to the offices of the **Centro Provincial de Selección PNR** ① *Tulipán y Boyeros, Mon-Fri 0830-1700*, to get permission.

Tip...
There are two other old forts in Havana: **Atarés**, finished in 1763, on a hill overlooking the southwest end of the harbour; and **El Príncipe**, on a hill at the far end of Avenida Independencia (Avenida Rancho Boyeros), built 1774-1794, now the city jail. The finest view in Havana is from this hill.

The Church of El Santo Angel Custodio ① *Compostela 2 esq Cuarteles, T7-8610469, Mon-Fri 0900-1730, Sun 0830-1130, Mass Tue-Thu 1700, Mon, Fri, Sun 0900, currently being repaired*. The Church of El Santo Angel Custodio was built by the Jesuits in 1689 on the slight elevation of **Peña Pobre**, with the tower added in 1704. The original church was largely destroyed by a hurricane in 1846 but was restored and became the parish church in 1852. It was rebuilt and enlarged in its present neo-Gothic style in 1868-1870. It has white, laced Gothic towers and 10 tiny chapels, no more than kneeling places, the best of which is behind the high altar. There is some interesting stained glass depicting *conquistadores*. During the Christmas period an impressive Nativity scene is placed at the entrance. Famous people baptized here include José Martí in 1853, Amelia Goire (La Milagrosa), Alicia Alonso and Julián del Casal. It is also the setting for the last chapter of the novel *Cecilia Valdés*, see Literature, page 424.

Museo de la Revolución
Refugio entre Monserrate y Zulueta, facing Av de las Misiones, T7-8624091/6, daily 0900-1600, CUC$8, guide CUC$2. Allow several hours, explanations are mostly in Spanish.

This huge, ornate building, topped by a dome, was once the Presidential Palace, but now contains the Museo de la Revolución. The history of Cuban political development is charted, from the slave uprisings to joint space missions with the ex-Soviet Union. The liveliest section displays the final battles against Batista's troops, with excellent photographs and some bizarre personal mementoes. The yacht *Granma*, from which Fidel Castro disembarked with his companions in 1956 to launch the Revolution, has been installed in the park facing the south entrance, surrounded by planes, tanks and other vehicles involved, as well as a Soviet-built tank used against the Bay of Pigs invasion and a fragment from a US spy plane shot down in the 1970s. Allow several hours to see it all.

★ Museo Nacional Palacio de Bellas Artes

T7-861 5777/863 9484, www.museonacional.cult.cu. Tue-Sat 0900-1700, Sun 1000-1400. Single museum ticket CUC$5 for foreigners, day pass to both museums CUC$8 (CUP$5 for Cubans), children under 13 free, accredited art students free, guide CUC$2 by prior reservation (T7-8639484 ext 105). No photography permitted in the galleries. Both museums have shops selling books, art and souvenirs.

This impressively extended museum has two separate buildings: the original 1954 Fine Arts Palace on Trocadero, which houses the Cuban art collection (Arte Cubano) from colonial times to the 1990s, including a section on the post-Revolution Art Schools; and the former Centro Asturiano, two blocks away on the east side of Parque Central, housing European and international art and ancient artefacts (Arte Universal). This is a truly spectacular museum and well worth a look

Arte Cubano ① *Trocadero entre Zulueta y Monserrate.* Cuban paintings include the 20th-century painter Victor Manuel's *Gitana Tropical*, considered an important symbol of the Cuban vanguard. There are masterpieces by José Nicolás de la Escalera and Victor Patricio Landaluze from the colonial period and representations of modern-era Cuban paintings from Wifredo Lam and René Portocarrero. Exhibited works of more recent Cuban artists include those of Roberto Fabelo and Zaida del Río and some artists who have left the country. Start on the third floor with the colonial art and work your way down to the present day. On the ground floor there are also temporary exhibitions, a small shop and toilets.

Arte Universal ① *Centro Asturiano, San Rafael entre Zulueta y Monserrate.* On the east side of Parque Central, the older building was designed by the Spanish architect Manuel del Busto in the early 20th century and was fabulously renovated at the turn of the millennium (at an estimated cost of CUC$14.5 million) with huge marble staircases giving access to five floors. The large collection of European paintings, from the 16th century to the present, contains works by Gainsborough, Van Dyck, Velázquez, Tintoretto, Degas et al. One painting by Canaletto, *Chelsea from the Thames*, in the Italian room on the fifth floor, is in fact only half a painting; the other half of the 18th-century painting is owned by the National Trust in Britain and hangs in Blickling Hall, Norfolk. It is believed to have been commissioned in 1746-1748 by the Chelsea Hospital, which is featured in the Cuban half, but the artist was unable to sell it and cut it in two just before he died in 1768. The left half was sold to the 11th Marquis of Lothian, whose family owned Blickling Hall, where it has stayed ever since. The right half was bought and sold several times until it ended up with a Cuban collector, Oscar Cinetas, who donated it to the museum before the Revolution.

A full-size photograph of the Blickling section of the panorama is now on display next to the Cuban section and a complete digital image of the two pieces has been shown at Blickling Hall.

The museum also has Greek, Roman, Egyptian and Etruscan sculpture and artefacts, many very impressive. The unharmed Greek amphora from the fifth century BC is considered remarkable.

> **Tip...**
> Between the two galleries on Avenida de las Misiones, between Empedrado and San Juan Dios, is the wonderful art deco former Bacardí building, topped by its signature bat. A great view of it can be appreciated from the roof terrace of the Hotel Plaza.

Additionally, there are rooms dedicated to Latin American art and 18th- and 19th-century paintings from the United States.

Among the museum's holdings are private collections left behind by rich Cuban families (including the Bacardí and Gómez Mena families and members of Batista's government) who fled Cuba soon after the 1959 Revolution. These include works by Spanish masters Sorolla and Zurbarán. However, it is rumoured that some of these collections were sold by the Cuban government during the economic crisis of the Special Period.

Parque Central

This is a very pleasant park with a monument to **José Martí** in the centre. The north side is entirely occupied by the **Iberostar Parque Central**, while the **Hotel Plaza** is in the northeast corner. On its west side are the **Hotel Telégrafo** and the historic **Hotel Inglaterra**, which celebrated its 125th anniversary in 2000. Now a National Monument, it has had many famous former foreign guests over the decades, including Sarah Bernhardt in 1887, General Antonio Maceo (one of the heroes of the Cuban Wars of Independence) in 1890, and the authors Federico García Lorca and Rubén Darío in 1910. Next door, the **Gran Teatro**, a beautiful neo-baroque monument dating from 1838, reopened on New Year's Day 2016 after three years' closure with a performance of *Giselle* by Ballet Nacional de Cuba. It is now known as the **Gran Teatro de la Habana Alicia Alonso**. It is used by the National Opera and National Ballet and also houses the Teatro García Lorca, where Sarah Bernhardt once performed when it was called the Teatro Tacón. José Martí wrote of her performance, "Sarah is flexible, delicate, svelte. When she is not shaken by the demon of tragedy, her body is full of grace and abandon, when the demon takes her over, she is full of power and nobility… Where does she come from? From poverty! Where is she going? To glory!"

3 Parque Central

Capitolio and around

*Paseo de Martí entre San Martín y Dragones.
Closed for renovation.*

South of the Parque Central, the Capitolio was built in the style of the US Capitol in Washington DC in 1929-1932 by the dictator Machado in an attempt to impress his US paymasters with his loyalty. The white dome over a rotunda is 62 m high, and inside is a 17-m statue of Jupiter, representing the state. This is the tallest

N

400 metres
400 yards

Where to stay
Iberostar Parque Central **11**
Saratoga **16**

Restaurants
A Prado y Neptuno **1**
El Castillo de Farnés **13**
El Floridita **14**
Hanoi **17**
La Piña de Plata **25**
Los Nardos **28**
Pastelería Francesa **33**

Bars
Bar Monserrate **4**
Casa del Escabeche **7**

⇒ **Havana maps**
1 Havana orientation, page 42
2 Plaza de Armas, page 44
3 **Parque Central, page 50**
4 Centro & La Habana Vieja, page 58
5 Vedado & Plaza de la Revolución, page 64
6 Miramar, page 68

interior statue in Latin America and the third largest in the world. A 24-carat diamond (or is it a fake?) is set into the centre of the floor in the entrance hall to pinpoint zero for all distance measurements in Cuba. The interior has large halls and stately staircases, all most sumptuously decorated.

The Capitol was initially used as the seat of parliament with the Senate and the House of Representatives meeting there, but these were dissolved after the Revolution. More recently it housed the Cuban Academy of Sciences and the National Library of Science and Technology.

South of the Capitolio, and landscaped to show off the building to the best effect, is the **Parque Fraternidad**. It was originally called Parque de Colón, but was renamed to mark the VI Panamerican Conference in 1892. At its centre is a ceiba tree growing in soil provided by each of the American republics. Also in the park is a famous statue, sculpted in 1837, of La Noble Habana, the Amerindian woman who first welcomed the Spaniards.

There is still a cigar shop near the Capitolio at the former site of the **Partagas cigar factory** ① *Industria entre Dragones y Barcelona, T7-8668060, Mon-Sat 0900-1900*, where you can buy rum, cigars and coffee, but the factory itself has moved (see Centro, below).

Calle Obispo and Calle Obrapía

From the Parque Central you can walk back to the Plaza de Armas along Calle Obispo, now closed to traffic and one of the streets of La Habana Vieja which has seen most restoration, with many shops lovingly restored to their former splendour. There is a small **handicrafts market** on Obispo between Aguacate and Compostela, where they sell leather goods, clothes, ceramics and jewellery. Avoid buying coral, which is protected internationally. Sundays are particularly busy. Calle Obrapía, which runs parallel, has some magnificent colonial buildings, many of which are now museums and galleries.

The **Museo Numismático** ① *Obispo 305 entre Aguiar y Habana, T7-861 5811, numismatica@patrimonio.ohc.cu, Tue-Sat 0930-1730, Sun 0930-1300, CUC$1, cameras with permission*, is a coin museum which exhibits and sells coins, medals and documentation. The extensive collection of more than 1000 pieces, including rare notes and valuable cold coins, dates from the colonial period up to the Revolution.

Farmacia Taquechel ① *Obispo 155 entre Mercaderes y San Ignacio, T7-862 9286*, displays all manner of herbs, remedies and concoctions stored in porcelain jars, glazed and gilded with herbal motifs and meticulously arranged on floor-to-ceiling polished mahogany shelves. The original 1896 building was the workplace of Francisco Taquechel Mirabal.

Just west of the Plaza de Armas, the **Museo de la Orfebrería (Casa de la Plata)** ① *Obispo 113 entre Mercaderes y Oficios, T7-8639861, plata@patrimonio.ohc.cu, Tue-Sat 0930-1700, Sun 0900-1300, CUC$1, guide CUC$2,* has a silverware collection and old frescoes on the upper floor.

Head south on Oficios to reach the **Casa de los Arabes** ① *Oficios 16 entre Obispo and Obrapía, T7-861 5868, arabes@patrimonio.ohc.cu, Tue-Sat 0900-1700, Sun 0900-1300, free, donations welcome*, in a lovely building built in Mudéjar style with vines trained over the courtyard for shade. The collection includes a mosque, jewels, Saharan robes, gold- and silver-painted weapons and rugs.

West of here are a cluster of museums on Obrapía. **Casa de México** ① *Obrapía 116 entre Mercaderes y Oficios, T7-861 8166, mexico@patrimonio.ohc.cu, Tue-Sat 0930-1645, Sun 0930-1245,* also called **La Casa de Benemérito de las Américas Benito Juárez**, is more of a cultural centre than a museum, housed in a pink building draped with the Mexican flag. Exhibits include pre-Columbian artefacts and popular arts and crafts including ceramics from Jalisco.

Works donated to Cuba by the late Ecuadorean artist Oswaldo Guayasamín are displayed at the **Casa de Guayasamín** ① *Obrapía 111 entre Mercaderes y Oficios T7-861 3843, guayasamin@patrimonio.ohc.cu, Tue-Sat 0930-1700, Sun 0900-1300, donations welcome*. Exhibits are, generally, paintings, sculpture and silkscreens, but there are occasionally other exhibitions. Guayasamín painted a famous portrait of Fidel Castro.

On 9 April 1958 a group of revolutionaries of the Movimiento 26 de Julio attacked the business of Compañía Armera de Cuba on Mercaderes between Obrapía and Lamparilla. They were unsuccessful and four members of the group were killed. After the Revolution, the site was declared a National Monument in their honour and on 9 April 1971 it became a museum. The **Museo Armería 9 de Abril** ① *Mercaderes entre Obrapía y Lamparilla, T7-861 8080, armeria@patrimonio.ohc.cu, Tue-Sat 0930-1700, Sun 0930-1300*, recreates the original business at the front, with some contemporary pieces, hunting and fishing accessories, including the collection of arms that Castro donated in the 1990s. At the back there is an exhibition on the events that took place there in 1958.

The **Casa de Simón Bolívar** ① *Mercaderes 156 entre Obrapía y Lamparilla, T7-861 3998, bolivar@patrimonio.ohc.cu, Tue-Sat 0930-1700, Sun 0930-1230, free, donations welcome*, contains exhibits about the life of the South American liberator and some Venezuelan art.

Casa de la Obra-Pía ① *Obrapía 158 entre Mercaderes y San Ignacio, T7-861 3097, obrapia@patrimonio.ohc.cu, Tue-Sat 0930-1630, Sun 0930-1230, no entry fee but donations welcome, photos free*, is a furniture museum, with examples from the 18th and 19th centuries, housed in a yellow building. It was built in 1665, then remodelled in 1793 by the Marqués de Cárdenas de Monte Hermoso, whose shield is over the door. The portico was made in Cádiz in 1793, but finished off in Havana. The building was restored in 1983.

The **Casa de Africa** ① *Obrapía 157 entre San Ignacio y Mercaderes, T7-861 5798, africa@patrimonio.ohc.cu, Tue-Sat 0900-1700, Sun 0900-1300, free*, is a small gallery of carved wooden artefacts and handmade costumes. Sculpture, furniture, paintings and ceramics from sub-Saharan Africa are on display, including gifts given to Fidel by visiting African Presidents. There is also an exhibit of elements of African-Cuban religions.

Plaza San Francisco and around

Calle Oficios runs south of the Plaza de Armas to the Plaza San Francisco, dominated by the **Iglesia y Convento de San Francisco de Asís** ① *Oficios entre Amargura y Churruca, T7-866 3638, sanfrancisco@patrimonio.ohc.cu, Tue-Sat 0930-1730, Sun 0930-1300, CUC$2 for museum and* campanario *(bell tower), guide CUC$3*. Built in 1608 and reconstructed in 1730, this is a massive, sombre edifice suggesting defence, rather than worship. The three-storey bell tower was both a landmark for returning voyagers and a lookout for pirates and has stunning views of the city and port. The **Basílica Menor de San Francisco de Asís** is now a concert hall (basilicamenor@patrimonio.ohc.cu, tickets for concerts are sold three days in advance) and the convent is a museum containing religious pieces. Restoration work continues. Most of the treasures were removed by the government and some are in museums.

The sculpture outside the church is of the eccentric *El Caballero de París* (Gentleman from Paris). The legendary vagrant with a deluded sense of grandeur was notorious throughout the city and affectionately embraced by Habaneros. He died in 1985 in Havana's psychiatric hospital. The sculpture was the work of José Villa who was also responsible for the John Lennon monument in Vedado, see page 67.

At the southern end of Plaza San Francisco, behind the church and convent, is the **Jardín de Madre Teresa de Calcuta** (Mother Teresa's Garden), and at the end of the garden is the Greek Orthodox Church.

Opposite San Francisco on the west side of the square, Nelson Domínguez, one of Cuba's most respected and prolific contemporary artists, has his own studio/gallery at the **Galería Los Oficios** ① *Oficios 166 entre Amargura y Teniente Rey, T7-863 0497, daily 1000-1700*. Working in various mediums, he is primarily influenced by the natural environment and draws heavily on indigenous and spiritual symbolism. There are several other artists' galleries in this area, such as **Galería de Arte Carmen Montilla Tinoco** ① *Oficios 162 entre Amargura y Teniente Rey, T7-866 8768, Tue-Sat 0930-1700, Sun 0930-1300*, housed in an early 18th-century building. It was originally used as a shop below and dwelling above, then briefly as the Consulate of Paraguay at the beginning of the 20th century, but it was ruined by fire in the 1980s. The **Oficina del Historiador**, with the help of the Venezuelan artist, restored it and opened it as an art gallery in her name in 1994. Nearby to the west is the **Museo de la Cerámica Cubana** ① *Amargura y Mercaderes, T7-861 6130, ceramica@ patrimonio.ohc.cu, Tue-Sat 0930-1700, Sun 0930-1300, free*, displaying Cuban ceramic art dating from the 1940s onwards.

On the northwest corner of the square, the Corinthian white marble building was once the **legislative building** where the House of Representatives met before the Capitolio was built. To the east, the newly restored Cuban Stock Exchange building, **La Lonja** (on the corner of Oficios and Plaza San Francisco de Asís), is worth a look, as is the new cruise ship terminal opposite.

Just north of the square, the British Embassy financed the construction of the **Diana Garden** ① *Baratillo, near Plaza San Francisco, daily 0700-1900*, in memory of Diana, Princess of Wales. It is dominated by a concrete tube covered in ceramics in the shape of liquorice all-sorts which don't reach to the top, symbolizing a life cut short. There is also a sculpture of the sun, representing the happiness in her life, but one triangle is missing, her heart. Around the base of the pole are rings for sadness.

Museo del Ron ① *Av del Puerto 262 entre Sol y Muralla, T7-861 8051, www.havana clubfoundation.com, Mon-Thu 0900-1700, Fri-Sun 0900-1600, CUC$7, includes a drink, under 15s free, multilingual guides included*. Southeast of Plaza San Francisco, the **Fundación Destilería Havana Club** has a museum that explains the production of rum, from the sugar cane plantation to the processing and bottling, with machinery dating from the early 20th century. The museum is well laid out, dark and atmospheric. There is a wonderful model railway which runs round a model sugar mill and distillery, designed and made by prize-winning Lázaro Eduardo García Driggs in 1993-1994 and restored in 1999-2000. At the end of the tour you get a tasting of a six-year old **Havana Club** rum in a bar that is a mock-up of the once-famous **Sloppy Joe's**. There is also a restaurant and bar next door, a shop and an art gallery where present-day Cuban artists exhibit their work.

Museo Humboldt ① *Oficios 254, esquina Muralla, closed for repairs in 2015*. The great explorer and botanist Federico Enrique Alejandro von Humboldt (1769-1857) lived here at the beginning of 1801 when he completed his calculations of the meridian of the city. His home is now a museum. Humboldt travelled extensively in Central and South America, paving the way for Darwin, who called him the greatest naturalist of his time. His scientific works were not confined merely to plants. His name has been given to the cold current that flows northwards off the coast of Chile and Peru, which he discovered and measured. He also made important contributions to world meteorology, to the study of vulcanism and the earth's crust and to the connection between climate and flora. In the process he discovered that mountain sickness is caused by a lack of oxygen at high altitudes. The last years of his life were spent writing *Kosmos*, an account of his scientific findings, which was soon translated into many languages.

Nearby, is the **Casa de la Poesía** ⓘ *Muralla 63 entre Oficios e Inquisidor, T7-862 1801, poeta@patrimonio.ohc.cu, Mon-Sat 0830-1730.*

★ La Plaza Vieja and around

This 18th-century plaza has been restored as part of a joint project by UNESCO and **Habaguanex**, a state company responsible for the restoration and revival of La Habana Vieja. The large square has a fountain in the middle and is overlooked by elegant balconies on many of the buildings.

The former house of the Spanish Captain General Conde de Ricla, who retook Havana from the English and restored power to Spain in 1763, can be seen on the corner of San Ignacio and Muralla. Known as **La Casona** ⓘ *Centro de Arte La Casona, Muralla 107 esq San Ignacio, T7-861 8544, www.galeriascubanas.com, Tue-Sat 1000-1730,* it is a beautiful blue and white building with friezes up the staircase and along the walls and trailing plants in the courtyard. There is a great view of the plaza from the balcony, but in 2015 the upper floor was closed for repairs and restoration works. The Galería Diago displays naïf art and has a shop selling books, cards, catalogues, prints and art reproductions. On the south side there is also a museum of playing cards, **Museo de Naipes 'Marqués de Prado Ameno'** ⓘ *Muralla 101 esq Inquisidor, T7-860 1534, naipes@patrimonio.ohc.cu, Tue-Sat 0930-1700, Sun 0930-1300.*

On the west side of the Plaza is the hugely popular microbrewery, **Cervecería La Muralla** (see page 86) and the **Centro de las Artes Visuales** ⓘ *San Ignacio 352 entre Teniente Rey y Muralla, T7-862 5279, Tue-Sat 1000-1700,* which has a variety of art exhibitions. There are two galleries, Siglo XXI and Escuela de Plata.

On the north side of the square, on Teniente Rey, is a posh and expensive restaurant, **Santo Angel**, which has tables outside and is a pleasant place for an evening cocktail. In the northeast corner (Mercaderes y Teniente Rey) is the **Café Taberna** (T7-861 1637), the first coffeehouse to be established in Havana by the English, after they took the city in 1762. The café was named after its owner, Juan Bautista de Taberna. It remained in operation until the 1940s and was known as a place where merchant traders congregated. It was reopened in 1999 as a Benny Moré theme restaurant. Unfortunately the food is nothing special, rather greasy, and the service is poor.

On the top floor of the Gómez Vila building is the **Cámara Oscura** ⓘ *Teniente Rey esq Mercaderes, Plaza Vieja, T7-866 4461, Tue-Sun 0930-1715, CUC$3, free for under 12s, presentations every 20 mins,* where lenses and mirrors provide you with a panoramic view of the city. Donated by Cádiz, this camera obscura is the first in the Americas and one of few in the world: there are two in England, two in Spain and one in Portugal.

In one of the converted mansions on the east side, the **Fototeca de Cuba** ⓘ *Mercaderes 307 entre Teniente Rey y Muralla, T7-862 2530, Mon-Sat 1000-1700,* showcases international photography exhibitions. The old post office, also on the east side, dates from 1909.

Academia de Ciencias de Cuba ⓘ *Cuba 460 entre Amargura y Brasil, T7-863 4824, closed for long-term renovations in 2015.* Housed in a strikingly ornate building northwest of the plaza, the museum contains displays about science in Cuba, the history of the Academy of Sciences and exhibits on the role of the medical profession during the Wars of Independence. It was previously known as the **Museo Histórico de las Ciencias Carlos J Finlay** after the eminent Cuban doctor who discovered that the mosquito was the vector of yellow fever in the late 19th century and helped to eradicate the disease in Cuba.

Convento de Santa Clara ⓘ *Cuba 610 entre Luz y Sol, closed for repairs*. The convent of Santa Clara was founded in 1644 by nuns from Cartagena in Colombia. It was in use as a convent until 1919, when the nuns sold the building. In a shady business deal it was later acquired by the government and, after radical alterations, it became offices for the Ministry of Public Works until the decision was made to restore the building to its former glory. Work began in 1982, with the creation of the **Centro Nacional de Conservación, Restauración y Museología** (CENCREM), and is still continuing. The convent occupies four small blocks in La Habana Vieja, bounded by Calles Habana, Sol, Cuba and Luz, and originally had three cloisters and an orchard.

Southern Habana Vieja

The area is rather off the beaten track. Renovation works have not yet spread this far south, so it looks scruffy, and some people find it intimidating. It is much more a residential area than a tourist attraction, and, while there are plenty of churches, you won't find the museums and palaces typical of the northern part of the old city.

Opposite the central railway station, the **Museo Casa Natal de José Martí** ⓘ *Leonor Pérez 314 entre Picota y Egido, T7-861 5095, nataljmarti@patrimonio.ohc.cu, Tue-Sat 0930-1700, Sun 0930-1300, CUC$2, guided tour CUC$3*, is the birthplace of the country's great hero (see box, page 426), with his full life story documented with photos, mementoes, furniture and papers. The tiny house has been devoted to his memory since a plaque was first put on the wall in 1899; it's been a museum since 1925 and was restored in 1952-1953.

Another attraction in the southern part of Old Havana is the vintage car museum, **Depósito de Automóviles** ⓘ *Desamparados (Av del Puerto) y Damas, T7-863 9942, automovil@patrimonio.ohc.cu, Tue-Sat 0930-1700, Sun 0930-1300, CUC$2, guided tour CUC$5*, which lovingly presents vehicles from the 19th and 20th centuries. There are a great many museum pieces including pre-Revolution US models, which are still on the road especially outside Havana, in among the Ladas, VWs and Nissans.

The church of **San Francisco de Paula** is on a traffic island on Avenida del Puerto (Desamparados). On the bay side of the road you will see some fine old steam engines, which have been put to rest outside the renovated warehouse, Almacenes San José. This is now the main handicrafts market in Havana (see Shopping, page 95), attracting coachloads of tourists to buy their souvenirs. There are hundreds of stalls where you can bargain for a good price and a waterfront café where you can get a drink overlooking the docks. Next door is another old warehouse, **Antiguo Almacén de la Madera y el Tabaco**, which has been converted into a microbrewery and restaurant/snack bar (see page 85).

two massive fortresses guard the entrance to the bay and afford lovely views of the city

From near the fortress of La Punta in the old city, a tunnel built in 1958 by the French runs east under the mouth of the harbour; it emerges in the rocky ground between the Castillo del Morro and the fort of La Cabaña, some 550 m away, where a 5-km highway connects with the Havana–Matanzas road.

Castillo del Morro
Ctra de la Cabaña, T7-8619727. Daily 0900-1900. CUC$6 plus CUC$1 for the guide, CUC$2 for the lighthouse (currently closed), children under 6 free, children 6-11 CUC$4. No charge for photos.

The Castillo del Morro (El Castillo de los Tres Reyes) was built between 1589 and 1630, with a 20-m moat, but has been much altered. It stands on a bold headland with the best view of Havana and is illuminated at night. It was one of the major fortifications built to protect the natural harbour and the assembly of Spain's silver fleets from pirate attack. The flash of its lighthouse, built in 1844, is visible 30 km out to sea. It now serves as a museum with a good exhibition of Cuban history since the arrival of Columbus.

On the harbourside, down by the water, is the **Battery of the 12 Apostles**, each gun being named after an Apostle. There is a bar here, open Monday to Saturday 1200-1900, which is worth a visit for the views of the harbour and the whole of Havana.

Fortaleza de San Carlos de Cabaña
T7-7911233. Daily 1000-2200, CUC$6, plus CUC$2 for cannon-firing ceremony 1800-2200. No charge for camera or video. Access as for Castillo del Morro, see above.

It is believed that around 1590, the military engineer Juan Bautista Antonelli, who built La Punta and El Morro, walked up La Cabaña hill and declared that "he who is master of this hill will be master of Havana." His prophecy was proved correct two centuries later when the English attacked Havana, conquering La Cabaña and thereby gaining control of the port. In 1763, after the English withdrew, another military engineer, Silvestre Abarca, arrived with a plan to build a fortress there. Construction lasted until 1774, when the fortress (the largest the Spanish had built until then in the Americas) was named San Carlos de la Cabaña, in honour of the king of Spain. It has a solid vertical wall of about 700 m with a deep moat connected to that of El Morro. The ditch is 12 m deep on the landward side and there is a drawbridge to the main entrance. From its position on the hill it dominates the city, the bay and the entrance to the harbour. In its heyday it had 120 cannon.

Essential Casablanca

Finding your feet

To cross the bay to Casablanca, join the left-hand ferry queue at Muelle Luz, opposite Calle Santa Clara. Security is very tight here since a ferry was hijacked in 2003 for an abortive attempt to get to Miami. Everybody is searched and there are metal detectors. The ferry crossing costs 10 centavos. Access to the Castillo del Morro is from any bus going through the tunnel (40 centavos or 1 peso): board at San Lázaro and Avenida del Puerto and get off at the stop after the tunnel, cross the road and follow the path up to the left. Alternatively, take the **HabanaBusTour** or a taxi, or it's a 20-minute walk from the Fortaleza de San Carlos de la Cabaña.

Inside are **Los Fosos de los Laureles**, where political prisoners were shot during the Cuban fight for independence. On 3 January 1959, Che Guevara took possession of the fortress on his triumphant arrival in Havana after the flight of the

Tip...
You can walk from the Christ statue to the Fortaleza in 10 minutes and then, from there, on to the Castillo del Morro.

dictator, Batista. Every night the cannon are fired in an historical ceremony recalling the closure of the city walls to protect the city from attack by pirates. In the 17th century the shot was fired from a naval ship in the harbour, but now it is fired from La Cabaña at 2100 on the dot by soldiers in 18th-century uniforms, with the ceremony starting at 2045. There are two museums here, one about Che Guevara and another about fortresses with pictures and models, some old weapons and a replica of a large catapult and battering ram from the 16th to 18th centuries.

Other sights in Casablanca

Casablanca is also the site of a statue of a very human-looking Jesus Christ, erected in white marble during the Batista dictatorship as a pacifying exercise. To get there from the ferry dock, go up a steep, twisting flight of stone steps, starting on the other side of the plaza. You can get a good view of the harbour and Havana's skyline from **Parque El Cristo**, particularly at night, but be careful not to miss the last ferry back. Also in Casablanca you will find the **National Observatory** and the old railway station for the **Hershey line** trains to Matanzas.

Centro *Colour map 1, A5.*

ornate but crumbling 19th-century buildings

The state of the buildings in Centro Habana can be a shock to the first-time visitor; some streets resemble a war zone, with piles of rubble and holes like craters on the streets and pavements. Centro is not a tourist attraction, although many visitors end up staying here in one of the many *casas particulares*, conveniently placed between the architectural and historical attractions of La Habana Vieja and the nightlife of Vedado.

Centro is separated from La Habana Vieja by the Prado (although we have included those buildings on the west side of the avenue in the old city text, above). Centro's main artery is Calle San Rafael, which runs west from the Parque Central and is initially closed to traffic. This was Havana's 19th-century retail playground but today is spliced by ramshackle streets strewn with rubble and lined with decrepit houses. To the north, Centro is bounded by the seafront drive, the Malecón, which is in a dire state of repair because of buffeting sea winds, although renovation is underway in parts.

Barrio Chino

At the cross-section of Amistad and Dragones stands the gateway to Barrio Chino, a Cuban-Chinese hybrid. In its pre-Revolutionary heyday, this 10-block zone, pivoting around the Cuchillo de Zanja, was full of sordid porn theatres and steamy brothels. Now, a handful of restaurants strewn with lanterns, a colourful food market and a smattering of Chinese associations are all that remains of what was formerly the largest Chinatown in Latin America.

④ Centro & La Habana Vieja

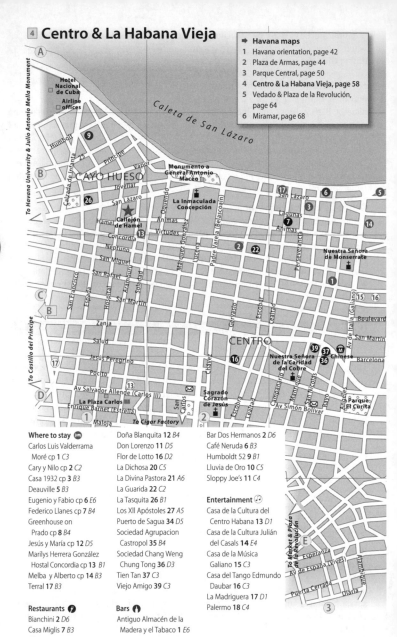

➡ **Havana maps**
1 Havana orientation, page 42
2 Plaza de Armas, page 44
3 Parque Central, page 50
4 **Centro & La Habana Vieja, page 58**
5 Vedado & Plaza de la Revolución, page 64
6 Miramar, page 68

Where to stay 🛏
Carlos Luis Valderrama
  Moré cp **1** *C3*
Cary y Nilo cp **2** *C2*
Casa 1932 cp **3** *B3*
Deauville **5** *B3*
Eugenio y Fabio cp **6** *E6*
Federico Llanes cp **7** *B4*
Greenhouse on
  Prado cp **8** *B4*
Jesús y María cp **12** *D5*
Marilys Herrera González
  Hostal Concordia cp **13** *B1*
Melba y Alberto cp **14** *B3*
Terral **17** *B3*

Doña Blanquita **12** *B4*
Don Lorenzo **11** *D5*
Flor de Lotto **16** *D2*
La Dichosa **20** *C5*
La Divina Pastora **21** *A6*
La Guarida **22** *C2*
La Tasquita **26** *B1*
Los XII Apóstoles **27** *A5*
Puerto de Sagua **34** *D5*
Sociedad Agrupacion
  Castropol **35** *B4*
Sociedad Chang Weng
  Chung Tong **36** *D3*
Tien Tan **37** *C3*
Viejo Amigo **39** *C3*

Restaurants 🍴
Bianchini **2** *D6*
Casa Miglis **7** *B3*

Bars 🍸
Antiguo Almacén de la
  Madera y el Tabaco **1** *E6*
Bar Dos Hermanos **2** *D6*
Café Neruda **6** *B3*
Humboldt 52 **9** *B1*
Lluvia de Oro **10** *C5*
Sloppy Joe's **11** *C4*

Entertainment 🎭
Casa de la Cultura del
  Centro Habana **13** *D1*
Casa de la Cultura Julián
  del Casals **14** *E4*
Casa de la Música
  Galiano **15** *C3*
Casa del Tango Edmundo
  Daubar **16** *C3*
La Madriguera **17** *D1*
Palermo **18** *C4*

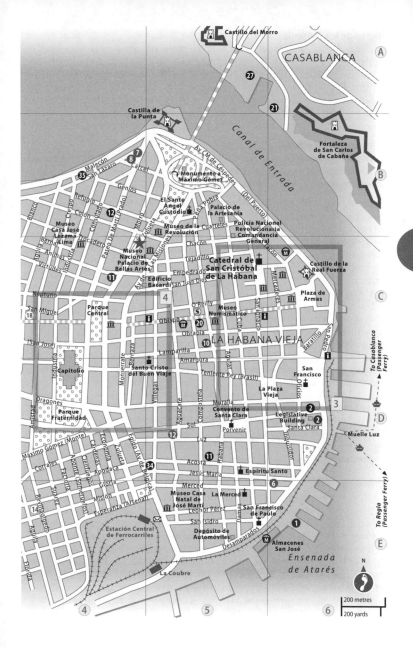

Castillo del Morro

CASABLANCA

27

21

Castilla de
la Punta

Canal de Entrada

Fortaleza
de San Carlos
de Cabaña

Malecón
7
8
35 San Lázaro

Cárcel

Genios

Av Cío de Céspedes (Del Puerto)

Monumento a
Máximo Gómez

Refugio
Blanco
Crespo
Colón

Paseo de Martí (Prado)

El Santo
Ángel
Custodio
Palacio de
la Artesanía

Morro

Zulueta

La Pobre

Cuba

Cuarteles

Policía Nacional
Revolucionaria
Comandancia
General

Museo
Casa José
Lezama
Lima

Museo de la
Revolución

Bernaza
Trocadero
Animas

Industria

Aguila

Paseo de Martí (Prado)

Museo
Nacional
Palacio de
Bellas Artes

Av de las Misiones

Chacón

Tejadillo

Catedral de
San Cristóbal
de La Habana

Castillo de la
Real Fuerza

Empedrado

Mercaderes

Tacón

San Ignacio

11

Edificio
Bacardí

San Juan de Dios

Plaza de
Armas

Virtudes

Neptuno

San Miguel

18 (San José)

Parque
Central

O'Reilly

Obispo

Museo
Numismático
20

Cuba

Obrapía

Baratillo

Oficios

Plaza de
Armas

LA HABANA VIEJA

Capitolio

Industria
Amistad

Bernaza
Monserrate

Villegas

Lamparilla

10

Amargura

Santo Cristo
del Buen Viaje

Teniente Rey (Brasil)

Compostela

Aguacate

Habana

San Francisco

Dragones

Parque
Fraternidad

Muralla

Convento de
Santa Clara

Sol

La Plaza
Vieja

Oficios

Legislative
Building
2
2

Santa Clara

To Casablanca
(Passenger Ferry)

3

Muelle Luz

Máximo Gómez (Monte)

Egido (Av de Bélgica)

Luz

Porvenir

12

Acosta

11

Jesús María

Espíritu Santo

6

Cárdenas
Cienfuegos
Apodaca
Gloria

34

Misión

Economía
Factoría

Suárez
Revillagigedo

Zulueta

Merced

Museo Casa
Natal de
José Martí

Leonor Pérez

San Isidro

La Merced

Damas

San Francisco
de Paula

1

14

Aguila

Esperanza (Arsenal)

Estación Central
de Ferrocarriles

Depósito de
Automóviles

Desamparados

San Francisco
de Paula

To Regla
(Passenger Ferry)

Florida

La Coubre

Almacenes
San José

Ensenada
de Atarés

N

4

5

6

200 metres
200 yards

Quinta de los Molinos

Handsome Avenida Allende runs west from the corner of Parque de la Fraternidad to the high hill on which stands **El Príncipe Castle** (now the city jail). At the foot of the hill, on the border of Centro and Vedado, is the Quinta de los Molinos, which once housed the School of Agronomy of Havana University. The main house now contains the **Máximo Gómez Museum**, with displays on the life of the Dominican-born fighter for Cuban Independence. Also here is the headquarters of the association of young writers and artists (Asociación Hermanos Saiz). The gardens are a lovely place to stroll.

Partagás cigar factory

San Carlos 816 entre Sitios y Peñalver, 40-min tours Mon-Fri 0900-1300, CUC$10; tickets must be bought in advance in hotel lobbies. English, Spanish or French-speaking guides available, but you may have to wait until a guide is free in your preferred language.

Relocated from its old position behind the Capitolio, the factory offers a behind-the-scenes look at cigar production. The tour can be interesting but is more often a shambles and not worth the entry free. You are taken up to the top floor where you stand in a corridor looking in through windows to where people are working. You briefly see the workers rolling cigars and get a cursory description of the components, but there is very little space and it is difficult to hear the guide over the loud music. Four different brand names are made here: *Partagás*, *Cubana*, *Ramón Allones* and *Bolívar*. These and other famous cigars can be bought at the Romeo y Julieta shop in a blue building a block away on the opposite corner (Mon-Sat 0900-1700), as can rum (credit cards accepted). Do not buy black market cigars from your guide. Cigars are also made at many tourist locations (for example Palacio de la Artesanía, the airport, some hotels). Also see Cayo Hueso box, opposite.

Tip...
If your stay is not restricted to Havana, then you are far better off visiting the cigar factory in Pinar del Río (see page 123).

Museo Casa José Lezama Lima ① *Trocadero 162 entre Industria y Consulado, T7-863 4161, mlezama@cubarte.cult.cu, Tue-Sat 0900-1700, Sun 0900-1300, CUC$1, CUC$5 with guide.* This is the house where José Lezama Lima (1910-76) lived, one of the most important Cuban writers. There is a collection of his personal belongings and art by Cuban painters of the vanguard movement (La Vanguardia).

★ Malecón

The Malecón is Havana's oceanfront esplanade, which links Habana Vieja to the western residential district of Vedado. The sea crashing along the wall here is a spectacular sight when the wind blows from the north. On calmer days, fishermen lean over the parapet, lovers sit in the shade of the small pillars and joggers sweat along the pavement. On the other side of the six-lane highway, buildings which from a distance look stout and grand, with arcaded pavements, balconies, mouldings and large entrances, are salt-eroded, faded and sadly decrepit inside. Restoration is progressing slowly, but the sea is destroying old and new alike and creating a mammoth renovation task. Parts of the sea wall are also being rebuilt meaning that there is always construction work somewhere along the Malecón.

ON THE ROAD
Cayo Hueso

Cayo Hueso is a run-down *barrio* lying in a triangle between Infanta, San Lázaro and the Malecón in Centro Habana. It was named by cigar factory workers returning from Key West and has nothing to do with bones (*huesos* in Spanish), although it was once the site of the Espada cemetery and the San Lázaro quarry. There are about 12,000 homes in the *barrio*, mostly tenements, which have been earmarked for restoration. As in La Habana Vieja, the renovation project also involves educating the community in its own particular culture and history.

In 1924, the cigar factory workers built a social club on San Lázaro, which became the site of the José Martí People's University. San Lázaro, with the University of Havana's wide stairway at its western end, was the site of fierce and determined student demonstrations from the late 1920s onwards. In the mid-1950s, Infanta was the Maginot line where the students faced Batista's troops. On 25 Jul 1956, Fidel Castro departed from Calle Jovellar 107 for the attack on the Moncada Garrison in Santiago de Cuba. There is a memorial plaque there now.

Cayo Hueso is now best known as a centre of *Santería* in the city, with Afro-Cuban art and music in abundance, especially on Calle Hamel (see below).

★ Callejón de Hamel

Among the alleyways of Cayo Hueso (see box, above) is Calle Hamel (an extension of Calle Animas, between Aramburu and Espada). It is the location of **Salvador González Escalona's art studio** ① *Hamel 1054 entre Aramburu y Hospital, T7-878 1661, www. afrocubaweb.com, www.havana-cultura.com, daily 0930-1800, free.* Salvador is a self-taught painter and sculptor, inspired by the history of the neighbourhood and its *Santería* traditions. He has painted large bright Afro-Cuban murals on the walls of Calle Hamel, combining a mixture of abstract and surrealist designs with phrases giving advice and warnings about danger, death and life. The project is affectionately called Callejón de Hamel and is recognized as the first open-air mural in Cuba dedicated to *Santería* and reflecting Afro-Cuban scenes. Salvador himself describes it as a community-based project, "from el barrio, to el barrio and with el barrio". As well as murals there are other surprises such as a typewriter pinned to the door of the gallery, painted drums and sculptures of corrugated iron and bike wheels.

Every Sunday 1200-1500 a free Peña Cultural Alto Cubana, known as **Peña de la Rumba del Cayo**, is held to honour the different Orishas. This is a very popular event, attracting large enthusiastic crowds (see box, page 442). Other community activities at Callejón de Hamel include children's activities every other Saturday from 1000. There are a couple of *paladares* here, and a small bar in the street sells a unique rum cocktail called El Negrón. There's also a stall selling herbs with spiritual and curative roles within Santería.

Hamel 1108 is the home of singer-songwriter Angel Díaz and the birthplace of the musical genre known as *filín* ('feeling'). Nearby, Calle Horno was the site of the first cultural circle dedicated to Carlos Gardel (the Argentine maestro of tango) and is another centre for cultural activities.

The largely residential district of Vedado was built in the mid 19th century, funded by the massive wealth generated by the sugar industry. According to Cuban historian Hugh Thomas, between 1917 and 1925 money flooded into the capital as Cuba supplied the United States with its entire sugar needs following the First World War. Prosperity and decadence went hand in hand, as opportunistic officials grew rich on non-existent projects and gambling was allowed. The grand hotels and sumptuous houses of Vedado reflected the opulence of life under the dictatorship. However, imagination is now required to conjure up the glory days of these beautiful residences, with their magnificent but crumbling staircases, twisted wrought-iron work and patched or broken stained-glass windows.

Plaza de la Revolución is the place to be for any demonstration, political rally or festive occasion. It was the scene for most of Castro's marathon speeches in the days when they lasted for hours. Vedado is also the place to come for nightlife. This is where you'll find all the hottest clubs and discos, bars and floor shows. If you are a night owl, find yourself a hotel or *casa particular* here so that you can walk home in the early hours, after enjoying salsa, jazz, *son*, boleros, cabaret, a show, theatre, cinema, ballet or a classical concert – whatever takes your fancy.

Plaza de la Revolución
This vast open space looks more like a car park than the venue for some of the nation's most rousing speeches and memorable gatherings including the May Day parade. Surrounded by imposing 1950s buildings housing most of the more important ministries, it is a focal point for anyone wanting to understand the charisma of Fidel and his marathon speeches. Suspended on the outside of the **Ministry of the Interior** is the 30-m steel sculpture of Che Guevara seen in all photos of Havana, a replica of the iconic image originally shot in 1960 by the celebrated photographer Alberto Korda. The long grey building behind the Martí monument is the former **Justice Ministry** (1958), now the headquarters of the Central Committee of the Communist Party. The plaza was completely transformed for an open-air Mass held by Pope John Paul II in January 1998 with huge religious paintings suspended over the surrounding buildings.

Memorial y Museo a José Martí ① *Plaza de la Revolución, T7-859 2347, Mon-Sat 0930-1630, CUC$3, children under 12 free, lookout CUC$2 extra.* Overlooking the Plaza is the 17-m statue of the national hero, José Martí, carved from white marble extracted from La Isla de la Juventud. The enormous base of the monument is where Castro stood to address the people. Inside it is a beautifully restored and most impressive museum. Don't miss the lookout accessed by mirrored lift. This is the highest point in the city with good panoramic views of Havana. You should receive a certificate from the lift attendant on your descent.

Museo Postal Cubano ① *Ministry of Communications, Plaza de la Revolución, T7-8828223, Mon-Fri 0800-1730, free.* The museum tells the history of the Cuban postal service. You will also find a collection of stamps and the story books of José Antonio de Armona (1765).

La Rampa and around

Calle 23, familiarly known as La Rampa, runs through Vedado from the Malecón at its eastern end, to the Cementerio Colón and the Río Almendares in the west. The eastern end is full of activity, overlooked as it is by the (in)famous **Hotel Nacional de**

Tip...
The garden of the iconic Hotel Nacional is the place to drink cocktails while watching the sun set and the moon rise over the Malecón.

Cuba and **Hotel Habana Libre** (see box, page 73). Airline offices and the International Press Centre cluster together alongside restaurants and nightclubs and the ice cream parlour **Coppelia** (see also page 83), which found movie fame in *Strawberry and Chocolate*. The parlour, which occupies a whole block, is a good example of the architectural creativity of the post-Revolution years. It was built by Mario Girona in 1966, based on an idea by Celia Sánchez Manduley, a heroine of the Sierra Maestra.

Tribuna Anti-Imperialista José Martí On the Malecón, close to the **Hotel Nacional**, the **Monumento al Maine** is a tribute to the 265 men who were killed when the *USS Maine* warship exploded in the bay in 1898. Close by, the Tribuna Anti-Imperialista José Martí was built during the Elián González affair and features a statue of Martí holding his son Ismaelillo and pointing towards the US Embassy, fronted by a veil of mirrored glass windows and patrolled by Cuban military personnel. The famous billboard of a fanatical Uncle Sam towering menacingly over a young Cuban patriot has been relocated behind the Embassy.

Pabellón Cuba ⓘ *Calle 23 entre N y M, T7-832 4925, Tue-Fri 1400-2000, Sat, Sun 1000-2000*. The Cuban Pavilion is a combination of a tropical glade and a museum of social history, with live music and dancing held regularly. It tells the nation's story through a brilliant combination of objects, photos and the architectural manipulation of space. It also hosts the annual *Feria del Libro* in February (the main site is at La Cabaña), the *Cubadisco* music convention in May, a showcase for the latest Cuban music, and *Arte en la Rampa* in July, August and the first two weeks in September, with handicrafts and souvenirs for sale, music and dancing.

Universidad de Habana Just to the south of Calle 23, on the edge of Centro and Vedado, is Havana University. The neoclassical building was constructed in the early 20th century and is reached by an imposing stone stairway. A monument to **Julio Antonio Mella**, founder of the Cuban Communist Party, stands across from the university entrance. This area is full of students, helping to make it a lively and happening part of town. Near the university the **Museo Napoleónico** ⓘ *San Miguel 1159 esquina Ronda, T7-879 1460, mnapoleonico@patrimonio.ohc.cu, Tue-Sat 0930-1700, Sun 0930-1230, CUC$3, guide CUC$5*, houses 7000 pieces from the private collection of sugar baron, Julio Lobo: paintings and other works of art, a specialized library and a collection of weaponry. Check out the tiled fencing gallery.

Avenida de los Presidentes

The Avenida de los Presidentes, or Avenida G, joins the Plaza de la Revolución in the south to the Malecón in the north, bisecting La Rampa on its way through to the sea. It is a magnificent wide boulevard with grand houses and blocks of apartments that are desirable places to live. Just north of the intersection with La Rampa is a statue of

Gulf of Mexico

Boca de la Chorrera

A

Malecón

Hotel Habana Riviera

9

10 ✉

(Calzada)

6

14

Iglesia del Carmelo ✝

Casa de la Cultura de Plaza

Línea

4

Catedral Episcopal ✝

11

B

13

15

To Miramar

Parque John Lennon

7

Casa de la Amistad

13

19

→ Havana maps
1 Havana orientation, page 42
2 Plaza de Armas, page 44
3 Parque Central, page 50
4 Centro & La Habana Vieja, page 58
5 Vedado & Plaza de la Revolución, page 64
6 Miramar, page 68

1

21

23

C

Entrance

Zapata

31

★

33

Cementerio de Colón

San Antonio Chiquito

D

35

San Antonio

2

37

Norte

1

39

Víazul Bus Station & Zoo

41

Av de Carlos M de Céspedes

E

Av de Rancho

3

Where to stay 🛏

Alicia Horta cp 1 *B6*
Casa Betty et Armando
  Gutiérrez cp 2 *B6*
Casa Caprí (Eugenia y Rudel)
  cp 3 *A5*
Colina 4 *C6*
Daysie Recio cp 5 *B4*
Gisela Ibarra cp 6 *A4*
Jorge Coalla Potts cp 7 *B5*
Martha Vitorte cp 8 *B5*
Meliá Cohiba 9 *A3*
Mercedes González cp 10 *B5*
Nacional de Cuba 11 *B6*

Restaurants 🍴

Adela 1 *C4*
Café Laurent 2 *B6*
Coppelia 3 *B5*
Decameron 4 *B3*
Gringo Viejo 5 *B4*
Hurón Azul 6 *C6*
La Casona de 17 7 *B6*
La Roca 8 *B5*
La Torre 9 *B6*
Le Chansonnier 10 *B5*
Los Amigos 11 *B6*
Starbien 12 *B6*
Unión Francesa 13 *B3*

Entertainment 🎭

Bar Bohemio 1 *C2*
Cabaret Las Vegas 2 *C6*
Café El Gato Tuerto 3 *B6*
Café Teatro Bertolt
  Brecht 4 *B5*
El Cocinero 5 *B1*
El Gran Palenque Bar 6 *A3*
El Submarino Amarillo 7 *B3*
Hurón Azul 8 *A3*
Imágenes 9 *A4*
Jazz Café 10 *A3*
La Casona de Línea 11 *A4*
La Zorra y El Cuervo 12 *C5*
Salón Rojo 13 *B6*
Tikoa 14 *B3*

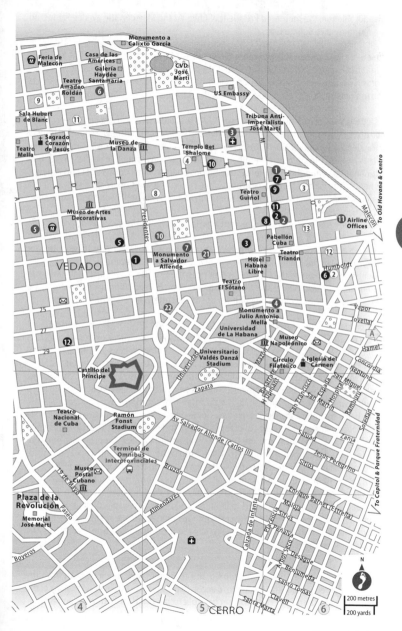

Feria de Malecón
M

Casa de las Américas
Galería Haydée Santamaría

Monumento a Calixto García

CVD José Martí

Teatro Amadeo Roldán
6

9

US Embassy

Sala Hubert de Blanc

11

Sagrado Corazón de Jesús

Teatro Mella

Museo de la Danza
III

Tribuna Anti-Imperialista José Martí

3

Templo Bet Shalome

4

10

8

8

1
7

Teatro Guiñol

9

3

8

Museo de Artes Decorativas
III

11
2
2

5
M

8

13

11 Airline Offices

5

Presidentes

10

Pabellón Cuba

12

VEDADO

1

Monumento a Salvador Allende

7

21

3

Hotel Habana Libre

Teatro Trianón

6 2

Humboldt

Teatro El Sótano

4

Monumento a Julio Antonio Mella

Vapor

Jovellar

25

22

Universidad de La Habana

Museo Napoleónico
III

Hamel

27

Universitario Valdés Danzá Stadium

Universidad

Mazón

Círculo Filatélico

Iglesia del Carmen

Concordia

Neptuno

29

12

Zapata

Castillo del Príncipe

Ronda

San Lázaro

San Francisco

San Martín

San Miguel

Espada

Hospital

Rambón

Teatro Nacional de Cuba

Ramón Fonst Stadium

Av Salvador Allende (Carlos III)

Salud

Zanja

Lealtad

Terminal de Omnibus Interprovinciales

Bruzón

Jesús Peregrino

Sitios

Museo Postal Cubano
III

10 de Mayo

Enrique Barnet (Estrella)

To Capitol & Parque Fraternidad

Plaza de la Revolución

Paseo

Almendares

Maloja

Franco

Sitios

Calzada de Infanta

Peñalva

Desagüe

Árbol Seco

Benjumeda

Santo Tomás

Memorial José Martí

Boyeros

N

200 metres
200 yards

4

5 CERRO

6

To Old Havana & Centro

Malecón

A

Salvador Allende, the murdered President of Chile. At the Malecón the avenue is blocked by a monument to Calixto García.

Museo de la Danza ① *Entrance on Línea esq G (Av de los Presidentes), T7-831 2198, musdanza@cubarte.cult.cu, Tue-Sat 1000-1700, CUC$2, guided tour CUC$1, CUC$5 to take photos*. The museum presents an engaging collection of items from the dancer Alicia Alonso's personal collection and from the Ballet Nacional de Cuba. See box, page 428.

Casa de las Américas ① *Calle 3 52 esq G, T7-838 2706, www.casa.cult.cu, Mon-Fri 0830-1600 except the last Fri in the month*. This active and welcoming centre was founded in 1959 by Haydée Santamaría (1923-1980) for pan-American cultural promotion and interchange. It hosts a varied programme of seminars workshops and investigative studies in addition to running its own publishing house. Exhibitions of art from all corners of Latin America are held in the Galería Latinoamericana, while contemporary Cuban art is shown in the Sala Contemporánea. On the ground floor is the **Librería Rayuela** book and music shop and a small peso bookstall.

Next door is the **Galería Haydée Santamaría** ① *Calle G entre 3 y 5, alongside Casa de las Américas, T7-838 2706, closed for renovation 2015*, which displays the work of Latin American artists. There is a good representation of mostly 20th-century styles with over 6000 works of art including sculptures, engravings and photography.

Built in 1961 opposite the Casa de las Américas, the **Estadio José Martí** (Malecón entre Avenida de los Presidentes y J), is a good example of post-Revolutionary architecture; the sports ground shows a highly imaginative use of concrete, painted in primary colours.

Museo de Artes Decorativas ① *Calle 17 502 esq E, T7-832 0924, artdeco@cubarte.cult.cu, Tue-Sat 0930-1700, CUC$5 including Spanish- or English-speaking guide, or 1100-1630, CUC$3 without a guide, CUC$5 to take photos, CUC$10 for videos*. European and Oriental art from the 16th to the 20th centuries has been displayed at this French Renaissance-style mansion since 1964. It was originally designed by Alberto Camacho (1924-1927) for José Gómez Mena's daughter, who belonged to one of Cuba's wealthiest families. Most of the building materials were imported from France and the interior decoration was by House of Jansen. In the 1930s the mansion was occupied by Gómez' sister, María Luisa, Condesa de Revilla de Camargo, who was a fervent collector of fine art and held elegant society dinners and receptions for guests, including the Duke of Windsor and Wallace Simpson. Her furniture included a desk that had belonged to Marie Antoinette. Her valuable collections were found in the basement after the family fled Cuba following the Revolution in 1959.

There are 10 permanent exhibition halls with works from the 16th to 20th centuries including ceramics, porcelain (Sévres, Chantilly and Wedgewood), furniture (Boudin, Simoneau and Chippendale) and paintings. The Regency-inspired dining room is recommended viewing and includes a sumptuous dinner service that belonged to the dictator Batista. The attendants are very knowledgeable and informative about the exhibits, but only in Spanish.

Paseo

Further west, this is another of Vedado's grand thoroughfares, running south from the Mafia-built **Hotel Habana Riviera** on the Malecón to the Plaza de la Revolución. Many of the elegant mansions either side of the street have been converted into offices or embassies.

Casa de la Amistad ⓘ *Paseo 406 entre 17 y 19, T7-830 3114 ext 103. Bar and café Sun-Fri 0900-2200, Sat 0900-0100 for 'Noche Cubana' (CUC$3 including a cocktail).* This former mansion dating from 1926 was built by a wealthy plantation owner for his lover, later his wife, who left her first husband for him. (They were the first couple to divorce when it became legal in Cuba.) A beautiful dusky, coral pink building with gardens, it is now operated by ICAP (Cuban Institute for Friendship among the Peoples), which has a reasonably priced bar and cafeteria, with a live show on Saturday nights. You can eat on the balcony overlooking the garden, serenaded by the resident quartet; the food is consistently good with large portions; there are two menus: one has lobster and shrimp, the other is a house menu. Indoors is the **Primavera** restaurant, to the right of the entrance, which has elegant furniture and is expensive (daily 1200-2400).

John Lennon Park ⓘ *Calle 17 entre 6 y 8.* The recently re-landscaped and renamed park just west of Paseo features a bronze statue of the Beatle sitting on a bench. It was sculpted by José Villa, who also sculpted the Che Guevara monument at the Palacio de los Pioneros in Tarará (see page 422). Words from Lennon's song 'Imagine' have been translated into Spanish and etched on the ground: *"dirás que soy un soñador, pero no soy el único"* ("You may say I'm a dreamer, but I'm not the only one."). It was inaugurated in December 2000 in a ceremony attended by Fidel Castro and Silvio Rodríguez (singer/songwriter and founder of the movement of *La Nueva Trova*). Theft of the statue's glasses has meant there is now a 24-hour security guard, and the replacement glasses have been permanently fixed in place. Classical guitar concerts are sometimes held here.

★ Cementerio Colón

Entrance on Zapata y 12, T7-830 4517, daily 0800-1700. CUC$5 entrance including photos, CUC$1 for good map.

Constructed in 1871, the 56-ha city of the dead is the second largest cemetery in the world. It was designed by the Spanish architect, Calixto de Lloira y Cardosa, who was also the first person to be buried there. The Colón cemetery should be visited to see the wealth of funerary sculpture, much of it in Carrara marble, from the 19th and 20th centuries. Cubans visit the sculpture of Amelia La Milagrosa (Amelia Goire) at Calle 3 entre F y G and pray for miracles. The Chinese cemetery is at Avenida 26 y 31.

Miramar and further west *Colour map 1, A5.*
this smart area is where diplomats and business people work and play

Miramar is some 16 km west of the old city on the west side of the Río Almendares and is easily reached via two road tunnels or bridges. Although there are many beautiful art nouveau and other houses from the early 20th century, the area is now being developed into a modern city with glossy new hotels for business people with state-of-the-art fitness and business centres. Most of the embassies are here, which always implies a certain status and level of comfort. It has the appearance of a wealthy suburb, with broad avenues and neatly aligned rectangular blocks.

Avenida Primera (first) runs closest to the sea, which is rocky and not recommended for bathing (use the hotel pool instead); Avenidas Tercera (third), Quinta (fifth) and Séptima (seventh) run parallel, with the tunnels to Vedado at the end of Avenidas 5 and 7. Some of the best restaurants are in Miramar and there are good nightlife venues too, including the internationally famous **Tropicana** cabaret show to the south.

To get a good idea of the layout of the city and its suburbs, visit the **Maqueta de la Ciudad** (scale model of Havana) ① *Calle 28 113 entre 1 y 3. T7-2027322, closed for renovation.* The 88-sq-m model covers Havana and its suburbs as far out as Cojímar and the airport. Every building is represented. Colonial buildings are in red, post-colonial pre-Revolution

6 Miramar

➡ **Havana maps**
1 Havana orientation, page 42
2 Plaza de Armas, page 44
3 Parque Central, page 50
4 Centro & La Habana Vieja, page 58
5 Vedado & Plaza de la Revolución, page 64
6 Miramar, page 68

Gulf of Mexico

MIRAMAR

Maqueta de la Ciudad

Santa Rita

Estudio Galería Rigoberto Mena

N

300 metres
300 yards

Restaurants 🍴
1830 **1** *B6*
El Aljibe **2** *C3*
El Palio **3** *A3*
El Tocororo **4** *B4*

La Cocina de Lilliam **5** *D2*
La Esperanza **6** *A4*
La Fontana **7** *B1*

Entertainment 🎵
Casa de la Música
  Egrem **1** *C4*
Club Almendares **2** *D5*
Don Congrejo **3** *A4*

buildings are in yellow and post-Revolution buildings are in white. Some of the model is difficult to see, especially in the middle, but there is an upper viewing gallery with two telescopes which makes it is a little easier.

Also worth a visit if you can read Spanish is the **Museo del Ministerio del Interior** ⓘ *Av 5 y 14, T7-2034432, closed for renovation*, which, through a series of photographs and lengthy explanations (all in Spanish), details the history of the police force and fire brigade as well as all the counter-revolutionary activity in Cuba since 1959 and plots to kill Fidel. Curious cases such as false money production, killer shampoo and airline terrorism through to the bombings of tourist hotels are all documented.

Rigoberto Mena is one of Cuba's most respected contemporary artists, and his studio, **Estudio Galería Rigoberto Mena** ⓘ *Calle 21 esq 54, T7-2025276, 5241 5737 (mob)*, just south of Miramar, houses a fantastic collection of abstract art. His style is deceptively simple: a meticulous composition of brilliant colours radiating from dark backgrounds.

Marina Hemingway
Off Av 5, Santa Fé, 20 mins by taxi (CUC$10-15) from central Havana.

The Marina Hemingway tourist complex in the fishing village of **Santa Fé** is the largest marina in the country and offers fishing and scuba-diving trips as well as other water- and land-based sports (see What to do). It also hosts numerous fishing competitions and regattas (see Festivals and events). The resort includes the hotel **El Viejo y El Mar**, restaurants, bungalows and villas for rent, shopping, facilities for yachts, sports and a tourist bureau. Also here is the Hemingway International Nautical Club, a social club for foreign executives based in Cuba. Founded in 1992, it currently has 730 members from 37 countries. The noticeboard is a good place to find crewing opportunities. Another club in this area is the **Club Habana** (Sol Meliá) ⓘ *Av 5 entre 188 y 192, Playa, T7-2750100, 7-2750300-9*. The main house dates back to 1928 and was the Havana Biltmore Yacht and Country Club. It is very posh but has lots of facilities on land and in the water.

El Río Club
  (Johnnie's Club) **4** *B6*
Salón Boleros en
  Dos Gardenias **5** *C3*

Salón Rosado Benny
  Moré, La Tropical **6** *E3*
Tropicana **7** *E3*

Instituto Superior de Arte (ISA)
Calle 120 1110 entre 9 y 13, Cubanacán, T7-208 8075, vrri@isa.cult.cu. Visits must be arranged by tour agencies (Paradiso), a specialist guide is provided. Independent visitors should phone or email at least 2 days in advance.

The Instituto Superior de Artes (ISA), which combines schools of visual art, modern dance, ballet, music and drama, is located in the grounds of the former Havana Country Club in Cubanacán, southwest of Miramar. Architects will be interested in this 'new spatial sensation', which was an ambitious project of the early 1960s. Three architects, Ricardo Porro, Roberto Gottardi and Vittorio Garati, were involved in the revolutionary design, which was to be constructed using domestic rather than imported materials.

Some parts of the scheme were not completed and others have since been abandoned (they were not entirely practical), but you can still visit the **Escuela Superior de Artes Plásticas**, which consists of a series of interlinked pavilions, courtyards and sinuous walkways designed by Porro. (Many people believe the layout takes the form of a woman's body, although some see it more as the womb itself, with a cervix-like fountain in the centre.)

There is also the **Escuela Superior de Artes Escénicas**, built by Gottardi, in the form of a miniature Italian hill-top town. It's rather claustrophobic and quite unlike Porro's sprawling, 'permeable' designs, which are full of fresh air and tropical vegetation. Porro's Dance School, although part of the same complex, is not accessible via the Country Club. The Clubhouse itself now serves as the Music School, since the 1960s Music School by Garati is now in ruins.

A lack of maintenance, water leaks, a faulty drainage system, structural defects, vegetation and vandalism have all contributed to the deterioration of both the finished and unfinished buildings and there is a lack of funds for planning a renovation programme and for carrying out repairs.

Parque Lenin
Northwest of Boyeros and the airport, T7-644 2721, Wed-Sun 1000-1700.

Parque Lenin is a huge green space on the edge of Havana, which is very popular as a weekend escape for Cuban families. There are lakes for boating, horses for riding, an amusement park (very popular) with a circus show, an aquarium and an upmarket restaurant. To the south is the botanical garden and Expocuba. Hiring bikes has been recommended as a good way to visit.

Jardín Botánico Nacional de Cuba
Km 3.5, Ctra Rocío, Calabazar, south of Havana beyond Parque Lenín, T7-697 9170, www.uh.cu/centros/jbn/index.html. Wed-Sun 0900-1600, but in practice you may not be allowed in after 1530. CUC$1, or CUC$3 if you take the 'train' with guide, children half price. Many hotel tour desks offer day trips with lunch for CUC$25. Taxi from Habana Vieja CUC$15-18 one way, good for groups.

The 600-ha botanical garden in Arroyo Naranjo is well maintained with excellent collections of Cuban and other tropical plants representing five geographical regions, including a Japanese area with tropical adaptations. It is part of the University of Havana and much scientific research takes place here. A multilingual guide will meet you at the gate, no charge, and you can take a 'train' tour along the 35 km of roads around the site in an open-sided, wheeled carriage towed by a tractor, which enables you to see the whole garden in about two hours. There are few signs, so it is not as informative as it might be, and a guide is helpful, describing unusual plants in the various zones. Several interconnected glasshouses are filled with desert, tropical and sub-tropical plants, and are well worth walking through. The garden's **organic vegetarian restaurant** uses solar energy for cooking (see Where to eat, page 85). There are also other restaurants and snack bars serving *criollo* food in CUP$ or CUC$.

Expocuba

Boyeros, T7-697 4401. Wed-Sun 0900-1700 (times subject to change), CUC$3, children under 12 CUC$1. Special trains leave from the main terminal in La Habana Vieja.

Past Lenin Park, near the botanic gardens, is Expocuba, a sprawling facility that was completed in January 1989. It features a score of pavilions showing Cuba's achievements in industry, science, agriculture and the arts and entertainment. It also hosts various visiting art and cultural exhibitions, sometimes including live bands. Telephone to confirm what's on; information on times is available from hotels in Havana.

Listings Havana *maps p42, p44, p50, p58, p64 and p68*

Tourist information

Oficina Nacional de Información Turística (Infotur)
Calle 28 303 entre 3 y 5, Miramar, T7-204 6635 and Guanabo, Av 5 entre 468 y 470, T7-796 6868, www.infotur.cu.
This is the headquarters of the national tourist board.

There is also a network of kiosks run by **Infotur**, which can provide you with information and maps. These are located at the **airport** (Terminal 3, T7-266 4094/642 6101, open 24 hrs); in **Habana Vieja** (Obispo entre Bernaza y Villegas, T7-866 3333, and Obispo y San Ignacio, T7-863 6884); in **Playa** (Av 5 y Calle 112, T7-204 7036, daily 0815-1615). At the **Santa María del Mar** office (Av Las Terrazas entre 11 y 12, Playas del Este, T7-797 1261/796 1111) you will find maps, excursions, internet, booking for hotels, souvenirs, but with no map of the area and with limited bus information, it remains to be seen how useful it's going to be.

The state tour agencies, such as **Cubatur** and **Havanatur**, are found in hotels and other locations. Their main task is to sell tours, but they can also make hotel reservations, sell tickets for buses, trains and planes and organize pick-ups and transfers. If you are staying in a *casa particular* you will probably find your host is a mine of useful information and can fill you in on all the gossip and background detail to enrich a stay in the capital.

Where to stay

Tourist hotels have a/c, 'tourist' TV (US films, tourism promotion) and restaurants with reasonable food, but standards are not comparable with Europe, and plumbing is often faulty or affected by water shortages. Payment for hotels used by tourists is in CUC$.

Several important hotel renovation projects have been completed by **Habaguanex** in La Habana Vieja and these are now elegant places to stay, becoming known as 'boutique' hotels. See www.habaguanexhotels.com for a full list of their hotels in Old Havana. Hotels in Vedado are some distance away from the colonial sights but are in a better district for nightlife. Miramar is further away still; hotels

Tip...
Always tell the hotel each morning if you intend to stay on another day. Do not lose your 'guest card', which shows your name, meal plan and room number.

here are designed for business travellers and package tourists, but there are good restaurants, *paladares*, bars, clubs and Teatro Karl Marx.

La Habana Vieja
Hotels

$$$$-$$$ Conde de Villanueva – Hostal del Habano
Mercaderes 202 esq Lamparilla, T7-862 9293/4, www.habaguanexhotels.com.
Named after Claudio Martínez del Pinillo, Conde de Villanueva (1789-1853), a notable personality who promoted tobacco abroad and helped to bring the railway to Cuba. Just 9 rooms and suites around a peaceful courtyard, attractive red and green colour scheme, cigar theme with cigar shop, café, bar, good restaurant, highly regarded, friendly staff.

$$$$-$$$ Iberostar Parque Central
Neptuno entre Prado y Zulueta, on north side of Parque Central, T7-860 6627/9, www.iberostar.com.
Rooms and suites of international standard in 2 buildings connected by an enclosed walkway, excellent bathrooms, business centres, Wi-Fi, 3 restaurants, 4 bars, great view of Havana from pools on 9th floor of the Torre section and on 8th floor of the Colonial section, fitness centre, sauna, charming and helpful multilingual staff.

$$$$-$$$ Santa Isabel
Baratillo 9 entre Obispo y Narciso López, Plaza de Armas, T7-860 8201, www. hotelsantaisabel.com.
Beautiful 18th-century mansion, 27 luxury rooms, 10 of them suites, well-equipped bathrooms, rooms on 2nd floor have balcony overlooking plaza and those on the 3rd floor have a terrace, central patio with fountain and greenery and lobby bar. Wi-Fi. Good views from the **El Mirador** restaurant and the café.

$$$$-$$$ Saratoga
Paseo del Prado 603 esq Dragones, T7-8681000, www.hotel-saratoga.com.
The 1879 neoclassical façade of this corner plot masks a smart, modern hotel, favoured by celebrities such as Mick Jagger and Beyonce. Suites and rooms are comfortable and spacious but can suffer from traffic noise. The food is good with several dining options, from a tapas bar to an upmarket restaurant, and there's Wi-Fi in the Mezzanine Bar. Breakfast is comparatively expensive. The rooftop pool is particularly popular with views of the Capitolio, Parque Fraternidad and the Prado, great for sunset cocktails. Spa 0800-2000. Service nothing special.

$$$-$$ Hostal Valencia
Oficios 53 esq Obrapía, T7-867 1037, www.habaguanexhotels.com.
Joint Spanish/Cuban venture modelled on the Spanish *paradores*. 10 suites and rooms – some rather past their best – named after Valencian towns. Tastefully restored building, nicely furnished, pleasant courtyard with vines, music, good restaurant. Sister hotel, **El Comendador**, next door. The restaurant and bar on the corner is open from 1200 and serves pizza, *tortillas, empanadas*, etc, for lunch.

Casas particulares

$$ Eugenio y Fabio
San Ignacio 656 entre Jesús María y Merced, T7-862 9877, fabio.quintana@infomed.sld.cu.
6 rooms, all well-equipped and spacious but some are dark, overlooking interior courtyard, a/c, fan. House is stuffed with antiques and bric-a-brac and meals are served family style in an ornate baroque dining room. Roof terrace for sunset

BACKGROUND
Hotel Habana Libre

The hotels in Vedado harbour many secrets and tales from the past, Some, such as the Nacional, were built with Mafia money and were frequented by the mob during the decadent years before the Revolution. The **Havana Hilton** was inaugurated on 19 March 1958; its huge tower symbolized everything that was luxurious and profligate in the capital and attracted a high-flying and wealthy clientele. However, it had been open for barely one year before it was taken over by the victorious revolutionaries in 1959 and renamed the **Habana Libre**. The Continental Suite, room 2324, was used as the Revolution Headquarters for the first three months of 1959 and press conferences for foreign journalists were given here. Later, the first Soviet embassy in Havana occupied two floors. In the 1960s it was used for international meetings. Castro stayed in La Castellana Suite, room 2224, for the Tricontinental conference in December 1961.

watching. Fabio and staff are very helpful and English is spoken. Breakfast CUC$8.

$$-$ Federico Llanes
Cárcel 156 Apto 3, entre San Lázaro y Prado, T7-861 7817, 5264 6917 (mob), fllanes@gmail.com.
Excellent location just off the Prado and a stone's throw from the Malecón. You have to climb 64 stairs up to the apartment on the 3rd floor but Federico, a former lawyer, is helpful with luggage as well as providing advice and information. 2 large, light rooms with tiled floors and heavy dark furniture, double beds, extra bed on request, a/c, fan, fridge, desk, safe box, English spoken, friendly household, good breakfast with lots of fruit and juice.

$$-$ Greenhouse on Prado
Cárcel 158 entre San Lázaro y Prado, T7-8617810, 5389 4652 (mob), jorgemc84@nauta.cu and on Facebook.
Jorge Muñoz Céspedes speaks English and is very helpful and friendly. Ground floor apartment in good condition. Large room with comfortable double and single bed, a/c, fan, good bedside lighting, safe box, desk, fridge stocked with water, beer and soft drinks, substantial breakfast, CUC$5.

$$-$ Gustavo Enamorado Zamora – Chez Nous
Teniente Rey (Brasil) 115 entre Cuba y San Ignacio, T7-862 6287, hostalcheznous@gmail.com.
3 spacious double rooms, 2 of which share a bathroom, the other is en suite, a/c, fan, TV, safe box, fridge, balcony overlooking street, roof terrace, parking, warm atmosphere. Gustavo and Kathy are kind and helpful, French, English and Russian spoken. In the building opposite they have another apartment with 3 rooms to rent with private bathroom and balcony – **Chez Nous Art Deco**, with the advantage of an elevator.

$$-$ Jesús y María
Aguacate 518 entre Sol y Muralla, T7-861 1378, jesusmaria2003@yahoo.com.
Upstairs above the family and very private, 5 a/c bedrooms on 2 floors with double and single bed, with fan, fridge, safe box. Top floor rooms are the nicest. There is a terrace where you have meals and a sunbathing area. More of a hostal than a family home.

$$-$ Yamelis Elizalde
Cuba 518 entre Muralla y Teniente Rey, T5331 9498 (mob), fllanes@gmail.com.
1 block from Plaza Vieja, this is a delightful apartment renovated in 2015 with high

ceilings and tall windows. 2 rooms, each with balcony overlooking the street, quiet a/c, fan, safe box, fridge. Yamelis speaks English and is a good cook, serving breakfast and other meals on request. She lives here with her little boy.

Centro
Hotels

$$$-$$ Terral
Malecón esq Lealtad, www. habaguanexhotels.com.
Stunning position on Malecón, all rooms have great view over the sea. Small new hotel in a contemporary, chic style with spacious rooms, good bathrooms and large windows. Even the breakfasts are modern. Very good service from cheerful staff. Only drawbacks are traffic noise and a longish walk to the sights (20 mins to Old Havana).

$$ Deauville
Galiano y Malecón, T7-866 8812, reserva@hdeauville.gca.tur.cu.
144 basic rooms, temperamental lifts, noise from Malecón but great view, balconies overlooking sea and fortress, breakfast included, helpful *buró de turismo*. Restaurant **Costa Norte** offers dinner 1900-2200, followed by a cabaret 2200-0230, Tue-Sun. The pool is open to non-guests for CUC$5 including CUC$4 *consumo* (food/drinks) in winter and CUC$10 including CUC$8 *consumo* in summer, children under 3 free, snack bar.

Casas particulares

$$-$ Carlos Luis Valderrama Moré
Neptuno 404 entre San Nicolás y Manrique, 2nd floor, T7-867 9842.
Carlos and Vivian are former teachers, friendly and helpful, he speaks English and loves to talk about football. 1930s apartment above a shop, 3 rooms, front room has balcony overlooking street, good bathrooms, a/c, fans, safe box, good food.

$$-$ Cary y Nilo
Gervasio 216 entre Concordia y Virtudes, T7-862 7109, caridadgf45@yahoo.es.
Beautiful house with high ceilings, quiet, spotlessly clean, Nilo has decades of experience of hotel work and knows how to treat his guests. 3 spacious rooms with bathrooms, antique furnishings, colonial style, quiet, good food, huge breakfasts. No English spoken.

$$-$ Casa 1932
Campanario 63 bajos entre San Lázaro y Lagunas, T7-8636203, 5264 3858 (mob), www.casahabana.net.
A living museum stuffed with art deco stained glass, antiques and a collection of musical instruments in this beautiful house. Luis Miguel speaks English and Italian and is extremely informative. 3 a/c rooms of different sizes and prices but all comfortable and stylish with en suite bathrooms, safe box, fan, fridge. Pleasant patio and terrace. Airport pickup in vintage taxi can be arranged.

$$-$ Melba y Alberto
Galiano 115 Apto 81 entre Animas y Trocadero, T7-863 5178, T05-264 8262 (mob), barracuda1752@yahoo.es.
Unprepossessing entrance on street but up on the 8th floor you're in another world with views of the sea and city. 2 bedrooms, 1 with balcony and double bed, the other with double and single bed, use of kitchenette and living room, good for families, charming hosts, excellent food, breakfast served on balcony, very comfortable and pleasant.

$ Marilys Herrera González – Hostal Concordia
Concordia 714 altos entre Soledad y Aramburu, T7-870 0608, http:// casaparticular.tripod.com.
3 a/c rooms with private bathrooms although not en suite, fridge, fan, safe box, use of kitchen, patio and roof terrace. All spotlessly clean and comfortable, laundry offered, Marylis (former Russian teacher) and

Miguel (former aircraft engineer) are very kind and caring, they have travelled abroad and speak English, French and Russian.

Vedado
Hotels

The better hotels in Vedado are used by package tour operators and business travellers and are of a reasonable international standard. The cheaper hotels are basic, with intermittent electricity and poor water pressure, variable levels of cleanliness and security. For comfort and ambience you might prefer to forego the facilities of a hotel and opt for a *casa particular*, where you will get better food and service.

$$$$-$$$ Meliá Cohiba
Paseo entre 1 y 3, T7-833 3636, www.meliacuba.com.
International grand high rise that dominates the neighbourhood, 462 rooms and suites with every comfort, the higher rooms have the best views, very good service, shops, gym, healthclub, pool, gourmet restaurant, piano bar and Habana Café nightclub.

$$$$-$$$ Nacional de Cuba
O esq 21, T7-873 3564, www. hotelnacionaldecuba.com.
429 rooms, some renovated, generally friendly and efficient service, faded grandeur, dates from 1930, superb reception hall, note the vintage Otis high-speed lifts, steam room, 2 pools, restaurants, bars, shops, business centre, exchange bureau, gardens with old cannons on hilltop overlooking the Malecón and harbour entrance, great spot for a sundowner, the hotel's tourist bureau is efficient and friendly.

$$ Colina
L y 27, T7-836 4071, commercial@colina. islazul.tur.cu.
Often used by students learning Spanish at the university opposite; there is no reason otherwise to stay here. 80 rooms, some of which have been renovated, others have

poor water pressure and broken fittings, street noise, reasonable breakfast.

Casas particulares

$$ Alicia Horta
Línea 53 entre M y N, Apto 2, T7-832 8439, aorta@infomed.sld.cu.
Alicia is a doctor, she and her daughter María are friendly and speak English, French and German, 3 rooms, 1 has an en suite bathroom, the other 2 share a bathroom, good for families. Large terrace/balcony overlooks Paseo.

$$ Casa Betty et Armando Gutiérrez
21 62 entre M y N, Apto 7, 4th (top) floor, T7-832 1876.
A penthouse with elevator which opens directly into the apartment. Very convenient for *paladares* and nightlife, very close to Hotel Nacional. Large and comfortable a/c rooms with 2 beds, big bathrooms, balcony. A delightful place to stay. Armando and his wife, Betty, have been renting for 20 years, they speak French, German and English and are knowledgeable on history and culture.

$$ Daysie Recio
B 403 entre 17 y 19, T7-830 5609.
Spacious, light and clean. 2 airy rooms with interconnecting bathroom, 1 has a terrace overlooking the backyard, both have double and single bed, a/c, fridge, English spoken. Daysie is a vivacious hostess and this is a good option for families or groups of up to 6.

$$ Gisela Ibarra
F104 altos entre 5 y Calzada, T7-832 3238.
Straight out of the 1950s, marble staircase, balconies, very high quality, wonderful old rooms with original furnishings, a/c, fan, fridge and safety box. Gisela is an excellent hostess, running a very proper, quiet and traditional home in a residential neighbourhood. Huge, filling breakfast for CUC$5, laundry service offered. If she is full, her daughter Marta Díaz runs another *casa* just round the corner on Calzada 452 Apto 5,

same price but rooms are smaller, darker and hotter.

$$ Jorge Coalla Potts
I 456 Apto 11 entre 21 y 23, T7-832 9032, 5283 1237 (mob), www.havanaroomrental.com.
2 a/c rooms on ground floor, 1 large with 2 beds, 1 smaller with double bed, comfortable, good mattresses, new bathrooms, lots of hot water, ceiling fan and fridge, ample breakfasts. Excellent location close to the bars and restaurants of Vedado. Generous and fascinating hosts, Jorge and Marisel, and their daughter, Jessica, are mines of information and speak English. If they are full, Jorge will find somewhere else for you to stay.

$$ Martha Vitorte
G 301 Apto 14, 14th floor, entre 13 y 15, T7-832 6475, martavitorte@hotmail.com.
High-rise building near corner with Línea, 1 apartment on each floor, referred to as 'horizontals', beautiful modern building, very spacious, 3 rooms, en suite bathroom, a/c, security safe in each room, balcony on 2 sides for panoramic views of Havana, sea and sunsets, Martha is a retired civil servant and speaks some English and French. She also rents an independent apartment on Línea 453 entre E y F, piso 10, with 2 bedrooms and a terrace.

$$ Mercedes González
21 360 Apto 2A, entre G y H, T7-832 5846, mecylupe@hotmail.com.
Mercedes runs 2 identical *casas* on the same floor of the apartment block, with terrace, elevator, laundry service. 5 airy rooms, a/c, fan, good bathrooms, 3 rooms have a balcony, smart, helpful and friendly, good location, near park.

$$-$ Casa Caprí (Eugenia y Rudel)
Calle 11 161 entre L y K, T7-830 5160, crisjo@infomed.sld.cu.
Right next to the US Embassy. 2 good-sized rooms with a/c and private bathrooms as well as 2 sitting areas for guests. Very cheerful and helpful family, some English spoken.

Miramar
Hotels
There is a string of 4-star hotels west along the coast that are used by package tour operators; guests are often here for the first and last nights of their stay in Cuba before being whisked off round the island. They are not particularly convenient for visiting the old city, but you do get a sea view. Miramar is also popular with business people; hotels are of an international standard and the area is quiet at night.

$$$$-$$$ Meliá Habana
Av 3 entre 76 y 80, T7-204 8500, www.meliacuba.com.
Not quite as luxurious as the Meliá Cohiba, but still the best in this area, with the biggest swimming pool in Havana and a free shuttle service to Old Havana 0930-2130. Rooms and beds are huge and sea view rooms have a balcony with lovely view, but the pool and garden view rooms are quieter.

Casas particulares

$$ Villa Reina
Calle 80 916 entre 9 y 11, T7-209 4951, 5280 2303 (mob), www.villa-reina.com.
Detached 1960s house in its own garden where you can sit and relax. Bedrooms are upstairs in 2 sections and living areas downstairs. Rosi, Carlos and Marielena are welcoming and helpful and provide a good breakfast. In a quiet residential area but within easy reach of *paladares*, hotels, Av 5 and transport to other parts of Havana.

$$-$ Nieves y Marlen
Calle 3 9401 entre 94 y 96, Apto 2, T7-203 5284.
Clean, spacious and modern apartment, a/c, fridge in room, balcony.

Where to eat

Snacks and fast food

In addition to the excellent and varied *paladares* and more predictable state restaurants listed below, there are many street stalls and places where you can pick up cheap snacks priced in CUP$. These are good for filling a hole at lunchtime, but don't expect a culinary masterpiece. One of the best options is pizza fresh from the oven, which usually costs over CUP$10 in a private cafeteria but is just CUP$3-5 in a state snack bar; they can be very greasy, so take plenty of napkins. Very sweet juice drinks cost CUP$2 per glass. There are also many fast-food outlets throughout the city: **El Rápido** (red logo) is clean with fast service and numerous locations; **Burgui** serves hamburgers and fried chicken. Branches of **DiTú** are all over the city, open 24 hrs, selling pieces of chicken by weight.

La Habana Vieja
Restaurants

$$$ A Prado y Neptuno
Prado y Neptuno, opposite Hotel Parque Central, T7-860 9636. Daily 1200-2400.
Italian and Cuban food, excellent tiramisu and good pizza and pasta. Sports on TV at the bar. Good views over Parque Central.

$$$ Dominica
O' Reilly esq Mercaderes, T7-860 2918. Daily 1200-2400.
Italian and international, very smart, set menus CUC$25-30, pasta from CUC$6, pizza CUC$5.50-9 depending on size, vegetarian options, outdoor seating nice for lunch, credit cards accepted.

$$$ El Castillo de Farnés
Monserrate 361 esq Obrapía, T7-867 1030. Restaurant daily 1200-2400, bar 0800-2400.
Tasty Spanish and international food, reasonable prices, good for tapas, *garbanzos* and shrimp, also Uruguayan beef and chateaubriand. Castro came here at 0445, 9 Jan 1959, with Che and Raúl. Very small restaurant, eat inside or on the street.

$$$ El Floridita
Obispo esq Monserrate, next to the Parque Central, T7-8671300. Daily 1130-2400.
A favourite haunt of Hemingway, this is now a very elegant bar and restaurant as reflected in the prices (CUC$6 for a daiquirí), but well worth a visit if only to see the sumptuous decor and 'Bogart atmosphere'. In the corner of the bar is a life-size bronze statue of Hemingway, and on the bar, also in bronze, are his glasses resting on a open book. Live music.

$$$ La Barca
Av del Puerto esq Obispo, T7-866 8807, comercial@templete.habaguanex.cu. Daily 1200-2400.
Just down from El Templete but cheaper, overlooking the road and the harbour opposite the old yacht club with outdoor seating. Good variety on the menu with some Spanish dishes, seafood and steaks.

> **Tip...**
> Although Havana's restaurants and *paladares* are more enlightened than those in the rest of the country, vegetarians will still have little choice of where and what to eat. The best bet is the restaurant in the Jardín Botánico, **El Bambú** (see page 85). Otherwise, many of the hotels, including the **Nacional**, see page 75, serve good all-you-can-eat lunchtime buffets, and Italian restaurants offer the usual meatless pizza and pasta. Some *paladares* will serve meatless meals with advance notice, and all offer eggs on the menu, but always ask for the *congris* to be cooked in vegetable oil.

$$$ La Bodeguita del Medio
Empedrado 207 entre Cuba y San Ignacio, near the cathedral, T7-867 1374.
Restaurant 1200-2330, bar 1030-2300. It is here that Hemingway allegedly inscribed the now famous line *"Mi mojito en La Bodeguita, mi daiquirí en El Floridita"*. It has since been claimed that one of Hemingway's drinking buddies Fernando Campoamor, the owner of *La Bodeguita*, hired a calligrapher to write the line as a lucrative tourist con, but it's still worth sampling a mojito at the bar (rum, crushed ice, mint, sugar, lime juice and carbonated water – CUC$5). The food is poor and expensive, but very popular.

$$$ La Mina
On Obispo esquina Oficios, Plaza de Armas, T7-862 0216. Daily 1000-2400.
Very much on the tourist trail but a lovely spot to sit and soak up the atmosphere, traditional Cuban food, sandwiches, lots of liqueur coffees, outdoor seating with live Cuban music.

$$$ Marinero El Templete
Av del Puerto 12-14 esq Narciso López, T7-866 8807, comercial@templete.habaguanex.cu. Daily 1200-2400.
Eat inside or outside with view over the road to the harbour, pleasant, understated elegance. Good food, international with Cuban flavours, meat, fish or lobster.

$$$ París
San Ignacio 54 esq Empedrado, Plaza Catedral, T7-867 1034.
Restaurant and snack bar daily 1200-2400. Expensive, small portions, slow service, but has selection of national dishes, tables outside take up most of the square, lovely location, worth stopping here for a coffee when visiting the cathedral.

$$$-$$ Europa
Obispo esquina Aguiar. Daily1200-2400.
International and Cuban food, the most expensive dish is *grillada de mariscos* at CUC$11.95. Lots of cheaper options CUC$3-6,

although sometimes things run out. Good music and dancing.

$$$-$$ La Piña de Plata
Bernaza esq Obispo, T7-867 1300 ext 134. Daily 1200-2400.
Small and smart a/c restaurant with Wi-Fi if you have a *tarjeta*. Full range of Cuban dishes, chicken, pork, fish, shrimp and lobster, also pasta, pizza. Good food, well presented. Piña colada is the bar's speciality.

$$$-$$ Mesón de la Flota
Mercaderes 257 entre Amargura y Teniente Rey, T7-863 3838.
Restaurant-cum-tapas bar with wooden tables and impassioned flamenco *tablaos* 1200-1500 and 2000-2200. Reasonably priced menu with wide selection of Spanish dishes and plenty of fish and seafood, including paella, but the tapas choices are better value than the main dishes. Try the feisty *patatas bravas*.

$$$-$$ Torre de Marfil
Mercaderes 115 entre Obispo y Obrapía, T7-867 1038. Daily 1200-2200.
Generally good-value Oriental cuisine with food surpassing anything that Chinatown has to offer in terms of authenticity, decked out with colourful lanterns and Chinese paraphernalia.

$$ Café del Oriente
Oficios y Amargura, T7-860 6686. Daily 1200-2400.
High-class food with a reasonably priced set menu and elegant surroundings.

$$ Café El Mercurio
Next to to Café del Oriente. Daily 1200-2400.
Informal, pleasant terrace.

$$ Los Nardos (Sociedad Juventud Asturiana)
Paseo del Prado 563 entre Dragones y Teniente Rey, opposite the Capitolio, T7-863 2985. Daily 1200-2400.
Not obvious from the street but look out for the waiters at the entrance. Dining room upstairs lined with cabinets containing old football trophies, cups from 1936, while

the heavy wooden furniture is reminiscent of a rancho. At one end are chefs in white hats busy in the kitchen while at the other you are overlooked by the stained glass windows of a pool room. Not a great option for vegetarians: plenty of meat, pork, lamb or Uruguayan steak, although there is also fish and assorted vegetables. Popular with Cubans and foreigners, large, filling portions, background music is limited to golden oldies played 2-3 times during the meal. In the same building are **El Trofeo**, 2nd floor, serving Cuban and international food, big portions, a little cheaper than Los Nardos, good mojito CUC$2.20, and **El Asturianito** for Cuban and Italian food, good pizzas CUC$3-7. If you find a queue outside for Los Nardos, explain that you are going to El Asturianito and they will let you through.

$$ Puerto de Sagua
Bélgica (Egido) 603 esq Acosta, T7-867 1026.
Nautical theme, a cafetería serving dishes such as *arroz Puerto de Sagua* for CUC$6, and a more upscale restaurant specializing in seafood.

$$-$ Hanoi
Brasil (Teniente Rey) 507 y Bernaza,
T7-867 1029. Daily 1200-2400.
A simple restaurant with plain furnishings but a little gem, serving typical Cuban food, excellent value for money with main dishes at less than CUC$5, mojito for CUC$2. Plenty of food, the rice and beans are good and the garlic on the potatoes will keep away vampires. Vegetarian option of beans, rice, salad and root vegetables with a *criollo* sauce, CUC$3.50. Live music after 1900, nice atmosphere, welcoming service, popular with Cubans and foreigners.

Paladares

$$$-$$ Don Lorenzo
Acosta 260A, entre Habana y Compostela,
T7-861 6733. Daily 1200-2400.
Not a cheap option with fish and meat dishes at CUC$5-15 and vegetarian options

for CUC$5-6, but one of the most extensive menus, with over 50 dishes offered, all types of meat and fish with a huge variety of sauces, Basque-style, French-style, cider, fruity, almond, etc. An entertaining night when it's full, good for people-watching from the 2nd floor. Watch out for tourist pricing and high service charges added to the bill.

$$$-$$ Doña Blanquita
Prado 158 entre Colón y Refugio, T7-867 4958.
Open from 1200.
Run by English-speaking lawyer, the dining room is upstairs, with a neon sign and a lovely view of the Prado. Eat inside with fan or on balcony if dry. Good location but food nothing special, consisting of simple Cuban food done to a formula: pork, chicken or eggs CUC$7-9, beer CUC$2.

$$$-$$ La Moneda Cubana
San Ignacio 77 entre O'Reilly y Empedrado,
T7-867 3852. Open 1200-2300.
Limited choice, good fish with salad, beans and rice with fried banana, and usually good salads prepared for vegetarians. Menus for around CUC$8-10. More notable for the rooftop terrace which gives spectacular views of Havana and particularly the firing of the cannon at 2100. There is also an elegant dining room in colonial style if it is raining.

Cafés and bakeries

Bianchini
Sol 12 entre Oficios y Av del Puerto (beside
the Rum Museum) and Callejón del Chorro,
San Ignacio 68, Plaza de la Catedral, http://
dulceria-bianchini.com. Daily 0900-2100.
For sweet and savoury baked goodies, delicious quiches, cakes, pastries, croissants, biscuits, all hand made. The chocolate is organic from Baracoa, every cup of coffee is made with freshly ground beans, and fresh juices are unsweetened. Happy hour 1400-1500 for cut-price coffees.

Café El Escorial
Mercaderes 317 esq Muralla,
escorial@enet.cu. Daily 0900-2100.
Coffees CUC$0.75-3.50, also coffee beans at
CUC$3.25 for 250 g, plus ice cream, juices,
soft drinks and sweets. Sit inside or out
overlooking Plaza Vieja, if you can get a seat.
Popular location.

Café O' Reilly
O'Reilly 203 entre Cuba y San Ignacio.
Daily 0900-2100.
Coffee in various forms, sandwiches, drinks
and cocktails. Coffee beans and ground
coffee also sold by weight. Upstairs bar being
renovated in 2015 as an Irish pub, with a
balcony and live music.

Café París
Obispo y San Ignacio. Daily 0900-0100,
live music 1200-2400.
Serves reasonably priced food and snacks,
prices vary, make sure you see a menu.
Seating inside with band or outside on the
street for watching the world go by, popular,
lively, fun.

Cafetería Jardín del Oriente
Amargura entre Mercaderes y Oficios.
Daily 1100-2300.
Comida criolla, sandwiches, wine, juices
and soft drinks at reasonable prices.

La Dichosa
Obispo esq Compostela. Daily 0900-2400.
Good place for breakfast, CUC$3.50, or a
snack, CUC$2-4. Full meals available for
lunch and dinner. Live music 1200-2200.

Panadería San José y Cafetería Santo Domingo
Obispo 161 entre San Ignacio y Mercaderes,
T7-860 9326. Daily 0700-2400.
Bakery and café.

Pastelería Francesa
Between the Hotels Telégrafo and Inglaterra
on the Prado.
Smorgasbord of pastries and cakes in a
peach-coloured dining room. Popular, some
of the better cakes have gone by lunchtime.

The hot *pan au chocolat* and *pan con pasas*
(raisins) are particularly good.

Casablanca
Restaurants

$$$ La Divina Pastora
Fortaleza de la Cabaña, T7-860 8341.
Daily 1200-2300.
Expensive, upmarket state restaurant, food
praised for its presentation but it tastes
good too. However, the view is what makes
this restaurant special. Sit indoors or in the
open air overlooking cannon pointing out
over the water towards La Habana Vieja and
along the coastline. Great at lunchtime or for
sunset-watching.

$$$-$$ Los XII Apóstoles
Near El Morro, T7-863 8295. Daily 1200-2345.
Fish and good *criollo* food, good views of the
Malecón. The 12 apostles are the 12 cannon
on the ramparts.

Centro
Restaurants

$$$-$$ Sociedad Agrupación Castropol
Malecón 107 entre Genios y Crespo, T7-861
4864. Daily 1200-2400.
Beautiful central patio on ground floor where
food is cooked over coals, the mixed grill
for 2 people is CUC$19.90. Upstairs, lobster,
fish or meat dishes and an extensive wine
list are served on a balcony overlooking the
Malecón or in a/c dining room with a show
at night Thu-Sun 2200-0300, cover CUC$5.

Paladares

$$$ Casa Miglis
Lealtad 120 entre Animas y Lagunas, T7-864
1486, www.casamiglis.com. Daily 1200-0100.
Swedish fusion cuisine, including Swedish
meatballs, although there are other
international dishes such as Mexican chilli,
Greek souvlaki, pizza or cous cous. There's a
small but excellent bar if you don't want to eat.
Eclectic Scandinavian design. Very popular.
Look for the Swedish flag hanging outside.

$$$ La Guarida
Concordia 418 entre Gervasio y Escobar,
T7-866 9047, www.laguarida.com.
Lunch daily 1200-1600, dinner 1900-2400
with reservation.
Film location for *Fresa y Chocolate* and
popular with tourists, many of whom would
not normally enter such a dilapidated
building. The grand old marble staircase
leads past drying laundry to a smart
but quirky historic dining room on the
3rd floor. Consistently good food, *filet
mignon*, seafood and vegetarian paellas
are delicious. Main courses are around
CUC$15, lobster is CUC$22, and, as you are
charged for everything, even bread, this is
more expensive than an average *paladar*.
It is always busy but you can go up to the
glamorous rooftop bar even if you don't
have a reservation, wonderful at sunset.
A Cuba libre is CUC$3.50. Don't miss a visit
to the bathroom.

$$$ La Tasquita
*Espada 208 entre Jovellar (27 de Noviembre) y
San Lázaro, T7-873 4916. Daily 1200-2400.*
Run by Santiagüera Aralicia. Wonderful
food and great atmosphere. House special
for CUC$8 is a pork steak stuffed with ham,
cheese and chorizo, served with a sweet and
sour sauce and all the trimmings, including
a drink, dessert and coffee. Other dishes
of chicken, fish, pasta, pork, etc. Good for
vegetarians with delicious sweet potato
and Cuban fried eggs, served on mountains
of rice and beans, plus good salads. Potent
mojitos. No smoking.

Barrio Chino
At Zanja y Rayo, 1 block west of Galiano,
there are several restaurants in a small street
with tables inside or outside and menus on
view; you will be pestered for your custom.
Food can be very good if there is sufficient
water, cooking gas and ingredients –
shortages affect all the restaurants around
here – but do not expect authentic Chinese

cuisine or you will be disappointed. Chop
suey or chow mein is about the most
Oriental you can get. 'Sweet and sour' dishes
are not recommended as they are very sweet
and fruity. Spring rolls bear no relation to
anything you might find in China. Lots of
flies during the daytime. All prices in CUP$
or CUC$. Meals around CUC$5-10.

$$$-$$ Flor de Lotto
*Salud 313 entre Gervasio y Escobar,
T7-860 8501. Daily 1200-2400.*
Although it looks Chinese from the decor,
in fact this is a good Cuban restaurant with
some Asian flavours such as sweet and sour
sauce or chicken with pineapple. There's
a wide-ranging menu with everything
from tasty staples such as *ropa vieja*, to
lamb, rabbit and lobster, all served in large
portions. Popular, with queues at weekends.
Main courses around CUC$4.50-8.

$$$-$$ Tien Tan (Templo del Cielo)
*Cuchillo 17, entre Zanja y San Nicolás, T7-861
5478, taoqi@enet.cu. Daily 1100-2400.*
Always full. The chef is from Shanghai, but
this is still Cuba so don't expect much in the
way of authenticity. Cheapest dish CUC$1,
most expensive around CUC$25.

$$$-$$ Viejo Amigo
*Dragones 356 entre Manrique y San Nicolás.
Daily 1200-2400.*
Combination Chinese/Cuban/international
restaurant and pizzeria. Good food, pleasant
service, nice restaurant upstairs with a
friendly atmosphere. Portions are huge so
ask them to box up what you can't eat.

$$ Sociedad Chang Weng Chung Tong
*San Nicolás 517 entre Zanja y Dragones,
T7-862 1490.*
Bar, café and restaurant, daily 1200-2400. Part
of the **Sociedad China de Cuba**, Chinese and
criollo food. They have an all-you-can-eat
international buffet upstairs including soups,
roast meats, vegetables, pizza, pasta, salads
etc for CUC$8.80, or you can order à la carte.

Vedado
Restaurants

$$$ La Torre
17 y M, Edificio Focsa, T7-838 3089.
Daily 1200-2400.
The a/c, glass-enclosed bar and restaurant on the 33rd floor of the Focsa building serves the best French food in Havana, about CUC$40 per person but worth it. Go for a drink at the bar even if you don't want to eat there: bar prices are no higher than elsewhere (mojito CUC$3); the view is free and, as this is the highest point in the city, you get the full panorama.

$$$ Polinesio
Hotel Habana Libre, with access from the street, T7-834 6100. Daily lunch 1200-1530, dinner 1900-2230.
Dark and cool, a mix of Chinese and Indonesian dishes, CUC$12-20, also a good happy hour 1700-2000.

$$ La Casona de 17
17 60 entre M y N, T7-838 3136.
Daily 0830-2400.
Elegant peach mansion with colonial terrace, once home to Castro's grandparents. House dish is *arroz con pollo a la chorrera*. Also good is *paella Casona*, or there is always a half roast chicken (a bit greasy) with bacon, rice'n'beans, chips and salad. Large servings. Adjoining Argentine *parillada* serves up mixed grills. Nice for a relaxing lunch. Owned by a cooperative, all staff have a stake and service is good.

$$ Unión Francesa
17 esq 6, T7-830 6515.
Attractive colonial building on the corner of Parque John Lennon, eat inside with a/c or on the veranda overlooking the garden, relaxed, nice atmosphere, photos of Fidel and Chirac, economical with set menus for CUC$5 (main course with bread, rice, vegetables and a drink) or CUC$10 (plus salad, dessert), but some items are not always available.

$$-$ La Roca
21 102 esq M, T7-8363219.
Daily 1200-0200. Fri, Sat CUC$10 cover includes CUC$7 consumo.
Restored 1950s building with stained-glass windows dating from when it was a guesthouse. Sleek but stark dining room serves an international menu for a range of budgets: onion soup CUC$1, spaghetti carbonara CUC$2.50, plus more expensive dishes. Set menu is excellent value at CUC$3.75-4.50 for drink, main course and dessert, plus piano music while you eat. It's very popular so best to get there before 1900. Evening entertainment on some nights.

Paladares

$$$ Adela
Calle F 503 entre 21 y 23, T7-832 3776.
Call ahead for opening hours. Adela is an artist and this *paladar*, though legal, is primarily an art gallery. Clients come to buy art and stay to eat. Appetisers include cinnamon-baked bananas, fried *malanga*, corn and chorizo stew, although the choice of main course is limited. A meal costs around CUC$20-25 per person.

$$$ Café Laurent
Calle M 257 entre 19 y 21, T7-8312090, see Facebook. Daily 1200-2400.
Smart penthouse restaurant much in demand so reservations are essential and are checked before you get in the lift. Get a table on the covered terrace if you can, to enjoy the view and the billowing white curtains. Light, bright decor during the day becomes chic and romantic at night. The international food is very good and nicely presented, not overly expensive with fish and shrimp around CUC$12.50, but you are charged for bread and side dishes so expect to pay CUC$25 per person without wine.

$$$ Decameron
Línea 753 entre Paseo y 2, T7-832 2444.
Unprepossessing on the outside but the dining room is pleasant and full of antiques.

Extensive menu and good wine list, Cuban and international dishes, large portions.

$$$ Hurón Azul
Humboldt 153 entre O y P, T7-836 3636.
Lunch and dinner.
The small, cosy dining room is decorated with works by local artists. Food and service are good, with large portions of Cuban dishes, reasonably priced.

$$$ Le Chansonnier
J 257 entre 15 y Línea, T7-832 1576,
www.lechansonnierhabana.com.
Very smart and contemporary bar and restaurant design in elegant 1890 building, fabulous international food and reasonable prices. Outdoor seating too. Dress up to come here.

$$$-$$ Gringo Viejo
21 454 entre E y F, T7-831 1946,
gringoviejocuba@gmail.com.
Daily 1200-2300.
Nice atmosphere with wall-to-wall cinema memorabilia, red checked tablecloths and hanging plastic grapes and strings of garlic, good portions, main course of fish, chicken, pork and other meats with fruity or spicy sauces accompanied by rice, beans and salad.

$$$-$$ Los Amigos
M entre 19 y 21, opposite Victoria,
T7-830 0880. Daily 1200-2400.
Good Cuban food, *ropa vieja* is recommended, but check your bill. Dine among Christmas decorations, religious artefacts and wind chimes. Convenient location for après-dining entertainment, popular with locals and ex-pats.

$$$-$$ Starbien
29 205 entre B y C, T7-8300711.
Mon-Sat 1200-1700, 1900-2400.
A 2-storey green and white 1930s house has been converted into a moden contemporary restaurant and bar, serving some of the best food in Havana. Chef Osmani has trained abroad but now offers elegantly presented Cuban food. A lunch special of 5 courses and a drink for CUC$12 can't be beaten. There's a bar upstairs with a small terrace. Service is excellent. Always full, reservations advised.

Bakeries and ice cream parlours

Coppelia
23 y L, T7-831 9908, 833 3160.
Tue-Sun 1000-2200, or daily Jul/Aug.
A visit to the most famous ice cream parlour in Cuba is recommended, see also page 63. It has capacity for 707 seated ice cream lovers, with several separate outdoor areas to eat in, each with its own entrance and queue in the surrounding streets, or inside in La Torre. It's extremely popular with Cuban families. If you pay in CUP$, you will almost certainly have to queue for an hour or so, particularly at weekends, but this is not unpleasant as the characteristic *copey* trees provide plenty of shade. A dedicated attendant (brown uniform) controls the queue and directs you into the seating area as tables become free. Alternatively, pay in CUC$ in the Fuente de Soda kiosks outside (said to be open 24 hrs but often closed after midnight), although this can work out extremely expensive. Bring your own plastic spoons for the tubs as they invariably run out. The ice cream (CUC$2 for small portion) comes in many different flavours depending on availability (chocolate is still the top flavour) and styles (all come with a glass of water): *ensalada* (mixture of flavours), *jimaguas* (twins), *tres gracias*. After devouring your 1st choice you can stay and order a 2nd portion without queuing. There is also an a/c area within Coppelia called Las Cuatro Joyas, where you pay by weight in CUC$. Alternatively, sample Coppelia ice cream in the tourist hotels and restaurants and in some dollar food stores.

Pain de París
Línea entre Paseo y A, also Plaza de la Revolución. Daily 24 hrs.
Good coffee served *cortadito* or *con leche*, croissants and *señoritas de chocolate* (custard slices).

Miramar and further west
Restaurants

$$$ 1830
Malecón y 20 (officially 7 1252 entre 20 y 22),
T7-838 3090/1/2. Daily 1200-2400.
Bar, restaurant and nightclub in a
wonderful setting at the mouth of the Río
Almendares, one of the best places for
dancing. International and Cuban cuisine,
from CUC$12 for a local dish, to CUC$16.25
for tenderloin with blue cheese sauce, and
lobster at CUC$30. Cabaret shows Mon-Sat
2200-0300, Sun 1800-2400, and local bands.

$$$ El Aljibe
7 entre 24 y 26, T7-204 1583. Daily 1200-2400.
Originally opened in 1947 as Rancho Luna,
it attracted '50s movie stars like Eva Gardner
and Errol Flynn with its secret recipe for
roast chicken with a bitter orange sauce.
The restaurant closed in 1961, but reopened
again as a state-owned restaurant in 1993
and the original owner Sergio García Macías
began to bring his famed *pollo al Aljibe* to
a new generation of movie stars, including
Jack Nicholson, Steven Spielberg and Danny
Glover. Open, breezy, framework design
with thatched roof and friendly atmosphere.
Generous portions of delicious black beans,
rice, fried potatoes and salad, with more if
you want, CUC$12 per person. Good wine
cellar. There is a cigar store attached if you
want a fine rum and a cigar after your meal.

$$$ El Rancho Palco
Av 19 y 140, Playa, T7-208 9346.
Daily 1200-2200.
Set in a lovely jungle garden west of Miramar,
near the Palacio de las Convenciones, this is
very popular with ex-pats for its Argentine
steaks, good barbecued chicken, meats,
typical *criollo* cuisine and international food.
Good live music is provided by a trio.

$$$ El Tocororo
18 302 esq Av 3, T7-204 2209. Daily 1200-2400,
bar 2000-0300.
Named after the national bird of Cuba.
Old colonial mansion with nice terrace
and a great house band. Prices fluctuate
between CUC$20 and CUC$30. It used to
be one of the best restaurants in town but
is now on the tour party circuit and quality
can be haphazard.

$$$ La Cecilia
5 entre 110 y 112, T7-202 6700. Daily 1200-
2400, dance shows Fri-Sun 2200-0300.
Good international and Cuban food, mostly
in an open-air setting. There are dance
shows by top-level companies in the **Sala de
Fiestas de la Cecilia** at the weekend and live
bands with dancing outside, cover charge
depends on who is performing. Can get very
busy with tour parties.

$$$ La Ferminia
5 18207 entre 182 y 184, T7-273 6555.
Daily 1200-2400.
A beautiful neoclassical residence with an
elegant atmosphere. Best for meat eaters as
this is a *churrasquería*. Salads are brought to
the table and then staff come round with
skewers of pork, beef, chicken and chorizo.
Vegetarians should call beforehand to
coordinate a menu.

Paladares

$$$ La Cocina de Lilliam
48 1311, entre 13 y 15, T7-209 6514.
Sun-Fri 1200-1500, 1900-2300,
closed 2 weeks in Aug, 2 weeks in Dec.
Very good, imaginative Cuban and Spanish
food with tables outside but under cover
in a lovely garden. Great appetizers and
fresh fish, lots of vegetables, all beautifully
presented. Popular with locals, reservations
recommended, main course plus beer
CUC$20-30, usually excellent service.

$$$ La Fontana
3-A 305 esq 46, T7-202 8337. Daily 1200-2400.
Lovely leafy setting with fish pools between
the tables outside, fountains, exposed
brickwork and stone, modern and chic.
Good Cuban food, extremely popular,
ask for the *menú de la casa*, about CUC$25
per person. Good grilled and barbecued

meat and fish, extensive wine list. Arrive early or make a reservation, essential at night. A contemporary basement lounge bar stays open late.

$$$-$$ El Palio
Av 1 entre 24 y 26.
Italian and Cuban cuisine, notably fresh fish and seafood with a choice of creative sauces and good vegetables. Portions can be rather small, however, and the atmosphere is lacklustre. Eat in the open air or indoors.

$$$-$$ La Esperanza
16 105 entre 1 y 3, T7-202 4361.
Mon-Sat 1900-2330.
Small sign, very popular, traditional food, excellent cocktails, meal and drinks CUC$10-15 per person, plus 10% service, reservations advisable, run by Hubert and Manolo in their inviting 1950s period living room surrounded by their paintings and antiques.

Southern suburbs
Restaurants

$$ El Bambú
Jardín Botánico Nacional de Cuba (see page 70). Lunch served daily 1400.
Cuba's only organic vegetarian restaurant. Eat as much as you like from a selection of hot and cold vegetarian dishes for CUC$12, including drinks. Water and waste food is recycled and the restaurant grows most of its own food.

$$-$ La Casa del Dragón
Cortina de la Presa y 100, Boyeros (off the main road to the right soon after entrance from Arroyo Naranjo, look for the sign), T7-6443713. Wed-Sun 1200-1700.
Chinese restaurant with bamboo furniture and good food priced in CUP$, making it cheap, beer priced in CUC$. There is also a *ranchón* where they serve *comida criolla*. Nice walks nearby.

Bars

Many restaurants listed above have bars attached. Ordinary bars not on the tourist circuit will charge you in CUC$, if they let foreigners in at all. Even so, the prices in most places are not high by Caribbean standards: national brands of beer usually cost CUC$1-1.50 (or CUP$10-18, Tínima being the most expensive); imported beers cost CUC$2-3.

You will find musicians in most bars. Many play only 3 or 4 songs, then come round with the collecting bowl trying to sell their CDs before moving on, to be replaced by another band who do the same thing. Have a ready supply of small change for tips.

La Habana Vieja

Antiguo Almacén de la Madera y el Tabaco
Desamparados (Av del Puerto) esq Paula.
An old timber and tobacco warehouse converted into a microbrewery and restaurant/snack bar. You can get a cold pint of beer for CUC$2 and sit inside with the machinery and vats or outside by the water. The service is slow and the food nothing special, but it is still a good place to stop for a break in a city tour or after shopping at the handicraft market next door. It is vast, so there will always be room for you.

Bar Dos Hermanos
Av del Puerto esq Sol, opposite the ferry terminals, T7-8613514 ext 104. Daily 1100-2300.
Beside the rum museum. A trio and a quartet alternate each night and play traditional Cuban music.

Bar El Louvre
Hotel Inglaterra, Prado 416, Parque Central, T7-860 8595. Daily 1200-2400.
A pleasant place for an outdoor evening drink, where you can watch the sun going down catching the cream stone of the Museo de Bellas Artes through the Royal

palms. Roving live musicians don't stay long and expect a generous tip, making your excellent CUC$3 daiquirí rather pricey. Slow service.

Bar Monserrate
Monserrate y Obrapía, T7-860 9751. Daily 1200-2400.
Draft beer CUC$2, imported beer about CUC$2.50, mojito CUC$3, plenty of flavour but not very generous shots of rum, food available, interesting to sit and watch comings and goings.

Café de París
Obispo 202 esq San Ignacio. Daily 0900-0100.
Predominantly tourist clientele but good location for people-watching.

Casa del Escabeche
Obispo esq Villegas, T7-863 2660. Daily 1000-2300.
Tiny bar but popular and welcoming, house quartet from 1200, cocktails CUC$3, Cristal and Bucanero CUC$1.50.

Cervecería La Muralla
Factoría Plaza Vieja, San Ignacio esq Muralla, T7-866 4433. Daily 1200-2400.
This popular microbrewery is a great place for a midday breather or a sundowner during or after your walk round the city. You can sit inside or out on the plaza listening to live music. Their own beer is CUC$2 in a pint mug, or you can buy a larger tube to share. Slow service.

El Floridita
Obispo esq Monserrate, next to the Parque Central, T7-8671300. Daily 1130-2400.
See Restaurants, above.

La Bodeguita del Medio
Empedrado 207 entre Cuba y San Ignacio, near the cathedral, T7-867 1374. Bar daily 1030-2300.
See Restaurants, above.

Lluvia de Oro
Obispo esq Habana. Daily 0900-2400.
Good place to drink rum and listen to loud recorded rock music or salsa, live music 1230-1600, 1830-2300, food is also served.

Museo del Ron
Av del Puerto 262 entre Sol y Muralla, T7-861 8051.
2 bars with nightly music, 0900-2100, serve good Cuba Libre and sometimes showcase quality live bands.

Sloppy Joe's
Zulueta 252 entre Animas y Virtudes, T7-866 7157.
A popular bar in the 1930s has been recreated by the state in a smarter guise aimed at the tourist market. The name comes from the sandwich served there, which is filled with *ropa vieja*, other food includes tapas and hamburgers. You'll pay CUC$5 or so for cocktails and CUC$2.50 for a beer. Drinks are cold and good, but service is extraordinarily slow.

Centro

Café Neruda
Malecón entre San Nicols y Manrique, T7-864 4159. Daily 1000-2400.
Habaguanex has used the shell of an old building for this modern open-air bar with artistic flair. It's very popular with young Habaneros, who queue at weekends when they're taking a break from a stroll along the waterfront. Reasonable prices: mojitos and daiquiris CUC$2, meals CUC$6-8, snacks available.

Humboldt 52
Humboldt 52 entre Infanta y Hospital, T5295 4893 (mob) and see Facebook. Daily 1700-0300.
Havana's first official gay bar is welcoming to all. There's entertainment on most nights, with drag shows, karaoke, salsa and DJ nights. Screens show music videos, there's a dance floor and plenty of seating, with a back room for smoking.

Cuban all stars

Celebrities have always had a fascination for Cuba and there has always been a steady stream of rich and famous visitors to the 'Pearl of the Antilles'. In 1898 the young Winston Churchill narrowly missed being hit by a bullet on his 21st birthday when he visited to see what the Spanish-American War was all about. He returned, older and wiser, to paint and to smoke cigars, creating the ever-popular image of the wartime British leader puffing on a great fat *Habano*.

The US Prohibition Act of 1919 gave tourism in Cuba an unexpected boost, when drinking customers and whole bars moved to the island. The Irish-owned Donovan's Bar was relocated, lock, stock and barrel to a building opposite the Capitolio in Havana, and Cuban bartenders became world famous for their cocktails. Constante Ribalaigua, at the **Floridita**, was already an established expert before Hemingway discovered his daiquirís (he allegedly regularly drank 11 double, sugarless daiquirís before 1100), but the author gave him the crowning touch by writing about his cocktails in the novel *Islands in the Stream*. He also invited his friend Marlene Dietrich to sample them and she became a regular visitor to Havana. Another actress visitor, Mary Pickford, had a cocktail created for her in the **Hotel Sevilla Biltmore**.

George Gershwin was so taken with the music and rhythms of Cuba that he composed the *Cuban Overture*, first performed in 1932. Frank Sinatra was a regular visitor and even had a modernist house in the former Country Club district. Many others came down in their yachts to sail around the cays and drink in the bars. Photos of Errol Flynn, Gary Cooper, Spencer Tracy, Ava Gardner, Carmen Miranda and other glamorous figures still grace the walls of the **Bodeguita del Medio** bar.

There were also, of course, the less salubrious visitors – gangsters like Al Capone, Lucky Luciano, Meyer Lansky and George Raft – who were attracted by the money to be made in the casinos and by bootlegging alcohol. George Raft had a penthouse apartment (now a restaurant) on top of the **Capri** casino hotel. The **Hotel Nacional** and the **Riviera** were also linked to mafia money. The bar of the **Nacional** has a rogues' gallery of photos of its famous guests.

Today, celebrities continue to flock to this last bastion of Communism in the Western world. Famous names have included Sir Paul McCartney, Francis Ford Coppola, Naomi Campbell, Kate Moss, Leonardo di Caprio (whose entourage was so large he took over whole hotels), Paris Hilton, Rihanna, Beyonce and Jay-Z, while the annual Latin American Film Festival attracts a clutch of actors and directors, notably Robert de Niro, Arnold Schwarzenegger, Ken Loach, Jack Nicholson, Helen Mirren, Kevin Spacey and Kevin Costner.

Vedado

Bar Bohemio
21 entre 12 y 14, T7-833 6918.
Former ballerinas from the Ballet Nacional de Cuba have created this beautiful tapas bar in a lovely Vedado mansion with huge windows, high celings and tiled floors, spacious and comfortable, also a terrace outside. Extensive list of some 60 cocktails and a cigar menu. Happy hour 2000-2200. Gay friendly.

Casa de la Amistad
Paseo 406 (see page 67).
Bar with a beautiful garden extension, tasty cheap light meals optional, very peaceful surroundings.

El Cocinero
26 entre 11 y 13, T7-832 2355. Daily 1200-0200.
Contemporary industrial chic at this rooftop bar under the chimney of a disused vegetable oil factory. A place for the young and fit, as you have to climb 3 flights of a spiral staircase to get there. Popular with affluent young Cubans. Food is available on a lower terrace, indoors or open air, but it's best for drinks and tapas. English spoken, good, friendly service.

Hotel Nacional de Cuba
O esq 21, T7-873 3564.
If it's a nice evening, opt for a sunset cocktail at a table in the garden overlooking the Malecón, an ideal spot for looking out for old cars and watching the moon rise over the sea.

La Torre
17 y M, at top of Edif Focsa, T7-838 3089. Daily 1200-2400.
Have a drink at the bar on the 33rd floor even if you don't want to eat at the restaurant (see above). Day or night, this is a terrific place for a cocktail.

Entertainment

Cabaret
Cabaret Las Vegas, *Calzada de Infanta 104, Vedado, T7-836 7939. Daily gay show 2300-0400, CUC$3, matinée Fri 1600-2000, CUP$20.*
Copa Room, *Habana Riviera, Paseo y Malecón, Vedado, T7-834 4225 for reservation. Thu-Sun 2030-0300.* Part of the nightclub scene since before the Revolution. Traditional music including the boleros of Benny Moré. Glitzy Cuban cabaret *A lo Riviera*, skimpy outfits and sequins.

Parisien, *Hotel Nacional, Vedado, T7-873 3564. Daily 2200-0200.* Excellent show for CUC$35, lasts longer than **Tropicana** and of equivalent standard, make a reservation.
Salón Rojo, *Hotel Caprí, 21 entre N y O, Vedado, T7-833 3747.* The country's best musical groups play here, 2200-0400, CUC$10-35 depending on who is playing, drinks extra. The Caprí was Meyer Lansky and Lucky Luciano's turf in the days of the Mafia wheeling and dealing in the 1950s. Scenes from the *Godfather II* were filmed here.
Tropicana, *72 y Línea del Ferrocarril, Marianao, T7-267 0110, reserves@tropicana.tur.cu. Daily 2030 until some time after midnight. Reservations 1400-2000. Tickets CUC$75, CUC$85 and CUC$95 (depending on location of seat), including ¼ bottle of rum, 1 bottle of cola and a small salad.* Internationally famous and open-air cabaret (entry refunded if it rains). Hotels sell entrance only, so it's best to take a tour, which will include transport, as a taxi from La Habana Vieja costs CUC$12. A snack or dinner can be added. Alternatively, if you fancy a cheap drink or snack go to **Rodneys** (daily 1200-0100), a 1950s bar and restaurant designed by Cuban painter, Nelson Domínguez, located just beyond the entrance.
Turquino, *Hotel Habana Libre, 25th floor, Vedado, T7-834 6100. Daily cabaret 2230-0300, CUC$10, last entry 0200, couples only.* Great setting with amazing views. The roof opens and you can dance under the stars. Expensive drinks at CUC$6.

Cinemas
Comprehensive weekly listings of all films posted in cinema windows Thu-Wed. There are several cinemas on La Rampa, Vedado; most have a/c.

Classical music and dance
Amadeo Roldán, *Calzada y D, Vedado, T7-832 1168.* The home of the **Orquesta Sinfónica Nacional** was closed for renovation in 2015.
Gran Teatro de la Habana Alicia Alonso, *Prado y San José, Parque Central, T7-861 3078,*

dir.gth@cubarte.cult.cu, CUC$10. First opened in 1838 and reopened in Jan 2016 after renovation, this wonderful baroque building, which seats 1500 with 2 galleries, has seen countless famous performers on its stage. It is home to the **Cuban National Ballet** and **Opera** companies, who perform in the Sala García Lorca. The **Conjunto Folklórico Nacional** and **Danza Contemporánea** dance companies also perform here, and it hosts the **International Ballet Festival**.
Sala Hubert de Blanck, *Calzada 654 entre A y B, Vedado, T7-833 5962 (Casa de Ensayos), T7-8301011.* Specializes in classical and contemporary music concerts but has also staged contemporary dance companies, **Danzabierta** and **Danza Contemporánea**.
Teatro Nacional de Cuba, *Paseo y 39, T7-878 4275.* Concerts are held in the main theatre, but there's also a piano bar, **El Delirio Habanero**, upstairs, and the **Café Cantante** in the basement (for both, see Music and dance clubs).

Drama
All productions are performed in Spanish. Tourists pay in CUC$.
Sala Hubert de Blanck, *Calzada 654 entre A y B, Vedado, T7-833 5962 (Casa de Ensayos), T7-8301011.* Has staged major works by García Lorca and Cuban playwright Abelardo Estorino.
Teatro El Sótano, *K 514 entre 25 y 27, Vedado, T7-832 0630.* Contemporary drama, fringe theatre and home of the **Rita Montaner Company**.
Teatro Guiñol, M entre 17 y 19, Vedado, T7-832 6262. A children's theatre that specializes in marionette shows.
Teatro Mella, *Línea 657 entre A y B, Vedado, T7-833 5651.* Specializes in modern dance but stages lots of drama performances as well.
Teatro Trianón, *Línea entre Paseo y A, Vedado, T7-830 9648.* Small theatre in good condition, headquarters of **Teatro El Público**. The seats have quirky pull-out extensions for you to rest your thighs on.

Music and dance clubs
Havana is buzzing with musical activity. Rumba, conga, *son*, danzón, charanga, salsa – you'll hear it all. Cuba's greatest musicians converge on the capital's theatres and clubs, but there are also plenty of less star-studded venues to discover.

Havana clubs are late night/early morning affairs with most Cubans arriving around midnight and staying late. Expect queues at the weekends. Cubans dress up for club nights and most clubs have a smart dress code, strictly enforced by the door staff. This includes no shorts or sleeveless T-shirts for men. No one under 18 is admitted. The emphasis is on dancing, be it salsa and Latin dance styles, R&B, hip hop, reggaeton, electronic or rock. Many places are frequented by *jineteros/as* and lone travellers have reported feeling uncomfortable with the unwelcome attention. Several venues now feature earlier shows, aimed at young Cubans, with entrance in CUP$. There are also some good jazz venues in Vedado.

Radio Taíno FM 93.3, an English- and Spanish-language tourist station, gives regular details of a wide range of venues and Cuban bands playing, particularly in the programme *El Exitazo Musical del Caribe*, daily 1500-1800 presented by Alexis Nargona. Information is also given on **Radio Ciudad de la Habana**, 94.9 FM, 820 AM, in Spanish, including up-to-the-minute salsa programmes and live music events on *Disco Fiesta 98*, Mon-Sat 1100-1300, and *Rapsodia Latina*, Mon-Fri 1630-1730. The newspaper

> **Tip...**
> For a quick glance at which music was popular in 2015, see https://www.cibercuba.tv/musica/2015/12/18/los-temas-mas-pegaos-del-2015; cibercuba.tv also has a list of 10 young Cubans to watch, covering all genres: https://www.cibercuba.tv/musica/2015/12/04/10-jovenes-de-la-musica-cubana-que-debes-escuchar.

Opciones has a listing of what's on and is sold in **Paradiso** (Calle 23 469 esq O, T7-8333921) and in the hotels where Paradiso has a office.

Centro

Callejón de Hamel, *Hamel entre Aramburu y Hospital, Centro Habana, T7-8781661.* A fast, kicking *rumba* show with invited guests and community artists every Sun 1200-1500. A responsive audience and electric jam sessions make this a hot venue, recommended (see page 61). Take lots of sun screen and water.

Casa de la Cultura del Centro Habana, *Av Salvador Allende 720 entre Soledad y Castillejo, T7-878 4727.* Phone for details as events vary considerably. Extensive programme from blasting rock to sedate *peñas campesinas*, frenetic rap to hip hop.

Casa de la Cultura Julián del Casals, *Revillagigedo entre Gloria y Misión, T7-8634860.* On the 4th Fri of every month 1600-1830 there is a Peña de Danzón with the Orquesta Siglo XX and others. On the 2nd Sat 1700-1900 there is a Peña de Boleros with different musicians of the genre.

Casa de la Música Galiano, *Galiano 255 esq Neptuno, T7-8608296/7, cmh-eco@egrem. cult.cu.* Music shop, restaurant and dance floor with popular salsa bands; the best place to come for salsa. Tue-Sun matinée 1700-2100, price depends on who is performing, evening performances daily 2300-0300, CUC$10-30.

Casa del Tango Edmundo Daubar, *Neptuno 309 entre Aguila y Italia, T7-863 0097.* Musical venue/museum with fascinating collection of tango memorabilia dating back to the 1940s, from record sleeves to all manner of Carlos Gardel idolatry. Also tango dance classes, ask for Ruben.

La Madriguera, *Quinta de los Molinos, Av Infanta esq Jesús Peregrino, entrance on Jesús Peregrino (Final), after crossing over Infanta. T7-879 8175.* This is the **Casa del Joven Creador de Ciudad Habana** and the headquarters of the **Asociación Hermanos**

Tip...
Many of the *comparsa congas* parade regularly throughout the year down Paseo Martí and through La Habana Vieja.

Saíz in Centro, with arts, crafts and musical workshops for all ages and talents. Hip hop, rap and traditional Cuban rhythms are all here; fascinating glimpse into Cuban youth culture. Sun 2000-2400 electronic music, free; alternate Fri and Sat 2000-2400, hip hop, free; once a month there is a Café-Teatro with different theatre groups.

Vedado

Café Cantante, *Basement, Teatro Nacional, Plaza de la Revolución, Paseo y 39, T7-878 4275. Matinées Tue-Thu 1700-2400, Mon 2100-0200, Fri, Sat 1600-2000, Sun 2000-0100, CUC$5-10 (depending on who is performing).* Highly regarded venue, top bands play here and it's popular with local musicians and others in the business. Live bands perform at the daily matinées except Sun when there is recorded music. Matinées are particularly popular with Cuban youth. At night there are live bands on Fri 2200-0300 and Sat 2200-0600. Start your night in **El Delirio**, see below, then head down to the basement for the last hour of **Café Cantante** (the doorman may let you in with no charge at this late hour).

Café El Gato Tuerto, *O entre 17 y 19, T7-838 2696. Daily 2200-0400, CUC$5. Son, trova, filín* and bolero are performed live at the 'One-eyed Cat' to a bohemian crowd. The funky, post-modern decor is bordering on pretentious. Local legends often perform on the intimate stage with audience participation encouraged. There is a restaurant upstairs open daily 1200-2400.

Café Teatro Bertolt Brecht, *Centro Cultural Bertolt Brecht, 13 entre I y J, T7-830 1354. CUC$2/CUP$50.* A large basement bar open every night, but for the latest music visit late on Tue, Thu, Fri nights for '*No se lo digas a nadie*' (Don't tell anyone), when contemporary fusion bands play live.

El Delirio Habanero, *5th floor, Teatro Nacional, Plaza de la Revolución, Paseo y 39, T7-878 4275. Matinée on Sat 1600-2000, CUC$5. Thu-Sun 2200-0300, CUC$5.* Piano bar upstairs (lift sometimes not working) where you can hear quality music by small traditional groups. Great views of floodlit José Martí monument and Plaza de la Revolución. Take the big red sofa seats under the windows. Busy at weekends with a mostly Cuban crowd; phone to reserve the best tables. Delicious cocktails, good-value snacks, attentive service. Recommended. Energetic clubbers leave here and head for the sweaty **Café Cantante** (see above) in the basement for the last hour.

El Gran Palenque Bar, *4 entre Calzada y 5, T7-830 3939/830 3060. Closed for repairs 2015.* On Sat at 1500-1700 the courtyard of this open-air café/bar is taken over by the acclaimed **Conjunto Folklórico Nacional de Cuba** for an upbeat rumba show: *Patio de la Rumba* (CUC$5).

El Submarino Amarillo, *17 esq 6, corner of Parque John Lennon. Mon 2100-0200, Tue-Sat 1400-1930, 2100-0200, Sun 1400-2200, CUC$5.* Beatle-themed decor, Pop Art on the walls, reasonable drinks prices, snacks available. No smoking. Some die-hard Beatles fans might find the cover bands a cringe, but it's all good nostalgic fun with music by the Beatles, Led Zeppelin, Queen, etc, plus plenty of heavy metal and lots of Cuban rock.

Habana Café, *Hotel Meliá Cohiba, Paseo entre 1 y 3, T7-833 3636. Daily show 2100-2400, CUC$20 minimum, CUC$30 with drinks, CUC$50 with dinner and drinks (buy tickets in advance in the hotel lobby).* Very touristy and largely frequented by Meliá guests. A 1950s American pastiche has replaced the bombed-out disco. Old cars, small Cubana plane hanging from the ceiling, memorabilia on the walls, Benny Moré and Buena Vista Social Club music and large screen showing brilliant film of old Cuban musicians and artistes. Show is followed by a DJ who plays until 0200. Food expensive and not recommended, overpriced cocktails from CUC$6.

Hurón Azul, *17 351 entre Av de los Presidentes y H, T7-832 4571.* The headquarters of UNEAC (artists' and writers' union) in a majestic, colonial mansion is an inviting hangout for the intelligentsia. The lovely, welcoming bar hosts regular upbeat afternoon *peñas*. Wed alternate between *Trova sin Traba* and *Peña del Ambia* 1700-2000. Sat bolero from 2100 onwards.
Imágenes, *Calzada 602 esq C, T7-833 3606. Daily 2130-0300. Matinée Fri-Sun 1500-2000, CUC$1. Comedy Mon, Tue CUC$3, Wed-Sun CUC$5.* Intimate, classy piano bar, great for low-key evening, also stand-up comedy, karaoke, recorded music and games. Very popular, few tourists, reservations recommended for tables.
Jazz Café, *Galerías del Paseo esq 1, T7-838 3556. Daily 1200-0200. CUC$10 consumo mínimo after 2030. 2 live performances at 2130 and 2300.* Sleek and savvy jazz venue with class acts, a laid-back welcoming ambience and a highly appreciative audience. Star-studded line-up includes legendary pianist Chucho Valdés. Excellent for jazz lovers.
La Casona de Línea, *Línea 505 entre D y E, T7-8305373, llaurado@cubarte.cult.cu.* A cultural institute in a grand old Vedado mansion, once the home of the family that owned the Cristal brewery, now the headquarters for the Teatro Estudio theatre group. On Sun at 2030 in the small patio, you can see up-and-coming singer/songwriters and bands performing. Cover CUP$10. Call to see who is playing.
La Zorra y el Cuervo, *23 y O, T7-8332402, zorra.cha@tur.cu. Daily 2200-0200, CUC$10 (including 2 cocktails).* 'The Fox and the Crow' is one of the best nights in Havana for jazz enthusiasts. The small, dark cellar space on La Rampa is entered through a fine reproduction of a red British telephone box. High-calibre jazz musicians play to an appreciative crowd. Get there before 2300 if you want a table with an unobscured view of the stage as there are pillars in the way. Cuban bands often feature visiting US musicians.
Tikoa, *23 entre N y O, T7-830 9973. Daily 2200-0300. Disco Fri-Sun CUC$3, Mon-Thu CUC$2.*

All types of music. Wed matinee CUC$1 1600-2000. Popular with travellers and locals, this small and sweaty basement club swings with a strong Afro-Cuban vibe.

Miramar

Casa de la Música Egrem, *Sala Té Quedarás, 20 3308 esq 35, T7-204 0447. CD shop daily 1100-2300. Music and dancing daily 1700-2100 (CUC$5-15) and 2300-late (CUC$10-25).* One of the top venues to listen to the cream of Havana's musical talent. The programme changes a lot so it's best to phone in advance to see who is on. Upstairs at the **Diablo Tun Tun** traditional and alternative music is played by small groups daily 2300-0600, CUC$5-15. Food service from the *parrilla* daily 1200-2400.

Club Almendares, *Márgenes del Río Almendares, 49 y Av 28, Kohly, Miramar, T7-204 4990/7502.* Salón Chévere (*Disco Temba*), daily 2200-0300, CUC$2 except Wed when it is CUC$5, all types of music. Swimming pool 0900-1800, CUC$10 including drinks of CUC$5. Mosquitoes can be troublesome as you are in the Bosque de la Habana.

Don Cangrejo, *Av 1 entre 16 y 18, T7-504 5002/204 3837. Daily 2300-0300.* A large open-air venue beside the sea with a rather inconvenient covered swimming pool in the centre. Cover CUC$5-20, depending on who is playing. Fri night is very busy and popular with young Cubans keen to see contemporary bands.

El Río Club, *A entre 3 y 5, T7-209 3389. Daily 2200-0400, CUC$5.* Locals still refer to it as *Johnnie's Club,* which it was called before the Revolution. The salsa disco is hot and sweaty, a favourite with Havana's dance crowd.

La Maison *Calle 16, 701 esq 7, T7-204 0124. Daily 2030-0050.* Live music in the lovely open-air patio of this luxurious mansion and fashion shows displaying imported clothes sold in their own boutique (see Shopping). The Piano Bar is open daily 2200-0400 for karaoke and comedy show as well as live music, CUC$5. There's also a swimming pool, bar and café open during the day.

Salón Boleros en Dos Gardenias, *7 esq 26, Miramar, T7-204 2353. Daily 2200-0500, CUC$5.* Upmarket *bolero* venue, 4-5 live shows every night, elegant, well-dressed crowd with popular Chinese and criollo restaurant and bars. Live singers with small bands.

Salón Rosado Benny Moré, *La Tropical, 41 y 46, T7-206 4799. Closed Mon-Thu.* Fri electronic music 1900-0400, CUC$2, Sat 2030-0300, CUC$2-5 depending who is on, Sun Discotemba 1700-2300, CUC$1 with live bands. Raunchy, popular dance venue with some of the best salsa in town.

Teatro Karl Marx, *Av 1 1010 entre 8 y 10, T7-203 0801, T7-209 1991.* Huge venue, famous for hosting the 1st rock concert by a Western band, Manic Street Preachers, who played here in 2001 in the presence of Fidel Castro.

Festivals

The most popular cultural events are the cinema and jazz festivals, but there are also several dance festivals as well as folk and classical music events. At the Marina Hemingway there always seem to be regattas and fishing tournaments in progress.

Jan Cubadanza is a twice-yearly dance festival with workshops and performances.
Feb Havana International Book Fair is held at La Cabaña castle. It's a commercial fair but is immensely popular with book-hungry families. Look out for new book launches. Also held in many cities around the island, www.cubaliteraria.com.
Cigar Festival, www.festivaldelhabano.com, is for true aficionados of *Habanos.* Held at the Palacio de las Convenciones. You can learn about the history of cigars and there are opportunities for visits to tobacco plantations and cigar factories.
Mar Bienal de la Habana is held over a month and takes place every 2 years (next in 2017), gathering over 200 artists from 40 countries in the Centro de Arte Contemporáneo Wifredo Lam, Centro de Arte La Casona, Parque Morro-Cabaña,

Pabellón Cuba and other venues, www. bienalhabana.cult.cu.

Spring in Havana The **International Festival of Electroacoustic Music** features workshops and performances.

Apr **Offshore Class 1 World Championship** and the **Great Island Speedboat Grand Prix** are usually held during the last week at the Marina Hemingway, attracting powerboat enthusiasts from all over the world.

May **Ernest Hemingway International Billfishing Tournament** is one of the major events at the Marina Hemingway, www. internationalhemingwaytournament.com. **Festival Internacional de Poesía de La Habana** is held at CubaPoesía, Hospital esq 25, www.cubapoesia.cult.cu.

Jun **Festival Danzón Habana** Latin American musicians and dancers celebrate *danzón* at the Teatro América, Centro Hispanoamericano de Cultura y Unión Fraternal, at the end of the month. Each year it is dedicated to a different Latin American country, ireartes@hotmail.com.

Jul **Cuballet de Verano** is a summer dance festival with workshops and courses for dancers and dance teachers, www.prodanza.cult.cu.

Aug **Cubadanza**, the 2nd of the year, with workshops and courses, see Jan for details. **Carnival** Conga parades through the city.

Sep **International Blue Marlin Fishing Tournament** at Marina Hemingway. The marina fills up with mostly US fishermen eager to pit their strength against marlin and their fellow competitors, with lots of après-fishing social events.

Oct **Havana International Ballet Festival** is held every other year (2016) in the 2nd half of the month at the Gran Teatro, Teatro Nacional and Teatro Mella. Run by Alicia Alonso, head of the Cuban National Ballet, www.festivalballethabana.cult.cu.

Havana Theatre Festival takes place at theatres and plazas all over the city at the end of Oct and into Nov, featuring contemporary international and Cuban drama, workshops and seminars, organized by Cuba Escena, www.cubaescena.cult.cu.

Nov **Havana Contemporary Music Festival** is held at UNEAC and theatres mid-month, www.musicacontemporanea.cult.cu. **Marabana**, Havana's marathon, takes place on the 3rd Sun of the month, www.inder.cu/marabana.

Dec **International Festival of New Latin American Cinema** shows prize-winning films (no subtitles) at cinemas around Havana. This is the foremost film festival in Latin America with the best of Cuban and Latin American films along with documentaries and independent cinema from Europe and the USA. The festival attracts big-name actors and directors, www.habanafilmfestival.com.

International Jazz Plaza Festival is held at theatres and at the Casa de la Cultura de Plaza. It is one of the world's major jazz festivals with the best of Cuban and international jazz for CUC$5-10 per show. There are also events at the **Nacional** and the **Habana Libre**. There are masterclasses and workshops available and the event is organized by Grammy winner Jesús 'Chucho' Valdés, http://jazzcuba.com.

San Lázaro Pilgrims flock to the church in the small town of El Rincón (just south of the airport) on 17 Dec to ask Lazarus to cure them.

Christmas Day The conga parade is another chance to go wild with the *farolas* and *tambores*.

Shopping

Art

You need documentation to take works of art out of the country or you may have them confiscated at the airport; galleries will provide the necessary paperwork and even vendors in the market can give you the required stamp. The following are all in La Habana Vieja.

Casa de los Artistas, *Oficios 6 entre Obispo y Obrapía. Mon-Sat 1030-1630.* Several leading

Cuban artists have their studios here which can be visited. There is also a gallery of contemporary art showcasing their work and that of others.

Centro de Desarrollo de las Artes Visuales, *San Ignacio 352 esq Teniente Rey, just off Plaza Vieja, T7-862 3533. Tue-Sat 1000-1700.* Exhibitions on 3 floors of established and up-and-coming artists. Experimental art has a home here.

Galería del Grabado, *at the back of the Taller Experimental de Gráfica de la Habana, Callejón del Chorro 62, Plaza de la Catedral, T7-864 6013, tgrafica@cubarte.cult.cu. Mon-Fri 1000-1630.* Original lithographs and other works of art can be purchased or commissioned directly from the artists. You can watch the prints and engravings being made and specialist courses are available for those who want to learn the skill for themselves, for 1 week, CUC$150, 2 weeks CUC$250, 1 month, CUC$500, contact Yamilys Brito Jorge, Especialista Principal.

Galería Forma, *Obispo 255 entre Aguiar y Cuba, T7-862 0123. Daily 0900-2100.* Formerly the bookshop, **Exlibris Swan** 1927-1960, now an art gallery belonging to the **Fondo Cubano de Bienes Culturales,** selling paintings, *artesanías,* ceramics, jewellery and sculpture.

Galería Víctor Manuel, *San Ignacio 56 esq Callejón del Chorro, Plaza de la Catedral, T7-861 2955. Daily 0900-2100.* A bit of a tourist trap selling mainstream representative art, rather than anything experimental, at high prices. However, you may still find something you would like to live with. The gallery is in the former Casa de Baños (public bath house).

Taller de Papel Artesanal, *Mercaderes entre Obispo y Obrapía, T7-861 3356. Mon-Sat 0830-1700, Sun 0830-1300.* Sells handmade paper as well as postcards and other items made from recycled paper. Workshops and courses in paper-making available.

Taller Serigrafía René Portocarrero, *Cuba 513 entre Teniente Rey y Muralla, T7-8623276, serigrafia@cubarte.cult.cu.* Another big workshop, making screen prints; again, you can watch them being made and buy things.

Terracota 4, *Mercaderes entre Obrapía y Lamparilla. Daily 1000-1800.* Studio and gallery of 2 ceramicists, Amelia Carballo and Angel Norniella.

Books

There are second-hand bookstalls outside on the Plaza de Armas where you may be able to pick up a treasure if you know what you are looking for.

El Navío, *Obispo entre Mercaderes y Oficios, La Habana Vieja, T7-861 3187. Mon-Sat 1000-1800.* Maps, road maps (*Guía de Carretera*), tourist maps in 3 languages and charts, both national and regional.

Fernando Ortíz, *L 460 esq 27, Vedado, T7-832 9653.* Quite a wide selection, mostly in Spanish, and some beautiful postcards.

La Moderna Poesía, *Obispo 527 esq Bernaza, La Habana Vieja, T7-861 6640, libreria@ lamodernapoesia. ohch.cu. Mon-Sat 1000-1800.* Biggest in Cuba, modern design, literature, sciences, art materials, CDs, posters, cards.

Flowers

Jardín Wagner, *Mercaderes 113 entre Obispo y Obrapía, La Habana Vieja, T7-866 9017. Mon-Sat 0900-1800, Sun 1000-1300.* Flowers for sale, including artificial flowers and pot plants.

Food

For food shopping, there is the **Focsa Supermarket** (on 17 entre M y N in Vedado, at the base of the big tower block) or the **Amistad** (on San Lázaro, just below Infanta in Cayo Hueso). The **Isla de Cuba** (on Máximo Gómez entre Factoría y Suárez), supermarket has the best selection of food in La Habana Vieja, with prices stamped on the goods to prevent overcharging. Farmers are allowed to sell their produce (root and green vegetables, fruit, grains and meat) in free-priced city *agromercados.* You should pay for food in CUP$. There are markets in Vedado at 19 y B and a smaller one at 21 esq J; in Nuevo Vedado, Tulipán opposite Hidalgo. There are busy food markets on the last Sun of every

month in other Havana neighbourhoods and a new state market on the Plaza del Cerro, Vía Blanca y Boyeros opposite the Ciudad Deportiva entrance, Tue-Fri 0800-1800, Sat 0700-1700 and Tue 0700-1200, with a **Cadeca** exchange bureau, car and bike park.
Museo del Chocolate, *Mercaderes entre Teniente Rey y Amargura, La Habana Vieja, T7-866 4431. Daily 0900-2200*. Sells chocolate candy made on the premises, also offers hot and cold chocolate.

Handicrafts
Asociación Cubana Artesanos y Artistas (**ACAA**), *Obispo 411 entre Compostela y Aguacate, La Habana Vieja. Office T7-862 0655, Mon-Fri 1000-1500. Gallery, T7-8678577, and market daily 1000-1900*. Handicrafts, clothing, humidors, glassware and musical instruments.
Casa del Abanico, *Obrapía 107 entre Oficios y Mercaderes, La Habana Vieja, T7-863 4452. Mon-Sat 0900-1800*. Beautifully decorated fans for sale from luxury silk to everyday cotton. Lots of historical details. You can have one customized to your own design, just as the *criollo* ladies used to.
Palacio de la Artesanía, *Palacio Pedroso (built 1780) at Cuba 64 entre Peña Pobre y Cuarteles (opposite Parque Anfiteatro)*. A mansion converted into boutiques on 3 floors with musicians in the courtyard. A large selection of Cuban handicrafts is available. It also has things not available elsewhere, such as American trainers, as well as clothing, jewellery, perfume, souvenirs, music, cigars, restaurant, bar and ice cream. Visa and MasterCard accepted, passport required.

Handicraft markets
Many open-air markets, handicraft and tourist souvenir stalls and *ferias de artesanías* have sprung up.

> **Tip...**
> It is illegal to import black coral into many countries, so avoid buying items made from it.

Feria Almacenes San José, *Desamparados (Av del Puerto) entre Damas y San Isidro, La Habana Vieja. Daily 1000-1800*. Havana's largest craft market has a multitude of products: tourist souvenirs, clothing, paintings, carvings, crochet, ceramics, boxes, jewellery, T-shirts and baseball bats – the list is endless; if you can't find what you want, someone will know someone who has it. A platform for many talented young artists to show off their skills. You may pick up a bargain, or you may be asked to pay Miami-type prices. Also on the market site is a CADECA, a small music shop, a rum, tobacco and coffee outlet, a shop selling coins and antiques, and an office of ETECSA for phone cards; a second hand book stall is planned.
Feria del 23, *23 entre M y N, Vedado. Daily 0900-1700*. A varied selection, but carvings and beads predominate.
Feria del Malecón, *Malecón, entre B y C, Vedado. Tue-Sat 0930-1730, Sun 1000-1400*. Items include shoes and costume jewellery.

Music, cigars and souvenirs
Artex, *L esq 23, T7-838 3162. Mon-Sat 1000-2100, Sun 1000-1900*. Excellent music section with instruments and tasteful T-shirts and postcards.
Casa Cubana del Perfume, *Teniente Rey 13 entre Oficios y Mercaderes, La Habana Vieja, T7-866 3759. Mon-Sat 1100-1800, Sun 1100-1400*. Perfumes mixed on the premises. On the mezzanine is a little cafetería.
Casa de la Música Galiano, *Galiano 255 esq Neptuno, Centro, T7-860 8296, cmh-eco@egrem.cult.cu. Daily 1100-2300*. Shop specializing in music, extensive list of titles, past and contemporary.
Casa del Habano, *7 y 26, Miramar, T7-204 2353. Mon-Sat 1030-1830*. Full range of cigars, one of many state cigar shops. See box, page 120.
Casa del Tabaco y Ron, *Obispo esq Monserrate, La Habana Vieja, T7-866 8911. Daily 0900-1900*. Wide range of rums of all ages, plus tobacco and coffee.

EGREM, *Casa de la Música, see Music and dance clubs, above.* A good selection of CDs and music.

La Maison *Calle 16, 701 esq 7, Miramar, T7-204 0124.* Luxurious mansion with shops selling cigars, alcohol, handicrafts, jewellery and perfume. There is live music (see Entertainment) and fashion shows in the evening, displaying imported clothes sold in the boutique. However, as with all shops depending on imports, the quantity and quality of stock is variable and can be disappointing.

Longina Música, *Obispo 360 entre Habana y Compostela, La Habana Vieja, T7-862 8371. Mon-Sat 1000-1800, Sun 1000-1300.* You can buy drums and other instruments here as well as CDs and stereos.

Perfumería Habana, *Mercaderes 156 entre Obrapía y Lamparilla, La Habana Vieja, T7-861 3525. Mon-Sat 1000-1900, Sun 1100-1400.* Manufacture and sale of perfumes and colognes from natural essential oils. Aromatherapy massages also offered.

Shopping centres/department stores

Shopping centres tend to get very busy at weekends. Taxis and *bicitaxis* wait outside. Bags must be left outside shops in designated storage areas called *guardabolsas*; you should receive a numbered badge to identify your bag. Items purchased will be checked against receipt by security when you leave each shop. The large department stores include: **Galerías de Paseo** (1 entre Paseo y A, opposite Meliá Cohiba, Vedado, T7-833 9888); **Harris Brothers** (O'Reilly 526 entre Villegas y Monserrate, La Habana Vieja, T7-861 1615); **La Epoca** (Av de Italia (Galiano) y Neptuno, Centro Habana, T7-866 9418), and **La Plaza Carlos Tercera** (Av Salvador Allende (Carlos III), entre Arbol Seco y Retiro, Centro Habana).

What to do

Baseball

Estadio Latinoamericano, *Pedro Pérez 302, Cerro, T7-870 6576.* South of the centre in Cerro district, this is the best place to see baseball (the major league level). Opened in the 1950s, it has a capacity for 55,000 spectators and is home to the 2 Havana teams, **Industriales** (Los Azules) and **Metropolitanos**. Days and times of games vary considerably, CUC$3 for the best seats and CUC$1 for the regular stand.

The *Serie Nacional* baseball season runs Aug-Nov, culminating in the national play-offs, followed a couple of weeks later by the *Liga Superior*, which lasts a month. Baseball games have a fanatical following and can last up to 3 hrs. Follow the evening's game by visiting the Parque Central in La Habana Vieja the next day, the traditional venue for groups of passionate fans to congregate and discuss match details using frantic hand gestures to illustrate their opinions.

Basketball

Estadio Ramón Fonst, *Av Independencia y Bruzón, Plaza de la Revolución, T7-881 4196.* Local team is **Capitalinos**. No fixed match dates.

Boxing

Sala Kid Chocolate, *Paseo de Martí y Brasil, La Habana Vieja, T7-861 1547.* The sports centre hosts regular matches during boxing season. Also here are judo, weightlifting, chess and handball; for international events it hosts tennis, boxing and badminton, when tickets are CUC$1. A monthly programme of events is on the noticeboard.

Golf

Club de Golf, *Calzada de Varona, Km 8, Capdevila, Boyeros, towards the airport, cgolf@continental.cubalse.cu.* The 9-hole course is par 35. CUC$30 for 18 holes (caddy charges CUC$6), CUC$20 for 9 (caddy CUC$3), CUC$10 for a 30-min lesson, club rental CUC$10. Nonmembers are welcome. For foreign residents or frequent visitors, club membership is CUC$45 a month after an initial fee of CUC$70, which gives you unlimited golf. There is also a 2-lane bowling alley, billiards (3 tables), tennis (5 courts, bring your own rackets, instruction available), squash and swimming pool, CUC$5 (CUC$8 in summer) including a drink, a bar (**Hoyo 19**, reserved for golfers and members) and a poor restaurant/snack bar, **La Estancia**.

Gyms
Some of the hotels have facilities that can be used by anyone. At the **Hotel Nacional** there is a small range of machines and free weights, sauna available. Lockers provided, CUC$15 including towel and shower (free to guests). The **Hotel Meliá Cohiba** has better facilities and range of machines, CUC$10 including sauna, massage from CUC$25. There is also a gym in the Barrio Chino, run by the **Sociedad Chang Weng Chung Tong** (San Nicolás 517 altos entre Zanja y Dragones, T7-862 1490, Mon-Fri 0800-2000, Sat 0800-1200), for aerobics, Taibo, apparatus, CUC$25 for monthly membership, restaurant attached, see page 81.

Horse riding
You can go riding at **El Rodeo** (near Las Ruinas in Parque Lenin, T7-644 1476, Wed-Sun 1000-1700, for CUC$15 per hr, including a guide). It is mostly for Cubans and you may be able to pay in CUP$, but book in advance to verify price. Horses are well cared for. There are also 3 cafes and a swimming pool.

Running
Entry to Havana's Marathon, **Marabana**, in Nov, is CUC$10, including a marathon jersey, see Festivals and events for details. Another race is **Terry Fox** on 2 Feb each year to raise money for cancer treatments.

Sports centres
Ciudad Deportiva, *at the roundabout on Av Boyeros y Vía Blanca, T7-881 6979.*

P2 bus passes outside. The 'Sports City' is a large circular sports stadium seating 18,000 spectators for volleyball (very popular), basketball, martial arts and table tennis. The stadium is enclosed by a dome with a roof diameter of 88 m and was designed by architects Nicolás Arroyo and Gabriela Menéndez. The complex was inaugurated on 26 Feb 1958 and at the time was considered one of the world's best indoor sports facilities. Entrance usually CUP$2 for a seat and CUP$1 for the concrete benches in upper tiers, but it depends on the event. Buy tickets in advance at venue. International matches are usually a sellout. Great atmosphere, crowded, limited food and drink facilities. Large neon sign outside *'listos para vencer'* (ready to win).

Tour operators
There are lots of state-owned travel agencies, which cooperate fully with each other and have bureaux in all the major hotels. As well as local trips to factories, schools, hospitals, etc, tours can be arranged to destinations all over Cuba by bus or air, with participants picked up from any hotel in Havana at no extra charge.

Examples include a tour of the city's colonial sites (CUC$15, 4 hrs); a trip to the Tropicana cabaret; Cayo Largo for the day by air with boat trip, snorkelling, optional diving, lunch; Cayo Coco for the day with flight, all-inclusive package and changing room; Cayo Levisa day trip by bus and boat with snorkelling and lunch; Guamá and the Península de Zapata with a stop en route at the Finca Fiesta Campesina, tour of crocodile farm, lunch; Viñales and Pinar del Río, visiting mogotes, caves and tobacco factory, lunch; a day on the beach at Varadero with lunch, 10 hrs, and you get a changing room with shower and towel; Trinidad and Cienfuegos overnight, visiting the colonial city and the Valle de los Ingenios; ecological tour of Las Terrazas with walking and river bathing, lunch. Prices vary slightly between agencies and you can negotiate a reduction without meals.

Watersports

Marina Hemingway has 140 slips with electricity and water and space for docking 400 recreational boats.

Centro de Buceo La Aguja, *Marina Hemingway, T7-204 5280*. The dive centre takes up to 8 divers on the boat.
Club Habana (Sol Meliá), *Av 5 entre 188 y 192, Reparto Flores, Playa, T7-275 0100*. A club for permanent residents with annual membership of CUC$1500. Tennis, squash, pool, diving (with certification), windsurfing, training golf course, child care, shops, meetings facilities, sauna and massage, bar and restaurant, expensive. All motorized watersports were withdrawn in 2003 following a security clampdown.
Club Náutico Internacional 'Hemingway' (Hemingway International Yacht Club), *Residencial Turístico 'Marina Hemingway', Av 5 y 248, Playa, T7-204 6653, yachtclub@cnih. mh.cyt.cu*. Offers help and advice to visiting yachties. The club organizes regattas, sailing schools and excursions, as well as the Hemingway Tournament.

Transport

Air

José Martí International Airport is 18 km southwest of the city and has 3 terminals: Terminal 1 for domestic flights; Terminal 2 for flights from Cancún and Terminal 3 for all other international flights (for details, see Practicalities, page 457). There are no buses from Terminal 3 to the other 2 terminals (although it's just 5 mins in a taxi) and no public buses from Terminal 3 into Havana, but there are lots of taxis and taxi organizers waiting for you. As many transatlantic flights arrive late at night it can be sensible to arrange the transfer from the airport to your hotel in advance with your travel agent. However, it is cheaper to get a taxi when you arrive: CUC$25 is commonly asked to the old city; sharing a taxi with someone else will reduce the fare a bit. On the way back to the airport it is possible to arrange a regular taxi, which may work out cheaper, if you negotiate with the driver. Travelling by bus is not practical.

Bus

HabanaBusTour is a hop-on, hop-off tour bus service for foreigners, CUC$5 per day, which travels 0900-2100 on 2 routes: T1 leaves from Almacenes San José (Feria de Artesanía on Av del Puerto) to the Plaza de la Revolución and out to Miramar (Av 5 y 112), while T3 leaves from the Parque Central and travels past the Fortaleza Cabaña, the Villa Panamericana and Alamar out to the Playas del Este.

Local Metrobuses (CUP$0.40) serve the suburbs, but the service has long been in crisis due to a lack of vehicles and fuel, and foreigners are not expected to use them. They are hot and sweaty and uncomfortably crowded at all times. *Habaneros* insist they carry more people than a Boeing 747 and refer to them as *La Película del sábado* (Saturday Night Movie) since they contain bad language, violence and sex scenes. This may be a slight exaggeration, but you should certainly be aware of pickpockets. If you insist on using the bus, then be sure to follow queuing etiquette at the bus stop. Discover who is last in line (*el último*, you have to shout loudly) for the bus you want, then ask him/her who they are behind (*¿detrás de quién?*). The queue may look disorganized, but it is actually highly functional: people mark their places and then wander off until the bus comes when everyone re-forms into an orderly queue. That's the theory. However, things may deteriorate at night, particularly if there has been a long wait, when the elbow becomes the preferred mode of queuing. We have included some useful bus routes in the listings, but in general you are advised to find alternative transport.

Long distance A/c tourist buses to most cities are run by **Viazul**, and leave from Av 26 entre Av Zoológico y Ulloa, Nuevo Vedado, T7-881 1413/881 1108/881 5652/881 5657,

Tip...
Some **Viazul** ticket sellers refuse to sell tickets until the bus arrives. Passengers in the waiting lounge are not told when it does arrive and it leaves without them. The 'helpful' ticket seller then tries to sell them a seat in a private taxi, for which he/she no doubt receives a commission.

www.viazul.cu, with lots of intermediate stops. See Practicalities, pages 461-465, for advance booking addresses, and timetable. Viazul's terminal is small, with toilets and a poor snack bar upstairs; outside there's an **Etecsa** cabin for local and long-distance calls. **Taxis** wait outside the terminal and will cost around CUC$5-6 to La Habana Vieja or Centro.

Astro buses leave from the Terminal de Omnibus Interprovinciales, Av Rancho Boyeros (Independencia) 101 entre 19 de Mayo y Bruzón, by the Plaza de la Revolución, T7-870 9401/870 3397. However, foreigners are not allowed to use this service any more. **Viazul** buses often call in here after leaving their own terminal, but you can't rely on seats being available.

Car

Most of the hotels have car hire agencies in the reception area and many streets around tourist locations have unofficial 'supervisors' who monitor car parking spaces and expect a CUC$1 payment on your return. However, hiring a car is not recommended for getting around Havana, as roads are badly signed and there have been many accidents involving tourists driving rental cars, see Practicalities, page 466.

Instead, if you want the real experience, **Gran Car**, T7-8788784, rents classic cars (including Oldsmobiles, Mercury '54, Buicks and Chevvy '55) with driver for a maximum of 4 passengers. Under new regulations, you must negotiate the price with driver, usually CUC$25-30 per hr or more for cars without roofs (go for the Oldsmobile '52).

Motos (scooters) can be hired from **Transtur**, Av 7 esq 26, Restaurante Dos Gardenias, Miramar, T7-204 0646, 1 day CUC$25, 2-4 days CUC$23 daily, 5-12 days CUC$21 daily, 13-20 days CUC$18 daily, 21-29 days CUC$16 daily, 30 days CUC$14 daily. Returnable deposit of CUC$50.

There are **Cupet-Cimex** petrol stations (green logo) at Av Independencia y 271, Boyeros (near Terminal 2); Av Independencia esq Calzada de Cerro, Plaza (near Plaza de la Revolución); Paseo y Malecón (near Hotel Riviera), Vedado; L y 17, Vedado; Línea y Malecón, Vedado; 86 y 13, Miramar; 7, entre 2 y 4, Miramar; 112 y 5, Miramar, and Vento y Santa Catalina, Cerro. All are open 24 hrs and sell drinks, snacks and food.

Cycling

Cycling is a good way to see Havana, especially the suburbs; you can reach the Playas del Este beaches and surrounding countryside quickly and easily, although some roads in the Embassy area are closed to cyclists. The tunnel underneath the harbour has a bus designed specifically to carry bicycles and their riders, from Parque El Curita, Aguila y Dragones, to Reparto Camilo Cienfuegos after the tunnel. Take care at night as there are few streetlights and bikes are not fitted with lamps. *Poncheros*, small private businesses that crudely fix punctures, are everywhere.

Ferry

There are ferries from La Habana Vieja to **Casablanca** and **Regla**, CUP$0.10, which depart from Muelle de Luz, San Pedro opposite Bar Dos Hermanos. If you are facing the water, the Casablanca ferry docks on the left side of the pier and goes out in a left curve towards that headland, and the Regla ferry docks on the right side and goes out in a right curve. There are lots of security checks with X-ray machines and body searches following the 2003 hijacking of a ferry.

Taxi

Bicitaxi/cocotaxi In La Habana Vieja and Vedado, bicycle or tricycle taxis are cheap and a pleasant way to travel. A short journey will cost at least CUC$2. There is also the *coctaxi/cocomóvil.* If you can handle being driven around in a bright yellow vehicle shaped like a coconut shell on a 125cc motor bike, then these are quick and readily available. They take 2 passengers, no safety belts, plenty of pollution in your face. The fare is fixed in CUC$, but agree the fare before the journey. A typical fare from the Hotel Nacional to La Habana Vieja is CUC$3. Less conspicuous are the **Rentar una fantasía** vehicles, using the same 125cc engine but the vehicle is designed as a pre-1920s motor car.

Cubataxi Regular taxis are plentiful and are a safe and easy way to travel around Havana, although they are relatively expensive. **Cubataxi**, T7-855 5555, is now the only company. They wait outside most hotels and at the airport, or you can ask your hotel to call one. Cubataxi also have minibuses, or big taxis, T7-8831587, which take 7 people, useful if you are a group with lots of luggage. From Centro to the airport costs CUC$25.

Peso taxis Taxi *colectivos* ply their trade up and down main thoroughfares, usually stopping at bus stops to pick up passengers. They are large old American gas guzzlers in variable condition, usually poor, and everyone is squeezed in. Fixed CUP$10 fare. These taxis can also be hired by foreigners if they have a licence.

Train

Rail services in Cuba are notoriously unreliable so the following departure and fare information is liable to change without

> **Fact...**
> The Estación Central has what is claimed to be the oldest engine in Latin America, *La Junta*, built in Baltimore in 1842.

warning. For further information, see Practicalities, page 460.

The **Estación Central on Egido** (Av de Bélgica) y Arsenal, on the edge of La Habana Vieja, is currently closed for renovation and trains for the east of the country are instead leaving from **Estación La Coubre** (Av del Puerto y Egido), nearby. Get your tickets in advance for trains, buses and the catamaran from different agencies, including Estación La Coubre, T7-8603165, Mon-Fri 0830-1600, Sat 0830-1130. Take your passport. The train to **Santiago de Cuba** leaves every 3rd day at 1800, about 14-15 hrs on a good day, returning 1530, CUC$30. Also every 3 days to **Bayamo**, CUC$25; **Manzanillo**, CUC$27.50, and **Guantánamo**, CUC$32. There is a train every other day to **Sancti Spíritus**, CUC$13, which passes through **Santa Clara**, CUC$10.50. The trains are very uncomfortable and stop at every town along the way; they also have to give way to goods trains, so there are always delays.

Trains to **Pinar del Río** depart from Terminal 19 de Noviembre, Tulipán y Factor, Nuevo Vedado, T7-883 2769, every other day, 7-8 hrs, CUC$6.50. However, a long-distance bus or dollar taxi will do the same journey in a fraction of the time.

The **Hershey** electric train (see page 104) with services to **Matanzas** starts from Casablanca departing daily 0445, 1221, 1635. Buy tickets at Casablanca booking office an hour before departure, CUC$2.80 single to Matanzas, CUC$1.40 to Hershey, but call first, T7-793 8888, because the service is 'informal'.

Around
Havana

Several places of interest in the provinces of Havana and Mayabeque can easily be reached as a day trip from the capital, with the option of staying a night or two if you wish. Readers of Ernest Hemingway novels will be fascinated to see his former home, now a museum dedicated to his memory, just as he left it, or Cojímar, the setting for his novel *The Old Man and the Sea*. Alternatively you can base yourself on the beach and come in to Havana for sightseeing. The best beaches are east of Havana, at Playas del Este, an easy cycle ride or taxi from the city, or further afield at Jibacoa where you can explore the countryside as well as the sea. For destinations west of the capital in Artemisa Province, see the West of Havana chapter.

East of Havana
Afro-Cuban and Hemingway attractions plus miles of beaches for city escapees

Cojímar
The former seaside village, now a concrete jungle, featured in Hemingway's *The Old Man and the Sea*, is an easy excursion (15 minutes by taxi) from central Havana. Hemingway celebrated his Nobel prize here in 1954, and there is a bust of the author opposite a small fort built in 1645. Unfortunately the wharf where he kept the *Pilar* was smashed by the hurricanes in 2008 and has not been repaired. The coastline (no beach) is covered in sharp rocks and is dirty because of effluent from tankers. La Terraza, founded in 1926, is a restaurant with a pleasant view, where Hemingway used to sit and pass time with the local fishermen upon whom he modelled his 'Old Man', see page 106.

Regla
Ferry from Muelle Luz (at the end of C Santa Clara), La Habana Vieja, or Ruta 6 bus from Zulueta entre Genios y Refugio, CUP$0.40.

Regla is to the east of La Habana Vieja, across the harbour. It has a largely black population and a long-standing and still active cultural history of Yoruba and *Santería* traditions (see page 431). The main street, Martí, runs north from the landing stage up to the church

BACKGROUND
Hemingway's Havana

Marlin fishing, gambling, beautiful prostitutes: these were the things that attracted Ernest Hemingway to Cuba in 1932. At first he stayed at the Hotel Ambos Mundos in Havana, but his visits became so frequent that he decided to buy a property. In 1940 he bought **Finca Vigía**, a 14-acre farm outside Havana. The staff included three gardeners, a Chinese cook and a man who tended to the fighting cocks Hemingway bred.

During the Second World War, Hemingway set up his own counter-intelligence unit at the Finca, calling it 'the Crook Factory'; his plan was to root out Nazi spies in Havana. He also armed his fishing boat, the *Pilar*, with bazookas and hand grenades. With a crew made up of Cuban friends and Spanish exiles from the Civil War, the *Pilar* cruised the waters around Havana in search of German U-Boats. The project surprisingly had the blessing of the US Embassy, who even assigned a radio operator to the *Pilar*. With no U-Boats in sight for several months, the mission turned into drunken fishing trips for Hemingway, his two sons and his friends.

When Hemingway returned to Cuba after more heroic contributions to the war effort in France, he wrote the book that was to have the biggest impact on the reading public, *The Old Man and the Sea*, which won him the Pulitzer Prize in 1953. This was a period of particularly heavy drinking for Hemingway: early-morning scotches were followed by numerous papa dobles (2½ jiggers of white rum, the juice of half a grapefruit, six drops of maraschino, mixed until foaming) at the **Floridita**, absinthe in the evening, two bottles of wine with dinner, and scotch and soda till the early hours in the casinos of Havana.

When the political situation under Batista began to grow tense in 1958, a government patrol shot one of Hemingway's dogs at the Finca. By then he was older and wearier than he had been during the Spanish Civil War and he quietly went back to his home in Idaho, from where he heard the news of Fidel Castro's victory. Hemingway made a public show of his support for the Revolution on his return to Cuba. He met Castro during the marlin fishing tournament, which the new president won.

Hemingway's last days at the Finca were taken up with work on *The Dangerous Summer*, a long essay about bullfighting, but his thoughts frequently turned to suicide, and he left for Florida in 1960. After the Bay of Pigs US-backed attempted invasion in 1961, the government appropriated the Finca. Hemingway committed suicide in the USA in 1961.

Bibliography: *Hemingway*, Kenneth S Lynn (Simon & Schuster, 1987).

on your left. In the church is the Santísima Virgen de Regla, the spirit (Orisha) who looks after sailors. Next to the church, the **Museo Municipal de Regla** ① *Martí 158 entre Facciolo y La Piedra, T7-797 6989, museoderegla@cubarte.cult.cu, Tue-Sat 0900-1800, Sun 0900-1300, CUC$2, with guide CUC$3, camera CUC$5, amateur video CUC$50,* has a room with information and objects of Yoruba culture. Three blocks further on is the **Casa de la Cultura** ① *Martí 208, T7-797 9905,* which has very occasional cultural activities.

Guanabacoa
5 km east of Havana and reached by a road turning off the Central Highway. Take a CUP$0.40 bus: Ruta 195 (1 hr) from Calle 23 esq J, Vedado; Ruta 5 (1 hr) from 19 de Mayo; Ruta 3 from Parque de la Fraternidad, or a direct bus from Regla.

Guanabacoa is a small colonial town. Sights include the old parish church, which has a splendid altar, the monastery of San Francisco, the Carral theatre, the Jewish cemetery and some attractive mansions. Housed in a former estate mansion, with slave quarters at the back of the building, is the **Museo Histórico de Guanabacoa** ① *Martí 108 entre Versalles y San Antonio, T7-797 9117, musgbcoa@cubarte.cult.cu, Mon-Sat 0930-1730, Sun 0900-1300, CUC$2, CUC$3 with guide, CUC$5 photos, amateur video CUC$25.* The **Festival de Raíces Africanas Wemilere** is held here in the last week of November, each year dedicated to a different African country. Museum staff offer a 45-minute guided tour of the town (in Spanish) and there's sometimes folk dancing for groups.

The **Cementerio de Judíos** (Jewish Cemetery) was founded in 1906-10 and is set back behind an impressive gated entrance on the left on the road to Santa Fé. There is a monument to the victims of the Holocaust and bars of soap are buried as a symbolic gesture. Saúl Yelín (1935-1977), one of the founding members of Cuban cinema, is buried under a large flamboyant tree and you can also see the graves of the *Mártires del Partido Communista*, victims of the Machado dictatorship.

Museo Ernest Hemingway
Finca La Vigía, San Francisco de Paula, San Miguel del Padrón, 12.5 km from central Havana, T7-691 0809. Mon-Sat 1000-1700, closed rainy days. CUC$5 plus CUC$5 for a guide, children under 12 free, amateur video CUC$50. Getting there: Bus P7 from Parque Fraternidad and P2 from Línea y G, Vedado. The signpost is opposite the post office, leading up a short driveway. No toilets at the site.

Hemingway fans may wish to visit **Finca La Vigía**, where the author lived from 1939 to 1961, now the Ernest Hemingway Museum. Visitors are not allowed inside the plain whitewashed house, which has been lovingly preserved with all Hemingway's furniture, books and hunting collections, just as he left it. But you can walk around the outside and look in through the windows and open doors. A small annex building is used for temporary exhibitions and from the upper floors there are fine views over Havana. The garden is beautiful and tropical, with many shady palms. Next to the swimming pool (empty) are the gravestones of Hemingway's pets, shaded by a shrub. For details of the extraordinary joint US-Cuban project to restore the house and preserve Hemingway's papers, see the website of the Finca Vigía Foundation, http://fincafoundation.org/. Hemingway tours that include Finca Vigía are offered by tour agencies in the city for CUC$35. See also box, opposite.

Playas del Este
Day trips (minimum 6 people) from Havana cost about CUC$15 per person, but for small groups it's worth hiring a private car or a taxi. The HabanaBusTour, CUC$5, stops at Villa Bacuranao, Villa Tarará, Villa Mégano, Hotel Tropicoco, Hotel Atlántico and Hotel Arenal (see Transport, page 98).

This is the all-encompassing name for a string of truly tropical beaches within easy reach of Havana, which arguably surpass Varadero's brand of beach heaven. The only blot on the picture-postcard landscape is the ugly concrete mass of hotels, which erupt sporadically along the coastline.

Travelling east, the first stretch is the pleasant little horseshoe beach of **Bacuranao**, 15 km from Havana, which is popular with locals. At the far end of the beach is a villa complex with restaurant and bar. Then comes **Tarará**, famous for its hospital where Chernobyl victims have been treated, and which also has a marina and vast hotel complex, and **El Mégano**.

Santa María del Mar is the most tourist-oriented stretch of beach. A swathe of golden sand shelves gently to vivid crystal-blue waters, lined with palm trees, and dotted with tiki bars, sun loungers and an array of watersports facilities; the hip spot to chill out, flirt and play. For more undistracted sun worship, continue further eastwards to the pretty, dune-backed **Boca Ciega**, a pleasant, non-touristy beach 27 km from Havana. At the weekend, cars roll in, line up and deposit their cargo of sun worshippers at the sea's edge transforming the beach into a seething mass of baking flesh.

For a more authentic seaside ambience, head to the pleasant, if rather more rough-hewn (avoid the sewage canals), beach of **Guanabo**. Most facilities here are geared towards Cubans and it can get very busy during the national holiday season of July and August. The small town of Guanabo is very laid-back, there is no hassle and it also has a lush, green park between Avenida 474 y 476 and a children's playground. Generally, it is cheaper than Santa María del Mar and it's where a cluster of *casas particulares* are located, although there is little to do in the evening. The quietest spot of all is **Brisas del Mar**, at the east end of the stretch.

Cheap packages and all-inclusive holidays can be booked to Playas del Este from Canada and Europe, which can be good if you want to combine a beach holiday with excursions to Havana. However, most people report getting fed up after a few days of sitting on the beach here and the food is monotonous, so if you are the sort of person who likes to get out and about, avoid the all-inclusive deals. For details of watersports, see What to do, page 107.

Santa Cruz del Norte and around

The main road along the coast towards Matanzas and Varadero is called the Vía Blanca. There are some scenic parts, but you also drive through quite a lot of industry, such as the rum and cardboard factories at **Santa Cruz del Norte**, a thermal electricity station and many smelly oil wells. The **Hershey Railway** runs inland from Havana, more or less parallel to the Vía Blanca, and is an interesting way to get to Matanzas. This electric line was built by the Hershey chocolate family in 1917 to service their sugar mill, which became known as the Central Camilo Cienfuegos after the Revolution; it was dismantled following the decline in the sugar industry.

From Santa Cruz del Norte, you can drive inland, via the former Central Camilo Cienfuegos, to **Jaruco** and the **Parque Escaleras de Jaruco**. The *escaleras* (stairs) are geological formations in the limestone, set in a very picturesque landscape with caves, forests and other rocks to see. There is a hotel in the park, but it is for Cubans only. The restaurant at the entrance is only open at weekends for lunch, but there is a nice coastal view from the terrace.

Jibacoa

Continuing east from Santa Cruz del Norte, some 60 km east of Havana is Jibacoa beach, which is good for snorkelling as the reefs are close to the shore. It is also a pretty area for walking, with hills coming down to the sea, making it a pleasant place to go for a weekend away from Havana.

Some 14 km east of Jibacoa is the **Marina Puerto Escondido**, at Vía Blanca Km 80, which has boat trips, fishing, snorkelling, scuba-diving and a cafetería.

Where to stay

Cojímar
Casas particulares

$ Casa Ferreiro
E entre 29 y 30, T7-765 0876.
Alejandro Ferreiro offers a large house
with lots of space for guests including
3 bedrooms, bathroom, a living and
dining room and a large terrace.

$ Villa Estrella
Martí 460 entre 32 y 33, jpy@infomed.sld.cu.
Independent, 3 rooms, a/c, 3 bathrooms,
fridge, kitchen, small swimming pool.

$ Yohana Ferra Veloso
30 96 entre E y F, T7-763 3907.
2 rooms, 2 bathrooms, a/c, hot water,
kitchen and living room for guests use
only, interior garden.

Playas del Este
Hotels

$$$ Villa Los Pinos
*Av de las Terrazas 21 entre 4 y 5, Santa María
del Mar, T7-797 1269, www.grancaribe.com.*
2- and 3-bedroomed houses, most with
pools or near the beach, grill restaurant,
café and pizzeria, popular with Italians,
Spanish and French in that order, lots of
repeat guests, comfortable, private, good
for entertaining friends or for families,
very flexible, friendly management,
multilingual staff.

$$$ Club Atlántico
*Av Las Terrazas entre 11 y 12, Santa María del
Mar, T7-797 1085.*
92 rooms, all-inclusive with all mod cons
and it's right on the beach. Friendly service,
food average in buffet, but the à la carte
restaurants and beach barbecue that
you have to book are better. Free shuttle

bus twice a day to Havana, a taxi costs
CUC$18-25 depending on where you go.

$$ Aparthotel Atlántico/Las Terrazas
*Av Las Terrazas entre 10 y Ronda and
entre 11 y 12, Santa María del Mar,
T7-797 1345, www.islazul.cu.*
Originally 2 hotels, now run as 1. Rooms
and apartments and 2 houses with a/c and
balcony, plus a restaurant, bar, tennis and
pool. Cooking facilities if you stay for more
than 2 months. The **HabanaBusTour** stops
outside, making it convenient for getting
into the city.

$$ Hotel Tropicoco
*Av Sur y Las Terrazas, Santa María del Mar,
T7-797 1371, recepcion@htropicoco.nor.tur.cu.*
The architecture here is ugly, with lots of
concrete and small windows, the rooms are
basic but adequate with sea view but no
balconies. It has a pool, restaurant and 3 bars
and is an all-inclusive. It is conveniently
placed opposite the beach where most
tourists are deposited on day trips from
Havana, so if you need drinks or the toilet,
best stop here.

Casas particulares
Prices here are high, starting at CUC$30 per
night for a double room with many at a lot
more than that if they are on the beach or
very close to the water.

$$ Nancy Pujol
*Av 1 50019 entre 500 y 504, Guanabo,
T7-796 3062.*
Right on the waterfront, this house has
2 bedrooms but is only rented to 1 couple or
2 couples travelling together as the bathroom
is shared. You also get your own kitchen and
living/dining room, but if you don't want to
cook Nancy will provide meals at the usual
rates. Lovely location only steps from the
sand, pleasant garden at the edge of the sea.

$$ Iriana Suárez y Rosa Machado
Av 1 50017 entre 500 y 504, Guanabo,
T7-796 3959.

Next door to Nancy and also on the
waterfront, with a lawn going down to
the seawall, Iriana and Rosa rent 2 rooms
upstairs with independent access, while they
live downstairs. Floor-to-ceiling windows
in the living area with kitchen/bar lead out
onto balcony overlooking the garden and
the sea with sun loungers. They also have
an apartment a the same address with
1 bedroom and bathroom.

$$-$ Alberto y Neisa
500 5 D 08 entre 5 y 7, Guanabo,
T7-7796 4503, 5291 2992 (mob),
maidarubio@infomed.sld.cu.

2 rooms, 1 in the house with own entrance,
the other in a cottage in the backyard, each
with a/c, fridge. Short walk to beach. Small
swimming pool.

Jibacoa
Hotels

$$ Memories Jibacoa
Playa Arrojo Bermejo, Vía Blanca Km 60,
T47-295122, www.memoriesjibacoa.com.
Price per person per night depending on
season and view, all-inclusive, no children
under 18.

250 rooms and suites in 2-storey buildings,
attractive setting with hilly backdrop and
curved, sandy bay, comfortable, good
bathrooms, nice beds, buffet, Cuban or
Italian restaurants, vegetarian options,
tennis, basketball, hiking, snorkelling,
diving, catamaran, sunfish, kayaks, gym,
windsurfing, no motorized watersports to
protect reef, excursions available, indoor
games room, pool, piano bar, nightclub,
beach bar, wheelchair accessible, 2 rooms
for disabled guests, evening entertainment
disappointing, but around the headland is a
Cuban camping resort where they know how
to party during the summer holidays.

Tip...
You can eat freshly caught lobster for
lunch on the beach, on specially laid
tables with white tablecloths.

$ Campismo Los Cocos
T47-295231.

About the best *campismo* in the country,
cabins of good quality, facilities for the
disabled, swimming pool, children's pool,
public phones, games room, TV room, lots of
activities such as dancing, horse riding, bar,
2 restaurants and 2 cafeterias, shop, 24-hr
first-aid station.

Where to eat

Cojímar

$$$ La Terraza
Real 161 esq Candelaria, T7-766 5150,
comercial@terrazaspalmares.cu.
Daily 1200-2300, bar 1000-2300.

Overpriced seafood meals, terrible fish,
paella is the house speciality. Photographs of
Hemingway cover the walls. Tourist trap for
tour parties.

Playas del Este

In addition to the hotel restaurants and
buffets, there are many reasonably priced
paladares in Guanabo and elsewhere.
You'll find cafés, bakeries, restaurants
and *heladerías* on Av 5 entre 478 y 480 in
Guanabo, including, **La Hatuey**, a chilled,
dark, wooden bar, and **La Cocinita**, which
has a pool table, on Av 5 esq 480, and **El
Piccolo**, quite a good Italian. There's also a
great little bakery just past the *Cadeca*.

$$ Maeda
Quebec 115 entre 476 y 478, Guanabo,
T7-962615. Daily 1800-2300.

This is a *paladar* in a beautiful setting on
hillside with outside seating under flower-
filled terracing. There is also seating in an
a/c room. International and Cuban food is
served as well as a *parillada* along with wines
and a selection of puddings. They also have

a wood-fired oven for baking. Run by the welcoming Miguel. Reservations advised for the evenings as it's a popular spot for visiting *Habaneros*. They also rent 2 rooms with a/c, fridge, TV.

Bars

Playas del Este
All the hotels have a/c bars indoors and open air bars on the beach, offering the usual range of Cuban cocktails or a cold beer.

Entertainment

Playas del Este
There are several cabarets and nightclubs on Av 5 in Guanabo, also the **Guanabo Club** (at 468 entre 13 y 15), and **El Tucán** (at the Hotel Bacuranao).

Shopping

Playas del Este
There is a farmers' market in Guanabo selling fresh fruit and vegetables 6 days a week and a supermarket for bread and tinned goods. The **Centro Comercial de Guanabo** shopping centre, behind Recreación Náutica, has a supermarket.

What to do

Playas del Este
The hotels provide non-motorized watersports. **Marina Tarará**, *run by Marinas Puertosol, Vía Blanca Km 18, Tarará, Playas del Este, T7-796 0242, VHF77*. Moorings for 50 boats, VHF communications and provisioning, yacht charters, deep sea fishing (CUC$200-550 for up to 4 people depending on number of hours and type of boat) and scuba-diving, all of which can be arranged through the hotel tour desks. Diving is surprisingly good here,

considering its proximity to the capital city. The seabed drops off in steps and there are wrecks to explore as well as coral gardens and reef fish.
Mi Cayito Recreation Centre, *Av de las Terrazas, Laguna Itabo, Santa María, near Boca Ciega, T7-797 1339. Daily 1000-1800*. A lake just behind the beach is used for pedal boats (CUC$1.50 per person per hr), waterskiing (CUC$10 for 15 mins) and kayaks (CUC$1 per person per hr). The **Restaurant El Pelícano** is on site but set back from the lake.

Transport

Playas de Este
Bus
The easiest, most comfortable, safest and quickest way to get out to the beach is to take the **HabanaBusTour** T3, which leaves every 35 mins from Parque Central 0900-1900, CUC$5. Alternatively, the 400 bus (CUP$0.40) from Egido near the Estación Central de Trenes can get you to **Bacuranao**, **Santa María** and **Guanabo**.

Cycling
Cycling is a good way to get to the **Playas del Este**. Use the *ciclobus* from Parque El Curita, Aguila y Dragones, Centro, via the tunnel under Havana Bay, or the CUP$0.20 ferry to **Regla** from near the Aduanas building, and cycle through Regla and **Guanabacoa**. Be careful of the very poor road surfaces and frequent roadworks.

Taxi
The standard taxi price from Havana to the **Playas del Este** is CUC$20-25 (fix the price before you set off or insist on the meter being used); opposite Hotel Miramar in Guanabo is a taxi stand, 478 esq 7B, open 24 hrs.

West of Havana

startling scenery, both on land and under the sea

The west of Cuba is dominated by one of the island's three main mountain ranges, the Cordillera de Guaniguanico, divided into the Sierra del Rosario in the east and the Sierra de los Organos in the west. A fault line creates a sharp boundary between these mountains, with a wide expanse of rolling farmland to the south.

The forested Sierra del Rosario encompasses the Biosphere Reserve at Las Terrazas, a must for anyone with an interest in tropical flora and fauna, as well as the orchidarium at Soroa. The Sierra de los Organos, meanwhile, is famous for the landscape of steep-sided limestone mogotes and flat, fertile tobacco fields around the Valle de Viñales. This is where you will find the world's best dark tobacco, which is hand-processed into the finest cigars. The valley attracts thousands of visitors, due to its spectacular scenery and good walking opportunities. The only major city west of Havana, Pinar del Río can be a good base for excursions to this area as transport starts from here. The coast offers undeveloped beaches and some sensational scuba diving, most notably in the far west, where María La Gorda is a diver's dream: low key, laid back and friendly.

Best for
Climbing ▪ Diving ▪ Landscapes ▪ Tobacco

Footprint picks

★ Las Terrazas, page 114

Hike through old colonial coffee plantations to waterfalls and sulphur springs.

★ Orchidarium, Soroa, page 115

The orchid farm at Soroa has examples of 700 different orchids from all over the world.

★ María La Gorda, page 129

Scuba dive in pristine waters with reef, walls, caves, tunnels and wrecks to explore.

★ Valle de Viñales, page 131

Take in the spectacular view from Hotel Los Jazmines, where you'll see mogotes rising out of the tobacco fields.

★ Cayo Levisa, page 138

A small, isolated dive lodge and nothing else.

Essential West of Havana

Finding your feet

Pinar del Río, 157 km from Havana, is the main transport hub for the area. It is connected to Havana by a slow and unreliable train service and by daily **Viazul** buses, which continue on to Viñales; they will stop on request at Las Terrazas and San Diego de los Baños. A dual-carriageway has been completed almost as far as Pinar del Río, although some of the slip roads are still unsurfaced mud and stones. It takes nearly three hours to get from Havana to Pinar del Río on the *autopista* (see page 113) or four hours 10 minutes on the old main road.

Getting around

From Pinar de Río, it is easy enough to get a bus to Viñales, but public transport to other destinations is limited to local peso buses. A local train runs from Pinar de Río to Guane but is not recommended. Apart from the long-distance **Viazul** buses (see above), there is very little public transport at all in the Sierra del Rosario. Car hire is available in Pinar del Río and Viñales and is recommended for independent excursions: driving distances from Pinar del Río are 159 km to María La Gorda, 103 km to Las Terrazas, 88 km to Soroa, 25 km to Viñales.

There are also plenty of organized tours to caves, cigar factories, tobacco farms and other local attractions. Long-distance travel by taxi is possible but you will need very good Spanish to negotiate effectively.

When to go

The driest time in the Sierra del Rosario is from January to April, when it is easiest to hike in the mountains. The orchids at Soroa are good then too. The wet season begins around May, but storms can be expected between September and November. This is also the wettest time in the Sierra de los Organos. Pinar del Río holds its carnival in July and Viñales has one in March.

Tip...
Take plenty of insect repellent to ward off mosquitoes and sand flies. Mosquito nets and screens are rare, and despite regular spraying by the authorities, there are lots of wet places in this region where mosquitoes breed.

Time required

Las Terrazas and Viñales are often visited as day trips from Havana, but to do the area justice you need at least three days. If you want to visit beaches or cays on the north coast, allow another day or two. María la Gorda is very remote, so even if you spend only one day diving, you will need a day to get there and a day to get back.

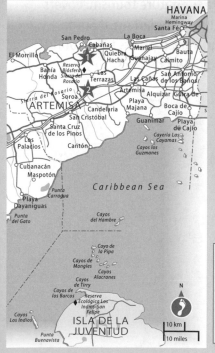

Footprint picks

1 **Las Terrazas**, page 114
2 **Orchidarium, Soroa**, page 115
3 **María La Gorda**, page 129
4 **Valle de Viñales**, page 131
5 **Cayo Levisa**, page 138

Artemisa
Province

Artemisa Province was created in 2011 from parts of La Habana and Pinar del Río provinces. Heading west from Havana the land is initially low-lying and unimpressive. Soon, however, the green mountains of the Sierra del Rosario come into view, stirring anticipation of exploration and discovery. The Sierra incorporates a 260-sq-km biosphere reserve, giving recognition to its ecological diversity and richness. Birdwatching is rewarding around Las Terrazas, the main centre for nature tourism. Lovers of flora will also appreciate the orchidarium at Soroa, although there are many and varied plants to be found by anyone who hikes up and down the hills.

Along the coast to Mariel

Heading out of the city west along the north coast, on the *autopista* La Habana–Mariel, you come to **Playa Baracoa** in the relatively new province of Artemisa, a nice place to go for some relaxation on the beach. There is another beach at **El Salado**, 25 km west of Havana; some parts are rocky, but there is good snorkelling as a result, although the water is slightly polluted because locals bring their pigs here for a bath. Further along the coast there is a completely abandoned holiday village with empty swimming pool and then the remains of a military coastal defence system, also deserted. There is a hotel here, described by one reader as a bungalow park, **Villa Cocomar**. Parties of day-trippers come to use the swimming pool and there are watersports on offer in season, including rowing boat hire and scuba-diving. The **Centro de Buceo Blue Reef** is based here, taking up to eight divers to 30 dive sites ranging from 5-35 m. In addition to the dive shop and other watersports, this is now a centre for karting, with international championships are held at the *kartódromo*.

Don't expect a beach at **Mariel**, further west from El Salado along the coast. This is a major industrial town, with the largest cement plant on the island, a shipyard, a thermal electricity plant and an industrial zone. It was the scene of the mass exodus in 1980 known as the Mariel boatlift. The port here has undergone a huge expansion and can be seen for miles around. If you continue along the coastal road, you eventually enter the province of Pinar del Río on the way to Viñales.

Towards Pinar del Río

The *autopista* journey from Havana to Pinar del Río is a rather surreal experience, with modern motorway junctions but virtually no traffic using them except horse-drawn buses running to nearby villages. Watch out for dogs sleeping peacefully in the fast lane or bicycles heading towards you in the wrong direction. Also take care when driving under bridges as people wait there for lifts and sometimes step out into the road to stop traffic, resulting in accidents. Vultures can be seen circling overhead. The *autopista* passes through flat or gently rolling countryside, with large stretches of sugar cane, tobacco fields and some rice fields, with scattered Royal palms and distant views of the Cordillera de Guaniguanico. There are also large uncultivated areas used as rough pasture, with hump-backed zebu and other cattle, as well as white cattle egrets which help rid them of parasites. You can see traditional houses built of palm planks, thatched with palm leaves, and plenty of *vegas*.

An alternative route is to leave the *autopista* at **Candelaria** or **Santa Cruz de los Pinos** and continue west on the Carretera Central, quite a good road. It passes through more intensively farmed countryside, with citrus and other fruit trees. Villages straggle along the road, with colonnaded single-storey traditional houses and newer post-Revolution concrete block structures.

San Antonio de los Baños

San Antonio de los Baños is a pleasant country town of some 30,000 people, set in an agricultural area southwest of the capital where citrus and tobacco are grown. The Río Ariguanabo flows through the town, going underground by a large ceiba tree near the railway station.

The town has an intriguing museum: the **Museo del Humor** ⓘ *Calle 60 y Av 45, T047-382817, Tue-Sat 1000-1800, Sun 0900-1300, CUC$2*, which has an unusual collection of cartoons, drawings and other humorous items including political satire; it's worth visiting if you are in the area. The **Galería Provincial Eduardo Abela** ⓘ *Calle 58 3708 entre 37 y 39, T047-384224, Tue-Sun 1200-2000, free*, is an art gallery displaying the work of local artists with changing exhibitions.

Outside the town, in the middle of a grapefruit plantation off the Vereda Nueva road, is the **International Film and Television School (EICTV)** ⓘ *www.eictv.org*, approached down an avenue of magnificent palm trees. It is not, unfortunately, open to the public unless you obtain prior authorization to visit with 24 hours' notice. This is one of the best film schools in the world, founded in 1986 by the triumvirate of Colombian novelist and journalist Gabriel García Márquez, Argentine poet and film-maker Fernando Pirri and Cuban film-maker Julio García Espinosa. Their aim was to create a school for the developing as well as the developed world; since its creation, thousands of students and professionals from over 50 countries have studied there.

Sierra del Rosario *Colour map1, B4.*
follow trails through thick forest and old coffee plantations, full of birds and butterflies

On the *autopista*, 51 km west of Havana, a roadside billboard announces the turning to Las Terrazas/Moka, 4 km north of the *autopista*. However, after that there is little signposting through a confusing series of side roads; you may have to ask the way.

A barrier marks the entrance to the **Biosphere Reserve** ⓘ *admission CUC$10 although it can be cheaper in low season*, which covers 260 sq km of the eastern Sierra del Rosario. Admission to the reserve includes a drink and all park facilities, including Río San Juan and Río Bayate. There is a map at the entrance so you can work out where you are in relation to what you want to do and see.

★Las Terrazas

Las Terrazas was built in 1971 as a forestry and soil conservation station, with nearby slopes terraced to prevent erosion. It is a pleasant settlement of white-painted houses and a long apartment block overlooking the lake of San Juan, which now houses an ecological research centre. On the hillside, **Hotel Moka** (see Where to stay) is run as an ecotourism centre. This is an unusual opportunity to stay in a nature reserve, with tropical evergreen forests, 850 plant species, 82 bird species, an endemic water lizard, the world's second smallest frog and world-class experts on tap. Elsewhere in Las Terrazas there is a vegetarian restaurant, a *paladar*, as well as craft workshops, a gym, a cinema and a museum which sometimes holds *canturías* or folk music sessions. Nearby there are waterfalls where you can picnic. Other

Essential Sierra del Rosario

Getting around

Public transport is negligible. Long-distance buses go along the *autopista*, occasionally to Las Terrazas, but not to other sites of interest. Taxis are expensive and can only be arranged in Havana, Pinar del Río or Viñales. Therefore, the easiest way of getting to Soroa or Las Terrazas is to book yourself on an organized tour from Havana. A day trip (10 hours) to Las Terrazas, with walking, river bathing and a ghastly lunch is around CUC$50 at any tour agency. Other trips include overnight stays at the hotels and some take in Soroa as well. Alternatively, hire a car and take your time, but note that rooms at **Hotel Moka** need to be booked in advance.

activities include riding, mountain biking, rowing on the lake and fishing. There is also a zip line, **Canopy Las Terrazas**, which crosses the lake into the trees (CUC$25 for foreigners, CUC$15 for hotel guests, CUC$7 for Cubans).

Following the death in a car accident of the popular singer, Polo Montañez in 2002, his lakeside house was opened as a museum, run by his brother. In nearby San Cristóbal, a clay statue of the singer has been put on display. Formerly a woodcutter, he rose to fame as a singer/songwriter and had many hits in the three years before his death, touring Latin America and Europe.

Hiking around Las Terrazas The hills behind Hotel Moka rise to the **Loma del Salón** (564 m). There are several easy hiking trails: to the partly restored 19th-century **Buenavista** coffee plantation (restaurant has *pollo brujo*, cheaper for hotel guests than for others); 3 km along the San Juan River to the old **La Victoria** coffee plantation and sulphur springs; 4 km along La Serafina path to the ruins of the 19th-century **Santa Serafina** coffee plantation, excellent for seeing birds like the Cuban trogon, the solitaire, woodpeckers and the Cuban tody; 8 km along the Cañada del Infierno valley to the **San Pedro** and **Santa Catalina** coffee plantations. There are also more demanding whole-day hikes with a professional ecologist as a guide (CUC$33-41 for one person, falling to CUC$14-18 per person with six people).

★Soroa

If travelling by car, you can make a detour to Soroa, a spa and resort in the Sierra del Rosario, 81 km southwest of the capital, either by continuing 18 km west then southeast from Las Terrazas through the Sierra del Rosario, or directly from the *autopista*, driving northwest from Candelaria. As you drive into the area from the south, a sign on the right indicates the **Mirador de Venus** and **Baños Romanos**. Past the baths is the **Bar Edén** (open till 1800), where you can park before walking up to the **mirador** ① *25 mins, free on foot, CUC$3 on a horse.* From the top you get fine views of the southern plains, the forest-covered Sierra and Soroa itself. There are lots of birds, butterflies, dragonflies and lizards around the path; many flowers in season and birdwatching is very popular here.

Further north is a **Jardín Botánico Orchidarium** ① *T48-522558, guided tours daily 0830-1140, 1340-1555, CUC$3, camera CUC$1, birdwatching, hiking and riding CUC$3 per hr, parking CUC$1,* with over 700 species of which 250 are native to Cuba, as well as ferns and begonias (check if the orchids are in bloom before visiting). Alberto at the desk speaks good English and some French, and there is also a restaurant, **Castillo de las Nubes** (1200-1900). There is an excursion to **El Brujito**, a village once owned by French landlords, where the third and fourth generations of slaves live. Across the road from the Orchidarium is a **waterfall** (250 m along a paved path, CUC$2), which is worth a visit if you are in the area. You can do a day trip from Havana or stay overnight.

San Diego de los Baños

Nearer Pinar del Río, another detour north off the Carretera Central at Entronque de San Diego is to the spa of San Diego de los Baños. (In the wet season a nearby irrigation lake, the **Embalse La Juventud**, often floods and then this diversion becomes compulsory.) San Diego de los Baños is a pretty little village in fine scenery, with colonnaded houses and a tree-lined square, right on the southern edge of the Sierra del Rosario. Its mineral waters were discovered in the 17th century and public thermal baths were opened in 1951, but the buildings are currently closed and the place is empty. The area was badly hit by Hurricane Ike in 2008 and has not yet completely recovered.

Parque Nacional La Güira

A few kilometres west of San Diego, an impressive neo-Gothic gateway leads to the Parque Nacional La Güira. Inside, there are extensive neglected 19th-century gardens, pools and statues, with the ruins of a Gothic mansion. There is a small bar near the entrance. Behind, the road winds up through the hills to an army recreation centre; behind this there is an enormous, cheap and rather run-down restaurant. The **Cueva de las Portales** just north of here was Che Guevara's HQ during the Cuban missile crisis and there is a small exhibition of military and personal relics. The national park covers an area of 22,000 ha and protects a number of endemic species.

Listings Sierra del Rosario

Where to stay

Las Terrazas
Hotels

$$$-$$ Hotel Moka
T48-578600, www.hotelmoka-lasterrazas.com.
Above the village is this 26-room hotel complex run in cooperation with the Cuban Academy of Sciences as an ecotourism centre. It is beautifully designed and laid out in Spanish colonial style with tiled roofs. Breakfast and dinner packages available, transfers from Havana, a/c, satellite TV. Staff are friendly and knowledgeable: even the hotel receptionist has an ecology PhD. Gardens behind have a tennis court and a pleasant pool where you can have food and drinks.

Casas particulares

All *casas particulares* are outside the park, a short distance away on the Cayajabos road.

$ Casa Hospedaje Villa Duque
Finca San Andrés, road to Cayajabos, T5322 1431 (mob).
2 km from Las Terrazas entrance, this 2-storey house is in a lovely rural setting on a hillside with views for miles over the countryside. 2 a/c rooms in very good condition with independent access, roof terrace for cocktails and star gazing. Delicious food from the garden and the home-grown, home-roasted coffee should not be missed. The owners have a 1955 Chevy if you want to go anywhere. Some English spoken.

$ Villa Juanita
Calle 1 601, Finca La Pastora, Cayajabos, 3 km from las Terrazas, T5221 0634 (mob).
3 a/c rooms with fridge, apartment upstairs has independent access. Meals available, good food, very welcoming *casa particular*, a little English and expressive, slow Spanish spoken. Parking.

Soroa
Hotels

$$$-$$ Villa Soroa
T48-523534.
Cabins and self-catering houses used mostly by tour groups, restaurant, disco, bar, Olympic-sized swimming pool, bike rental, riding nearby. A peaceful place on a hillside but the rooms and bathrooms are in need of renovation. The hotel runs 1-day, 17-km, gently paced hikes around the main sights of the area with picnic.

Casas particulares

$ Casa Los Sauces
Jorge y Ana Lidia, on the road up to Villa Soroa, about 1 km from the autopista, T5228 9372, lossauces@nauta.cu.
Ana Lidia works at the orchidarium and her own garden is a mini botanical garden. 3 a/c rooms each with double and single bed, fridge, rocking chairs on shady terrace, the 3rd room is upstairs, meals available. A good *casa*, experienced hosts.

$ Hospedaje Estudio de Arte
*Km 8.5, 300 m outside Soroa next to
a primary school in converted church,
T48-598116, infosoroa@hvs.co.cu.*
Jesús is an artist and has a contract with
UNEAC; the hotel organizes tours to his
Estudio de Arte in the house, where he
sells his paintings. His wife, Aliuska, runs
the house, 1 room, large and decorated
with Jesús' art, excellent *comida criolla*,
food recommended by Cubans.

Where to eat

Las Terrazas

$$ El Romero
T48-578555. Daily 0900-2200.
Vegetarian restaurant, exceptional for Cuba.
Service and food suffer if a large party is in
and sometimes menu items are not available,
but overall it is a pleasant change from
regular Cuban food with liberal use of fresh
vegetables, fruit, herbs and their own honey.
Pleasant view from the terrace.

$$ La Fonda de Mercedes
Edif 9, Apto 2, T48-578647. Daily 0900-2100.
Best to make reservations as this small
paladar is very popular. Mercedes prepares
excellent meat dishes to traditional recipes
and serves them on her patio in the
apartment block just below Hotel Moka.

$ Café de María
Las Terrazas.
This is the place to come for coffee, locally
grown, home-roasted, ground and brewed.
María ran this café for 40 years and now her
family continue in her memory. Generally
considered to serve the best coffee in Cuba.

Pinar del Río
Province

Pinar del Río province grows about 70% of Cuba's tobacco crop. Almost every agricultural area is dotted with *vegas*, curious tent-shaped windowless structures made of palm thatch, which are used for drying tobacco leaves. The cigar factory in Pinar del Río city has regular tours and in the harvest season it is possible in most villages to visit an *escogida de tabaco*, where the best leaves are selected for further processing. The flat lands of San Juan y Martínez are where the very best tobacco is grown. For further details, see Cuban cigars, page 120. Other highlights of the province include the exotic scenery around Viñales and the dive sites off the west and north coasts.

The capital of Pinar del Río province gives a good taste of provincial Cuba. It is a lively city and there is always something going on, but it is not particularly attractive. The centre consists of single-storey neoclassical houses with columns, some with other interesting architectural details. Under the porches are thriving one-person businesses, ranging from selling snacks to repairing cigarette lighters. Horse-drawn vehicles vie for space alongside bicycles and battered old cars on the roads, while the pavements are full of people jostling and weaving in and out of the pillars and other obstacles.

Sights

The main shopping street and centre of activities is José Martí, which runs west-east through the town. At the west end is the **Centro de Artes Visuales** ① *Martí, opposite Parque Independencia, T48-752758, Mon-Fri 1000-1700, Sat 0800-1200, CUC$1*. Walk along José Martí to the east to a renovated building opposite the Wedding Palace: the **Palacio de Computación** ① *Martí esq González Coro, Mon-Sat 0800-2100, theatre, cafetería and classrooms for teaching computer skills*, which was inaugurated by Fidel Castro in January 2001. It is very photogenic if seen from Parque de la Independencia. The **Casa de la**

Essential Pinar del Río

Finding your feet

There is a **train** from Havana, which is cheap but has the disadvantage of being very slow with lots of stops and is very dark, so there is a risk of theft. You have to hang on to your bags all the time and take particular care of your pockets in the tunnels. The **bus station** is reasonably central and all buses use the same terminal. **Viazul** air-conditioned buses come from Havana on a route that continues to Viñales. On arrival in Pinar del Río you must expect to be hassled by crowds at the bus or train stations, who are touting for your business (see Where to stay, page 123). Even if you come in by car they will be waiting for you at the road junctions. Young men on bicycles are a particular hazard and very persistent. Always say you have a reservation. See also Transport, page 126.

Getting around

The town has changed its street names, but locals continue to use the old ones as well as the new official names. It can be confusing when names on the map conflict with what people really call the streets: for example, 20 de Mayo is now Primero de Mayo; Vélez Caviedes is also Ormani Arenado, while Virtudes is also Ceferino Fernández. Pinar del Río is not large and it is easy to walk around the centre and to most of the places of interest, such as the rum and tobacco factories.

When to go

Carnival is in July but it is not on the scale of Santiago's or Havana's. At any time of year you can find something going on in and around the city. Expect storms between September and November, although heavy showers can happen at any time, usually in the afternoon. This area was badly hit by the hurricanes in 2008 but is now largely rebuilt.

During Columbus' second journey to the New World, he landed at Gibara in Cuba. Forays inland brought reports that the local inhabitants were smoking roughly rolled dried leaves for ceremonial or religious purposes, which they called *cohibas*. The Spaniards soon acquired the taste for tobacco and in the 17th century introduced it to the European market with great success. The first tobacco plantations in Cuba were established by the Río Almendares (Havana), in the centre of the island and around Bayamo. Tobacco planting spread in the 18th century, becoming particularly successful in the west, and by the 19th century tobacco planters and merchants were extremely prosperous. By the time Cuba achieved its independence, there were 120 cigar factories around the island.

Nowadays tobacco is cultivated in the west of Cuba in the province of Pinar del Río, in the centre in the provinces of Villa Clara and Sancti Spíritus, and in the east in the provinces of Granma and Santiago de Cuba, although the tobacco regions are known as Vuelta Abajo, Semi Vuelta, Partidos, Remedios and Oriente. Only Partidos and Vuelta Abajo can grow tobacco of a high enough quality for the Grandes Marcas of cigars (*Habanos*), and only Vuelta Abajo (Pinar del Río) produces all the leaves necessary to make a cigar. Lower quality tobacco is made into cigarettes.

Tobacco is extremely labour intensive, and in Cuba it is grown, harvested and processed entirely by hand. Seedlings are transplanted from the nursery between October and December when they are 18-20 cm, and great care is taken not to damage the delicate roots. After a week they are weeded and after two weeks they are earthed up to maintain humidity and increase the plants' assimilation of nutrients. This is done with the help of oxen rather than a tractor, to avoid compacting the soil. When the plant reaches 1.4-1.6 m, side shoots are removed and the plant is encouraged to grow tall with only six to nine pairs of leaves. Harvesting takes place between January and March, during which time the leaves are collected by hand, two or three at a time, every five days, starting at the bottom. They are then taken to a *vega*, a huge, thatched barn, where they are sewn together in pairs and hung on a pole to dry. The leaves turn yellow, then reddish gold and are considered dry after about 50 days. They are then piled in bundles or stacks for about 30 days, during which time the first fermentation takes place at a temperature not exceeding 35°C, before being classified according to colour, size and quality for wrappers or fillers. At this stage the leaves are stripped off the main vein, dampened, flattened and packed in bigger stacks for up to 60 days of fermentation at a temperature not exceeding 42°C. Finally they are stored and aged for months, or maybe years, before being taken to be rolled by the expert hands of factory workers.

Five types of leaves are used in the manufacture of a cigar. In the middle (*tripa*) are a mixture of three types, *ligero*, *seco* and *volado*. These are wrapped in the *capote*, which is then enveloped in the *capa*, which is the part you see and determines the appearance of the cigar. There are two types of tobacco plant: the *corojo*, and the *criollo*. The former produces only the *capa*, but it comes in several colours. It is grown beneath vast cotton shrouds to protect it from the sun's radiation and keep it soft and silky. The latter provides the other four leaves needed to make up the cigar, which determine the flavour. It is grown in full sunlight to get intense flavours. Each of the five leaves is processed and aged differently before reaching the factory floor for mixing according to secret recipes and rolling.

Hundreds of workers sit at tables in the factory, equipped only with a special knife called a *chaveta*, a guillotine and a pot of gum. A skilled artisan (*torcedor*) makes an average of 120 cigars a day. They used to sit and listen to readings from the press or novels, a tradition which started in 1865 but has recently been replaced by the radio or recorded music. Although many of the people rolling cigars are women, it is unfortunately a myth that Cuban cigars are rolled on the thighs of dusky maidens. The women sorting the leaves do, however, place them across their laps on each leg and this may have been where the erotic image originated.

Quality control is rigid. Any cigars which do not meet the standards of size, shape, thickness and appearance are rejected. Those which do make it are stored at a temperature of 16°-18°C and at a humidity of 65-70% for several weeks until they lose the moisture acquired during rolling. A specialist then classifies them according to colour (of which there are 65 tones) and they are chosen for boxes, with the colours ranging from dark to light, left to right. They have to remain exactly as they are placed in the cedar wood box and the person who then labels each cigar has to keep them in the same order, even facing the same way.

Finally the boxes are stamped and sealed with the government's guarantee, which looks rather like a currency note and carries the words: 'Cuban Government's warranty for cigars exported from Havana' in English, French and German as well as Spanish.

Always buy your cigars from a state shop, not on the street, where they are bound to be fakes, no matter how good a deal they appear. Check the quality of each cigar. They should be tightly rolled, not soft; they should have no lumps or other protuberances; if you turn them upside down nothing should come out; the colour should be uniform and the aroma should be strong. The box should be sealed with the four-language warranty, which should not be a photocopy, and on the bottom you should find the stamp: Habanos s.a. HECHO EN CUBA *Totalmente a mano*. You may take only 20 cigars out of the country without a receipt, but if you buy them in a state shop and get a formal sales invoice you can buy cigars up to a value of CUC$5000 (unless you are returning to the USA, of course, where the embargo forbids you to import Cuban cigars of more than US$100).

Cigars are like fine wines or whiskies and there are many different types from which to choose. Castro used to smoke *Cohiba* cigars, which were created in 1966 exclusively for the diplomatic market. In 1982 the *Cohiba Lanceros*, *Coronas Especiales* and *Panatelas* were created for public sale, followed in 1989 by the *Espléndidos*, *Robustos* and *Exquisitos*, which together make up the Classic Line (*La Línea Clásica*). In 1992, to mark the 500th anniversary of the landing of Columbus, they brought out the 1492 Line (*La Línea 1492*), with its five centuries: *Siglo I, II, III, IV, V*. The *Espléndidos* now sell for up to CUC$385 a box.

As well as the *Cohiba* brand, there are *Montecristo*, *Romeo y Julieta*, *Bolívar*, *Punch*, *Hoyo de Monterrey*, *H Upmann*, *Partagás*, *Quintero*, *La Flor de Cano*, *El Rey del Mundo* and *Rafael González*, all of which have their company histories and logos, mostly dating from the 19th century.

Cultura Pedro Junco ① *Martí esq Rafael Morales, Mon-Sat 0800-1800*, is in a huge colonial house and includes an art gallery, a hall for parties and seven classrooms for teaching dancing, painting, singing, etc. There are evening activities according to scheduled programmes. The old **Globo** hotel, right in the centre near the corner of José Martí and Isabel Rubio, is only for Cubans, but it has a beautiful tiled staircase worth a peep, and its clock is a local curiosity for its accurate time-keeping. The **Museo Provincial de Historia** ① *Martí 58 entre Isabel Rubio y Colón, T48-754300, Mon-Fri 0830-1830 Sat 0900-1300, CUC$1*, renovated and reopened in 2015 details the history of the town and displays objects from the Wars of Independence. On the same side of the street is the **Teatro José Jacinto Milanés** ① *Martí esq Colón*. Built in 1883, this is one of the most beautiful theatres in the country. Renovated and reopened in 2006, it is true to its original style and decor, with its three-tiered auditorium and antique chairs. Further along Martí is the **Museo de Ciencias Naturales Tranquilino Sandalio de Noda** ① *José Martí 202 esq Av Comandante Pinares, T48-753087, Mon-Sat 0800-1700, CUC$1*, with geological and natural history exhibits: not large, not much explanation, not much on typical Cuban animals. The great thing,

Pinar del Río

Where to stay
Casa Colonial Jose
   Antonio Mesa cp 1
Vueltabajo 2

Restaurants
Doña Neli 1
El Gallardo 2
El Mesón 3

Entertainment
Bar La Esquinita 1
Casa de la Cultura 2
Casa de la Música 3
Casa del Joven Creador 4

however, is the eclectic building, formerly the Palacio Guasch, which is the most ornate in the region, with Gothic towers, spires and all sorts of twiddly bits.

The cigar factory, **Fábrica de Tabaco Francisco Donatién** ⓘ *Maceo 157 y A Tarafa, T48-723424/773069, Mon-Sat 0800-1700, CUC$5 for a short visit, no photos or videos allowed*, is one of the town's main tourist attractions. It reputedly makes the

Tip...

Avoid the youngsters selling cigars outside. Workers in the factory will also try and sell you cigars. Remember there is a limit on the number of cigars you can take out of the country without a receipt so any illegally bought cigars should be smoked in Cuba.

best cigars in Cuba, and it will give you a better appreciation of how cigars are made than you would gain on a tour in Havana. Even when the factory is shut, you can still buy the very finest cigars in the town from the shop opposite, Casa del Habano: you'll get the genuine article, even if it is pricey.

Also worth a visit, if you're interested, is the rum factory, **Fábrica de Guayabita** ⓘ *Isabel Rubio 189 entre Ceferino Fernández y Frank País, Mon-Fri 0900-1530, Sat 0900-1230, CUC$2 for a tour and stop at the tasting room*, which makes a special rum flavoured with miniature wild guavas, *Guayabita del Pinar*, which comes in either dry or sweet varieties. The bottles on sale are cheaper than those in the shops. Between the two is the pretty cream-coloured cathedral of **San Rosendo** ⓘ *Maceo 2 Este esq Gerardo Medina*.

Listings Pinar del Río *map p122*

Tourist information

Tour agencies such as **Cubatur**, **Cubanacán** and **Havanatur** operate as tourist information offices, although their main purpose is to sell tours. They can help with hotel reservations, tickets and transfers.

Where to stay

Hotels

$$ Hotel Vueltabajo
C José Martí 103 y Rafael Morales, T48-759381, carpeta@vueltapr.co.cu.
Pleasant hotel, nice rooms with very high ceilings, but those facing the street can be noisy, particularly at weekends, internal rooms are quiet, safety deposit box, satellite TV. Pricey meals of poor quality but fast service, restaurant open 0715-0930, 1200-1445, 1900-2145. Bar open 1700-2330, very crowded with locals, who offer cigars to foreigners (beware fakes), drink inside or outside, but the porch is close to the road. Car rental, excursions, tourism bureau, currency exchange.

$$ Finca La Guabina
Carretera a Luis Lazo Km 9.5, T48-757616.
Outside Pinar del Río is this 1000-ha ranch where they breed horses and other animals. There are 5 a/c rooms in the main house and 3 in cabins overlooking the lake, which are very peaceful and relaxing. Lots of outdoor activities such as walking, riding, trips in horse-drawn carriage, taking a boat out on the lake and watching traditional rural pastimes. The restaurant serves fresh and tasty food and the breakfasts are substantial. English-speaking guides available for tours. Horse riding CUC$7 per hr through the mountains and countryside on good horses. Tour parties come here for the day from Viñales and Pinar del Río and there are rodeo shows Mon, Wed, Fri 1000-1200, 1600-1800.

Casas particulares

There is a mafia of young men on bicycles who will meet you on arrival, whether by car, bus or train, and pester to take you to a *casa particular, paladar,* or whatever. Sometimes they say they are from **Formatur**, the tourism school. Sometimes they tell you there is a salsa festival in town to get you to stay here rather than go on to Viñales. They are after a commission, set by them at CUC$5 per person per night and have been known to be violent with Cuban landlords who refuse to pay. Avoid them if you can and make your own way using the map. If you accept any help with directions they will ask the Cuban family for money. Taxi drivers are in the same game; if your driver says he can't find the address, refuse to pay unless he goes to the right house. He will try and take you somewhere else to get his commission.

$ Casa Colonial José Antonio Mesa
Gerardo Medina 67 entre Adela Azcuy y Isidro de Armas, T48-753173.
A gem of a colonial building, single storey with pillars and decorative topping, spacious, high ceilings, stained glass, tiled floors, rooms have fridge and fan, lovely courtyard garden with jacuzzi in a gazebo, meals available.

$ Casa Villa Maury
Ceferino Fernández 186 entre Antonio Tarafa y Antonio Guiteras, T48-771735, 5371 4505 (mob), domipimientav@gmail.com.
Maura Padrón Cruz rents 2 rooms with a/c and fan, terrace, patio, parking, English and Portuguese spoken. The house is recognizable by its orange and pink paint.

$ Villa Manuela
Garmendia 10 entre Antonio Guiteras y Volcán, T48-773274, www.casaparticular-manuela.sitew.com.
Rental rooms upstairs above the multi-generational family quarters. Friendly and welcoming, French and English spoken, Manuela is Cuban and Gérard (Pepe) is French. However, the house is run by Sandy and other staff, as the owners live in France

part of the year. Good home cooking eaten under the thatched palapa on the multi-level terrace, chairs outside for street-watching, all clean, spacious and well cared for. Parking CUC$2.

Where to eat

$$$-$$ Rumayor
2 km on Viñales road.
Open 1200-2200, closed Thu.
State-run restaurant which specializes in *pollo ahumado* (smoked chicken), at CUC$6.50. Also *Tropicana*-style show, Fri, Sat and Sun (see Entertainment, below).

$$ El Gallardo
José Martí 207 entre Comandante Pinares y Celestino Pacheco, opposite the Museo de Ciencias Naturales, T48-778492, 5283 3603 (mob), restaurantgallardo@nauta.cu.
Good comida *criolla*, attentive and prompt service. Good for lunch or dinner, also rooms to rent, **Casa Roger**.

$$ El Mesón
José Martí 205, opposite the Museo de Ciencias Naturales, T48-822867.
Mon-Sat, 1200-2200.
Good, fresh food served in this *paladar*, run by Rafael, a former teacher, Cuban menu popular with local families, grilled pork with vegetables CUC$5.50.

$ Doña Neli
Gerardo Medina 24.
Bakery. Open daily 0700-1900 for bread, 0830-2300 for pastries and cakes.

Entertainment

The town is very lively on Sat nights and, to a lesser extent, on Fri, with music everywhere: salsa, *son*, Mexican music, international stuff.

Music
During the day you can hear traditional music (mambo, rumba, cha-cha-cha, *danzón*) in Parque Roberto Amarán. Baseball fans gather here for heated discussions about

sport. Parque de la Independencia is quieter and a place to enjoy the breeze at night, a popular hangout for the young crowd.

Opposite the **Hotel Vueltabajo** is a bar where locals gather to drink draft beer made from grapefruit and perform *canturías*. Open daily but best on Fri evening. Other places to try include **Artex** (Martí 36, daily 0900-0200), and **Bar La Esquinita** (Isabel Rubio, daily 2000-0200), for live guitar music.

Casa de la Cultura, *Rafael Morales esq Martí*. Band play every Sun evening with a dance contest for the elderly, fantastic, free, photos allowed.

Casa de la Música, *on Gerardo Medina next to Coppelia*. Live music daily except Mon.

Casa del Joven Creador, *José Martí 113A, opposite the Chess Academy, T48-774672*. An organization for music and the arts where young musicians gather at night and arrange concerts. A band that rose up through this system is the ethno-metal **Tendencia**, led by singer and director Kiko, a former high school English teacher. They have travelled abroad and now have a national reputation.

Nightclubs
Disco Pista Rita, *on González Coro*. An open-air venue popular with teenagers, where they play loud, US-style disco music and rock, entry CUP$2, the only drink on sale is neat rum at CUP$25 a bottle. **Pinar Rock**, a national rock festival, is held here the 2nd weekend of Mar.

Rumayor, *2 km on road to Viñales. Restaurant (1200-2200, closed Thu)*. A *Tropicana*-style show, Fri, Sat and Sun CUC$5, very good, lots of security. Starts 2300 (get there before 2200 to get a table) and lasts about 1½ hrs, followed by disco until 0300 or so. Held in small amphitheatre with proper sound and lighting system. No photography or videos allowed. The complex is in a pleasant garden with lots of trees.

Theatre
Teatro José Jacinto Milanés, *Martí entre Isabel Rubio y Colón, T48-753871*. There are 3 theatre groups, 1 for children and 2 for adults, which give occasional performances.

Festivals

Festivals
1st week of Jul Carnival lasts for for 5 days, Wed-Sun.

Shopping
Art gallery
Galería de Arte Yoruba, *Rafael Ferro 119. Open 0900-1900, CUC$1, coffee or tea included*. Local artists displaying and selling Afro-Cuban cultural works. Run by Enrique Machín, a Babalao, who is also a painter. Many languages spoken here.

Cigars and rum
Casa del Habano, *opposite the cigar factory*. For all brands of cigar from the Vueltabajo region. Smart, upmarket bar at the back, open same hours as the factory.

Casa del Ron, *Maceo esq Antonio Tarafa, 50 m from cigar factory*. For all your rum needs.

Markets
There is a fruit market opposite the railway station on Av Rafael Ferro, Mon-Sat 0800-1600, Sun 0800-1300, pay in CUP$. An even better farmers' market is on Av Alameda, near Parque Independencia, on the left before the cemetery on the road to Luis Lazo, Tue-Sat 0800-1800, 0800-1200 Sun. A newer a/c market is opposite the Banco Financiero Internacional, next to Coppelia on the corner of Gerardo Medina and Isidro de Armas, daily 0900-1700.

What to do

Tour operators
Cubanacán, *Chucho Valdés y M Gómez, T48-773015*. Tours, reservations, tickets, internet 0830-2100.

Cubatur, *Martí 115, T48-778405. Daily 0800-1700*.

Ecotur, *Casa del Veguero, Km 24 Ctra a Viñales, T48-796120, ecoturpr@enet.cu*. Contact them for full-day tours taking in birdwatching, hiking, trips to tobacco plantations, the crocodile farm, horse riding, fishing, jeep safaris, caving and hunting. **Havanatur**, *Martí, T48-778494.*

Transport

Bus

The bus station is on Colón, north of José Martí, near Gómez. It has been recently renovated and is under constant police surveillance. Head downstairs for tickets for provincial buses and trucks, upstairs for buses to **Havana**. A new boulevard has opened at the bus terminal, where you can get a quick lunch for CUP\$30 (just by the stop for buses from Havana). There's also a 24-hr café opposite the bus station.

Viazul, T48-752572/755255, runs a daily bus service from Havana continuing to **Viñales**, see page 131. It stops on request at **Las Terrazas** and **San Diego de los Baños**. There are no buses to María La Gorda; you have to get an official transfer from Havana with a package tour or rent a car.

If you get a local peso bus your name has to be on the list. Prices are CUP\$2-4 to **La Palma**, 1730, **Bahía Honda**, 1820, **Puerto Esperanza**, 1930, **Sandino**, 1800, **Guane** and **Mantua**.

Car hire

Transtur, Martí 109 near Restaurant La Casona, T48-750104, commercial.pri@ transtur.cu. **Servi Cupet** station on C Rafael Morales esq Frank País, on the road to San Juan y Martínez.

Taxi

Cubataxi has an office in the bus station with an a/c waiting room and an officer who can show you a brochure of trips and fares (no English spoken), Mon-Sat 0700-1800, Sun 0700-1200. Taxi to **Havana** bus terminal, CUC\$100, to **María la Gorda**, CUC\$120 (4 passengers), to **Viñales**, CUC\$20 one way, CUC\$60 round trip with waiting time.

Train

The railway station in Pinar del Río is on Av Comandante Pinares, T48-752106/752272. From **Havana**, departs 19 de Noviembre (Tulipán) station at 0610 every other day, arriving at 1325. It returns the next day at 0900, getting in at 1455, CUC\$7. This service is not recommended as it is very slow and robberies are common: take a torch for the tunnels and hang on to your luggage; don't sleep. The line continues to **Guane**, CUC\$3.

La Coloma and Cayos de San Felipe

The nearest beach, 25 km to the south of Pinar del Río, is **Las Canas**, near **La Coloma**. From La Coloma you can take a boat trip to the **Cayos de San Felipe**. The cays are unspoilt and fabulous, and have been protected as a national park since 2002. The protected area of 26,250 ha covers not only the cays and mangroves, but also a large marine reserve. Turtles and iguanas nest here; there are also manatee and lots of birds, endemic and migratory. There are white-sand beaches, dunes, crystal-clear water, coral gardens, reef and 20 dive sites. See What to do, page 128.

Boca de Galafre and Bailén

The Carretera Central continues southwest from Pinar del Río through pleasant farming country with villages strung along the road, sugar and tobacco fields, citrus trees and pasture. There are distant views of the mountains to the north and clearly marked side roads lead south to the fishing town of **Boca de Galafre** and the beach at **Bailén**. Bailén has a sprawling camping resort for Cubans stretching 2 km along the sand, with small A-frame cabins on the beach and concrete houses with self-catering facilities behind, T48-496145. It is very popular with Cubans from April to September for a very basic beach holiday. The beach is spoilt by the run-off from the Río Cuyaguateje, which makes the water muddy, and there is no reef to snorkel on. It is cleared at the beginning of April but then left to get dirty, muddy and smelly. Further east, away from the river, the beach is nicer. There is a bus from Pinar del Río in the morning, returning in the afternoon, but it often fails to appear.

Several kilometres down the road to Playa Bailén and 1 km before you get to the beach, there is a **crocodile farm** ① *daily 0900-1700, CUC$2, photographs CUC$3, video cameras CUC$5*, where they breed the American crocodile (*Crocodrylus acutus*). You can get uncomfortably close to the babies and can hold them. However, unless you are lucky, or come at feeding time, you are a 500 m telephoto lens away from the 4- to 5-m beasts. Note that small cars are likely to get bogged down on the sandy drive to the farm.

Isabel Rubio, Guane and the Valle de San Carlos

Back on the Carretera Central, **Isabel Rubio** has a gas station with a shop selling drinks, toiletries and canned foods. There is car rental in town and a place to buy pizza at the junction of the road to Sandino. From Isabel Rubio, a very pretty way to return to Pinar del Río (about one hour) is through Guane, Los Portales and Sumidero.

Guane, a large, attractive village with old houses and a little baroque church, is also the railway terminus (see Transport, above). The road runs through limestone hills, crossing the pretty **Río Cuyaguateje** several times and passing through the **Valle de San Carlos**, a spectacular narrow valley with cliffs and steep wooded hills rising on either side. Farmers grow fruit, vegetables and tobacco, with ox-drawn ploughs furrowing the bright red soil and tent-shaped tobacco drying sheds, *vegas*, everywhere.

West towards the coast

After Isabel Rubio the countryside becomes completely flat. The villages are less lively and the agricultural landscapes less varied, with plantations of Caribbean pine in some stretches. On the north side of the road, 7 km west of Isabel Rubio, is the turning for **Laguna Grande**, a lake where you can fish or swim. A few miles further on at **Punta Colorada** is a small beach.

The main road continues through **Sandino**, 68 km from Pinar del Río, where there are ten schools for Latin American students to study medicine, nursing and engineering, and **La Fé** to **Manuel Lazo**. The latter is a convenient place to stay if you want to visit the Guanahacabibes peninsula and go diving without staying at the hotel in María la Gorda, which is about an hour's drive, 75 km, away. After this village, potholes are more common. The last 15 km or so to the coast are through semi-deciduous dry coastal woodland.

Listings Southwest of Pinar del Río

Where to stay

West towards the coast
Casas particulares

$ Villa Edilia
Zona M 41, Sandino, T48-423843, 5263 7359 (mob), tonyg@princesa.pri.sld.cu.
Edilia and Tony have comfortable and quiet a/c rooms with fridge in a modern house with stone cladding on the front. Tony speaks good English and they are both very hospitable. The house is also a *paladar* so even if they don't have room for you to stay, you can eat here, good food, large portions.

What to do

La Coloma and Cayos de San Felipe
Boat trips

Ecotur, *Casa del Veguero, Km 24, Ctra a Viñales, T48-796120, ecoturpr@enet.cu.* From Coloma there are boat trips to the cays. Prices for a day trip range from CUC$38, if there are 10 of you, to CUC$166 per person if there are only 2, including a visit to a lobster ground, a coral reef for snorkelling, Cayo Sijú, birdwatching, fishing, lunch and a spell on the beach. In winter you can watch turtles and at any time you can see crocodiles and iguanas watching you while you have lunch. The boat doesn't always run, so make sure you confirm beforehand.

Transport

There are local buses from Pinar del Río to **Guane**, CUP$2, and very slow trains, CUC$3, but car hire is advised.

The Península de Guanahacabibes, which forms the western tip of Cuba, is a Natural Biosphere Reserve. The reserve covers 1175 sq km but has not yet been developed for ecotourism.

The peninsula is formed of very recent limestone, with an irregular rocky surface and patchy soil cover. There are interesting fossil coastlines, caves and blue holes; but with dense woodland on the south coast and mangrove on the north, the peninsula is uninviting for the casual hiker. However, for keen naturalists there are 12 amphibian species, 29 reptiles including iguana species, 10 mammals (including *jutia carabalí* and *jutia conga*) and 147 bird species, including nine of the 22 that are endemic to Cuba.

La Bajada and around
On reaching the coast at **La Bajada**, a very desolate little village, you will be asked to show your documents at the immigration post. There is a visitor centre at La Bajada, from where a 1.5-km trail leads to **Cueva Las Perlas**, a 300-m-long cavern with eight galleries, best done with a guide. Permits are required for entering the reserve. The Science Academy offers a Safari Tour with an English-speaking guide, Osmani Borrego, for CUC$25 per person. You can climb to the Radar for CUC$1 for a good view of the forest and the sea.

Cabo San Antonio
To the west of La Bajada, a good new road continues for 52 km to Cabo de San Antonio, where there is a new hotel, a few houses and a lighthouse built in 1849 and named after the then Spanish governor, Roncali. A marina opened in 2009, offering provisioning and refuelling for yachts, fishing and a dive shop. The coastline has several pretty white-sand beaches and clear waters with several suitable spots for snorkelling, but is otherwise lonely and desolate. There are some caves to explore, the main one being **Cueva La Sorda**, 1 km northwest of the lighthouse, where three different levels have collapsed into a central hole. There are many legends attached to the cave, where archaeological finds have been made. More recently an endemic frog was discovered after Hurricane Ivan: the 20-mm *Eleutherodactylus guanahacabibes*.

★María La Gorda
The main road continues 12 km south, hugging the coast, to María La Gorda, in the middle of nowhere, reputedly the best scuba centre in Cuba and an idyllic spot for relaxing, diving and birdwatching. There is good snorkelling with small coral heads close to the white-sand beach, or you can go out on the dive boat, but from September to December there are sometimes jellyfish. These inflict only a mild sting, but they make swimming uncomfortable.

Diving There are several wrecks off the western peninsula and freshwater cave diving in the blue holes is also possible, though not on offer as an organized activity. The dive boat tours usually go a short distance to dive sites, mostly reef or wall dives with caves, tunnels, drop-offs and even sections of old Spanish galleons, where there are lots of fish of all sizes, rays, moray eels, lobsters, grunts, groupers, turtles, barracuda and maybe whale sharks. The sea is very clear, very warm and calm, even when it is too rough to dive anywhere else in Cuba. See What to do, page 130.

Where to stay

Hotels

$$$-$$ Villa Cabo San Antonio
Playa Las Tumbas, T48-757655,
www.villacabosanantonio.com.
Simple resort of tasteful wooden lodges,
16 rooms with verandas, no disco or noise,
just peace and quiet except for mosquitoes
at sunset. On white-sand beach with
crystal clear water, very remote, you may
share the beach with pigs and cows. Lots
of wildlife around. Marina 4 km from hotel
with bar, scuba diving, fishing, although
activities only take place if the right member
of staff is on duty. Car and bicycle hire,
excursions, restaurant serves good lobster
and other seafood, but most things are
frozen and expensive.

$$$-$$ María La Gorda
T48-771316, www.hotelmarialagorda-
cuba.com.
Buffet meals and diving can be included in
packages. Lovely location, some rooms open
onto the beach, while other *cabañas* are in
the forest, but take plenty of repellent for
sandflies and mosquitoes. Expansion works
in 2013 cleared parts of the forest. Service and
cleanliness have been criticised as hit or miss.
You might want to take some snacks with
you as the buffet is poor and expensive, or
have sandwiches in the bar. Note that if you
eat outside, cats will try to steal your food.
There are no places to eat outside the hotel.

What to do

Diving
Dive shop at María La Gorda, T48-771306, see
page 129. Doctor specializing in hyperbaric
medicine. Good boat with shade, pleasant
Spanish-speaking staff. The dive boat
leaves 0930 and 1530 for the offshore reef
(CUC$40 per dive, plus CUC$10 a day to rent
equipment for those not on a package).
Some boats are very crowded.
　　The marina at Cabo de San Antonio has a
dive centre with 27 dive sites to explore but
it is not always staffed. They also offer fishing
at the marina and berths for yachts.

Sailing
For visitors arriving by yacht, **María La Gorda**
is a port of entry. There are 4 moorings, max
draft 2 m, VHF channels 16, 19, 68 and 72.
The **Marina Gaviota Cabo de San Antonio**
has refuelling facilities for visiting yachts,
T48-750123, www.gaviota-grupo.com.

Transport

Bus
There are no buses to **María La Gorda**; you
have to get an official transfer from Havana
with a package tour or rent a car. There is a
local peso bus from Pinar del Río to **Sandino**
at 1800.

Taxi
A taxi from Pinar del Río to **María La Gorda** is
CUC$120 for up to 4 passengers.

an area of outstanding natural and man-made beauty

North of Pinar del Río, the road leads across pine-covered hills and valleys for 25 km to Viñales, a delightful small town in a dramatic valley in the Sierra de los Organos. The area has a distinctive landscape, with steep-sided limestone mogotes rising dramatically from fertile flat-floored valleys, where farmers cultivate the red soil for tobacco, fruits and vegetables. This unique countryside is recognized as a UNESCO World Cultural Landscape. As in so much of rural Cuba, horses, pigs, oxen, zebu cattle and chickens are everywhere, including on the main road.

Viñales town

Viñales itself is a pleasant town, with single-storey houses with red-tiled roofs and wooden colonnades along the main street. Visitors come here to relax, hike in the hills and maybe visit a beach on the north coast. The main street is Salvador Cisneros and a walk along it will reveal nearly all the attractions Viñales has to offer. Streets running parallel or across it are residential and contain many *casas particulares*. **Viazul** drops you off half way along the street, opposite the main square with a little-used church. This is the Wi-Fi hotspot for the town so there are always people about (buy Etecsa cards at the office around the corner). There is also a little municipal museum on Salvador Cisneros and a **Casa de la Cultura** on the square with an art gallery. An informative curator here speaks English. There are several bars and restaurants along Salvador Cisneros, but hardly of the quality to warrant the thousands of visitors who come here every year.

On the edge of Viñales is **Caridad's Garden** ① *turn left at the gas station at the end of Salvador Cisneros on the road to Cueva del Indio, no entry fee, but a tip of CUC$1 is appreciated.* The garden contains a beautiful collection of flowers and fruit trees from Cuba and around the world. Chickens scratch about in the shady undergrowth with their chicks. The garden was first planted in the 1930s. A guide will show you around, pointing out all the different species and you will be invited to try all the different fruits. They are generous with their produce but appreciate contributions to the upkeep of the garden.

Mural de la Prehistoria

Two kilometres west of Viñales is the Mural de la Prehistoria, painted by **Lovigildo González**, a disciple of the Mexican Diego Rivera, between 1959 and 1976, generally disliked as a monstrous piece of graffiti. If you are fit and active you can climb up the rocks to the top for a great view. No guide needed. One hundred metres before the mural is **Restaurant Jurásico**, from where you can see the paintings; there is a swimming pool nearby. A new attraction in this area is a zip line, **Fortín Canopy Tours** ① *CUC$7 for Cubans, CUC$25 for foreigners*, which opened

Essential Valle de Viñales

Finding your feet

Viazul has a daily bus service from Havana via Pinar del Río. The nearest train station is at Pinar del Río.

Getting around

Viñales town is small and easy to walk around, although there's also a hop on/hop off bus that runs between the hotels, daily 0830-1800, CUC$5 for a 40-minute round trip. Many visitors hire a car or scooter to get around the nearby attractions, although there are also horses for hire and local buses between villages.

in September 2015 and is only the second in the country after Las Terrazas (see above). The zip line runs for 1100 m between the mogotes, over the tobacco fields and across the valley.

Los Acuáticos

Four kilometres from Viñales is the community of **Los Acuáticos**, where the villagers worship water. It was founded in 1943 by Antoñica Izquierdo, a *santera*, who recognized the importance of hygiene and clean water for health. The few families in the hamlet on the mountainside are self-contained and they bathe three times a day. Despite excellent rural healthcare in Cuba, the community refuses medical assistance for anyone who has an accident or is sick. It is recommended that women do not come here on their own.

Caves

Six kilometres north of Viñales is the **Cueva del Indio** ① *avoid 1130-1430 when tour parties arrive and there are long delays, CUC$5,* a cave which you enter on foot, then take a boat, with a guide who gives you a description, very beautiful. There is a restaurant nearby where tour parties are given a lunch of suckling pig (*lechón*). The tour includes lunch but not the cave, and no drinks; even water is an 'extra'. Beyond the restaurant is a small farm, well kept, with little red pigs running around, oxen and horses. There are trips to a disco

Viñales

Where to stay 🛏
Casa Deborah Susana cp 1
Casa El Cafetal cp 2
Casa Oscar Jaime cp 3
Casa Ridel y Claribel cp 4
La Ermita 5
Los Jazmines 6

Villa Renga y Julia cp 7

Restaurants 🍴
3 J Bar de Tapas 1
Casa de Don Tomás 2
El Olivo 3
La Cocinita del Medio 4

Entertainment 🎵
Artex 1
Bar Polo Montañez 2
Patio del Decimista 3

N
Not to scale

ON THE ROAD
Rocks, caves, valleys and mogotes

The rocks around Viñales are pure limestone formed in the Jurassic period around 160 million years ago. Unlike most other rocks, limestone can be dissolved by rainwater. Rivers and streams often flow underground through extensive cave systems; most of the 10,000 recorded caves in Cuba are in Pinar del Río province and one cave system in the Valle Santo Tomás consists of a total of 25 km of underground passages. Where a valley is formed in tropical limestone, often by downwards faulting of the rock, it may be filled with fertile red soil. Rotting vegetation increases the acidity of the groundwater on the valley floor. This 'aggressive' water eats into the valley sides, undercutting the rocks and producing steep cliff-like features. The valley floor is broken by isolated steep-sided hills, known to both English- and Spanish-speaking geologists by their Cuban name: mogotes. Other valleys (narrow gorges) are produced when the roof of a large cave collapses. Similar tropical limestone landscapes can be seen in parts of Puerto Rico and Jamaica.

Rapid drainage of rainwater into the rock produces dry growing conditions for plants. The limestone hills have a distinctive vegetation type, with palms (including the curious cork palm), deciduous trees, succulents, lianas and epiphytes. More than 20 species are endemic, found only in the Viñales area. The isolation of the mogotes has also produced distinctive animal species, with some types of snail found only on a single mogote.

in the **Cueva de San Miguel**, west of Cueva del Indio (much better to go on your own and have the cave to yourself), short hiking trips to a mogote, visits to various caves and **El Palenque de los Cimarrones**, a restaurant and craft shop with a display of Cuban folklore. These are advertized as daily events, but don't rely on it. See Entertainment, page 136.

The **Valle de Santo Tomás** (with 25-km cave system) contains the **Gran Caverna Santo Tomás** 17 km southwest from Viñales in a community called El Moncada. A guide will show you the cave; prices depend on which walk you choose. Near El Moncada is the 3-km ecological path, **Maravillas de Viñales**.

Listings Valle de Viñales *map p132*

Tourist information

There is a visitor centre, **La Casa del Visitante**, on the main road heading out to Pinar del Río, near **Hotel Los Jazmines**, daily 0730-1800.

Where to stay

Hotels

$$$-$$ La Ermita
Ctra de la Ermita, Km 2, 3 km from town with magnificent view of the valley and town,

especially at sunset, T48-796122/796071, www.hotelescubanacan.com.
62 rooms, a/c, shop, tennis court, wheelchair access, pool (not always usable), food not recommended, better to walk into the village for evening meal, breakfast included, nicer public areas than at **Los Jazmines**.

$$$-$$ Horizontes Los Jazmines
Ctra de Viñales, Km 23.5, 3 km before the town, in a superb location with travel brochure view of the valley, T48-796123/796205, www.hotelescubanacan.com.

62 rooms and 16 *cabañas*, nightclub, breakfast buffet CUC$5 if not already included, unexciting restaurant, bar with snacks available, shops, swimming pool (CUC$5 including towels for day-visitors and CUC$5 in vouchers for bar drinks), riding, easy transport.

Casas particulares

There are more than 500 registered *casas particulares* in Viñales. Many were rebuilt after the 2008 hurricane and are of a good standard. Tourist rooms tend to be built on to the side of houses with their own, independent entrance. Most charge CUC$20-25 a night, with breakfast at CUC$3-4 and dinner at CUC$7-10, depending on your menu choice. Many offer juice, coffee or *mojito* but do not say whether it is free or not; ask to avoid nasty surprises on the final bill. *Casa* owners will meet you at the bus station.

$ Casa Deborah Susana
Calle C Final 1, T48-796207, T5283 2018 (mob), deborahsusana7@nauta.cu.
Deborah Alfonso and Juan Carlos (barman at **Don Tomás**) are very caring and friendly and both speak English. They offer 2 airy rooms at the back of the house with a/c, fan, fridge, lots of power points, good bathrooms and independent access, which open out onto a pretty patio garden with comfy chairs and hammock under cover. The *casa* is very quiet, behind the main street at the back of Banco Nacional, and there is no traffic noise, despite being very central.

$ Casa El Cafetal
C Adela Azcuy Norte Final s/n, T5223 9175, 5331 1752 (mob).
Lovely rural and peaceful location, last house on the road, detached cottage in a lush garden which produces lots of fruit and coffee for the household. The food is wonderful and you eat overlooking the garden and the mogotes. Marta and Amador Martínez run this *casa* with Marta's son, Edgar Rivery, a climbing guide who speaks

English. 2 a/c bedrooms with 2 double beds and private bathroom.

$ Casa Oscar Jaime
Adela Azcuy 43, T48-793381.
Oscar Jaime Rodríguez and Leida Robaína Altega offer a friendly and welcoming home shared by 3 generations of family, including cousins, which is a mecca for climbers. Oscar was one of the first local people to get involved in climbing the mogotes and is very experienced and knowledgeable about routes. He can lend you equipment. 3 new rooms and a *paladar* built in 2015, making 6 in total on different levels and all to a high standard. Great food and delicious juices and (strong) mojitos.

$ Casa Ridel y Claribel
C Salvador Cisneros (Pasaje B), on western outskirts of town, T48-695127, 5823 3677 (mob), www.ridelyclaribel.altervista.org.
Very friendly and helpful hosts who can arrange trips and transport, and go out of their way to make your stay memorable. 2 comfortable a/c rooms, 1 has its own patio but there is also a roof terrace for sunset watching looking over the town roofs to the mogotes. Good food: you won't go hungry.

$ Villa Renga y Julia
C Salvador Cisneros Interior 1a, T48-798333, 5331 1817 (mob), http://casavinales.jimdo.com.
Immaculate house run by Julia's daughter Meily. Modern furnishings, disco lighting around the beds in the a/c bedrooms, jacuzzi outside. Excellent mattresses, safe box, large new bathrooms, all good quality. Very good food too, with huge and varied breakfast. Very close to Casa Deborah Susana, so also quiet but central.

$ Villa Tery
Calle 4 31 entre 5 y 7, Rpto La Colchonería, T48-696662.
Simple house in quiet, rural area, a short walk to centre, large comfortable rooms with a/c, fan and fridge, the room at the back has its own entrance. Very friendly, kind and

informative family. Guillermo, the father, will answer all your questions, Jolie, his daughter is an excellent cook and speaks English, while her grandfather has a tobacco farm and will show you how to make cigars. Parking. Bicycle hire.

Where to eat

$$$-$$ 3 J Bar de Tapas
Salvador Cisneros 45, T48-793334, 5531 1658 (mob).
A tapas bar with a good menu. Rum cocktails as strong as you like and they'll top up your glass with rum until you're happy. Modern, stylish decor in a renovated old house. Sit on the veranda or inside. Pleasant staff and friendly owner. A good place to sit with a book for a couple of hours, day or night.

$$$-$$ Buena Vista
On the road to Hotel Los Jazmines, T5223 8616 (mob), buenavista@nauta.cu.
Look for the blue and white thatched and tiled house. Tables outside on the veranda or inside, with glorious view over the valley to the mogotes, quiet and peaceful. Very good *comida criolla*, tasty lobster, plentiful side dishes. There are also rooms to rent so you can wake up with the same view in the mornings.

$$$-$$ Casa de Don Tomás
Salvador Cisneros 140, T48-796300. Open 1000-2200.
The oldest house in Viñales (1879), totally renovated after the 2008 hurricanes, very pretty with a spectacular orange climbing begonia (*lluvia de oro*) on a pergola at the back. Food very average, eggs the only option for vegetarians, but the cocktails are good and it's pleasant to sit and listen to live music with a Ron Collins or Mary Pickford. Most cocktails are CUC$2, but the house special, *Trapiche*, is CUC$2.20 (rum, pineapple, sugar cane syrup, served with ice and a stick of sugar cane). A bottle of rum is not much more than in a shop and a shot of rum starts at CUC$0.30.

$$$-$$ El Olivo
Salvador Cisneros 89, T48-696654, olivo.vinales@nauta.cu. Open 1200-2200.
A small, smart town centre *paladar* with a wide range of menu options including Mediterranean food and professional service. Good fish, paella, spaghetti, plenty of vegetarian options and interesting starters. Rabbit in chocolate sauce is worth trying and the goats cheese salad with raisins and hazelnuts (all imported) has very crisp, fresh lettuce. Most pasta dishes CUC$5-6, cocktails CUC$2.50-3.50. Eat inside or on the veranda. Always popular, queues outside.

$$$-$$ Fernando's
Ctra de la Ermita, Km 1, T48-696628.
Paladar within walking distance of the town centre, tables al fresco on patio among plants overlooking countryside and mountains. Lunch and dinner, with live music at night, good *criollo* food, lobster at CUC$15 the most expensive dish, several courses included, excellent service.

$$$-$$ La Casa Verde
50 m from Hotel Los Jazmines, T5223 8626.
Friendly, rustic, open air *paladar* with a great view over the valley to the mogotes, simple food but much better than anything on offer in the hotel and well worth the short walk for lunch or dinner. Usually a choice of chicken, fish or pork and sometimes lobster, with rice, beans, salad, sweet potato or plantain, followed by fresh fruit salad laced with liqueur. Vegetarians catered for. Meals usually CUC$10-12.

$$$-$$ La Cocinita del Medio
Salvador Cisneros 122, T48-796414. Open 1200-2300.
Good, simple *comida criolla*, grilled or stewed meat comes with all the usual trimmings: rice and beans, salad, yuca or plantain, generous portions.

Cafés

Mogote Café
Pasaje Ceferino Fernández 1, T5440 7238.
Drinks with a view. Lovely open-air seating on a veranda overlooking the mogotes, very peaceful. Good coffees and cocktails with happy hour in the afternoon. Soak up the mojitos with bruschetta or canapés. Sometimes live trios, otherwise international music.

Entertainment

Live music
Artex, *Salvador Cisneros*. Bar, live music, shop 1000-2000.
Bar Polo Montañez, *next to Casa de la Cultura on the plaza, CUC$2*. Live music every night from 2100-2400 with different bands, followed by DJ until 0200. Valle Son plays Tue and every other Sat, Afro-Cuban night Wed. Large dance floor.
Los Jazmines, *see Where to stay, above.* Disco 2000-0300, CUC$5.
Palenque de los Cimarrones, *4 km north of Viñales at Km 32 Ctra a Puerto Esperanza, T48-796205.* Fri-Sat there is a cabaret show and after midnight a disco, very popular. Take a sweater with you in case you stay until very late.
Patio del Decimista, *Salvador Cisneros 112A, T48-796014.* Tables on the pavement or in the courtyard. Live music 1730-2030 in the open-air courtyard and from 2100 until late in the inner patio. Bands switch every other night, good mix of locals, tourists and professional salsa dancers. Good fun, small and intimate, everyone gets up to dance, no cover charge.

Festivals

Mar Carnival and **Semana de la Cultura** are in the middle of the month lasting for 4 days, Thu-Sun. Lots of music and other activities, starting at 0600.

What to do

Climbing
The mogotes are a magnet for climbers. There is a local climbing group of men and women, very enthusiastic, who are equipped mostly with gear left behind by foreign climbers. Possible contacts include **Oscar Jaime Rodríguez** (C Adela Azcuy 43, T48-793381), who has a *casa particular* (see Where to stay) which is often used as a base camp by visiting climbers. He knows all the best climbing (*escalando*) spots in Viñales and the rest of the country. Be wary of *jineteros* who offer to take you to a man called Oscar, but actually take you somewhere completely different for a commission. Alternatively, Edgar Rivery at **El Cafetal** (see above), is very experienced. For more information on routes and hazards, see www.cubaclimbing.com.

Hiking
Hiking in the valleys is perfectly safe, but it is sensible to take a guide if you are venturing into the mountains themselves; this is particularly advisable for single women. Note that not all guides speak good English. You can find one at the visitor centre for CUC$10-20, depending on the chosen trail, or at the museum opposite **Artex**, or ask at your *casa particular*.

Riding
Ask around before choosing a guide. Most offer a 5-hr tour taking in the Cueva del Indio, which is probably more than enough on a horse. 3-hr tours also offered. Well worthwhile and a good way to see the countryside, but do inspect the horse beforehand. Most of the horses are in poor condition, very thin with sores, bites and cuts. Many tourists are far too heavy for the little Cuban horses and, as most do not know how to ride, they bump around on their backs like a sack of potatoes, causing further injury. If in doubt, walk.

Tour operators

Cubanacán, *Salvador Cisneros 63C, next to the bus terminal, open 0800-1700*. Excursion to Cayo Jutías including lunch and a drink. **Havanatur**, *Salvador Cisneros 65, T48-796161*. Tours, reservations and ticket sales. **Paradiso**, *bureau in the bookshop beside Cubanacán, T48-796164*. Wide variety of tours and excursions around town.

Transport

Bus

Bus terminal at Salvador Cisneros 63A. **Viazul**, T48-793195, daily from **Havana** via Pinar del Río, see page 118. Local buses from **Pinar del Río** to **Puerto Esperanza**, **La Palma** and **Bahía Honda** all pass through Viñales. Tour buses from Havana will drop you off if you want to stay more than a day and collect you about 1600 on the day you want to return.

Bicycle/scooter

On the plaza **Cubanacán**, daily 0900-1900, rents bicycles by the hour, the day or longer. Alternatively rent a bike on the street for CUC$10 for the afternoon. It is illegal to rent bicycles from *casas particulares*, but it happens and is cheaper. Scooters and bicycles can be rented from **Don Tomás** restaurant.

Car hire

Havanautos and **Transtur** at the end of Salvador Cisneros by the gas station, T48-796305/796330, Mon-Fri 0830-1800, hire cars and small jeeps. **Cubacar**, also by the gas station, T48-796060, Mon-Fri 0800-1700, Sat 0900-1300, is not always open but has good rates.

Taxi

Taxi fares vary and can be negotiated for long distances. To **Cayo Jutías** is CUC$60-70, depending on waiting time, with a surcharge later in the afternoon. To **María la Gorda** costs CUC$75 (tour agencies charge CUC$90-100 with commission).

It is a lovely drive southwest through the valley, via El Moncada, and then north through Pons and the former copper mining centre of Minas de Matahambre up to Cayo Jutías on the north coast near Santa Lucía, 50 km. The road is well signed on the way there, but not at all on the way back.

Cayo Jutías
Day trip to Cayo Jutías with a tour operator from Viñales, CUC$50 per person including lunch; or taxi transfer, CUC$60-70 (up to 4 people), 1 hr.

Cayo Jutías, a 6.7-km cay, is attached to Cuba by a long causeway through mangroves. There is a restaurant/bar on the beach (very busy with groups at lunchtime), plus thatched shade umbrellas, a beach volleyball pitch and a toilet. Sunbeds cost CUC$1.50 per day. You can also rent towels and pedalos.

Tip...
The coastal road west of Santa Lucía through Mantua to Guane is long and rather tedious. It is too far inland to see the sea and is also full of potholes and other surprises.

There is no hotel, and the beach therefore remains an undeveloped narrow strip of curving white sand with mangroves at either end. The far west end is quieter and better. The sea is calm, warm and multi-coloured with starfish, but there are patches of weed and not much snorkelling unless you can swim quite far out to the reef, which is marked by buoys. There is a lot of sand and sea grass on the way out to the reef, which can get stirred up with poor visibility, depending on the weather, but the reef itself is shallow with excellent visibility, especially when the sun is shining. There is some good brain coral and anemones here but, although there is a good variety, the fish are quite small. **Mégano**, an islet just offshore, is reached by boat, 12 minutes.

Tip...
Ask your *casa particular* for a packed lunch to save the bother of a long wait and poor service at the restaurant.

Puerto Esperanza
The road east of Santa Lucía to San Cayetano is in very poor condition and travellers have to detour through Viñales to regain the coast. **Puerto Esperanza**, 24 km from Viñales, is a fishing town and not a beach destination, although it does have *casas particulares* and plenty of seafood on offer.

★Cayo Levisa
Ferries depart from Palma Rubia daily 1000 and 1800 (15 mins), returning from Cayo Levisa at 0900 and 1700, CUC$15 uding drink. Hired cars can be left at the terminal building at Palma Rubia.

Cayo Levisa is part of the **Archipiélago de los Colorados**, with a long, sandy beach and reef running parallel to the shore that offers good snorkelling and scuba diving (lots of fish). The ferry jetty is on the south side of the island from where you follow a boardwalk through the mangroves to get to the hotel on the north side. The island is very quiet and peaceful with nothing much to do on land except walk a circuit of the island, which takes about three hours. It is very relaxing and charming, but take insect repellent.

Diving There are about 23 dive sites between 15 m and 35 m deep and none is more than 30 minutes away by boat. The underwater scenery is characterized by big sponges and enormous black coral trees. Angel fish are very numerous, as are barracuda and schools of jacks. The current is generally quite gentle, so it is an ideal place for beginners and experts alike. There are several bits and pieces of old galleons, most of which have been covered by corals. In season you can windsurf or go on sailing and snorkelling trips to other cays and beaches, but from September when the sea gets rougher there is less available, so check beforehand.

Listings North coast

Where to stay

Cayo Jutías
Some people choose to lodge in Santa Lucía, which is closer to the cay than Viñales, but is not a particularly nice place to stay.

Casas particulares

$ Villa Cayo Jutías
Entronque Cayo Jutías (El Punto), Santa Lucía, T5336 5574, 5419 1595 (mobs), aylen.vento@nauta.cu.
A few km from Cayo Jutías, but with transport to the beach as well as diving and boat trips. 3 a/c rooms with independent access, 1 double and 2 twins, each with fridge. Parking.

Cayo Levisa

$$$ Cayo Levisa
T48-756501, www.hotelescubanacan.com.
Book in Havana through any tour agency that deals with **Cubanacán**; packages include transport from Havana, some or all meals and often watersports. Cabins on beach, thatched, with verandas, built in 2 rows but staggered so that each gets a sea view, a/c, TV, fridge, comfortable but not luxurious, spacious, also newer apartments further along the beach and more being built. The restaurant serves bland and boring food and service is awful, the beach bar at the far end serves fresh fried fish or chicken which is preferable, bar, live music. Even on an all-inclusive package you will probably have to pay for your drinks and beach towel rental.

There are lots of day-trippers from Havana, but the beach doesn't feel crowded and once they've gone back, you could be on a desert island. Take plenty of insect repellent against mosquitoes and sand fleas/*jejenes*.

What to do

Cayo Jutías
A kiosk rents snorkelling equipment for CUC$2.50 per hr or CUC$5 per day (individual bits can be rented separately) on production of identity documents. You can also go diving for CUC$35, good, but try and discourage the divemaster from touching everything underwater.

Cayo Levisa
Cayo Levisa Diving Centre. Dives at 0830, 1100 and 1430. 1 large boat for up to 20 divers and 1 smaller one for 10 out to 23 dive sites: coral, wall and wreck diving. Diving costs CUC$40, including a drink and a packed lunch, snorkelling trips are CUC$14, equipment included. Snorkels and fins can also be hired for CUC$5 per day, but get to the dive shop early to make sure of a set. SSI courses are available for Open Water and Advanced qualifications. The nearest hyperbaric chamber is at the Naval Hospital in Havana, 35 mins away by helicopter.

> **Tip...**
> In the off-season, from September check weather conditions before paying for a dive trip; it is difficult to get a refund if the boat doesn't go out.

Matanzas

beaches, birds and botched invasions

Matanzas province, to the east of Havana, is mainly associated with the mega-resort of Varadero beach. This tourist enclave is squeezed onto a finger of land stretching out into the Caribbean. The white sand, handsome palm trees, watersports and all-inclusive deals make this a popular holiday spot. However, for all that it represents of Cuba it might as well be another country.

Close to Varadero and in contrast to it are the low-key towns of Matanzas and Cárdenas, where there is no engineered tourism. Both have had their heyday. The outstanding Cuevas de Bellamar and the luscious Valle de Yumurí, studded with thousands of Royal palm trees, are also worth visiting.

The south coast has one of Cuba's most notable geographic features, the Ciénaga de Zapata, a huge marsh covering the entire coast and the peninsula of the same name. It is a nature reserve, protecting many endemic species of flora and fauna, as well as numerous migrating birds. The diving in the deep-blue sea off Playa Girón and Playa Larga is exceptional. Also here, the disastrous American-backed invasion at the Bay of Pigs is remembered in a fascinating museum.

Best for
Beaches ■ Birdwatching ■ Diving ■ Revolutionary history

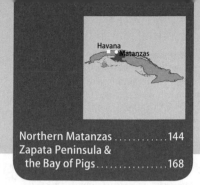

Footprint
picks

★ **Matanzas**, page 144

An elegant colonial city with impressive theatres and museums on the banks of two rivers.

★ **Parque Nacional Ciénaga de Zapata**, page 170

Go birdwatching for rare endemics and flocks of migratory species in winter.

★ **Shore diving in the Bay of Pigs**, page 171

Wrecks, reef and wall create a beautiful underwater environment around Playa Larga and Playa Girón.

★ **Museo Girón**, page 171

Relics of the battle tell the Cuban version of the history of the CIA-backed invasion.

★ **Snorkelling at Caleta Buena**, page 171

The pale blue natural swimming pools are teeming with colourful fish.

Essential Matanzas

Finding your feet

There is an **international airport** at Varadero, which receives scheduled and charter flights from Europe and Canada. Matanzas is on the main railway line between Havana and Santiago. The Hershey electric railway line, which used to service the Hershey chocolate factory before the Revolution, also runs between Havana and Matanzas, but it breaks down frequently and timings are very approximate. More reliable than the train is the excellent bus service provided by **Viazul**, which uses the good road out from Havana along the north coast to Matanzas and Varadero. **Viazul** also stops at Entronque de Jagüey and Playa Girón (for the Zapata Peninsula) en route between Havana and Cienfuegos.

Tip...

Public transport is notoriously scarce outside the main towns and tourist areas. Tourists from Varadero are herded on to tour buses for excursions, but to do your own thing, hire a car or pay a driver to take you around in his old Chevrolet taxi.

Tip...
Some places in Varadero accept euros (€).

Getting around

There are local trains from Matanzas to other towns in the province, but service is poor. Local buses run from Matanzas and Varadero to other towns such as Cárdenas, but public transport to the Zapata Peninsula is limited. Taxis are available from Entronque de Jagüey and Girón, and there are plenty of tour buses to take you to the peninsula on an excursion, but car hire is recommended if you want flexibility. See also Essential Matanzas city, page 145, Essential Varadero, page 153, Essential Cárdenas, page 163, and Essential Zapata Peninsula, page 169.

When to go

The winter season between December and April has the best weather, although, if there is a cold front off the eastern seaboard of the USA you can expect rough seas and a smaller expanse of sand as a result. This is also the most expensive season in the resorts. The wettest time of year is between September and November. The Bay of Pigs is more protected from the weather than the north coast but has been hit in the past by hurricanes at this time.

Time required

The province can be seen in three or four days on a whistle-stop tour, with day trips from Varadero to Matanzas, Cárdenas, Bay of Pigs and the Zapata Peninsula, but you will only be skating over the surface. It's better to spend a night in Matanzas to take in some of the cultural activities on offer. Allow a couple of days for birdwatching in Zapata, and another couple for snorkelling and diving in the Bay of Pigs. A sun, sea and sand holiday in Varadero can last as long as your boredom threshold allows.

> **Best** *casas particulares*
> **Hostal Alma**, Matanzas, page 151
> **Beny's House**, Varadero, page 157
> **Casa de Yeni**, Playa Larga, page 172
> **Hostal Luis**, Playa Girón, page 173

Northern
Matanzas

palaces and theatres, castles and caves

Matanzas (population 115,000) is a sleepy city with old colonial buildings, a remarkable pharmacy museum and a legendary musical history. It sits on the Bahía de Matanzas and is freshened by the sea breeze.

On the opposite side of the bay is the busy, ugly industrial zone, consisting of oil storage facilities, chemical and fertilizer plants, sugar, textile and paper mills and thermal power stations. Both the rivers Yumurí and San Juan flow through the city; walk along the riverside at dusk to watch the fishermen or to take in the tranquillity of your surroundings and listen to the murmur of fellow observers. Most of the old buildings are between the two rivers, with another colonial district, Versalles, to the north of the Río Yumurí. This area was colonized in the 19th century by French refugees from Haiti after the revolution there. The newer district, Pueblo Nuevo, also has many colonial houses.

Parque de la Libertad
Parque de la Libertad is the main square, with a statue of José Martí in the middle and dominated by the former **Palacio del Gobierno** on its eastern side. The **Sala de Conciertos José White** is on the northern side, and next to it is the newly renovated Hotel E Velasco, built in 1902 and very grand. Just beside the hotel is the **Teatro Velasco**, now a cinema.

Sala de Conciertos ⓘ *Contreras (79) entre Ayuntamiento (288) y Santa Teresa (290), T45-267032.* The Sala has been beautifully restored by Atenart, a local group of artists and conservationists, who also worked on the restoration of the Museo Farmacéutico. Every detail of the neoclassical decor has been faithfully preserved or replicated; you would never know what a terrible state the building had fallen into prior to its restoration. The Sala de Conciertos reopened in 2015 as the home of the Matanzas symphony orchestra. It is on three levels and has space for a huge orchestra with 120 musicians accompanied by a choir. There is also a reception area, a gallery of photos of the city and a café. The interior patio contains a ceramic mural and a bronze, homage to the first *danzón*, performed here in 1879. See also Music in Matanzas, page 146.

Museo Farmacéutico ⓘ *Milanés (83) 4951 entre Santa Teresa y Ayuntamiento, T45-223197, Mon-Sat 1000-1700, Sun 1000-1600, CUC$3, camera charge, CUC$1.* On the south side of the plaza is this beautifully preserved museum containing the original equipment, porcelain jars, recipes and furnishings of the Botica La Francesa, opened in 1882 by the Triolet and Figueroa family. Both men founded a pharmacy in Sagua la Grande before visiting Matanzas together and establishing the new pharmacy; Triolet later married into the Figueroa family. It was a working pharmacy until 1964, when it was nationalized and then converted into this fascinating museum, believed to be unique in Latin America. The pharmacy shelves are all made of cedarwood and divided by Corinthian columns – all made from one tree trunk. The shelves are filled with 19th-century French porcelain jars, which contain medicinal plants, imported European products and North American goods. The museum exhibits lists of formulas, pill makers, the original telephone, baby bottles, gynaecological equipment and scorpion oil. You can also go upstairs to see the living quarters. Curator Patria Dopico is very helpful.

Calle Milanés

East of the plaza, on the street that bears his name (Calle 83), is the former home of local poet José Jacinto Milanés (1814-1863); it is now the **Archivo Histórico**. There is also a statue of the poet on Milanés, outside the elegant **Catedral de San Carlos Borromeo**. The cathedral was first built in 1693 but rebuilt in a neoclassical style in 1878 after a fire, with frescoed ceilings and walls. It is now undergoing restoration that will cover up the frescoes. The **Museo Provincial Palacio de Junco** ⓘ *Milanés entre Magdalena y Ayllón, T45-243195, Tue-Fri 1000-1800, Sat 1300-1900, Sun 0900-1200, CUC$2,* is a royal blue building that houses the provincial museum, built by a wealthy plantation owner and dating from 1840. The historical exhibition includes an archaeological display and exhibits on the development of sugar and slavery in the province. It includes the remains of a slave who was thrown into a pit with his chains still attached and stocks to hold the feet of slaves. There are guns and pistols from the capture of silver boats of Dutchman Piet Heyn on 8 September 1628.

Plaza de la Vigia

Teatro Sauto ⓘ *T45-243420, daily 0830-1600, CUC$2, 14 performances per month; ticket prices vary.* This magnificent neoclassical building dominates the Plaza

Essential Matanzas city

Finding your feet

The town lies 104 km east of Havana along the Vía Blanca, which links the capital with Varadero beach, 34 km further east. If you are travelling by car the drive is unattractive along the coast and can be smelly because of the many small oil wells producing low-grade crude en route, but once you get into the hills there are good views of the countryside. Long-distance buses between Havana and Varadero all pass through Matanzas and you can request a stop here. You can also get here by train, although this is unreliable, either en route from Havana to Santiago, or on the Hershey Railway, the only electric train in Cuba. The 2½- to four-hour journey from Havana to Matanzas is memorable and scenic if you are not in a hurry.

Getting around

Most of the places of interest are within walking distance, but if you get tired you can board a horse-drawn *coche* or hail a bicitaxi. Taxis can be hired for day trips out of town. Some of the city's historic sights (San Severino fort, Cuevas de Bellamar and Tropicana) can be reached using the hop-on hop-off **MatanzasBusTour** between Varadero and Matanzas, which passes through the city centre. See also Transport, page 152.

Tip...

The **Mirador de Bacunayagua** is a spectacular lookout on the route between Havana and Matanzas, where the highest bridge in Cuba spans the gorge of the Yumurí valley. Most buses make this a rest stop.

Music in Matanzas

Matanzas is a quiet town in all senses but one. If you listen carefully you can hear its unique heartbeat: one, two, one two three.

With its docks and warehouses, Matanzas provided the ideal birthplace for the rumba and it is still the world capital of this exhilarating music and dance form. Families here are virtually born into the rumba: the latest incarnation of the *Muñequitos de Matanzas* has a young boy keeping the beat on the bamboo *guagua*. The *Muñequitos* are the fathers and mothers of contemporary rumba, having set the standards for *rumberos* on their tours across the globe. Of course, the *rumba Matancera* bears not the slightest resemblance to its ballroom namesake.

The rumba at the Casa de la Trova was famous for its intricate drumming, vocal improvisations and dancing, which is by turns graceful, audacious, devotional and downright dirty. Rumba is a communal art form – the *Columbia* style was created by workers on the Columbia railway line; however, great names of the past are recalled in *Columbias* such as '*Malanga Murió*'. On your way to a rumba, don't forget to stop at a bar and put a record by Matanzas' own Arsenio Rodríguez on the 1950s jukebox. Without Arsenio, there would have been no *conjunto son* and thus no Latin salsa. If you've got time, go and pay homage at the site of the dance hall where on a hot January night in 1879 Miguel Faílde created the *danzón cubano*, still the only authentic, unselfconscious marriage of orchestral sounds with African rhythms. It is now the Sala de Conciertos José White de Matanzas, Calle 79 entre 288 y 290. *Danzón* is currently enjoying a revival: across Cuba, music is being reissued and orchestras formed. The world has much to thank Matanzas for.

de la Vigía south of Milanés. It was designed by Daniel Dallaglio, an Italian, who won the commission by competition; Dallaglio also built the church of San Pedro Apóstol, see page 148. The theatre dates from 1862-63 and seats 650 people in cream, wrought-iron seats in three-tiered balconies. Performances in the past have included Enrico Caruso and Anna Pavlova, who toured Cuba in 1917. French actress Sarah Bernhardt, musician José White, singer Rita Montaner and Alicia Alonso, director of the Cuban National Ballet, have all appeared here. It was restored after the Revolution and further renovation works take place from time to time. In the entrance there are Carrara marble statues of Greek goddesses and a painting of Piet Heyn, the Dutch admiral (see box, page 148) and, in the hall, the muses are painted on the ceiling. Most unusually, the floor can be raised to convert the auditorium into a ballroom.

Opposite the theatre is the restored, pale orange **Palacio de Justicia**, built in 1826 and rebuilt in 1911.

There are several bridges in the town, but the one you are most likely to notice is the steel **Puente Calixto García**, built in 1899 at the edge of Plaza de la Vigía and next to the neoclassical fire station, **Parque de los Bomberos**. Just below the bridge is a **mosaic memorial** to Che Guevara. Opposite the fire station is **Ediciones Vigía** ① *daily 0900-1600*, founded in 1985, where you can see books being produced, ranging from fairy tales to those commemorating important events, embracing a variety of formats: books, magazines, loose sheets and scrolls, mostly poetry, short stories, literary criticism and

1 Matanzas

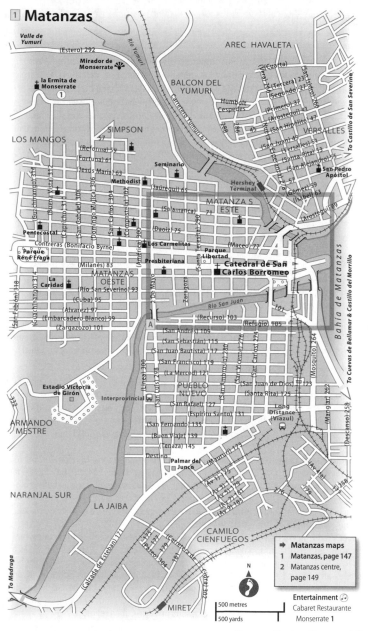

Valle de
Yumurí

(Estero) 292

Mirador de
Monserrate

la Ermita de
Monserrate

Río Yumurí

AREC HAVALETA

BALCON DEL
YUMURÍ

(Cuarta)

(Tercera) 23
(Segundo) 27

(Primero) 33
(Arosteguí) 41
(San Hipólito) 47

Humbolt
Cespedes

Carretera Yumurí

To Castillo de San Severino

SIMPSON
57

LOS MANGOS

(Reforma) 59

(Fortuna) 61

(Jesús María) 63

Seminario

Methodist

(Jaúregui) 65

(Salamanca) 71

Pentecostal

Contreras (Bonifacio Byrne)

Parque
René Fraga

(Milanés) 83

La
Caridad

(Río San Severino) 93

(Cuba) 95

(Alvarez) 97

(Embarcadero Blanco) 99

(Zargazozo) 101

MATANZAS
OESTE

Estadio Victoria
de Girón

Interprovincial

ARMANDO
MESTRE

NARANJAL SUR

To Madruga

MIRET

(San Juan) 49
VERSALLES

(Santa-Rita) 55
(San Alejandro) 55

San Pedro
Apóstol

(Gómez) 59
(Isabel) 63

(Arosteguí) 69

Hershey
Terminal

MATANZAS
ESTE

(Daoiz) 75

(Maceo) 77

Los Carmelitas

Presbiteriana

Parque
Libertad

Catedral de San
Carlos Borromeo

Río San Juan

2 de Mayo

(Recurso) 103

101

(Refugio) 105

A

(San Andrés) 109

(San Sebastián) 115

(San Juan Bautista) 117

(San Francisco) 119

(La Merced) 121

PUEBLO
NUEVO

(San Juan de Dios) 123

(Santa Rita) 125

(San Rafael) 127

(Espíritu Santo) 131

(San Fernando) 135

Long
Distance
(Viazul)

(Buen Viaje) 139

(Tenaza) 145

Destino

Palmar del
Junco

(Murillo) 173

(Av 11) 175

(Av 23) 179

(Av 77) 181
(Av 91) 183

CAMILO
CIENFUEGOS

LA JAIBA

(Paseo) 364

Calzada de Esteban 171

(Carretera de Cuba) 102

Bahía de Matanzas

To Cuevas de Bellamar & Castillo del Morrillo

(Mosquito) 264

(Mangari) 262

(Descanso) 258

N

500 metres
500 yards

→ Matanzas maps
1   Matanzas, page 147
2   Matanzas centre,
     page 149

Entertainment 🎵
Cabaret Restaurante
Monserrate 1

Matanzas Northern Matanzas • 147

BACKGROUND

Matanzas

The town dates from 1693, when immigrants from the Canary Islands founded a settlement they called San Carlos y Severino de Matanzas, between the rivers San Juan and Yumurí. Before that, the Bahía de Matanzas was known mainly for an attack on the Spanish fleet by the Dutch Admiral Piet Heyn, which took place in 1628. The fleet was considered war booty, and the four million ducats of gold and silver that were captured were used to finance further battles between Spain and Holland. The name Matanzas, meaning 'slaughters' or 'massacres', is thought to come from the mass slaughter of wild pigs to provision the fleets, but it could also refer to the killing of the Amerindians who lived here and called the bay Guanima. Around the time of the founding of the city, a fortress, the Castillo de San Severino, was built on the northern shore of the bay to keep out pirates and any other invaders.

The town became prosperous with the advent of sugar mills in the 1820s, followed by the railway in 1843; most of the buildings date from this time. By the 1860s it was the largest town in Cuba after Havana, with all the trappings of an important city, such as a theatre, newspaper and library. It even became known as the 'Athens of Cuba' because of all the musicians and writers living there. The Sala de Conciertos José White de Matanzas on the plaza, was formerly the Lyceum Club and is famous for being the place where the *danzón* was danced for the first time in 1879; see box, page 146.

children's literature. These are all handmade and in first editions of only 200 copies, so they are collectors' items, particularly if you get one signed. The **Galería de Arte Provincial** ⓘ *also on the plaza, daily 0900-1700*, has rotating displays of contemporary Cuban art.

Northeast of the centre

North of the Río Yumurí in Reparto Versalles near the Hershey terminal is the **Iglesia de San Pedro Apóstol** ⓘ *Calle 57 y 270, open Mon-Sat mornings and 1530-1930*. Cross the park in front of the terminal and walk up the street in the far corner; the church will soon be towering above you on the left. The interior is mustard yellow and has an imposing altar piece with four Ionic columns and a rather lovely stained glass of Saint Peter.

Museo de la Ruta de los Esclavos ⓘ *Castillo de San Severino, Av del Muelle, Tue-Sat 1000-1900, Sun 0900-1200, CUC$2, CUC$1 for pictures, CUC$5 for a video camera*. Beyond Reparto Versalles, towards the northeast, is the **Castillo de San Severino**. This muscular, colonial castle was built in 1693 as a solid lookout post on the Bay of Matanzas to prevent pirate attack. The original coat of arms is still above the main entrance. Originally water lapped at the castle entrance but a road was built in front of it in 1910. The moat, however, was never filled with water. This was the place where slaves were unloaded from ships, having crossed the Atlantic in appalling conditions, before being sold. San Severino was also used as a prison until the 1980s. (One man was incarcerated here for six years for being a Jehovah's witness.) It is said the prison was divided by a wall, with political prisoners on one side and homosexuals on the other. With UNESCO support, the castle has been turned into a **museum of slavery**, including displays of ceramics and pipes and other materials found at the castle as well as exhibits on Afro-Cuban religion.

Northwest of the centre

La Ermita de Montserrate, a good hike north up Domingo Mujica (306) from the Parque de la Libertad (or take the hourly bus No 12 from beside the Museo Farmacéutico), was built in 1872 in honour of the Virgin of Monserrat. The roof caved in after storm damage but has now been rebuilt. From the hilltop it is perched on, you can see the city and the bay rolled out before you and, on the other side, the verdant **Valle de Yumurí**, although the perfection of the view is slightly marred by the pylons marching towards the horizon. This is an excellent place to walk, and there is a bar and restaurant in the park for refreshment.

South of the city

The road out to Varadero goes past the university and the Escuela Militar. One kilometre past the university you come to the **Río Canímar**, which flows into the Bahía de Matanzas. (Trips along the river can be arranged from Varadero.) Just before the bridge over the river, take the road running alongside the river towards the bay to the **Castillo del Morrillo**.

Castillo del Morrillo ① *Tue-Sun 1000-1700, CUC$1 entrance, CUC$1 for guide.* Built in 1720 to protect the area, the castle is now a museum in memory of Antonio Guiteras Holmes, who was shot, along with the Venezuelan revolutionary Carlos Aponte Hernández, by Batista's troops near the bridge. Bronze busts of the two men can be seen underneath a mahogany tree. Guiteras Holmes was a student leader who started a revolutionary group called *Joven Cuba* (Young Cuba) in 1934. He served briefly in the government that replaced Machado, but fell foul of the rising Batista. It was when he and Aponte came to Matanzas

2 Matanzas centre

➡ **Matanzas maps**
1 Matanzas, page 147
2 Matanzas centre, page 149

Where to stay 🛏	Restaurants 🍴	Entertainment 🎭
Casa Rabelo cp **1**	Bistro Kuba **1**	Casa ACAA **1**
Hostal Alma cp **2**	Le Fettucine **2**	Teatro Sauto **2**
Hostal Azul cp **3**	Restaurante Romántico	
Hotel E Velasco **4**	San Severino **3**	

in 1935 to try and find a boat to take them into exile in Mexico that they were caught and executed. The castle also has a *sala* of aboriginal archaeology and a large rowing boat.

Cuevas de Bellamar ① *Southeast of town at Finca La Alcancía, T45-261683. Mon-Sat 0900-2030, Sun 0900-1700. Tours daily at 0930, 1030, 1130, 1315, 1415, 1515, 1615, CUC$5, CUC$8 includes the extra 100-m stretch, parking CUC$1, CUC$5 for cameras, no bags allowed in. Take bus No 12, CUP$1, from Parque Libertad to the caves, leaves every 2 hrs. Tours from Varadero including brief city tour, CUC$30.* This cave system, discovered in 1862 by somebody working the land, stretches for 23 km, and is stuffed full of stalactites, stalagmites (one 12 m tall) and underground streams. Tour parties come from Varadero, so you may get herded along with a bus load. In any case, all visitors must be accompanied for the 750-m walk through the caves; you can go a further 100 m with torches. There are 154 steep steps down into the cave. Wear appropriate footwear because the caves can be wet, muddy and slippery, and the surface is uneven. The complex has a small museum with items found in the caves and explanations in English and Spanish, plus a restaurant, shop and children's playground.

Other caves around Matanzas There are also caves at **Las Cuevas de Santa Catalina**, near Carbonera, 20 km east of Matanzas, where there are believed to be 8 km of tunnels. The caves were used as an Amerindian burial site and feature paintings close to the entrance. **Refugio de Saturno** is a large cave often visited by scuba-divers, although anyone can enjoy a swim here. It is 1 km south of the Vía Blanca, 8 km east of the Río Canímar.

Listings Matanzas city and around *maps p147 and p149*

Where to stay

Hotels

$$$-$$ Hotel E Velasco
Contreras entre Santa Teresa y Ayuntamiento, Parque de la Libertad, T45-253880, www.hotelescubanacan.com.
Newly renovated with a beautiful reception hall, intricately painted and with marble columns. 17 a/c rooms which open onto central atrium, except for suites, which are more spacious and have windows onto the square. Rooms are not large but are well-equipped and comfortable. Wi-Fi in the lobby. Reserved parking in the square. Food is fine and service is friendly.

$$ Canimao
Km 4.5 Ctra Matanzas a Varadero, T45-261014, www.islazul.cu.
A modern, but nice-looking hotel on the outskirts of Matanzas opposite the **Tropicana** cabaret. It has 120 rooms on a hill above the Río Canímar, with excursions

offered on the river or to caves. Nearby is a natural canyon, the Cueva de Los Cristales, which had evidence of aboriginal infanticide. The hotel is past its best but the food and service are OK and the location makes up for its shortcomings.

Casas particulares

$ Casa Rabelo
Zaragoza (292) entre Milanés (83) y Medio (85), T45-243433, morirabelo@gmail.com.
Moraima (Mori) Rabelo, speaks English, is very helpful and full of advice. She has 3 rooms with a/c and fan, all on ground level, although there are steps. Walk through the house to the pretty courtyard garden where you have breakfast, dinner or just relax. This *casa* is popular with cyclists; Mori can recommend routes with lodging and will store bike boxes for the return flight if you are leaving from Varadero airport. Garage for parking.

$ Hostal Alma

Milanés (83) 29008 Altos entre Sta Teresa
(290) y Zaragoza (292), T45-290857,
5283 1479 (mob), hostalalma@gmail.com.
Huge and grand 19th-century house with
beautiful *vitrales*, large, multi-level terraces
for drinks, meals or just sunbathing, and
fabulous roof view, with 3 rooms on the
2nd floor with private bathroom, fridge,
minibar. 1 room can hold a couple and child.
Dinner is also offered to non-guests, but
ring beforehand to book. Mayra, her friendly
family and their attractive house make this a
very popular option.

$ Hostal Azul

Milanés (83) 29012 entre Santa Teresa (290)
y Zaragoza (292), T45-242449, T5-273 7903
(mob), hostalazul.cu@gmail.com.
Well-preserved 1870s mansion with original
tiles. Very spacious, 4 rooms with high
ceilings; the room up a spiral staircase has
a balcony. There is a bar/café with vaulted
ceiling in the front room of the house
overlooking the street. Sometimes live music
here. Run by husband and wife team Yoel
Baez and Aylin Hernández, who are very
helpful. Having worked for many years in Sol
Meliá hotels in Varadero, Yoel is experienced
in hospitality and speaks English and Italian.

$ Hostal Villa Mar

Calle 127 (San Rafael) 20809 entre 208 y 210,
Rpto Playa, T45-288132, 5296 9894 (mob),
lictik87@gmail.com.
A stylish 1950s villa on the waterfront away
from the city centre, offering 2 rooms, one
of which is an independent unit. English-
speaking hosts, charming and hospitable
and maintaining an excellent standard of
accommodation. You have the option of
dining overlooking the sea or relaxing with
a cocktail enjoying the view but there are
paladares in walking distance if you want to
go out. If you fancy a swim, there are steps
down through the rocks, coming out on a
rocky overhang at the water's edge.

$ Villa Costa Azul

Calle 127 (San Rafael) 20817 entre 208 y 210,
Rpto Playa, T45-261460, 5244 5223 (mob).
A modern house on the waterfront with
2 rooms, one on top of the other, with private
entrance. The upstairs room has a terrace
overlooking the sea, but the downstairs
room also has a sea view and access to the
garden. Meals can be taken in the gazebo
by the sea. Teresa and Fernando are very
hospitable and helpful and their son, Fernán,
speaks good English. There is no access to the
water, but a small beach is only a block
away. Several *paladares* close by, although
Teresita is a good cook.

Where to eat

$$$-$$ El Bukan

Calle 110 entre 127 y 129, Playa, T45-289999,
www.elbukan.com. Thu-Tue 1200-2230.
On the top floor of a building overlooking
the bay. The young men running this
bar and restaurant with home-delivery
service are professional and friendly. The
cocktails are great, the beer frosty and the
wine selection good. The food is varied,
appealing to any member of a family,
although some dishes are a heart attack
waiting to happen and the portions are
vast, so ask for leftovers to be bagged up
for another meal or share one (meat skewer,
for example) between 2 people.

$$$-$$ Mallorca

Calle 334 7705 entre 77 y 79, T45-283282.
Wed-Sun 1230-2130.
A smart, modern *paladar* with screens for
music videos or sports, but there is also live
music and entertainment. The chef used to
work for Meliá and the food is beautifully and
professionally presented. Plenty of variety,
fusion food, generous portions, menu in
English. Quite a distance from the centre,
a taxi is CUC$3.

$$$-$$ Restaurante Romántico San Severino
Calle 290 7903 Altos entre 79 y 83, T45-281573, Thu-Tue, 1200-late.

Upstairs in a grand old building overlooking Parque de la Libertad, sensitively renovated keeping the old tiles, light fittings and other fixtures. The best tables are the 3 on the balcony overlooking the plaza, good for people-watching by day but particularly in the evening when all the birds come to roost in the trees. Food is average to good. Cash only.

$$-$ Le Fettucine
C Milanés 29018 entre Zaragoza y Santa Teresa, T5412 2553 (mob), see Facebook. Fri-Wed 1200-2130.

New in 2015, starting small but bound to expand because of its instant popularity; queues outside. Home made pasta and pizza, limited selection but all delicious and menu changes according to availability of ingredients. Cash only. Takeaway service.

Bars

Bistro Kuba
C Milanés 29014 entre Zaragoza y Santa Teresa, T45-261465, see Facebook. Open 1100-0200.

Bar and café serving tapas and larger dishes. Modern and stylish, this is a great bar open after Le Fettucine has closed. Good cocktail list, cold beer, live music.

Entertainment

The **Centro de Promoción y Publicidad Cultural** (Independencia (85) entre Ayuntamiento (288) y Sta Teresa (290)), has a *cartelera* in the window displaying all entertainment fixtures. The Plaza de la Vigía is the place to go in the evenings; locals congregate here to chat, play dominoes or draughts, or make music. The **Teatro Sauto**, see page 145, usually has live performances at the weekends.

Cabaret

Cabaret Las Palmas (Artex), *Calle 254 (Levante) esq 127 (Gen Betancourt), T45-253252. Tue-Thu 2000-2400, Fri, Sat 2100-0200, Sun 1700-2100.* Mostly Cuban clientele, live shows, comedy or recorded music. Sun afternoon dancing. Entry usually CUC$2-4 per couple, depending on the event.

Cabaret Restaurante Monserrate, *Mujica (306) final, T45-244222. Wed, Fri, Sat, Sun 2100-0200. CUC$1 or pay in CUP$. Bus No 12 takes you there.*

Tropicana Matanzas, *Autopista Varadero Km 4.5, T45-265380, reservas@tropimat.co.cu. Show Thu-Sun 2200-2330 then disco until 0200, adults CUC$49 (children CUC$34) which includes ¼ bottle of rum and cola and snacks. A lesser show Tue, Wed is CUC$39.* The Matanzas version of the famous cabaret is in a spectacular outdoor setting opposite the **Hotel Canimao**. CUC$5 to use a camera.

Live music and dance

Casa ACAA (Asociación Cubana de los Artistas Artesanos), *Calle 85 entre 282 y 280.* Live music with trios and pianists. Also has a café.

Festivals

20-26 Aug Carnaval de Matanzas.

Transport

Bus
The bus station, T45-291473, open 24 hrs, is at Calle 131 y 272, Calzada Esteban esq Terry (Coppelia is opposite the terminal). **Viazul**, T45-916445, passes through on its **Havana–Varadero** route, 3 daily, see timetable, page 463. There are taxis and *coches* at the bus station.

The hop-on hop-off **MatanzasBusTour** leaves Matanzas' Parque Libertad at 1115, 1445, 1545 and 1715. It passes the city centre historic sights and goes on to the San Severino fort, Cuevas de Bellamar and Tropicana arriving at Varadero at 1245, 1415,

1715 and 1845. It returns from Varadero at 0930, 1100, 1400 and 1530. CUC$10. **Transtur** operates the service and passengers wishing to return from Varadero later can take any **Transtur** bus heading to the city.

Train

There are 2 stations: the Hershey terminal and main terminal. The Hershey terminal is north of the Río Yumurí in Versalles at 282 y 67. There are no facilities here and the ticket office, T45-244805, has erratic opening hours. There are 3 trains daily on this electric line to and from Casablanca in **Havana**. Trains from Casablanca to **Hershey** leave at 0445, 1221, 1635. Tickets CUC$2.80, children half price, but you may never get charged. If there is no electricity it doesn't run.

The newer, main station south of the town at Calle 181, Miret (open 24 hrs, T45-292409), receives trains from Havana en route to **Santiago**.

Varadero	Colour map 2, A1.

life's a beach

Cuba's chief beach resort, Varadero, is built on the Península de Hicacos, a thin, 23-km-long peninsula. Two roads run the length of the peninsula lined with dozens of large all-inclusive hotels, some smaller ones, and several chalets and villas, many of which date from before 1959. Sadly, some of the hotel architecture is hideous.

Varadero is still undergoing large-scale development, and joint ventures with foreign investors are still being encouraged. However, with the relaxation of restrictions on self-employment, it is no longer a state monopoly. You can now sleep in a *casa particular* and eat in a *paladar*.

Essential Varadero

Finding your feet

Varadero's **international airport** is 26 km west of the hotel strip, so, if you are booked into one of the new hotels at the far eastern end of the peninsula, you will have a journey of some 40 km to get there. The **Viazul** bus pulls in to the airport on its way to the central bus terminal and has recently opened a ticket office here. If you are travelling by car from Havana there is a good dual carriageway, the Vía Blanca, which runs to Varadero, 142 km from the capital. The toll at the entrance to the resort is CUC$2 for cars. The easiest way to get to and from Havana is on a tour or transfer bus, booked through a hotel tour desk, which will pick you up and drop you off at your hotel. There are daily buses from Havana, and also from Santiago de Cuba, from Trinidad via Sancti Spíritus and Santa Clara with **Viazul** (see timetable, page 462).

Getting around

Distances should not be underestimated. Avenida 1, which runs southwest–northeast along the peninsula, has a tourist bus service (see Transport, page 161) that takes about an hour to cover the entire length, taking into account dropping-off times. Calle numbers begin with lowest numbers at the southwest end and work upwards to the northeast. Car rental is available at the airport and at numerous hotel and office locations along the peninsula. Most hotels also rent bicycles or mopeds, which will allow you to get further, faster. Taxis wait outside hotels, or you can phone for one. There are also horse-drawn carriages for a leisurely tour and a handful of *cocotaxis*. See also Transport, page 161.

The southwestern end of the resort is the more low key, with hustlers on the beaches by day and *jineteros* in the bars at night. The village area feels like a real place, not just a hotel city, and, in contrast to some other tourist enclaves (such as the northern cays), Cubans do actually live here. The far northeastern end is where the international hotels are located. Most are all-inclusives, although you can pay to use their facilities even if you are not staying there.

Tip...
Between Cárdenas and Varadero there are oil wells, which release gas into the air, often in the middle of the night. The smell of sulphur drifts as far as Varadero if the wind is in the wrong direction; it is particularly obvious if you stay at the southwestern end of the peninsula.

Sights

The relatively recent development of Varadero means there is little of historical or architectural interest; visitors spend their time on the beach, engaging in watersports or taking organized excursions. The **Museo de Varadero** ① *C 57 y Av de la Playa, daily 1000-1900, CUC$1*, is worth a visit if you want something to do away from the beach. The house itself is interesting as an example of one of the first beach houses. Originally known as Casa Villa Abreu, it was built in 1921 by architect Leopoldo Abreu as a summer house in blue and white with a lovely timber veranda and wooden balconies all round, designed to catch the breeze. Restored in 1980-1981 as a museum, it has the usual collection of unlabelled furniture and glass from the early 20th century, stuffed animals in a natural history room (a revolutionary guard dog, Ima, appears to be suffering from mange), and an Amerindian skeleton (male, aged 20-30, with signs of syphilis and anaemia). However, the most interesting exhibit is a two-headed baby shark washed up on these shores. There are several old photos of the first hotels in Varadero, including Dos Mares (1940), Internacional (1950) and Pullman (1950), as well as items of local sporting history, a shirt of Javier Sotomayor and a rowing boat from the Club Náutico de Varadero. The house is in serious need of renovation again and the upstairs floor can no longer be used for exhibits.

The **Parque Josone**, Avenida 1 y 57, is a large park with pool and several restaurants. You can take a pedalo out on the boating lake. The bar/café closest to the entrance is renowned for its piña coladas, made with fresh ingredients.

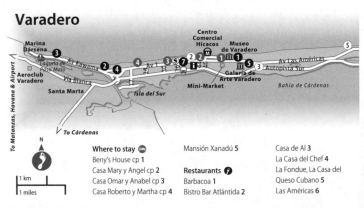

Varadero

Where to stay
Beny's House cp **1**
Casa Mary y Angel cp **2**
Casa Omar y Anabel cp **3**
Casa Roberto y Martha cp **4**
Mansión Xanadú **5**

Restaurants
Barbacoa **1**
Bistro Bar Atlántida **2**

Casa de Al **3**
La Casa del Chef **4**
La Fondue, La Casa del Queso Cubano **5**
Las Américas **6**

BACKGROUND

Varadero

Salt was the first economic catalyst in the area, followed by cattle, timber and sugar. A plan was drawn up in 1887 for the foundation of a city, but development of the peninsula did not really begin until 1923, when it was discovered as a potential holiday resort for the seriously rich. The Dupont family bought land in the 1920s, sold it for profit, then bought more, constructed roads and built a large house, now the Mansión Xanadú. There are some old wooden houses left from this period, with rocking chairs on the verandas and balconies, but the village area at the western end of the peninsula was not built until the 1950s.

At the far end of the peninsula 450 ha of the land has been designated the **Varadero Ecological Park** (Parque Ecológico Varahicacos) ① *Centro de Visitantes at the road entrance to Hotel Paradisus Varadero, daily 0900-1630, CUC$5; the tourist bus stops nearby*. The reserve includes 700 m of shoreline with different plant species, including scrub and cactus, a lagoon where salt was once made, several kilometres of sandy beach and two caves. The **Cueva de Ambrosio**, 30 minutes' walk from the main road, is where dozens of Amerindian drawings were discovered in 1961. **Cueva de Musulmanes** contains aboriginal fossils. You can see hummingbirds and other birds, lizards, crabs and bats in the caves. Allow 1½ hours for the walk. Wear stout footwear because the paths are rough, and take water, insect repellent, hat and sunscreen because it is fiendishly hot.

Beaches

Varadero's sandy beach stretches the length of the peninsula, broken only occasionally by rocky outcrops which can be traversed by walking through a hotel's grounds. Some parts are wider than others; as a general rule, the older hotels have the best bits of beach. The **Internacional**, for instance, which was the **Hilton** before the Revolution, has a large swathe of curving beach, whereas the newer **Meliá Las Américas** and its sister hotels, **Meliá Varadero** and **Sol Palmeras**, have a disappointingly shallow strip of sand and some rocks. That said, all the beaches are beautifully looked after and cleaned daily, and the

Paladar Nonna Tina **7**

Entertainment ☺
Cabaret Cueva del Pirata **1**
Casa de la Música **2**

La Comparsita **3**
Mambo Club **4**
Palacio de la Rumba **5**

ON THE ROAD
Diving around Varadero

Varadero is one of the most developed areas in Cuba for diving. There are several sites around the offshore cays suitable for novice or advanced divers. Interesting sites include the wreck of the *Neptune*, a 60-m steel cargo ship thought to be German, lying in only 10 m. This is home to a number of fish including massive green moray eels and very large, friendly French angelfish. The wreck is very broken up, but the boilers are still intact, and there are places where the superstructure (shaft and propeller) is in good condition and interesting to explore with good photo sites. Among the many reef dive sites in the area are Clara Boyas (Sun Roof), a massive 60-sq-m coral head in 20 m of water, with tunnels large enough for three or four divers to swim through. These connect with upward passages where the sunlight can be seen streaming through. Another site, Las Brujas (the Witches), is only 6 m deep. Large coral heads protrude from the sandy bottom, with coral holes and crevices, adorned with sea fans, home for large schools of snapper. Playa Coral is a site on a 2-km barrier reef west of Varadero, beginning at Matanzas Bay, with a large variety of fish and coral. This is usually a shore dive, although if you go over the wall, where you can find black coral and gorgonians in deep water, it can be a boat dive. If you are based in Varadero on a dive package, you may be offered a trip to Playa Girón (see page 171) for good shore diving, and to the Refugio de Saturno for an inland cave dive (see page 150), as part of your package.

water is clean and nice for swimming. For good **snorkelling**, however, you're advised to take one of the many boat trips out to the cays (see below).

Cays

The cays around the **Hicacos Peninsula** were once the haunt of French pirates, and it is supposed that the name 'Varadero' comes from *varados* (stranded), due to the fact that ships ran aground here. There are many **sailing tours** to the offshore cays, which usually include lunch, an open bar and time for swimming and snorkelling. **Cayo Mono** lies five nautical miles north-northeast of Punta de Morlas. During the nesting season in mid-year it becomes a bird sanctuary for the brown noddy (*Anous stolidus*; known as the *gaviota negra* in Spanish), the sooty tern (*Sterna fuscata; gaviota monja*) and the bridled tern (*Onychoprion annaethetus*), during which time you can only pass by and watch them through binoculars. **Cayo Piedra del Norte** is two miles southeast of Cayo Mono and has a lighthouse. Other cays visited by tour boats include Cayo Blanco, Cayo Romero and Cayo Diana. See What to do, page 160.

Tourist information

State tour agencies can be found in all the hotels. Although their main purpose is to sell tours, they operate as tourist information offices and can help with hotel reservations, tickets and transfers. **Infotur** has an office at Calle 13 esq Av 1, T45-662966. There are also offices in the airport and at Centro Comercial Hicacos, Av 1 entre 44 y 46, T45-667044. Most are open daily 0800-1700.

Where to stay

The building of new hotels and renovation of older ones is continuing all along the peninsula and there are now some 18,000 rooms, with some encroaching on the edge of the nature reserve. Overdevelopment is a real issue. The newer international hotels are located at the northeastern end of the peninsula, very remote from the shopping area and independent restaurants. Unless you specifically want an all-inclusive beach holiday in an international hotel, it is best to stay in the village area, where restaurants, bars and shops are within walking distance, hotels are smaller and more intimate, and the beach is just as good. We do not list the all-inclusives in this guide.

It is now legal for Cubans to rent rooms to foreigners in Varadero; *casas particulares* are generally a better option than the few small hotels (cleaner, friendlier, better food). You could also choose to stay in Matanzas and get the bus in to Varadero.

$$$$ Mansión Xanadú
Ctra Las Americas, Km 8.5, T45-668482, www.varaderogolfclub.com.
The beach house built for the Du Pont family in the 1920s is now the clubhouse for the golf course, offering the smartest, boutique type accommodation in Varadero. The mansion sitting on a bluff overlooking the sea and

Tip...
Note that booking a hotel package from abroad will get you a better deal than booking from Havana where you'll get the rack rate.

backed by the golf course offers 5 doubles and 1 single room, each with balcony. Furnished with period pieces and very prettily decorated, golf is usually included in the package. Restaurant and bar. Away from the hustle and bustle of the beach resorts. Guests use all the facilities and the beach at the next door **Meliá Las Américas**.

$$ Beny's House
Calle 55 124 entre Av 1 y 2, Varadero, T45-611700, www.benyhouse.com.
Very good, very popular house within 80 m of the beach, Parque Josone and the Beatles Bar. Spacious rooms and an apartment with quality fixtures and fittings, pleasant garden and patio. Food is tasty and plentiful. English spoken. Friendly and helpful family and staff. Sunbeds provided for you to take to the beach.

$$ Casa Mary y Angel
Calle 43 entre Av 1 y 2, Varadero, T45-612383, marisabelcarrillo@yahoo.com.
Good location, short walk to beach, 3 rooms with good bathrooms around a patio. Friendly and helpful family, English spoken. Plenty of outside space for relaxing, plus outdoor shower when you come back from the beach. Parking.

$$ Casa Omar y Anabel
Calle 31 104 entre Av 1 y 3, T45-612587, sherlyday@yahoo.es.
A suite with its own entrance, very comfortable, immaculate, a/c, kitchenette and fridge, TV, patio with table and chairs outside the door, convenient location, beach towels provided. Omar and Anabel are experienced hosts, very friendly and helpful and will do their best for you. English spoken. Good food. Parking.

$$ Casa Roberto y Martha
Calle 17 102A entre Av 1 y 2, T45-612958, varr@nauta.cu.

Roberto is the epitome of a genial host: he's a mine of information about where to eat and what to do and can sort out accommodation all over the island. 3 rooms, of which 1 is a suite with kitchen, 1 is rather small, but all are well-equipped and spotless. Rooms have own access. Close to the beach but also close to a night club which can be noisy Sat night. Delicious food and particularly good breakfasts. Special diets catered for.

Where to eat

$$$ Barbacoa
Calle 64 esq Av 1, T45-667795. Daily 1200-2300.

Good surf and turf with indoor and alfresco dining. Huge lobster tails will feed 2 for CUC$22, or a smaller one for CUC$18. The steak is Canadian. Extensive wine list. Reservations advised in high season, but they will usually find room for you.

$$$ Casa de Al
Villa Punta Blanca.

A stone building with blue painted wooden attributes, which used to belong to Al Capone. It's a quiet spot for a sunset drink (with outdoor tables on the terrace) or a meal of Mafia Soup, Godfather Salad, Fillet Mignon "Lucky Luciano" and cold blood ice cream. The service is a little on the slow side but not annoyingly so. Worth a visit.

$$$ La Fondue
La Casa del Queso Cubano, *Av 1 entre 62 y 64, T45-667747. Daily 1200-2300.*

Powerful a/c and smart tables. Serves a variety of fondues including lobster fondue and chocolate fondue as well as breaded pork, chicken and grilled fish. Service often lacking.

$$$ Las Américas
Mansión Xanadú, Av Las Américas, T45-667388, www.varaderogolfclub.com. Daily 1200-1600, 1900-2230.

International food that is acceptable but not outstanding. You come for the beautiful setting in the lovely old mansion (built between 1928 and 1930) and upstairs bar with wide, sweeping views.

$$$-$$ Bistro Bar Atlántida
Av 1 entre 6 y 7, Santa Marta, T5283 6972, atlantidabistro@gmail.com.

A great bar and bistro with a wide range of drinks and a good Spanish menu. Welcome cocktails, tapas as well as main dishes, all beautifully presented and tasty. Owner Félix is friendly, and the service is exemplary compared with the state restaurants.

$$$-$$ La Casa del Chef
Av 1 y 12, T45-613606. Daily 1230-2200.

Seafood restaurant with good value lobster, indoor or outdoor seating, pleasant live music.

$$$-$$ Paladar Nonna Tina
38 5 entre Av 1 y Playa, T45-612450, www.paladar-nonnatina.it. Daily 1200-2300.

Tina is Italian married to a Cuban and cooks authentic Italian food, delicious pizzas and pastas. Very popular, especially with Italian visitors, queues outside. Resort hotels are worlds away.

Bars

Every hotel has several bars to choose from and it can be fun to work your way through the barman's list of cocktails during your holiday. Even here, however, you may be told 'no hay', with tomato juice and other mixers often unavailable. Stick to the traditionally Cuban and you won't be disappointed.

Outside the hotels, the **Bar Mirador Casa Blanca**, on the top floor of the **Mansión Xanadú** at the Golf Club is worth a visit for the view and relaxed atmosphere, if not the prices. Several *paladares* have good bars for before or after your meal, while *casas particulares* often have a cocktail list for a relaxing evening on the patio.

Beatles Bar
Calle 59 y Av 1.
You can't miss it thanks to the statues of John, Paul, George and Ringo outside. An after-dinner bar where you can catch tribute bands to the fab four and other rock music in an outdoor setting. It is also open during the day for a salad lunch and to look at all the old photos on the walls. Reasonably priced cocktails.

Entertainment

Live music
Buena Vista Social Club, *at Plaza América, call Paradiso travel agency to reserve, T45-614759.* A group performs live every 1st and 3rd Wed of the month at 2200.
Casa de la Música, *Av Playa entre 42 y 43, T45-668918. Tue-Sun 2230-0300, CUC$10 entrance.* Lots of live bands every night, good for dancing, also DJ. *Jineteros* can be pushy. Run by EGREM, the state music company. A *cartelera* in the window advertizes events.

Nightclubs and cabaret
Cabaret Cueva del Pirata, *Autopista Sur Km 11, T45-667751. Show in a cave, CUC$10. Check opening times.* Music is a mix of traditional Cuban with more modern Cuban and international music. Lots of dancing. Cool on a hot night. Toilets are unhygienic. Take toilet paper.
La Comparsita, *Calle 60 y Av 3, T45-667415.* Dancing under the stars at this nightclub. A mix of entertainment, from live salsa band to DJ playing European music. Most nights cover is CUC$7 and drinks are free, although limited in choice and availability is restricted by the tiny size of the bar, more like a window. Upstairs there is karaoke for an extra charge.
Mambo Club, *Ctra Las Morlas Km 14, T45-668565. CUC$15. Temporarily closed in 2015, so call ahead.* A club stuck in a 1950s time warp.
Palacio de la Rumba, *Av Las Américas, Km 4, T45-668210. Daily 2200-0300. CUC$10-15, depending on whether drinks are included.*

Indifferent staff at bar, live salsa bands at weekends. Frequented by Cubans and foreigners but often empty mid-week.

Festivals

Jan Carnival involves lots of tourist participation, encouraged by the hotel entertainment teams.
Nov Some years an **arts festival** is held in Varadero, lasting a week, which attracts some of the best artists in South America.

Shopping

Arts and handicrafts
Handicraft markets offer all manner of souvenirs, from elaborately decorated wooden *humedores* to keep your cigars temperature-controlled, to T-shirts and keyrings, which are easier to pack. The main market area is in the Parque de las Mil Taquillas.
Artesanía, *Av 1 entre 12 y 13, Av 1 entre 15 y 16, Av 1 esq 47 and Av 1 esq 51.*
Galería de Arte y Taller de Cerámica Artística, *Av 1 entre 59 y 60. Daily 0900-1900.* On one side is the workshop where you can see the ceramicists at work and on the other side is the gallery and shop where you can buy original pieces, both utilitarian and decorative pottery.

Cigars
Cigars are available from **Casa de Habanos** (Av 1 esq 39) and from **Casa del Habano** (next to La Casa del Queso Cubano, Av 1 esq Calle 64, daily 0900-2300).

Rum
Casa del Ron, *Av 1 esq 62. 0900-2100.* No bargains to be had, but they have the best selection of rums, including some unusual ones. Staff are very knowledgeable and will guide you through tastings of many different rums. There is a scale model of Matanzas' Santa Elena distillery and it's a nice old building.

Shopping centres
Centro Comercial Caimán (Av 3 entre 61 y 63); **Plaza Caracol** (Av 1 esq 54); **Plaza América** (by the Sol Meliá hotels). The **Centro Comercial Hicacos** (Av 1 entre 44 y 46), originally the Parque 8000 Taquillas, has 6 modules that include a variety of shops, **Etecsa** office and an **Infotur** office.

What to do

There are 3 **marinas**, all full service (see below), offering sailing tours, restaurants, deep-sea fishing and diving. All activities can be booked through the tour desks in hotels. You can indulge in almost any form of watersport, including windsurfing and kitesurfing and non-motorized pedalos but these are not practised in the open sea for environmental and safety reasons (you might get blown over to Miami). If you are not staying in any of the Varadero hotels you may organize activities yourselves, but it will be a bit more difficult.

Diving
Diving is offered at all 3 marinas (see below). Equipment is well-maintained but old, so, if you can, you are advised to bring your own. A full range of courses is offered, and, as diving has now been opened up to private enterprise, there are also some very good private instructors with equipment that is usually newer than that offered by the marinas. However, private operators can only offer shore diving as they are not allowed boats in case they use them for trips to Miami. For details of dive sites in the area, see box, page 156.
Orestes Sánchez, *C 42 113 entre Avs 1 y 2, T5271 7001, orestes.sanchez@inbox.com.* Affiliated with **Adventure Divers in Canada**, www.adventuredivers.ca. Orestes is professional and entertaining, very popular with divers and snorkellers. No boat. Shore diving is offered at Coral Gardens, where there are caves, coral and a lot of fish; at Bacunayagua, where there is more beautiful

coral, and at the Bay of Pigs, where there is Cueva de los Peces, a wall, more coral and more marine life. He offers a great trip to the Bay of Pigs in his Chevrolet truck for shore diving, followed by lunch in a family *paladar* with local meats and seafood accompanied by live music.
Varadiving, *C 38 entre Av 1 y Playa, T5487 9091, 5263 6525, www.varadiving.club.* A small, privately owned club offering snorkelling and diving, instruction and circuits around Cuba. No boat. They take a maximum of 6 divers per instructor, depending on the level of experience, and 8 snorkellers. A 2-tank dive at Coral Beach, Varadero is CUC$70, at Bacunayagua CUC$80 and at Bay of Pigs CUC$90, including pickup and transport. Snorkelling at the Bay of Pigs is CUC$45, 2 hrs drive each way and 3 hrs at the snorkelling site. Discounts for Cubans training to be instructors. A professional and safety-conscious club with good equipment.

Fishing
Contact the marinas for fishing, usually including open bar and equipment.
Offshore fishing: *peto* (wahoo) Oct-Feb; *dorado* Apr-Sep; *sierra* (sailfish) Apr-May; *atún, bonito* Apr-Sep. **Reef fishing**: barracuda all year; *aguají* (grouper) all year; *pargo* (snapper) May-Jul best, Aug-Apr good. **Bay fishing**: *sábalo* (tarpon); *jinawa* (yellow jack) Feb-Apr best, rest of year good.

Golf
Varadero Golf Club, Av *Las Américas Km 8.5, T45-668482, www.varaderogolfclub.com. Daily 0700-1900.* The Canadian-designed golf course has 18 holes, par 72, and stretches east from the original Du Pont mansion, built in 1928-30, which is now the **Mansión Xanadú**, past the **Sol Meliá** resorts. There are 2 putting greens, a chipping green and a driving range and Pro-shop and equipment rental at Caddie House. Green fee 18 holes, CUC$120 including cart and balls. Beginners' lessons available. Special offers are available at certain times of the year with shared

powered golf carts (which are compulsory) thrown in. Reservations with 24 hrs' notice are advised especially Sep-Dec.

Hotel sports

The large hotels all offer tennis courts; some also have squash courts, and volleyball is played on the beach, usually organized by the hotel entertainment staff. Table tennis, billiards and other indoor games are available if the weather deteriorates or you have had enough sun.

Marinas

Marina Chapelín, *Autopista del Sur, Km 12.5, T45-667550. VHF 16 and 72, daily 0800-1900.* Moorings for 20 boats, maximum draft 30 m, boat rental and laundry. There's an on-site restaurant and staff are friendly. Ring at least 1 day beforehand to book your activity. This is by far the busiest marina. Activities include: snorkelling at a coral beach and in Saturno Cave; a full-day seafari to Cayo Blanco, with a dolphin show, transfer, equipment, open bar, lunch and an Afro-Cuban show (CUC$75 per person); a boat adventure through the canals (CUC$39), and a jeep and boat **Discover Tour**, which involves off-roading, swimming in a cave and speedboating along the river Canimar (CUC$73).
Marina Dársena Varadero, *Ctra de Vía Blanca Km 31, T45-667550. VHF 16.* Moorings for 113 boats, maximum draft 4 m, boat rental, showers, laundry, internet, restaurants, bar, fishing, shops, day charters, diving, liveaboard for 20 people.
Marina Gaviota Varadero, *Peninsula de Hicacos Km 21, T45-664115, www.gaviota-grupo.com. VHF 16.* Moorings, 3 m draft, showers, laundry, restaurant, bar. Sea safaris in catamarans with a visit to Cayo Cangrejo, yacht rental, fishing, swimming with dolphins and diving.

Sky diving and parachuting

Centro Internacional de Paracaidismo de Varadero, *Km 1.5, Vía Blanca, opposite Marina Dársena Varadero, T45-662828,* http://skydivingvaradero.com. Courses or tandem jumps are on offer, see the price list on the wall at the airstrip. It is approximately CUC$180 for a jump/fall/fly.

Tour operators

Every hotel has a tour agency on site offering local and national excursions to Havana, Cárdenas (see page 162), Valle de Yumurí, Pinar, Cayo Largo, Bay of Pigs, Guamá–Cienfuegos–Trinidad, Tropicana and Santa Clara, plus boat trips, multilingual guides, transfers, booking and confirmation of air tickets, air charters, car rentals, reception and representation service. Excursions can all be booked at all hotel tourism bureaux and through tour operators. Note that most agencies close for lunch.
Cubanacán, *C24 entre Av 1 y Av Playa, T45-667836, www.cubanacan.cu.*
Gaviota, *Calle 56 y Av Playa, T45-611844, www.gaviota-grupo.com.*

Transport

Air

The **Juan Gualberto Gómez airport** (VRA), T45-247015, www.varadero-airport.com, receives international scheduled and charter flights.

Bus

The interprovincial bus station is at Autopista Sur y C 36. **Viazul**, T45-614886, has daily buses to/from **Havana**, **Trinidad** and **Santiago de Cuba**, via **Santa Clara** and **Holguín**, see timetable, page 462. There is also a ticket office at the airport, just outside **Arrivals**, T45-663396.

The hop-on, hop-off, open-topped tourist bus, **Varadero BeachTour** (**Transtur**, T45-668212) runs every 30 mins daily 0930-2100, along Av 1 southwest–northeast the length of the peninsula, with 45 stops at hotels and shops, CUC$5 per day. Don't lose your ticket or hand it in on alighting, or you will have to pay again. There is also the **MatanzasBusTour**, which leaves Varadero at 0930, 1100, 1400 and 1530, arriving in **Matanzas** at 1100, 1230, 1530 and 1700. It returns to Varadero at 1115, 1245, 1545 and 1715; CUC$10 per day.

Car/moped hire
Agencies have offices all over town and in nearly all the hotels. **Cubacar** at many of the hotels, main office: T45-667326. **Transtur**, T45-667715. **Vía Rent a Car**, T45-619001. **Havanautos**, T45-614409. Hiring a moped is a good way to see the peninsula but you will have no insurance and no helmet. The **Servi Cupet** petrol station is at 54 y Autopista, 17 y Autopista, Vía Blanca Km 31.

Tip...
Hire a car rather than a jeep to avoid having your spare wheel stolen; insurance covers four wheels, not the spare.

Taxi
Cubataxi, T45-614444. Most trips cost CUC$5-15 depending on where you need to go along the peninsula. The best place to hail a taxi is at any hotel, as they usually wait there for fares. Horse-drawn vehicles act as taxis, usually just for a tour around town.

Cárdenas and beyond *Colour map 2, A1.*
experience a real Cuban town away from the crowds

Cárdenas is 18 km southeast of Varadero on the Bahía de Cárdenas. The town's architecture is in the traditional 19th-century Spanish colonial style: houses with tall windows, intricate lattices, high ceilings, ceramic tiled floors and interior gardens. However, its glory days are over, and it's a good place to come to see a working Cuban town. It is trapped in a time warp, empty of tourists, friendly and a good place to meet Cubans. There is none of the aggressive hustling found in hotel districts or more tourist-oriented cities and no police harassment of Cubans associating with foreigners. However, the flip side of this relaxed attitude is that romantic 'liaisons', which once took place in Varadero, are being squeezed out to Cárdenas.

Sights
Cárdenas is a city with a sense of humour: it commemorates the mundane with bizarre memorials. On Calle 13 there is a *coche* statue, equipped with a white, stone horse. Behind the **Fuerte Roja** bar is a bicycle that stands high on a thin metal plinth as if it were balancing on a gymnastics beam. Outside the hospital a large, fibreglass nose provides a bus shelter; its giant nostrils welcoming passengers in to the waiting area. And, at the entrance to the city (approaching from Varadero) a giant crab welcomes visitors. However, the sculptor's lack of marine knowledge has left a biological mutant on the roadside: the Cárdenas crustacean has a large right pincer, whereas normal *cangrejos* sport the large claw on the left.

Where Avenida Céspedes ends at the sea, there is the **Monumento a la Bandera** with a huge flagpole commemorating the flag-raising event on 19 May. There is also a plaque at the **Hotel Dominica**, which Narciso López occupied with his men and which is now a National Monument. Unfortunately, the General's attempts to free Cuba from colonial rule were unsuccessful, as he failed to get local support.

One of the town's other claims to fame is that it contains the oldest **statue of Christopher Columbus** in the Western Hemisphere, now in front of the cathedral in Parque Colón on Avenida Céspedes, five blocks from the flagpole. It was the work of a Spanish sculptor, Piquier, in 1862.

Plaza Malacoff is worth a visit to see the decaying, iron market building, unique in Latin America, which was put up in the 19th century on Avenida 3 oeste and Calle 12. The two-storey building is in the shape of a cross and is surmounted by a 15-m dome made in the USA. The market is a great public gathering place for gossip and beer-drinking.

On Calle 2, overlooking the water, is the **Fábrica de Ron Arrechabala**, which makes both the *Varadero* and *Bucanero* label rums. The site has been a rum factory since 1878, when the *Havana Club* company was founded here.

In July 2001, Fidel Castro opened the **Museo a la Batalla de Ideas** ① *C 12 y Plaza Echeverría, Tue-Sat 0900-1700, Sun 0900-1300, CUC$2, kids free, camera CUC$5, guide CUC$2, mirador CUC$1.* This small museum, housed in the 1873 fire station, is a veritable shrine to the boat boy Elián González (see Background, page 165). The display includes the T-shirt worn by the fisherman, Sam Ciancio, who hauled Elián out of the sea. There are also letters from the likes of Guatemalan Nobel Prize-winning author Rigoberta Menchú and the late Uruguayan exiled writer Mario Benedetti saying that Elián must be reunited with his father. A *maqueta* (model) of the Tribuna Antiimperialista José Martí, which was erected in front of the US Interests section in Havana during the saga, is also included, along with the large bronze statue of José Martí that served as the centrepiece (the one now in Havana is a replacement; see page 50). There is also a large display about the Miami Five. The *mirador* on the top floor is the highest point with public access in the city.

The **Museo Municipal Oscar María de Rojas** ① *Plaza Echeverría entre Av 4 y 6 este, Tue-Sat 0800-1600, Sun 0800-1200, CUC$2,* exhibits art, geology specimens and local and natural history. **Museo Casa Natal José Echeverría** ① *Av 4 este y Plaza Echeverría, Tue-Sat 0900-1700, Sun 0800-1200, CUC$1,*

Essential Cárdenas

Finding your feet

Most long-distance transport is via Varadero, where you will find the nearest airport. The railway is for local services only, and there is not much in the way of long-distance bus transport, although there are **Astro** services from Havana, Matanzas and Varadero, and **Viazul** stops here on its way between Varadero and Trinidad.

Getting around

Cárdenas is a slow city, with traffic moving at the pace of the horse. Transport is limited to *coches*, bicycles and pedestrians. The city is set out in very regular grid form, with Calles running parallel to the sea in consecutive numbers and Avenidas crossing them. The main street is Avenida Céspedes. Avenidas are numbered from here: those running northwest start from Avenida 1 oeste and proceed in odd numbers, and those running southeast start from Avenida 2 este and proceed in even numbers. However, as in many places, people refer to the old street names rather than the numbers. The three main museums are around Plaza Echeverría, just two blocks from Avenida Céspedes.

When to go

Hurricane season can be wet and stormy, although there are plenty of fine, bright days. Between December and April is the driest time.

Tip...
Use the TV tower on Avenida Céspedes y Calle 11, called Coronel Verdugo, as a landmark.

Cuban rum

Sugar was first introduced to Cuba by Christopher Columbus, who brought sugar cane roots from the Canary Islands on his second transatlantic voyage. The first rudimentary mills produced sugar cane juice, but as they became more sophisticated the juice was turned into alcohol. A clear wine was made, which, when distilled several times, became a basic rum. In the 19th century a new manufacturing process was developed, which considerably improved the quality of Cuban rum, and the industry rapidly expanded with the construction of hundreds of sugar mills all over the country. The cities of Havana, Santiago de Cuba, Cienfuegos and Cárdenas all produced rum of export quality under the labels of *Havana Club* (founded in 1878), *Bacardí, Campeón, Obispo, San Carlos, Jiquí, Matusalem, Bocoy* and *Albuerne*.

The family firm of Bacardí was the largest in Cuba for nearly 100 years, building substantial wealth on the back of rum. After the 1959 Revolution, when the sugar industry and the distilleries were taken over by the state, the family left the island and took the Bacardí name with them. The Bacardí rum, now found worldwide, is not distilled in Cuba. Many labels can be found in Cuba, including the venerable *Havana Club, Caribbean Club, Caney, Legendario, Matusalem, Varadero, Bucanero* and *Siboney*.

Rums of all different ages can be found. Generally, the younger, light rums are used in cocktails and aged, dark rums drunk on the rocks or treated as you might a single malt whisky. Light, dry rum in Cuba is aged (*ron añejo*) for three years, has little body and is between 40° and 60° proof. Old gold, dry rum is aged for five years, is amber in colour and can be drunk straight or added to cocktails for an extra kick. Extra aged rum is aged for seven years and is usually drunk neat in a brandy glass or on the rocks.

Cocktails first became popular after the development of ice making in the USA in 1870 and were introduced to Cuba soon afterwards. The first Cuban cocktails were the Cuba libre and the daiquirí, the former developed when US intervention forces brought in bottled cola drinks during the War of Independence against Spain at the end of the 19th century, and the latter invented by an engineer in the Daiquirí mines in eastern Cuba.

Cocktails boomed in the 1920s with an influx of bartenders and global visitors, many of whom were escaping prohibition in the USA. Recipes were named after visiting film stars and other dignitaries and developed at La Bodeguita del Medio or El Floridita, bars still flourishing today. The Hemingway Special was created for the writer by the famous bartender, Constante, at El Floridita. Others include a Greta Garbo, Lilian Gish and a Mary Pickford.

guide CUC\$2, CUC\$1 per photo, dates from 1703, but the local 20th-century hero Echeverría was born here in 1932. He was a student leader killed by Batista's troops in 1957. Exhibits are scarce but those on show relate to 19th-century independence struggles and the 20th-century Revolution upstairs. Of note are a giant doll used to hide clandestine objects and a photo of the man himself, blood-drenched in the street after being mown down. The park outside is named after Echeverría and there is a monument to him in the park.

BACKGROUND
Cárdenas

Cárdenas was founded in 1828. It was once one of the most important cities in Cuba, with its wealth built on sugar. It had the first alcohol refinery, the first electricity plant and the first gynaecological hospital in the country. The town's main claim to fame, however, is that the Cuban flag was first raised here in 1850 by the revolutionary General Narciso López, a Venezuelan who tried unsuccessfully to invade Cuba by sailing from New Orleans and landing at Cárdenas with an army of 600 men (only six of whom were Cuban). Cárdenas was also thrust onto the world stage in 1999-2000, when a young resident of the city, Elián González, was shipwrecked off the Miami coast. His mother was drowned, and the six-year-old was placed with family members in Miami, despite the protestations of his father in Cuba. Elián finally returned home to Cárdenas after seven months of geopolitical wrangling between the USA, Cuba, the boy's family and the law. Elián resumed near-normal life in school, but remains one of Cárdenas' most celebrated residents. His story is commemorated in a museum, see page 163.

The **Salón Massaguner art gallery** ⓘ *Av Céspedes 560, 1 block south of the TV tower*, has high-quality works from Matanzas province artists. There is the *art naif* of Olga Vallejo and political works by Francisco Rivero, among others, including sculptures.

About 10 km from town is the museum and sugar mill **Central Azucarero José Smith Comás**, where an 1888 steam engine is still used for tourist trips. Take the road to Santa Clara and turn right at the fork by an old paper mill.

Jovellanos and central Matanzas

Some 24 km south of Cárdenas is Jovellanos, a large town with a pleasant colonial centre, Parque Central and church. It is a junction on the roads from Varadero to the Zapata peninsula and from Matanzas to Santa Clara. It is of no particular interest to travellers except that as a result of slavery and enforced migrations, the Arara people of Benin came here via Haiti and brought the sort of music with them that is normally only heard around Santiago de Cuba. Due south of Jovellanos you head towards the Zapata peninsula (see page 168), and the countryside becomes flat and uninteresting. This area was particularly badly hit by Hurricane Michelle in November 2001, with lots of houses damaged or destroyed.

The main road east, meanwhile, continues from here to **Colón**, which is on the main railway line from Havana. This is another 19th-century town with abundant neoclassical architecture and faded grandeur. For adventurous independent travellers exploring rural Matanzas, it is well off the tourist trail, so you can spend *pesos cubanos* in restaurants and on transport. Carnival is celebrated 15-17 October.

Where to stay

Cárdenas

$$ Chez France y Pedro
Palma (Av 31) 785 entre Minerva (Calle 16) y Mercedes (17), T5311 9152 (mob), queenyfrances@hotmail.com.
France is from Quebec and Pedro is Cuban and together they run this smart house, renting 2 a/c rooms with kitchen, lounge with TV, balcony and plunge pool.

$ Hostal Angelo's
Spriu (Av 14) 656 entre Velázquez (14) y Cristina (15), T5284 9108, estangel01@yahoo.es.
Owner Angel Luís Renoso is a Varadero guide and speaks English, French and Italian, but if he is not there, his family is also multilingual and helpful. There is independent access to the rooms upstairs, which are good, a/c. There is parking, luggage storage and a small pool. There is a small *paladar* in the patio and food is good.

$ Hostal Ida
Calzada (13) 368 entre Phinney (Av 15) y Saez (Av 13), T45-521559.
Idiana and her husband Lulu speak English and French and rent 1 very large and smart room with private entrance and balcony for street watching. Parking.

$ Casa Grillo
Coronel Verdugo 314 entre Anglona y Spriu, T5823 1107.
Rolando and Idalmis and their family live downstairs while upstairs is an apartment with private entrance, a/c bedroom, kitchen, lounge and terrace. At the back of the house, upstairs, is another room with fridge and comfy chairs. Small swimming pool for communal use. Garage.

$ Casa Hostal Relax
Saez 323 entre Aranguren y Jenez, T5821 1395.
A 1940s house which has been modernized to a high standard with granite tiled floors throughout. There are 2 smart a/c rooms with private entrance, kitchen, parking, a large courtyard with jacuzzi and a mango tree with hanging chairs. English spoken.

Where to eat

Cárdenas

There has been an explosion of *paladares* in town and there is no longer a problem finding somewhere to eat. The public market has seasonal fresh fruit and vegetables if you are staying in an apartment with a kitchen.

$$$-$$ Don Qko
Céspedes 1001 entre 21 y 22, T45-524572, 5271 7450 (mob), see Facebook.
Wed-Mon 1200-2300.
A large and elegant *paladar* and bar which has proved very popular with locals and guests from Varadero. In a romantic garden setting with a pool and outdoor grill, diners can watch their meal being prepared in the kitchen while listening to live music. The food is traditional but beautifully presented and the portions are large. The house speciality is roast pork but there is also seafood. Family-run by Alexeis Padrón and his father Jesús (Cuco – Qko).

$$$-$$ Don Ramón
Av 4 564 entre Calles 12 y 13, overlooking Parque Echevarría, T45-522169.
Open 1100-2200.
In an elegant colonial building, this is a smart and professional *paladar* offering very good food and exceptional value while the service is friendly and efficient. The food is imaginatively presented and there are Italian specialities on the menu. Really good espresso too. Reservations advised in high season when *aficionados* flock here from Varadero.

$$ Hard Rock Café
Spriu 659 entre Velázquez y Cristina, T5294 7671. Open 1200-0200.

Nothing to do with the US version, this is a good bar and *paladar* on 2 floors. Much of the food is cooked on an open barbecue, great ribs and chicken. Service is polite and helpful, some of the staff speak English.

Bars

Cárdenas

Studio 55
Coronel Verdugo (12) 111 entre Vives (4) y Jenez (6), T45-522172, 5263 3097 (mob), see Facebook. Mon-Thu 1200-2400, Fri, Sat 1200-0200.
Modern industrial chic, this bar and café is unlike anything else in Cárdenas and very popular. Indoor and open air seating in a converted old building. A good place for lunch after sightseeing, with tapas, sandwiches, good snacks and cold drinks. Tourists come here when visiting the museum across the square. At night it has a lively vibe with international music and a young crowd.

Transport

Cárdenas
Bicycles or *coches* are the only form of local transport.

Bike
Cárdenas is an easy bike ride from **Varadero**, and there are bike park areas where a guard will watch your bike for CUC$1.

Bus
The bus station is on Av Céspedes y 22, with services to **Matanzas**, **Colón**, **Jagüey Grande**, **Havana** and **Santa Clara**. To get to **Varadero**, catch a bus from the corner of Av 13 oeste y Calle 13; they should leave every hour, but as the principal demand is from hotel workers, they are more likely to run according to shifts.

Viazul stops in Cárdenas on its **Trinidad–Varadero** route. Get there early, or buy a reserved ticket.

Taxi
Taxi from **Varadero**, CUC$40 round trip with waiting time.

Zapata Peninsula
& Bay of Pigs

This is one of the most famous places in the Caribbean: for every Cuban it signifies a great victory; for the Americans, a failure of monumental proportions. Historian Hugh Thomas said the disaster of the CIA-backed invasion at the Bay of Pigs in April 1961 was so politically dismal for JFK that he went out and ordered the US space agency to land a man on the moon before the decade was out. In his history epic *Cuba*, Thomas wrote, "perhaps a victory for the US in Cuba might have deprived mankind of that achievement in 1969".

There is little to see at the Bahía de Cochinos relating to the air and sea attack except a fascinating museum about the invasion and monuments on the roadside marking the fallen. However, there is a sense of achievement in making it to such an important historical site that is a little off the beaten track.

There is more to the region than its 20th-century history, however. The coast of the Bahía de Cochinos is lapped by sapphire-coloured water that teems with tropical fish. Diving here is highly rated, with reefs, wrecks, caves and cenotes to tempt you underwater. On land, the whole of the south of the province is taken up with the Zapata Peninsula, an area of swamps, mangroves, beaches and prolific bird and animal life that forms the largest ecosystem on the island and is protected as the Parque Nacional Ciénaga de Zapata.

Jagüey Grande and around

Jagüey Grande lies just north of the central highway that runs from Havana to Santa Clara. Some 38 km west of Jagüey Grande, at Km 102, is the launch site for a one-hour boat trip along the Río Hatiguanico (CUC$19 per person), which can be organized by Cubanacán or by the national park office at Playa Larga (see page 170).

Just to the south of the Entronque de Jagüey is the settlement of **Central Australia**, named after the Central Australia sugar mill, which looks like an ailing dinosaur. Built in 1872 and decommissioned in 2002, it had its moment of fame when Castro used the administration office (built 1915) as his centre of operations to repel the Bay of Pigs invasion (Operation Pluto). The office is now the **Museo Memorial Comandancia de las FAR** ① *T45-912504, Mon-Sat 0900-1700, Sun 0800-1200, CUC$1 plus CUC$1 with guide plus CUC$1 to take pictures.* It is a singularly unimpressive museum considering its historical importance. There are photos of destroyed planes and victory pictures, including one showing the name Fidel written on a wall in the blood of one of the Cuban victims. There are also some pictures of José Ramón Fernández, Director of Operations, who was a Vice President of the Council of Ministers 1978-2012. The phone used by Fidel is still in situ and there is an anti-missile machine in the lobby. Outside the museum is the wreck of a plane shot down by Castro's troops. The guide will tell you that the dead American pilot was kept frozen in an institute in Havana as the US did not want to claim him and thereby admit responsibility for the invasion. The serviceman was not reclaimed until his daughter came to collect him in 1989.

Essential Zapata Peninsula

Getting around

The Entronque de Jagüey (junction) on the Autopista Nacional between Havana and Santa Clara marks the 'entrance' to the peninsula. There is also a road from Cienfuegos in the southeast. Public transport on the peninsula is limited: **Viazul** runs a Havana–Entronque–Girón–Cienfuegos route and a few local buses run to Playa Girón and Playa Larga. Tour buses and taxis are the usual method of transport, but the most convenient way of getting around is to hire a car so that you can get to out-of-the-way places and stay as long as you like. Between Playa Girón and Playa Larga in a car is 30 minutes; from Playa Larga to Guamá is 10 minutes; from Guamá to Entronque de Jagüey is 15 minutes. Hiking is good in the national park, but you will need to carry water as it is very hot in the swamps.

When to go

The dry season is from December to April. Winter is also the time when migratory birds visit the peninsula so birdwatching is especially rewarding.

Time required

A stay of a few nights would be plenty to explore the area, visit the Bay of Pigs museum and take advantage of the scuba diving and snorkelling. Keen ornithologists should add another couple of days to go birdwatching in the Ciénaga de Zapata.

A nearby attraction is the **Finca Fiesta Campesina** ① *daily 0900-1800*, a large country farm, displaying examples of Cuban plants and wildlife, including the *Majá de Santa María* snake, a large-eared rat known as a *jutía*, and a prehistoric fish called a *manjuarí*, which has a long bill with lots of teeth and eyes set far back, making it look a bit like a platypus crossed with a crocodile. You can watch a man push sugar cane through a mangle so that you can try a glass of *guarapo* (sugar cane juice) mixed with lime (and rum if you want it). There's also a bar, shops, toilets and a *cabaña* complex in the grounds providing accommodation.

Boca de Guamá and Laguna del Tesoro

Boca de Guamá is a tourist centre of shops, a ceramic factory, a restaurant and a crocodile farm, **Criadero de Cocodrilos** ① *T45-913224, daily 0900-1800, CUC$5, CUC$3 for children, shows 0900-1630,* where they successfully breed the native Rhombifer (*cocodrilo*; see also box, page 450). The farm is also home to turtles (*jicotea*), *jutía* and the *manjuarí* fish.

The main attraction, however, is the boat trip from Boca de Guamá to the Laguna del Tesoro, a 9.1-sq-km lagoon over 10 m deep. The **boat trip** ① *8 people minimum, return after 1 hr, CUC$12 per person, CUC$5 for children under 12,* goes to **Villa Guamá**, a hotel of thatched cabañas on stilts in need of renovation, and on to **Aldea Taína**, a recreation of an Amerindian complex in the **Laguna del Tesoro**. (There's also a speedboat at 0900.) On one of the islets a series of larger-than-life-size statues of Amerindians going through their daily routines has been carved by the late Cuban sculptor Rita Longa, which you can see by following a boardwalk. In the middle is a replica of a *caney*, a large house belonging to the *cacique* (chief), where (if there is a large tour group) actors do a lot of wailing, blow a conch, daub your face black and expect you to give them a generous tip. This is not obligatory.

Birdwatchers are advised to spend a night or two in the area, as the lagoon is an important winter home for flocks of migrating birds. You could go on a tour one day and return with the next tour the following day. You will see most at dawn before the tour buses arrive. Take insect repellent.

Tip...
The best time to see flamingos and migratory birds is from December to March.

Playa Larga *Colour map 2, B1.*

The road south down the peninsula meets the coast at Playa Larga, at the head of the Bahía de Cochinos, commonly known as the **Bay of Pigs**. The US-backed invasion force landed here on 17 April 1961 but was successfully repelled (see page 169, for more information). There is a small monument here, but most of the commemorative paraphernalia is at Playa Girón (see below). The beach, however, is open and better than that at Playa Girón. Two kilometres southeast of Playa Larga is **Playa de la Máquina**, a sandy beach frequented by locals where you can see lots of old trucks, caravans and other 'machines'.

★ Parque Nacional Ciénaga de Zapata

Playa Larga is a good place from which to explore the Parque Nacional Ciénaga de Zapata, also known as Gran Parque Natural Montemar. The park is a bird lover's paradise, with over 21 endemic species, the smallest of which is the hummingbird. Other sightings include flamingos, magnificent frigates, sandhill crane, Cuban parakeet, nighthawks, owls and pied billed grebe. There are also 16 species of reptile, including crocodiles, and more than 1000 species of invertebrate, of which more than 100 are spiders. Mammals include the *jutía* and the manatee.

The **national park office** ① *T45-987249, pnacionalcz@enet.cu, daily 0800-1630,* is just north of Playa Larga on the main road, indicated by a sign. It can organize guided trips into the park with bird specialists (see page 174). West of Playa Larga, a track leads to **Santo Tomás** where, in addition to waterfowl, you can see the Zapata wren, the Zapata rail and the Zapata sparrow. The **Laguna de las Salinas**, 25 km southwest of Playa Larga, is the temporary home of huge numbers of migratory birds from December to April. The rest of the year it is empty. At the end of the road, at the forest technical station at La Salina, you can get a boat to one of the outlying islands, **Cayo Venado**, where there are iguanas and *jutías*.

★ South of Playa Larga

Halfway between Playa Larga and Playa Girón, is **Cueva de los Peces** ① *daily 0900-1600, CUC$3 (but not always applied),* a *cenote* that is full of fish and is good for diving (CUC$40) and snorkelling (CUC$5), particularly early in the day. To the south is **Punta Perdiz** ① *1100-1700, entry CUC$15 includes lunch and open bar,* where there is more excellent snorkelling via a ladder over the rocks into the water. The **Punta Perdiz Centro de Buceo** offers spectacular dives over wrecks from the invasion (CUC$25 per dive) and boat trips.

Playa Girón *Colour map 2, B2.*

At the southeastern end of the bay, Playa Girón is named after a 17th-century French pirate, Gilbert Girón, who frequented the area and presumably appreciated its isolation. It was the main landing site for the US-back invasion in 1961 (see History, page 405). Located at the site of national pilgrimage is the ★ **Museo Girón** ① *T45-984122, daily 0800-1700, CUC$2, plus CUC$I for Spanish-speaking guide, under 12s free, video show CUC$1, use of camera CUC$1, video camera CUC$5.* It shows how the invasion was repelled within 72 hours, with 200 CIA-trained Cuban exiles killed, 1197 captured and 11 planes shot down. Monuments to those who died are scattered along the coast. Outside the museum is a British Sea Fury fighter aircraft, used by Castro's air force against the invaders. The tank outside is a replica of the original in Havana that destroyed *USS Houston*. The remains of an American B-26 that came down on the *pista* on 17 April 1961 are also in the gardens. There are also tanks and boats belonging to the mercenaries (Brigade 2506).

Today, Playa Girón is favoured as a ★ **dive centre**. The beach is walled in and therefore protected, and, although the seabed is rocky, you can walk to the reef from the shore. Further along is another long sandy beach, and nearby is a Fisheries Division shipwreck, sitting in 20 m of water on a sand slope. The wreck was one of numerous vessels built in the early 1980s from concrete and wire. The boats were expected to last for around 10 years and were then stripped, with everything of value being reused on a newer model. These 'throw away' boats used to be sunk in deep water, but as diving developed as a sport, the wrecks were placed in shallow waters to allow divers to explore them. This wreck was intentionally sunk by the government in 1995. The dive operation at the resort offers courses and packages of dives which can be tied in with accommodation, see What to do, page 174.

★ Caleta Buena and around

Southeast of Girón by 8 km is **Caleta Buena** ① *T45-984110, daily 1000-1700, CUC$15 (CUC$7.50 children) including lunch (1230-1500) and all drinks; snorkelling CUC$5 per day, diving CUC$25 for 1 dive,* a pretty cove that is excellent for snorkelling. The small tourist centre is perched on some craggy rocks above the pale blue, natural swimming pools, which are teeming with coral and shoals of multi-coloured fish. It's highly recommended as a day or half-day trip, but you'll need your own car or a taxi to get there. There are also **caves** in the area for divers to explore. If you have your own transport, find a beach along the road between Playa Girón and Caleta Buena: there will be no people and good snorkelling 100 m offshore.

Tourist information

The **Centro de Información La Finquita** is at Entronque de Jagüey, on the national highway, T45-913224, daily 0800-2000, and provides local information and sells a map of the zone. It can arrange taxis down to Playa Larga, CUC$20, and to Playa Girón, CUC$30. For national park information, visit the office near Playa Larga, page 170.

Where to stay

Jagüey Grande and around
Hotels

$$ Bohío de Don Pedro
Autopista Nacional Km 142, T45-91-2825.
Next to the **Finca Fiesta Campesina** is a complex of 10 very attractive fan-cooled *cabañas*. It's a lovely relaxed spot close to nature with a restaurant (0700-2130) and is great for families with young children who need to run around. Used by groups for birdwatching or fishing tours, within easy reach of Guamá and Playa Girón. Room rate usually includes breakfast and evening meal.

Casas particulares

$ Casa Bertha
Calle 52 1727 entre 17 y 19, Jagüey, T45-912116, 5244 2128 (mob), bertamery90@nauta.cu.
Bertha Cabrera offers 2 a/c rooms which share a bathroom. There's a swimming pool and patio area where meals are taken and a garage for parking.

$ Violeta Pita
Calle 58 1718 entre 17 y 19, Jagüey, T45-912690.
1 room above the family's quarters, with dining area, Violeta cooks wonderful fried bananas.

Playa Larga
Hotel Playa Larga is used by tour groups and is conveniently located, but facilities are often out of order, and the restaurant food is awful. There are *paladares* in walking distance which are much better. *Casas particulares* are more comfortable and friendly; they can arrange tours and some have beach access.

Casas particulares
All the *casas particulares* are in Barrio Caletón, which is just west of the public park in Playa Larga. When you arrive in Playa Larga take an immediate right in front of the public park and swing round the edge until you arrive at the small residential area; ask directions as you go.

$$-$ B&B El Varadero
Barrio Caletón, T45-987485, www. bbelvaradero.com and Facebook.
Tony and Osmara offer 2 newly decorated rooms with a/c, safe box and fridge stocked with water, beer and wine. There is a little beach beside this waterfront property and a sea view from every window. Meals are taken on the veranda and Tony is a brilliant chef. Both hosts speak excellent English and can arrange tours, transport and help in any way. A lovely place to relax.

$$-$ Casa de Yeni
Barrio Caletón, T45-987385, 5247 6096 (mob), yenyjcarlos@nauta.cu.
2 comfortable rooms, a/c, fan, secure parking, not far from the beach. Hosts Juan Carlos and Yeny and their two children make sure your stay is as good as it possibly could be. Juan Carlos is an enthusiastic chef and food is excellent and plentiful. After dinner (CUC$10-15) he is happy to sit and chat over a rum, and both of them are very helpful and informative. Any excursion can

be booked for you, bikes rented, transport arranged, nothing is too much trouble. This professionally run *casa* is a delight.

$$-$ Kiki Hostal
Barrio Caletón, T45-987404, www.hostalkiki.com.
Very friendly and welcoming family with 3 a/c rooms, well-stocked fridge and access right on to the beach. The room up a spiral staircase is newer, bigger, with a large balcony and worth paying extra for. *Comida criolla* for supper, fresh and tasty local produce. Kiki used to be a fisherman and still likes to fish and play chess with guests.

$ Ernesto Delgado Chirino
T45-987278, ernestodccz@gmail.com.
Waterfront property, with waterside patio and great views of the boats. He has rooms in 2 houses with 3 more new rooms for 2016 and a high standard of furnishings. You eat on the patio in the primary house, the second one is 5 mins walk away, very close to the beach. If there are enough guests, a band comes in to play during dinner. Visiting vendor friends can be pushy, but other friends, such as a taxi driver with an old Chevrolet can be useful.

Playa Girón
The resort hotel at Playa Girón is run down, isolated, insecure and hasn't got much to recommend it. Local *casas particulares* are better in all respects.

Casas particulares
When you enter the village from the north, on your left are 2 apartment blocks. The 1st block is edificio 2, while the one behind, at an angle, is edificio 1. Opposite are a line of houses, some of which are *casas particulares*.

$ Hostal Luis
Ctra a Cienfuegos esq Ctra a Playa Larga, T45-984258, 5238 1264 (mob), hostalluis@yahoo.es.
This is the best house in the Zapata area recognizable by its lion-topped columns on the gates. It is close to the hotel. Owners Luis and Marleyn have 2 comfortable bedrooms in their house and 3 suites in a new building alongside, each with bedroom, living room and bathroom, 2 of which can connect, all with independent access. They also offer secure parking. It's a lovely, super-friendly and helpful household. The food is delicious too and plentiful, CUC$17 for dinner and breakfast. Good English spoken.

$ Ivette y Ronel
Camino Principal, 1st house on the left, T5311 7389 or T5311 8699 (mob), www.playagironcasa.com.
A modern house off the main road with 2 rooms; 1 in the front with 3 beds and 1 at the back behind the kitchen, both of a very high standard with well-stocked fridge. Ronel is the lead dive instructor at the Playa Girón International Dive Centre and can take guests diving at CUC$25 per dive, or snorkelling. Both he and Ivette speak English well and take good care of their guests' needs.

$ Lidia y Julio
Camino Principal, second house on the left, T5398 5833 (mob), lidia-julio@videotron.ca.
Lidia is a translator and speaks very good English. Julio is the founder of the local dive school, a great underwater photographer and head of diving in the area. Dive packages are available for guests. This is a new, smart house with 1 large room to rent with a/c, good bathroom and fridge. Food is served indoors or outside. Covered car parking.

Where to eat

You may be offered turtle meat in some *paladares*; you should politely refuse to eat it as all turtles are protected species.

Playa Larga

$$ Don Alexis Bar & Grill
Calle 10 19 entre 1 y 5, Pálpite,
T5366 0928 (mob).
A popular place for lunch when on a private tour of the area. Alexis is friendly and entertaining and there are usually musicians on hand if enough people are in the outdoor restaurant. Food is cooked fresh on the grill and there are lots of seafood options as well as farmed crocodile, but please discourage him from serving turtle.

$$ Edel Orlando
T45-987540. Lunch and dinner.
Coming into town from the north, the restaurant is on the right. The chef is often outside on the road trying to attract customers. The house is unassuming, but once inside the ambience is very pleasant. There are usually all sorts of things to try, including unusual fish and farmed crocodile but, again, please avoid the turtle meat or soup. Food is cooked fresh on the grill and comes with a plentiful supply of side dishes.

$$ La Terraza de Mily
Opposite Hotel Playa Larga, T45-987376.
Popular with people fleeing the awful food at the hotel, who come here for some good home cooking, fresh and tasty. Mily and her husband, Alain, make a good team and are very welcoming. They also have rooms to rent.

Playa Girón
Most people eat in *casas particulares*, many of which are open to non-guests by prior reservation, see Where to stay, above.

$$ Bar Brig
Opposite Museo de Girón.
A bar and grill with surprisingly good food and cocktails. Good for watching the world go by at the road intersection.

What to do

Birdwatching and wildlife watching
Orestes Martínez Garcías, *known as El Chino), T45-987373, T5253 9004 (mob), chino.Zapata@gmail.com.* Has been working in the Zapata peninsula for 35 years and has expert bird knowledge. He also rents rooms in his *casa particular.*
Parque Nacional Ciénaga de Zapata, *Playa Larga, T45-987249, pnacionalcz@enet.cu. Daily 0800-1630.* The office runs guided trips to the Río Hatiguanico, Las Salinas, Los Sábalos, Bermejas and Santo Tomás for CUC$10 per person. The guides are all bird specialists and some speak English. Visitors need their own transport and tips are not included. Call beforehand if you want a particular specialist. Sport fishing is also offered but you need to ring the office for information and prices (minimum CUC$190).

Diving
There are several state-run dive operations in the area and once they have reached their quota of divers for the month, dive instructors are allowed to operate independently as self-employed dive guides (*cuentapropistas*). All dives cost CUC$25 for a single tank (or 1 hr's diving), including all equipment. Private instructors usually have better equipment than the state dive shops. Dive centres include the **Centro Internacional de Buceo Octopus** (at Hotel Playa Larga), with 13 dive sites just offshore; **Cueva de los Peces** (very busy); **Punta Perdiz** (more spread out and less crowded); the **Centro Internacional de Buceo Azul** (at Hotel Playa Girón), and **Centro Internacional de Buceo El Pirata** (at Caleta Buena), where there are 19 dive

sites, some of which are in cenotes and caves. Private dive instructors include Ronel Almeida, Playa Girón, T5311 7389 (mob), and Julio Ruiz, T5398 5833 (mob), who are neighbours and both have *casas particulares*.

Tour operators
Both hotels **Playa Girón** and **Playa Larga** have tour desks. See also **Cubanacán**, page 161.

Bus
Viazul runs a daily bus **Havana–Jagüey Grande–Guamá–Girón–Cienfuegos–Trinidad**; see timetable, page 462.

Car hire
Havanautos is opposite Hotel Playa Girón, daily 0800-1200 and 1300-2000. There's a **Servi Cupet** petrol station opposite Museo Girón, open 24 hrs, and another outside Boca de Guamá.

Taxi
For **Playa Larga**, organize a taxi at Entronque de Jagüey. **Playa Girón** can also be reached by taxi from **Cienfuegos** (1½ hrs).

Centre West

The three provinces of Cienfuegos, Villa Clara and Sancti Spíritus share the lush, forested Montañas de Guamuhaya, their boundaries meeting close to the highest point, Pico San Juan, in the Sierra del Escambray.

The mountains are a habitat for many birds, butterflies, frogs and other creatures of the forest and offer great hiking, river bathing and birdwatching. To the north, the low-lying coast is protected by an archipelago of cays with some spectacular white-sand beaches.

From the early Spanish settlements and sugar plantations to magnificent 19th-century merchants' mansions and opulent theatres, this region is also generously endowed with architectural delights. Sancti Spíritus was one of the seven towns founded by Diego Velázquez in 1514, but the star attraction is Trinidad, awarded UNESCO World Heritage Site status to protect its cobbled streets, its single-storey houses, its churches and its planters' mansions. It also has the advantage of being close to a beach, having access to the mountains and enjoying some outstanding live music. The 1958 battle for the city of Santa Clara was crucial to the outcome of the Revolution. This lively university city is now a shrine to the Argentine *guerrillero* and icon, Che Guevara.

Best for
Architecture ▪ Birdwatching ▪ Festivals ▪ Hiking ▪ History

Footprint picks

★ **Jardín Botánico de Cienfuegos**, page 192

A gardener's dream, with fine collections of palm trees, orchids and medicinal plants.

★ **Che Guevara monument, Santa Clara,** page 200

Last resting place of the poster-boy *guerrillero* and his comrades-in-arms.

★ **Remedios**, page 209

An attractive colonial town with Carnival pageants, fireworks and an ebullient spirit in the lead up to Christmas.

★ **Playa Las Gaviotas, Cayo Santa María**, page 216

Backed by a National Park, this undeveloped beach is glorious and the clear, shallow water is divine.

★ **Trinidad**, page 226

Little has changed since the 19th century in this colonial town with its cobbled streets and sugar barons' mansions.

★ **Parque Natural Topes de Collantes**, page 240

Mountain trails wind through the rainforest to picturesque rivers and waterfalls.

Essential Centre West

Finding your feet

Santa Clara lies at the heart of this region and is the main transport hub. There is an **international airport** just outside the city, or you can fly to Havana or Varadero and transfer from there overland. On the cays, an airstrip receives short-hop flights and air taxis (**Gaviota**). Santa Clara is on the main east–west highway from Havana to Santiago and communications by land are excellent, with frequent buses in both directions. Direct buses also run daily from Havana to Cienfuegos, continuing to Trinidad, Sancti Spíritus and Santiago de Cuba. If travelling by car, turn off the Autopista Nacional at Aguada de Pasajeros to reach Cienfuegos

and Trinidad. Alternative routes to Trinidad are from Varadero, via Santa Clara and Sancti Spíritus, or from Santiago de Cuba, with several stops along the way. Santa Clara, Cienfuegos and Sancti Spíritus can be reached by train from Havana, although services are unreliable. Trinidad is not on the main line and only a tourist service operates from here.

Getting around

A good road leads northeast from Santa Clara through Camajuaní to Remedios and Caibarién, from where a stone causeway (toll road) has been built to link several cays. Another road heads south from Santa Clara

towards Trinidad. There are daily bus services between Santa Clara and the other regional centres, but hiring a car or a taxi is the best way of touring the region as local public transport is intermittent and unreliable (and non-existent on the cays). Car hire is

available in Cienfuegos, Santa Clara, Sancti Spíritus and Trinidad, or there are guided tours from some of the travel agencies in these towns. Hiring a taxi is also an option, as long as you agree the terms and the price before you set off. If you are staying in a *casa particular* ask if anyone in the family offers their services as a driver and/or guide, which will be cheaper.

When to go

The driest time of year is from December to April, generally considered high season with the best weather, but if a cold front comes down from the north, then the cays and the north coast can get cool and windy. Later in the year the weather gets hotter but wetter. If you enjoy watersports and festivals related to the sea, then March is a good time to go to Cienfuegos. May is busy in Santa Clara, as there are film, music and dance festivals, but the best time is around 28 December, when the populace celebrate the end of the Revolution and the Plaza de la Revolución is alive with revellers enjoying a concert. The week leading up to Chrismas Eve is the time to be in Remedios, when the *parrandas* are in full swing, and September is ceremonial in Trinidad, with followers of Catholicism and *Santería* joining parades through the streets in honour of the Virgen del Cobre, patron saint of Cuba, whose day is 8 September.

Time required

Each of the cities in this area needs at least a day to see all the sights. Excursions from Trinidad into the mountains or to the beach make a three-day stopover the optimum. Also leave time to visit the cays north of Remedios.

Cienfuegos
Province

magnificent 19th-century buildings reflect the port's former maritime glory

Cienfuegos (population 386,100), on the south coast, is an attractive, breezy seaport, with a Caribbean feel, sometimes described as the pearl of the south. Once known as Fernandina de Jagua, it has its fair share of legends about pirates and corsairs. A couple of dive lodges to the south, a marina and a naval museum add to its nautical atmosphere.

French immigrants at the beginning of the 19th century influenced the development and architecture of the city, which is a fascinating blend of styles, including a density of art deco buildings in the residential streets. Highlights are the Tomás Terry theatre and the Ferrer palace, both remarkable buildings from the 1890s, the heyday of Cienfuegos' prosperity. The city was granted UNESCO World Heritage Site status in 2005.

The bay of Cienfuegos, at 88 sq km, is the third largest in Cuba and has attracted industry and shipping. A large shrimp fleet sails from here, and the port is also a major exporter of sugar with 12 cane refineries in the area as well as the largest cement plants and oil refineries in Cuba. A huge nuclear plant lies unfinished on the western side.

Essential Cienfuegos city

Finding your feet

The city lies on the eastern side of the Bahía de Cienfuegos, 80 km from Trinidad and 70 km from Santa Clara. There are regular buses from both these cities as well as from Havana, Varadero, Santiago de Cuba and Camagüey. The bus station is on Calle 49, esquina Avenida 56, close to the railway station. Trains run to and from Santa Clara, where you connect with trains to Havana or to the east.

Getting around

The city is designed on a grid system with even-numbered Avenidas running from west to east and odd-numbered Calles running

south to north. Part of Avenida 54, from Calle 29 to Calle 37, is closed to traffic. Known as the Boulevard, it has small trees, cafés and restaurants as well as many shops, banks and other services and is the hub of city centre life. The main street is Calle 37, called the Prado in the centre and the Malecón further south, between Avenida 40 and Avenida 22, where it runs beside the water. The bay can be seen from quite a few places in the centre of the city, but there is no beach and the land by the water is usually dirty. Much of the city can be seen on foot, or you can use a horse-drawn *coche* for longer distances. For excursions out of the city, car hire is the most convenient, or hire a taxi to take you around, or take a tour. See also Transport, page 189.

Parque José Martí and around

The central square is **Parque José Martí**, formerly the Plaza de Armas, which is a pleasant plaza with benches, a rotunda bandstand and a statue of the ever-present José Martí. The first 25 blocks of the city were laid out from here and all the most important colonial buildings are around it. The arch on the west side of the square symbolizes the entrance to the city and is supposed to be similar to the Arc de Triomphe in Paris, having been built by the French founders of Cienfuegos.

On the north side, on Avenida 56, is the majestic building of the old **Colegio San Lorenzo,** a site of former resistance. A civilian and naval uprising in Cienfuegos was quashed by Batista on 5 September 1957, and there are several memorials and references to the event across the city. The building is now a secondary school and is not generally open to the public, but if you do get permission to enter, there is a memorial to the martyrs who died and their pictures are in a glass cabinet.

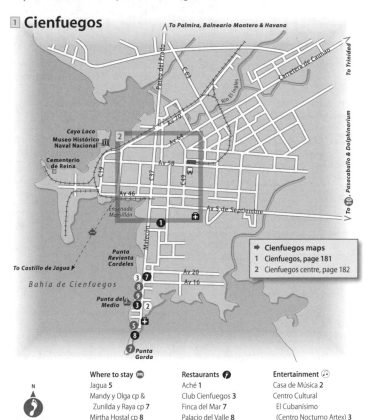

1 Cienfuegos

➡ **Cienfuegos maps**
1 Cienfuegos, page 181
2 Cienfuegos centre, page 182

500 metres
500 yards

Where to stay 🛏
Jagua **5**
Mandy y Olga cp &
  Zunilda y Raya cp **7**
Mirtha Hostal cp **8**
Palacio Azul **9**
Rancho Luna **10**

Restaurants 🍴
Aché **1**
Club Cienfuegos **3**
Finca del Mar **7**
Palacio del Valle **8**

Entertainment ☺
Casa de Música **2**
Centro Cultural
  El Cubanísimo
  (Centro Nocturno Artex) **3**

Next door is Cienfuegos' *pièce de résistance*, the **Teatro Tomás Terry** ① *Av 56 2701 entre 27 y 29, T43-551772, www.teatroterry.azurina.cult.cu, daily 0900-1700, CUC$1 including a guided tour, CUC$2 photos/video, see also Entertainment, page 188*, built in 1889 after the death of the Venezuelan Tomás Terry, with the proceeds of a donation by his family. It was inaugurated in 1890 in front of an audience of 1200 with a performance of *Aída*. Great artists such as Enrico Caruso, Sarah Bernhardt and Ana Pavlova all performed here. The lobby has an Italian marble statue of Terry and is decorated with fine paintings and ornate gold work. The interior is largely original with wooden seats. Note the ceiling, with exquisite paintings of muses and also two portraits of Cuban writers. Over the stage is a large grinning mask representing comedy. The two sets of theatre boxes nearest the stage were traditionally used by mourners who were not supposed to be at the theatre, but did

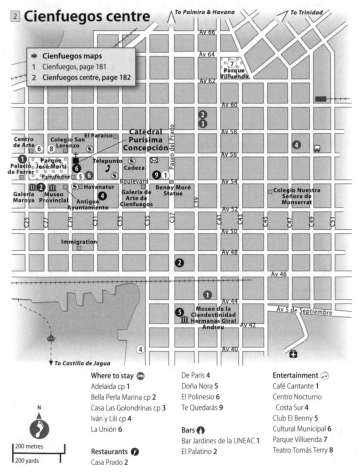

2 **Cienfuegos centre**

➡ **Cienfuegos maps**
1 Cienfuegos, page 181
2 Cienfuegos centre, page 182

Where to stay
Adelaida cp 1
Bella Perla Marina cp 2
Casa Las Golondrinas cp 3
Iván y Lili cp 4
La Unión 6

Restaurants
Casa Prado 2

De París 4
Doña Nora 5
El Polinesio 6
Te Quedarás 9

Bars
Bar Jardines de la UNEAC 1
El Palatino 2

Entertainment
Café Cantante 1
Centro Nocturno
Costa Sur 4
Club El Benny 5
Cultural Municipal 6
Parque Villuenda 7
Teatro Tomás Terry 8

not wish to miss the performance. They had a separate door so that they could enter and leave the theatre and watch the performance unseen by the rest of the audience.

On the east side of Parque José Martí, on Calle 29, is **La Catedral Purísima Concepción** ① *Mon-Fri 0700-1200, Mass daily at 0730, at 1400 on Sat and at 1000 on Sun*, built in 1868, which has a somewhat neo-Gothic interior with silvered columns.

The grand grey and white building on the south side of the square is the **Antiguo Ayuntamiento**, the former town hall where Fidel Castro spoke to the people on 6 January 1959. Also here is the **Museo Provincial** ① *Av 54 2702 entre 27 y 29, T43-519722, patrimonio@ azurina.cult.cu, Tue-Sat 1000-1800, Sun 0900-1300, CUC$2, tour CUC$1, photos CUC$1*, formerly the Casino Español, a cultural-political institution built in 1894 for meetings and gatherings and now a Monumento Nacional. It has a grand staircase with lots of marble, and its rooms contain furniture and art as well as displays on the archaeology and history of the region. Exhibits include an aboriginal skeleton, a necklace made from vertebrae, small zoomorphic statues and stones, art nouveau doorways, a *maqueta* of the 5 September 1957 uprising and plenty of explanations about the event, but one of the most interesting things in the museum is a gigantic pair of red, fibreglass, high-heeled shoes – the vast heels hanging over the toilet walls.

The most notable building on the west side is the Palacio de Ferrer, now the **Casa de Cultura Benjamín Duarte** ① *T43-516584, closed for renovation for years but now in the final stages of restoration*. It is a beautiful building dating from 1894, with a magnificent tower on the corner designed to keep an eye on the port and shipping; there are great views of the park and the sea if you climb the tower. The opera singer Caruso stayed at the Palacio de Ferrer when he came to Cienfuegos to sing at the theatre in 1920. It is worth seeing for the marble floor, staircases and walls, carved in Italy and assembled at the palace. Also note the Italian ceramic wall tiles in gold, white and blue, which change colour in the sunlight, and the plasterwork on the walls and ceiling.

Paseo del Prado

The main street is Calle 37, called the Paseo del Prado, which has a central promenade down the middle of the road where people stroll or sit. At the junction with the Boulevard (Avenida 54) is a bronze lifesize statue of Benny Moré, who looks like he's strolling down the Prado. The musician was born in the province, and Cienfuegos was his favourite city. Other famous musicians from here include the Orquesta Aragón, which unleashed the cha-cha-cha upon the world, and Los Naranjos, the oldest band in the country, founded in the city in the 1930s.

Ten minutes' walk south along Prado is the **Museo de la Clandestinidad Hermanas Giral Andreu** ① *Av 42 entre 37 y 39, Tue-Fri 0900-1800, Sun 0900-1200, free*, which has a few exhibits about the Revolution and some grainy black-and-white pictures of the 5 September 1957 uprising. Revolutionaries Lourdes and Cristina Giral were born here but later moved to the capital to earn a living, getting involved in raising funds and obtaining medicines for the revolutionaries. The sisters were murdered in Havana in 1958 during the Batista regime. The museum preserves their bedroom, some photos and a few personal possessions.

West of the centre

Some 10 minutes walk west along Avenida 62 on the waterfront is the **Museo Histórico Naval Nacional (Naval Museum)** ① *Cayo Loco, T43-516617, Tue-Sat 0900-1800, Sun 0900-1300, CUC$1 for foreigners, free for Cubans*, painted a dusky pink and white like a fairy tale castle. This is a much more interesting museum than it looks and is not entirely military, including many exhibits with more commercial links to the sea. Outside, there are old weapons in the garden. Inside, rooms are dedicated to the 1957 uprising and contain a number of interesting exhibits, such as Cuba's declaration of war against Germany, Tokyo and Rome; the flags from the *Maine* and the *Granma*; items and documents relating to the Playa Girón invasion; pre-Columbian indigenous artefacts; models of boats, fishing memorabilia; items relating to the Wars of Independence; natural history, lighthouses and local artwork.

Southwest of here in Reparto Reina is the **Cementerio de Reina** ① *daily 0800-1700*, opened in 1839 as the municipal burial ground. It has some interesting 19th-century tombs with lots of marble and works by local sculptors. You can find here the tombs of the French founders of the city and Spanish soldiers who died in the Wars of Independence on the left of the entrance, as well as relatives of Batista. The largest statue is that of the Sleeping Beauty, commemorating a woman who died in 1907 aged 24; she has some opium plants in one hand and a poisonous snake in the other. Although it was declared a Monumento Nacional in 1986, the cemetery suffered from lack of maintenance and fell into a poor state; it is currently being renovated.

South of the centre
Paseo el Prado (Calle 37) runs straight from the town centre down the peninsula to **Punta Gorda** as the **Malecón**. The palm trees and the view across the Bahía de Cienfuegos make this a lovely walk.

In this area are hotels, restaurants, nightlife and some of the largest houses, built for wealthy families in the first half of the 20th century. One of the most photographed buildings, **El Palacio del Valle** ① *T43-551226, daily 1000-2300, terrace bar 1100-0200, entry CUC$1 includes a drink on the terrace*, is right at the end of Calle 37 in a beautiful location with sea views all around. The building dates from 1894, with a mixture of architectural styles but with Arab influences predominating. It has incredibly ornate ceilings and other decorations. Designed by Italian architect Alfredo Collí Fanconetti, it was created with the help of Cuban, French and Arab artists. Materials were imported from Spain, Italy and the USA. The building was bought by Alejandro Suero Balbín and given to his daughter as a wedding present upon her marriage to Sr Valle. It is now used as a restaurant, but you can wander in during the day for a look around.

Another interesting building is the **Club Cienfuegos** ① *Calle 37 entre 10 y 12, T43-512891*. Inaugurated in 1920 as the Cienfuegos Yacht Club, it is painted a brilliant white and can be identified by the twin domes on the towers at the front, linked by a balcony and a grand staircase. It is still a centre for sailing, but also has tennis courts, a swimming pool, a playground, a *sala de fiestas* for public events, two restaurants, free parking and scooter rental.

East of the centre
About 3 km east of the centre is the **Cementerio Tomás Acea** ① *Av 5 de Septiembre entre Km 3 y 4, Mon-Sat 0700-1800, free or CUC$1 with guide*, built by one of the most powerful families in the city and noted for its grand replica of the Parthenon at the entrance. There is a striking monument to the fallen of 5 September 1957 inside and there are avenues of fruit trees and ornamental trees.

Tourist information

Infotur has an information desk on the Parque Martí outside Bar El Palatino with a few leaflets. You can also contact the **Ministerio de Turismo** (in Cienfuegos, T43-551631, www.cubatravel.cu). If you are staying in a *casa particular*, you will find your hosts very knowledgeable about what is going on in the area.

Where to stay

Hotels

$$$ La Unión
Calle 31 entre 54 y 56, T43-551020, www.hotelescubanacan.com.
Built in 1869, this very attractive hotel in colonial style is painted in duck-egg blue with white, wrought-iron balcony railings. 49 rooms and some suites are equipped with pleasant, dark-wood furniture and all mod cons. The hotel is decorated in pretty tiles and the swimming pool is beautifully sunken into the patio. There's also a sauna, jacuzzi, gym, laundry, pharmacy, internet centre, tourism bureau, car hire, shop, 3 bars and the **1869** restaurant, see Where to eat, below. Non-guests can use the pool for CUC$10 including food and drinks (*consumo*) of up to CUC$7.

$$$ Jagua
Calle 37 entre 0 y 2, Punta Gorda, T43-551003, www.gran-caribe.com.
Modern block design but in great location at the tip of the peninsula. 147 a/c rooms (most with twin beds), 2 suites, with views over the bay. **Restaurant Escambray** and 24-hr café next to a very nice pool. Non-guests can use the pool for CUC$10, which includes food and drinks (*consumo*) to the value of CUC$9. The **Palacio del Valle** restaurant is also next door to the hotel. There is a shop, internet access and nightly cabaret (except Wed), 2200, CUC$5 includes 1 cocktail, which is extremely colourful, good and worth the entry fee.

$$$-$$ Palacio Azul
Calle 37 1202 entre 12 y 14, Punta Gorda, T43-555828, www.hotelescubanacan.com.
Designed by an Italian architect in 1920 as a private home, this delightful little hotel is definitely the best in town (Venezuelan president, the late Hugo Chávez once stayed here). 7 rooms, all individually named after flowers, double, twin or triple beds, some with balconies, very comfortable, high standard of fixtures, fittings and furnishings, TV, safe, minibar, room service, parking, dining room for breakfast and snacks only, bar, roof terrace for sunbathing. Painted blue and white outside, the building is distinguished by a turret, from where you can get a fabulous view of the bay.

Casas particulares

$ Adelaida
Avenida 44 3925 entre 39 y 41, T43-513595.
Colonial-style house with high ceilings and tiled floors, 2 a/c rooms off passage with no external windows, 1 room larger than the other, double or twin beds, firm mattress. Tables and chairs on roof terrace, under cover or in full sun. Parking.

$ Bella Perla Marina
Calle 39 5818 esq 60, T43-518991, wrodriguezdelrey@yahoo.es.
Unlike the usual *casas particulares*, this 1950s house was designed by the Dean of the Faculty of Architecture in Havana and built by a former mayor for his niece as a wedding present. There are 2 internal rooms downstairs and a smart new suite upstairs (**$$$**), which is light and bright with modern bathroom and jacuzzi. It sleeps up to 6 but is popular with couples for its space and enormous bed. Multi-level terraces have plants, including an orchid collection, and there are views of the city and sea from the mirador at the top, good for sunset watching. The bar and dining room overlook the street

and roof tops, good chef and solicitous waiter employed for evening meals. Billiard table, book swap, secure parking, Amileidis and Waldo are helpful and informative hosts, English and Italian spoken.

$ Casa Las Golondrinas
Calle 39 5816 entre 58 y 60, T43-515788, drvictor61@yahoo.es.

Dr Víctor Sosa Rodríguez del Rey and his family offer 2 rooms in a lovely colonial house with tiled floors and high ceilings with antique chandeliers and light fittings. Excellent mattresses for a good night's sleep. Lovely terrace and sunbathing area on the roof with lots of plants around the dining tables where you have breakfast and dinner. Good food, friendly and helpful family.

$ Iván y Lili
Calle 47 5604 entre 56 y 58, T43-597245, 5247 3192 (mob).

Iván speaks good English and the family lives downstairs while guests have the whole of the 1st floor, 2 a/c rooms and bathrooms, dining room, terrace with tables and chairs, also huge roof terrace with sunbeds and shade. Not a grand *casa*, but spotless with friendly and helpful hosts. Good food and mojitos too. Walking distance from Viazul bus terminal.

$ Zunilda y Raya
Calle 35 14 entre 0 y Litoral, T43-523330, 5275 7289 (mob).

Lovely old timber house painted deep red and white, very pretty, backs onto the water with tree-shaded patio for romantic dining and sunset view. 2 a/c rooms, 1 upstairs with view over the bay, the other downstairs. Food here is particularly good for lovers of seafood, but vegetarians are well fed too.

$$-$ Mirtha Hostal
Calle 37 1205 entre 12 y 14, Punta Gorda, T43-526286, T5292 9936 (mob), dailynh12@yahoo.es.

Mirtha Bango Trujillo is an efficient hostess at this spacious modern house next to Palacio Azul, set back off the road in its own garden

with safe car parking. 1 room with double and single beds on ground floor, 2nd room upstairs with terrace and sea view. A balcony upstairs has chairs and is great for drinks, sunbathing, etc. Plenty of storage space, laundry service, lots of good food. The family is not the friendliest, but the location and views are great.

$ Mandy y Olga
Calle 35 apto 4D entre Litoral y 0, Punta Gorda, T43-515951.

Independent access via a staircase to an apartment upstairs, with 2 bedrooms, 1 bathroom and balcony with a lovely view over the parque to the sea. Nicely kept and Mandy and Olga are excellent hosts. The family lives downstairs.

Where to eat

$$$ Aché
Av 38 4106 entre 41 y 43, T43-526173. Mon-Fri 1200-2200.

In operation since 1996, this is a professional establishment, very well appointed with matching tables and chairs, local artwork on the walls, rustic decor, comfortable, nice bar, indoor or open air dining, pleasant garden with fishpond and caged birds. Seafood, fish and meat dishes, shrimp is the house speciality, most dishes CUC$8-10. Try *cascas de huevo con queso* for dessert. Excellent cocktails, very generous with the rum and will add more to your daiquirí if you want it, Chilean or Spanish wine (Cuban wine is used in the sangria). Service is a little over-attentive, but English is spoken.

$$$ Casa Prado
Calle 37 4626 entre 46 y 48, T5262 3858. Daily 1130-2230.

Small and cosy a/c restaurant, popular, often queues in the street. Extensive menu of *comida criolla*, well cooked food and good service. Some English spoken. A few doors down, the same family owns a cafetería which is good for breakfast and snacks.

$$$ Finca del Mar
Calle 35 entre 18 y 20, Punta Gorda,
T43-526598. Daily 1230-0030.
Fresh and tasty seafood, meat and vegetarian
dishes, international cuisine washed down
with a good mojito. Open-air dining under
cover by seafront, just across the road from
the water, elegant decor, with furnishings
and equipment brought from the USA, very
popular but more expensive than other
paladares. The owners also have **$$ Hostal
Bahía**, next door. The rooms upstairs have
a wonderful view over the bay but avoid
weekends when the local night club noise
deters sleep.

$$$ Palacio del Valle
Calle 37 y Av 0, next to Hotel Jagua, T43-551226.
Daily 1200-2200, terrace bar 1100-0200.
The place to go for its style, if not for the
food. Speciality seafood, including *paella
Cienfuega* and lobster, with cheaper options
such as fried shrimps and omelettes. There
is a lovely view of the bay from the bar on
the terrace. Live music at weekends and the
pianist, Carmencita, plays in the restaurant.

$$$ Te Quedarás
Avenida 54 (Boulevar) 3509 entre 35 y 37,
T5826 1283.
Upstairs in a grand colonial house with
original tiled floors and high celings.
Elegant dining room with dark wood
furniture and bar. A balcony with bar
stools is a lovely place to sit and have a
drink overlooking the street, people-
watching. Food is good: pasta, shrimp,
fish, lobster, beef, chicken and vegetarian
options come with all the usual Cuban
trimmings, main course prices CUC$10-18.

$$$-$$ Club Cienfuegos
Calle 37 entre 8 y 12, Punta Gorda, T43-512891.
Daily 1000-0100.
Beautiful white building formerly the
Cienfuegos Yacht Club, opened in 1920. This
is a lovely place to come for a sunset beer.
You can still arrive by boat and dock for a
few days. 2 government-run restaurants,

1 is a cafetería and bar by the salt-water
pool (open from 1100) offering fast food and
comida criolla. Get a day pass for CUC$7 to
swim and lounge, with food and drinks of up
to CUC$6 included. Evening entertainment.

$$$-$$ De París
Calle 31 5212 entre 52 y 54, T43-514229.
Daily 1130-2330.
Small a/c restaurant, friendly service,
pleasant atmosphere and good food. If you
want a change from the usual Cuban fare,
they do pasta and pizza too. Several options
for vegetarians.

$$$-$$ Doña Nora
Calle 37 (Prado) 4219 entre 42 y 44, T43-
523331, 5290 3019 (mob). Lunch and dinner.
Eclectic decor with impressive marble pillars
in the dining room, open to the street. Also
open-air dining on the roof terrace with a
view over the harbour and city. The food
is good and includes more unusual items
such as rabbit and lamb. Good cocktails.
Live music.

$ El Polinesio
Calle 29 5410 entre 54 y 56, T43-515723.
Daily 1200-1500, 1800-2200.
State restaurant, a/c, Cuban food, priced
in CUP$. Chicken, pork or beef with sides
of rice and cabbage salad should cost the
equivalent of less than CUC$2.50. Sometimes,
however, staff charge in CUC$ with higher
prices. Try the appetizer, *mariposa*.

Bars

El Palatino
On the south side of Parque José Martí,
Avenida 54 entre 25 y 27, T43-551244.
Bar open 0900-2200.
Built in 1842 as a private residence, it has
been used as a bar and restaurant since the
beginning of the 20th century, decorated
with the works of local caricaturists. Snacks
available. Live traditional music and jazz.
Good drinks and very friendly.

Palacio de Valle
Calle 37 y 0. Roof bar daily 1000-1700.
The roof bar has good views of the bay and the town, great for photos. The restaurant is popular with tour parties, food is OK: the speciality is spit-roast pork.

Entertainment

Live music
Bar Jardines de la UNEAC, *on the west side of Parque José Martí, Calle 25 5411 entre 54 y 56, T43-523272, www.uneac.co.cu. Daily 0900-2200 or later, depending on event.*
Set in a tranquil garden/patio covered in bougainvillea. A centre for cultural nightlife with live music (trova, Afro-Cuban, folk) on Sat nights, *peña folklórico* on Sun, film shows 3 nights a week and an art gallery for more experimental art. Always something going on, events are posted on the gates. No entry fee for the bar, but they sometimes charge depending on the activity.
Café Cantante, *Calle 37 esq Av 54.* Traditional Cuban music with cocktails, you may be charged in CUP$.
Casa de la Música, *Calle 37 entre 4 y 6, T43-552320.* This is a large venue on the seafront with afternoon and evening entertainment posted outside the entrance. Entrance price varies according to band/show. Fri 1800-late is gay night with a show and fiesta. There is a rather lovely seafront stage with great views across to the Escambray mountains. Also a music shop with helpful staff, Mon-Sat 0830-1700, Sun 0830-1200.
Centro Cultural El Cubanísimo (Centro Nocturno Artex), *Calle 35 entre 16 y 18, Punta Gorda, T43-551255. Daily 0930-0200, CUC$1.* Also known as the **Patio de Artex**. Live music. The place for the most important musical events in Cienfuegos, including the **Festival Internacional Benny Moré de Música Popular** and **Cubadisco**.
Centro Nocturno Costa Sur, *Av 40 entre 33 y 35. Restaurant open 1100-140, 1800-2100. Nightclub 2200-0100 weekdays and until 0200 at weekends. Cabaret CUC$2.* Live music and disco.
Club El Benny, *Av 54 2904 entre 29 y 31. Mon-Fri 2100-0100, Sat 2100-0200, CUC$3 per person, couples CUC$8, minimum charge.* Nightclub with live entertainment. Nightly offerings of comedy, karaoke and *bolero*. Men must dress smartly, no T-shirts or sandals.
Cultural Municipal, *Av 56 entre 25 y 27. Boleros, peñas* and *danzón.*
Parque Villuenda, *between 62 y 64.* Live music by *Guajiros* in this park on Sun at 1000.

Theatre
Teatro Tomás Terry, *Av 56 2701 entre 27 y 29, T43-513361. See page 182. Cartelera* is posted outside. Tickets usually cost CUC$5 for a *silla* and CUC$40 for a *palco*.

Festivals

Most of the city's festivals are based on seafaring activities, with many regattas and races for yachts, power boats, kayaks and rowing boats.
Mar Late in the month there is a national motor boat competition for the **Copa 26 de Julio**.
Apr International **rowing** competition. On 22 Apr there are celebrations for the **founding of the city** of Villa de Nuestra Señora de los Angeles de Jagua, or Cienfuegos.
End of May A **sailing** tournament.
Jul In the 1st week is the **Fiesta de los Amigos del Mar**, with sailing regattas and races as well as exhibitions of watersports, including sailing, rowing, water skiing, motor boating, kayaking, swimming, as well as cycling, beach volleyball, karting, etc. The bay of Cienfuegos roars to the sound of speed boats mid-Jul when the **Grand Prix, Formula T-1**, is held, with competitors from the USA, Mexico, Venezuela, Costa Rica and Cuba, among others.
Jul/Aug Carnival, with stalls and plenty of boozing along the partially shut off Malecón.
Sep **Festival Internacional Benny Moré**, every other year, celebrating Cuban music

in honour of the great *sonero*, who was born in Santa Isabel de las Lajas in Cienfuegos province.

5 Sep Fiesta in Parque José Martí and a procession to the Tomás Acea cemetery to commemorate the fallen heroes of the failed insurrection of that day in 1957.

Dec Christmas is celebrated with a huge street party; rum is drunk from all manner of containers and there is dancing to a band on the **Hotel Jagua** promenade.

Shopping

Art and souvenirs

Artex, *Av 54 entre 35 y 37. Daily 0800-1800.* Music, clothing, drinks and souvenirs.

Casa del Fundador, *Av 54 esq 29. Daily 0900-1900.* Rum, music, handicrafts, cigars.

El Embajador, *Av 54 esq 33. Daily 0930-1900.* Cigars, rum and coffee.

Galería Maroya, *Fondo Cubano de Bienes Culturales, Av 54 2502 entre 25 y 27, south side of park. Mon-Sat 0900-1830, Sun 0900-1300.* The courtyard at the back of a large colonial house dating from the 1890s is a showcase for local artists and is a magnet for tour parties. As well as original artwork, there are papier mâché goods, wooden items, jewellery, clothes, T-shirts, bags, baskets, leather and antiques. The appropriate export documents for works of art are available.

What to do

Sailing and watersports

Club Cienfuegos, *Calle 37 entre 10 y 12 Av, Punta Gorda, T43-512891, contacto@club.cfg. cyt.cu. Sun-Fri 1000-0100, Sat 1000-0200.* A pure white Parisian-style mansion built in 1920 is now this club/marina where you can arrange excursions on a catamaran or yacht. There are 2 restaurants, tennis, pool, a shop selling sporting and fishing equipment, billiard table, bumper boats, go-karts and minigolf.

Marina Puertosol (also known as **Marlin Cienfuegos**), *Calle 35 entre 6 y 8, T43-551699/ 551241, VHF 16, operativo@nautica.cfg.cyt.cu.* Full-service marina 1 km from town centre with 36 slips, maximum length 60 m, maximum draught 30 m, dinghy dock, fuel, water, electricity, chandler, car hire, taxis, restaurant, bathrooms, waste disposal. Cienfuegos is a port of entry so Customs are here too. You can rent catamarans, pedalos and kayaks. Sailing and diving excursions also available.

Tour operators

Excursions and tours usually depend on a minimum number of people. Typical tours focus on Cienfuegos city centre or travel further afield to the Jardín Botánico, Castillo de Jagua, cigar factory, El Nicho, Hanabanilla or Topes de Collantes. There are also tourst to Trinidad, Varadero, Havana, Guamá and Santa Clara.

Cubanacán, *Av 54 2903 entre 29 y 31, T43-551680, cuba.viajes@cfg.cyt.cu. Mon-Fri 0800-1700, Sat 0800-1200. Also at Calle 37 1208 entre 12 y 14, T43-551191.* Reserve tours a day in advance. Can arrange taxis, diving and fishing.

Cubatur, *Calle 37 5399 entre 54 y 56, T43-551242 and in Hotel Jagua, T43-551242.*

Ecotur, *T43-550575, www.ecoturcuba.tur.cu, contact Francisco Román.*

Havanatur, *Boulevard (Av 54) 2906 entre 29 y 31, T43-511393. Mon-Fri 0830-1200, 1330-1630, Sat 0830-1200. Also at Hotel Jagua.* They also offer tours to Yaguanabo, Hacienda La Vega and Finca La Isabela.

Transport

Bus

Terminal at Calle 49 esq Av 56, T43-515720/516050. **Viazul** office is to the right of the main building: follow the path round, go in the white door and the ticket office is on the right, T43-518114/515720, daily 0800-1700. Viazul buses pass through Cienfuegos on the **Havana–Trinidad** route. For Trinidad it is best to buy tickets in advance, but if you want to travel immediately you can join a waiting list to see how many people get off, freeing up seats. Viazul also has a daily service from Cienfuegos to **Remedios**, **Caibarién** and **Cayo Santa María**, departing 0845, CUC$15 one way, return 1400.

Car/moped hire

Havanautos, Calle 37 entre 16 y 18, Punta Gorda, in front of Servi Cupet, and at the Hotel Jagua T43-551154, 551211. Daily 0800-1200, 1300-2000. As well as car hire, you can also hire mopeds at CUC$22 per day.

The **Servi Cupet Cimex** petrol station is at Calle 37 entre 16 y 18, and also on the way to Rancho Luna. The **Bahía** filling station, at Autoimport, is at Calle 37 esq Av 40.

Taxi

Cubataxi, T43-519145. Taxi drivers all charge much the same: to **Rancho Luna**, CUC$20 return; to **Pasacaballo** CUC$25-30; to **El Nicho**, CUC$50; to **Playa Girón** CUC$45; to **Playa Larga**, **Playa Girón** and **Caleta Buena**, CUC$60; to **Trinidad**, CUC$30; to **Santa Clara**, CUC$30; to **Varadero**, CUC$50; to **Havana**, CUC$60.

Train

Terminal at Calle 49 esq Av 58, T43-528328. All services are via **Santa Clara** (see Transport, page 208) and are generally slow, unreliable and uncomfortable.

Laguna Guanaroca
CUC$10. A taxi from Cienfuegos costs CUC$20-25 with waiting time.

The road from Cienfuegos to Rancho Luna crosses a narrow branch of the Bahía de Cienfuegos; east of the bridge is the Laguna Guanaroca, a lovely place to see flamingos, pelicans and other wildlife. You are given a guided nature walk to a jetty, from where rowing boats take visitors out into the Laguna and to the mangroves where you can see crabs and other creatures that live there. The flamingos come and go, but are a spectacular sight if they are there. Bring binoculars. Guides speak English and tours leave at specific times, so you may have to wait until the next one is ready; early morning, at about 0800, is best.

Playa Rancho Luna and around
If you are in need of some sea and sand, the Playa Rancho Luna is about 16 km south of Cienfuegos, a CUC$10 taxi fare, on a road lined with mango trees. The beach is quite nice and popular with local families; vendors sell snacks to beachgoers. Close by is one of Cuba's controversial **Dolphinariums** ① *Km 17 Cienfuegos–Pasacaballo, T43-548120.* See page 449 for further details about dolphin shows in Cuba. If you continue northwest along the road for about 3 km you get to the **Hotel Pasacaballo** and its jetty on the Bahía de Cienfuegos. There's another jetty further along a rough track to the left, from where you can get a little **ferry** ① *regular departures, 5-min crossing, CUC$1,* across the mouth of the Bahía de Cienfuegos to the village and castle of Jagua on the western side (see below).

Castillo Nuestra Señora de los Angeles de Jagua
Daily 0900-1600, CUC$1, guides are available. As well as the ferry from Hotel Pasacaballo, there is also a ferry from Av 46 entre 23 y 25 in Cienfuegos to the castle daily at 0800, 1300, 1700, 45 mins, returning 0630, 1000, 1500, CUC$1.

The castle was built at the entrance to the bay in 1733-1745 by Joseph Tantete of France. There is only one entrance via a still-working drawbridge across a dry moat. There are views of the narrow entrance to the bay and the Escambray mountains beyond. The vista is impressive minus the eyesore of the **Hotel Pasacaballo** on the opposite shore and the eerie structures and housing projects of Ciudad Nuclear, which were built for a nuclear power station whose construction was abandoned after the fall of the USSR. The courtyard of the castle has a prison and a chapel. Inside the castle is the **Museo Nuestra Señora de los Angeles de Jagua** ① *T43-965402,* with five exhibition rooms full of legends and historical explanations. It does not compare in size and grandeur with El Morro in Havana, but it is an interesting trip for the view and also for the ferry ride across the bay if you're coming from Cienfuegos.

Palmira
About 12 km north of Cienfuegos, the town of Palmira has a rather unusual Parque Central: the church looks as though it has been decorated with segments of *Terry's Chocolate Orange*, and the southern side of the square is dominated by an ornate Grand Masonic Lodge. The lodge interior features statues of Minerva, Venus and Hercules, the severed head of John the Baptist, as well as unusual swords. There are human skulls on display, although questions about their origins are sidestepped. Ask at the lodge social club next door if you would like to be shown around.

ON THE ROAD
Dive sites around Cienfuegos

There are lots of reef sites and a variety of modern wrecks around Cienfuegos, including seven sunk as diving sites just outside the harbour. One of the best is *Camaronero II*, a shrimp boat. Most of the wrecks have been stripped of everything, but the *Camaronero II* still has her propellers which makes an interesting photo. Built in 1974 from steel, she is 22 m long and was sunk deliberately between 1983 and 1984 in 18 m of water, totally intact. The wreck is adorned with small coral growth, small gorgonias and sponges; seasonally, large schools of red snapper, grouper, hog fish and jacks are found there. However, during the rainy season the visibility is not good because she lies near the mouth of the river. Other wrecks include: the *Camaronero I*, an 8-m wreck lying in shallow water close to shore but very broken up; the cargo ships, *Panta I* and *II*, sunk in 1988; the *Barco R Club*, a 20-m cement and steel passenger ship sunk in 1992 in 8 m; also the 20-m passenger boat *Barco Arimao* sunk in 1992 in 18 m, and the steel fishing boat *Itabo* sunk in 1994 in 12 m. The best reef sites include *El Bajo* in 4 m, *El Laberinto*, *La Guasa* and *Rancho Luna II* all in 12 m, and *La Corona* in 15 m (divers often see whale sharks here).

Palmira is famous for its *Santería* processions, especially at the beginning of December (see Festivals, opposite). At the **Museo Municipal de Palmira** ① *southeast corner of the park, T43-544533, Tue-Sat 1000-1800, Sun 0900-1300, CUC$1*, the very friendly staff will explain all the exhibits in the three sections dedicated to *Santería*, especially the three principal sects in the area: Cristo (dating from 1913), San Roque (1915) and Santa Barbara (1917). The museum also arranges folkloric shows. Ring for information or ask at one of the tour operators in Cienfuegos.

Balneario Jesús Montane Oropesa Ciego Montero
North of Palmira, open all year except the last 2 weeks of Dec, T43-542236. There is a train from Cienfuegos (0700) on alternate days, 1 hr, to Baños station, which is a few mins' walk from the balneario, return train 1700; daily bus at 1420 from Cienfuegos, returning 0600.

These thermal baths are close to the famous water factory from where millions of bottles of mineral water are transported around the country. The sulphurous waters, with temperatures of 37-38° are supposed to be good for rheumatism, arthritis, psoriasis and traumas. Treatments include acupuncture, hydromassage, body massage, fangotherapy and immersion in thermal pools alone or in groups. There are no facilities nearby.

★ Jardín Botánico de Cienfuegos
Pepito Tey, between the villages of San Antón and Guaos, T43-545115. Daily 0800-1700, CUC$2.50, children CUC$1. Bus from Cienfuegos, CUP$0.20; taxi, CUC$30 including waiting time, or take an organized tour. The entrance is marked by 2 rows of palm trees leading to the garden.

Some 23 km east of Cienfuegos, on the road to Trinidad, is the Cienfuegos botanical garden, a national monument founded in 1901 by Edwin F Atkins, the owner of a sugar plantation called Soledad, nowadays called Pepito Tey. Atkins turned over 4.5 ha of his sugar estates to study sugar cane, later introducing other trees and shrubs that could be used as raw materials for industry. In 1919 Harvard University became involved in the studies and the site became known as the Harvard Botanical Station for Tropical Research and Sugar Cane Investigation. After the Revolution, the State took charge of the gardens in 1961, renaming them and employing scientific personnel to preserve and develop the many tropical species now found there. Different sections of the gardens are devoted to areas such as medicinal plants, orchids, fruit trees, bamboos and one of the world's most complete collections of palm trees. It is a fine garden and a nice place to wander around, although don't expect manicured paths, and there are few signs. See if you can get an English-speaking guide (tip welcomed) as it will be much more interesting. There is a good café for lunch or refreshments.

El Nicho
46 km east of Cienfuegos.

In the east of the province, a detour on the way to Trinidad, El Nicho is a series of cascading waterfalls up to 35 m high surrounded by the forested Escambray mountains. The falls are situated on the Río Mamey, west of the Embalse de Hanabanilla. This is a beautiful spot on the edge of the Parque Natural Topes de Collantes (see page 240), with pools, caves and paths to explore. Take your swimsuit for a very refreshing dip in the cold water. There is almost no public transport to the lake despite assurances of the occasional bus from Manicaragua, so car hire or private transport is essential. A shared taxi from Cienfuegos should cost around CUC$10 per person, while official tours cost CUC$75.

Listings Around Cienfuegos

Where to stay

$$ Villa Guajimico
Ctra a Trinidad Km 45, T43-420646.
Best to book through a tour agency.
Overlooks the mouth of Río La Jutía in a great location, surrounded by cliffs, caves, coral reefs and small beaches accessible only by boat or by walking through a cave. 51 simple cabins, white with red-tiled roofs, a/c, bathroom, pool, a/c restaurant serving adequate food, good bar, parking, hobicats, good for excursions, but more than anything it is a great dive resort, see Diving, below.

Festivals

Palmira
Dec The time to be in town is 3-4 Dec for the **Santería** celebrations. On 3 Dec animal sacrifices are made; on the following day processions can be seen in the streets.

What to do

Diving
Centro Internacional de Buceo Faro Luna, *18 km southeast of Cienfuegos near the lighthouse at the entrance to the bay,* T43-548020. English, French, German and Italian spoken. Diving 0900-1130 daily, 1 dive CUC$30, 2 dives CUC$59, 3 dives CUC$87, equipment rental CUC$10 daily. Courses available.
Villa Guajimico, *Ctra a Trinidad Km 45, T43-420646, best to book through a tour agency.* Offers various dive packages with accommodation.

Villa Clara
Province

The capital of Villa Clara Province, Santa Clara, is a pleasant university city lying in the heart of Cuba, famous for its conclusive role in the Revolution and for being the final resting place of Che Guevara. Aside from Santa Clara, the province has plenty of lesser known attractions to offer. South of the city, the land rises gently to the Alturas de Santa Clara, a range of hills that merge into the magnificent Sierra de Escambray. There are lakes and reservoirs where you can hike, birdwatch or fish in a peaceful and picturesque landscape. Northeast of Santa Clara, the delightful 500 year-old town of Remedios is famous for its Christmas-time festival but is a pleasant place to visit at any time of year and is a fine example of an unspoilt provincial town. Caibarién, an old fishing port on the coast, has fewer charms but suits those looking for off-the-beaten-track Cuba. The northern coast is low lying and there are mangroves and swamps, but it is fringed with coral cays with sandy beaches and crystal clear water in the Archipiélago de Sabana. Some of the cays have been developed into major beach resorts, with more hotels being built all the time.

Che Guevara's last resting place

Santa Clara (population 238,000) is best known for being the site of the last and definitive battle of the Revolution, when Che Guevara and his men captured an armoured troop train and subsequently the city. Che's body is interred here and his mausoleum is a major visitor attraction.

Long underestimated by tourists on their way to somewhere else, Santa Clara is a cultured city with several art galleries, museums and parks, plus any number of clubs and music venues where you can take in traditional or more contemporary Cuban styles. There is also a beautiful old theatre where you can find dance or drama performances of an international standard.

Parque Leoncio Vidal

Parque Leoncio Vidal is the central plaza of the city, a pleasant park with trees, a central bandstand and a bronze statue of **Marta Abreu de Estévez**, one of the benefactors of Santa Clara. It is busy day and night with local people listening to the band playing or just strolling around with their friends and families. The municipal band plays a variety of music for about an hour Thursdays and Sundays at 2000. There are plenty of benches where you can sit and take in the atmosphere, but be prepared to be joined by interested Cubans. Until 1894 the park was racially segregated, with a fence dividing the inner and outer footpaths: white people walked in the centre of the park, while black people were only allowed around the edge. In one of the fountains on the north side of the Parque is a sculpture of a young boy by José Delarra dating from 1989 (replacing a statue placed here in 1925 which was damaged in 1959), called '**El Niño de la Bota Infortunada**'. It represents those who, during the war of secession in the United States, used their boots to carry water to the sick and injured, much of it often spilt or lost through holes in the shoe. There are plans to renovate some of the buildings around the square and turn one or two into hotels and shops.

Essential Santa Clara

Finding your feet

Abel Santamaría airport is located north of the city. There are no domestic flights but international charters come from Canada, France, Germany, Italy and the USA, while **Copa** flies from Panama City with connections from Latin America. Santa Clara is on the main cross-island railway line. Train services join the city with Havana and Santiago de Cuba and with most of central Cuba's towns but buses are more efficient and reliable. If you are travelling by car, the arterial *autopista* running from Havana to Santiago de Cuba links the city with these two major urban centres and other provincial capitals.

Getting around

The railway station is quite near the middle of the town; local services are slow and designed for commuters to get to work in Santa Clara, rather than for tourist excursions. The long-distance bus station is about 2.5 km from the centre (a taxi to the centre is CUC$3-4). It is easy enough to walk round the town centre but the main attraction, the Che Guevara mausoleum in Plaza de la Revolución, is some way out (20 minutes on foot).

Tip...

Cartelera is a pamphlet detailing what's on in Santa Clara, Remedios and Caibarién.

BACKGROUND

Santa Clara

The village of Santa Clara was founded on 15 July 1689, when 17 families from San Juan de los Remedios migrated from the coast to the interior. Land was parcelled out and a powerful landholding oligarchy was formed. The settlement grew, and the economy prospered on the fortunes of stockbreeding, tobacco, sugar and other crops and the exploitation of the Malezas copper mines; the town also took advantage of its favourable location on the main trading route through the island. In 1827 when the island was divided into three departments, Santa Clara became part of the central department. In 1867 the town became a city, and in 1873 the railroad arrived, linking it with Havana. In 1895 when the island was further divided into six provinces, Santa Clara became the capital of Las Villas, which included within its boundaries what is now Villa Clara, Cienfuegos, Sancti Spíritus and the Península de Zapata. The 1975 administrative reorganization sharply reduced the provincial territory, renaming it as Villa Clara, with Santa Clara as its capital and dividing it into 13 municipalities.

Santa Clara was the site of the last battle of the Revolution in December 1958 before Castro entered Havana. Batista had sent an armoured train with guns, ammunition and soldiers to Santiago de Cuba to counter-attack the revolutionaries. However, when the train arrived in Santa Clara on 24 December it could go no further because the rebels had destroyed several bridges. Che Guevara had his command post in the university and his troops were hiding on the outskirts of the city. When the train parked near the Loma El Capiro the soldiers on board climbed up the hill to see Che's troops advancing; they opened fire but were defeated, and the rebels took the Loma. Che moved his command post to the building which is now the seat of the PCC Provincial and from there made plans to derail the train, which took place at dawn on 29 December. At around 1500 the same day, the train retreated but was ambushed by 23 men. Fighting for the train was over within an hour, but the battle for the city lasted until 1 January 1959 when news spread that Batista had fled the country. It is said that the capture of the train was the decisive factor in the triumph of the Revolution and it is now a major tourist attraction (see page 199).

On the west side of the Parque is the **Hotel Santa Clara Libre**, an ugly green towerblock, whose bullet-marked, art deco façade is a reminder of Che's battle for the city. Art exhibitions and cultural events are held during the day and evenings at the **Casa de la Cultura** ① *T42-217181, daily 0800-2300.* The building is architecturally interesting and worth a look.

Tip...

Handicrafts and fresh flowers are sold on Calle Lorda just off the square.

Teatro La Caridad ① *Parque Vidal, T42-205548, Mon-Sat 0900-1600, CUC$1, tickets for performances around CUC$5-10.* On the north side of the Parque, on the corner of Calle Máximo Gómez, is the theatre, built in 1884-85 with money raised by Marta Abreu de Estévez. In its heyday it attracted artists such as Enrico Caruso, Libertad Lamarque, Lola Flores, Alicia Alonso, El Ballet Nacional de Cuba, Chucho Valdés, etc. It is a Monumento Nacional and has been restored several times, most recently in 2009, but contains more original features than any other theatre in Cuba, including frescoes by artist Camilo Salaya (Philippines), furniture, mirrors, paintings and busts in the lobby. You can also see the original stage machinery, with over 4.5 km of ropes, levers, pulleys and counterweights, possibly the only machinery of this period still in use anywhere in the world.

Galería Provincial de las Artes Plásticas ① *Máximo Gómez 3 entre Marta Abreu y Barreros, T42-207715, Tue-Thu 0900-1700, Fri-Sat 1400-2200, Sun 1800-2200, free.* Round the

Santa Clara

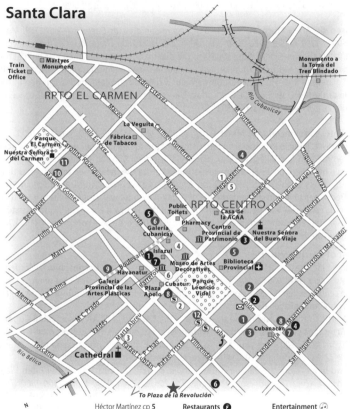

Where to stay
Alba Hostal cp **1**
América **2**
Casa Mercy cp **3**
Casa Mercy 1938 cp **4**
Héctor Martínez cp **5**
Hostal Auténtica
  Pergola cp **6**
Hostal Florida Center cp **7**
Hostal Florida Terrace cp **8**
Hostal Las Jimaguas cp **9**
José Ramón de Zayas
  Lara cp **10**
Olga Rivera Gómez cp **11**
Santa Clara Libre **12**

Restaurants 🍴
1878 Colonial **1**
Coppelia **2**
El Alba **3**
Florida Center **4**
La Aldaba **5**
La Casona Guevara **6**
Santa Rosalía **7**

Bars 🍸
Salón Juvenil **8**

Entertainment 🎵
Bar Club Boulevard **1**
Casa de la Cultura **2**
Club Mejunje **3**
Piano Bar **4**
Teatro 2 **5**
Teatro La Caridad
  & La Marquesina **6**

corner from the theatre is the largest art gallery outside Havana. Originally built in the 19th century as a family house, it became the headquarters of the Colonia Española at the beginning of the 20th century. After the 1960s it was used for other purposes and has recently been rebuilt in all its former glory. There are three rooms for temporary exhibitions of paintings, drawings, crafts, sculpture and other works by national and international artists. There is sometimes live music in the form of *peñas culturales*, with professional musicians playing Cuban music at weekends (Friday 1700, first Saturday 1700, second Saturday 2100, other Saturday 1800, Sunday 1800), with food available.

Museo de Artes Decorativas ① *Parque entre Lorda y Luis Estévez, T42-205368, Mon-Thu 0900-1800, Fri-Sat 0900-2200, Sun 0900-1200, 1800-2200, check times as they can vary, CUC$2.* On the same side of the square as the theatre is this house, which was built at the end of the 18th century and belonged to a *criollo* family. Furniture, paintings, porcelain and glassware are exhibited in rooms around a central courtyard, each furnished in the style of the 18th, 19th or 20th centuries. The courtyard is also used for small concerts, fashion shows and the like, CUC$2.

Biblioteca Provincial José Martí ① *T42-206222, Mon-Fri 0800-1800, Sat 0800-1600.* The neoclassical **Palacio Provincial** on the east side of the square was the seat of the provincial government of Las Villas (see box, page 196). General Máximo Gómez addressed the people from here on 13 February 1899. Under Batista the palace became the one-time headquarters of the city's police force, which was attacked by the Revolutionaries on 29 December 1958 and surrendered the next day. A 72-hour wake for Che Guevara and his guerrilla comrades was held here in 1997. The palace is now a library; although its stock of books is limited, the architecture rewards a visit. There is also a concert hall; check the *cartelera* on the door for events.

East of Parque Vidal

Half a block east of the Parque is the **Centro Provincial de Patrimonio** ① *Céspedes 10 y Plácido, T42-205051, Mon-Fri 0900-1630, free,* dating from the beginning of the 19th century when it was a domestic building on two floors; the first floor is now an art and photographic gallery.

A little further on and round the corner is the **Casa de la ACAA (Asociación Cubana de Artesanos y Artistas)** ① *Maceo 7 entre Bulevard y Céspedes, T42-223969. Mon-Fri 0900-1600, Sat 1900-2200.* Here you can find locally made high-quality cultural handicrafts and works of art for exhibition and sale in a recently restored colonial house (1840).

Two blocks from the Parque is the Catholic church, **Nuestra Señora del Buen Viaje** ① *Pedro Estévez (Unión) esq Buen Viaje, T42-206332, Mon 0800-1200, 1400-1800, Tue-Fri 0700-1800, Sat 1100-1800, Sun 0700-1200, 1400-1600, 1900-2100, Mass Mon-Fri 0800, Sat 1630, Sun 0900, 2000.* Some of its architectural elements date from the 18th century, although the building was deeply modified later, especially during the 20th century and it is a mixture of styles. Next to the church, the former monastery built by the priests is now the Bishopric of Santa Clara.

Another Roman Catholic church to the south of the Parque is **la Santísima Madre del Buen Pastor**, or 'La Divina Pastora', built in the 19th century and part of the Capuchin Order.

West of Parque Vidal

Iglesia Parroquial Mayor de las Santas Hermanas de Santa Clara de Asís ① *C Marta Abreu, entre Alemán y Lubián, T42-202078, Mon-Fri 0830-1200, 1400-1700, Sat 1400-1600.*

Mass Tue, Thu 1700, Sat 1500, Sun 0800, 1000, 1700. The 20th-century cathedral was consecrated in 1953 after a decade of works, and has some interesting stained-glass windows donated in the memory of loved ones. It became the cathedral of the new Diocese of Santa Clara in 1995. The main attraction is the 3-m-high white marble statue of the Virgin Mary at the main door, officially known as La Inmaculada Concepción, but also called La Virgen de la Charca (Virgin of the pond). The statue was commissioned by a local association of Roman Catholic women and blessed on Mother's Day, 12 May 1957. It stood originally at the entrance to the city, but in the 1960s it was discarded in a ditch. It remained there until 1986 when it was disturbed by road building machinery and attracted huge interest with hundreds of people helping to clean up the Virgin. However, it was not until 1995 that the rather damaged and soiled Virgin was put inside the cathedral.

El Bulevar

Just behind Teatro La Caridad runs Santa Clara's main commercial thoroughfare, best known as 'the Boulevard', which heads east as Calle Independencia to the Tren Blindado. If you walk two blocks away from the Parque along Marta Abreu and then turn right along Zayas, heading up to Bulevar, you enter what has traditionally been the Chinese part of town. The architecture ranges from traditional colonial to art deco and you won't find Chinese temples here, but around 20% of the residents are of Chinese origin and until recently the Chinese Consulate was here (now a school, 13 de Marzo).

The **Casa de la Ciudad Atípica** ① *Boulevard esq Zayas, T42-205593, closed since 2012 for renovation with no known date for reopening,* was built in the 19th century and has beautiful stained-glass windows and colonial architecture. It was initially a family house belonging to a man from Barcelona, called Rivalta, but became an exhibition space in 1990.

Monumento a la Acción Contra el Tren Blindado

Independencia, heading east towards Camajuaní, between Río Cubanicay and the railway line, T42-202758, Mon-Sat 0830-1730, CUC$1, photos inside the wagons CUC$1.

Three of the five carriages of Batista's troop train and a bulldozer used to derail the train are preserved here. (Is Cuba the only place in the world where a bulldozer sits on a plinth?) The train, carrying 408 heavily armed troops and weapons, was attacked and taken on 29 December 1958 by 23 guerrillas under the command of Che Guevara in a heroic battle lasting only one hour. The carriages are arranged in a small park among clusters of angular pillars; an inscription on an obelisk describes the event. There is a museum inside the wagons showing weapons and other things carried on the train as well as photos of the aftermath.

El Carmen

Some 360 people, of which three quarters are women, work at the **Fábrica de Tabacos** ① *Maceo entre Julio Jover y Berenguer, T42-202211, guided tours Mon-Fri 0900-1330, CUC$4,* the largest cigar factory outside Havana occupying most of one block north of the centre. It produces Cohiba, Montecristo, Partagás, Robaína and Romeo y Julieta cigars. Tours are available during working hours; get a ticket in advance from a tour agency (Havanatur, Cubatur, Infotur) or from the shop opposite, **La Veguita** ① *T42-208952, Mon-Sat 0900-1900, Sun 1100-1600,* which sells rum, cigars and coffee; then wait your turn at reception. Note the cigar labels used as paper chain decorations.

Nearby is the small church of **Nuestra Señora del Carmen** ① *Parque El Carmen, T42-205217, daily 0900-1200, 1500-1700, Mass Mon-Tue 1700, Fri 0830, Sat 1430, Sun 0730, 2100,* which was built in the 18th century on the hill where the founders of Santa Clara had celebrated the first Mass, in 1689. It was used as a prison for women from 1868 to 1878.

Part of the Silesian Order, it has connections with Don Juan Bosco and Italian saints, whose portraits adorn the walls. Father José Vandor, a Silesian priest and deeply holy man, was a mediator in the historic Battle for Santa Clara in December 1958. He was much loved by his parishioners, and the process for his canonization has recently started.

In the pleasant square outside, **Parque El Carmen**, there is a 1951 marble monument to the 12 families who founded the city. It is a semi-circular spiral construction supported by 12 pillars; in the middle is a tamarind tree. Also in the square is a monument to Roberto Rodríguez 'El Vaquerito', a troop commander who was killed here in one of the battles for Santa Clara in December 1958.

★ Plaza de la Revolución
About a 20-min walk from the city centre. A bicitaxi or coche should cost CUC$1 per person, but agree on a price in advance.

The Plaza de la Revolución Ernesto Che Guevara is the focal point of the national obsession with the Argentine *guerrillero*. On one side of the Plaza (on Prolongación Marta Abreu after the Carretera Central forks to the south) is the **Complejo Escultórico Comandante 'Ernesto Che Guevara'** ① *entrance on C Rafael Tristá, T42-205985*. A huge bronze statue of Che carrying a machine gun stands on top of a large concrete plinth, a bas-relief scene depicting Che in battle and an inscription of a letter from Che to Fidel when he left Cuba. The monument complex, inaugurated on 28 December 1988, was designed by **José Delarra** (1938-2003), who went on to construct 14 further sculptures symbolizing the feats of the guerrilla and his invading forces in Villa Clara province. Major speeches and commemorative events take place here on May Day and 8th October, the day of Che's death. On 28 December there is an annual concert with Cuban and Latin American singers.

Under the monument is a **Mausoleum** where the remains of Che and his comrades who fell in Bolivia have been interred. The architecture is designed to be in keeping with the harsh surroundings in which they fought. Fourteen Royal palms to the left represent Che's birthday, 14 June, while the additional 14 Royal palms to the right, making a total of 28, represent the year of his birth: 1928. The mausoleum is open to the public (numbers limited to 20) and the chamber is a place of contemplation and calm. There are now 39 tombs but only 31 are occupied.

Beside the mausoleum is the **Museo Histórico de la Revolución** ① *Tue-Sun 0930-1630, free, bags should be left at the entrance.* The museum has good displays in Spanish and sometimes a video about Che's life and role in the Revolution, with many photos, uniforms and personal effects, including his famous leather jacket and the clothes he was wearing when he was murdered in Bolivia, as well as displays of the battle in Santa Clara. Recommended.

Behind the complex construction work is underway on a cemetery for all the guerrillas under Che's command during the Revolution.

El Che de los Niños
On the outskirts of Santa Clara as you head towards the cays (opposite the PCC offices, which were Che's HQ in 1958), there is another statue of Che, a bronze cast by Casto Solano of Spain. It is known as El Che de los Niños and shows Che striding along holding a small child in one arm, a cigar in the other hand and lots of tiny details reflecting events in his life: on his shoulder is an Amerindian man on a goat; on one of his boots is the motorbike he rode around South America; Don Quijote is on one of his pockets, and his Bolivian comrades in arms are depicted on his belt.

BACKGROUND

Ernesto 'Che' Guevara: rise and fall of the 'New Man'

Every visitor to Cuba learns to recognize the face of Che Guevara, the Cuban Revolution's unofficial emblem. Born in Rosario, Argentina, Ernesto Guevara was a medical student when he began travelling around Latin America by motorcycle, bus, truck and even as a stowaway on ships. In 1954, Guevara was in Guatemala when the CIA toppled that country's elected government. His hopes for peaceful change in the hemisphere were dashed and Guevara found his enemy: imperialism. Months later in Mexico he met his natural ally, the exiled Cuban lawyer, Fidel Castro. Guevara joined Castro's invasion force as a doctor, but once in Cuba quickly showed himself a brilliant field commander as well and rose during three years of warfare to lead the guerrilla army's second column.

Repeatedly wounded, Che led from the front lines and was lionized by his Cuban soldiers, many of whom would follow him for the rest of their lives. On 27 December 1958, Che's badly outnumbered *guerrilleros* ambushed a troop train at Santa Clara, Cuba, the victory that sealed the fate of the Batista regime. It was the apogee of Guevara's career. Within days he had entered Havana and revolutionary politics, a field of battle far more dangerous than the mountains of the Sierra Maestra.

Following the triumph of the Revolution on 1 January 1959, Cubans rallied to Guevara. Nicknamed 'Che' after an Argentine figure of speech, Guevara routinely spoke at Castro's side and was seen as the Revolution's second leader. His position was won through public support; a charismatic orator, Guevara appealed to the idealism of the young, calling for the birth of a 'New Man', or a revolutionary society based on moral, rather than material incentives. His eloquence on behalf of the poor and dispossessed made him a global spokesman for the Third World.

Once in power, Guevara endorsed show trials and summary executions of opponents and later, as head of the Central Bank and the Ministry of Industry, his Socialist economic reforms produced chaos even by his own account. Frustrated by Fidel Castro's increasing reliance on the Soviet Union, Guevara quit Cuba in 1965, first to join a doomed rebellion in the Congo, then, in late 1966, to launch his own guerrilla column in Bolivia.

On 8 October 1967, in an operation coordinated by the CIA, Guevara was captured and executed by Bolivian troops. His remains were repatriated to Cuba 30 years later, to be interred in a bronze mausoleum at the site of his great victory in Santa Clara.

Despite his position as the Revolution's greatest hero, Guevara remains an enigmatic figure, seen as both an inspiring idealist and an inflexible ideologue. See also box, page 420.

Tourist information

The **tourist office** is at Cuba 68 entre San Cristóbal y Candelaria, T42-201352. Several state tour agencies (**Cubatur**, T42-208980, **Gaviotatur**, T42-201515) in town can also give you information on trips and excursions, as well as make hotel reservations and reconfirm flight tickets. If you are staying in a *casa particular* you will probably find your hosts to be a mine of information worth tapping into. They will usually make phone calls for you to arrange transfers or accommodation at your next destination. The hotels all have a *buró de turismo*, which sells organized tours and little else.

Where to stay

Hotels

\$\$\$ América
Domingo Mujica 9 entre Colón y Maceo, T42-201585, www.hotelescubanacan.cu.
Smart new hotel with modern decor and clean lines, buffet breakfast, reasonable restaurant and great bar. Rooms are not large but well organized, very green, and have good hot showers and a fridge. A lift is planned for the upper floors. Pool, which can be noisy with groups of children. Parking.

\$\$ Santa Clara Libre
Parque Vidal 6, T42-207548, www.islazul.cu.
Central, 1956 dilapidated metal and concrete building on Parque Vidal with bullet holes on the façade, preserved from the Dec 1958 battle when some of the police were using the building to defend the city from the revolutionaries. 142 spartan rooms, but comfortable, with a/c, phones, TV, water shortages, lifts also erratic and ancient, straight out of Batman's Gotham, noisy, observation deck with bar on top of the building from where you get a great view of the city, cinema.

Casas particulares

Casas charge CUC\$20-30, although occasionally you can negotiate a lower rate, depending on the season and demand. All those listed offer meals, private bathrooms, hot water, a/c, fan, fridge. Beware of *jineteros* outside who may tell you the house is full and offer to take you somewhere else, or concoct some other story so they can get a CUC\$5 commission. Ring the bell and get the facts from someone inside. If you come by bus with a prior reservation, the *casa* owner may meet you at the terminal with a taxi, CUC\$3-4.

\$ Alba Hostal
San Cristóbal (E Machado) 7 entre Cuba y Colón, T42-294108.
A beautiful old house, high ceilings, tiled floors, colonial style, lovingly renovated and run by Wilfredo Alba Contreras and his family. 2 rooms each with 2 antique beds (new mattresses) which open on to a small patio with tables and plants. Period furniture and light fittings complete the restoration. Breakfast is a feast. Other meals at nearby **Hostal Florida Center**, where Wilfredo is the chef.

\$ Casa Mercy
San Cristóbal (E Machado) 4 entre Cuba y Colón, T42-216941, 5283 6076 (mob), casamercy@gmail.com.
Very central *casa* run by experienced hosts, Omelio and Mercedes Moreno, who speak several languages and are helpful, knowledgeable and friendly. 2 comfortable rooms upstairs sleep 3 or 4 with good quality furniture and fridge, private and separate from the rest of the house, laundry, good home cooking, vegetarians and children catered for, extensive cocktail menu and rum tasting, roof terraces with view of the Che mausoleum in the distance. Parking nearby, taxis and tours arranged. Free Wi-Fi 1800-2000.

$ Casa Mercy 1938

Independencia (Bulevar) 253 entre Unión y San Isidro, T42-216941, 5283 6076 (mob), casamercy@gmail.com.

Beautifully restored 1938 house in traditional style with a central courtyard run by Arnaldo Moreno and family. Several languages spoken. Helpful and knowledgeable, Arnaldo grew up in his parents' *casa* and can anticipate guests' needs. 2 bright rooms with 2 double beds in each. Breakfast CUC$5 and evening meal CUC$8-12 with good home cooking, catering for special diets and children. Rum tasting and cocktails CUC$2.50. Parking, taxis and tours arranged. Laundry service, hand-washing area, internet service.

$ Hostal Auténtica Pergola

Luis Estévez 61 entre Independencia y Martí, T42-208686, carmenrt64@yahoo.es.

Magnificent colonial house run by Carmen and Obregón with ornate exterior and *rejas* on the windows, 3 rooms, high ceilings, huge garden patio and roof terrace, all bursting with plants. Excellent food and generally very highly regarded.

$ Héctor Martínez

Rolando Pardo (Buen Viaje) 8 entre Maceo y Parque, T42-217463.

Room in house dating from 1902, original floor tiles, double and single beds, good fixtures and fittings, pleasant patio with tables, rocking chairs, plants.

$ Hostal Casa Bonsái

EP Morales (Síndico) 67 entre Juan Bruno Zayas y Villuenda, T42-206996, 52624507 (mob), http://hostalbonsai.blogspot.com.

Friendly and pleasant house south of the centre, with bonsai trees and other ornamental plants. 2 rooms, 1 with double bed and 1 twin room, fridge in the living room stocked with drinks, terrace with jacuzzi. Meals and cocktails offered. Parking outside on the street is free, or there is a car park 3 blocks away, CUC$2.

$ Hostal Florida Center

Candelaria (Maestra Nicolasa) 56 entre Colón y Maceo, T42-208161.

Delightful colonial house dating from 1876; it was the first ever private house to win the architectural conservation prize in 2008. 2 rooms with antique furniture open on to large, verdant patio garden where there are orchids. The house is also a *paladar* and is busy at night with tables beside the rooms. The food is very good and you get a huge breakfast with an enormous plate of seasonal fruits and loads of pastries. Hospitable host Angel Rodríguez Martínez speaks some English, French and a little Italian. Parking for CUC$2.

$ Hostal Florida Terrace

Candelaria (Maestra Nicolasa) 59 entre Colón y Maceo, T42-221580, florida.terrace@yahoo.com.

New in 2015, Angel Rodríguez Martínez has built a larger hostal across the road with 6 light and airy rooms, each with 2 beds, a/c, good bathrooms, excellent hot showers, terrace with a bar, sunbathing area, good view over the city from a mirador, city tours offered. Evening meals at Florida Center.

$ Hostal Las Jimaguas

Independencia 104 entre Zayas y Esquerra, T42-215471, lasjimagua104@yahoo.es.

English-speaking Carlos and Belkis and their 2 daughters offer 1 room in a colonial house on the corner of the Boulevard and are kind, warm and generous. Garage available.

$ José Ramón de Zayas Lara

Máximo Gómez 208 entre E Yanes y Berenguer, T42-207239, T5281 4972 (mob), josedzayas@yahoo.es.

Short walk from Parque Vidal and train station. Private and independent suite upstairs with kitchen/diner, alcove with child's bed, fenced in and tiled terrace with good view. Ideal for long stays or for people with a small child who need to self-cater. Meals available. Family lives downstairs.

$ Olga Rivera Gómez

Evangelista Yanes 20 entre Máximo Gómez y Callejón del Carmen, T42-211711.
Lovely art deco house in front of Nuestra Señora del Carmen church. A lush green vineyard in the inner patio is home to a dozen parrots and canaries singing in their cages. 2 rooms, TV, parking, terrace, helpful owner.

Around Santa Clara
Hotels

$$$-$$ Los Caneyes

Av de los Eucaliptos y Circunvalación, T42-218140, www.hotelescubanacan.cu.
Thatched public areas with 96 rooms in cabins designed to look like Indian huts in a park-like setting. It all could do with renovating but service is friendly and everything works, a/c, hot showers, internet access, facilities for disabled people, pool, disco Fri-Sat 2200-0200, enthusiastic evening entertainment by the pool, adequate buffet food, medical services, shop, popular hotel for tour parties and hunters. Day passes (1000-1700) are available whereby you can use the pool for CUC$7, including CUC$5 of food and drink, anything you eat or drink over that amount will be charged at the end of your visit.

$$$-$$ Carrusel La Granjita

Outside town at Km 2.5 on Maleza road, T42-218191, www.hotelescubanacan.cu.
73 rooms in thatched *cabañas* among fruit and palm trees, emphasis on nature and tranquillity with lots of farm animals around but also bugs, so take insect repellent, a/c, internet access, bar, shop, buffet restaurant, breakfast included, horses, nighttime entertainment around the pool. Pool open to visitors for CUC$7, which includes food and drinks of CUC$5 (*consumo*) *Sala de fiestas*. 24-hr medical services, massage. The hotel is a long way out of Santa Clara, CUC$10 one way by taxi.

Where to eat
Restaurants

$$$ Florida Center

Maestra Nicolasa (Candelaria) 56 entre Colón y Maceo, T42-208161. Daily 1830-2200.
Delightful colonial house, see above for rooms to rent. Romantic setting with candlelit tables around and in the middle of a lush courtyard garden with orchids. House speciality is lobster or fish with shrimp in sauce, or you can have grilled fish, smoked pork, roast chicken or beef; the *ropa vieja* is particularly good. Reservations advised.

$$$ La Casona Guevara

JB Zayas 160 entre E Machado (San Cristóbal) y Candelaria, T42-224279. Daily 1200-2400.
A colonial house with a little interior patio, offering good Cuban dishes very attractively presented. Vegetarian options are more interesting than usual too. English spoken, friendly service. Live music.

$$$-$$ La Aldaba

Luís Estévez 61 entre Independencia (Bulevar) y Martí, T42-208686.
Rooftop terrace above La Auténtica Pérgola *casa particular*. Open air dining but under tarpaulin cover, romantic at night. Good breakfast, lunch and dinner, also pleasant bar and live music, you can go for just a drink if you want. Service is attentive and there is a nice atmosphere. Reservations advised.

$$$-$$ Santa Rosalía

M Gómez 2 entre Martha Abreu y Independencia, T42-201438. Open 1100-2300.
A lovely old blue and white building with ornate white metal grills on the windows. A surprisingly good state restaurant with prompt service and reasonable prices. Somehow they manage to cater for large tour parties as well as couples. All you can eat buffet for CUC$8 or à la carte Cuban and international food. There is a huge central patio with a bar which is open until 0200, live music and an Artex shop.

$$$-$ 1878 Colonial
Máximo Gómez 8, near the Boulevard,
T42-202428. Daily 1200-1500 lunch,
1900-2245 dinner.
Offers a variety of *criollo* dishes, mainly pork
in different styles, bar in the patio, long
trousers required for men at night, charges
in CUP$ only.

$ Coppelia
Colón esq Mujica just off Parque Vidal,
T42-222288. Tue-Sun 1000-2330.
Ice cream, seriously cheap, sweets and drinks.

$ El Alba
Rolando Pardo (Buen Viaje) 26 entre
Maceo y Parque. Daily 1130-2230.
Meals are mostly pork dishes, chicken,
seafood, with *congrí* or white rice and salad,
although you can order sides of fried plantain
or *potaje de frijoles* if you are extra hungry,
a cheap and practical *paladar* charging in
CUC$ or CUP$: *ropa vieja* is CUP$70 while
stewed pork is CUP$35.

Bars

La Marquesina
Attached to La Caridad theatre,
M Gómez y M Abreu.
Snacks and drinks, tea and coffee charged
in CUP$, beer, rum and other drinks in
CUC$, pleasant place for a drink, popular
with young people at night, live traditional
music 2100-2400.

Salón Juvenil (Palmares)
Marta Abreu 10 entre Máximo Gómez y
Villuendas, T42-200974. Daily 1000-2200.
Dinos Pizza, cafeteria, drinks, cocktails,
part bar, part restaurant.

Entertainment

Cartelera is a pamphlet detailing what's on
in Santa Clara, Remedios and Caibarién.

Cinema
Cine Teatro Camilo Cienfuegos, *on the*
ground floor of the Hotel Santa Clara Libre on
Parque Vidal, T42-203005. Check billboard
outside for show times and what's on. This is
Santa Clara's only cinema and entering is like
stepping back in time. Seriously cheap: CUP$2.

Live music
You don't have to go to a club or bar to
hear live music in Santa Clara as there are
regular performances in the parks: the
municipal band plays Thu and Sun evenings
in Parque Vidal, and there is dancing to a
good band playing Cuban music from the
1950s on Sat at 2100 in Parque Las Arcadas
(Independencia y Luis Estevez). Aimed
mainly at senior citizens, it is wonderful
to watch even if you don't join in.
Bar Club Boulevard (Carishow),
Independencia 225 entre Maceo y Unión,
T42-216236. Daily 2000-0200. CUC$1-3. Small
nightclub offering phenomenal dancing and
lethal supplies of rum, although drinks more
expensive than other places, also used for
social occasions, birthdays, etc.
Casa de la Cultura, *Parque Vidal, T42-217181.*
A variety of cultural activities with local and
provincial artists, including *Los Fakires,* with
dancing every Sun 1600, very popular party
on the street outside.
Club Mejunje (mishmash), *2½ blocks west*
from Parque Vidal, Marta Abréu 107 entre
Alemán y Juan Bruno Zayas, T42-282572.
Cultural centre in a backyard full of trees,
ruins, artefacts and graffiti-covered walls.
The best place to go to sample what Santa
Clara has to offer in the way of nightlife.
Composers, singers, musicians and friends
sing, play and drink together, friendly,
welcoming, enjoyable. Bar/cafetería open
weekdays at variable hours, very cheap at
CUP$2-5. Regular events range from jazz to
rock to very good *trova* and *filín*, both live and
recorded music. Larger events are staged in
the courtyard (popular at weekends).
El Bosque, *Centro Cultural Artex, Av El Sandino*
y Ctra Central, Vigía, 1 km from Parque Vidal,
T42-204444. Tree-ringed, outdoor venue for
live and recorded music (including *trova, filín*
and *danzón*), nightlife and shows, CUP$25.

Patio bar 1800-2000. Film salón showing 3-D films 1700-1900.

Piano Bar, *Luis Estévez 13 entre Independencia y Parque, T42-215215*. Restaurant daily 1045-2245, *comida criolla*. Piano bar daily 1200-1800 for drinks, cocktails and snacks and Wed, Sat and Sun 2100-0100 for live music, with the pianist Freyda Anido and band, invited singers, national and international music.

Theatre

Teatro 2, *Independencia entre Maceo y P Estévez, T42-204038*. Base for Teatro Estudio Teatral from Santa Clara. Experimental or alternative theatre, occasionally visiting companies from abroad. Varied programme, see billboard at the theatre, CUC$2.

Teatro la Caridad, *C Máximo Gómez, Parque Vidal, T42-208548*. Look in *Cartelera* or the billboard outside for what's on; you might catch a performance by a top ballet company and the annual National Dance Festival is held here. Tickets CUC$5-10, performances Mon-Sat 2100, Sun 1700.

Festivals

The dates of festivals vary from one year to the next and new festivals may be added.

Jan Festival Longina Canta a Corona.
A *trova* festival, with subsidiary events in Caibarién.

Mar Festival 'A Tempo' con Caturla. Santa Clara is the base for this chamber music festival; a young people's concert is also held in Remedios.

Apr Festival Nacional de la Danza.
Traditional music and dancing in theatres and all around Parque Vidal; international groups participate every 4 years.

12 Aug La Verbena de la Calle Gloria.
A popular jazz festival, celebrated since the beginning of the 20th century in honour of Santa Clara de Asís, patron saint of the city.

End Oct Festival de Rock Ciudad Metal.
A week-long festival held on Plaza Sandino.

Dec Festival a Bailar en Casa del Trompo.
Dance festival.

28 Dec Lots of commemorative activities in the Plaza de la Revolución and in the Parque Vidal, celebrating the last successful battle of the **Revolution** in 1958 with concerts and music festivals attracting Cuban and Latin American singers and musicians. 28-30 Dec, early in the morning, hundreds of children dressed in rebels' uniform commemorate the battle, marching from the Monumento al Tren Blindado to different parts of the city, including Parque Vidal.

Shopping

The pedestrianized street behind the theatre, between Maceo and Juan Bruno Zayas, is known locally as *Boulevard/Bulevar*. Locals shop here in CUC$ for clothes, electrical, domestic and household goods, some food and other items. Shops are open daily 0900-1700 unless otherwise stated.

Cigars/rum/coffee

La Veguita (Cubanacán), *Maceo 176 entre Berenguer y Martí, opposite the tobacco factory, T42-208952, veguita@vcl.cyt.cu*. Mon-Sat 0900-1900, Sun 1100-1600. Sells cigars, rum and coffee, English spoken, very informative, large stock.

Markets

Agromercado Buen Viaje, *Rolando Pardo (Buen Viaje) Final*. Mon-Fri 0900-1800, Sat 0800-1700, Sun 0800-1200. Sells fruit, vegetables and pork, in CUP$.

Souvenirs

Artex Mi Ilusión, *Colón 18 entre Machado y Parque, T42-214397*. Mon-Sat 0900-1700, Sun 0900-1200. Sells *artesanías*, Che souvenirs, percussion (drums, bongos) instruments, CDs, toiletries, T-shirts and nicknacks. There is another Artex, **El Bazar** (Carretera Central y Prolongación de Marta Abreu s/n, near the Plaza de la Revolución, T42-206505), which has a good choice of books, drinks and biscuits.

Galería Cubanicay, *Luis Estévez 9*. Mon-Sat

0830-1630. Wide choice of handicrafts and art as well as furniture and shoes made locally.
Plaza Apolo, *Villuendas entre Martha Abreu y C Barreros.* More than 400 sq m of kiosks selling *artesanías*, shoes, handmade clothing, wooden items, leather goods, paintings, etc.

What to do

Baseball
Played from Nov until around Apr at the **Augusto César Sandino** stadium (Av Sandino y 6, T42-206461. Tickets CUP$1-2). Take drink and snacks. The local team is Villa Clara. Nearby is the **Natilla Jiménez** mini-stadium built for children's baseball, great matches, unforgettable.

Tour operators
Prices of tours at all the agencies depend on numbers in the party and any additional features added.
Cubanacán, *Colón 101 esq Maestra Nicolasa, T42-205189, Mon-Fri 0830-1730, Sat 0830-1230.* Excursions, hotel reservations, transfers, car hire.
Cubatur, *Marta Abreu 10 entre Máximo Gómez y Villuendas, T/F42-208980, cubatur@ tur.cu. Mon-Fri 0900-1800, Sat 0800-1200. Also at Cayo Santa María.* Excursions to every possible tourist site in west and central Cuba as well as **Viazul** tickets, flight confirmations, etc. Helpful and informative personnel.
Ecotur, *Hotel Santa Clara Libre, T42-201598, and in Caibarién, T42-353906, www.ecotur cuba.tur.cu. Mon-Sat 0900-1799.* Expeditions are organized for shooting and fishing with guide and all equipment if necessary. Also other excursions and tours to Rancho Querete, Lago Hanabanilla, Caleta Buena at Playa Larga etc.
Havanatur, *Máximo Gómez, 13 entre Independencia y Barreras, T42-204001, Mon-Fri 0830-1730, Sat 0830-1230.* Air tickets, tours, etc. Excursions to Cayo las Brujas (transfer, lunch and beach time), Cienfuegos (city tour, lunch and beach), Trinidad (city tour, lunch and beach), to Hanabanilla on demand.

Islazul, *Lorda 6 entre Parque Vidal y Boulevard, just off Parque Vidal by the theatre, T42-217338, Mon-Fri 0800-1130, 1300-1600.* Hotel reservations.

Transport

Air
Abel Santa María international airport is on Ctra de Malezas, Km 11, north of the city, T42-214402. Charter flights come in from Canada, France, Germany, Italy and the USA, while **Copa** fly twice a week from Panama City with connections to South and Central America. At the moment there are no domestic flights.

Bus
Local There are some buses, CUP$1, but horse-drawn *coches*, or taxis are more plentiful and go all over town, including down Marta Abreu to the bus stations, CUP$2-3. They stream up and down some main streets, taking 8 passengers.

Long distance The provincial bus station for destinations within Villa Clara is in a white building on Ctra Central esq Pichardo, T42-203470, 1 km from centre. The interprovincial bus station for long distances is 1 km further out on Ctra Central (Av Cincuentenario) 483 entre Independencia y Oquendo, Virginia, T42-222524 for reservations.
For **Viazul** services, see page 462, to **Havana**, **Santiago**, **Varadero**, **Camagüey**, **Trinidad**, **Cayo Santa María**, and to most of the provincial capitals. **Astro** services are usually not available for tourists.

Car hire
Havanautos/Cubacar, *Unión 250 entre San Miguel y Nazareno, T42-218177, daily 0800-1700; Tristá y Amparo, T42-202040, daily 0800-1730; Abel Santamaría airport, T42-209118, open when there are flights.* Small cars CUC$70-85 per day for up to 6 days, less for each subsequent week, CUC$45 per day for over 30 days, including insurance and 20 litres of fuel. Motos CUC$20-25 per day.

Rex, at the airport, T42-222244, daily 0830-1730 or when there are flights, more upmarket than the other companies with the best cars, good service, rates variable over 1-30 days, with or without driver.

Vía, Ctra Central (Banda Esperanza) and at the airport, T42-201558. Similar service to Cubacar.

Taxi
Cubataxi, T42-222555/T210363, good drivers, reasonable prices, about CUC$150 for a whole day's tour to the cays and Remedios.

A **bicitaxi** costs CUC$2-5 to most places in town; fix a price beforehand or they will overcharge you.

Train
The **Martha Abreu** railway station is north of Parque Vidal on Estévez at Parque Mártires, and is much more central than either of the bus stations. It is a very impressive station, with a shady square outside, the usual bust of Martí and a monument to martyrs that looks like a stone totem pole that someone has taken a bite out of where it has eroded at the top. The ticket office (and a post office) is across the square: information T42-202895-6, reservations T42-200853, Mon-Fri 0830-1800, Sat 0830-1200. There are trains to **Havana** (CUC$10) and to **Santiago** (CUC$20); also trains to **Bayamo** (CUC$15.50), **Camagüey** (CUC$9), **Sancti Spíritus**, **Cienfuegos**, **Holguín** and other towns; timetables are unreliable and the train may not even appear at any time, so call beforehand. In 2015 they were running every 3 days, to eastern towns at 0225 and 2350, and to the west (Havana) at 0832, 1032 and 0015.

South of Santa Clara

forests, mountains and lakes

The Sierra del Escambray, part of the Montañas de Guamuhaya, occupies most of the land between Santa Clara and Trinidad and can be visited from either city. Although not the highest mountain range in Cuba, it is one of the most beautiful, coated in forest and home to a variety of plant and animal species. The peaks are intersected by streams, waterfalls and fertile valleys, where thatched *bohíos* are home to farming families eking out a living from growing bananas, coffee and livestock. There are several lakes and dams in the province of Villa Clara. Man-made Embalse Hanabanilla, the third largest, is very attractive and used for recreational purposes as well as water supply, with hunting and fishing both popular.

Embalse Hanabanilla
Some 40 km south of Santa Clara, the road to Trinidad passes through **Manicaragua**, a large town of 80,000 inhabitants set in rolling hills covered with tobacco fields, and then rises into the mountains. The town provides access to the Embalse Hanabanilla, the third-largest reservoir in the country. It has Cuba's largest hydroelectricity station, but looks like a natural lake set in a very attractive landscape with lovely views. The lake is stocked with largemouth bass and other fish and there are plenty of wild duck, quail, pheasant and other game birds. You can take a boat trip on the lake to the **Restaurante Río Negro** (7 km from the **Hotel Hanabanilla** and accessible only by boat). There are several options and tours available. Private boat operators will take you to beauty spots

Fact...
Villa Clara Province boasts the longest river in Cuba to drain into the Atlantic, Río Sagua la Grande, at 144 km long.

including the Trucha Falls, or fishing. The resort area can get crowded with Cubans at the weekends and during the summer holidays, but you don't need to walk far to get peace and quiet. Embalse Hanabanilla can be visited as a day trip from Santa Clara, Cienfuegos, Trinidad or Sancti Spíritus, but an overnight stay would be more rewarding, and it is a convenient place to stay between the towns.

Northwest of Santa Clara

thermal spa off the beaten track

Baños de Elguea
North of El Corralillo on the Circuito Norte, T42-686292, www.islazul.cu.

In the extreme west of the province, 136 km from Santa Clara, is Elguea *balneario*, a hotel and health resort with sulphur springs which are used to treat arthritis, rheumatism, skin diseases and tourists in need of pampering. The waters healing properties were discovered accidentally when a slave of the Elguea family was freed. He had a skin disorder and it was feared he might contaminate the rest of the slaves. He was later found to be cured after he had frequently bathed in the springs. A small hotel was then built to exploit the waters' beneficial properties, now replaced by the hotel and spa. Thermal waters are different temperatures (average 45°C) and there are medicinal muds for a variety of complaints including stress and obesity. The waters at the hotel's Thermal Centre are claimed to be hyper-mineralized, with chlorine, sodium, bromine, and a small amount of radon and sulphur. Qualified medical assistance is available, along with masseurs for general pampering.

To say that the hotel is remote is understated and you will need your own transport and a good road map to get there. It is also seriously run down, few of the hotel rooms are in operation, and it is desperately in need of funding to renovate what could be a great attraction.

There are beaches at **El Salto** and **Ganuza**, nearby, and accommodation at local resorts and *campismos* (if there is space for non-Cubans).

★ San Juan de Remedios and around   *Colour map 2, B4.*

a delightful town with many historic charms and unmissable street parties – well worth a visit

The colonial town of San Juan de Remedios (population 30,000) is 43 km northeast of Santa Clara. It has many beautiful colonial buildings, particularly around the pleasant Plaza Martí, which has some Royal palms and a gazebo in the centre. Remedios is an interesting side trip for tourists staying on the cays, and also takes some of the pressure off Trinidad as the main colonial attraction in the region. Traffic is very light and moves at the pace of the many *bicitaxis*, which can be found for hire around the Plaza.

Sights
Plaza Martí This is the only town in Cuba where there are two churches on the plaza. **Iglesia Buen Viaje** was in a poor state and leaking for many years, but it is now under renovation and will be brought back into use. The **Iglesia Parroquia Mayor San Juan Bautista de Remedios** ① *visitors Mon-Fri 0900-1200, 1400-1700; Mass Mon-Wed 0830, Thu-Sat 0800, Sun 1630, donations requested,* was built in 1692 on the remains of a 1570

BACKGROUND
San Juan de Remedios

San Juan de Remedios was the eighth *villa* founded by the Spaniards, around 1513-1515, by Vasco Porcallo de Figueroa, and for 160 years it was the main settlement in the area. However, it was never given the status of one of the original *villas*, because Porcallo de Figueroa refused to allow the construction of a city hall. Its location was changed in 1544 and again in 1578, and when pirate attacks and other commercial incentives encouraged some of the inhabitants to move inland to Santa Clara, Remedios' importance began to wane. A fire in 1692 hastened its political decline. The present town was built following the fire and many of its buildings still date from this time. Despite the discrepancies in historical dates, the government decided to celebrate Remedios' 500th anniversary in 2015, investing large sums in renovation, new hotels and other tourism projects, Wi-Fi access and road resurfacing.

church, making it one of the oldest churches in Cuba. It was renovated in 1944-1953 by an American millionaire who traced his family roots to Santa Clara. He found birth records in the church that confirmed that one of his ancestors had been a founding member of the town. He spent US$1 million renovating the roof, walls and altar, taking off a false ceiling and whitewash to reveal gloriously painted and carved beams. The altar is cedar and was covered in gold leaf, but it shone so much you couldn't see the detail, so some of it is now painted over to give more definition and contrast. Buried in the church are Juan de Loyola (parish priest 1685-1775) and 17 of his relations.

Museo de Música Alejandro García Caturla ① *Mon-Sat 0900-1200, 1300-1700, Sun 0900-1300, CUC$1.* Housed in a recently restored house on the square, this museum remembers García Caturla, who was born in 1906 and studied both music and civil law at the university of Havana in the 1920s. He formed the jazz band *Caribe* with a group of students but was strongly influenced by the Grupo Minorista, which contributed to bringing African influences into Cuban mainstream music. Caturla met the writer Alejo Carpentier and went to Paris under his protection, where he continued his cultural education by going to the *Ballets Russes* and the *Folies Bergères*. On his return to Cuba he created the *Orquesta de Conciertos de Caibarién*, which gave its first concert in 1932. His music then took a back seat and he concentrated on law, rising through the ranks of the local judiciary until he was murdered in 1940, aged 34, shot by an unknown assassin allegedly for upsetting the local social order by working with the poor. The museum has copies of newspaper articles about his death, including one by Nicolás Guillén, the poet. There are also displays on other prominent local musicians and bands with lots of photo boards, and art exhibitions.

Museo de Arte Popular Las Parrandas ① *Alejandro del Río 74 entre Enrique Malaret y Máximo Gómez, Tue-Sat 0900-1200 and 1300-1800, Sun 0900-1300, CUC$1, with guide CUC$2, photos CUC$1 each.* This interesting museum in a restored mid 19th-century mansion should not be missed. It is dedicated to the *parrandas* (street parties) that take place in Remedios and other regional towns in the lead up to Christmas. Two sections of the town compete against each other in games and festivities in the week leading up to 24 December, with the winning district being the one to make the most noise, although no one really wins. The event traces its roots to a local priest who told the children of the town to wake everyone for midnight mass by making as much noise as possible; it soon became a tradition. The mayor complained to Spain about the "music from hell" and asked for it to be banned, but the *parrandas* continued and developed into what they are today.

The two districts, named Carmen and San Salvador, prepare long in advance, building towers in secret, which have a different theme each year and are transported and erected at the corners of the plaza. There is music, based on the *polka*, which varies slightly between Carmen and San Salvador, fireworks and floats. However, in contrast to carnival elsewhere, the people on the floats do not dance, in fact they do not even move, they are there simply as a tableau.

An informative guide will explain all about the *parrandas* in English or Spanish, starting with a model and map of the city showing how the festival boundaries have changed over the years from eight groups to two, Carmen and San Salvador. There are replicas of several towers constructed during the 20th century, photos, costumes, musical instruments and mascots.

Camajuaní

West of Remedios on the road from Santa Clara, Camajuaní is a typical 19th-century town stretching along the main street, Independencia. All the houses in Camajuaní have columns and verandas, and there's an extremely grand railway station that evokes the town's prosperous shoe-making past.

Museo de Agroindustria Azucarero Marcelo Salado (Museo del Vapor)
Central Marcelo Salado, Reforma village, 400 m on the left of the road from Remedios to Caibarién, T42-363586. Mon-Sat 0900-1600, CUC\$3, or CUC\$9 with return steam train trip to Remedios.

This redundant sugar mill has been converted into an interesting museum dedicated to the history of the sugar industry in Cuba, with an exhibition area made up of all the different installations of a sugar mill, its tools, machinery and boiling rooms. There are 38 working steam engines (the largest collection of steam locomotives in Latin America) and a video room, and you can even clamber up on to some of the machinery. You can travel by steam train back to Remedios, stopping at the **Finca la Cabaña** for a farm visit with a typical *criollo* lunch, but call early to find out what time the steam train leaves, as its operation depends on visitor numbers.

Listings Remedios and around

Where to stay

Hotels

\$\$\$-\$\$ Hotel E Barcelona
José A Peña 67 entre La Pastora y Antonio Maceo, T42-395144, www.hotelescubanacan.cu.
Sister hotel to **Mascotte**, opened end 2012, renovated colonial house just off the square with high ceilings, arches and balconies. 24 rooms on 3 floors (no lift) around central courtyard including one for the disabled, good a/c, showers and minibar. Some rooms are a bit dark. Restaurant and bar quite good. Pleasant staff.

\$\$\$-\$\$ Hotel E Mascotte
Máximo Gómez 114, T42-395144, www.hotelescubanacan.cu.
Recently restored to former glory, 10 lovely rooms in colonial mansion, those in front are the largest and overlook the square, those at the back look over old tiled roofs, bar, restaurant, charming inner patio used

for occasional entertainment. Friendly staff, multilingual receptionist.

$$$-$$ Hotel E Camino del Príncipe
Camilo Cienfuegos 9 entre Montalván y Alejandro del Río, www.hotelescubanacan.cu.
New in 2015, formerly the home of a very rich family, the mansion was restored and converted to a hotel for the 500th anniversary celebrations. Overlooking the plaza, 25 beautiful colonial rooms.

Casas particulares

$ Hostal Buen Viaje
Andrés del Río 20 entre Enrique Malaret y Máximo Gómez, Remedios, T42-396560, hostal.buenviaje@gmail.com.
Lester and Naty run this traditional colonial house with loving care and attention and are full of advice for excursions to the cays, beaches or waterfalls. Pretty patio garden with fountain for relaxing in, good mattresses and a/c, excellent food, suitable for families as well as couples. Secure parking round the corner for a small fee. Lester is renovating a large colonial house nearby which will have 5 rooms to rent when finished.

$ Hostal Las Chinitas
Independencia 21 entre Brigadier González y Maceo, Remedios, T42-395784/395316, perezandro@yahoo.ca.
Greisy Fong Gómez offers rooms in a colonial house, with double and single beds, new bathroom and high ceilings, windows on to street, or opening on to the dining room and the patio. Next door, her parents Deisy Gómez Montenegro and Gregorio Fong Seuc have another room on the street with small but adequate bathroom in the corner. The family is friendly and keen to please and their food is a delight, with seasonings not normally common in Cuba. Don't miss the Chinese chicken. Car parking.

$ La Casona Cueto
Alejandro del Río 72 entre Enrique Malaré y Máximo Gómez, Remedios, T42-395350, luisenrique@capiro.vcl.sld.cu.

Spectacular colonial house from the 18th century with its original façade, floors and roof, beautiful interior windows and wooden spiral staircase leading from the vast living room with piano and antiques to wood-panelled room upstairs, as well as medallions symbolizing the Soles y Rayos de Bolívar conspiracy. Jenny Cueto (Kaky) has 2 other large rooms with 2 beds in each and modern bathrooms off the dining room, interior patio with fountain as well as roof terrace, dogs, doves and turtles, safe car parking.

$ Hostal El Chalet
Brigadier González 29 entre Independencia y José A Peña, in front of the old post office, T42-396538, jorgechalet@nauta.cu.
Jorge Rivero Méndez and his family run this *casa* in a smart house dating from 1950. The rooms are upstairs on the roof, with double and single beds, one is a suite with sitting room, all in very good condition, fabulous views over the town and the tiled roofs around, terraces up and downstairs, lots of space for sitting and relaxing, laundry service, parking for 2 cars with a guard at night, good meals, including for vegetarians.

$ Hostal Villa Colonial Frank y Arelys
Antonio Maceo 43 entre Av Gen Carrillo y Fe del Valle, T42-396274, villacolonial.frank@nauta.cu.
Frank and Arelys are very friendly hosts at this wonderful colonial home with a front room stuffed with antique furniture and beautiful tiles. 3 bedrooms each with 2 double beds, a small patio where *mojitos* are made for guests and a dining room where delicious dinners are served.

Where to eat

Restaurants

$$$-$$ Taberna los Siete Juanes
Máximo Gómez esq Parque Central. Mon-Fri 1000-2300, Sat, Sun 1000-2400.
Another renovated building, opened in 2015 as a wine and tapas bar, with tables outside overlooking the plaza and the church, all

very pleasant. There is an extensive cellar for storing wine.

$$ El Pirámide
Andrés del Río 9A, Remedios.
Excellent restaurant run by Marelys, who used to work in one of the all-inclusives on the cays. Dining room upstairs, beautiful and very professionally run. Large portions of very good food, a full meal with wine or beer will be about CUC$15 per person.

$$-$ Curujey
1 km from the steam and sugar museum, also known as La Finca de la Cabaña, T42-395764. Daily 1000-1700.
Tour parties are taken here. Good Cuban food. Rural location, farm surroundings, large grove of trees, turkeys, chickens and you can watch them milking the cows.

$$-$ El Louvre
Overlooking the square, Remedios, T42-395639. Daily 0700-0200.
Said to be the oldest restaurant in Cuba, colonial building with wooden bar and counter, tables inside and out, snacks and drinks, terrible coffee, nice place to stop for lunch or a drink and watch the school children on their break. Popular bar in the evenings too.

$ Cafetería Doña Lala
Máximo Gómez esq Alejandro del Río. Daily 1000-2200.
Another of Cubanacán's new projects, selling breads, ice cream, pastries and sweets, a good place to come for dessert at night, a/c, quiet.

Entertainment

Live music
Centro Cultural Las Leyendas (Artex), *on the square next to Louvre bar.* Tables outside or inside, walk through the building to the stage at the back, live music at night, also recorded music, depending on the event.

El Golazo, *Maceo esq Independencia (formerly El Guije). Tue-Sun 1400-0200.* During the day this is a café and restaurant serving pasta, pizza and drinks. There is a sports bar showing live international football or baseball, a/c and comfortable. Then at night it opens as a disco, the best and most modern in the whole province, a/c.

Festivals

Dec Apart from its architecture, Remedios' other claim to fame is its **carnivals** (*parrandas*), held on **16-24 Dec**; the best night being **24 Dec**, when celebrations go on until dawn. This is a once-in-a-lifetime experience and well worth attending. Personal safety is not an issue (apart from the thousands of home-made fireworks), but do watch out for your personal belongings, particularly when the fireworks are let off: the resulting crush and excitement is the perfect setting for wallets and cameras to go missing. Either make sure you hang on to your bags, or get out of the crowd before the mayhem starts.

Shopping

Casa de Ron y el Habano Los Tres Reyes, *Máximo Gómez esq Pi y Margall, annexed to the Hotel Mascotte, T42-396447, daily 0900-1900.* Now completely renovated, the building was for many years the town's main pharmacy. This is the only *casa* in the province of Villa Clara, showcasing a variety of rums and cigars. You can see cigars being rolled and try the rum.

Transport

Bus
The bus station is at the entrance to the town on the right coming from Santa Clara, T42-395185. **Taxis** and **bicitaxis** wait outside.

Car hire
Havanautos/Cubacar, T42-395555.

Fidel Castro used to fish here off the Villa Clara coast when he was younger, and for many years he kept the cays undeveloped. A 48-km stone causeway from Caibarién to the three cays off the north coast was completed in 1996, having taken seven years to build, and now there is extensive development offshore, with many all-inclusive resorts. If you want a few days of peace and quiet on unspoilt beaches, then the cays are perfect, but they are remote and you need to be aware that there are no facilities outside the hotels, which sell day passes (Villa Las Brujas has the cheapest). You can use the public beaches – Las Salinas, Perlas Blancas and Playa Las Gaviotas – but you'll need to take your own food and drink.

Caibarién
Gateway to the cays, Caibarién is a fishing town and the main port for the province. It has been bypassed by tourism, which is focused on the cays, and so the visitor can wander around unmolested by hustlers. Founded in 1832, the small town has distinctive 19th-century architecture, but has become rundown and scruffy in parts. Many buildings have fine wooden porches with a French influence, and some are quite grand, but there is an atmosphere of the Wild West, emphasized by the number of horses in the streets. The pavements, unusual in Cuba, are made of large stone slabs set in concrete.

The Malecón is lined with numerous warehouses used for storing sugar cane in the 19th century, most of which are now in ruins. Recent investment in the seaside boulevard has led to the construction of a new Malecón to the fishing zone in the east with a new road, coconut palms and several bars and cafés where you can sit and admire the view. There is a neglected (or unspoilt) beach on the edge of town.

At the centre of the town is a large square, with an 1850 church and the impressive neoclassical Lyceo (1926), with the **Museo Municipal de Caibarién María Escobar Laredo** ① *Av 9 entre 8 y 10, Parque Central, T42-352189, Tue-Sat 1000-1800, Sun 0900-1300, free*, is on the second floor. There are permanent and temporary exhibitions as well as the furniture belonging to María

Essential Caibarién and the cays

Getting around

It is 116 km from **Abel Santamaría airport** (see page 195) to Cayo Santa María, the furthest resort. On the cays, an airstrip receives short-hop flights and air taxis. If you are travelling by car, a good road leads northeast from Santa Clara through Camajuaní to Remedios and Caibarién, from where a stone causeway has been built to link several cays. The causeway is a toll road (see page 215). There are no buses to the cays, so hiring a car or a taxi is your only option if you're not on a package deal.

When to go

High season is December to April. The sea is calmest from June to August. It can be rough from September onwards if there is a cold front off the eastern seaboard of the USA, and the waves can be positively huge in January and February.

Fact...
The town's full name is Cayo Barién, but it is always referred to as Caibarién.

There is a legend that says recently transported slaves who escaped from their masters in Santa Clara fled northwards, believing that they were still in Africa and had merely been shipped along the coast of their continent. Upon reaching Caibarién, they despaired to find that they could not go any further, and reluctantly settled there. Certainly, much of the local culture is influenced by slavery and African traditions, including the *parrandas* festivities on Christmas Eve. This is a non-religious celebration, inaugurated in 1892 with the banging of a drum by a 110-year-old former slave called Juan de Jimagua. The public followed him around the town, accompanied by many other conga players, creating a tradition that is still maintained today. After the procession members of each *barrio* build an artistic creation on the plaza, based on local legends and folklore; they are ostensibly judged, but this is usually just a friendly, heated discussion of which is the best creation.

Escobar Laredo, who was one of the benefactors of the city. The gazebo in the centre of the plaza was built in 1915; it's the largest in Cuba and famous for its excellent acoustics. There are concerts by local bands on Thursday and Sunday nights. Also on the plaza is a store, which was formerly a bespoke tailor's called **London City**.

Cayo Conuco
The nearest cay to Caibarién is Cayo Conuco, accessible by ordinary road (not the causeway) just offshore. This is a biosphere reserve with lots of flora and fauna, and a campsite. Take insect repellent. There are the ruins of a former cholera hospital, built by the slaves in the 19th century to quarantine victims of the disease.

Causeway to the cays
To reach the cays from Santa Clara or Remedios, turn right at the statue of a huge crab on the edge of Caibarién, and then right again at the next junction, avoiding the town centre. Carry on as far as a bridge: go under it and then turn right in order to go over it, effectively turning left. (There are signs.) There is a toll booth (*peaje*) at the start of the causeway (CUC$2 per vehicle, one way), and passports are checked. The road takes you on an impressive drive across mangroves and open water.

Cayo Las Brujas
At bridge 36 is the air strip on Cayo Las Brujas, the first of the cays to be developed for tourism. There is a small hotel, **Villa Las Brujas**, on the cay, which has pleasant restaurant and bar, open to non-guests, and a wooden observation deck up on the rocks overlooking the pretty beach and the sea. You can buy a day pass to visit the hotel and make use of their facilities; this a recommended way to experience the cays. Watch out for biting insects at dawn and dusk. **Scuba-diving** trips can be arranged for around CUC$40 at the adjacent **Marina Gaviota Las Brujas**, and there are other trips which leave from the jetty, including to the 132-m *SS San Pasqual*, a moored American cargo ship made of concrete and launched in 1920, which has been here since it ran aground in 1933. It was once used as a molasses warehouse; barrels of molasses (*miel*) in the hold are still used as ballast. During World War II it was fitted out with guns and cannon to keep a look out for German

U boats. It was also a prison ship after the Revolution but then converted to a 10-room hotel, now closed.

Las Salinas beach is undeveloped, although a new hotel is being built at one end. (Take the turning north of the airport, which is signed, then fork left before reaching the new hotel.) There is parking here and shade, but the thatched palapas look tired, and the area appears neglected rather than unspoilt, with a ruined jetty and the rusting hulk of a boat on the shore. Look out for flamingos in the lagoon behind the beach.

Cayo Santa María

The last and largest cay, Cayo Santa María, is now almost wall-to-wall all-inclusive hotels managed by international hotel chains. They are low rise but not beautiful. There is little to do outside the hotel enclaves, but you can get food and drink at El Pueblo, about half way along the road, which is a 'replica' colonial plaza with souvenir shops and a café; it's about the only place to eat outside the hotels. The beach here is long and sandy, but the sea does get rough at certain times of the year.

For an undeveloped beach, drive to ★ Playa Las Gaviotas at the very end of the road; the last section is a dirt track and then there's a parking area. The beach is in a protected area, and you have to pay the guards CUC$4 to walk the 750-m path through dry tropical forest to the sea. It is an interesting walk, with lizards of all colours and sizes and plenty of birds including hummingbirds flitting about. Once over the dunes you find a lovely, open, unspoilt beach at the end of the hotel strip, with no shade, no bars and no bathrooms. The sea is shallow, particularly at low tide when the water gets very warm over the palest, finest sand ever. The sea is a range of colours at different depths, becoming a rich blue at its deepest. The beach is not empty, as hotel guests walk along it too, but it is peaceful.

Listings Caibarién and the cays

Where to stay

There are many all-inclusive hotels on the cays, operated by international management companies such as Barceló, Meliá or Iberostar, usually sold as package holidays from abroad, although short stays and day passes are available.

Caibarién
Casas particulares

Many families offer rooms in their houses, although without the charm and style of Remedios; touts will find you when you get off the bus or stop you as you drive into town.

$ Casa Hostal El Carretero
Calle 18 2112 entre 21 y 23, T42-363675.
Fernando and Mayra are friendly and helpful and speak English and Italian. They offer 1 double and 1 twin room with a/c, fridge,

TV, terrace and patio, laundry service, parking on the premises and good, plentiful food.

$ Hostal Calle 12
Calle 12 1116 entre 11 y 13,T42-364274, caibarienhostalcalle12@gmail.com.
Juanito and Rosa (La China) rent 3 double a/c rooms on the ground floor with fan, fridge, TV. There is a patio with flowers and chairs to relax in. Laundry service offered, parking available, English spoken. A very friendly and helpful household maintaining a good standard of accommodation.

$ Hostal La Nena
Av 13 1415 entre 14 y 16, T42-364463, hostallanena@gmail.com.
English-speaking owner, Noemi, lives downstairs (with Roberto) and rents out 2 rooms upstairs with good beds, a/c, fan, fridge, TV, a shared sitting and dining area with balcony as well as a roof terrace giving

a good view of the town. Noemi has been in hospitality for a long time and is very helpful and friendly. Good food, plenty of variety. Central, with safe parking on the street.

Cayo Las Brujas

$$$ Villa Las Brujas
T42-350199, www.gaviota-grupo.com.
One of the nicest small beach hotels in the country and the only one on the cays which isn't all-inclusive. A complex of 24 red-roofed, wooden *cabañas* connected by a wooden boardwalk above rocks and between mature bushes. All have balconies and verandas on stilts, but go for one of the 19 sea view rooms. Don't expect luxury and don't expect everything to work. Come for the location, which is quiet and peaceful, with access to a good sweep of curving beach, soft, pale sand and lovely water. Restaurant with open air or a/c seating and view down to the beach. Pity about the food, but the staff are friendly, unlike the unhelpful reception staff. Marina close by for watersports.

Festivals

Caibarién
Aug Carnival on the last weekend.
Oct Caibarién has an annual **fiesta**, dating from 1999, celebrating the founding of the town on 26 Oct.
Dec Like Remedios, Caibarién also has *parrandas* on Christmas Eve (see box, page 215).

What to do

Cayo Las Brujas
Marina Gaviota Las Brujas, *T42-350013, www.gaviota-grupo.com/en/marina/marina-gaviota-las-brujas. Daily 0900-1700.* For scuba-diving, fishing and sailing excursions. Avoid the tours to the dolphinarium.

Cayo Santa María
Heart of Cuba Tours, *T5825 4399, http://heartofcubatours.wix.com/heart-of-cuba-tours.* Yasmany specializes in tailor-made tours from the hotels in Cayo Santa María, visiting Santa Clara, Remedios, Caibairién or anywhere you want to go, including his own house! He covers all the regular sights but also several that are off-the-beaten track doing everything at your own pace. Yasmany speaks good English and some Italian and French. Yordany, the driver, has an old Chevrolet with the advantage of a/c, seating 4, but a larger van is available for groups of 6. You pay by the car load rather than per person, making it cheaper than the hotel tours for 2 or more people.

Transport

Air
Cayo Las Brujas airport, T42-350009, receives **Aerocaribbean** charter flights. International flights use the airport north of Santa Clara (see page 195).

Bus
The Caibarién bus terminal, Calle 1 entre 6 y 8, has regular buses to **Remedios** and **Santa Clara**, if you can get on. *Carros particulares* (private cars) can be found for trips to other destinations. Fares are all in pesos, get a numbered ticket when you arrive at the terminal, seats are sold only when the bus arrives. If going to **Santa Clara**, many private cars will take you from outside the terminal for about CUC$2-3 per person. There is no public transport out to the cays, so you have to arrange car hire or taxi.

Sancti Spíritus
Province

The architectural riches of Sancti Spíritus and, most
notably, Trinidad were built on the profits of sugar
production in the province. Sugar is no longer grown in
commercial quantities here, but many ruined sugar mills,
plantation houses and slave quarters from the 18th and
19th centuries can still be seen in the San Luis valley (or
Valle de los Ingenios) between the two towns. Above the
valley rise the Montañas de Guamuhaya, whose rich flora
and fauna can be explored in the Parque Natural Topes
de Collantes. The mangroves and flatlands of the north
coast are pockmarked with caves, but there are beaches
and watersports on the south coast, easily accessible from
Trinidad. In the east of the province is Embalse Zaza, the
largest man-made reservoir in the country, through which
flows the 145-km Río Zaza.

steeped in history but off the beaten track

Sancti Spíritus, the provincial capital (population 133,000), is one of Cuba's seven original Spanish towns. It has a wealth of buildings from the colonial period, although many of them have been altered and there has been lots of new building. Tourism is now being developed around the town. Hotels have been renovated and remodelled and coach parties come for day trips. So far, foreign tourists get little unwanted attention.

Parque Serafín Sánchez and around
Parque Serafín Sánchez is the centre of activity in the city where all major roads converge. Around the square are the cinema, library, banks, Havanatur/Havanautos and the beautiful baby-blue **Hostal del Rijo**, renovated to its colonial splendour.

The **Museo Provincial de Sancti Spíritus** ① *Máximo Gómez 3, T41-327435, Tue-Thu 0900-1700, Fri 1400-2200, Sat 0900-1200, 2000-2200, Sun 0800-1200, CUC$1,* has the usual exhibits on local history and culture in a building that dates from 1740. There are collections of Amerindian artefacts, items from the colonization and African slavery, the Wars of Independence and the Revolution plus coins and decorative arts.

Just north of the square **El Lyceo/Sociedad Cultural de Negros** on Calle Luz Caballero was the first school for blacks, opened in 1859. It is now a society for veterans of the Revolution.

The **Galería de Arte Universal Oscar Fernández Morera** is in the house of the local artist Oscar Fernández Morera on Céspedes 126 Sur, whose works are on permanent display. There are exhibits of originals as well as reproductions.

Essential Sancti Spíritus town

Finding your feet

There are no scheduled flights to the airport north of town. Mainline trains from Havana to Santiago stop at the train station 15 km away at Guayos, where you will be met by taxis. The town can be reached by road from Cienfuegos, Santa Clara (80 km northwest) or Trinidad (70 km southwest). Long-distance buses come to Sancti Spíritus from both ends of the island. See Transport, page 224.

Tip...
Trinidad can be visited as a day trip by bus or car, but it is better to stay in Trinidad and visit Sancti Spíritus as a day trip.

Getting around

The bus station is 2 km from the centre, so if you are not up to walking with your luggage you will have to get a taxi. The old city can be toured on foot without much difficulty; there are also horse-drawn *coches* and bicitaxis for short journeys. For excursions by taxi ask at a *casa particular*, or find one outside the bus station and negotiate a price.

Tip...
Many of the excursions included in the Trinidad section, page 236, can also be done from here, particularly the Valley of the Sugar Mills (see page 242), which lies between the two towns.

South of Parque Serafín Sánchez

Iglesia Parroquial Mayor del Espíritu Santo ① *Plaza Honorato, Jesús Menéndez 1 entre Honorato y Agramonte, Tue-Sat 0900-1100, 1400-1700.* The church dates from 1522 when it was a wooden construction. The present Romanesque and Baroque stone building replaced the earlier one but is nevertheless acknowledged as the second oldest church in Cuba because it still stands on its original foundations. It was finished in 1680, having taken 60 years to build, and is now a National Monument. Fray Bartolomé de las Casas gave a famous sermon here, marking the start of his campaign to help the indigenous

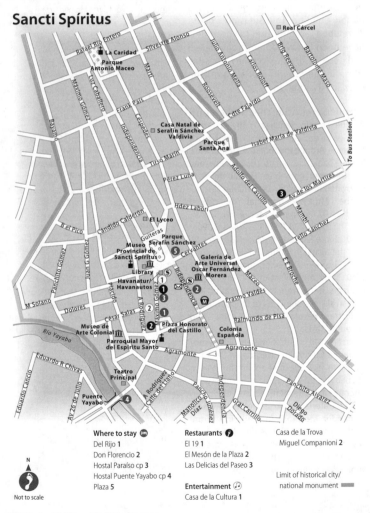

Sancti Spíritus

Where to stay	Restaurants	Casa de la Trova
Del Rijo **1**	El 19 **1**	Miguel Companioni **2**
Don Florencio **2**	El Mesón de la Plaza **2**	
Hostal Paraíso cp **3**	Las Delicias del Paseo **3**	
Hostal Puente Yayabo cp **4**		
Plaza **5**	Entertainment	Limit of historical city/
	Casa de la Cultura **1**	national monument ▬▬

N

Not to scale

The town was founded by Diego Velázquez in 1514. Originally situated on the Río Tuinicúe, it was moved to its present location on the Río Yayabo in 1522. The town was sacked by pirates in 1665, but during the following decades its geographical position made it an increasingly important market town for the burgeoning sugar and livestock trade. There are many sites around town commemorating those who fought in the 19th-century Wars of Independence, the local hero being Major General Serafín Sánchez Valdivia. At the end of the Cuban Revolution in 1958, rebel forces were led into the city under the command of Armando Acosta Cordero. Sancti Spíritus was liberated on 23 December, and Fidel Castro arrived on 6 January 1959 and spoke from the balcony of the library. With the administrative changes in 1976, Sancti Spíritus became the capital of the new province of Sancti Spíritus.

people. He was a Dominican missionary and polemist, who devoted his life to the cause of Amerindian liberty. He spent many years on Hispaniola (now the Dominican Republic and Haiti), where he wrote the *Brief Relation of the Destruction of the Indies*, a horrifying catalogue of atrocities that took place at the time. He was appointed Protector of the Indians in 1516 and spent the next 10 years trying to prove that free Amerindians could be converted to Christianity without use of force or enslavement. However, the experiment came too late for the Amerindians of the Greater Antilles, as the Spanish could not do without slave labour, and the Amerindians would not work without coercion.

East of the church, a shopping mall has been established in the renovated **Colonia Española**, on Independencia Sur esquina Agramonte. It is a fine building, constructed in 1926 in the eclectic style with neoclassical ceilings and CE on the windows. It was once a cultural centre for high society.

Museo de Arte Colonial ① *C Plácido 74 Sur entre Guairo y Pancho Jiménez, T41-325455, Tue-Sat 0900-1700, Sun 0800-1200, CUC$2, photos CUC$1.* The museum is housed in the former palace of the Iznaga family, who made their fortune out of sugar and were hugely influential with links to the military and bureaucracy of the province. Built in 1744, the house has 100 doors. It contains the family's collections of porcelain from France, England, Germany and Spain, oil paintings and decorative fans, and in the music room there is one of the oldest pianos in Cuba.

Puente Yayabo and around The **Puente Yayabo** is considered a particular feature of Sancti Spíritus and is the only bridge of its type left on the island. It was built in 1831 with five arches made of limestone, sand and bricks, which, according to legend were mixed with donkey milk. It is now also a National Monument. The river itself has given its name to the *guayaba*, or guava, which grows along its banks, and also to the *guayabera*, a loose man's shirt without a tail, worn outside the trousers and without a tie.

The former **Teatro Principal** next to the bridge was built in 1839 and was the scene of all the major cultural, social and political events of the city. **Calle Llano** is a twisty street with cobblestones right to the edge of the river.

North of Parque Serafín Sánchez

Walk up Céspedes and you will pass the **Casa Natal de Serafín Sánchez Valdivia** ⓘ *Céspedes 112 Norte, entre Sobral y San Cristóbal, T41-327791*. Sánchez Valdivia was born here on 2 July 1846. He went on to fight in three wars in the 19th century, collaborating with José Martí and reaching the rank of Major General before being killed in battle in 1896.

To the northwest, **Parque Antonio Maceo**, on which stands the **Iglesia de la Caridad**, was the place where the Communist Party of Sancti Spíritus was founded on 7 December 1930.

If you head east along Frank País out of the historic centre, you will come to the old prison, **Real Cárcel (Royal Prison)** ⓘ *Bartolomé Masó entre Anglona y Mirto*. The building has been preserved as a site of historical interest. It was built in the mid-19th century and used initially to incarcerate runaway slaves and then to imprison hundreds of Cubans who fought for independence.

Jardín Botánico de Sancti Spíritus

1.5 km from the town centre, CUC$2 including guided tour, bus 0900, 1200, 1500 in the summer holidays from the Casa de la Cultura on Parque Serafín Sánchez.

Covering an area of 97 ha, 7 ha of which are protected natural forest, this has the appearance of a park, rather than a garden. It contains 4000 different plants, including many endemics, among them medicinal as well as ornamental plants.

Listings Sancti Spíritus *map p220*

Tourist information

There is no tourist office in Sancti Spíritus, but the office of **Havanatur** on the square can provide information.

Where to stay

Hotels

$$$ Del Rijo
Honorato del Castillo 12 esq Máximo Gómez, T41-328588, www.islazul.cu.
Built in 1818-1827 overlooking Plaza Honorato, the building has been converted from the ruins of the old family home of a doctor, Rudesindo García Rijo. It is a typical example of colonial architecture with stained-glass windows, arches downstairs for shade and balconies with wrought-iron fretwork upstairs, all painted in a variety of beautiful blues. An inner courtyard has a fountain, plants and dining tables outside, overlooked by the landing giving access to the 16 spacious (some bigger than others) and well-furnished rooms with wooden

shutters at the windows (difficult to open), high ceilings, fridge, restaurant, *cafetería*, snack bar, internet, laundry.

$$$ Don Florencio
Independencia 63 Sur, T41-328588, www.islazul.cu.
Opened in 2014, a striking blue and white colonial mansion with 11 rooms on 2 floors around a central courtyard where, bizarrely, there are 2 small jacuzzis and some sun beds. Rooms are attractive with colonial-style furniture and good bathrooms, all of a good standard. Some upstairs rooms have external windows and shared balconies overlooking the Bulevar, but most open out onto the courtyard. There is a very good bar for cocktails but as yet no restaurant, so you take meals at Hotel Plaza down the road.

$$ Plaza
Independencia 1, Plaza Serafín Sánchez, T41-327102, www.islazul.cu.
25 rooms in an old colonial building, first built in 1854 but destroyed by fire in 1973

and subsequently restored and opened to the public in 1994. High-ceilinged rooms, refurbished in colonial style, some with balconies overlooking the plaza which can be noisy. Bar, restaurant: food varies in quality but breakfast is usually good.

Casas particulares

$$ Hostal Las Américas
Ctra Central (Bartolomé Masó) 157 Sur entre Cuba y Cuartel, T41-322984, hostallas americas@yahoo.es.
10-min walk to the centre. Modern house with spacious rooms, stocked fridge, safe box in wardrobe, hair dryer, garage for 2 cars. Large, lush garden with fruit trees and ornamental plants and several seating areas where you can have a Las Américas mojito. Snacks, breakfast, lunch and dinner are available, any special requirements or tastes catered for, typical dishes of the region with lots of fruit and veg, house speciality *cordero espirituano*. English and Italian spoken.

$ Hostal Paraíso
Máximo Gómez 11 Sur entre Cervantes (Parque Central) y Honorato (Parque Honorato), T41-334658, 5271 1257 (mob), hectorluisparaiso64@gmail.com.
A very central *casa* with professional and friendly hosts offering 2 a/c rooms with large bathrooms and great showers. Meals are good and breakfast is ample, served in the patio garden. Parking is in the street in front of the house.

$ Hostal Puente Yayabo
C Jesús Menéndez 109 entre Padre Quintero y Río Yayabo, T01-5240 8545, puente.yayabo@yahoo.es.
This hostal officially dates from 1840 but could be earlier. It is right beside the old bridge, and the rooms have lovely views over the river. Elena and Víctor are most hospitable and offer unusual touches such as fishing rods, free tea, coffee, mojitos. Their son speaks English and French. Double and single beds, roof terrace with tables and benches under cover, garage.

$ Hostal Santa Elena
Santa Elena 42 (C del Gas) entre Ctra Central y Onza, T41-329218.
Under new management in 2015, this remains a great place to stay, clean and immaculate. Thania is a cheerful and enthusiastic host, anticipating the needs of her guests. The rooms are spacious and well-equipped with good bathrooms, good lighting, fridge, a/c. Food is simple but well cooked *comida criolla*. There are plenty of places to sit and relax, with a terrace upstairs. 20 mins walk into town centre or take a bicitaxi.

Where to eat

$$$-$$ El Mesón de la Plaza
Máximo Gómez 34, on Plaza Honorato del Castillo, T41-328546. Daily 1000-2200 if there are customers.
In a building that was the 1st post office, furnished with heavy wooden tables and chairs. *Criollo* food, probably the best restaurant in town, crowded at lunchtime, popular with tourists, live music. Good seafood, or try *garbanzo* soup or *ropa vieja*.

$$-$ El 19
Máximo Gómez 9, T41-331919.
Old colonial house with high ceilings, pleasant *paladar* charging in CUC$ or CUP$. *Comida criolla*: the usual shrimp, pork, chicken with sides of rice, plantain and salad, with some vegetarian options. Nothing out of the ordinary but you'll get a decent meal.

$$-$ Las Delicias del Paseo
Av de los Mártires 255, T4132 1325 (mob).
2 menus, if you get the English one you pay in CUC$; the menu for Cubans is in CUP$ and much cheaper. There's a fast food section too. Good pasta and pizza. Very popular at weekends with local families.

Entertainment

Most nightlife happens around the Parque where the **Casa de la Cultura** holds ad hoc art exhibitions, poetry readings and live music. There is usually rock music on Sat night and irregular performances of more traditional *boleros* on other nights.

Live music
Casa de la Música, *Padre Quintero 32, T41-324963*. Open-air seating and a stage, with terrace overlooking Río Yayabo, CUC$1, shows Fri and Sat nights.
Casa de la Trova Miguel Companioni, *Máximo Gómez Sur 26*. Walk through a grand house past photos of all the local musicians, past and present, to the patio where there is a bar and stage and a mango tree in the centre. Live music. Artex shop.

Shopping

There are **CUC$ stores** on Independencia Sur (Boulevar) and a **peso market** on Erasmo Valdés, good for meat, fruit and vegetables. **Fondo de Bienes Culturales**, *Independencia Sur 55*. Art and handicrafts.

What to do

Tour operators
On the square, at Cervantes 1, are **Havanatur** (T41-328308), for flights and tours; **Havanautos** (T41-328403), for car hire, and **Islazul** (T41-326390), for hotels and tours. **Ecotur** (T41-357419, www.ecotur.tur.cu), offers countryside tours, birdwatching, hiking, horse riding, fishing or jeep safaris.

Transport

Bus
The bus station is 2 km east of town on the Ctra Central. Walk out of town along Cervantes; follow signs to Ciego de Avila along Ctra Central for about 5 blocks past the zoo and the bus station is on your right. There are daily **Viazul** buses on the **Havana–Santiago** or **Trinidad–Santiago** routes, but you may not get a seat.

Taxi
Bicitaxis will get you around town if you don't want a taxi. For longer journeys a taxi will take you to **Trinidad** for CUC$25 or less, and to **Santa Clara** for around CUC$30, depending on the quality of your Spanish. Find a driver outside the bus station.

Train
The station is at Guayos, 15 km north. Taxi into town CUC$10. Touts offer transport and accommodation. Sancti Spíritus is on the mainline service between **Havana** and **Santiago** and there are additional daily trains to **Camagüey**, 2-3 hrs, in theory.

For those with their own transport, you can tour the north coast of the province along the Circuíto Norte to Morón, although this is easier from Remedios and Caibarién (see pages 209 and 214). Parque Nacional Caguanes, a UNESCO Biosphere Reserve on the north coast, contains mangroves and a cave system. The park is just 25 m above sea level at its highest point and is notable for its caves, pictographs and underground treasures rather than its scenic beauty. Lago Martí in the park has freshwater sponges.

Rancho Querete
Near Yaguajay, T41-554044, Tue-Sun 0900-1600, CUC$10 all day including lunch, other packages available.

The ranch is popular with Cuban families in summer as well as jeep tour parties from the cays. There are two rivers on the property, one of which comes up in a cave and forms a waterfall where you can bathe. Right by the reception and café is a deep pool of clear water where you can usually swim July to March. However, in the dry season there is no water at all and even in the wet season it is not guaranteed, so check beforehand. There is also hiking along paths to the Cueva de Valdés and Solapas de Genaro, horse riding and good birdwatching. Wardens have put up nest boxes for the trogon to distract them from using woodpecker holes. Take insect repellent.

Mayajigua and around
This is the main town in this area, founded in 1820, and a reasonable place to take a break from driving. A few kilometres east of Mayajigua along the Circuíto Norte is **San José del Lago**, a fairly non-descript place notable only for the country hotel **Villa San José del Lago**. Its centrepiece is a permanent small lake fed by natural springs. The lake is surrounded by pleasant lawns and palm trees, and a few flamingos pose for photos in the water. The hotel has a swimming pool, thermal pool, bar and restaurant.

North of Mayajigua, on a road which stops just short of the coast, is **Punta de Judas**. Here is the Cueva Grande de Judas, one of several caves in the **Parque Nacional Caguanes**; others are Cueva del Pirata, Cueva Humboldt and Cueva de los Chivos. There are archaeological sites in the caves and pictographs.

Listings Northern Sancti Spíritus

Where to eat

$$-$ Papo's Paladar
Calle D esq Martí, Altos, Zaza del Medio, T41-785 7360.
About 15 km northeast of Sancti Spíritus heading for the autopista, on the main plaza by the old railway station. The restaurant is upstairs. Good for a lunch stop if you're in the area but also open in the evenings with live music. Cuban and Italian food, large portions, plenty of rice, plantain and other sides. Popular for local celebrations, when it can get lively.

Trinidad (population 60,000), 133 km south of Santa Clara, is a perfect relic of the early days of the Spanish colony, with beautifully preserved streets and buildings and hardly a trace of the 21st century anywhere. The whole city, with its fine palaces, cobbled streets and tiled roofs, is a national monument. Architecturally, Trinidad is perhaps Cuba's most important town: its colonial buildings are suspended in a time warp and since 1988 it has been a UNESCO World Heritage Site.

Many of the families who live in the old houses rent out rooms, making this one of the best places to lodge privately. There is good hiking among picturesque waterfalls and abundant wildlife in the forests up in the mountains overlooking Trinidad. Playa Ancón, nearby, is a reasonable beach to relax on and a good base for boat trips and watersports.

Essential Trinidad

Finding your feet

There is a small **airport** that only receives charter flights. Trinidad is not connected to the national rail network. The most convenient independent way of getting to Trinidad is by **Viazul** bus (see timetable, page 462), with services from Havana via Cienfuegos, or from Varadero via Santa Clara and Sancti Spíritus. Most visitors to Trinidad arrive on tour buses from Havana and Varadero and do a day trip, although it is possible to extend your stay and rejoin the bus a day or two later. Transport (other than **Viazul**) to the east of Cuba is difficult from Trinidad as it is not on the Carretera Central, so it's best to go to Sancti Spíritus and take the bus or train from there; the drive through the Valley of the Sugar Mills between the two towns is very attractive. See also Transport, page 237.

Getting around

The old city should be toured on foot. The cobbled streets make wheeled transport rather uncomfortable, and all the main sights are within easy walking distance of each other. For local excursions many people hire a driver and car, although some prefer to cycle to the beach (fine on the way there, harder work on the way back), and organized tours are recommended for hiking in the mountains to avoid getting lost and to make sure you go to all the right places.

Maps of Trinidad can be unbelievably difficult to follow because of the use of old and new street names. Locals of course switch from one to the other. The old ones are printed in capital letters and the new ones in lower-case letters.

When to go

September is good for religious processions around the eighth of the month, Cuba's patron saint's day, but at any time of year you can find music, dance and other festivities. Semana Santa (Easter) is another good time for processions, with a huge event on Good Friday; Semana de la Cultura is the second week of January and Carnival is in June. Expect heavy rain between September and November, when the cobbled streets become awash with water, but in the mountains it can rain any day, turning paths into muddy slopes.

BACKGROUND
Trinidad

Trinidad was founded in 1514 by Diego Velázquez as a base for expeditions into the 'New World'; Hernan Cortés set out from here for Mexico in 1518. A thriving economy soon grew up around the settlement, originally based on livestock, exporting leather, meat and horses. This prize inevitably attracted the attention of adventurers and there was a particularly severe period of attacks between 1660 and 1688. Mansfield from Port Royal in Jamaica and Legrand from Tortuga, off Hispaniola, looted and set fire to the town, destroying the original archives of the church and the city hall. Unlike other populations who moved inland to escape pirate attacks, the inhabitants of Trinidad decided to stay and defend their wealth with their own fleet, inflicting several defeats on British and Dutch corsairs in the 17th and 18th centuries. After taking Havana in 1797, the British tried and failed to invade Trinidad and Sancti Spíritus, an event which is portrayed in the coats of arms of both cities.

By this time there were 56 sugar mills around Trinidad and 11,697 slaves had been imported to work in the sugar cane fields. Trade, art and science all expanded on the back of the sugar prosperity: Alexander von Humboldt visited and studied the fauna and flora around Trinidad; the first printing press was opened and the first newspaper began to circulate; schools of languages, music and dance were opened; a wide variety of artisans set up businesses, including gold and silversmithing; and in 1827 the Teatro Cándamo opened its doors. The well-off patricians built huge mansions for themselves (now museums) and sent their children to European universities. However, the Industrial Revolution and the increased production of sugar beet in Europe sounded the death knell for an economy based on slave labour. In the second half of the 19th century Trinidad went into decline. Construction ceased and the city remained frozen in time with its cobbled streets and red-tiled roofs. The town's five main squares and four churches all date from the 18th and 19th centuries.

Plaza Mayor
The Plaza Mayor is the centre of the town, an elegantly adorned square with white wrought-iron railings and ornate lamp posts, shaded by a few towering Royal palms. Some of the very few two-storey buildings can be found here, denoting the importance of the plaza, and all are painted in pretty pastel colours with red-tiled roofs.

Iglesia Parroquial de la Santísima Trinidad ① *Visit the Casa Parroquial at Fco J Zerquera 456, opposite the church, T41-993668, daily 1030-1300 for sightseeing and photos; Mass daily at 2000, Sun at 0900, during which no sightseeing is allowed.* On the east side of the plaza, the cathedral was built between 1817 and 1892. It is the largest church in Cuba and is renowned for its acoustics. Inside, the altars are made of precious woods, such as cedar, acacia, mahogany and grenadine, and were built in 1912-22 by a French priest, Amadeo Frieory, a Swiss Brother Lucas and two Cuban carpenters. On the left of the altar is a crucifix of the brown-skinned Christ of Veracruz, who is the patron of Trinidad. The church choir, called **Piedras Vivas**, composes and sings religious music and hymns with a Cuban rhythm, wonderful to hear on Sundays and holidays. Visitors who can play an instrument or sing are welcome to participate in rehearsals and then performances. Travelling

Trinidad

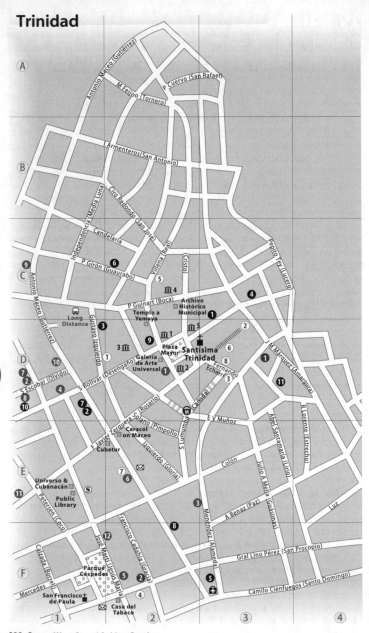

Antonio Maceo (Gutiérrez)
M Felipo (Tornero)
P Cuervo (San Rafael)

Armenteros (San Antonio)

Cro Redondo (San José)
Independencia (Media Luna)
Candelaria

P Girón (Guaurabo)
Villena (Real)
Cristo

Pepito Tey (Lucero)

Antonio Maceo (Gutiérrez)
Long Distance
P Guinart (Boca)
Templo a Yemayá
Archivo Histórico Municipal

Plaza Mayor
Santísima Trinidad
Galería de Arte Universal
Fernando Echerri

S Bolívar (Desengaño)
Gustavo Izquierdo

M Márquez (Amargura)
R Lorente (Estrecho)

E V Muñoz
Jununú (Cababa)

F Javier Zerquera Solano (Pimpollo)
Caracol on Maceo
Cubatur
Izquierdo (Gloria)
C (Rosario)

Colón

Abel Santamaría (Lirio)
Julio A Mella (Guásimas)

Universo & Cubanacán
Public Library
Petersen (Coco)

A Benaz (Paz)
Menéndez (Alameda)

Luz

Calzada Borrell
José Martí (Jesús María)
Francisco Cadahia (Gracia)

Gral Lino Pérez (San Procopio)

Parque Céspedes
Mercedes
San Francisco de Paula
Casa del Tabaco

Camilo Cienfuegos (Santo Domingo)

100 metres
100 yards

Where to stay

Casa Carlos Sotolongo cp **1** *D2*
Casa Muñoz cp **2** *D1*
Casa Orbea cp **3** *E3*
Casa Rogelio Inchauspi Bastida cp **4** *D1*
Grand Hotel Iberostar Trinidad **5** *F2*
Hostal Lola cp **6** *E2*
Hostal María y Enddy cp **7** *D1*
Hostal Marilú y Carlos cp **8** *D1*
Hostal Sandra y Víctor cp **9** *C1*
Hugo P Bastida Saenz
 de Buruaga cp **10** *D1*
José y Fátima cp **11** *E1*
La Ronda **12** *F1*

Restaurants

1514 **1** *C2*
Cubita **2** *D1*
Don Antonio **3** *D1*
Estela **4** *C3*
Guitarra Mía **5** *F3*
La Ceiba **6** *C2*
La Redacción **7** *D1*
San José **8** *F2*
Sol Ananda **9** *D2*
Sol y Son **10** *D1*
Vista Gourmet **11** *D3*

Bars

Bar Las Ruinas de Segarte **1** *D3*
Floridita **2** *F2*

Entertainment

Bar Yesterday (Casa de los Beatles) **1** *D1*
Casa de la Música **2** *D3*
Casa de la Trova **3** *D3*
Centro Cultural Artex **4** *F2*
La Chanchánchara **5** *C2*
La Escalinata **6** *D3*
Las Ruinas de Brunet **7** *E2*
Palenque de los Congos Reales **8** *D3*

Museums

Museo de Arqueología Guamuhaya **1** *D2*
Museo de Arquitectura Colonial **2** *D2*
Museo Municipal de Historia **3** *D2*
Museo Nacional de
 Lucha Contra Bandidos **4** *C2*
Museo Romántico **5** *D2*

⑤

musicians have included members of the London Philharmonic Orchestra. If you want to make a charitable donation of any sort, the church is the place to do it.

Museo Romántico ⓘ *Hernández 52, T41-994363, Tue-Sun 0900-1700, CUC$2, cameras CUC$1, no bags allowed, you have to leave them at the entrance.* Next to the church, the museum has an excellent collection of porcelain, glass, paintings and ornate furniture, which belonged to several families from the area. The ground floor was built in 1740 by Santiago de Silva and in 1808 the second floor was added by Don José Mariano Borrel y Padrón. The Conde de Brunet family lived there from 1830 to 1860, during what is known as the Romantic period. The Conde de Brunet, a local dignitary, whose full name was Nicolás de la Cruz Brunet Muñoz, made his fortune from sugar and cattle. At his death he owned 700 slaves and two sugar mills as well as lots of land and cattle. The exhibits are displayed in the colonial mansion, with beautiful views from the upper-floor balconies. Locals come here for their wedding photos.

Museums

Other museums worth visiting in the centre include the **Museo de Arqueología Guamuhaya** ⓘ *Simón Bolívar 457, esq Villena, Plaza Mayor, T41-993420, Sat-Thu 0900-1700, CUC$1, use of camera CUC$1,* which presents a general view of developments from pre-Columbian to post-conquest times. **Museo de Arquitectura Colonial** ⓘ *Desengaño (Ripalda) 83, T41-993208, Sat-Thu 0900-1700, CUC$1,* has exhibits specifically on the architecture of Trinidad, particularly aspects of the 18th and 19th centuries. It also offers tours of the city and the Valley of the Sugar Mills with a guide and video showings. The **Museo Nacional de Lucha Contra Bandidos** ⓘ *Hernández esq Piro Guinart, T41-994121, Tue-Sun 0900-1700, CUC$1,* is housed in the old San Francisco de

Asís convent and features exhibits on the 1960s conter-revolutionary campaign in the Escambray mountains. It has a small shop selling T-shirts of Che, postcards and the like. **Museo Municipal de Historia** ① *Simón Bolívar 423, T41-994460, Sat-Thu 0900-1700, CUC$2,* is an attractive building, but with rather dull displays; walk up the tower for a good view of Trinidad instead.

Cultural venues

The **Galería** ① *Plaza Mayor, free,* exhibits local art. Upstairs, a shop sells paintings, clothes and handicrafts. Neaby is the **Casa de la Cultura** ① *Francisco Javier Zerquera 406 entre Muñoz y Lumumba, T41-994308, daily 0700-2300,* which has an art gallery and a *sala* for teaching drama, painting, music and dance, open for special events. The **Casa del Música** and the **Casa de la Trova** are also close to the plaza, just east of the cathedral. For further details, see Entertainment, page 235.

Templo a Yamaya ① *Villena 59 entre P Guinart y S Bolívar.* This is an Afro-Cuban shrine with dolls on the altars and Afro-Cuban symbols on the walls. It is open to the public, who can watch *Santería* celebrations take place. Initiations are held here for anyone who wants to become a *Santero*. On 8th September 2003 the first procession was permitted through the streets of Trinidad to celebrate the Día de la Caridad de Cobre, patron saint of Cuba. After lighting candles in the temple, the Virgin was paraded around the block to the accompaniment of trumpet and drums, similar to many Catholic processions. However, it was followed by ceremonies back at the Templo involving *Santería* drumming when dancers became possessed by spirits.

South of the centre

Parque Céspedes Parque Céspedes to the southwest of the centre has shaded archways of vines and trailing plants. To the west is the fine building of the local government, **Poder Popular Municipal**, and to the south is the **Iglesia de San Francisco de Paula**. There is also a cinema

> **Tip...**
> There's a Wi-Fi hotspot outside Etecsa in the park, so you will see lots of people on their phones or tablets talking to friends and family abroad.

and telephone offices. The corner of the park at Calles Francisco J Zerquera y Martí is known as La Esquina Caliente (the hot corner) because it is where heated discussions are held between sports fans as they argue over baseball. In the middle of the park towards the local government building is another area where people argue about everything except sport.

Plaza Santa Ana At the extreme southeast of the colonial zone this square has the ruined church, the **Ermita de Santa Ana**, on the north side, and on the east, a yellow colonial building that houses the **Restaurante Santa Ana**.

> **Fact...**
> Cuba is known for its old 1950s American cars, but the Santander family owns a 1914 Ford model T car, which has been used in several movies.

La Casa del Alfarero (Casa Chichi) ① *C Andrés Berro 51, T41-993146, Mon-Sat 0730-1200 and 1300-1600.* South of Parque Céspedes is a ceramics factory, making earthenware pots. (To get there, go east on Maceo until one block after the hospital, and turn left when you get to a blue house on a corner. Go down a side entrance to the left of the house to reach the workshop at the back.) There is no organized tour, but the factory is open for you to wander around, watch the pots being thrown and glazed, and buy anything if you want. The Santander family has been operating for 150 years; for many years the factory was in the hands of the government, but the family has now been allowed to produce its own pots and souvenirs for sale.

Listings Trinidad *map p228*

Tourist information

There is an **Infotur office** (Gustavo I\quierdo, beside Bar Yesterday, T41-998257/8, daily 0800-1800. Information is also freely available from the state tour operators: **Cubatur** and others (see Tour operators, below). However, they are concerned to sell their own tours, so for impartial advice and for how to get off the beaten track it is worth asking your hosts, if you are staying in a *casa particular*. They will know of private, usually illegal, taxi drivers and guides who can show you something a bit different from the organized tours.

Where to stay

Hotels

$$$ Grand Hotel Iberostar Trinidad
José Martí y Lino Pérez, T41-996070,
www.iberostar.com.
35 rooms and 4 suites with view from balcony of the plaza, very good standard, smart and elegant with efficient and friendly service, good restaurant with international cuisine, buffet breakfast, piano bar, smokers' bar with cigars and rums available.

$$$ La Ronda
José Martí 238 entre Lino Pérez y Colón, T41-998538, administradorronda@cuevas.co.cu.
Small hotel, built 1868, renovated in 2012, full of character and with staff to match, already famed for the towel art on the beds. Rooms on 2 floors around a central courtyard, rooftop bar for sunset watching, good a/c and decent showers. Good breakfast, not a buffet.

Casas particulares

There are over 950 *casas particulares* in Trinidad but even so, at peak times they can all be full and you will need to book ahead. They are generally more expensive than in other towns, so expect to pay around CUC$30 for a room. Always reconfirm your booking a couple of days before you arrive. If arriving by bus you will be met by a throng of *casa* owners and touts using any number of scams to get your business. Ignore them and make your own way to your lodging.

$$ Casa Muñoz
José Martí 401 entre Fidel Claro y Santiago Escobar, T41-993673, www.casa.trinidadphoto.com.
Very friendly, English speaking, run by Julio Muñoz Cocina and Rosa Orbea. Great house, one of the grandest in Trinidad, built in 1800 with lofty ceilings and cool, intricately tiled floors, 4 rooms with new bathrooms, minibar, safe box, a/c. 1 is a suite with 2 levels, 1 king-sized bed, 2 double beds and 2 bathrooms, patio where you have a substantial breakfast, roof terrace, parking, Wi-Fi (with Etecsa card), very popular so book in advance. Base for photographers and film makers; Julio is a photographer specializing in street photography. He offers workshops, CUC$100, and photo tours, CUC$25 per person. He is also a horse whisperer, runs a charity project

> **Tip...**
> Do not believe anyone who tells you your *casa* is overbooked or closed until you have been there to check.

for horse welfare and offers horse riding tours on some of the best horses in the area (see below).

$$ Casa Rogelio Inchauspi Bastida
Simón Bolívar 312 entre Jose Marti y Antonio Maceo, T41-994107.

A large colonial house formerly the Spanish Consulate, on 2 floors offering 2 large a/c rooms, one of which is huge, with 2 comfy beds, high ceilings and balconies overlooking the street. Terrace on the roof is higher than most and ideal for sunset watching with something from the well-stocked fridge. Good breakfast in the patio downstairs. Rogelio and Barbara are very hospitable and friendly; he has an old motorbike with side car in excellent condition.

$$ Gisela Borrell Bastida
Frank País (Carmen) 486 entre Fidel Claro y Santiago Escobar, about 200 m from bus station, T41-994301.

2 rooms with double and single bed on ground floor, use of own dining room, sitting room, own entrance, lots of space, patio garden with fountain in the middle and spiral staircase up to roof terrace.

$$ Hostal Lola
Maceo 415 entre FJ Zerquera (Rosario) y Colón, T41-994513, see Facebook.

Artist-owned, this chic hostal is more like a hotel than a *casa particular*, with no family atmosphere but efficient service. 9 spacious a/c rooms on 2 floors around a courtyard, each individually decorated and furnished, very stylish and comfortable. Restaurant for guests only serves good food at regular prices. The staff are very friendly, making extra efforts for special occasions.

$$ Hostal Marilú y Carlos
Santiago Escobar 172 entre Frank País y José Martí, T41-992899, hostalmarilu@yahoo.es.

3 rooms, on ground floor and upstairs; 2 have 2 beds, room 3 has bunk beds and sleeps 3, all with a/c, fan, fridge, good bathrooms. Eat outdoors upstairs on terrace or indoors downstairs. There is also a roof terrace for

sunbathing. Marilú, Carlos and family are very friendly and pleasant and serve good food and drinks.

$$ Casa Carlos Sotolongo
Rubén Martínez Villena 33, overlooking the Plaza Mayor, T41-994106.

A huge colonial house, prettily painted and in immaculate condition with antique furniture. 2 rooms open onto delightful interior patio garden. Carlos is the curator at the Museo Romántico. Friendly and helpful family, English spoken, good food.

$$ Hostal María y Enddy
Jose Marti 407, T41-993597, T5289 4821 (mob), enddymar@yahoo.es.

Lovely old house with entrance hall full of antiques going through to courtyard behind with rooms off it for guests. Currently 4 rooms, 2 downstairs and 2 newer ones upstairs, above the bar and dining area, with more under construction. All of a good standard with comfortable mattresses. Friendly hosts, very helpful, good food, cooking lesson on request. Enddy was born into the Santander pottery family and the courtyard has lots of earthenware pots around rocking chairs.

$ Casa Orbea
Sonia Orbea, Jesús Menéndez 95 entre Colón y Smith, T41-994577.

A large colonial house, not as grand as some, but comfortable, with 2 rooms to rent, interior patio with lots of climbing plants and trailing greenery, terrace, parking.

$$ Hostal Sandra y Víctor
Maceo (Gutiérrez) 613 entre Piro Guinart (Boca) y Pablo Pichs (Guaurabo), T41-996444, hostalsandra@yahoo.com.

There are 2 rooms upstairs with balcony to the front and large terrace to the rear plus dining area, all for the exclusive use of guests, private and secure, also 1 smaller, noisier room downstairs in the family's quarters. Well-cared-for property, good bathrooms, fridge, spacious and comfortable with friendly hosts who provide delicious and hearty meals.

$$ Hugo P Bastida Saenz de Buruaga
Maceo 539 entre Santiago Escobar (Olvido) y Piro Guinart (Boca), name above the door, T41-993186.
Typical dark colonial home with high ceilings run by elderly gentleman, 1 lovely room, Sr Bastida speaks English and his wife is an excellent cook, good-value meals.

$$ José y Fátima
Francisco J Zerquera 159 (Rosario) entre Frank País y Francisco Petersen, T41-993898.
Upstairs rooms, 1 with double bed, the other with double and single beds, both spacious, door and windows open onto balcony for lots of fresh air, table on the patio for meals and roof terrace with laundry facilities and washing machine and a great view over the rooftops. The food is excellent and very stylishly presented, restaurant quality, while José mixes a mean cocktail. José speaks very good English and is extremely helpful in organizing things. More rooms are being built.

Where to eat

$$$ 1514
Simón Bolívar 515 entre JM Márquez y Hernández Echerrí, T41-994255.
Romantic setting in colonial house with candles and flowers on the tables, a patio decked with plants, antiques and heirlooms, underground wine cellar, live music and professional dancers. Food is beautifully presented and served on elegant china, while drinks are in cut glass.

$$$ Estela
Simón Bolívar 557, T41-994329. Open from 1900 Mon-Fri.
Garden setting among trees and variegated shrubs, surrounded by very high walls at the back of a colonial house. Excellent and plentiful food, lots of variety with salads, rice, beans, vegetables, well-cooked meats,

friendly hosts, get there early to avoid queues in high season, this is a popular place to eat. Menu changes according to what's available and fresh. All main dishes priced at CUC$10.

$$$ Guitarra Mía
Jesús Menéndez 19 entre Lino Pérez y Camilo Cienfuegos.
Stylish Cuban food and international dishes although relatively expensive for what you get. The decor is a fusion of old style and contemporary, everything music-themed, guitar on the walls, musical notes on the plates.

$$$ La Ceiba
Pablo Pich Girón 263 entre Lino Pérez e Independencia, T41-992408. Daily 1200-2300.
A large restaurant in a courtyard around a huge and very old ceiba tree. The setting is very attractive, particularly at night when you are serenaded by musicians. The food is a mix of *criollo* and more international cuisine; the house speciality is *pollo Melozo*.

$$$ La Redacción
Maceo 463 entre Simón Bolívar y FJ Zequera, T41-994593, www.laredaccioncuba.com. Daily 1030-2300.
Opened in 2015, the owners have brought their experiences of living in Europe to the menu but the food is still mostly Cuban. You can have tapas to start followed by roast pork, which is perfectly cooked with delicious crackling, or have lobster which, unusually for Cuba, is not overcooked. Plenty of options for vegetarians, such as stuffed pancakes or veggie burgers. An historic house which was formerly the editorial offices of a local newspaper and the newspaper theme is prominent. Live music.

$$$ San José
Maceo 382 entre Colón y Smith, T41-994702, T5283 4737 (mob), www.sanjosetaste.com. Daily 1200-2230.
Bar and restaurant, part of which is a/c. Wide selection of drinks at the bar, which is popular, and good rum cocktails.

The restaurant is busy, which may have something to do with the wood-fired pizza oven, but all the food is good and of an international standard. Smart decor with pictures of old cars on the walls, live music. Service is very good. Even the toilets are upmarket.

$$$ Sol Ananda
Real 45 entre Simón Bolívar y Piro Guinart, T41-998281. Lunch and dinner.
Typical colonial house with antique furnishings including a brass bed. Bar and *parrillada* with a variety of local and international dishes, including vegetarian, Japanese, Indian, Italian. Live music in the bedroom.

$$$ Vista Gourmet
Callejón de Galdós 2B entre EV Muñoz y Callejón de los Gallegos, T41-996700, tahiri_bolo@yahoo.es.
Certainly the restaurant with the loveliest setting in town, on the terrace of a colonial house 3 blocks from the Plaza Mayor with a magnificent view. Bar, wine cellar, self-service buffet for first course and dessert; choose your main course from menu: criolla and international cuisine. Professional service. Live music and entertainment (can be a bit intrusive) with cooking shown on large screen.

$$$-$$ Cubita
Maceo 471 entre FJ Zerquera y Simón Bolívar, T52-711479, luanis76@nauta.cu. Daily 1100-2300.
Comfortable restaurant and bar decorated with traditional pottery from the renowned Santander family. Tasteful decor of wood and wrought-iron furniture, partly exposed stone walls, modern use of traditional materials. *Criollo* and international food, including vegetarian options. Price includes bread and dipping sauce, *amuse bouche*, salad, rice and vegetables with the main course, mostly CUC$10-15. Huge *brochetas* of lobster and seafood, generous portions. Excellent drinks list with vodka cocktails as well as rum.

Helpful, English-speaking staff. Musicians not too dominant.

$$$-$$ Don Antonio
Izquierdo 118 entre Piro Guinart y Simón Bolívar, T41-996548. Daily 1100-2300.
A nice old colonial house with ornate columns and tiled floors and walls. Food is simple but very good with all the usual side dishes; the fish and seafood are delicious.

$$$-$$ Sol y Son
Simón Bolívar 283 entre Frank País y José Martí, T41-992926, www.paladarhostalsolyson.com. Daily 1200-2400.
Lovely setting in 19th-century house, nice decor, courtyard, popular, vegetarian special, excellent pork, tasty fish. Live music.

Bars

Bar Floridita
Lino Pérez entre Cadahía y José Martí. Daily 0900-2300.
Beer CUC$1.15, mojito CUC$2, daiquirí CUC$4.

Bar Las Ruinas de Segarte
Alameda entre Márquez y Galdós. Open 1000-2400.
Set in a ruined courtyard, also does snacks.

Círculo Social de Obreros
Martí.
Serves rum in CUP$, tourists welcome, an authentic drinking experience.

Entertainment

Music and dance
Lots of people offer 'unofficial' salsa lessons for about CUC$4 an hr; Trinidad is a good place to learn and you'll soon be dancing with Cubans in local bars.
Bar Yesterday (Casa de los Beatles), *Gustavo Izquierdo entre Simón Bolívar y Piro Guinart. Open 1600-2400.* Local groups play live rock in English, although it is principally a tribute to the Beatles. You can't miss it for the statues of the fab four at the entrance.

Casa de la Música, *up the steps past the church in Plaza Mayor, T41-996622. Restaurant daily 1000-2200, show 2200-0200, piano bar 1800-0600.* Full of tourists and Cubans, salsa, live performers, shop selling CDs, cassettes, music magazines, with a small display of the history of music in Trinidad. The 2nd entrance on JM Márquez leads to a large 'greenhouse' venue.

Casa de la Trova, *entrance on Fernando Echerrí. Daily 0900-0100. Entry free during the day, CUC$1 at night.* Located in an open-air shell of a house 1 block from the church. Excellent live Cuban traditional music and *trova* with a warm, vibrant atmosphere. There are mostly Cubans here, of all age groups, and it's a great place to watch and join the locals having a good time. Excellent fresh lemonade, local cocktails, refreshing pit stop after a stroll through the *artesanía* market. Live music day and night.

Centro Cultural Artex (formerly **Casa Fisher**), *Lino Pérez 306 entre Cadahía y José Martí, T41-996486. Outdoor bar 0900-0100.* In a nice old colonial house built in 1870, CUC$1 for show at 2200 with *parrillada*, dancing, live music and karaoke.

La Canchánchara, *Villena 78. Daily 1000-2245.* Another venue for live music, fast food, serves a drink of the same name created out of rum, honey and lime in small earthenware pots. More touristy than **Casa de La Trova** (cigar and souvenir shop), but good traditional music with different groups playing.

La Escalinata, *T41-996622, on the terrace leading up the steps next to the church, before you get to the Casa de la Música. Bar 0900-0200, cafetería 1600-0400, show 2100, live bands 0900-2000, but not when it rains.* Great place for a sunset cocktail.

Las Cuevas, *Finca Santa Ana, T41-996133, www.cubanacan.cu.* Hotel on a hill 10 mins' walk from town (good road), with caves in the grounds and a caving museum, nice view of the sea and lovely sunsets, bar with excellent daiquirís and great view, show in

the hotel 2100. Good disco, dance merengue and salsa with Cubans between the stalactites in a cave below reception, from 2230, entrance CUC$3.

Las Ruinas de Brunet, *Maceo entre Colón y Francisco Javier Zerquera. Daily 0900-2400.* Nightly Afro-Cuban show at 2100 for tourists in ruined colonial courtyard, very tacky and unauthentic, also *trova* from 1600, percussion classes 0900-1100, dance classes 1300-1600. Bicycle and scooter rental.

Palenque de los Congos Reales, *Fernando H Echerri entre La Escalinata y Casa de la Trova, T41-994512. Bar daily 1000-2400 (Sat until 0100).* During the day there are sometimes groups playing and an Afro-Cuban show. Nice shady open-air space for day time or evening drink.

Festivals

Jan Semana de la Cultura is in the 2nd week of the month, with art exhibitions, live music in the streets and other cultural activities. Following Semana de la Cultura there are several Santería festivals, including **Mamalroko**, a rite where offerings are made to the Orisha Iroko living in the Ceiba tree to ask for health and peace, which often include street parades and the beating of Batá drums.

Mar/Apr Semana Santa (Easter) is celebrated with an enormous procession on Good Fri. Special attention is given to the statue of Cristo de la Veracruz, which is thought to work miracles, and the choir sings its heart out.

Jun Carnival, with traditional festivities and contests, including one for the Carnival Queen.

18 Aug Santa Elena, the patron saint of Casilda, is celebrated with a Mass in the ruins of the church, festivities, fairs and horse competitions.

8 Sep Día de la Caridad de Cobre, Cuba's patron saint's day. There are lots of religious processions around the town, accompanied by music and dance.

22 Nov Santa Cecilia, the patron saint of music, is a fiesta with music on the streets and a special mass in the church.

Dec Santa Bárbara (Chango), an important Santería festival, with a Velada on 3 Dec and procession and Bembé (drum beating for the saints) on 4 Dec. **San Lázaro** (Babalú Ayé) on 17 Dec, another of the principal Orishas, with procession and Bembé. The week before Christmas you will see **Posadas**, nativity processions when children dress up as Mary, Joseph and shepherds and sing carols on the streets with Mary on a donkey.

Shopping

Art

Casa de los Conspiradores, *Cristo 38, to the right of La Escalinata.* Gallery-cum-studio of the painter and sculptor, Yami Martínez. The name of the house comes from being the base, in 1848, of Cuban patriots fighting against the Spanish government in a conspiracy known as the Conspiración de la Mina de la Rosa Cubana.

Galería de Arte Universal, *Villena 43, opposite the Plaza Mayor, T41-994432. Fri-Wed 0800-1700.* Contemporary Cuban art for sale.

Tienda de Arte Amelia Pelaez, *Simón Bolívar esq Valdés Muñoz, T41-993590.*

Handicrafts

In front of the Casa de la Trova on Fernando Echerrí are handicraft stalls, especially crochet and needlework, with jewellery, beads, carvings, hats, baskets and boxes. It is called **Candonga**, or **Mercado Popular de Artesanía**. The standard of handicrafts has improved and they are cheaper than in Havana, but avoid coral, shell or any other items taken from the sea.

Souvenirs

Tienda La Cochera, *on Simón Bolívar, round the corner from the Museo Romántico.* A small selection of souvenirs, drinks, postcards, toiletries, T-shirts.

What to do

Horse riding

There are many people offering horse riding tours of the area and all *casa* owners will know of someone with access to horses. Prices are CUC$15-30 depending on the guide and where you go.

Casa Muñoz, *José Martí 401, entre Fidel Claro y Santiago Escobar, T41-993673.* Julio Muñoz and his partner maintain a string of good horses on a farm just outside Trinidad. They charge CUC$26 for 4-5 hrs (includes entrance to the waterfall), but the price reflects the quality of horses and service. Only the quietest horses are used to carry tourists, accompanied by 2 guides. Lunch and drinks at local farms at additional cost. Trips to waterfall with swimming, good for novice riders. Experienced riders can ask for more challenging tours or multi-day riding. All riders given helmets and have to sign a disclaimer. Check your travel insurance covers horse riding.

Tour operators

There are 4 tour operators and all offer the same tours at the same prices. Trinidad has access to the sea, mountains, valleys, rivers, waterfalls, etc, so just head for the nearest agency and see what takes your fancy. Prices vary according to what options you choose, such as lunch and transport. Opening hours vary according to the season, but they are usually 0830-1700. Prices for the most popular excursions are as follows: Valley of the Sugar Mills on the steam train, 5 hrs, CUC$10; 5-hr horseback ride in the Valley CUC$23; truck safari to the Parque el Cubano, 6 hrs, CUC$35; jeep safari to Guanayara (Topes de Collantes), 6 hrs, CUC$55; truck safari to Topes de Collantes, CUC$45; jeep safari to Salto del Caburní, CUC$29; Salto de Javira, 6 hrs, CUC$16. Excursions further afield include Guamá and Playa Larga, 12 hrs, CUC$69; Santa Clara, 8 hrs, CUC$45; Sancti Spíritus, 8 hrs, CUC$39; nature tour including the Valle de los Ingenios, Parque Natural Jarisco in Banao, CUC$55; Cienfuegos, 8 hrs, CUC$43.

Cubanacán, *Colón esq Frank País, T41-996320/996590, with bureaux in the Universo store on Martí entre Colón y Francisco J Zerquera, T41-996142; at Cubacar, Lino Pérez 366 entre Maceo y Cadahía, T41-994753; and at Dulcinea, Simón Bolívar esq Maceo, T41-996736.*

Cubatur, *Maceo esq Zerquera, T41-996314, with a bureau at Simón Bolívar 430 esq Maceo, T41-996368, and in all the beach hotels.*

Julio César Muñoz Cocina, *José Martí 401 entre Fidel Claro y Santiago Escobar, T41-993673, www.trinidadphoto.com.* A photographer specializing in street photography (John Wayne style of rapid fire anticipating shots). He offers workshops, CUC$100 and photo tours, CUC$25 per person.

Infotur, *Gustavo Izquierdo, next to Bar Yesterday, T41-998258. Open 0800-1800.*

Paradiso, *Lino Pérez 306 entre Cadahía y José Martí in the Centro Cultural Artex (formerly Casa Fisher), T41-996345, paradiso@artextdad.co.cu.*

Watersports

Sea Sports, *José Mendoza (Alameda) 577, T41-992288.* Pedro Sánchez offers diving, snorkelling and fishing and includes equipment and transport in his tours.

Transport

Bicycle/scooter hire

Cycling on cobbled streets is difficult, to say the least. Scooters and bicycles can be hired from **Las Ruinas de Brunet**, see Entertainment, page 235. Bicycles can also be hired through tour companies or *casas particulares*. Trinidad is on a hill, so cycling to the beach is easy; coming back is hard work. Make sure your bike is in good condition.

Bus

Long distance Terminal entrance on Gustavo Izquierdo, near the corner with **Piro Guinart**, T41-992214, T44-996676 (after 2000), T53-5251 2165 (mob, for international calls and text messages), economica@trin.palmares.cu, office daily 0700-1700. For **Viazul** timetable and prices, see page 462. In addition, **Viazul** runs an irregular transfer service to **Havana airport**, to **Varadero** and to **Viñales**, using minibuses. Go to the **Viazul** office a couple of days in advance to organize it.

Transtur also runs a bus service from Parque Céspedes. You can make reservations at any tour agency or go straight to Parque Céspedes if you want to travel the same day. To **Havana**, 0715, CUC$25, stopping in **Cienfuegos**, CUC$6; to **Viñales**, 0700, CUC$35.

Car hire

Cubacar, at Servi Cupet fuel station on the way out of Trinidad towards Casilda, T41-996301; at the Cubatur office, Maceo esq Zerquera, T41-996110; at Lino Pérez 366 entre Maceo y Cadahía, T41-996633; at Simón Bolívar 430 esq Maceo, T41-996257. **Rent a Car Vía** (Gaviota), Frank País entre Fidel Claro y Santiago Escobar, T41-996388.

Taxi

Cubataxi, Camilo Cienfuegos on the way out to Casilda, T41-998080, or at the bus station. Also *cocotaxis* and taxis parked on Maceo entre Simón Bolívar y Colón.

Train

The station is south of the town: walk south straight down Lino Pérez until you get to the railway line, then turn right, T41-993348. Tourists can take a trip on a 1907 steam train to **Manaca Iznaga** daily in high season at 0900, CUC$10. Call beforehand to see if it is running as it does sometimes break down.

the beaches aren't the best in Cuba but offer a welcome break from sightseeing

La Boca

About 8 km west of Trinidad is the small, pleasant fishing village of La Boca. The beach here is not cleaned daily, as it is on Playa Ancón in front of the hotels, but Cubans come here on holiday and there is a cheerful if rough-and-ready atmosphere about the place. Many people prefer it to Playa Ancón as it is lively, with *casas particulares* and places to eat. There are some buses to La Boca or you can get a taxi, or rent a bicycle from local people for about CUC$3 a day. You can also hire a private car or taxi for about CUC$5 one way or a *cocotaxi* for CUC$2 to take you from Trinidad to La Boca. In summer there is a bus stop and taxi rank on Simón Bolívar by the railway line.

Casilda

Casilda is a rather scruffy fishing village 5 km south of Trinidad across a tidal flat where there are lots of birds. It is a run-down port used mainly for exporting sugar. Its sights include the ruined Catholic

Tip...
There's a Servi Cupet petrol station on the way out of Trinidad towards Casilda.

Ermita de Santa Elena. There is private accommodation available, but it is still about 11 km to the beach. If you are cycling this route you may be pleased to know that there is a breezy bar at the point where the road La Boca–Ancón meets the road Casilda–Ancón.

Playa Ancón

Bus from Havanatur's office in Trinidad at 0900, 1100, 1400, 1700 (in theory), but don't rely on it. A taxi fare is CUC$8 one way, but you can share the car between 4 people.

The best beach resort near Trinidad is Playa Ancón, not a town as such, just three resort hotels of varying quality. The beach is white sand with clean turquoise water, but sandflies appear after 1600. Inland there are swamps and lakes, so be prepared for mosquitoes at certain times of the year. The best part of the beach is right in front of the **Hotel Ancón**, where there are straw sunshades, some seagrape trees and beach loungers (CUC$2). The rest of the beach has little shade, but there is a beach bar for drinks and snacks. There is good diving less than 300 m offshore. The drop-off is at about 25 m and there is plenty to see.

People are sometimes disappointed when they come here and expect something more spectacular, but it is very pleasant for a day trip out of Trinidad. There are usually plenty of taxis and *cocotaxis* waiting in the public car park next to the hotel for the return journey.

Cayo Blanco de Casilda

Offshore and southeast of Playa Ancón, 1½ hours by boat, is Cayo Blanco de Casilda, where there is a beautiful beach with lovely white sand. A small cay to the east, **Cayo Macho**, is excellent for watching seabirds and pelicans, while to the west of Cayo Blanco there is some lovely coral 18 to 40 m deep where you can find a wide variety of fish, turtles, lobster and crab. In places the coral has been damaged by storms, but in other patches it is plentiful with brain coral, sea fans and lots of fish and starfish. A day trip on a catamaran with snorkelling is organized by hotels and tour companies for CUC$50 to Cayo Blanco. It is also possible to visit **Cayo Iguanas** (CUC$45), another white-sand island where huge iguanas and hermit crabs clean up all the the tourists' leftovers. You get a lovely view of the Sierra Escambray from the sea and it is a worthwhile excursion. See What to do, page 240.

Where to stay

La Boca
Casas particulares

$$-$ Hostal Cuba
Calle 2A entre C Real y Av del Mar, T41-993651, 5261 7921 (mob), www.hostalcuba.net.
Smart modern house, recently extended and upgraded, kitchenette in the suite upstairs and minibar fridge in the room downstairs. The room upstairs has its own balcony and is more private than the room downstairs. Dining upstairs on covered terrace, great seafood, lots of fruit for breakfast, smiley eggs, view of the bay, which is even better from the roof terrace where there are sunbeds. Very welcoming hosts, Elpidio and Norma, Parking, bike rental, laundry.

$ Hostal Vista al Mar
C Real 47, T41-993716.
Owned by Manuel (Manolo) Menéndez and his wife Sylvia. Traditional Caribbean design with the roof extending over the wraparound veranda overlooking the mouth of the river, the sea and the mountains behind. Very relaxing. Meals are taken on the veranda, wonderful freshly caught fish, mangos from the tree. 2 a/c rooms, parking,

$ Casa Hostal Valledares
Calle D 1 entre Av del Sol y Av del Mar, T41-996883, 5313 0281 (mob), christhian_dares@yahoo.com.
House within metres of the sea. Excellent food with organic produce from their garden, friendly, English spoken, 1 a/c room with 2 double beds, separate from the owners' quarters with private entrance, sitting room with extra single bed, parking. Excursions offered and watersports including diving and fishing.

Casilda
Casa particular

$ Villa Dalia
Real 158 entre Iglesia y Perla, T41-995382, 5244 7903 (mob), juanmayor@yahoo.es.
New house, 3 modern rooms with good facilities, quiet a/c, minibar fridge, hair dryer, patio, terrace, parking. Multilingual hosts also rent a whole apartment in a modern building 100 m away. Delicious food beautifully presented.

Playa Ancón
Hotels

$$$ Brisas Trinidad del Mar
Playa Ancón, T41-996500-7, www.hotelescubanacan.com.
Satisfactory place to stay if you want to be on the beach and do day trips in to Trinidad. Supposed to be 4-star but isn't; all-inclusive hotel, 241 rooms and junior suites in need of renovation in 2/3-storey multicoloured blocks in a circle around free-form pool, 2 rooms for wheelchair users, a/c, internet access, car and bike rental, tourism desk, buffet and à la carte restaurants, jacuzzi, tennis, gym, sauna, games room, watersports, entertainment including, disco 2230-0200, on reasonable beach, reef-protected sea, nice sand with sea grapes behind.

$$$ Club Amigo Ancón
Playa Ancón, T41-996120, www.hotelescubanacan.com.
Concrete block of 279 rooms, Soviet style, showing its age, all-inclusive. Most of the rooms are very small and it is worth upgrading to something better. The hotel has a disco and many facilities, including watersports, best beach here, lots of families stay, but lots of complaints. Offices of **Cubanacán** and **Transtur** for excursions.

$$$-$$ Club Amigo Costa Sur
Playa Ancón, T41-996174-8,
www.hotelescubanacan.com.
Standard (73) or superior rooms (39) in a
block or better chalets/bungalows (20) in
front of them, built above rocks with beach
to north of hotel where there is a natural
swimming pool and bar on the sand. Price
all-inclusive. Gym, nightclub show at 2145.

What to do

Playa Ancón
Cubatur, has a desk in all the beach hotels.
Marina Marlin Trinidad, *Península*

Ancón, opposite Hotel Ancon, T41-996205,
marinastdad@enet.cu, VHF 16, 19, 68, 72.
6 moorings, 1.8-m draft, showers, laundry,
rental. All boat excursions and water
activities are based here and you can buy
direct from the marina or through any tour
operator. A seafari to Cayo Blanco on a
catamaran costs CUC$50, 5 hrs with lunch,
open bar and snorkelling; to Cayo Macho
on a catamaran is CUC$45, 5 hrs with lunch,
open bar and snorkelling. Diving costs
CUC$35 for 1 dive, CUC$64 for 2, night diving
CUC$45 for qualified divers. All types of
fishing available including deep-sea fishing,
CUC$280 for 6 hrs for 6 people.

★ Parque Natural Topes de Collantes

waterfalls and hiking trails surrounded by luscious vegetation

Inland from Trinidad are the beautiful, wooded Escambray mountains, whose
highest point is Pico San Juan, also known as La Cuca, at 1140 m. Rivers have cut
deep valleys, some of which, such as the Caburní and the Guanayara, have attractive
waterfalls and pools where you can swim. The Parque Natural Topes de Collantes is
a 110-sq-km area of the mountains which contains many endemic species of fauna
and flora. There are several paths in the area and walking is very rewarding, with
lovely views and lush forest. You can see lots of wildlife, butterflies, hummingbirds
and the *tocororo*, the national bird of Cuba. These are great days out in luscious
surroundings. The visitor centre is in the settlement of Topes de Collantes, 20 km
from Trinidad, where the park entrance fee is collected (CUC$9).

Hiking in the park

The most popular hike is to the **Salto de Caburní**, a waterfall that plunges into appealing
forest pools. The path starts at the **Hotel Escambray**: walk from the village to the hotel
and ask for directions there. Guides can be picked up in the village, or take an official tour
at the hotel, which is much better value as you go to all the right places. The path is steep
and slippery; you may find horses for hire half way up the hill if the climb back up is too
much for you. A walking stick is recommended, as is a guide.

To get to the **Salto Vegas Grandes**, another waterfall, turn right immediately after the
barrier when entering Topes village from Trinidad. You go into a cul-de-sac with several
high-rise apartments. Continue along the track at the end of the last block for about
1.5 km. Eventually the track descends steeply along a narrow path (very tricky, good
footwear required – do not attempt after rain).

Another 2-km walk leads west from the hotels to **La Batata**, a cave with an underground
river making pools in which you can swim. The temperature of the water never exceeds
20°C. Just northwest of here, but best reached on another path, is the restaurant at
Hacienda Codina, T42-540117 (serving *comida criolla*). A visit here is often combined with
a trip to the Cueva del Altar, the orchid gardens and a *mirador*.

Some 12 km north of Topes near Guanayara, there is another less accessible waterfall, the **Salto El Rocío**, with swimming in the Poza del Venado by the Río Caballero. There is a restaurant nearby, the **Casa de la Gallega**, where you can have a chicken lunch Galician style.

Parque El Cubano and the Salto Javira

This park is part of the Topes de Collantes protected area but is closer to Trinidad and off the beaten track. At its heart is the **Salto Javira**, which can be reached on horseback or on foot from Trinidad. It's a very pretty and pleasant trip through farmyards, bean fields and other crops. You can go on horseback as far as the national park entrance and from there you have to walk, 40 minutes.

Heading west out of town on the Cienfuegos road, take a track next to the Río Guaurabo after 5 km to reach **Restaurant El Cubano**, where you buy your CUC$9 park entrance ticket. From here the attractive 40-minute walk is marked along a tributary of the river; you cross pretty streams in the forest until you climb a rocky path to get to the waterfall. At one point you pass a cliff face covered with hundreds of hanging wasps' nests. The river cascades down a smooth rock face into a deep green pool, surrounded by cliffs and caves inhabited by bats, which fly in and out of the darkness. It

Essential Topes de Collantes

Finding your feet

There is no public transport, but recommended day trips are organized by **Cubatur** or **Cubanacán**. A six-hour jeep safari costs CUC$55 per person, minimum two passengers, lunch included. The trip includes a stop at a farm house for fruit, mashed plantain with garlic and lime, *guarapo* (sugar cane liquor) and coffee for an extra CUC$1. A truck safari, minimum eight passengers, including lunch, costs CUC$45. All take in swimming in a waterfall. Hiring a private car with driver to Topes de Collantes and the Salto de Caburní will cost you about CUC$25-35 with up to four people. Private tours do not go to the same places as jeep tours, whatever anybody tells you. Bargain hard for a good price and make sure the driver takes you to the right place.

When to go

Do not go if it has been raining recently. It gets very muddy and can be dangerous to walk in the hills. For further details, see What to do, page 21.

is great for a cool swim and very photogenic. If you don't want to go to the waterfall, you can carry on through the valley on horseback. There is a nice ride passing farmers' houses so you can see how they live and work, chat with them, maybe be offered a cup of coffee, and there are several rivers where you can bathe.

BACKGROUND
Alberto Delgado

About 4 km from Trinidad, on the Cienfuegos road, before the turning for the Topes de Collantes Natural Park, there is a small monument to Alberto Delgado. Turn south on the road by the stone wall with his name on it to reach a small monument and cave by the Río Guaurabo. Alberto Delgado was a revolutionary who infiltrated the group of US-backed counter-revolutionaries known as G2, working from the Escambray mountains. As a result of his activities, a group of 90 counter-revolutionaries was caught in the early 1960s. However, intelligence sources in Cuba and Miami identified him as a spy and a message to that effect was sent from *Radio Swan* (on Swan Island near Miami) to G2 in the mountains. Delgado was captured and executed by the counter-revolutionaries by being hung from a tree in the vicinity of the monument. On the other side of the river from the monument is the Finca Maisinicú, where Alberto Delgado lived.

Listings Parque Natural Topes de Collantes

Where to stay

Hotels

\$\$ Kurhotel Escambray
Topes de Collantes, T42-540180,
www.gaviota-grupo.com.
A huge, multi-storey hotel in the mountains, formerly a hospital for TB victims built in the 1950s. The rooms are basic and it is completely out of keeping with the forest that surrounds it. Lots of Cuban art from the 1980s displayed on the walls of public areas. Excursions, disco, pool, squash court.

\$\$ Los Helechos
Southwest of Topes de Collantes village,
T42-540330, www.gaviota-grupo.com.
48 rooms, restaurant, bar, *cafetería*, all right for a night, but very run down.

Valle de los Ingenios

a story of sugar and slavery

On the road to Sancti Spíritus, 5 km from Trinidad, is a mirador, from where you get a fine view of the Valley of Sugar Mills and the Escambray mountains, with the sea on the opposite side. There is a nice bar at the *mirador*, and if a tour group turns up there is often a demonstration of a sugar press. This area was a centre for sugar production in the 18th and 19th centuries, with more than 50 mills processing sugar from the surrounding plantations. The sugar was transported by train to be loaded onto ships at Casilda (see page 238).

Torre de Manaca Iznaga
15 km from Trinidad on road to Sancti Spíritus, daily 0900-1600 or 1700, CUC\$2.

The Torre de Manaca Iznaga in the village of the same name has now been given UNESCO World Heritage status alongside Trinidad city because of its historical importance. The legend goes that there were two rival brothers, one who wanted to build a tower and

ON THE ROAD
Horse riding around Trinidad

Horse riding is a popular excursion around Trinidad and a good way of covering long distances into the countryside, giving access to rivers, waterfalls, mountains, forests and other natural attractions. Within a relatively short time you can also get a feel for the way local farmers live and work and see what they produce. Many of the routes take in rivers and waterfalls where you can bathe, cool off and relieve any aches and pains from the exercise. The drawback is the quality of the horses, which would often be regarded as rescue cases in Europe or the USA. This is partly through ignorance and lack of education about horse welfare and partly because of a lack of funds for veterinary medicine, including basic items such as wormers. Veterinary care has not kept pace with the standard of health care enjoyed by the Cuban people.

As a visitor to the country, you can encourage the owners to look after their horses better by refusing to accept animals or tack that are in poor condition. Think also of your own safety (and travel insurance): a thin, unhealthy animal is more likely to fall; a horse with sores may make a sudden movement in pain and may unseat its rider.

Some Cuban riders and owners have linked up with charities, trainers and vets overseas to improve horse welfare. For further information on a project supporting horse welfare in the Trinidad area, see www.diana.trinidadphoto.com.

the other who wanted to dig a hole as deep as the tower was high. In fact there is only a tower, which was built between 1835 and 1845. It is 43.5 m high, has seven floors and 136 steps to the top. It was built as a lookout to watch the slaves working in the sugar cane fields. There were two bells in the tower: one was rung when it was time for the slaves to stop work and take a meal in a communal eating house; the other was rung if an escape was discovered, alerting the slave catchers, or *rancheros*. One of the bells, dating from 1846, can be seen on the path leading to the tower. There is a great view of the surrounding Valle de los Ingenios (Valley of the Sugar Mills) and the Escambray mountains as well as the rooftops of the village below. Look out for the large sugar cauldrons lying around the village. The **Manaca Iznaga** restaurant is in the old plantation house, a yellow colonial building (daily 0900-1700, meals CUC$6-15) and there is a small shop. Tour operators offer day trips, see page 236, or you can hire a taxi to take you for about CUC$15-20. Tourists can take a trip on a 1907 steam train from Trinidad to **Manaca Iznaga** daily in high season at 0900, CUC$10, but call beforehand to see if it is running, as it has been known to break down.

Centre East

The three provinces of Ciego de Avila, Camagüey and Las Tunas are largely flat and agricultural with few natural features of outstanding beauty, although the landscape is pleasing with livestock grazing in the meadows.

The city of Ciego de Avila, also known as the pineapple town, is not a tourist attraction, but the centre is being improved with many changes for the better. North of the city is one of the island's main resorts, Cayo Coco and Cayo Guillermo, where extensive beaches of pale sand are a magnet for the all-inclusive tourist market.

Camagüey, a UNESCO World Heritage Site since 2008, is an ideal place to stay a few days if travelling from one end of the island to the other. The old colonial heart of the city, with its labyrinthine streets, has been restored to its former splendour, and its magnificent 19th-century buildings have stood the test of time better than those in seaside cities such as Havana or Santiago. North of the city is the long-established, low-key beach resort of Playa Santa Lucía, where the diving is superb, especially if you like sharks. Further east, the north coast of Las Tunas Province is so far relatively undeveloped with attractive beaches but few facilities.

Best for
Beaches ▪ Birdwatching ▪ Diving ▪ Escaping

Footprint
picks

★ Playa Los Flamencos, page 258

Flamingos still populate the beach and starfish can be seen in the shallow, translucent water.

★ Camagüey city, page 263

Five hundred years of history can be discovered in the delightful colonial plazas and labyrinthine streets.

★ Playa los Cocos, page 278

A couple of beach bars are the only tourist facilities on this unspoilt bay.

★ Cayo Sabinal, page 279

See flamingos, dolphins and an imposing lighthouse on this idyllic wildlife reserve.

★ Playa Covarrubias, page 286

Powder-white sand, turquoise water and not another soul in sight.

Essential Centre East

Finding your feet

There are **international airports** on Cayo Coco (Jardines del Rey) and near Camagüey (Ignacio Agramonte) and **domestic airports** at Las Tunas and Playa Santa Lucía. Charter flights from Canada, Argentina and the UK bring visitors to the cays. The three provincial capitals are linked by both rail and road on the main routes from Havana to Santiago de Cuba. Trains are unreliable and some services are not available to foreigners. Viazul has a good daily bus service from Havana, Varadero or Trinidad to Holguín or Santiago, stopping at all the major towns along the way. See also Essential Ciego de Avila, page 249, Essential Camagüey city, page 263, and Essential Las Tunas, page 283.

Getting around

Provincial bus services tend to be limited. The resort hotels all offer tours and excursions to destinations inland, but this can be time-consuming as they are often located on remote cays. Car hire is available from resort hotels, airports and city centres. Hiring a car will give you the flexibility to explore on your own, although you might not have access to the same range of activities as the tour groups. Another alternative is to hire a taxi with a reliable

driver for the day; most *casa particulares* should be able to advise you on this.

When to go

You will find plenty of wet weather if you come here between June and November, with most of the rain falling in the three months at the end of that period

Tip...
If you break your bus journey in one of these central provinces, make sure you have made an onward reservation, as most of the long-distance buses are full when they arrive in these towns.

Best places to eat
El Crucer, Ciego de Avila, page 251
Maite La Qbana, Morón, page 256
Restaurante 1800, Camagüey, page 272
Casa Austria, Camagüey, page 272
Rocola Club, Camagüey, page 273

when there is also a significant hurricane risk. Canadian tourists come in the winter months to the north-coast beaches but there can be rough seas bringing weed and debris from November to February if there is a cold front further north. Generally the driest time of year is between December and April.

Time required

Camagüey warrants a day of exploration, but the sights of Ciego de Avila and Las Tunas can be seen in a few hours. Allow time for day trips to beaches on the cays north of Morón and to Playa Santa Lucía north of Camagüey.

Atlantic Ocean

Ciego de Avila
Province

The Province of Ciego de Avila is most often visited for the beach resorts off its northern coast. Sandwiched between the provinces of Sancti Spíritus and Camagüey, it is the flattest province with none of its land rising above 50 m. The northern coastline is low-lying and swampy with mangroves. Offshore, but connected to the mainland by a long causeway (*pedraplen*), are the islands of Cayo Coco and Cayo Guillermo, which make up part of a 400-km coral reef. The cays have excellent deep sea fishing, diving and snorkelling. Many new luxury hotels have opened for package tourism, but they are very remote and isolated from the rest of Cuba. Scuba divers also rate highly the cays off the south coast that make up the western half of the Jardines de la Reina archipelago. Dive packages must be organized in advance, but the unspoilt underwater environment makes the effort well worthwhile.

The two main cities of Ciego de Avila and Morón lie in the centre of the province. The main road from Havana to Camagüey and Santiago passes straight through the middle of Ciego de Avila, and most people just keep going. Birdwatching in the countryside is good, with 234 species, of which 18 are endemic; there is also some freshwater fishing.

Ciego de Avila (population 130,000) was founded in 1840 on the site of a hacienda granted to Alonso de Avila, one of Velázquez' commanders. Today, the provincial capital is an agricultural market town with a large thermal electricity plant and little of architectural merit, although there are plenty of columns, portals and tiles to decorate the 19th-century buildings.

Sights

The main square is the **Parque Martí**, with a statue of José Martí dating from 1925 in the centre. On the south side are the church, **Iglesia de San Eugenio de la Palma**, dedicated to the patron saint of the city, and the former **Ayuntamiento**, built in 1911 and now the municipal government headquarters. The **Teatro Principal** ⓘ *Joaquín Agüero y Honorato del Castillo, T33-222086*, built in 1927, is considered one of the best on the island for its acoustics and is an interesting eclectic style. Also on Parque Martí is the **Museo de Artes Decorativas** ⓘ *T33-201661, Sun-Tue 0800-1600, Wed-Sat 0800-2100, CUC$1.* Dating from 1930, when it was opened as the Liceo society, it now showcases Cuban and foreign furniture, china, porcelain, silver, marble and ivory from the 19th and 20th centuries.

Just north of the square, the **Museo Provincial Simón Reyes** ⓘ *Honorato del Castillo entre Máximo Gómez y Libertad, T33-204488, Mon-Tue 0900-1700, Wed-Sat 0830-2200, Sun 0830-2100, CUC$1*, is in a restored building that was formerly the seat of the Spanish Army Command during the War of Independence. It contains many items of local historical significance.

Calle Independencia runs along the southwest side of the square. From Honorato del Castillo to José María Agramonte it is now pedestrian and known as the Boulevard. As in many other Cuban cities, it is the focus of regeneration and beautification in the city, with statues, benches and decorative plants along the busy commercial street. For an insight into local artists, visit the **Galería del Consejo Provincial de las Artes Plásticas** ⓘ *C Independencia entre Honorato del Castillo y Maceo, T33-223900, Sun-Fri 0830-2100, Sat 1400-2200*.

South of Independencia, at Marcial Gómez y Joaquín de Agüero, is the place where the city was founded. There is a 19th-century **Mapa Mural here**, depicting the first 25 blocks of the rising town. It shows the Spanish command headquarters and some of the forts that were part of the Júcaro to Morón military line (see Background, page 253).

Essential Ciego de Avila

Finding your feet

The railway station in Ciego de Avila is central; trains on the Havana to Santiago route stop here but are unreliable. **Viazul** buses are more convenient, running several times daily from Havana to Santiago and Holguín, from Varadero to Santiago, and from Trinidad to Santiago. However, if you break your journey here, make sure you have a reservation well in advance for the onward bus, as the long-distance buses are usually full when they go through town.

Getting around

Much of the city can be seen on foot, or you can use a bicitaxi or *coche* for longer distances. For excursions out of the city, car hire is the most convenient, or you can hire a taxi to take you around, or take a tour.

Tourist information

The hotels have *burós de turismo* which can give information, although their main purpose is to sell tours. These can be convenient if you do not have a car.

Infotur has an office beneath the Edificio de 12 plantas, **Honorato del Castillo esq Libertad** (T33-309109, www.infotur.cu). Maps and phone cards are for sale; information and leaflets are free.

Where to stay

Hotels

$$-$ Ciego de Avila
Ctra de Ceballos, about 2 km outside Ciego de Avila, T33-228013, www.islazul.cu.
143 standard, functional rooms in a modern, 5-storey block, large pool, taxis, car hire. All right for a night or two, but food and service are inadequate and it is noisy. Shooting arranged with guide and dog.

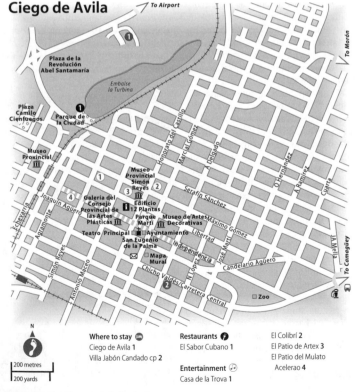

Ciego de Avila

Where to stay ●
Ciego de Avila 1
Villa Jabón Candado cp 2

Restaurants ●
El Sabor Cubano 1

Entertainment ●
Casa de la Trova 1

El Colibrí 2
El Patio de Artex 3
El Patio del Mulato
Acelerao 4

Casas particulares

$ Casa Yolanda/La China
*Calle 5 15 entre República (Joaquín Agüero)
y Callejón (Hicacos), Rpto Díaz Pardo, T33-
225641, yol.wong@hotmail.com.*
In a quiet area, but within easy walking
distance of the bus station and Parque Martí.
2 rooms, 1 larger than the other, comfortable,
welcoming, patio, terrace, meals are better
than in local restaurants, breakfast excellent,
parking, bike rental, laundry.

$ Iris Marrero Cano
*Cuba 265 entre 5 y Soto, T33-225571,
bellkiss265@yahoo.es.*
A 1966 yellow and chocolate brown home
with a spacious double room and plenty
of facilities. Guests have use of a kitchen.
Parking, bike rental.

$ Villa Jabón Candado
*Chicho Valdés 51 esq Abraham Delgado, T33-
225854, https://rentroomcuba.wordpress.com.*
The villa was built in 1935 by a company that
made soap and was given away as a prize to
a family that bought a lucky bar of soap. Still
retaining 1930s charm, there are 2 rooms to
rent. Downstairs is the smaller, with patio. Up
a steep staircase is the larger, with balcony for
people-watching, kitchenette and laundry
area. Solar hot water, a/c, TV, good breakfasts
and evening meal available. Parking.

Where to eat

$$$-$ El Crucer
*Libertad 366 entre 2 y 3, Rpto Vista Alegre,
T33-279405.*
Top floor of extraordinary house with
different architecture on each of the 3 floors.
However, once you're up the stairs you find
a smart bar and restaurant with an enviable
view over the city. The food is very good,
including lobster or paella, but ask what the
chef recommends as that will be the freshest
dish of the day. Good *tostones* and other
side dishes, delicious ice cream and good
cocktails and Chilean wine.

$$$-$ El Sabor Cubano
Parque de la Ciudad, T33-211523.
Decent restaurant and bar with good
cocktails, Chilean wine. Typical Cuban food
such as *ropa vieja* and all the trimmings.

Bars

El Patio del Mulato Acelerao
*Independencia entre Simón Reyes y
José M Agramonte, T33-227786.
Mon-Thu 0900-2000, Fri-Sun 0900-2400.*
Bar with recorded music, drinks, sodas,
sweets. Sometimes live music; one of the
venues for the Festival Nacional de Música
Fusión Piña Colada.

Entertainment

Music and dance
Batanga, *Hotel Ciego de Avila, T33-228013,
Wed-Mon 2200-0200, Sun 1600-2100.* Hotel
disco. Admission CUC$5 per couple including
drinks of CUC$3, or CUC$3.50 per person
including drinks of CUC$2.50.
Casa de la Trova, *Libertad 130 y Simón Reyes,
T33-222107. Fri-Sun until 2100.* Traditional and
folklore live music.
El Colibrí, *Honorato del Castillo y Máximo
Gómez, T33-266219. 2200-0200.* Cuba
Ritmos show, dancers, singers, comedy
and cabaret. Admission per couple
Mon-Thu CUC$3 including drinks of
CUC$2, Fri, Sat CUC$5 (*consumo* CUC$4),
Sun CUC$7 (*consumo* CUC$5).
El Patio de Artex, *Libertad entre Honorato del
Castillo y Maceo, T33-266680. Daily 1000-0200.*
Shows, *boleros*, singing, comedy, circus,
dancing, a wide range of artistic and cultural
events, lively, entertaining, attractive and
very Cuban atmosphere. Admission varies
according to the event. Cafetería serves
light food, snacks, fries and drinks.

Festivals

**Apr Festival Nacional de Música Fusión
'Piña Colada'.** Held in the 1st week, with lots

of bands playing a variety of genres: jazz, rock, *nueva trova*, fusion and dance music.

What to do

Tour operators
Contact **Cubanacán** (T33-301215/212600); **Cubatur** (T33-265636), or **Havanatur** (T33-308235/301371).

Transport

Bus
Ciego de Avila bus station is on the Ctra Central just east of the zoo. **Viazul**, T33-225109, stops here on its **Havana–Santiago** route, with buses to **Havana**, **Trinidad**, **Varadero**, **Holguín** and **Santiago**. For timetable and prices see page 462. Only tour buses go to **Cayo Coco**, there are no public buses. There are inter-municipal buses from Ciego de Avila to **Morón**, 7 daily, or you can take a taxi, CUC$10-15, 36 km.

Car hire
Cubacar is at Hotel Ciego de Avila, T33-200102; on Libertad s/n entre Honorato del Castillo y Maceo, T33-212570; on Candelario Agüero entre Arnaldo Ramírez y Onelio Hernández, T33-207133, and at the Terminal de Omnibus, Ctra Central Este, T33-225105. **Rex** is at Hotel Ciego de Avila, T33-228013, and has the best cars.

Taxi
Taxi OK, T33-308202, T33-302222; **Taxis Cuba**, T33-301414. To **Morón**, CUC$10-15; to **Cayo Coco** hotels or airport, CUC$60; to **Cayo Guillermo** hotels, CUC$80.

Train
In theory there are daily trains from **Havana** (arr 1230) and from **Santiago** (arr 0440), pay in CUC$. A local train runs to **Morón**, daily 0600, 1215, 1605, 2000.

Morón and the northwest

mangroves, lagoons and waterbirds

Morón *Colour map 2, B6.*
Morón (population 60,000) was founded in 1750 and is about 36 km northeast of Ciego de Avila. It is promoted as the Ciudad del Gallo (Cockerel City), with a monument to the bird by sculptor Rita Longa which is a replica of the rooster at Morón de la Frontera in Spain.

The centre of the town is the Parque Martí, dating from 1877. A key meeting point for all ages, the municipal band plays here on Sunday mornings. On the corner of Parque Martí is the Plaza de los Artesanos, where local handicrafts are sold daily 0900-1600. There is a **Museo de Arqueología e Historia Caonabo** ⓘ *C Martí 374, T33-504501, Tue-Sat 0900-1700, Sun 0800-1200, CUC$1*, showcasing Indo Cuban and Meso-American archaeology as well as the archaeology and history of the city, with a good panoramic view. The grand building was originally a bank, then the headquarters of the telephone company, before becoming the municipal museum. The railway station on Vanhorne, between Tarafa and Narciso López, is also considered architecturally important and is a National Monument. Built in 1923 in an eclectic style with a neoclassical influence, it is typical of many buildings constructed in the first years of the Republic.

Laguna de Leche and around
The system of lakes, marshes and low-lying wetlands north of Morón forms an ideal habitat for a number of endemic and migratory water and game birds; birdwatching is excellent thanks to the range and quantity of species. The lakes are also a popular destination for fishing and shooting.

Ciego de Avila Province

During the First War of Independence the Spanish built a road, railway line, fence, sentry towers and other fortifications north–south from Morón to Júcaro via Ciego de Avila to try and prevent independence fighters infiltrating the western half of Cuba. This was the largest fortification in the Spanish colonies in the 19th century, and the ruins can still be seen in places. The Spanish were unsuccessful in keeping out the rebels: in 1876 General Manuel Suárez took Morón, and in 1895 General Antonio Maceo crossed the line north of Ciego de Avila, as did Camilo Cienfuegos in 1958.

The rise in sugar production in the 20th century attracted many immigrants to the province both from Spain and other Caribbean islands. They brought with them their music, dances and other cultural traditions. At Baraguá, southeast of Ciego de Avila, there is a Jamaican community, which celebrates its Afro-Caribbean heritage and emancipation from slavery with La Cinta festival on 1 August, with singing, dancing, games and eating typical food and sweets, all dating from 1917. At Venezuela, south of Ciego de Avila, Haitian immigrants formed the OKAY group, which celebrates its festival in the second half of October with drumming, congas and *merengues*, as well as traditional Haitian food and drink.

About 3 km north of Morón to the west of the road is the Laguna de la Leche (Milk Lake), Cuba's largest natural lake at 68.2 sq km. It is so called because of its cloudy white appearance, caused by lime deposits under the water. Its salinity makes it very popular with several thousand flamingos. It is the location for the **Aquatic Carnival** of Morón held in August or September.

On the opposite (east) side of the road is **Laguna La Redonda**, which covers an area of 26 sq km, with four main canals and a channel network at an average depth of 1 m. Red mangroves grow in abundance and you may see the *tocororo*, the national bird. You can arrange fishing trips at the lake and hire rods, boats and guides (T33-302489). A guided 45-minute motorboat tour to see the fauna and flora costs CUC$7 per person (minimum four passengers). Fishing (principally for catfish) is available all year (see What to do, below). There is a restaurant/bar where you can sit and watch the water if you don't want to fish.

Florencia

About 40 km west of Morón, turn south off the Circuíto Norte to reach the pleasant rural town of Florencia. This is a place where organized excursion parties come from the cays to sample Cuban country life in a hilly and picturesque landscape. You can go horse riding in the hills, swim in the mineral waters of a river pool, have a lunch of suckling pig on the banks of the river and watch a rodeo. Independent travellers who time their visit to coincide with a tour party should be able to join in with these activities in peaceful surroundings. The Boquerón caves near the town have stalactites and stalagmites as well as pictographs showing that aboriginal people used them for shelter.

Chambas to Máximo Gómez

Turning north off the Circuíto Norte at Chambas, a road heads north through flat farm land to Punta Alegre and Máximo Gómez on the coast. By the radio masts there is a police control point where officers will check your passports. At the end of the road a dirt track leads to a *campismo* and a small beach. It is a long drive for little reward unless you are really keen on archaeology or exploring rural Cuba.

Los Buchillones ① *At Punta Alegre, take the right fork through the village and then it is 2 km to the Fábrica Yeso, opposite which is a very small museum.* This archaeological site is the only destination of note in the area. The site has not yet been fully developed and has been little publicized outside the world of academia, but it is believed to be one of the most important Taíno sites in Cuba. The settlement of late ceramic age agriculturalists dates from 1220-1620. British and Cuban researchers have discovered 1000 wooden objects, intricately carved, as well as 500 items of stone, shells, bone and pottery. It is believed that when the settlement was abandoned, the houses and their contents collapsed into the lagoon, where the mud preserved the wood. The objects came to light when fishermen brought up axe handles, dishes, needles and ceremonial items from the waters. Six houses have also been discovered. The site was declared a National Monument in 2011.

Most of the relics are now held in provincial museums elsewhere or in storage. The display at the little site museum is limited, but there are plenty of explanatory boards in Spanish, with photos of the archaeology. Staff will be delighted to see you and will show you the path through the mangroves around the lagoon where excavations took place. Most of the excavations were carried out by using barrages to hold back the water, but now that these have been removed, there is nothing to indicate where the digs took place. There was once a project to bring visitors by boat from Cayo Coco, but the half-finished jetty and bar are now abandoned.

Listings Morón and the northwest

Where to stay

As the nearest urban centre to the Jardines del Rey archipelago, Morón is a less expensive alternative to the mega hotels on the cays.

Morón
Hotels

$$-$ La Casona de Morón
Cristóbal Colón 41, by the railway station, T33-502236, www.islazul.cu.
A very attractive, yellow colonial building with wrap-around verandah and balcony, now a boutique hotel. Friendly staff, large and comfortable rooms with good showers and a/c. Pool in the rear garden. Food available, but lots of *paladares* in easy reach. Free parking.

$$-$ Morón
Off Av de Tarafa, T33-502230, www.islazul.cu.
3-star, concrete block type of hotel, 144 rooms and suites with balcony, restaurant, coffee shop, bars, disco, large pool, games room, good a/c, tourism bureau, medical service, car hire, shop, shooting arranged with guide and dog. Choose your room carefully to make sure everything works and you are not near to the nightclub.

Casas particulares

$ Alojamiento Maite
Luz Caballero 40B entre Libertad y Agramonte, T33-504181, maite68@enet.cu.
Large house overlooking park with excellent accommodation in 4 spacious rooms and suites with large bathrooms, a/c, fan, comfortable beds with good quality linen and independent access to the rooms, all

well kept by knowledgeable Maite Valor Morales, her partner Idolka and their staff. There is a small, walled pool and a very good *paladar* on site (see below). Parking. English and Italian are spoken. Very professional business. On the other side of the road beside the park is **Alojamiento Vista al Parque**, run as an overspill or alternative *casa* by Idolka María González Rizo, 2 rooms with shared kitchen, fridge with drinks, terrace with table and chairs, food available at **Maite La Qbana** and use of pool and parking.

$ Casa Particular Carmen
Gen Peraza 38, T33-505453.
Magaly and Alfonso offer great food and hospitality at their spacious colonial home with parking (CUC$3). One room is larger than the other. The fridge is always full, there's a nice garden with mango tree where you can have your meals and drink mango juice, and they are happy to arrange any transport or trips you want. The house is in the town centre and can be noisy with traffic, but convenient for banks and restaurants and at weekends there is a fruit and veg market next door.

$ Hostal Alicia
Libertad 90 entre Martí y Castillo, T33-505194, mob 5327 6404, katiavaz@enet.cu.
Giraldo and Katia run a comfortable, friendly household with a good standard of accommodation. Very helpful, they can arrange taxi excursions to the cays and elsewhere. Guest rooms upstairs, 1 double and 1 family room sleeping 4, host family lives downstairs, a/c, mini bar, TV, safety box. Good food served on rooftop terrace. Parking.

$ Hostal Dra Mirtha Carballo González
Dimas Daniel 19 entre Castillo y Serafina, T33-503036.
Lovely, spacious apartment upstairs with terrace, or room at the back of the house downstairs. All smart and clean with good furnishings and good water pressure. Mirtha and her staff are attentive and helpful, while Alvis is a great chef on the barbecue. Large

breakfasts and excellent evening meals, also run as a *paladar*.

$ Hostal Lalita
Av Tarafa 174, esq 7, T33-503523.
A lovely *casa* right on the main road run by a friendly family. The ample accommodation is upstairs with large terrace overlooking the street, large bathroom, huge sitting room, kitchen and dining area. There's also a sun terrace surrounded by bougainvillea. Food is available and parking.

$ Hostal Oasis Papito
Luz Caballero 38 entre Libertad y José M Castañeda, T5254 8595, oasispapito@nauta.cu.
2 rooms upstairs, 1 double and the other with 2 double beds, a/c, fridge, sitting area, use of kitchen, terrace at the back overlooks roofs. The family lives downstairs and are helpful, with lots of information. The owner is a barman on Cayo Coco and makes good cocktails. Pretty breakfast, evening meal on request. Parking.

Where to eat

Morón

$$$-$$ Dra Mirtha Carballo González
Dimas Daniel 19 entre Castillo y Serafina, T33-503036.
Paladar attached to a *casa particular* offering great food cooked on the grill, such as fresh fish cooked over coals, vegetarian dishes as well as the usual pork and pasta. Beautifully presented and lots of dishes. You won't go hungry. Reservations essential if you are not lodging there.

$$$-$$ Liberluz
Luz Caballero 42B entre Libertad y Agramonte, T33-505054.
1830 until late. Reservations only. *Paladar* attached to a *casa particular* serving a variety of Cuban and international dishes including lobster, crab or octopus and pastas with a prix fixe menu. Pleasant open air garden setting with most tables under cover,

capacity for 60 diners. Rather loud music can hinder conversation sometimes.

$$$-$$ Maite la Qbana
Luz Caballero 40B entre Libertad y Agramonte, T33-504181.
Paladar attached to a *casa particular* serving breakfast 0730-1000, lunch with prior reservation and dinner 1800-2200. Special diets can be catered for with advance notice. Probably the best food in the area, very popular, huge helpings and lots of dishes on the table, not just Cuban fare. All fresh ingredients with tasty fish and seafood. Substantial breakfasts. Professional service, good wine as well as cocktails. Reservations advised.

Laguna de la Leche and around

$$$-$$ La Atarraya
on the Laguna de la Leche, T33-505351.
Tue-Sun, 4 sittings, 1230, 1400, 1600, 1800.
Dishes are based on seafood and fish. Lovely setting.

$$$-$ Ranchón La Boca
Laguna de la Leche, T33-504420.
Tue-Sun 1200-1800.
Lots of fish dishes, known for its fried fish.

$$$-$ La Redonda
Laguna La Redonda, T33-302489. Tue-Sun.
Overlooking the water, boats go out from here for trips around the lagoon. Tables outdoors or under cover. Popular at weekends for family outings, food acceptable. Pleasant just to sit and gaze over the water with a cold beer on your way back from Cayo Coco.

Entertainment

Morón
Buenavista Social Club, *Martí 382 entre Dimas Daniel y Enrique José Varona. Tue-Sat 1800-2400, Sun matinee 1400-0200.*

Music in the style of the popular Buenavista Social Club.
Casa de la Trova (Centro Cultural El Patio del Gallo), *C Libertad 74 entre Martí y Narciso López, T33-504602. Thu-Sat 1200-1600, Fri 1200-2100, Thu-Sun 2200-0200.* Traditional music with local *trova* singers. Admission varies according to the event.
Casa del Bolero, *Martí entre Libertad y Agramonte, T33-505758.* Live boleros, drinks and fast food.
El Patio de Artex, *Libertad esq Narciso López.* Open-air entertainment, *boleros*, comedians, dancing, national and local artists.
El Patio del Gallo, *Narciso López 272 esq Libertad. Mon-Thu 0800-1200, Fri, Sun 0800-0100, Sat 0800-0200.* Music, comedy and shows, most night-time activities start at 2030, entrance CUP$10, Wed comedy night 2300, CUP$25, other shows begin 2130-2200.

Festivals

Morón
Mar Feria Internacional del Libro, with book sales, lectures and seminars. Every year it is dedicated to the work of a single author.
Jun Festival Internacional del Bolero at the Teatro San Carlos, Calle Martí 225 entre Castillo y Serafín Sánchez, during the 1st fortnight, usually dedicated to a single singer and his works.

Laguna de la Leche and around
Sep Carnaval Acuático is an aquatic festival held in the first 2 weeks of the month on the Laguna de la Leche, where some 14 floats from all over the country compete.

What to do

Morón
Tour operators
Contact **Cubanacán** (T33-504720/502230 in Hotel Morón); **Cubatur** (Martí 169 entre Libertad y Agramonte, T33-505519); **Havanatur** (T33-505866).

Laguna de la Leche and around
Fishing and shooting

Hotels can organize freshwater fishing trips to Laguna La Redonda, where you can hire rods, boats and guides. Non-fishing visitors can hire *lanchas*. Fishing is available all year, there is no closed season. Freshwater fishing is not as good as it used to be, due to the disappearance of the trout and their replacement by catfish. The shooting season for pigeon is 15 Jul-1 Sep; for duck 15 Oct-31 Mar.

Horse riding

At the **Isla de Turiguanó** north of Morón you can visit the International Centre for Quarter Horses, where horse riding is possible. It's often included on tours of the area.

Transport

Bus

Morón bus terminal is at Martí entre Poi y Céspedes, but **Viazul** does not come here. Get off the bus in Ciego de Avila and take a taxi, CUC$10-15, 36 km. Inter-municipal buses leave from the train station to neighbouring towns and villages, with 7 a day to **Ciego de Avila**.

Car hire

Cubacar is at Hotel Morón, T33-502028, and at Av Tarafa, T33-502222.

Taxi

A taxi from Morón to **Cayo Coco** hotels or airport, CUC$40; to **Cayo Guillermo** hotels, CUC$60; to **Ciego de Avila**, CUC$10-15.

Train

Morón is on the **Santa Clara–Nuevitas** railway line; the train runs one day to Santa Clara (dep 1720, passing through Morón at 1421) and the next day to Nuevitas (passing through at 0021), uncomfortable but if you can get on you pay in CUP$. You can also get to **Camagüey** daily 0310, returning 1530, paying in CUP$; and to **Ciego de Avila**, daily 0600, 1215, 1605, 2000.

Cayos Coco and Guillermo

sand, sea and all-inclusives

The Jardines del Rey archipelago was named by Diego de Velázquez in honour of the king of Spain. The cays were isolated and visited only by fishermen until the white-sand beaches and turquoise water attracted the attention of the tourist industry and a causeway was built in 1988 allowing access by land.

Since then, Cayo Coco has become a focal point for tourism development. The hotels are large, luxury all-inclusive resorts built and operated with foreign investment. The cays are very remote and nearly all foreigners are here on a package of a week or so. Development is now in progress on Cayo Paredón and Cayo Cruz (both in Camagüey Province) and roads and bridges are currently being constructed. In addition, a couple of *pueblos* are planned at Playa Flamenco and Playa Pilar to offer restaurants, bars, entertainment and shops outside the resorts.

Cayo Coco *Colour map 2, B6.*

Cayo Coco is the largest cay in the archipelago at 374 sq km. The landscape is mostly mangrove and bush and shelters many migratory as well as resident birds, some of which are considered endemic. In fact, Cayo Coco gets its name from the Coco Blanco, or white ibis, which stands

Fact...
Flamingos nearly died out here in the 1970s but, with some encouragement, the population in the cays has now increased to some 30,000 birds.

Essential Cayos Coco and Guillermo

Finding your feet

The **international airport** on Cayo Coco is convenient if that is your destination, saving a long bus ride out to the cays. So far it is receiving scheduled international flights from Argentina, the UK and Canada, as well as domestic flights and charter flights according to season and demand. Travelling by land, the first hotels on Cayo Coco are 62 km from Morón. The island is connected to the mainland by a 27 km causeway (*pedraplen*) cross the Bahía de Perros, which continues to Cayo Guillermo and Cayo Paredón Grande. Drivers must stop at the checkpoint, show passports and pay a CUC\$2 one-way toll. At the rotonda on Cayo Coco there is a gas station, shop and fast food bar. All the hotels on Cayo Coco and Cayo Guillermo are along the north coast. Contact tour operators, see What to do, page 260, to arrange excursions.

less than 50 cm tall and lives in remote areas of Cayo Coco and Cayo Romano.

The Atlantic side of the island has 22 km of excellent beaches, although many are quite difficult to get to and some of the hotels restrict access to guests only. ★**Playa Los Flamencos** has good public access, with some 5 km of white sand and shallow, crystalline water. At the eastern end, beyond the hotels, you can walk a long way out at knee depth, looking for starfish along the way. There are mangroves and the beach is unspoilt and uncrowded. Year round it is possible to see Roseate flamingos (*Phoenicoterus ruber ruber*), after whom the beach is named. There's a beach bar and grill with car parking and a couple of unobtrusive hotels.

Anyone looking for solitude can explore **Playa Prohibida**, appropriately named as the government has banned construction here in the interests of ecology. Nearby, a nature trail leads into the centre of Cayo Coco, ending at the dune, **Loma del Puerto**, the highest point in the area.

Parque El Bagá ① *Ctra a Cayo Guillermo Km 17, T33-301062 ext 103, baga_director@ fica.inf.cu*, is a protected 70-ha area designed to preserve the wildlife as well as make it accessible to visitors. It is named after a local tree, the roots of which are used for floats in fishing nets. You can take a guided tour through the forest along trails or a boat trip through the mangroves and canals, good for birdwatching.

Sitio La Güira ① *animal show at 1000 and 1500 Mon-Sat, children's circus show 0900-1300 Thu*, is an attractive purpose-built ranch in the middle of the cay offering horse riding, fiestas, animal shows and *bohíos* where you can stay. The site takes its name from the local name for calabash; there are many calabash trees growing here, the fruit of which are used to make maracas. There used to be a charcoal maker on the site at the beginning of the 20th century. **El Parador de la Silla**, near the entrance, is a rustic mirador from where you can see water birds, flamingos and the local topography.

Cayo Guillermo

Cayo Guillermo, a 13-sq-km cay with 5 km of beach, is connected to Cayo Coco by the causeway. The cay is protected by a long coral reef which is good for diving, with plentiful fish and crustaceans, while on land there are lots of birds. The sand dunes, covered in palms and other vegetation, are believed to be among the highest in the Caribbean.

Playa Pilar at the far western tip is one of the best beaches in Cuba. Resorts on Cayo Coco arrange day trips to the beach or it is 1½ hours' drive from Morón. There's a large restaurant and bar for drinks and food, plus toilet facilities and parking (CUC\$1 until 1700). Sunbeds and shade can be rented for CUC\$1 up to CUC\$10 for a four-poster bed and three drinks. Most of the beach is cleaned daily of weed and litter. The sand is soft and pale; the water is clear and not very deep, making it good for children. There are boat trips out to the reef for snorkelling, or you can walk along the beach to the headland for a stunning view from the top of the cliffs, but take shoes as the rocks are painful on bare feet.

> **Fact...**
> Ernest Hemingway came here to fish, which is why there are frequent references to him on the cays. Fishing is still superb around here.

Across a narrow channel to the north of Cayo Guillermo is **Cayo Media Luna**, a small islet with excellent snorkelling on the reef offshore, where you can see a wide variety of fish and coral as well as a few wrecks. The dictator Fulgencio Batista had his holiday home here.

Listings Cayos Coco and Guillermo

Tourist information

The hotels have *burós de turismo* which can give information, although their main purpose is to sell tours. These can be convenient if you do not have a car. Infotur has an office in the international airport in Cayo Coco. Maps and phone cards are for sale while information and leaflets are free.

Where to stay

All the hotels on Cayo Coco and Cayo Guillermo are all-inclusive. Some of them are huge, with the largest being the new Meliá Jardines del Rey, at 1176 rooms. More are being built with the aim of reaching 32,000 rooms on the cays. All hotels offer several restaurants, entertainment and watersports. The rate will vary depending on how long you are staying and the time of year. Although most people who stay here are booked on packages from abroad, independent travellers can book their own stays at short notice once they are in the country. In high season there is limited availability for rooms of less than a week's rental, but out of season rooms are filled on a daily basis. There are lots of 2- to 3-day packages or weekend breaks offered from Havana. A day pass is available from all the hotels, allowing you use of all the facilities, meals and drinks, usually around CUC$40-50, depending on the hotel and how late you are allowed to stay.

Cayo Coco

$$-$ Sitio La Güira
Cayo Coco, T33-301208.
The only option apart from all-inclusives, but not on the beach. 4 thatched *cabañas* sit in this delightful, peaceful rustic setting worlds apart from the resorts, where horses, ducks, turkeys and other animals roam around and a sad crocodile doesn't. The *cabañas* come with a small private bathroom, fridge and a/c. Restaurant on site (open 0800-2300) serves decent food. Best to reserve in advance. You'll need your own transport to get to the beach. Bring mosquito repellent.

Where to eat

Cayo Coco

$$$-$ Ranchón Las Dunas
Playa Academia, just north of the rotunda. Open 1100-2300.
Seafood served under a thatched roof. One of several state-run beach bars (*ranchón*) offering lunch, snacks and drinks for beachgoers and not usually too busy as hotel guests eat in their hotels.

$$$-$ Ranchón Playa Flamenco
Playa Los Flamencos. Open 0900-1600, food served 1200-1500.
Attractive beach bar and grill run by friendly staff. A full lobster meal will cost you around CUC$18 but a fried fish lunch is about CUC$6. Pleasant just to sit in the shade

overlooking the beach with a cold beer or ice cream. Parking.

Cayo Guillermo

$$$-$ Ranchón Media Luna
On a little cay off Playa Pilar, reached by boat.
Bar and grill, seafood, drinks and natural juices.

$$$-$ Ranchón Playa Pilar
Playa Pilar.
Overlooking idyllic sands, this fairly large beach bar gets very busy at lunch time with coach loads of visitors on day trips from the hotels, so get your table early.

Entertainment

Cayo Coco
All the hotels offer activities, night clubs, discos, piano bars, etc.
Cueva Jabalí, *Ctra a Cayo Guillermo Km 5, T33-301206. Daily 2200-0200.* A cave with several interconnecting rooms where shows and discos are held. Usually CUC$5 for transport from your hotel, then you pay admission with open bar, although there are packages on offer. Tue CUC$20 with live music and open bar, Thu CUC$10 for recorded music and open bar. Good club atmosphere but be prepared for bats and spiders as well as insufficient toilet facilities – it is a natural cave.

What to do

Diving
Diving is rewarding in the Jardines del Rey, with 32 km of coral reef made up of pillars, walls and sandy channels, including 28 dive sites of between 4 and 30 m where you can see coral gardens, invertebrates, lots of fish, turtles, dolphins, sharks and other large pelagics. The dive centres on Cayo Coco and Cayo Guillermo are run by **Marlin Náutica y Marinas** (www.nauticamarlin.com). They are **Blue Diving**, **Hotel Meliá Cayo Coco**, **Coco Diving**, **Tryp Cayo Coco** and **Green Moray**, at Meliá Cayo Guillermo, all of which offer resort courses and open water certification

with CMAS, ACUC, SSI. Staff are attentive and safety conscious, as well as fun, but they do allow fish feeding and touching of fish and coral, which should be discouraged if you encounter it. 1 dive costs CUC$40; dive packages are cheaper per dive, CUC$450 for 20 dives. An Open Water course costs CUC$310 and a Resort course CUC$70.

Fishing
Deep-sea fishing offshore can be arranged at the marinas on Cayo Coco and Cayo Guillermo (see below) and costs around CUC$290 per boat (up to 4 people) for a half day (4 hrs) or CUC$450 for a full day (7 hrs) including lunch and open bar. Inshore fishing for fish such as mackerel and snapper to the east of Cayo Paredón Grande costs CUC$129 per boat for 2 passengers for 4 hrs and CUC$179 for 7 hrs (T33-301323). There is an annual International Fishing Tournament mid-Oct from the **Marina Internacional de Cayo Guillermo**. Hotels can also organize freshwater fishing trips to Laguna La Redonda (see page 253).

Marinas
Marina Aguas Tranquilas, *Cayo Coco, T33-301323, www.nauticamarlin.com.* VHF 16 and 72, commissary, minor repairs, fuel, water, boat rental, fishing, dive centre.
Marina Internacional Cayo Guillermo, *Faro Paredón Grande, Cayo Guillermo, T33-301411/301323, www.nauticamarlin.com.* VHF 16, 19. 6 berths, 30 m draft, fuel, water, electricity, commissary, restaurant, bar, boat rental, fishing, diving, snorkelling, excursions.

Sailing
Catamaran tours from **Marina Aguas Tranquilas** to **Playa Pilar** and the coral reef, with snorkelling, lobster lunch and open bar, cost CUC$75 for adults and CUC$38 for children under 12 for a full day or CUC$43 and CUC$22 for a half day (T33-301516); a 4-hr sail to **Cayo Baliza**, on the route described by Hemingway in *Islands in the Stream*, costs CUC$29 for adults and

CUC$14.50 for children with lunch, open bar and snorkelling. You can drive your own motorboat in guided tours, 2 hrs, CUC$41 adults, CUC$20.50 children under 12, through the canals and mangroves south of Cayo Guillermo, with snorkelling (T33-301516). Private charters for up to 6 people with crew, fishing tackle, snorkelling equipment, open bar and lunch cost CUC$290 for a half day and CUC$480 for a full day (7 hrs). A trip to **Cayo Paredón Grande** with a visit to the Diego Velásquez lighthouse, Playa Los Pinos and a beach bar, followed by a boat trip around the cay is CUC$25pp, children half price (T33-301323). You can also go by boat on a 3-hr birdwatching trip from either Cayo Coco or Cayo Guillermo to see the flamingos, CUC$29 adults, CUC$22 children. There are several other options, including sunset cocktail trips with live music.

Spa
Centro Spa-Talaso Acuavida, *Av de los Hoteles, T33-302157, www.servimedcuba.com*. At the eastern end of the hotel strip on Cayo Coco, this spa offers mud therapy, massages and hydro treatments.

Tour operators
For general information and tours, contact **Cubanacán** (Hotel Tryp Cayo Coco, T33-301215, combinado@viajes.cav.cyt.cu); **Cubatur** (T33-301338/301436, cleon@cubatur.cu); and **Havanatur** (Hotel Sol Cayo Coco, T33-266342, vgomez@cimex.com.cu). **Ecotur**, *Parque El Baga, Cayo Coco, T33-301062/5, www.ecoturcuba.tur.cu*. Organizes freshwater fishing and shooting for game birds and waterfowl at Presa de Chambas and other lakes close by, as well as sea fishing. They also offer jeep or scooter tours of Cayo Coco and Cayo Paredón, CUC$39 adults, CUC$20 children by jeep, CUC$29 adults, CUC$15 children by scooter, minimum 2 people with guide. **Gaviota Tours**, *Hotel Playa Coco, T33-302259/60, gaviotatourscc@playacoco.co.cu*.

Self-drive jeep tours to the Quarter Horse centre on Isla Turiguanó, including the Casa de la Trova, lunch at the Loma de Cunagua, and visit to a crocodile farm, CUC$69 adults, CUC$52 children.

Watersports
Kite surfing is available at the hotels **Allegro Cayo Guillermo**, **Sol Cayo Guillermo** and **Iberostar Mojito Cayo Coco**, where equipment rental is CUC$50 and a course is CUC$250. El Paso beach on Cayo Guillermo is the longest and best beach for kite surfing, with sustained winds of 20-40 km.

Transport
Air
The Jardines del Rey international airport is on **Cayo Coco**, T33-309161-5. It receives **AeroCaribbean** flights from **Havana** as well as international flights from Canada, the UK and Argentina. International airlines landing here include **Cubana**, **Sunwing**, **Thomas Cook**, **Airtransat**, **Canjet** and **Air Canada**. The terminal has banking services, tourist information and shops selling handicrafts, cigars and rum.

Bus
Only tour buses go to **Cayo Coco**; there are no public buses.

Car hire
Cubacar is represented in most of the hotels. **Rex**, which has the best cars, is at Hotel Sol Cayo Coco, T33-302244. Mopeds can be hired on the cayos at most of the hotels for CUC$15 per hr or CUC$40 for 24 hrs.

Taxi
A taxi from the airport on Cayo Coco to Cayo Coco hotels is CUC$15; from the airport to **Cayo Guillermo**, CUC$35; from Cayo Coco to **Morón**, CUC$40; to **Ciego de Avila** CUC$60; from Cayo Guillermo to Morón, CUC$60; to **Ciego de Avila**, CUC$80.

Camagüey
Province

Camagüey is the largest of Cuba's 14 provinces, covering more than 14,000 sq km, and is an excellent place to break your journey if you are crossing the island from one end to the other. The attractive countryside is flat and fertile, rising gently to the Sierra de Cubitas north of Camagüey city, where there are caves and rocky spurs. Cattle roam the grasslands, which are dotted with Royal palms. Cowboys on horseback, wearing wide-brimmed hats and with machetes dangling at their sides, are a common sight on the road, as are horse-drawn carts, the commonest form of transport in rural areas. The colonial capital city of Camagüey is recommended for a stay of a few days, as it has many historical buildings and sites of revolutionary interest from the 19th and 20th centuries. However, most tourists head instead for the north coast to Santa Lucía beach resort for sun, sea and sand. On the southern coast of the province there is a fishing port at Santa Cruz del Sur but otherwise little habitation. Offshore, the sea is dotted with tiny uninhabited cays, part of the Jardines de la Reina archipelago (see box, page 286).

a largely undiscovered jewel in the heart of the country

Declared a UNESCO World Heritage Site in 2008, Camagüey is a little-visited colonial treasure, whose unique maze of streets reveals architectural gems at every turn. Significant restoration work is taking place in the old city, restoring the churches, plazas and mansions to their former glory. However, this is not a city preserved for the benefit of tourists: colonial buildings of the 17th to 19th centuries are used for everyday purposes and are interspersed with more modern constructions from the 20th century.

The city has been politically and historically important since the beginning of the 16th century. Many generations of revolutionaries are associated with Camagüey and several key figures are commemorated here, the most notable being Ignacio Agramonte, who was killed in action in 1873. Culturally, Camagüey also has plenty to offer, with an excellent ballet company, music venues and art exhibitions.

Parque Ignacio Agramonte and around

The Parque has lots of marble and a statue of Ignacio Agramonte on horseback. **Santa Iglesia Catedral** is on the south side. Construction was started after the town fire of 1616 with the intention that it should be the largest parish church in Puerto Príncipe, with two chapels and a cemetery. In the 19th century the chapels were demolished and a different shape was given to the building in 1875. In 1937 the sculptor Juan Albaijez carved a statue of Christ, which was placed inside the church. The Casa de la Trova Patricio Ballagas Palacios is on the west side of the square, together with the library.

Essential Camagüey city

Finding your feet

The city is located squarely in the middle of the province and all major routes pass through it, making transport and communication easy. The **international airport** is 9 km north of the city and you may be lucky enough to find a bus that will bring you into Parque Finlay, otherwise you will have to catch a taxi, CUC$5. Most tourists arriving at the airport are taken by bus straight to their resorts on the north coast, not into the city. There are flights from Havana and international scheduled and charter flights, although these vary with the season. The city is on the main railway line between Havana and Santiago. There are also long-distance buses from Havana and Santiago, as well as good connections with neighbouring towns.

Getting around

The **railway station** is just north of the city centre, within walking distance of several hotels and *casas particulares*. The **bus station** is further out, on the other side of the river from the centre (taxi CUC$5). The active will be able to walk to most sites of interest in the city; otherwise you can pick up a bicitaxi. Note that many streets have two names, one an old colonial religious name and the other a replacement from the early 20th century. People use both (see map, page 264). Many provincial towns and Playa Santa Lucía can be reached by bus from the city, but check your return journey before setting off. Car hire is available.

Camagüey

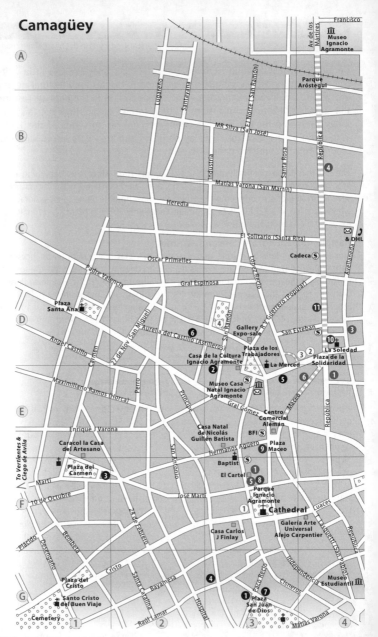

Francisco

Av de los Mártires

Museo Ignacio Agramonte

Parque Aróstegui

Lugareño
Santayana
Norte (San Ramón)
MR Silva (San José)
Industria
Santa Rosa
República
Matías Varona (San Martín)
Heredia
El Solitario (Santa Rita)
Oscar Primelles
& DHL
Cadeca (S)
Padre Valencia
López Recio
Gral Espinosa
Avellaneda

Plaza Santa Ana
San Ramón
❹
Aurelia del Castillo (Astilleros)
Gallery Expo-sale
San Esteban
❸
2 de Nov (San Miguel)
❻
Plaza de los Trabajadores
10
La Soledad
Angel Castillo
Carmen
Casa de la Cultura Ignacio Agramonte
❷
3 2
Plaza de la Solidaridad
Maximiliano Ramos (Horca)
Perto
Principe
La Merced
❺
❻
❶
Museo Casa Natal Ignacio Agramonte
(S)
República
Gral Gómez
Maceo
Enrique J Varona
Centro Comercial Alemán
Casa Natal de Nicolás Guillén Batista
BFI (S)
To Vertientes & Ciego de Avila
Caracol la Casa del Artesano
San Antonio
Hermanos Agüero
Plaza Maceo
❾
Plaza del Carmen
❸
Baptist
(S)
Martí
El Cartel
❶
❺ ❽
10 de Octubre
José Martí
Parque Ignacio Agramonte
❶
Cathedral
Luaces
Galería Arte Universal Alejo Carpentier
21 de Febrero
Casa Carlos J Finlay
Independencia
Lescano (San Pablo)
Placido
Desengaño
Bembeta
Cristo
Santa Catalina
Bayamesa
Hospital
Paco Recio
Cisneros
República
Museo Estudiantil
Plaza del Cristo
Santo Cristo del Buen Viaje
❹
Plaza San Juan de Dios
❶ ❼
Cemetery
Raúl Lamar
Matías Varona

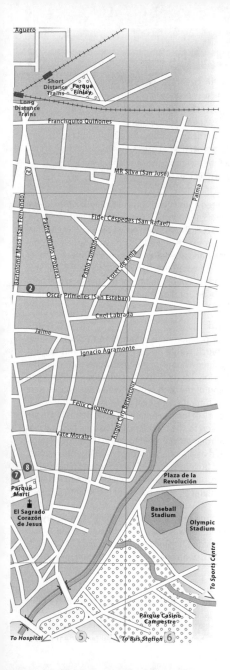

Where to stay 🛏

Avellaneda **1** *E4*
Casa Caridad cp **2** *C5*
Casa Láncara cp **3** *D4*
Colón **4** *B4*
El Marqués **5** *F3*
Gran Hotel **6** *E4*
Hospedaje Colonial
  Los Vitrales cp **7** *F4*
Natural Caribe cp **8** *E4*

Restaurants 🍴

1800 **1** *G3*
Casa Italia **2** *E3*
El Paso **3** *F1*
La Casa Austria **4** *G3*
La Isabela **5** *E3*
Mesón del Príncipe **6** *D2*
Parador de los
  Tres Reyes **7** *G3*

Bars 🍸

Bar el Cambio **8** *F3*
Bar Las Ruinas **9** *E3*
Bodegón San Cayetano &
  Callejón de la Soledad **10** *D4*
Club Oxio **11** *D4*

Entertainment 🎵

Casa de la Trova Patricio
  Ballagas **1** *F3*
Cine Encanto **2** *D4*
Cine Casablanca **3** *D4*
Teatro Principal **4** *D3*

N

Not to scale

ON THE ROAD

Tinajón – vessel of love and bondage

The logo of Camagüey is the *tinajón* and the city is known as the city of the *tinajones*. This story goes back to the time when the first settlers had serious problems with their water supply. However, it rained a lot in the region and the Spanish potters found a solution by storing water in pots similar to those brought from Spain containing wine and oil. From that time on the *tinajón* became a feature of every Camagüeyan house or patio. Legend has it that if a girl offers a visitor water from a *tinajón* he should not refuse it but, before accepting, he should know that if he drinks he will fall in love with the girl and never leave the city.

A famous son of Camagüey is remembered at the **Casa Carlos J Finlay** ① *Cristo 5 entre Lugareño y Callejón del Templador, T32-296745*. Born in 1833 in the city of Puerto Príncipe, as it then was, Finlay was of French and Scottish descent and studied in Philadelphia, Havana and Paris. As a result of his scientific research in the 1870s, he was the first to come up with the theory that a mosquito of the genus Aedes was the vector for yellow fever and that the mosquito population should be controlled. From 1902 to 1909 Finlay was the chief health officer of Cuba, and his findings were used to control the spread of both malaria and yellow fever during the construction of the Panama Canal at the beginning of the 20th century. He died in Havana in 1915.

Parque San Juan de Dios and around

A couple of blocks south of Parque Ignacio Agramonte is **San Juan de Dios**, another National Monument, built in 1728 as a church with a hospital attached. It was the first hospital in the town for men and also contained a home for the aged. Apparently this is the only church in Latin America that has the Holy Trinity as its central image. The **Plaza San Juan de Dios** was created at the beginning of the 19th century when two houses were bought to make the plaza. At around this time the San Juan de Dios church tower was moved to the front. On 12 May 1873 the body of Ignacio Agramonte was deposited in the hospital for identification before being taken to the cemetery. In 1902 the hospital was closed and later converted to a military infirmary. It was used to house the homeless after the hurricane in 1932 and was inaugurated as a modern hospital in 1952. Cobblestones were laid in the plaza in 1956. The hospital building changed hands several times before the **Centro Provincial de Patrimonio Cultural** occupied it. The plaza is closed to traffic. There is a small handicraft market, **Tienda Caracol**, and a couple of restaurants. Calle San Juan de Dios is stuffed with art galleries.

Nearby, the **Casa Jesús Suárez Gayol**, now the **Museo Estudiantil Camagüeyano** ① *República 69, T32-297744, closed lunchtime*, was the home of one of the Cuban guerrillas who lost his life in Bolivia alongside Che Guevara. The museum has exhibits about Camagüeyans, particularly students, who were active revolutionaries in the struggle for independence.

Parque Martí

East of the cathedral along Luaces is the Parque Martí, also known as the **Plaza de la Juventud**. The **Sagrado Corazón de Jesús**, on Luaces, overlooking the Parque Martí, is a beautiful neo-Gothic church built in 1920. It used to have wonderful stained-glass windows depicting scenes from the gospel, but most were destroyed by stone throwing

BACKGROUND
Brother Olallo

José Olallo Valdés (1820-1889) was abandoned as a tiny baby in an orphanage in Havana but at a very young age joined the Order of St John of God and spent the rest of his life helping the sick and wounded. At the age of 15 he was moved to Camagüey to tend to those suffering from the cholera epidemic of 1835 and continued to work in the San Juan de Dios hospital, later taking care of the wounded from both sides of the war. It is believed that he attended the body of Ignacio Agramonte in 1873. Religious orders suffered persecution under Spanish law but because of his popularity at the hospital the civil authorities allowed him to remain, thus becoming the only remaining Brother of St John of God in Cuba. He was beatified in the Plaza de la Caridad on 29 November 2008 in the first such ceremony ever to take place on Cuban soil.

after the Revolution. Restoration work in recent years has included a new roof for the church and the repainting of the whole plaza.

Plaza Maceo and around

If you walk north up Independencia from Parque Ignacio Agramonte, you come to Plaza Maceo, a busy junction of several roads with shops, banks and places to eat. One block west is the **Casa Natal de Nicolás Guillén Batista** ① *Agüeros 58 esq Cisneros, T32-293706*. The building may have been the poet's birthplace, but he only lived here until he was two. The building is now used as an art and cultural studies school, although staff are very happy to show you round and there are a few pictures and some of his poems on the walls. See also page 424. One block north of Plaza Maceo is the **Plaza de los Trabajadores**.

Plaza de los Trabajadores

Nuestra Señora de la Merced Located on the eastern edge of the plaza, this National Monument was built in 1747 as a church and convent at what was then the edge of town but is now in the centre. Over the years it has been transformed into a baroque church and a diocesan house. In the courtyard there are abandoned cannon used by the Spanish military in the 19th century. In 1906 a fire burned the altar, which was reconstructed in Spain in a neo-Gothic style. As the city expanded, the cemetery had to be closed, but the catacombs can still be seen. The entrance is either side of the altar; you will be followed by a warden down the steps into the mini-museum. The original wooden cross on the bell tower was moved into the catacombs in 1999. You can also see bones, skulls and several 18th-century artefacts from the church. The ceiling of the church shows early 20th-century paintings in a swirling pre-Raphaelite style. On the walls are four 17th-century and eight 18th-century paintings, but the most important treasure in the church is the Santo Sepulcro, a silver coffin, constructed in 1762 with the donation of 23,000 silver coins. Before the Revolution, it was carried in procession along the streets of Camagüey; now it is kept inside the church. The church has been under restoration for many years and is still not completed. It has an external clock, which was the first public clock in Camagüey, and a library. There is always someone around to show visitors the church and provide information.

Museo Casa Natal Ignacio Agramonte ① *Av Ignacio Agramonte 459, opposite the church on Plaza de los Trabajadores, T32-297116, Mon-Sat 0900-1645, Sun 09030-1430, CUC$2, musical activities Sat 0800-1500*. The museum is for students of revolutionary history but comes alive if you take the guided tour. Ignacio Agramonte y Loynaz, one of the national heroes of the struggle against the Spanish, was born here on 23 December 1841. Agramonte, a lawyer and cattle rancher, led the rebellion in this area. In 1868, shortly after finishing his studies at university in Spain and Havana, he took up arms against the colonial power, and in July 1869 forces under his command bombarded Camagüey. However, he died on 11 May 1873 after being wounded in action, and all his goods were confiscated by the state. The ground floor and courtyard of this lovely house were turned into a market while the second storey was occupied by the Spanish council. Later the ground floor became a bar and a post office. In the second half of the 20th century the house was restored, and now the top floor is a museum exhibiting objects relating to the life of this revolutionary, while other rooms are used for lectures, art exhibitions and offices.

East of Plaza de los Trabajadores

The area east of Plaza de los Trabajadores, along Ignacio Agramonte and Callejón de los Milagros, is devoted to the cinema: there are several film houses, plus cafés, galleries and restaurants on every corner (although they are not all worth trying). At the next junction is the tiny Plaza de la Solidaridad, formerly Plaza del Gallo, little more than a junction of five roads. (República is pedestrian up to and just beyond the railway line several blocks to the north.)

Nuestra Señora de la Soledad ① *República esquina Ignacio Agramonte on the edge of the Plaza de la Soledad*. This is the oldest church in town. In 1697 the Presbyterian Velasco started the construction of a hermitage, which was completed in 1701 and transformed into a parish by the bishop Diego Evelino de Compostela. In 1733 the current church was started, although construction was not finished until 1776. The outside is of brick, while inside there are attractive painted friezes on the arches, a carved wooden roof and a painted cupola (which needs renovation).

Plaza Santa Ana

Iglesia Nuestra Señora de Santa Ana, west along General Gómez, was started in 1697 with a single nave. Over the years it was gradually enlarged with a tower added in the middle of the 19th century.

Quinta Amalia Simoni ① *Gen Gómez 608 entre Simoni y Plaza de la Habana, T32-292469, Mon-Sat 0900-1645, Sun 0900-1430, CUC$1*. This was the family residence of the woman who became the wife of Ignacio Agramonte. The Spanish set fire to the house during the Ten Years' War, damaging most of its opulent furnishings, such as the Carrara marble, and it never fully recovered its former glory. After the war, the Simoni family had their property restored to them, but Agramonte's widow and two children lived there only intermittently, spending much of their time in the USA. The house was opened as a museum in 2005 and then underwent further restoration works before reopening in 2014 with three new exhibition rooms (ten in total): one deals with the history of the house; a second displays objects relating to the family; a third is dedicated to the role of women in Cuban society. It is considered the symbolic home of the Camagüeyan family and activities take place here for local women and children.

BACKGROUND

Camagüey city

The village of Santa María de Puerto del Príncipe was first founded in 1515 at Punta del Guincho in the Bahía de Nuevitas, but the site was unsatisfactory for development because of a lack of water and poor soil fertility. In 1516 the first settlers moved to Caonao (an Amerindian word for gold or place where gold can be found), an aborigine chiefdom near the Río Caonao. However, in 1527 enslaved Amerindians rose up against the Spanish colonizers and burned down the town. The settlers then moved again, further inland, between the Río Tínima and the Río Hatibonico, where the village was finally established.

Moving inland was no protection against pirates. During the 17th century, as the settlement became prosperous on the back of livestock and sugar, it was the target of the Welshman Henry Morgan in 1668 and of French pirates led by François Granmont in 1679. However, despite the looting, the town continued to grow throughout the 18th century. In an attempt to foil pirate attacks, the town's architects rejected the usual colonial grid system and took the precaution of creating a highly irregular urban plan, which, according to the 2008 UNESCO report, "contains a system of large and minor squares, serpentine streets, alleys and irregular urban blocks, highly exceptional for Latin American colonial towns located in plain territories… The Spanish colonizers followed medieval European influences in terms of urban layout and traditional construction techniques brought to the Americas by their masons and construction masters". On 12 November 1817, Fernando VII, the king of Spain, declared Puerto Príncipe a city with a coat of arms. The city retained its original name until 9 June 1903.

Several revolutionary events of the 19th century are remembered in Camagüey. In 1812 eight black slaves fighting for independence under the command of José Antonio Aponte, were executed. In 1826, revolutionary Agüero Velazco was hanged in what is now Parque Agramonte. Joaquín de Agüero y Agüero and his followers took arms against the colonial power in 1851, but their movement failed and they were executed by firing squad. In 1868, when Carlos Manuel de Céspedes initiated the struggle for independence, many Camagueyans supported him, including Ignacio Agramonte, Salvador Cisneros Betancourt, Maximiliano Ramos, Javier de la Vega and others who are remembered in street names, monuments and museums.

Plaza del Carmen

Nuestra Señora del Carmen, on the west side of Plaza del Carmen, was started in 1732 by Eusebia de Varona y de la Torre, who wanted to build a three-nave temple for the Jesuits. However, they did not like its location, which at that time was on the outskirts of the town, so they demolished it. One hundred years later, her heirs, with the help of Padre Valencia built a women's hospital on the site, which was finished in 1825. A church was built alongside the hospital, originally with only one tower, but a second was added in 1846, making it the only two-towered church in Camagüey. Part of the church collapsed in 1966 but restoration started in January 2001. The façade has been replastered and work continues inside. The hospital is now the **Sede del Historiador de la Ciudad**.

The whole of the Plaza del Carmen has been renovated to improve housing as well as to create smart new restaurants and tourist shops. Look out for the life-size statues modelled on real people going about their ordinary tasks: women gossiping over coffee, a man pushing a cart, another man reading a newspaper and a couple with their arms around each other. It's pleasant to sit on a bench with them and watch the world go by.

Plaza del Cristo
The square (also known as **Parque Gonfaus**) at the west end of Calle Cristo is not as interesting as some of the older squares in the centre of town as it has no buildings of architectural interest. The church of **Santo Cristo del Buen Viaje** was built as a small hermitage in 1794 by Emeterio de Arrieta with one nave. In the 19th-century two naves and a tower were constructed. It is rather dilapidated, but the large cemetery behind it is kept very smart with grand tombs.

North of the centre
From Plaza de la Solidaridad, Calle República heads directly north and is pedestrianized until just past the railway crossing by the train station, where it becomes Av de los Mártires. Here is **Museo Provincial Ignacio Agramonte** ① *Av de los Mártires 2 esq Ignacio Sánchez, T32-282425, Tue, Wed, Thu and Sat 1000-1800, Fri 1200-2000, Sun 0900-1300, CUC$2,* first built as a cavalry barracks in 1848. It was converted into the **Hotel Camagüey** from 1905-1943 but still has cannon, water troughs and *tinajones* in the garden. After considerable restoration the museum was inaugurated on 23 December 1955 (the anniversary of Agramonte's birth). There are exhibitions of archaeology, with copies of drawings and artefacts found in the caves of the Sierra de Cubitas (see page 276), natural history (lots of dusty stuffed animals and birds), paintings and furniture of the 19th and 20th centuries, including art by local painters.

At the far end of Avenida de los Mártires is Plaza Joaquín de Agüero (Plaza de Méndez), the second largest square in the city. Joaquín de Agüero and his followers were shot by a firing squad here on 12 August 1851. In 1913 a monument was erected to honour the heroes.

East of the centre
The **Parque Casino Campestre**, on the eastern side of the Río Hatibonico, was the first place in Cuba to hold cattle shows. In the 19th century it was used for fairs, dances and other social activities, but in the 20th century its purpose and structure was changed. Trees have been planted, and it is now a popular, green open space with monuments to independence fighter Salvador Cisneros Betancourt, to the Unknown Soldier, and to teachers. Next to the park there is a monument erected in 1941 to Barberán and Collar, the first pilots to cross the Atlantic at its widest point, in a flight from Seville. It took them 39 hours and 55 minutes.

Tourist information

All the main hotels have tourist agencies who can provide information, although their main aim is to sell tours. *Casas particulares* are usually better informed than agencies in Camagüey and often more helpful.

Where to stay

Camagüey centre
Hotels

$$$-$$ Gran Hotel
Maceo 67, entre Ignacio Agramonte y General Gómez, T32-292093-4, www.islazul.cu.
Colonial style, built 1939, when it was the most luxurious hotel in the country, perhaps even in Latin America. It is still attractive, with a lovely roof terrace, but service and cleanliness are unreliable. The 24-hr bar has live music until about 0200 at weekends, so avoid rooms above. Central, on a pedestrianized street, so rental cars are parked a block away. Small swimming pool with children's area, open to general public. Several dining options but all poor.

$$$-$$ Hotel E Avellaneda
República 226 entre Ignacio Agramonte y Callejón del Castellano, T32-244958, www.hotelescubanacan.com.
Only 9 rooms, all on ground floor in this restored mansion that was once the home of a doctor. Lovely central covered courtyard with columns and rooms off it. Friendly staff. No restaurant but lots of eating options nearby.

$$$-$$ Hotel E El Marqués
Cisneros 222 entre Hermanos Agüero y Martí, T32-244937, www.hotelescubanacan.com.
Charming colonial mansion converted to a 6-room hotel. Comfortable and good beds, well-equipped bathrooms with bathtub and rain shower, quiet a/c, all fresh and new, attractive patio for breakfast, parking on street outside (tip the caretaker).

$$ Colón
República 472 entre San José y San Martín, T32-283346/241727, www.islazul.cu.
Old style built in 1920s, beautifully painted in blue and white, marble staircase, long thin hotel on 2 floors around central well, rocking chairs overlook patio bar and restaurant, renovated 2015 with new wing. Small breakfast included, rooms with 1 or 2 beds, a/c, lobby bar, good cocktails, friendly staff. No parking.

Casas particulares

$ Casa Caridad
Oscar Primelles 310 A entre Bartolomé Masó y Padre Olallo (Pobres), T32-291554, abreucmg@enet.cu.
Caridad García Valera runs this colonial house with 3 rooms. Very clean, regularly fumigated, excellent water pressure in the shower. Delightful garden at the back with climbing and trailing plants over high walls and arbour, rocking chairs, eat indoors or outside, more than enough food, garage, safe parking.

$ CasAlta
Cisneros 160 Altos entre Luaces y San Clemente, T32-274712, 5466 0291 (mob), orlandohg@nauta.cu.
Kind and helpful Orlando and Alba offer 2 spacious rooms in an upstairs apartment with high ceilings, huge doors and windows in colonial style with artworks on the walls. Well-equipped with a/c, fan, TV and fridge.

$ Hospedaje Colonial Los Vitrales
Avellaneda 3 entre Gen Gómez y Martí, T32-295866, requejobarreto@gmail.com.
Run by Rafael Requejo and his family. Rafael speaks English and is full of stories about the architectural history of the house, which has a courtyard. Good traditional meals are served. 3 rooms with very high ceilings which open out onto patio with lush foliage, garage. In case of overspill, Rafael's sister has

a suite for rent through the garage so he can accommodate groups.

$ Casa Láncara
Avellaneda 160 entre Ignacio Agramonte y Jaime, T32-283187, T528 10375 (mob), casalancara@yahoo.es.

Built 1910 in colonial style with high ceilings and wonderful blue and yellow tiles on walls. Patio with trailing plants and rocking chairs. Cool, comfortable rooms with a/c, fridge, good shower. Friendly owners Alejandro and Dinorah speak English and are very helpful. Good food for breakfast and dinner.

$ Natural Caribe
Avellaneda 8 entre Gen Gómez (Keiser) y Martí, T32-295866, 52767598 (mob), requejoarias@nauta.cu.

Run by Rafael Requejo Arias, another architect and son of the owner of Los Vitrales, above. This colonial house has been completely modernized in a minimalist design with bold tropical colours and modern lighting. Comfortable rooms, good bathrooms, patio garden, bar, a sun terrace and plunge pool are planned for the roof.

$ Reyes y Carolina
Damas (Sabino Monte) 221 entre Horca y Medio, T32-298907.

West of the centre. Amazing decor with ornaments, plastic flowers and soft toys everywhere. 2 rooms, 1 in house with double bed, TV, fridge, brown bathroom, good quality fittings, the other upstairs at the back of the house, more independent and private with white bathroom, off terrace with view over tiled roofs, lots of plants. Carolina, a former history teacher, serves very good food and specializes in cocktails, particularly Canchanchara. Parking available opposite.

North of the centre
Casas particulares

$ Casa Miriam
Joaquín de Agüero 525 entre 25 de Julio y Perucho Figueredo, Rpto La Vigía, T32-282120, 052703252 (mob), miriamhouse29@yahoo.com.

Modern house, excellent accommodation upstairs with outside staircase. Well-maintained with good fixtures and fittings, 2 light and airy rooms each with private bathroom (1 has bathtub), large wardrobes, TV/DVD, internet. Large terrace on roof with lots of plants, dog and cat, great views of city, ideal for sunset watching. Miriam is a knowledgeable and efficient English-speaking hostess, she will collect you from the bus terminal or guide you in if you come by car, arrange excursions and transport and serves good, hearty 3-course meals with lots of fruit and fresh veg. Secure off-street parking opposite, CUC$1.

$ Casa Raúl Pérez Bahamonde
Alfredo Adán 355 entre Joaquín Agüero y Capdevila, Rpto La Vigía, T32-243574, 5450 7198 (mob), raulp.b@nauta.cu.

Independent studio apartment with separate staircase up from family sitting room, bedroom, living room, balcony overlooking street, bathroom and kitchenette, TV, fridge, rocking chairs, garage. Food available if you don't want to cook on limited facilities.

Where to eat

Restaurants

$$$-$$ 1800
Pl San Juan de Dios, T32-283619, www.restaurante1800.com. Daily 0900-0100.

High-class design with lovely, varnished bar, solid wood tables and chairs with white table linen. The tables out on the square are the most popular but you have to be early for them. *Criollo* cuisine accompanied by traditional bands of musicians and staff in uniforms. You can eat à la carte or from the buffet, which is greatly superior to the average hotel buffet.

$$$-$$ Casa Austria
Lugareño entre San Rafael y San Clemente, T5328 5580.

Austrian food is unexpected in Camagüey but can come as a welcome break from standard Cuban fare. Chef Josef serves up the most authentic dishes he can with the ingredients available in a pleasant open air setting around the patio at the back of a colonial house. He is renowned for his pastries and sweets, worth buying even if you're not eating there.

$$$-$$ Casa Italia
San Ramón 11 entre Gral Gómez y Astilleros, T32-257614, T5271 2654 (mob), erenia. piazza@yahoo.es. Daily 1200-2400.
Attractive setting with tables around a courtyard garden with tinajas, painted turquoise and cream. Wood-fired oven for pizza, plenty of pasta, but the main courses are not particularly Italian. Variations on the usual pork, chicken, shrimp, fish and lobster. Also room rental.

$$$-$$ El Paso
Hermanos Agüero 261, Pl del Carmen, T5239 0939.
Pleasant location at the entrance to the Plaza opposite the gallery of Martha Jiménez Pérez. Convenient for a lunch stop but sometimes full with tour parties. Traditional Cuban menu with better-than-average cooking and service.

$$$-$$ La Isabela
Ignacio Agramonte, near Pl de los Trabajadores, T32-221540.
Open 1100-1600, 1830-2200.
Unprepossessing from outside but the restaurant is dark and cosy, black and red decor, good a/c. Italian food, good pasta, risotto and thin-crust pizzas, although they are not particularly Italian. Named in honour of an actress from Camagüey; the chairs bear the names of Cuban film makers and there are film posters, photos and old film reels on the walls.

$$$-$$ Mesón del Príncipe
Astilleros 7 entre San Ramón y Lugareño, T32-293770, T5240 4598 (mob), mesondelprincipe@gmail.com. Daily 1200-2400.
Grand colonial building with seating in patio or a/c indoors. Traditional Cuban cuisine with

some twists on combinations of ingredients. Quality and service generally good.

$$$-$$ Parador de los Tres Reyes and Campana de Toledo
T32-286812, and T32-286812.
2 small colonial-style restaurants on Pl San Juan de Dios serving Spanish food, pleasant, live music. The latter has tables overlooking the square or in the courtyard. The former is cheaper but has smaller portions. Open for lunch and dinner, but tour parties mean they are busy at lunchtime.

$$$-$$ Rocola Club
Av Carlos J Finlay 462, T32-261144, rocolaclub@nauta.cu. Open 1200-2345.
Interesting building in a residential area, designed by the Brazilian architect Oscar Niemeyer in the 1950s; the decor still dates from that time. The restaurant is upstairs on a covered, open-air terrace, family-run, great attention to detail, Cuban and Italian food including pizza, with a good wine list. Parking available. Also rooms to rent.

Bars and clubs

Bar El Cambio
On the northeast corner of Parque Ignacio Agramonte. Open 24 hrs.
This one-time gambling den now has lottery artwork on the walls, designed and decorated by artist Oscar Lasseria. You can expect to be approached here with offers of 'private' restaurants. A good view of the cathedral.

Bar-café Las Ruinas
On west side of Pl Maceo.
Set in ruins and shady trees.

Bodegón San Cayetano and Callejón de la Soledad
República y Callejón de la Soledad, T32-291961, both at same location, the former open 1230-2300, the latter 1030-2300.
Musicians will play at night if asked, but they will wait for a tip.

Club Oxio
República 277 entre San Esteban y Finlay, T32-287384.
A complex with bar, grill, dancing, small pool, barbecue, 1000-1800, CUC$6 includes drinks up to CUC$5 (children 5-12 half price, under 5 free), games room, bowling CUC$1 per hr, billiards CUC$3 per hr, photo studio, electronic games for children and adults. **Rincón del Bolero** every Sat, Sun 2100-2400, free. **Spot Café** 1000-2200 Mon-Fri, 1000-2400 Sat, Sun.

Gran Hotel
See Where to stay.
Has several bars with entertainment: **Piano Bar Marquesina**, **Bar Piscina 1920**, **Bar El Mirador**. Cover charges are applied depending on the entertainment and whether food is included.

Entertainment

To see what is on, check www.pprincipe. cult.cu/actividades.

Cinema
There are 3 cinemas, none of which has a/c and so can be very hot, entrance CUP$0.60-1: **Casablanca** (T32-292244), and **Encanto** (T32-295511, next door on Ignacio Agramonte), and **Guerrero** (T32-292874).

Live music
Casa de la Trova Patricio Ballagas, *on the west side of Parque Agramonte between Martí and Cristo. Tue-Sun 0900-1900, Tue-Thu 2030-2400, Fri-Sat 2030-0200, CUC$3 including a drink.* Folk and traditional music. Courtyard and bar, while at the entrance is a souvenir shop where you can buy music.

Theatre
Teatro José Luis Tasende, *Popular entre Padre Valencia y López Recio, T32-292164.* The Camagüey Dramatic Company performs here.
Teatro Principal, *Padre Valencia 64, T32-293048.* The Ballet de Camagüey, ranked

2nd in the country after Havana's ballet company, often performs here.

Festivals

Feb The 1st week celebrates the foundation of the village with lots of street parties. **24-29 June** Carnival.

Shopping

Artex and other shops are on Maceo, Agramonte, República and on Cisneros, just north of Parque Agramonte. Maceo is a particularly busy street, with the **Centro Comercial Alemán** (on Pl Maceo) selling clothes, furniture and electro-domestic goods, plus other stores, **Coppelia** ice cream, fast food outlets and the **Gran Hotel**.

Art
Casa Taller de Cerámica Yasmín, *C Primera 33 entre 1 y 2 transversales, Rpto San Miguelito, on the road out to Vertientes, T32-273254.* Ceramics workshop where you can see how the *tinajón* is made as well as other domestic pottery.
El Cartel, *Cisneros entre Hermanos Agüero y Martí.* Marvellous collection of original screen prints from the 1960s and 1970s, many featuring Che and Fidel, as well as countless movie posters in the distinctive Cuban style. Some of the original prints are for sale, kept in a dusty cupboard and in poor condition. The owner will show you around the workshop if you ask.
Estudio Nazario Salazar Martínez, *Padre Valencia 74 entre Tatán Méndez y Lugareño, T32-297682, nsm@anec.cmw.inf.cu.* A noted artist with over 40 years of experience in drawing, painting, pottery and graphic design, his works are collected worldwide. He is known principally for his ceramics.
Galería Taller Larios, *Independencia 301 esq Gen Gómez, T32-291575, larios@pprincipe. cult.cu.* Gallery and workshop where you can see artists working on paintings, ceramics, ironwork, etc, under the direction of local artist, Orestes Larios Zaak, who specializes

in drawing and painting and has been exhibited in Europe and the USA. Free entry, works for sale.

Galería Taller Lorenzo Linares Duque, *Pintor 56*. Internationally exhibited painter since the 1970s, known for his landscapes and paintings of cockerels.

Galería Taller Martha Jiménez Pérez, *Gen Gómez 274B entre Masvidal y Lugareño, T32-291696, Martha@pprincipe.cult.cu*. A painter and sculptor, Martha's sculptures of real local people can be seen in Plaza del Carmen. Some of the models actually sit beside their representation, seeking tips from tourists.

Jardín del Edén, *Bellavista 420 entre Alfredo Adám y 25 de Julio, Rpto La Vigía, T32-286909*. Workshop and gallery of Oscar Lasseria, a painter, sculptor and ceramicist. If he is there he will show you around and you can buy anything he has for sale. Lasseria's works can be found decorating places such as Bar El Cambio, Cafetería La Bigornia and several ceramic murals around the city.

What to do

Most tours start from Playa Santa Lucía and it is often difficult to arrange anything from Camagüey unless you are in a group.

Tour operators

Ecotur, *San Estéban 453 entre Lope Recio y Popular, T32-243693, commercial@cmg.ecotur.tur.cu*.

Transport

Air

Any bus/truck going to Nuevitas, Minas or Playa Santa Lucía from Parque Finlay by the railway station will pass the **Ignacio Agramonte International Airport** (CMW). The airport is 9 km from the centre on the road to Nuevitas, T32-261010. There are 2 terminals, for domestic flights, T32-267202, and for international flights, T32-267150. **Cubana** flies daily from **Havana**, and once a week from **Toronto** and **Montréal**. There are also charter flights from **Toronto**, **Venezuela**, **Miami** and **Europe** depending on the season.

Bus

The Interprovincial bus station is southwest of the centre along the Ctra Central Oeste, esq Perú. **Viazul**, T32-270396 (24-hr service for reservations at the terminal or go to Cubatur), stops here on its **Havana–Santiago**, **Havana–Holguín**, **Varadero–Santiago** and **Trinidad–Santiago** routes. Buses and trucks to Playa Santa Lucía and other municipalities leave from opposite Parque Finlay. Bus to **Playa Santa Lucía** daily 0500 and 1400, CUP\$3.25.

Car hire

Havanautos is at Céspedes y Carretera Central opposite Hotel Camagüey, T32-272239, at Plaza Joaquín de Agüero (Pl de Méndez), T32 257537, and at the airport T32-261010/287068. **Cubacar** has an office at Av Jayama y Ctra Central este, opposite the fuel station near Hotel Camagüey, with branches at Hotel Plaza, T32-282413, at Parque Casino Campestre beside Restaurante DiMar on the edge of the Río Hatibonico, T32-297472, at Pl de los Trabajadores, Ignacio Agramonte 448, T32-285327, at Martí y Ctra Central oeste T32-257538, and at the airport, T32-287067. **Rex** at the airport, T32-262444, is the best for luxury cars such as Audi, with prices from CUC\$70-160 a day, although other makes are available for less. **Vía Rent-a-Car Transgaviota**, at the airport, T32-241806, is probably the cheapest in the city, with good deals on weekly rentals.

There are **Servi Cupet** 24-hr fuel stations by the river on the corner of Ctra Central and Av de la Libertad; on Vía Blanca, a couple of blocks further south on the other side of the Ctra Central; at Ctra Central este, beside Hotel Camagüey; at Av Saratoga, 300 m from Av Finlay; at Ctra Central oeste y Gen Gómez by the hospital; at Ctra Central este by the provincial bus station, and several others around the city.

Taxi

Cubataxi, Av de los Mártires in the same block as Hotel Puerto Príncipe, T32-281247/298721 in Camagüey. A taxi will cost CUC$50-60 to **Playa Santa Lucía**, 1 way. You can probably negotiate a round trip with waiting time for CUC$70, depending on your bargaining skills, as the driver can earn extra money while you are at the beach. Ask at your *casa particular* for a reputable taxi driver.

Bicitaxis in the city charge CUC$0.40 per block, double that at night (plus surcharge after midnight), see list on back of bike.

Horse-drawn carriages are used for local taxi journeys; official routes around town are charged at CUP$1-2; fix the price in advance.

Train

Schedules and fares must be confirmed as the train system cannot be relied upon. Railway station, T32-292633/281525. Train ticket agency, T32-283214. Foreigners pay in CUC$ at **Ladis** office above the main ticket office opposite Hotel Plaza. The station is divided into long distance services, south of the railway by Hotel Plaza, and provincial services (eg to **Nuevitas**), north of the railway between Joaquín de Agüero and Manuel Benavides. Camagüey is on the routes **Havana–Santiago**, **Havana–Bayamo** and **Havana–Guantánamo**.

Around Camagüey

excursions into the countryside for hiking, riding, fishing and birdwatching

North of Camagüey

A road heads northeast out of Camagüey past the airport through pastures and chicken farms to the coast. The first town of any size is **Minas**, with a population of about 20,000. There is no reason to stop here except to see the **Fábrica de Instrumentos Musicales** ① *C Camilo Cienfuegos, Minas, T32-696232*, where they make and sell violins, guitars and percussion instruments. Just northwest of Minas is a **crocodile farm** ① *9 km from Senado, Mon, Wed, Sat 0900-1700, CUC$1, other days with prior reservation through Ecotur, CUC$14*, where endangered species are preserved. There is also an Amerindian village and cave burial site on the farm. You can take a boat trip on the Río Máximo and watch a *Santería* ritual being performed. The farm has a restaurant for lunch, offering traditional Cuban dishes for CUC$6-8.

Tour operators offer walking tours of the **Sierra de Cubitas**, a protected area 35 km north of Camagüey, where you can visit caves with Amerindian drawings and see much endemic wildlife and lots of birds. The tours last all day and are hot and tiring, minimum eight people, two expert guides; take a hat, good walking boots and lots of water.

Fidel Castro sometimes stayed at **Rancho King**, 80 km from Camagüey on the road to Santa Lucía. The tourist farm, now offers rodeo, horse riding and tours of a local school and village with a chance to eat fresh fruit and try local coffee. This is a popular excursion from the Playa Santa Lucia hotels.

West of Camagüey

Some 46 km northwest of Camagüey on the road and railway to Ciego de Avila, is **Florida**, a town of some 40,000 inhabitants, with hospitals and clinics, a museum, art gallery, Casa de Cultura, cinema, hotel and restaurants. Tour buses pass through here, but few foreigners stop long, unless they're on a shooting or fishing expedition to the **Porvenir** and **Muñoz** reservoirs nearby or to the **Mañana de Santa Ana reservoir**, southeast of Camagüey. (If you stay at the local hotel, **La Casona de Florida**, you may find your fellow guests are hunters.) The other hotel, **Hotel Florida**, is used by Viazul as a lunch stop on the way from Trinidad to Santiago, but the guests are all Cubans on a family holiday.

South of Camagüey
Head east from the city on the Carretera Central as far as Jimbambay, and then turn south to reach **Najasa** and **Hacienda La Belén** ① *5 km from Najasa (54 km from Camagüey), T32-274995, www.ecoturcuba.tur.cu, entrance CUC$5, horse riding CUC$6, lunch CUC$8, see also Where to stay, below.* The hacienda covers 4500 ha in the Sierra de Najasa, a protected area of geological and biological diversity, including caves, a petrified forest and the second finest forest reserve in the country. You can go horse riding and birdwatching through the reserve and the forest, where you might see the *tocororo*, the national bird, as well as other protected endemic species. Introduced non-native animals such as antelope and zebras also roam. Tours of the area include a visit to a typical farmer's house and to the Gaspar-Najasa caves.

East of Camagüey
Heading southeast by road towards Las Tunas, you can stop in **Guáimaro**, just before the provincial border. It is a small town about 80 km from Camagüey, with a population of about 20,000 and a lively agricultural fair, *Feria Agropecuaria* in early October, when stalls are set up in the park and rows of people sell roast pork at the side of the street. However, the town is most notable for its historical connections: Carlos Manuel de Céspedes was elected first president of the Republic here by the constituent assembly of 1869. The assembly's other task was to draw up the first Cuban constitution. Seventy years later the town got round to commemorating the event with a monument in Parque Constitución dedicated to the men who fought for Cuban Independence including Céspedes and José Martí.

Listings Around Camagüey

Where to stay

South of Camagüey

$$$ Hacienda La Belén
5 km from Najasa, 54 km southeast of Camagüey, T32-864349/274995.
Small hotel operated by **Ecotur** (www.ecoturcuba.tur.cu). 10 double rooms for nature lovers, a/c, private bathrooms, breakfast included, meals available, pool, lovely rural location, horse riding, hiking, birdwatching.

Transport

Car hire
If you're driving through Camagüey province, there are **Servi Cupet** 24-hr gas stations in **Florida** on the junction of Ctra Central y Francisco V Aguilera and in **Guímaro** at Ctra Central y Martí.

The Atlantic north coast is broken by a series of large coral cays, which make up the Archipiélago de Camagüey. There are long sandy beaches, crystal-clear water and fantastic diving on the reef, but so far there has been little development except at Playa Santa Lucía in the east. Nuevitas is the main port on the north coast and there is considerable heavy industry in the area.

Playa Santa Lucía

Santa Lucía is a low-key beach resort 112 km northeast, or two hours by road, from Camagüey, where the sand stretches some 20 km along the northern coast at the mouth of the **Bahía de Nuevitas**.

This is a beautiful beach, protected by an offshore reef that contains over 50 species of coral and is much sought after by divers. The water is clear and warm, with some large patches of seaweed and an average temperature of 24°C. You can sometimes see dolphins near the shore and there are flamingos on the *saliñas* (salt flats) just inland, which are surrounded by scrub and swamp.

> **Fact...**
> Camagüey Province is the second largest salt producer in the country (after Guantánamo).

Santa Lucía is a lovely place to come and relax but be aware that it is remote, and excursions inland can therefore be time-consuming and expensive. There is no real town as such, and most people who stay here are on all-inclusive package tours for a week or so and see little of Cuba. Having said that, hotel tour desks can offer you day trips or longer excursions by land, sea or air to anywhere in Cuba. If you arrive by car and want public access to the beach, try parking at the Centro Comercial and walking between the hotels to the shore. Alternatively, the hotels offer day passes for the use of all their facilities.

★ Playa Los Cocos

Eight kilometres from Santa Lucía, this beach is even better. Horsedrawn carriages bring visitors along the sandy, pot-holed road from the hotels, but if you have your own transport, stop along the way to reach untouched beaches through the casuarina pines or to look for flamingos in the lagoon on the other side of the road. There is a broad sweep of sand at Playa Los Cocos with a fishing village of single-storey, waterfront houses, **La Boca**, at one end and beach bars at the other end, next to the channel which leads to Nuevitas. Shark feeding takes place near wrecks in the channel, see What to do, page 280. The beach is backed by the coconut palms from which it takes its name, and although there are a few rocks on the shoreline, it is mostly very white sand, which gently slopes to crystal clear water. The beach is safe for children, although it gets deep quite quickly and is good for swimming. Watch out for broken glass. The bars and seafood restaurants will rent you sunbeds from CUC$1 or four-poster beds with food and drinks packages. There is some shade under palapas. People selling handicrafts are not too pushy if you show no interest.

> **Tip...**
> Use insect repellent to protect against the small, black sandflies known as a *jejénes*; their bites hurt and start to itch like mad the next day.

Toilets are across the sandy track but bring your own paper. From La Boca a partly paved, mostly gravel and pot-holed road runs south of the lagoon and eventually meets the main road back to Camagüey.

★ Cayo Sabinal

Across the channel, west of Playa Los Cocos, Cayo Sabinal is reached by road from Nuevitas in about 40 minutes (there is no road from Playa Santa Lucía). The drive is possible in an ordinary car, although high clearance is best because of pot holes in the gravel road. The alternative way to get there is on a boat trip organized by hotel tour desks in Santa Lucía (to include snorkelling, beach time and exploration as well as lunch). You may see dolphins along the way and there is a starfish breeding spot where you can see hundreds of starfish.

Hemingway wrote that Cayo Sabinal was "a marvellous place where the wind from the east blows night and day, and the territory as virgin as when Columbus arrived on these shores." Things haven't changed much since then. The beautiful beaches of white sand are practically deserted, and the cay is a wildlife reserve housing the largest colony of pink flamingos in the Caribbean (zoom lens required on your camera), plus many other birds that are rare or endangered elsewhere. (There are also lots of mosquitoes, so take repellent.)

The island has historical links to piracy and was used as a base to attack shipping in the Old Bahama Channel to the north. The Spanish built **San Hilario fortress** in 1831 to deter pirates and protect shipping heading to Havana or Florida. The most obvious landmark, however, is the lighthouse, **Faro Colón**, built on Punta Maternillas to guide shipping past the cay and down the channel to Nuevitas. Built in 1847, it is Cuba's tallest lighthouse and is still in active use. Minor roads on the island are poor, and there is no accommodation available after cabins were blown away in a hurricane.

Listings Playa Santa Lucía and around

Tourist information

All the main hotels have tourist agencies who can provide information, although their main aim is to sell tours.

Where to stay

The Santa Lucía resort is part of the **Cubanacán** group (www.cubanacan.cu), including joint-venture hotels, restaurants, shopping centre, watersports, discos and other amenities. All the hotels are all-inclusive and prices are per person sharing a double room. Standards vary and none warrants more than 3 stars at most, but they all offer a/c, TV, entertainment, sports and tours. In the winter months the hotels are full of Canadians and other snow birds on a cheap break. In the summer months (Cuban holiday season) the hotels fill up with Cuban families, particularly at weekends, and foreigners take a back seat. It is now possible to stay in *casas particulares* at Playa Santa Lucía and Playa Los Cocos, although these are inland and require a slightly longer walk to the beach. Even if you're staying in a *casa* you can still book excursions and activities at the hotels.

Playa Santa Lucía

$ Casa Doña Bárbara
Barrio Obrero, T5304 0764 (mob).
Pleasant house in residential area 100 m from beach with 2 rooms, one in the house

Tip...
Very cheap hotels and some *casas* are used for prostitution and should be avoided.

and the other in the garden, a/c, fan, stocked fridge, laundry service, parking. Rubén was formerly a barman at one of the hotels and speaks good English.

$ Casa Martha Santana
Residencial 32, T32-336135, 5297 5765 (mob), rentasantalucia@gmail.com.
Martha and her family are very welcoming and prepare good meals and cocktails for visitors to their home, about 200 m from the beach. Simple accommodation in house with garden where you can park your car. The room has a double bed, a/c, stocked fridge and bathroom. To get there, turn right/east at the roundabout by the petrol station, take the next left, the next right and the house is on your right a bit further along.

Where to eat

Playa Santa Lucía
As well as the state-run restaurants and cafés, there are also *paladares*; ask *coche* drivers to recommend which are the best value. If you arrive by car, *paladar* owners will stop you and offer a card and information.

$$$-$$ Luna Mar at the Centro Comercial
T32-336146.
Pleasant a/c restaurant overlooking the sea. Makes a change from the hotels. Simple menu of chicken, pork, shrimp, lobster with all the usual accompaniments.

$ Organic Restaurant & Gardens
Teraraco, T5335 9708/5440 8810, www.organicocuba.com.
In a residential area, 10-15 mins from the hotels (for directions, see the website). Although the restaurant was closed in 2015, there are plans to reopen it in some form. In the meantime, owner Braulio is operating an organic juice bar with a few snacks. Ring the bell and wait for him to come from his garden. All ingredients are fresh, seasonal and organic.

Playa Los Cocos

$$$-$$ Bucanero
Daily 0800-2000.
Pleasant beach bar serving lobster CUC$18, shrimp CUC$8, fish CUC$7 or chicken CUC$3.50 as well as cold drinks. They do packages of 4-poster beds on the sand with drinks and meals from CUC$10. There are a couple of other beach bars at Playa los Cocos, serving good fish and seafood at reasonable prices.

What to do

All the hotels have tourism *burós* offering excursions.

Diving
Shark's Friends, Playa Santa Lucía, T32-365182. Dives cost CUC$40 for a single dive, cheaper for more, CUC$175 for 5 dives, CUC$300 for 10 dives, CUC$69 for shark dive. ACUC and SNSI courses are offered with 5 instructors. They use a 41-ft yacht, tanks and weight belts included, other equipment available.

Snorkelling
Catamarans leave for the reef twice daily at 1000 and 1400, weather permitting, from the pier just north of Escuela Santa Lucía, CUC$30 including all gear and soft drinks on board and transfers from your hotel, about 3 hrs from collection to drop-off.

Transport

Air
Ignacio Agramonte International Airport (CMW) is located between Camagüey and Nuevitas, T32-261010 (see page 246 for flight information). Most foreign visitors get a transfer bus direct to their hotel. If you're not on a package tour, you can still negotiate with the transfer buses and fill an empty seat for about CUC$18. Talk to hotel tour desks to book the return journey to the airport; Transtur will usually collect you from your

ON THE ROAD
Diving at Playa Santa Lucía

There are 37 dive sites within reach of Santa Lucía at depths of 5-40 m, including a controversial shark feeding site in the channel between Playa Los Cocos and Cayo Sabinal about 20 m offshore. A concrete area by the *guardia* station has steps down into the water, where up to 20 bull sharks congregate at a depth of some 26-30 m, next to the wreck of a Spanish merchant ship at 35 m. (The 66-m *Mortera* sank in 1905 on a slope of 7-27 m and is home to a host of marine life.) The sharks have been hand fed by the dive masters from Shark's Friends Dive Shop since the early 1980s and now swim freely amongst the divers. It is very exciting to watch, as the divers wear no body armour, but the practice is ethically unsound as it encourages dependency and aggression. Shark feeding can only take place between August and February when the tide is on the turn, giving a short 45-minute window of opportunity. The sharks migrate elsewhere for the rest of the year.

Other dive sites include caves, tunnels and a very picturesque and healthy coral reef. Wrecks include the *Sanbinal* in 17 m and the British steel ship, *Nuestra Señora de Alta Gracia*, sunk around 1973 and completely intact, allowing divers to penetrate the entire ship, including the engine room where all the machinery is still in place. An exciting historical site is Las Anforas, under an old fort dating from 1456. The fort was attacked several times by pirates, and artefacts from Spanish ships, including four anchors, are scattered across the sea bed.

casa particular. There is also a small airstrip at Playa Santa Lucía called **Joaquín de Agüero**.

Bus
Buses and trucks to Nuevitas and Playa Santa Lucía depart from Parque Finlay in Camagüey; all go via the airport.

Car hire
At Playa Santa Lucía, there are rental desks at the hotels or just outside them. **Havanautos**, T32-26188, commercial office at Av Residencial, T32-336368. **Cubacar**, T32-336109, commercial office, T32-365216. Also office at Martí y Medrano, Nuevitas, T32-416486. There is a **Servi Cupet** 24-hr gas station at the junction as you arrive at Playa Santa Lucía.

Taxi
Cubataxi, Av Principal La Concha, Santa Lucía, T32-336196. A taxi will cost CUC$50-60 to/from **Camagüey**, 1 way. Ask at your *casa particular* for a reputable taxi driver. To **Playa los Cocos**, expect to pay CUC$5-6. **Horse-drawn carriages** are used for local taxi journeys: to **Playa los Cocos**, CUC$20 return; a 2-hr tour is also CUC$20.

Train
A railway line runs from **Santa Clara** to Nuevitas via **Morón**, although services are infrequent and unreliable; there are also trains from **Camagüey** to Nuevitas.

Las Tunas Province

Travellers could be forgiven for not noticing this small, agricultural province on their way from Camagüey to Holguín or Bayamo, as only about 65 km of the road actually passes through it. Having said that, the provincial capital would make a convenient break in the journey, or you could get well off the beaten track by visiting the beaches of the irregular northern coast, indented by three large bays. Las Tunas boasts 35 virgin beaches, of which the main one, Playa Covarrubias, has fine, white sand and is protected by a 3-km coral reef. The rest of the province is mostly low-lying farming land, although the central part around the city is part of the Holguín ridge and is more undulating. The southern coast opens onto the Golfo de Guacanayabo and is marshy with mangroves.

Las Tunas city   Colour map 3, B4.

a provincial city of quiet charms

Victoria de las Tunas, also known as Las Tunas, or even just Tuna, was founded in the 1750s, but was never more than a market town until Las Tunas became a province in its own right in 1975 and needed a provincial capital.

The old centre of Las Tunas, the *casco histórico*, has received a certain amount of investment recently and has been beautified considerably, with the introduction of some 70 sculptures permanently exhibited around town. One, by Rita Longa, is of a naked woman lying in the shape of the island of Cuba, called 'Venus Stretching Out'. Las Tunas is known as the Cuban capital of sculpture and every two years has a major sculpture festival. Buildings, such as the 1945 Hotel Cadillac, have been completely renovated and an attractive pedestrian boulevard has been created, linking Plaza José Martí with the theatre, the provincial museum and the Memorial Mayor General Vicente García González (see below).

Sights
The town centre is effectively the junction of three roads – the tree-lined Vicente García (the Carretera Central), Angel Guardia and Francisco Varona – at the **Parque Vicente García**, where there is a small church. There is a memorial to General Vicente García just off the Parque and his name crops up frequently in the town, because he led the struggle

for independence in the area in 1868 and captured the town in 1876.

In 1976 a **Cubana** plane en route from Caracas to Havana was blown up just after leaving Barbados by a device left under a seat. Seventy-three people, including the Cuban fencing team, were killed. To this day no one has been charged in connection with the incident. Three members of the fencing team came from Las Tunas and the home of one of them is now a museum housing the **Memorial a los Mártires de Barbados** ⓘ *C Lucas Ortiz 344 entre Teniente Peiso y Mártires de Barbados, T31-347213. CUC$1.* The museum is in a park along Vicente García by the river and contains photos of all the victims around the walls. The 25th anniversary of the bombing, in 2001, coincided with the terrorist attack on the World Trade Center in New York, providing Cuba with extra publicity in its campaign for justice.

Opposite the Parque, the **Museo Provincial General Vicente García** ⓘ *C Francisco Varona entre Angel Guerra y Lucas Ortiz, T31-348201,* displays local history. Built in 1921, it was originally the Town Hall, before becoming the municipal public library in 1951, a high school after the Revolution in 1959 and a museum in 1984 after extensive remodelling. The **Memorial Mayor General Vicente García González** ⓘ *C Vicente García 5 entre Francisco Vega y Julián Santana, T31-345164,* is the birthplace of the General, although the original house was burned down in 1876 on Vicente García's orders, before he turned the city over to the Spanish. The present building dates from 1919 and is used for local ceremonies. It houses various historical exhibits, old weapons, documents and art.

The **Casa Natal Juan Cristóbal Nápoles y Fajardo** on Lucas Ortiz is the birthplace of a local 19th-century poet. Nápoles was one of the greatest exponents of the Cuban *cucalambé* style, which started in the 19th century but continues today as a niche cultural genre based on improvisation. Nápoles wrote *décimas*, songs of ten lines. He vanished in 1862 and no one knows what happened to him. Every year a music festival is held in Las Tunas, *La Jornada Cucalambeana*, at which performers of country music, improvisation and other musical forms honour Nápoles and fellow writers of *cucalambé* (see Festivals, page 285). There is also plenty of salsa and dancing, local food stalls and lots of beer and rum.

Essential Las Tunas

Finding your feet

The Carretera Central linking Havana with the east of the country runs through the middle of town, although there is now a Circunvalación to the south so that you can avoid the centre altogether if you want to. There is a **domestic airport** outside Las Tunas, but no international flights land here. Las Tunas is on the long-distance bus and train routes from Havana to Santiago de Cuba. It is easy enough to get there but more difficult to get out, as most of the buses are full when they pass through. See also Transport, page 285.

Getting around

The town of Las Tunas is small and you can walk around it in a day at a leisurely pace. The long-distance bus terminal is 1 km from the town centre and the railway station is 2.5 km away, but both are within walking distance if you haven't got much luggage. Bicitaxis, taxis and *coches* are available. The provincial bus station for bus services to local towns and villages is beside the railway station. Taxis will take you on excursions.

Where to stay

Hotels

$$$-$$ Hotel E Cadillac
Angel Guardia entre Francisco Vega y
Francisco Varona, T31-372790,
www.islazul.cu.
Small, central 3-star hotel. Built 1945 in the
shape of ship which looks like it is anchored
to the boulevard. Large rooms, some with
balcony overlooking the square which can
be noisy at night, no lift, 1 hr Wi-Fi access
per day included in rate, bar faces the plaza
and good for people-watching, **Balcony
Restaurant** on top floor, roof terrace.

Casas particulares

$ Casa Haydee
Luis Ramírez López 24 entre Joaquín Agüero y
Frank País, Rpto Velázquez, T31-347905.
A 1970s house in a quiet residential area with
a garden. 2 rooms, a/c, mosquito screens on
windows, fridge, TV, garage space for 2 cars,
English, Russian and Italian spoken.

$ Casa Karen y Roger
Lico Cruz 93 Altos entre Villalón y J W Gómez,
T31-343868.
Modern house with artistic design, 3 rooms
upstairs in family home with access to
garden at the back of the house, English,
French and Italian spoken, good food,
laundry service, parking available, CUC$2.

$ Villa Rosalba
Av 2 de Diciembre 3 entre Frank País y
Joaquín Agüero, Rpto Velázquez, T31-349042,
enobarguerra@yahoo.es.
1 room with bathroom, central location not far
from bus station, Rosalba Guerra Cruz is very
kind and hospitable as well as a good cook.

Tip...
Most restaurants price their menu in
pesos cubanos then convert to pesos
convertibles on the bill.

Where to eat

$$$-$$ Cache
Francisco Varona entre Nicolás Heredia y
Joaquín Agüero, T31-995557. Daily for lunch
and dinner.
Modern decor with red and black furniture,
small bar and lounge area. Good food
with nice salads, washed down with tasty
cocktails at CUC$3 each. Good a/c.

$$$-$$ La Romana
Francisco Varona 331, T31-347755.
Daily lunch and dinner.
Italian restaurant in a typical single-storey
colonial building with high ceilings, tall
windows and doorways a couple of blocks
from the plaza. Italian owned, perfect
bruschetta, homemade pasta cooked
al dente with delicious sauces, depending
on what's available.

Entertainment

Cabaret El Taíno, *Ctra Central esq Vicente*
García. Open 2000-0100. Entry in CUP$, best
on Fri, Sat, show with dancing, magicians
and comedians.
Casa de la Cultura, *Vicente García 8 entre*
Francisco Vega y Francisco Varona. As well
as entertainment here, there are often live
bands outside on the plaza or the boulevard.
El Ranchón, *at the roundabout on road to*
Holguín. 24 hrs. Open air, good for music and
drinks at the bar any time, but especially
popular at 0300 when the discos shut.

Hotel Cadillac, *Colón esq Francisco Vega, on the plaza*. Has a pleasant bar where there is often live music. The terrace bar is popular for sunset cocktails.

La Bolera (Discoteca Luanda), *Vicente García, near the bus station*. Tue-Sun 2200-0300. The largest disco in town playing salsa, rap and reggaeton.

Piano bar, *on the corner opposite Hotel Cadillac*. 2030-0200. A/c bar with live piano and/or violin music, couples preferred, good cocktails.

Festivals

Jun/Jul Fiesta Cucalambé at the Motel El Cornito, 7 km west of town off the Ctra Central, for folk music.
Dec Agricultural fair.

Transport

Air
Aeropuerto Hermanos Ameijeiras (VTU), T31-342484, 11 km from Las Tunas, receives **Cubana** flights twice a week from **Havana**.

Bus
The bus station is just south of the main Parque on Francisco Varona, T31-342444. Long-distance buses are already full when they pass through Las Tunas and you just have to hope that someone is getting off here. Local buses use the terminal near the railway station. There are 2 buses daily to **Puerto Padre**.

Car hire
There is a **Havanautos** desk in the Hotel Las Tunas, Av 2 de Diciembre y Carlos J Finlay, on the outskirts of town, T31-349328. The **Servi Cupet** fuel stations is at Ctra Central Oeste Km 2. **Oro Negro** service station at Francisco Varona entre Lora y Menocal.

Taxi and local transport
Most local transport is by horse and cart or other non-motorized vehicles such as *bicitaxis*.

Train
The railway station is northeast of the centre, with trains to **Holguín**, **Santiago** and **Havana**. Unreliable.

North coast   *Colour map 3, B4.*

wetlands, bays and empty beaches off the beaten track

There are three large bays on the northern coast: Bahía de Manatí, Bahía de Malagueta and Bahía de Puerto Padre de Chaparra, which offer safe harbour and fishing ports.

Bahía de Malagueta
You can see flamingos and other waterbirds in the Bahía de Malagueta, which is one of the largest protected areas in the country, at 23,262 ha, of which 9210 are underwater. It includes the Cerro de Caisimú and Yariguá hunting reserve (Coto de Caza), where shooting and fishing are permitted in season. To get there, drive yourself, hire a driver for the day or see if there is an organized tour from one of the hotels.

Puerto Padre
The main town on the north coast, 56 km from Las Tunas, is **Puerto Padre**, tucked in at the end of the bay of the same name. Unusually, there are freshwater springs here, right next to the sea shore. Overlooking the water is the **Fuerte de la Loma**, a stone fortress built in 1869 with four circular towers, a moat and a drawbridge. It saw active service during the Wars of Independence and during the Revolution, when it was used by Batista's troops until it was taken on 25 December 1958. Some colonial buildings dating from the 1860s remain in the town, which has a wide boulevard, Av Libertad, leading down to the Malecón. The

ON THE ROAD
The Queen's Gardens

The Jardines de la Reina archipelago consists of 3000 sq km of cays and mangroves along the south coasts of the provinces of Ciego de Avila, Camagüey and Las Tunas. Unapproachable for years, because they were Fidel Castro's favourite fishing spot, these islands have now been declared a natural park protecting birds, iguanas, turtles and loads of fish. The archipelago of virgin cays with empty beaches is uninhabited and generally visited only by liveaboard dive boats and fly fishermen. Dive boats leave from **Júcaro** on the coast of Ciego de Avila, where **Marlin** also operates the largest fly-fishing fleet in the country. Fishing and diving is promoted by **Avalon** (cubandivingcenters.com, www.avalonfishingcenter.com), which has liveaboard boats and offers complete packages for several days of dedicated diving or fishing. It also has a small floating hotel, **Hotel Tortuga**.

There are about 40 dive sites along the southwest side of the archipelago. The reef runs parallel to the shore and usually drops down in three 'steps': the first at 10-15 m, very exposed to the surf; a second at 20 m on a sandy bottom, and a third that starts at 40-45 m and drops downward. You will find all the reef fishes here including tarpons. The sea is often rough.

Galería de Arte José Martínez Ochoa ⓘ *C 24 de Febrero 74,* exhibits work by local and national artists. The former Liceo building on Av Libertad now houses a museum.

There are now several *casas particulares* where you can stay and a couple of decent restaurants. It is a quiet and pleasant place with few tourists and is a good place to base yourself to explore remote beaches. The Malecón extends west along the shore about 1 km to the district of La Morena and then the road curves around the bay 18 km to the village of **El Socucho**, facing Playa La(s) Boca(s) across the mouth of the inlet (see below). Small boats take people and goods the 300 m across the channel.

Playa La Boca and around

You can drive to the north coast beaches of **Playa La Boca, Playa Uvero** or **Playa La Herradura** by taking the road to Holguín and turning north (left) at Lora. There are no buses and little tourist development along this stretch of coast and you are likely to have the place to yourself. Playa La Boca is on the eastern bank of the mouth of the Bahía de Puerto Padre on a small bay with golden sand and a few palm trees. Crowds are almost non-existent, although in summer buses and truck-loads of Cubans arrive for their beach holiday. A basic beach bar sells pizza and soft drinks for pesos, but don't rely on it; take some supplies of your own. Playa La Herradura is east of here and is another unspoilt sandy beach with few facilities.

★ Playa Covarrubias

Playa Covarrubias, 26 km northwest of Puerto Padre, but best reached direct from Las Tunas, has one all-inclusive hotel, **Brisas Covarrubias**. The beach is white sand and protected by a reef which has created sand banks and shallow water, beautifully clear and safe. The Laguna Real, at the end of the resort, has pink water, coloured by the micro-organisms which live in it, attracting flamingos among other water birds.

Where to stay

Puerto Padre

$ Casa Villa Velázquez
Bartolomé Masó 55, T5313 7457 (mob).
2 modern a/c rooms on top floor in
residential neighbourhood, large terrace
for sitting and watching the world go by.
Good food, helpful owners.

Playa Covarrubias

$$$-$$ Brisas Covarrubias
T31-515530, www.cubanacan.cu.
All-inclusive hotel, 180 spacious rooms in
cabañas on the beach with lots of sporting
facilities available on land and in the water,
massages and mud therapy, and a nightclub.
Saltwater pool. Remote, so excursions can be
time-consuming. Busy and noisy in summer
with Cuban families; the food deteriorates at
this time. Otherwise it is somewhere to relax
and enjoy the extensive sand.

Where to eat

Puerto Padre

$$-$ El Bodegón
C Lenín 54. Daily lunch and dinner.
Usually referred to as 'Polito's' after the
owner, Hipólito. Small bar and restaurant
downstairs, better ventilated dining room
upstairs and roof terrace with barbecue and
views to the sea. Good *criollo* food.

$$-$ Villa Odalis
C Cuba 29, T5284 1719 (mob).
Several different seating areas under cover
but open air, also bar upstairs with view
to the sea from the balcony. The menu
comprises the usual chicken and pork dishes
found everywhere but also some very good
fish and seafood, particularly the octopus, all
cooked fresh so be prepared to wait with a
cold beer or glass of Spanish wine.

Entertainment

Puerto Padre

All the usual facilities and entertainment of
a small town can be found here, with the
large **Salón de Fiestas 1913**, beside San José
church, and the **Casa de Cultura Enrique
Peña** offering live music and cultural events.
There's also a nightclub, **Anacaona**, at the
west end of the Malecón esq Paco Cabrera.

Festivals

Puerto Padre

18-25 Dec La Semana de la Cultura,
culminating in the anniversary of the liberation
of the town by the revolutionary forces.

Transport

Puerto Padre
Bus
There are 2 daily buses to/from **Las Tunas**,
but it is easier to hire a car or a driver for a day
trip and take in a beach as well.

Car hire
If you're driving yourself, there is a **Servi
Cupet** fuel station at Av Libertad 156.

Taxi and local transport
Most local transport is by horse and cart or
bicitaxi. A small boat crosses the channel
east of Puerto Padre to **Playa La Boca**.

Holguín & Granma

The countryside of Holguín is attractive, hilly and covered with luxuriant vegetation. There are picture-book views of hillsides dotted with Royal palms, towering over thatched cottages, called *bohíos*, while the flatter land is green with swathes of sugar cane.

The city of Holguín is unassuming and pleasant. Guardalavaca on the north coast is indented with pretty horseshoe-shaped bays and sandy beaches, each now occupied by a huge tourist resort.

Columbus is believed to have landed at the Bahía de Bariay on 28 October 1492, which he claimed was the most beautiful country he had ever seen. The indigenous people probably thought so too, since archaeological explorations have shown that there were primitive cultures here some 6000 years ago. Seboruco man is thought to have been the first inhabitant of what is now the province of Holguín.

The province of Granma occupies the western end of the Sierra Maestra and the flatlands and swamps to the north of the mountains. It was named after the boat that brought Castro and his comrades to Cuba to launch the Revolution. The area is studded with memories of the guerrilla struggle, but it has been largely neglected as far as tourism is concerned. The capital of the province is Bayamo, which has good transport links and access to the mountains for hiking.

Best for
Archaeology ▪ Beaches ▪ Hiking ▪ History

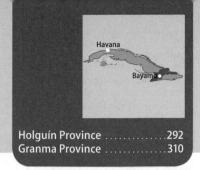

Footprint
picks

⭐ **La Loma de La Cruz, Holguín**, page 296
Make the hot, steep ascent for a commanding view over the city.

⭐ **Gibara**, page 301
Take time out at this attractive old fishing town with caves to explore.

⭐ **Banes**, page 305
See the area's archaeological discoveries on display at a fascinating museum.

⭐ **Jardín Botánico de Cupaynicú**, page 317
Visit one of the best botanical gardens on the island.

⭐ **Parque Nacional Sierra Maestra**, page 318
Join a guided hike to Fidel's revolutionary hideout or up Cuba's highest peak.

⭐ **Parque Nacional Desembarco de Granma**, page 324
Soak up the revolutionary history at *Granma's* landing site.

Essential Holguín and Granma

Finding your feet

Holguín's **international airport** is a useful starting point for a circuit of the eastern end of the island, taking in Holguín, Bayamo, Manzanillo, Santiago, Guantánamo and Baracoa. It affords easy access to both the north coast resorts and Bayamo. Bayamo and Manzanillo also have airports with a very limited service from Havana. Rail connections to Holguín and Bayamo have largely been replaced by more efficient bus services on the main Carretera Central from

Havana to Santiago de Cuba. Manzanillo is less accessible, as you have to change bus or train in Bayamo.

Getting around

Transport links are good, with Viazul buses for foreigners and Astro for Cubans. A hired car will give you more flexibility to reach out-of-the-way places. Cycling is another option, although you'll need to be fit to tackle the mountains of the Sierra Maestra. See also page 299 and page 316.

When to go

The driest season is from December to April. Hurricane season technically starts in June, but most storms arrive between September and November. Rain can fall at any time of year, usually in the afternoons. Holguín is developing a reputation as a good venue for festivals, with a local cultural event in January, the Romerías de Mayo in the first week of May and an Ibero-American festival in October. Gibara's Festival Internacional de Cine Pobre in April is now world famous within the film industry.

Favourite small hotels
Hotel E Ordoño, Gibara, page 302
Villa Don Lino, Playa Blanca, page 305
Villa Cayo Saetía, Cayo Saetía, page 309
Villa Pinares de Mayarí, page 309

Time required

The sights of the cities of Holguín, Bayamo and Manzanillo can be seen in half a day each, but there are lots of places to explore requiring day trips out of town. Hiking in the Sierra Maestra takes one to three days, as do trips to Gibara, Guardalavaca and other beaches on the north coast.

Footprint picks

1 **La Loma de La Cruz, Holguín**, page 296
2 **Gibara**, page 301
3 **Banes**, page 305
4 **Jardín Botánico de Cupaynicú**, page 317
5 **Parque Nacional Sierra Maestra**, page 318
6 **Parque Nacional Desembarco de Granma**, page 324

Holguín
Province

The province of Holguín is in the east of the country and incorporates the most beautiful part of the north coast, indented by many bays. The capital, Holguín, lies in a range of hills that stretches from Las Tunas in the west to the coast at Punta de Mulas. To the southeast are the foothills of the Sierra del Cristal and the Montañas de Nipe-Sagua-Baracoa. The highest point is Pico Cristal, at 1813 m, on the border with the province of Santiago de Cuba. Further east is the hugely important nickel and cobalt plant with shipping facilities at Moa.

Holguín city

a commercial hub characterized by its many parks and plazas

The city of Holguín was founded in 1545 and was named after García Holguín, a captain in the Spanish colonization force. It officially received the title of Ciudad de San Isidro de Holguín on 18 January 1752, but most of the architecture in the centre dates from the 19th and 20th centuries. There are numerous statues and monuments to national heroes, especially around Plaza de la Revolución on the edge of the city, the location of the modern City Hall and the Provincial Communist Party building.

Holguín is known as the 'city of the parks', five of which — **Parque Infantil**, **Parque Carlos Manuel de Céspedes** (also known as Parque San José), the **Plaza Central** (Plaza Gen Calixto García), **Parque Gen Peralta** and **Parque José Martí** — lie between the two main streets: Antonio Maceo and Libertad (Manduley). It also has a university, two big hospitals, a brewery and a baseball stadium and is busy, although all traffic moves at the pace of the thousands of bicycles that throng the streets. There are several attractive excursions to be made from the city, with easy access to some of the best beaches in the country.

Tip...
Very few streets in the city centre have name signs and it can be difficult to find your way around. There used to be metal signs fixed to the walls, but these were melted down to make cooking pots when times were hard.

Plaza Central

The Plaza Central is named after **General Calixto García Iñiguez**, who was born in Holguín in 1839 and took part in both wars of independence. He captured the town from the Spanish in 1872 and again occupied it in 1898 after helping US forces defeat the colonial power in Santiago de Cuba. His statue is in the centre and his birthplace, one block from the plaza, is now a national monument and museum, **Casa Natal de Calixto García** ⓘ *Calle Miró 147, T24-425610, Mon-Fri 0830-1700, Sat 0800-1300, Sun 0800-1700, 1800-2100, CUC$1*. The museum has a collection of dusty, faded exhibits and newer models of battles for lovers of army games.

Around the plaza are the **Commander Eddy Suñol Theatre** (he fought against Batista) and the **library** ⓘ *Mon-Fri 0800-2100, Sat 0800-1800, Sun 0800-1300*, a modern building with a spiral staircase, which hosts special events on Sundays. Adjacent, on Maceo 180, is the Centro de Arte y Pentagrama-Egrem. Also on the plaza is **Galería Bayado** where you can buy ceramics, carvings and furniture. To the rear of the *Galería*, there is a courtyard where you can enjoy music and singing in the evening. At the **Casa de Cultura** ⓘ *T24-422084, 0800-2100*, there are handicrafts for sale, and dancing (*danzón*).

On the north side of the square is the **Museo Provincial** ⓘ *Mon-Fri 0900-1700, Sat 0900-1300, CUC$1, CUC$3 with camera*, known as *La Periquera* (parrot cage) because of the brightly coloured soldiers known as *periquitos* (parakeets) who used to stand guard outside when the building was used as an army barracks in the 19th century. It was built between 1860 and 1868 and is now a National Monument. On 30 October 1868, 500 armed *independistas* attacked the building shouting ¡Viva Cuba! but failed to take it because of its strategic defences. The most important item on display here is the Hacha de Holguín, a pre-Columbian axe head carved with the head

Essential Holguín

Finding your feet

The **Frank País García international airport** is a 12-km taxi ride from the centre of Holguín city. Most foreigners are on their way to the Guardalavaca beach resort and are transported by tour bus to their hotels. Holguín city is 19 km from the main Havana–Santiago railway line with daily train services in each direction, but rail connections have largely been replaced by more efficient bus services: **Viazul** stops here on its Havana–Holguín, Havana–Santiago, Varadero–Santiago and Trinidad–Santiago routes. See Transport, page 299.

Getting around

It is recommended to walk around the centre of Holguín as traffic is very slow and there is very little motorized public transport; instead the city is choked with bicitaxis, horse-drawn buses and taxis. The family vehicle of choice is a bicycle with side car – dad does all the work, mum sits alongside with the baby, while seats on the cross bar and behind are for older children. To go further afield, hop on a horse-drawn coche, or hire a bicitaxi. There are also *colectivos* to Guardalavaca for CUC$2-5 or Gibara for CUC$1-2.

The road from Holguín past Rafael Freyre to Guardalavaca is broad with a good surface, lined with trees and empty of traffic. The *Amarillos* are at every junction, organizing lifts on trucks; other people improvise with bikes or motorbikes. Tour agencies offer organized excursions around the region, but if you want to go on your own, car hire is available.

Holguín

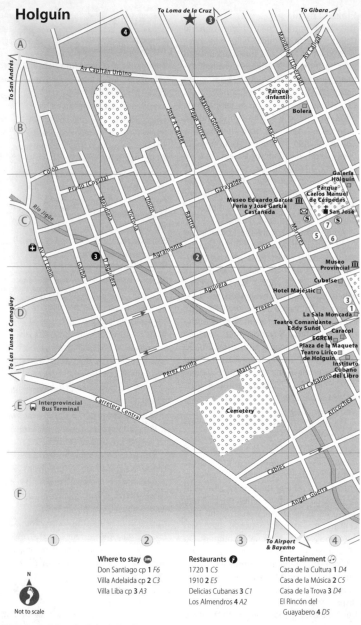

To Loma de la Cruz

To Gibara

To San Andrés

Av Capitán Urbino

Parque Infantil

Bolera

José A. Cardet

Pepe Torres

Máximo Gómez

Mandez de Libertad

Av Cajigal

Colón

Prado (Coyula)

Galixalde

Galería Holguín

Parque Carlos Manuel de Céspedes

San José

Museo Eduardo García Feria y José García Castañeda

Río Jigüe

Av V I Lenin

Garbo

D'Iguilera

Mejarda

Unión

Victoria

Rastro

Agramonte

Aguilera

Arías

Martires

Museo Provincial

Cubalse

Hotel Majestic

Frexes

La Sala Moncada

Teatro Comandante Eddy Suñol

Caracol

EGREM

Plaza de la Maqueta

Teatro Lírico de Holguín

Instituto Cubano del Libro

Pérez Zorilla

Martí

Carretera Central

Cemetery

Luz Caballero

Aricochea

Interprovincial Bus Terminal

To las Tunas & Camagüey

Cables

Ángel Guerra

To Airport & Bayamo

N

Not to scale

Where to stay 🛏
Don Santiago cp **1** *F6*
Villa Adelaida cp **2** *C3*
Villa Liba cp **3** *A3*

Restaurants 🍴
1720 **1** *C5*
1910 **2** *E5*
Delicias Cubanas **3** *C1*
Los Almendros **4** *A2*

Entertainment 🎵
Casa de la Cultura **1** *D4*
Casa de la Música **2** *C5*
Casa de la Trova **3** *D4*
El Rincón del
  Guayabero **4** *D5*

Ilé (Casa) de la Rumba **5** *C4*
La Caverna
 (The Beatles) **6** *C4*
Peña del Tango **7** *C4*
Salón de Beny Moré **8** *D5*
UNEAC **9** *D5*

of a man, measuring 350 mm in length and 76 mm at its widest point. It was found in 1860 on a hill near the city and is believed to be about 500 years old. It has become the symbol of Holguín. A replica is given to visiting dignitaries as the highest honour bestowed by the province.

The plaza is most active at night when families, friends and lovers sit on benches enjoying the cooler air, rollerskaters skim through the crowds and children leap all over the place, while music from the **Casa de la Trova** competes with a heavy-duty sound system on another corner. **Calle Manduley**, which runs along the eastern side of the square, has been converted into a pedestrian boulevard (between Luz Caballero and Martí, and between Frexes and Arias) lined with banks, cultural venues, restaurants and cafés; most charge in pesos cubanos.

North of the Plaza Central

Calle Manduley gives access to **Parque Carlos Manuel de Céspedes** where there is a monument to the great soldier: he is remembered for freeing his slaves on 10 October 1868 and starting the war of independence, becoming the first president of the Republic at Arms. The 1820 church, **Iglesia de San José**, is in the **Parque**. The **Museo Eduardo García Feria y José García Castañeda** ⓘ *Maceo esq Agramonte, free,* is dedicated to the archaeologist and natural scientist who created the Museo de Ciencias Naturales (see below). Also on the park is the **Galería Holguín** ⓘ *Manduley 137 entre Arias y Agramonte, free,* where local artists exhibit their work.

South of the Plaza Central

Off the Plaza Central, the **Museo de Ciencias Naturales** ⓘ *Maceo 129, Sun-Thu 0900-1700, Sat 1300-1700, CUC$1,* is full of stuffed animals, including a manatee, snakes, giant turtle, nearly all the indigenous birds of Cuba and a huge shell collection. It's rather macabre, with human and horse foetuses in jars, but remains popular. The building is almost more interesting than the exhibits, with neoclassical pillars, pretty turquoise tiles on the outside, sitting lions and two 'moorish' turrets.

Parque Peralta is another square between Maceo and Manduley, named after Julio Grave de Peralta, who led the Holguín independence struggle against Spain in 1868, although it is usually called the Parque de las Flores because flowers are sold here. The **Cathedral** is on this square, built in 1720 but frequently altered or improved. A statue of Pope John Paul II has been erected in memory of his visit in 1998. On 8 September there is a procession celebrating the day the Virgen de la Caridad appeared in the Bahía de Nipe, before she was taken to the Santuario del Cobre outside Santiago.

The oldest house in Holguín is nearby. It was the first house where the Governor lived and is now the **Museo de Arquitectura** ① *Morales Lemus entre Arecochea y Cables.*

The **Plaza de la Maqueta,** southwest of Plaza Central between Mártires and Máximo Gómez, contains the old market and has been reconstructed to become a Centro Comercial y de Artesanía. Around the square telegraph poles are carved like totem poles; a statue depicts a woman with a shopping basket, and on a balcony is another statue of a man looking over the railing. On the south side is the **Instituto Cubano del Libro** ① *Mon-Sat 0800-2000, Sun 0900-1200*, a printing house and an art shop stocking oils, acrylics and other art materials, as well as the Tienda Mona Lisa (Artex) for music, books and souvenirs. On the north side, EGREM has a music shop, La Flor de Holguín, selling CDs and musical instruments, while next door is Caracol's La Cohoba, for cigars, rum and coffee.

Beyond the centre

★ **La Loma de la Cruz** Above the city is this strategic hill and emblem of Holguín. It used to have a cross on top until Hurricane Georges blew it down in 1998. On 3 May 1790, a Franciscan priest, Antonio de Alegría, came with a group of religious people and put up the cross, 275 m above sea level, 127 m above the town. All the streets of the town were laid out from that strategic point, which has a lookout tower, built by the Spanish during the 10 Years' War. In 1929, a flight of stone steps was begun but was not finished until 3 May 1950. Every 3 May locals celebrate the **Romerías de la Cruz de Mayo**. There is a road round the side of the hill, but if you wish to walk straight up the 458 steps, there are lots of benches for resting on. The way is lit up at night with street lights. Candles are lit and offerings of coins are made, but you are more likely to meet gangs of boys waiting for tourists than religious devotees. A policeman is usually on patrol in the morning.

Factory tours For an insight into the local tobacco industry, visit the **Fábrica de Tabaco** ① *C Gen Rodríguez in the southeast before you get to Agropecuario Dagoberto Sanfiels, Mon-Fri 0900-1600, CUC$5. Tickets are available from the Buró de Turismo in the cafetería in the Pico Cristal building*. You can also visit an organ factory, **Fábrica de Organos** ① *Av Cajigal, about 2 km from the Parque Infantil on the road to Gibara, Mon-Fri 0800-1500, CUC$1*, to see how they make the instruments.

Mirador de Mayabe The Mirador de Mayabe is a popular excursion. A restaurant and hotel have been built on a hillside 8 km out of town with a splendid view over the valley and the whole city. Water towers stand out in the distance. The open-air restaurant has good Cuban food and the usual strolling musicians. There is a swimming pool perched on the edge of the hill and, beside it, a bar, where Pancho, the beer-drinking donkey entertains guests. It is unlikely that the quantity of beer does him any good, but apart from an air of boredom he seems reasonably healthy and happy. La Finca Mayabe has a second restaurant, normally open only for tour parties, with a *bohío* and a selection of chickens, turkeys and ducks.

Tourist information

Infotur has an office in Edif Pico Cristal, Holguín. Tour operators are another source of information, but you will get better advice from your *casa particular*, if that is where you are staying.

Where to stay

Hotels

Renovation work in the city centre is ongoing and includes the restoration of historic hotels, such as the Majestic (for Cubans only). Famous guests include Fidel Castro, who stayed in room 13, and the actor Jorge Negrete.

$$ El Mirador de Mayabe
T24-422160, www.islazul.cu, several kilometres outside the town.
Has 24 comfortable rooms in cabins under the trees, tiled floors, a/c, fridge, adequate bathroom, quiet, fantastic view. Take insect repellent for the evenings. A taxi to Holguín is CUC$10.

Casas particulares

$ Don Santiago
Narciso López 258 Apto 3, p2, entre Gen Rodríguez y Segunda, T24-426146, 5466 7433 (mob), donsantiago@nauta.cu.
Santiago Andraca Roblejo (formerly a civil engineer in the nuclear power industry) and his wife, Consuelo (architect), have been renting since the late 1990s. They offer 1 unexpectedly good room in an unprepossessing apartment block in walking distance of town centre. Double bed, reading lights, everything works, very homely. Excellent food, genial hosts, well-travelled in former Soviet block, very friendly and helpful, extremely knowledgeable about local tourism, can find alternative accommodation if they are full.

$ La Palma
Maceo 52A entre 16 y 18, T24-424683.
Enrique Interian Salermo offers 2 spacious rooms in this neo-colonial house built in 1945 in the shadow of the Loma de la Cruz. Large front garden, parking, patio to the rear. The paintings and sculptures are by Enrique's son, Ernesto.

$ Miriam Grave de Peralta Bermúdez
Av de los Libertadores 22, esq Roosevelt, Reparto Peralta, T24-427425, miriamgdep@yahoo.es.
Large modern house on a corner of busy road with a garden in front. 1 big room with double and single beds, large bathroom, TV, all very spacious and popular with long-stay visitors.

$ Sara Suárez y David Lamber
Peralejo 23 entre Gen Marrero y Cervantes, Reparto Peralta, T24-425175, 5324 0391 (mob).
Both owners are botanists and maintain a lovely patio with countless ornamental plants. 3 independent rooms, competitively priced, charming hosts.

$ Villa Adelaida
Rastro 30 Altos entre Arias y Agramonte, T24-461708, adelaida10@nauta.cu.
2 large rooms in modern apartment on 1st floor overlooking street, light and bright, lots of windows, TV. Adelaida Arias Ramírez is friendly and helpful with lots of contacts.

$ Villa Liba
Maceo 46 esq 18, T24-423823, hostalvillaliba@nauta.cu.
Modern house in quiet residential area within walking distance of the centre. Jorge Mezerene has 20 years' experience of renting his *casa particular*. He offers 2 rooms with double and single bed, a/c, fan, bedside lights, good wardrobe, phone interconnects with kitchen for room service, TV and video if you want it, patio with tables and rocking chairs under mariposa flowers and

grapevines. Huge tank for constant water. Small swimming pool. Jorge's wife, Mariela Góngora, offers yoga and massages. Excellent Arab and Criollo food, good for vegetarians.

Where to eat

Restaurants

$$$-$$ 1720
Frexes esq Miró.
Restaurant and bar, with shows, information and souvenirs, in a nicely restored blue and white building. The restaurant, on the right as you go in, is called **Les Parques** and is gloriously elegant with tablecloths, white china and roses on the table, but you don't need to dress up. The food is average but the service is OK. The menu ranges from chicken, pork and lamb at CUC$5-6 to beef at CUC$8 and lobster at CUC$22. Plenty of wine on display. The bar is on the other side of the courtyard.

$$$-$$ 1910
Mártires 143 entre Aricochea y Cables, T24-423994, 5326 7098 (mob). Wed-Mon 1200-2300.
Elegant restaurant in an old house, very nice setting. The menu is varied with both local and international styles of cuisine, including imported items such as *jamón Serrano*. Lamb is good, as is the seafood, prettily decorated plates. For something different, choose a flambéed house special cooked at your table.

$$$-$$ Delicias Cubanas
Dositeo Aguilera 78 (3rd floor) entre Agramonte y Garayalde, T24-464397. Daily 1200-2400.
Currently considered the best in the city, with *criollo* and international cuisine, good seafood, elegant and a/c or open air. Pleasant service.

$$$-$$ Loma de la Cruz
On the hill of the same name, T52-855647. Daily 1200-2145.
Panoramic view of the city, lovely during the day or night. It is a state-run Palmares

restaurant. The food is alright: local and international dishes, with lobster at CUC$16.

$$$-$$ Los Almendros
José A Cardet 68 (at the back behind a garage), T24-429652. Daily 1200-2300.
In the style of a *Ranchón* (country inn), serving large portions of *criollo* dishes, including staples such as chicken, pork, lobster and shrimp, all fresh and tasty. You can also get good beef and onions, served with *congrís*, fried plantain and salads. Pleasant service.

$$$-$$ Mirador de Mayabe
Villa Mirador de Mayabe, 9 km south of Holguín, see above, T24-422160. Daily 0700-1000, 1200-1500, 1800-2100.
Rural, panoramic views, country atmosphere. Popular with tour parties for lunch. The road is twisty and not in good condition so take particular care coming down.

$$-$ Taberna Pancho
Close to Plaza de la Revolución on Av Jorge Dimitrov, round the corner from the Hotel Pernik, T24-481868. Daily 1215-1600 and 1815-2200.
Serves beer and a reasonable burger, rustic style, heavy wooden furniture and lots of barrels, traditional music.

Entertainment

Las Noches Holguineras are held alternate Sat and Sun 2000-0100 all along Av de los Libertadores as far as the Pediatric Hospital, with music, food and drink, a celebration of local culture.

Music
Cabaret Nocturno, *on road to Las Tunas, Km 2.5, T24-425185. Wed-Mon 2100-0200.* Show with different Latin American music followed by salsa and dance music disco. It is open air, so if it rains there is no show. **Casa de la Música**, *Frexes esq Libertad, T24-429561.* Lots of different options. The **Salón Santa Palabra** (CUC$3, 1500-1900, 2200-0400) has live or recorded music with

food available; **Terraza Bucanero** (CUC$3, 1900-0200) serves food with national and imported beers; **Video Piano Bar Las Musas** (CUC$3, 1600-0400); **El Boulevar EGREM** (free, 24 hr). Buy entrance tickets in the EGREM shop on Maceo esq Martí, 1400-0200.
Casa de la Trova, *Plaza Calixto García between Casa de la Cultura and La Begonia, T24-453104. Daily 1100-0200, CUC$1.* Good music and dance, notice board outside announces what's on that night, small stage, bar, *salón*.
El Rincón del Guayabero, *Miró 102 esq Martí. Daily 1400-0200. CUC$1.* In the basement underneath Cafetería La Marieta. Cuban and Guayabero music, dance floor, bar.
Ilé (Casa) de la Rumba, *Maceo entre Aguilera y Arias, T24-422741. Wed-Mon 1400-1800, 1800-0100, CUC$1.* The Compañía Folklórica La Campana, directed by Chichío, puts on shows with music and dancing. Bar but no food. During the week there is also a 30-45-min show for tourists 0900-1230. Dance classes (salsa, folkloric, traditional, Yoruba/Orishas) are CUC$10 per hr.
La Caverna (The Beatles), *Maceo 107 esq Aguilera. Mon-Thu 1400-2400, Fri-Sun 1600-0200.* Dedicated to the fab four with statues and the words of *Imagine*.
Peña del Tango, *Arias 173 esq Maceo on Parque Céspedes. Free. Daily in high season 0900-1200, Thu-Sat rest of the year.* Very elderly musicians, all around 90 years old, sing tangos for tips. Very enjoyable.
Salón de Beny Moré, *Maceo esq Luz Caballero. Daily from 2100, CUC$1.* A tribute to Beny Moré.
UNEAC, *Libertad entre Martí y Luz Caballero, open until late, depending on the event.* A magnificent restored colonial building with tables and chairs in central courtyard and now the major cultural venue in town. Art exhibitions, video shows daily except Mon, cultural and artistic events.

Theatre

Teatro Comandante Eddy Suñol, *on Parque Calixto García, T24-454932.* Renovated with a high level of technology and comfort, this is now the cultural pride and joy of the city. Productions are posted on the daily *cartelera*.

Festivals

Jan **Semana de la Cultura Holguinera** is a week of cultural activities with artists invited from other provinces. Prizes are given in poetry, art, video, theatre, etc.
Feb/Mar The **Feria del Libro**, a book fair.
3-10 May **Romerías de la Cruz de Mayo**, see page 296.
Oct In the last week the **Fiesta de la Cultura Iberoamericana** is held, which each year is dedicated to one Latin American country and one province in Spain. There is a parade through the city and cultural events, organized by the Casa Iberoamericana, Arias entre Libertad y Maceo, Parque Céspedes.

Shopping

Art and crafts

La Sala Moncada (on the Parque Central), **Centro de Artes** (Martí 180 entre Maceo y Mártires, T24-422392) and **Galería Holguín** (on Parque Céspedes), under the chess academy, all host art exhibitions and sales.
Fondo de Bienes Culturales, *Frexes, on Parque Central next to museum.* Sells high-quality arts and crafts, prints and original art work in a renovated mansion with a patio café at the rear.

Transport

Air

The **Frank País International Airport** (HOG; T24-474525, international flight information T24-474630, national flight information T24-474629) is 12 km from town, best reached by taxi. It receives scheduled and chartered flights from abroad and from **Havana** to take visitors out to the beach at **Guardalavaca**. **Cubana** has a weekly flight from London and another from Toronto, but is only 1 of 14 airlines flying here with

22 flights a week from Canada, the UK, Germany, Italy and the Netherlands.

Bus

The interurban bus terminal, notable for the number of horses, rather than vehicles, is on Av de los Libertadores opposite the turning to Estadio Calixto García. Buses or shared taxis to **Gibara** leave from Plaza 4 de Abril on the road to Gibara. Cubans pay CUP$20-30, but foreigners will have to pay CUC$2-3 depending on their appearance and language. Private taxis and colectivos to **Guardalavaca** leave from behind the 18-storey buildings on Av XX Aniversario before you get to the Plaza de la Revolución, fare for Cubans is CUP$25 and for tourists anything up to CUC$3 until the car is full. On the return journey they wait under the bridge at the entrance to Guardalavaca beach.

The interprovincial bus terminal for **Viazul** (T24-426822) and **Astro** buses is west of the centre on the Carretera Central. You can walk along Frexes from the centre, but it is a hot walk with luggage; a *bicitaxi* costs CUC$2.

Car hire

Car hire is available at the large hotels, the airport and other locations depending on the company: **Transtur** inc **Cubacar** and **Havanautos** (T24-468412-4 at the airport, T24-468196 at Hotel Pernik, and T24-461212 at Holguín call centre); **Vía** (T24-468421 at the airport and T24-430075 at the call centre); **Rex** (T24-464644 at the airport).

Taxi

Taxis are yellow with a white roof and, although state-owned, they are rented by the drivers and are in direct competition with privately owned taxis. Prices are negotiable for long journeys; always determine the price before getting in the taxi.

Train

The main **Havana–Santiago** railway line is 19 km from Holguín at the village of **Cacocum**, with daily services in each direction but no public transport to or from the city.

an artistic fishing town with beaches and caves to explore

About 32 km north of Holguín on the coast is the pretty little town of Gibara (population 35,000), which has been restored and repainted following hurricane damage in 2008. The area is noted for its unspoilt coastline and its extensive network of caves, tunnels and pools.

It is believed that Columbus first landed near here at Cayo Bariay on 28 October 1492. The saddle-shaped hill nearby, the **Silla de Gibara**, became a landmark and navigation reference point. The town was not founded until 1817, when it became an

Tip...
There are cable cars to the top of the Silla de Gibara for those who prefer not to climb but who want to enjoy the views.

important port for the area. Gibara has a thriving fishing industry, specializing in lobsters, and is also known for its links with cinema, hosting the annual **Festival Internacional del Cine Pobre** (low-budget movie festival) in April, a project of the late Humberto Solás, who died in 2008.

Sights
Hike up to the mirador at the ruined fort, **El Cuartelón**, from where you get an excellent view of the Bahía de Gibara and the town with its higgledy piggledy red-tiled roofs punctuated by palm trees and the beach to one side. You will also be able to see the **Batería Fernando VII**, another important defensive fortification against attack from the sea. It still has cannon and a moat but now serves as a Centro Cultural. The town has a sweeping Malecón and many large, pleasant old houses with open porches and stained-glass windows dating from the 19th century. Many of these are being renovated and redeveloped as boutique hotels. The main square has a fine row of big African oak trees around it and a pretty yellow church with two red domes; in front is a Carrara marble replica of the Statue of Liberty. On Independencia are two museums, the **Museo Municipal** ① CUC$1, and the **Museo de Historia Natural** ① CUC$2, which have exhibitions about the area. Also on Independencia at No 32 (T24-423934) is the gallery of one of the foremost artists in Cuba, Cosme Proenza Almaguer (1948-). He was born in Tacajó, east of Holguín, and is a post-modernist painter, taking his inspiration from legends and fantasies, His paintings feature phantasmagorical creatures, gnomes, medieval lakes and caravels.

If you walk up the hill from Independencia and ask for directions you will come to the **Cavernas de Panaderos**, consisting of 19 galleries and an underground trail (see Caving and climbing, page 19).

Playa Caletones
About 18 km northwest of Gibara along the coast past wind turbines on a dirt road, you come to **Playa Caletones**. Most of the coast is rocky, but this little patch of powder soft, pale sand is unspoilt and a world away from the resort beaches. Weed and detritus wash up on the beach while horses graze along the shoreline, but efforts are made from time to time to clear it up. There is a small village of single-storey houses in various states of repair hugging the coastline and if you sit on the beach someone will come and offer you a seafood lunch in a *paladar* overlooking the cove with fishing boats at anchor.

Cayo Bariay

Cayo Bariay is not an island, but a round peninsula hanging onto the main island by a spit of land. At the tip is the **Monumento Encuentro Dos Culturas**, a monument erected in 1992 to commemorate Columbus' landing and the meeting of two cultures in 1492. There is a beach, **Playa Cayo Bariay**, and a restaurant, **El Mirador**, with a good panoramic view of the coast. The area is popular with Cubans on holiday. Across the water are Playa Blanca and the **Hotel Don Lino** (Islazul) on Playa Don Lino.

Listings Gibara

Where to stay

Hotels

A 3rd small hotel and a grand house were under development in 2015.

$$$-$$ Hotel E Arsenita
Sartorio 22 entre Martí y Luz Caballero, T24-844400, www.hotelescubanacan.com.
New in 2015, an imposing red and white, 2-storey, newly restored building by the cathedral, dating from the beginning of the 20th century with neoclassical columns on both the ground floor and the 1st floor. 12 spacious rooms with 1 or 2 beds, 1 room is wheelchair accessible with a connecting room for carers. There is a lobby bar with breakfast restaurant and room service so you can have your morning coffee on your balcony.

$$$-$$ Hotel E Ordoño
J Peralta y Donato Marmol, Gibara, T24-844448, www.hotelescubanacan.com.
Very grand and beautifully restored small hotel with ornate plastering and stained glass, huge arches and open lobby with a convenient bar serving decent coffee and clean toilets as well as computers for internet access. Wonderful rooftop bar for sunbathing or a sunset mojito overlooking the town and bay. A spiral staircase leads up to a mirador with coin-operated binoculars so you can appreciate the view. 27 very large, comfortable and well-equipped rooms and bathrooms, good food and excellent, friendly service.

Casas particulares

$ Hostal Doble Roble
Francisco Vicente Aguilera (Calle Cemento) 18 entre Maceo y Bernabé Varona, T24-844747.
Grand old house, beautifully restored by owners Juliet Almaguera and Armando Capó Ortega, patio and terrace, garage. 2 a/c rooms, 1 with own terrace, the other takes up the whole of the upstairs, with its own sitting and dining rooms and terrace. The owners are very attentive and their son, Armando Capó Ramos, is an award-winning film-maker (Cannes, San Sebastián).

$ Hostal El Patio de Lily Merino
J Mora 19 entre Cuba y Joaquín Agüero, T24-844269, 2282 7279 (mob).
2 double rooms. Lily is cheerful, helpful and is a good cook. The house is on the road leading up to the steps to the Mirador.

$ Hostal Las Brisas
J Peralta (Malecón) 61 entre Juan Mora y Mariano Grajales, Gibara, T24-845134.
Great location on seafront with sea view from bedroom and roof terrace, comfortable house, friendly host, Eleana Batista Lorenzo. 2 a/c bedrooms with bathrooms, expansion planned, a swimming pool is being built. There is a tiny sandy beach nearby and good snorkelling around rocks and rocky islets where young men fish.

$ Hostal Los Hermanos
Céspedes 13 entre J Peralta y Luz Caballero, T24-844542, odalisgonzalezgurri@gmail.com.
A block inland from the Malecón, this is a good, professional *casa* in a traditional old

house with tiled roof and central patio where tables are set out under cover for breakfast and other meals. Spacious a/c rooms with double and single bed, good bathrooms, rooms upstairs with vaulted ceilings and fan have 1 bed, the one at the back has a lovely view. Run by Odalis and her sisters and niece, while male family members take care of the farm and fishing boat. Food is excellent here, but they now also have a *paladar* a few doors away providing fresh, organic food.

Where to eat

$$ La Cueva
Calle 2, 52, Pueblo Nuevo, Gibara, in the northeast of the town.
Not in a cave, but open air under a thatched roof. Nicely presented food on earthenware crockery. Specialities typical of the area, such as Canoa India, and a particular way of preparing octopus as well as the usual chicken, fish, *ropa vieja*. Owner Jorge Luís grows his own ingredients in his herb garden. Can accommodate large groups, so tour parties often come here for lunch during excursions to the area.

$$ La Esperanza
Playa Caletones.
Seafront *paladar* run by Nelson Escalona overlooking the little fishing boats. Menu depends on what the fishermen come back with. Good catch of the day accompanied by *moros y cristianos*, salad and fried plantain. Also octopus in a tasty sauce.

$$ La Perla del Norte
Céspedes 18, T24-844542. Daily 1100-2200.
Run by the owners of Hostal Los Hermanos a few doors away, who also have a family farm and fishing boat to supply the restaurant. Central and only a short walk from the hotels, with a rooftop terrace for cocktails and appetizers as well as an a/c dining room. Excellent food, imaginatively presented. Several menu options for how you'd like your chicken, pork, fish, shrimp or octopus, and sides include *boniato* as well as plantain and

various rice dishes. Huge portions, but they will box up leftovers for you to take away.

$$ Las Terrazas
Calixto García 40, Gibara, T24-844461. Open 1200-2300.
Criollo food with seafood and fish specialities. Granny is the chef at this family restaurant.

Entertainment

Centro Cultural, *Batería Fernando VII*. Artex stages events here, and there is music Fri and Sun 1000-1900, 2100-0100.

Festivals

Apr The **Festival de Cine Pobre de Gibara**, a cinema festival for low-budget films, of worldwide importance, www. festivalcinepobre.cult.cu.

What to do

Caving and climbing
CIERIC, *Independencia 40, T24-844620/844457.* Can arrange hiking excursions to Los Panaderos cave, with its 19 chambers and a 270-m underground passage. You can bathe in the underground river. Alternatively contact the chief guide and naturalist, José Corella Varona, T5397 9096 (mob) direct, who can put cavers in touch with a local group of speleologists to explore the underground rivers and pools found in caves about 10 and 18 km from Gibara. An adventure park covering 36 sq km has been built by **Gaviota**, which includes a *rocódromo* for vertical climbs, cave exploration, potholing and cave diving, and there are other activities for the less experienced too.

Transport

Bus
There are buses or shared taxis to **Holguín**; Cubans pay CUP$20-30, but foreigners will have to pay CUC$2-3 depending on their appearance and language.

The beautiful stretch of coastline around Guardalavaca, indented with horseshoe bays and sandy beaches, has been developed as a tourist resort. The number of visitors has risen fast as new hotels have been built and, in the winter season, some 10,000 tourists arrive on up to 50 flights a week. Guardalavaca encompasses resorts on Playa Guardalavaca, Playa Esmeralda, Playa Yuraguanal and Playa Pesquero. The hotels and beaches are clearly signed off the road from Holguín.

The beaches

Playa Guardalavaca is the oldest resort and is a popular day trip from Holguín. There are apartments for workers (many now rent out rooms), a few shops, a small craft market, discos,

Tip...

Guardalavaca and Esmeralda are the easiest beaches for access by non-hotel guests.

a bank, petrol station, restaurant, pizza place (**Pizza Nova**) and bus stop. The beach has bars and outlets where you can hire surfboards and sailboats.

The other beaches are very isolated, and there is nothing to do outside the hotels, most of which sell day passes. **Playa Pesquero** is dominated by a gigantic hotel, whose reception is 1 km from the beach; you have to make a detour west of the hotel to gain access to the sand, which is difficult. **Playa Pesquero Nuevo** is considered the best beach, for its clear and shallow water.

Bahía de Naranjo

The lagoon in the Bahía de Naranjo has been developed as a small marina. Near the mouth of the lagoon is an **aquarium** ① *10 mins by boat from the dock, T24-430132,* which has a dolphin and sea lion show, not recommended, and a **restaurant**. A visit here is often included in tours of the area. On the eastern shore of Bahía de Naranjo is a nature trail, **Sendero Ecológico Las Guanas**, which has a cave and a mirador, with lots of information in English and Spanish on the vegetation, fauna and Amerindians. Although it's interesting, there have been many complaints about the CUC$10 fee. Just before the entrance is a path down to your left to **Playa El Tiburonario**, a nice beach – despite its name, there are no sharks. At the mouth of the bay on the west side is **El Birancito**, a replica of the finca where Fidel Castro was born.

Chorro de Maita

From Guardalavaca the road east is signed to Banes. After a few kilometres you pass through Cuatro Caminos and then turn right to Chorro de Maita, situated on a hill with a wonderful view. The **Museo Aborigen Chorro de Maita** ① *T24-430201, Mon-Fri 0900-1700, Sun 0900-1300, CUC$2 entrance, extra charge for photos,* is a well-presented museum displaying a collection of 56 skeletons dating from 1490 to 1540, exactly as they were found. One is of a young Spaniard with his arms crossed for a Christian burial, but the rest are Amerindians, buried in the Central American style, lying flat with their arms folded across their stomachs. Excavations took place in 1986 and a total of 108 skeletons were found. The aborigines had malformed skulls from birth, which can be seen clearly. The tallest was 1 m 75 cm, although the average was 1 m 56 cm.

Almost opposite the museum is a replica of a **Taíno village** ① *T24-430422, daily 0900-1700, CUC$5, extra charge for photos,* with statues of Amerindians going about their daily activities. If you are on an organized tour you may be taken to see the little village primary school just down the hill. You will pass the rural clinic where the doctor lives and works, looking after his allotted 120 families.

A left turn off the main road after Cuatro Caminos will take you down a poor road to the **Marina de Samá**, from where boat excursions originate. An even worse stretch of potholed track leads to Boca de Samá at the mouth of the inlet. **Boca de Samá** is very pretty with steep hillsides on either side. People come here to swim, but there are only very small patches of sand. The bar and restaurant, **Bahía del Sol**, are busy with Cuban families at weekends; fresh oysters are sold here for CUC$1.

★ Banes

It is a pleasant drive over the hills for about 30 km from Guardalavaca to Banes, through rolling fields of sugar interspersed with Royal palms. This town is not usually on the itineraries of tour parties, even though its church, **Iglesia de Nuestra Señora de la Caridad**, was the site of the marriage of Fidel Castro to Mirta Díaz Balart on 12 October 1948. Banes was also the birthplace of the dictator Fulgencio Batista, giving it a second claim to fame with Cuba's leaders. When the Spanish gave way to the Americans in 1898, Banes became a dependency of the United Fruit Company and was owned by them until the Revolution.

Banes is considered the archaeological capital of the country and was originally the site of the Bani chieftancy. The **Museo Indocubano Bani** ⓘ *Gen Marrero 305 y Av José Martí, T24-802487, Tue-Sat 0900-1700, Sun 0800-1200, CUC$1,* contains treasures discovered on the many archaeological digs in the area. If you've visited the Museo Aborigen Chorro de Maita (above), it is interesting to see the museum's collection of pre-Columbian artefacts, probably the best in Cuba, and a sizable collection of malachite. Explanations can be given by the curator, Luis Quiñones, who speaks English and French.

Listings Guardalavaca and around

Tourist information

All the hotels around Guardalavaca have tourist desks which can provide information as well as tours.

Where to stay

Guardalavaca
Hotels

Hotel construction continues apace and by 2017 there will be some 7500 hotel rooms available in the area. We do not include the large all-inclusives in our listings.

$$ Villa Don Lino
Playa Blanca, 8.5 km north of Rafael Freyre, T24-430259, www.islazul.cu.
Good for the price (all-inclusive), quiet and charming, although it can be noisy during the Cuban summer holidays. There is a block of rooms or 2-storey 'bungalows' with lovely

sea views from the top floor balconies. Good beach, although you may need shoes to get in the water as there can be sea urchins. Reasonable food, depending on what's in season. Car, motorbike and bicycle rental, excursions, sports and entertainment.

Casas particulares

$ Argeni Pérez García
Edif 17 Apto 17, 4th floor, T5246 9728 (mob).
Independent apartment with 2 rooms. Professional service and very attentive. If full, the owner will help you find another place.

$$-$ Villa Bely
Casa 262, Los Pozos, at the entrance to Guardalavaca opposite 'los Amarillos', T5228 7295, 5261 4192 (mob).
Abel Acosta y Mircelia rent 2 rooms: 1 with a double bed and 1 with a double and single

beds plus a kitchenette, which is spacious, comfortable and independent on the upper floor. Helpful in finding alternative hotels if full. Laundry service. Food available.

Bahía de Naranjo

$$ Bungalow Birancito
Cayo Naranjo (Gaviota), T24-430132, www.villacayonaranjo.com.
2 rooms available.

Banes
Casas particulares

$ Cary Hernández y Jorge Mulet
Augusto Blanca 1107 esq Bruno Meriño, T24-802905.
Modernized colonial house, 2 bedrooms, independent and comfortable, terrace with pergola and sunbeds, car parking, nice people. They have a *paladar*, **Las Delicias**, serving good food.

$ El Chino Lao
Bayamo 78 entre Augusto Blanca y José María Heredia, T24-803049.
2 rooms in a modern and central house, friendly and helpful service, will try and resolve any problems guests might have, happy family atmosphere. A 1-bedroom apartment on the upper floor is well-equipped and airy.

$ Gilma Quiñones Hernández
Calle H 1526 F entre Carretera de Veguitas y Francisco Franco, T24-802204.
Colonial building dating from 1920 and in the same family ever since, 1 independent bedroom at the back of the house, with kitchen, parking, terrace, good facilities, charming hosts.

$ Sonia Díaz Abaleen
Céspedes 119 entre Flor Crombet y Augusto Blanca, T24-802358.
1 large bedroom and bathroom, patio with ornamental plants, garage, centrally located, friendly and helpful hosts offering good food and service.

Where to eat

Guardalavaca

$$$-$$ El Ancla
At the western end of Playa Guardalavaca on a rocky outcrop, T24-430381. Daily 0900-2230.
Nice location with steps going down to the water, dining overlooking the sea, speciality seafood. Lots of hotel guests come here for a lobster or shrimp dinner to escape all-inclusive hotel food.

$$$-$$ La Maison
On the hill overlooking the beach, T5348 0839. Lunch and dinner.
Open air dining on terrace with beautiful and expansive view. Lovely setting for a good Cuban meal away from the hotel buffets. Good lobster, crab, shrimp and catch of the day as well as tasty chicken and other dishes, with all the usual trimmings of rice, plantain and salad.

Bahía de Naranjo

$$$-$$ Conuco de Mongo Viña
On the eastern shore of the Bahía de Naranjo. Daily 0700-1700.
There's a lovely view of the bay. Chef's choice includes chicken, *congrís* and salad. Hotel guests who sign up for reef fishing trips have their catch cooked for them here.

Banes
There are restaurants open for breakfast, lunch and dinner, offering standard fare for full meals or snacks.

Shopping

Guardalavaca
Handicraft stalls are set up daily outside the **Club Amigo Hotel**. Lots of wooden carvings and crochet work. There are 2 Centro Comercial shopping arcades, one next to the Club Amigo, the other closer to Hotel Las Brisas.

Guardalavaca
Diving

There are boat dives on the offshore reef and wall, cave diving for more experienced divers and an unusual artificial reef created by sunken tanks, anti-aircraft gun and armoured vehicles. Marine life is plentiful and includes lobsters, moray eels, huge crabs and angelfish, as well as a variety of small, colourful, tropical fish, grouper, snapper, triggerfish, eagle rays, tarpon, the predatory lionfish and, sometimes, sharks. However, diving is not recommended during the wet season when the sea is rough, visibility deteriorates, and entry and exit are tricky. There are dive shops on the beaches (including **Marlin Náutica**; see Sailing and watersports, below), and most of the big resort hotels offer diving as a package or on an individual basis; prices are all much the same, depending on the package you choose: a Resort Course is CUC$70 (introductory pool dive), while an Open Water course is CUC$370.

Eagle Ray, *western end of Playa Guardalavaca, T24-430316, marling.hlg@tur.cu.* Has a capacity for 11 divers and visit 32 named sites between 5 and 40 m, CUC$35 for 1 dive. It has 2 small boats and entry is by roll back, with a small ladder for re-entry. The staff are very experienced and good fun.

Sea Lovers Diving Centre, *Playa Esmeralda, T24-430060.* Several good dive sites on the reef offshore, but it can be rough at times. Good, well-maintained equipment and safety record, CUC$30 for 1 dive.

Sailing and watersports

Hobie cats, windsurfers, kayaks and pedalo bikes are available at Guardalavaca, but safety is not good and life-jackets not always offered or worn. Catamaran trips from Playa Guardalavaca cost CUC$42 with lobster lunch. For details of diving, fishing and boat excursions, contact **Marlin Náutica**, *Playa Guardalavaca, T24-430491, marling.hlg@tur.cu.*

Marina Bahía de Naranjo. The small marina in the lagoon has 9 moorings, fuel, water and electricity (VHF16). Sailing trips and fishing expeditions can be arranged.

Marina Gaviota Oriente, *Bahía de Vita, Carretera a Guardalavaca Km 38, T24-430445/430475, www.gaviota-grupo.com.* VHF 16, has 38 slips, fuel and water, 220 and 110V power supply, small repair shop and customs office. Deep-sea fishing trips leave from here, 0730 and 1300, boat rental CUC$270 plus CUC$20 per passenger, all equipment and lunch provided.

Tour operators

Tour desks in the hotels have lots of excursions on offer along the coast or inland, even to Santiago de Cuba. Alternatively you can hire a car, scooter or bike, or contract a local private driver to take you wherever you want. *Casa particular* owners will usually be able to recommend an English-speaking guide for private tours.

Ecotur, *Hotel Guardalavaca, T24-430755, www.ecoturcuba.tur.cu.* Ecotourism, hiking, shooting and fishing.

Transport

Guardalavaca
Air

The **Frank País International Airport** (see page 299) receives scheduled and chartered flights from abroad. Most visitors are transported by tour bus direct to their hotels in Guardalavaca.

Car hire

Hire cars are available at the large hotels, the airport and other locations depending on the company: **Transtur inc Cubacar** and **Havanautos** (T24-468412-4 at the airport, T24-430389 in Guardalavaca); **Vía** (T24-468421 at the airport and in most of the beach hotels); **Rex** (T24-464644 at the airport, T24-430476 in Guardalavaca). Scooters (motos) can be rented for CUC$24 for 24 hrs.

Taxi
Private taxis and colectivos to **Holguín** charge CUP$25 for Cubans and anything up to CUC$3 for tourists until the car is full. They wait under the bridge at the entrance to Guardalavaca beach.

Mayarí and around   *Colour map 3, B5/6.*

hills, forests, glorious views and the Castros' birthplace

Mayarí

On the road from Holguín to Baracoa is the small town of Mayarí (population 23,000) founded in 1814 on the river of the same name. It is the sort of place people pass through either on their way east around the coast to the industrial port of Moa (see page 377 for the route from Moa to Baracoa) or inland through the mountains to Santiago de Cuba, but hardly anyone bothers to stop, which is a shame as the setting is very pretty, with the Sierra del Cristal as a backdrop. North of Mayarí, there are some lovely beaches around the **Bahía de Nipe**, with good snorkelling. Six kilometres from Mayarí is a large cave, **Farallones de Seboruco**, where, in 1945, an archaeological exploration revealed evidence of human habitation dating back 5000 years.

Parque Nacional Jardín de Pinare

Inland and up in the hills the soil, known as *mocarrero*, turns a deep red due to its 85% iron content. To learn more, visit the scientific station in the **Jardín de Pinare National Park**. There are trails in the park through 12 different ecosystems. The **Salto de Guayabo** is 96 m high, making it one of the highest permanent waterfalls in Cuba (El Berraco is 127 m, but it dries up seasonally). There is a tremendous view across the fall, down the valley to the Bahía de Nipe. A guide service takes people on either a short walk (200 m downhill) or a longer, more difficult walk (1200 m downhill).

Museo Sitio Histórico de Birán

Finca Birán, for visitor information call T24-286102, to speak to Sulmari Vargas. Tue-Sat 0900-1600, Sun 0900-1200. CUC$10 adults, CUC$5 children, CUC$10 cameras, CUC$20 video cameras. You need your own car to get here as it is well off the beaten track, and there is no food available, so take your own refreshments.

In the foothills of the Sierra del Nipe, southwest of Mayarí, is the birthplace of Fidel (and Raúl) Castro: Finca Birán. If coming from Holguín or Santiago de Cuba, take the turning east to Birán at Marcané Uno (just south of Loyaz Hechevarría) along a road with pot holes like caverns. If you can take your eyes off the road, the sierra provides a fantastic backdrop. On arrival in the village take the first left and drive for 1.5 km until, on your left on the corner, you come to a little white house with brown shutters and cactus in the fence. Turn left and drive to the end, where you'll arrive at the gateway of the finca, formerly knowns as Las Manacas, where Fidel and Raúl grew up.

Although he has written of happy childhood memories, Fidel Castro has shown little attachment to the place. It was the first farm to be expropriated after the Revolution, and Castro had signed plans to flood the buildings under a reservoir in the 1960s before Celia Sánchez intervened to save them. It was only in November 2002 that the site was quietly opened to the public. It was declared a National Monument in 2009.

The original house on stilts where Fidel Castro was born and raised until he was 14 was destroyed by fire, but there is a faithful reconstruction with family photos lining the walls. In the grounds are the former school house, the teacher's house, bakery, cinema, and huts for the Haitian cane cutters. The tombs of Castro's parents are adorned by marble angels and can be clearly seen at the entrance to the buildings. In 2003 the finca marked the centenary of the birth of Castro's mother, Lina, by presenting the President with a book by journalist Katiuska Blanco about the birth of the estate and its development by his father, Angel Castro: *Todo el Tiempo de los Cedros*.

Listings Mayarí and around

Where to stay

Hotels

$$$-$$ Villa Cayo Saetía (Gaviota)
*On an island in the Bahía de Nipe,
T24-516900, www.gaviota-grupo.com.*
This is one of the nicest small beach hotels on the island, with 12 spacious rooms in rustic bungalows. It's a quiet, beautiful and relaxing place to stay. The suite is the best, with a breezy balcony overlooking the bay. There is a restaurant on the beach for lunch and another in the hotel for supper; the food is average. There are some lovely beaches here, with good snorkelling, and facilities for visiting yachts at the Base Náutica, VHF 16, plus boat rental. The island is popular with day-trippers from Guardalavaca, who arrive in noisy Russian helicopters, but most of the time you will have the place to yourself. You are surrounded by wildlife, principally introduced animals such as zebra, antelope, camel and ostriches, which can be seen on a jeep safari a surreal experience. Passports are required, as entrance to the cay is controlled.

$$$-$$ Villa Pinares de Mayarí
*La Mensura National Park, T24-521412,
www.gaviota-grupo.com.*
Isolated spot surrounded by pine trees near a lake. Mountain lodge in rustic timber and stone, with 2-star rooms and cabins for couples and families, plus pool, tennis, volleyball, gym, massage, bike rental, nature trails, restaurant, bar, billiards, horse riding. It's mostly used by eco-tour groups, so check that they are open before arriving as they sometimes close if no party is expected.

Casas particulares

$ Luís Majín y Chabela
*Coronel Despaigne 14, Barrio El Naranjal,
Mayarí, T5340 6817 (mob).*
2 comfortable rooms, plus food and laundry service available. Owner is friendly, professional and knowledgeable about the area. If full, he will find you somewhere else to stay. Used by cyclists doing the Guardalavaca–Banes–Mayarí–Moa–Baracoa route. To get there, find the main street in town, Leoncio Vidal, turn left and go to the end; turn left for 1 block and then turn right; go over Puente Naranjal and then turn left.

Granma
Province

The province occupies the western end of the Sierra Maestra and the flatlands and swamps to the north of the mountains. It is named after the boat that brought Castro and his comrades to Cuba to launch the Revolution. The history of the guerrilla struggle is palpable throughout the area, with constant reminders of the landing in 1953. Most visitors come to hike in the Sierra Maestra, although there are also several resort hotels clustered around Marea del Portillo on the south coast. Otherwise the area has been largely neglected as far as tourism is concerned.

Bayamo   *Colour map 3, C4.*

a provincial town steeped in patriotic symbolism

Capital of Granma province, Bayamo is a low-key, unexciting sort of place, where tourism is of little importance. For that reason it is worth stopping here to get a feel for local Cuban life. The city is clean, organized, friendly, cheap and undergoing renovation and beautification.

Bayamo was the second town founded by Diego Velázquez in November 1513. However, it was burnt to the ground by its own population in 1869 as an act of rebellion against the colonial Spanish and consequently has little to offer in the way of colonial architecture. Instead there are many uninteresting, low, box-like buildings reminiscent of provincial suburbs in Spain. Nevertheless, it is a cheerful town and there is often something going on, with makeshift stages put up for concerts or other festivities.

Plaza del Himno Nacional and Parque Céspedes
The National Anthem of Cuba (*Himno Nacional*) was written by a poet from Bayamo, as commemorated by the Plaza del Himno Nacional. On 20 October 1868, Bayamo was declared capital of the Republic in Arms. However, on 12 January 1869, the patriotic inhabitants set fire to the town rather than let it fall into the hands of the Spanish colonial rulers. This patriotism has led Bayamo to be called the 'birthplace of the Cuban nation' and it has been declared a National Monument. To find out more, visit the **Casa de la Nacionalidad Cubana** ⓘ *Plaza del Himno 36 entre Antonio Maceo y Padre Batista, T23-424833.*

The **Iglesia de Santísimo Salvador** in the Plaza del Himno Nacional is a 16th-century church which was badly damaged by the 1869 fire, but has been restored. It is a nice, cool, quiet place for a sit down. Beautifully painted, it is light and airy with a marble altar and a heroic and patriotic scene painted on the arch over it. The first Baptist church in Cuba, founded 17 May 1705, is on the corner of Maceo and Marmol.

The local museum is the **Museo Provincial** ① *Maceo 55, T23-424125, Tue-Sat 0800-1400, Sun 0900-1300*, which has one room on natural history, an exhibition of architectural history, and a room on the War of Independence. Next door is the **Casa Natal de Carlos Manuel de Céspedes** ① *Maceo 57 entre Donato Mármol y José Joaquín Palma, T23-423864, Tue-Sat 0900-1700, Sun 0900-1200, CUC$1*, a museum dedicated to the life of the main campaigner of the 1868 independence movement. The 'Father of the Homeland' was born here on 18 April 1819. It is the only two-storey house to survive the fire of 12 January 1869. There are exhibits on the history of the founding of Bayamo up to the death of Céspedes in combat. **Parque Céspedes** is named in his honour.

Calle General García and south

Running southeast from Parque Céspedes, is General García, the main street, now converted into a pedestrian boulevard known as Boulevard or Paseo Bayamez. It is a showcase for local artwork, with intriguing and amusing street lights and

Finding your feet

There is a small airport, **Carlos Manuel de Céspedes** (BYM), 6 km from the centre of Bayamo, but it only receives flights from Havana, twice a week. Most international air passengers fly to Holguín (see page 292) and get the bus or hire a car from there. Bayamo is on the main road between Havana and Santiago, so there are regular **buses** from both ends of the island. Holguín is only 70 km away and there is frequent traffic between the two cities. There is also an irregular **train** service, which should not be relied upon. There are international charter flights from Canada to **Manzanillo airport** bringing holidaymakers to Club Amigo Farallón del Caribe at Marea del Portillo on the south coast, but all other long-distance transport to Manzanillo is via Bayamo, unless you want to try for the once a week flight to and from Havana.

Getting around

Car hire is available in both Bayamo and Manzanillo for excursions, or there are organized tours from Bayamo. Local buses are slow and unreliable. Cycling is a great way to see the countryside if you're fit enough. See Transport, page 316.

benches. The Boulevard is lined with banks, museums, restaurants and cafés, the majority of which charge for their services in pesos cubanos. Among the new sites of interest along the Paseo are **La Galería de Cera** (waxworks) ① *Tue-Fri 1000-1800, Sat 1000-1500, 1900-2200, Sun 1000-1500, 1900-2130*), a small aquarium, an **archaeological museum** ① *Gómez 252 esq Masó, CUC$1)* and a Maqueta (scale model) of the city. Every Saturday there is a **Fiesta de la Cubanía**, when the whole of General García fills with stalls, ad hoc bars and pigs on spits, and the restaurants all put tables on the boulevard. At other times, you can enjoy a drink at a bar overlooking the plaza at one end of the Boulevard unmolested by *jineteros*; here your *mojito* or *cuba libre* will cost you CUP$5 (not pesos convertibles).

On the corner of Amado Estévez and José Martí is the site of the first cemetery established in Cuba on 5 January 1798. Also here is the ruin of San Juan Evangelista,

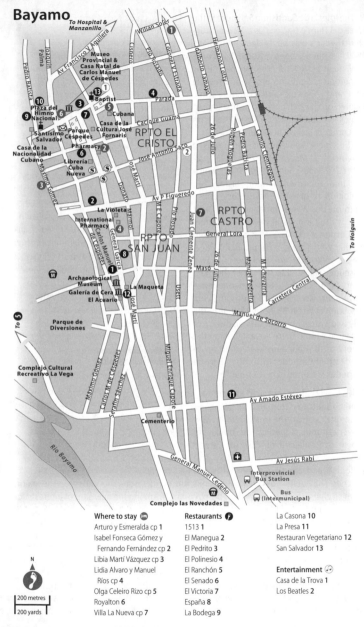

Bayamo

To Hospital & Manzanillo

RPTO EL CRISTO

RPTO CASTRO

RPTO SAN JUAN

To Holguín

To 5

Museo Provincial & Casa Natal de Carlos Manuel de Céspedes

Baptist

Cubana

Casa de la Cultura José Fornaris

Plaza del Himno Nacional

Santísimo Salvador

Parque Céspedes

Pharmacy

Casa de la Nacionalidad Cubano

Librería Cuba Nueva

La Violeta

International Pharmacy

Archaeological Museum

Galería de Cera
La Maqueta
El Acuario

Parque de Diversiones

Complejo Cultural Recreativo La Vega

Cementerio

Río Bayamo

General Manuel Cedeño

Interprovincial Bus Station

Bus (Intermunicipal)

Complejo las Novedades

Streets: Willan Soler, Cisnero, Pío Rosado, Coronel J Estrada, Alberto Tamayo, Hermanos Loti, Joaquín Palma, Pedro Batista, Av Francisco V Aguilera, Parada, Cacique Guamá, 26 de Julio, Rubén Noguera, Pedro Batista, Camilo Cienfuegos, José Antonio Saco, Maximo Gómez, José Marti, Donato Marmol, Av P Figueredo, M E Capote, Pío Rosado, Juan Clemente Zenea, General Lora, Carlos Manuel de Céspedes, General García, Maso, 26 de Julio, Manuel Pedreira, M E Chevarría, Carretera Central, Usert, Manuel de Socorro, Serafín Sánchez, Miguel Enrique Capote, Av Amado Estévez, Av Jesús Rabí

N
200 metres
200 yards

Where to stay

Arturo y Esmeralda cp **1**
Isabel Fonseca Gómez y
  Fernando Fernández cp **2**
Libia Martí Vázquez cp **3**
Lidia Alvaro y Manuel
  Ríos cp **4**
Olga Celeiro Rizo cp **5**
Royalton **6**
Villa La Nueva cp **7**

Restaurants

1513 **1**
El Manegua **2**
El Pedrito **3**
El Polinesio **4**
El Ranchón **5**
El Senado **6**
El Victoria **7**
España **8**
La Bodega **9**

La Casona **10**
La Presa **11**
Restauran Vegetariano **12**
San Salvador **13**

Entertainment

Casa de la Trova **1**
Los Beatles **2**

founded at the same time as the city, but destroyed by the 1869 fire. Only the tower survived. In the park is a monument to Francisco Vicente Aguilera, 1821-1877, one of the rebels in the 1868 war, and a *retablo* to *'los héroes'*.

Riverside

It is a pleasant stroll down through a well-tended park to reach the river. A large, open green space with plenty of trees also houses a market and kiosks, which sell fruit, vegetables, meat and snacks. Open-air events are often held here, and there is a good swimming area in the river. It is very popular with Cubans, particularly at weekends.

Listings Bayamo *map p312*

Tourist information

The tourist bureau at the **Hotel Sierra Maestra**, see Where to stay, below, is very helpful with information on all tours in this area. **Islazul** has an office on Gen García 207, daily 0830-1700. The private travel agency, **Bayamo Travels**, see page 316, is also helpful. Alternatively, if you are staying in a *casa particular*, your host family will probably know everything you want to find out.

Where to stay

Hotels

$$$ Hotel E Royalton
Maceo 53 y Joaquín Palma, T23-422290.
The building dates from the 1940s and has recently been done up. Very central location. Smart and comfortable, it also has a roof terrace for sunset cocktails.

$$$-$$ Sierra Maestra
Ctra Central Km 1.5 via Santiago de Cuba, 2 km from city centre, T23-427973, www.islazul.cu.
Post-Revolution 1960s building, kitsch interior, avoid rooms overlooking noisy pool, 3 bars, disco is the place for locals to go on Fri night, mostly Cubans, helpful staff, car hire, credit cards accepted. Buffet restaurant open 0730-2230 for breakfast, lunch and dinner, food average to poor. For CUC$5 you can use the pool 1000-1800 as a non-guest.

Casas particulares

$ Arturo y Esmeralda
Zenea 56 entre Wiliam Soler y Capote, T23-424051, www.casa-bayamo.com.
Double or twin beds, 4 rooms newly equipped, nicely decorated and comfortable, TV, roof terrace, laundry service, one of the best *casas* in town. Friendly family, Arturo is very helpful and knowledgeable about tourism in the area and can arrange tours and transport. Good food and lots of it.

$ Isabel Fonseca Gómez y Fernando Fernández
Donato Mármol 158A entre Canducha Figueredo y Maceo, T23-4111220.
Upstairs apartment with terrace overlooking Baptist church and plaza, 2 nice rooms, comfortable, friendly and helpful couple.

$ Libia Martí Vázquez
Máximo Gómez 56 Int entre Saco y León, T23-425671.
1 good-sized room upstairs at the back of the house with door to balcony and lovely view of a mature tree, gardens and the river. Bathroom in corner of room, walls do not reach to ceiling, double bed. Libia's family also rent in Santiago.

$ Lidia Alvaro and Manuel Ríos
Donato Mármol 323 entre Figueredo y Lora, T23-423175, http://lydia.freeservers.com, nene19432001@yahoo.es.
2 old colonial houses in 1, family lives in 1 half, the other is rented to visitors, 1 room with double bed, extra bed when needed,

sitting room with door to street, patio with flowers and caged birds, dachshund, use of kitchen, very private but family is there if you need them, charming elderly couple and their son.

$ Olga Celeiro Rizo
Parada 16 (altos) entre Martí y Mármol, above Cubana office, T23-423859.
Olga and her husband José Alberto are most hospitable and helpful in arranging excursions. 2 bedrooms with private bathrooms, 1 with 2 beds, comfortable, balcony off sitting room for watching the world go by in the plaza below. Good food, excellent sweet potato chips, substantial breakfast.

$ Villa La Nueva
Zenea 330 entre Lora y Figueredo, T23-424395.
Norma Ginarte Miranda and family live downstairs, while upstairs they have built 2 rooms with bathrooms, kitchen, dining room and 2 terraces, private, comfortable, good for family or groups.

Where to eat

There are a large number of restaurants along Gen García offering Cuban or international food, charged in CUP$. State restaurants are cheaper than *paladares* because of the currency difference, but the food is generally better in private restaurants.

Always order from a menu with prices on it and check your bill. It is a common scam to overcharge tourists by telling them what is available and then making up a price later. Dress smartly, no shorts or sandals at night, and men should wear long-sleeved shirts.

$$$-$$ La Bodega
Plaza del Himno Nacional, by the church, close to Parque Céspedes. Daily 1100-0200.
Colonial atmosphere, nice location overlooking the river, attractive, snacks and light meals, lunches, dinner, usual Cuban fare, good food but a bit overpriced, aimed at tourists. If a tour party is in, the menu is restricted to whatever they are having.

$$$-$$ Don Quijote
Maceo 116 entre Rafael María de Mendive y 2.
A *paladar* serving Cuban and international dishes.

$$$-$$ El Polinesio
Parada entre Pío Rosado y Cisneros, T23-423860.
Manolín runs this *paladar* on the upper floor of his house, serving Cuban and international dishes. At night a small group plays traditional Cuban music on the terrace outdoors.

$$$-$ El Trebol
23 56A entre 16 y Milanés, Rpto Camilo Cienfuegos, T23-427042. Daily 1200-late.
Upstairs in a private house, wide range of good value Cuban and international dishes.

$$$-$ San Salvador
Maceo 107 entre Donato Mármol y Martí, T23-426942. Daily 1200-2400.
Private restaurant and bar beside the Casa de la Trova run by former teachers in an old house with high ceilings and gothic arches and original paintings on the walls. Good variety of traditional Bayamesa, national and international dishes. Very good live music.

$$-$ 1513
Gen García esq Masó, T23-425921. Daily 1200-2330.
Small and simple but recommended by Bayameses. Cuban and international cuisine, wide choice of dishes, good music.

$$-$ El Manegua
Figueredo entre Céspedes y Gen García. Daily 1200-2400.
Wide choice of good-quality local dishes in CUP$.

$$-$ El Pedrito
Maceo entre Gen García y Donato Mármol. Open 24 hrs.
Pizzas and international food, bar, CUP$ accepted.

$$-$ El Ranchón
On the banks of the Río Bayamo at Balneario La Vega. Daily 1200-2100.
Specializes in *comida criolla* and is a great place to try Cuban roast pork, country style. Food priced in CUP$, drinks in either currency.

$$-$ El Senado
Canducha Figueredo entre Gen García y Céspedes. Open 1200-0600.
Offers *comida criolla* using meats such as goat, lamb and rabbit, good quality, high-class atmosphere.

$$-$ El Victoria
Gen García esq Maceo at the start of Blvd Bayamez opposite Parque Céspedes.
Very nice a/c restaurant offering tasty *criollo* food in a very Cuban atmosphere. Lobster, shrimp, pork and beef dishes, prices in CUC$ but sometimes cheaper than in *paladares*. Live traditional music at times.

$$-$ España
On Paseo Bayames in the middle of Gen García. Daily 1200-2300.
Very small and friendly, specializes in fish, look out for fish in *salsa perro*, a sauce made with fish stock, potatoes and chillies, typical of the Caibarién region in Villa Clara and apparently favoured by Fidel Castro. House or international wine. Charges in CUP$.

$$-$ La Casona
Plaza del Himno Nacional, behind the church in a corner. Daily 1200-0100.
Nice wooden bar, pasta, pizzas or meat dishes, very cheap, courtyard at the back covered with flowering vine, lots of green lizards, delightful.

$$-$ La Presa
Amado Estévez y Carretera Central. Daily 1200-2400.
Specializes in seafood and fish dishes, even lobster and shrimp can be found here for CUP$18-20 – less than a dollar!

$$-$ Restauran Vegetariano
Gen García esq Masó. Open 1200-2400.
Very cheap vegetarian food, good selection of dishes.

Bars and clubs

La Taberna
Gen García entre Saco y Figueredo.
A locals' bar charging in CUP$, although you will be asked to pay in CUC$. Draught beer in large, cold mugs is excellent value at CUP$10 or CUC$0.50. Square, central bar with tables around it; sit and wait for service. Loud music.

Entertainment

Cultural centres
Casa de la Cultura José Fornaris, *Gen García 15, T23-422209.*
Galería Provincial, *Gen García 174 esq Luz Vázquez, T23-423109.*

Live music and dancing
Cabaret Bayam, *opposite Hotel Sierra Maestra, on Carretera Central, T23-421698. Daily 2100-0200.* There is a restaurant at the entrance for a meal before the show, offering Cuban and international food in CUP$, drinks in either currency. Run by EGREM.
Casa de la Trova, *on the corner of Maspote and José Martí.* Outdoor patio covered with creeping vine or a/c at the back. Shows during the afternoon and every night, quite touristy in high season. You can watch local groups such as Chacho y Sus Muchachos, who also tour abroad.
Complejo Cultural Recreativo Bayam, *Carretera Central on the way out to Santiago.* Live music, dancing, comedy, food. Also activities for children Sat and Sun mornings, ice cream parlour Tue-Thu during the day, becomes a restaurant at night.
Los Beatles, *Juan Clemente Zenea esq Saco.* Lifesize statues of the fab four standing outside the door waiting to go in. Live music and the cheapest mojito in Cuba at only CUP$5. Mostly golden oldies played here, popular with the young and old.
Salón de Baile a Bayamo en Coche, *Hotel Sierra Maestra, T23-427970.* Disco, Thu-Sun 2100-0200. Dancing, popular with young

Bayameses, dancing, recorded Cuban and international music.

Festivals

Sat nights all year round are given over to the Fiesta de la Cubanía, when Gen García becomes an open-air bar and eating place with dozens of stalls setting out tables in the street and selling food and drinks in pesos, accompanied by traditional and modern music. It also takes place at Plaza de la Patria, on the opposite corner of Teatro Bayamo.
17-20 Oct La Fiesta de la Cubanía culminates in the **Día de la Cultura Nacional** on 20 Oct, celebrating the events of 10-20 Oct 1968 with the **Grito de la Demajagua** and the **Himno Nacional**. A host of cultural events are laid on, including theatre, ballet, concerts, art exhibitions, handicraft sales and book sales.

Shopping

Markets
Complejo Cultural Recreativo La Vega, *on the banks of Río Bayamo*. A large open recreation area with swimming in the river, fishing, restaurant, cafeterias, snack bars, toilets, children's play area and market stalls at El Chapuzón for food, selling whatever is in season. On Sat, Sun they hold a *feria agropecuario*, or farmers' market, which is hugely popular. People come from far and wide, even Santiago, to buy meat, fish, fruit and veg, returning with their vehicles bulging.
Complejo las Novedades, *just south of bus station*. Lots of kiosks, selling food and refreshments.

What to do

Tours
Bayamo Travels, *Ctra Central 478, opposite Astro bus station, T5292 2209, 5420 5813, anley82@yahoo.es, see also Facebook*. Anley Rosales Benítez runs tours to the Sierra Maestra, Comandancia de la Plata and Pico Turquino, going down to Las Cuevas on the other side if you want to. Also guided tours to Desembarco del Granma National Park, Manzanillo, La Demajagua, Celia Sánchez' house and Cabo Cruz. Bike rental and cycling tours also available. Transport, lodging and information can be arranged with contacts all over the island.

Transport

Traffic is slow-moving. You will be able to walk around the centre, which is quite small, but a *coche* or *bicitaxi* is useful to get out to the **Hotel Sierra Maestra**. Car hire is available for excursions or there are organized tours.

Air
Carlos Manuel de Céspedes domestic airport is 4 km out of town, T23-423695; 2 flights to **Havana** a week.

Bus
The terminal is on the corner of Ctra Central and Jesús Rabí, T23-424036. A *bicitaxi* from the bus station to the centre is CUC$2-3. **Viazul** (T23-421438) passes through Bayamo on its **Havana**, **Trinidad** and **Varadero** to **Santiago** routes, see page 462 for timetable and prices.

Car hire
Transtur offices outside Hotel Sierra Maestra. **Petrol stations**: **El Especial**, Ctra Central y 2, T23-427331.

Train
Station is at Saco y Línea. Daily trains, in theory, to **Santiago**, **Havana**, **Camagüey** and **Manzanillo**.

Guisa

This pretty little town in the foothills of the Sierra Maestra is bedecked with colourful plants and gardens. It was the site of a battle in the War of Independence and again during the Revolution. The **Mirador de Guisa**, on top of the hill, is where Calixto García took up his position on 28-29 November 1897. The restaurant complex now on the hill affords lovely views of the mountains and across to a dam in the far distance which provides water and energy to the town and to Bayamo. The indoor restaurant and outdoor bars charge in CUC$ or CUP$ and provide a useful pit stop on a day trip from Bayamo, although they are very busy at weekends.

★ Jardín Botánico de Cupaynicú

12 km from Bayamo on the outskirts of the town of Guisa. Look for signpost to Guisa on the right just after the electricity sub-station on the road to Santiago. Car or bicycle hire or private driver required to get here. CUC$2, Spanish-speaking guide, 2-hr tour, tip appreciated.

The Jardín Botánico de Cupaynicú is just outside the village of Guisa in a very mountainous region. It's difficult to get to but worth the effort for the beautiful setting and fascinating tour. There are 13 botanical gardens in Cuba, of which the most important is in Havana, followed by the gardens outside Cienfuegos and then these. It was started in 1981, but seems entirely natural, containing trees of over 300 years old, and is good for birdwatching. Of the total 104 ha, 54.5 ha is a protected reserve, while the rest is divided into different specialities. The garden has a lot of ornamental plants but also a collection of edible and medicinal plants and 72 palms of all shapes and sizes, of which 16 are native Cuban. There is a large area of native forest, and scientists are studying the flora to see what benefit they can be to man.

Dos Ríos

Ctra Jiguaní–San Germán Km 21, to the northeast of Bayamo, reached by bus to Jiguaní at 0710, CUP$0.80, 50 mins, then bus from Jiguaní to Dos Ríos at 0900, CUP$1; it arrives at 0950 and returns at 1015, but this gives you enough time to see the memorial.

José Martí was killed on 19 May 1895 at **Dos Ríos.** The national monument can be visited in a morning from Bayamo. The memorial path is lined with *lluvia de fuego* flowers and lots of yellow mariposas, the national flower. Note that the bus does not depart from where you got off, but from further up the road. You will probably see people waiting at the departure point along the former runway, now the road, created for Fidel's centenary memorial visit in 1995.

Bayamo to Villa Santo Domingo

From Bayamo the road passes **Camping La Sierrita** on the left after 4.5 km, then crosses Río Providencia at 11 km. (You can stay at La Sierrita, but you will have to book at the *campismo* office in Bayamo first, see below, which is not always open.) In Providencia village, turn left at the T-junction and begin a steep 4.5-km climb. There are excellent views at the top and time for cyclists to get their breath back before the very steep descent, with a left-hand bend at the bottom crossing the bridge over the Río Yara, leading to **Villa Santo Domingo**.

Alto de Naranjo and Comandancia de la Plata

This trip is a highlight of any tour of Cuba and not to be missed. From the park office, the jeep takes you for the 5-km drive up the steepest road in Cuba to the car park at **Alto de Naranjo** at 950 m. You can walk to this point, but you would have to be at the park office by 0800, and there is no guarantee that guides would be available at this time.

From Alto de Naranjo, there is a path to the left to Pico Turquino (see below) and a path to the right for the 3-km walk to the **Comandancia de la Plata**, Castro's mountain base during the Revolution. Three kilometres does not sound like a lot, but this hike is not for the unfit. Parts are steep and can be either bone dry or very muddy. You need to be prepared to wash everything you stand up in afterwards, including your shoes. Take lots of water and snacks.

Tip...
If there are only fit and fast walkers in your group, you could walk to Comandancia and be back at the park office by 1400, but it is likely to take longer than that.

Halfway along the path you come to the **Casa Medina**, where you rest for a bit in the shed where they dry coffee beans. The Medina family was the first to help the guerrillas during the Revolution, and the Osvaldo Medina Quintet, which entertained the troops, still continues to perform. It is alleged that even now, Castro drinks coffee from this region to the exclusion of all others.

Once you get to the command station you are shown a small museum and other wooden buildings in the camp. Castro's bedroom, campbed and kitchen are all still here. Some guides try to get home early by not showing you the whole site, so ask to see the hospital and the Radio Rebelde installations, which are a further 15-minute walk to the top of the hill. It is all very evocative and atmospheric, helped by beautiful mountain surroundings; you may see the Cuban trogon and other birds in the forest. Photography was previously not allowed at the camp, ostensibly because Castro wanted people to come and see for themselves what it was like to hide out in the mountains during the Revolution, but now there is a CUC$5 charge for photos.

Pico Turquino

Pico Turquino, the highest peak in the Sierra Maestra at 1974 m, can be visited from Alto de Naranjo or from Santiago (see page 359). From Alto de Naranjo it is a usually a two- or three-day hike. It takes one day to get up to the peak and the second day to come back the same way or to carry on over the mountains to the coast west of Santiago. (The route can be done in one day, even from Santiago.) **Camping Joaquín** is the overnight stop. With some persuasion, it is also possible to do Pico Turquino one day and the Comandancia de la Plata the next, camping overnight rather than coming down to Santo Domingo.

Essential Parque Nacional Sierra Maestra

Finding your feet

From Bayamo the quickest way of getting into the mountains is to take one of the daily tours offered by **Bayamo Travels**, see above, with a one-hour drive. You can also hire a taxi, best with a group of you to share costs. Alternatively, if you want to cut costs, you need to catch a local bus (if they will let you aboard, two a day) to Bartolomé Masó and hitch a lift from there (not much traffic) 20 km up into the hills to the village of Villa Santo Domingo. This is time consuming and hard work. A taxi will cost about CUC$40 to and from Bayamo and will take you direct to the National Parks office (uphill from Villa Santo Domingo) in time to get a guide for the day.

Cycling

Cycling is strenuous: you will need a good level of fitness and cycling experience. The road is mountainous and there are several demanding hill climbs and steep descents. Take care to control your speed.

Tours and hikes

All trips in the national park have to be fully guided, so if you want to do a two-day hike, it is essential to arrange it in advance, often up to two weeks beforehand as only a limited number of people are allowed on the mountain overnight and it is often fully booked. The guides are all knowledgeable but don't expect them to speak any languages other than Spanish. Bayamo Travels can arrange an English-speaking guide or, once you are at Santo Domingo, go to Flora y Fauna information centre at the entrance to the national park. All tours start at 0900 from the national parks office, and you need to get there before that to guarantee a place. To the Comandancia de la Plata costs CUC$27 per person (including guide and jeep service to Alto del Naranjo trailhead and sandwich lunch), while to Pico Turquino it is CUC$57 for a two-day hike (including guide, jeep, lunch and dinner the first day, overnight accommodation, and breakfast and lunch the second day). There are other walks available on demand, depending on your abilities and what you are interested in.

Listings Parque Nacional Sierra Maestra

Where to stay

Hotels

$$ Villa Santo Domingo
Santo Domingo, Bartolomé Masó,
www.islazul.cu.
20 rooms in cabins, some of which are damp, a/c, TV, bar, restaurant, parking. Chickens, pigs and horses roam around the garden eating the plants. There is good walking in the area along paths and trails and it is a great place to get close to nature with lovely views up in the mountains, but the local *casas* and *paladares* are better places to stay and eat.

Casas particulares

$ Mirador de Arcadia
Santo Domingo, T5292 2209 (Bayamo Travels).
Arcadia Verdecia Blanco and Ernesto Anaya Torres have 3 rooms with hot water and private bathroom just beyond Villa Santo Domingo.

$ Heidi en la Montaña
Ctra la Plata Km 19, Santo Domingo, the other side of the river from Villa Santo Domingo, T5442 2597 (mob, very poor signal) or T5292 2209 (Bayamo Travels).
Heidi and Lukas have 2 rooms with a/c and fan, a large and a small with interconnecting

door, 2 bathrooms but the bathroom for the single room is outside, not en suite.

Camping

$ La Sierrita
Ctra Santo Domingo Km 8, Bartolomé Masó, T23-565584, reservations at Campismo Popular in Bayamo, T23-424200.

The only *campismo* in the area authorized to accept foreigners; it is the base camp for hiking up Pico Turquino. You get a basic cabin with bathroom, cold water, fan, fridge. Rural, beside the river, but Cubans on holiday can be noisy. This river is prone to flash flooding during rainstorms.

Manzanillo *Colour map 3, C3.*

hassle-free port town and budget destination

Manzanillo is a small seaside town (population 100,000) on the Golfo de Guacanayabo and is the principal port of Granma province. During the Special Period the port was closed, imports ceased and 3000 men were made redundant. Although imports have recently picked up a bit, the harbour has silted up preventing big cargo from using it, so nowadays Manzanillo is principally a fishing town. The universities are thriving and attracting foreign students

Manzanillo does not have much to offer the foreign tourist, but this means that visitors will not be subject to the constant attention and hassle common in more popular destinations; the people of Manzanillo seem completely uninterested

> **Fact...**
> Many of the country's major rivers drain into the Golfo de Guacanayabo, the longest being the Río Cauto.

in the activities of foreigners in their midst and you can stroll about the town at your leisure virtually ignored. Another advantage is that you can pay for nearly everything in

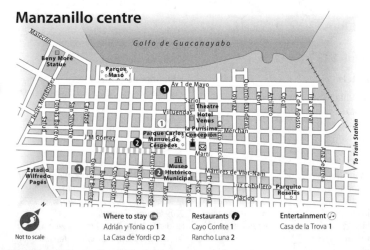

Manzanillo centre

Where to stay
Adrián y Tonia cp 1
La Casa de Yordi cp 2

Restaurants
Cayo Confite 1
Rancho Luna 2

Entertainment
Casa de la Trova 1

Not to scale

pesos cubanos, so for the budget traveller who wants to hang onto pesos convertibles for later, Manzanillo is a good stop-off point.

Sights

The centre of town is the **Parque Céspedes**. Here is the **glorieta** (gazebo), maintained in pristine condition and considered a symbol of the city, where concerts are held on Sunday afternoons. The square is surrounded by restaurants and snack bars, all of which charge in pesos cubanos. A small, colonial church, the **Iglesia de la Purísima Concepción**, is on Maceo, overlooking Parque Céspedes. On José Martí there are cheap stalls selling essential commodities for Cubans, also the usual mini-*paladares*. The **Museo Histórico Municipal** is on José Martí 226, with artefacts of the *conquistadores* in one section and relics of the clandestine struggle in the other. The **Casa de la Trova** on Merchan is the centre of nightlife on Saturdays, where you can mingle with Cubans in a natural environment, without feeling segregated in a tourist-only exclusion zone, as in the big cities.

North of Parque Cespedes, is the theatre, reopened after being closed for 30 years, together with the small **Hotel Venus** opposite for visiting stage artists. The **Malecón** stretches along the seafront out to the Proyecto Recreativo, where there are night clubs, cabaret and lots of open air night life. Along the seafront you will find **El Ranchón** restaurant, fish restaurants and kiosks selling *minuto pescado*, small fillets of fried fish, while offshore little fishing boats bob about on the water.

> **Tip...**
> Some streets in the centre are actually steps and therefore traffic-free.

Listings Manzanillo *map p320*

Tourist information

Tourism is not promoted in Manzanillo, so your accommodation is your best source of information, or talk to local people. Bayamo Travels (see above) can also help with tours and information.

Where to stay

Hotels

$ Guacanayabo
Av Camilo Cienfuegos, T23-574012, www.islazul.cu.
A multicoloured block hotel with 112 basic a/c rooms with private bathroom although only about 70 are in use, Visa/MasterCard, car hire, post office, 24-hr doctor, very helpful, views of pool (questionable cleanliness) from most rooms, full of noisy children during holidays, very loud disco music all day and evening. To get to town centre, walk down

steps to the right of the entrance, down the street to seafront and catch a horse and cart.

Casas particulares

$ Adrián y Tonia
Mártires de Vietnam 49 esq Caridad, T23-573028.
1 room with small but good bathroom, pleasant roof terrace with shady vines from where you get a good view down to the town and the bay. Quiet street, Caridad is a pedestrian street of steps. Charming hosts.

$ La Casa d'Ruben
León 256 entre Concordia y San Salvador, T23-575160, casadruben@nauta.cu.
Very comfortable house with 3 rooms, the room upstairs is small but has a kitchen and large terrace. Garage. Meals available. Lots of information and taxi service offered. Quite a walk to the town centre.

$ La Casa de Yordi
Pedro Figueredo 121 entre Luz Luz Caballero y Mártires de Vietnam, T23-572127.
A well-kept house with 2 rooms, run by helpful Caridad Romero Arias and her son Abelardo.

Where to eat

$$-$ Cayo Confite
Av Masó, Malecón.
Good fresh fish. Try the *liseta*, a small mullet found in the Golfo de Guacanayabo. They also offer the local rum, *ron Pinilla*, which is definitely worth trying.

$$-$ Lisetera
Av Masó entre 9 y 10. Open 1200-2200.
Eat indoors or outdoors, near the seafront, specializes in fish, all priced in pesos (CUP$).

$$-$ Rancho Luna
JM Gómez 169 esq Narciso López, T23-573858. Open 1200-2300.
Typical Cuban food, pork, chicken, beef, fish, lobster and shrimp with the usual side dishes, well cooked, a decent meal with friendly service, the best in town.

Entertainment

The **Casa de la Trova** is on the corner of Masó y Merchan. **Costa Azul** (on Av 1 de Mayo y Narciso López, T23-573158), has a cabaret show 2100-0100. There is also a folklore music show at the art gallery building on the south corner of Parque Céspedes on Thu at 2030. The Danzón orchestra, **La Original de Manzanillo** and singer Cándido Fabré come from Manzanillo.

Transport

The town is not very big, so you can walk around it or take a **bicitaxi** or **coche** for longer distances. **Car hire** is available for excursions to the *Granma* landing site and other local attractions.

Air
The **Sierra Maestra** (MZO) airport is 12 km from the city, T23-577520. It has international status and receives charter flights from Canada and from Caracas. It receives 1 scheduled **Cubana** flight a week from **Havana**.

Bus
The bus station is at Km 2 on the Bayamo road. To **Bayamo** at 0600, 1500, CUC$2.50; also daily buses to **Havana** and **Santiago de Cuba**. No **Viazul** services here.

Car hire
Transtur, Hotel Guayacanabo. **La Bujía** fuel station is on Ctra Central y Circunvalación, Manzanillo, T23-577202.

Taxi and coche
Plenty of 1950s American cars at the bus station operate as local taxis. *Coches* from the hotel to the centre cost CUP$1.

Train
Station is 10 blocks east of Parque Céspedes on José Martí. It is at least 2 hrs to **Bayamo** where the train links up with the **Havana–Santiago** line and all stations in between. The train to **Santiago** is 2nd class, so services are limited, no snacks available; take everything you need for a long journey. Departs 0625, should be daily but technical problems mean it is usually every other day, 8 hrs, CUC$5.75 (sometimes you can pay in pesos). If you have a bicycle go the day before to buy ticket, CUC$7.95, at the **Comercial de UB Expreso** office next to the train station, Mon-Fri 0800-1130, 1330-1700, Sat 0800-1130.

From Manzanillo a road follows the coast along the Golfo de Guacanayabo to the tip of the peninsula at Cabo Cruz. There are several police checks along the way. The *Granma* landing site and Cabo Cruz are part of the Parque Nacional Desembarco de Granma, which extends around the coast from the western end of the Sierra Maestra. The stunning limestone cliffs are among the largest and best preserved coastal limestone terraces in the world and have been declared a UNESCO World Heritage Site.

Parque Nacional de Demajagua
10 km south of Manzanillo. Mon-Sat 0800-1700, Sun 0800-1300, CUC$1, CUC$2 with guide.

Built in 1840, the **Demajagua** sugar mill is the place where, in 1868, Carlos Manuel de Céspedes cast the first stone in the First War of Independence by liberating his slaves and shouting *¡Viva Cuba Libre!*. The mill didn't produce sugar, only molasses (*miel*), and was named after the bell used to call the slaves to work. When Céspedes set off to rebel against Spanish rule, the bell became the symbol of the Revolution. The ruins are preserved in a park with neat lawns, palm trees and a visitor centre at the entrance. There is not a lot to see nowadays and a tree is growing up through the old machinery, but it is a pleasant stop on the hill with a view down to the sea and the cays offshore. The small one in the distance is Cayo Perla.

Media Luna
After 50 km driving past fields of sugar cane you come to the small, neat town of Media Luna, with hedges of hibiscus, bougainvillea and other flowering plants. The sugar mill still operates here. The town is notable for the **Museo Casa Natal Celia Sánchez Manduley** ① *Mon-Sat 0900-1700*, in a green and white traditional 1908 wooden house on the main road. Renovated in 2015 to commemorate the 95th anniversary of her birth on 9 May 1920, this is a small but worthy memorial to an influential player in the Revolution.

Celia Sánchez was born in Media Luna, one of nine children of a local doctor. In 1940 the family moved to Pilón. She was a key figure at the beginning of the Revolution, and it was partly because of her support that the *Granma* landing was not a complete disaster. Contrary to expectations, Batista's troops were waiting for the yacht, and the revolutionaries had to scatter into the hills. Despite being in great danger, Sánchez managed to get messages to the different groups, enabling them to reunite. Sánchez died in 1980, at which time the government renovated the house, turning it first into a Museo Municipal, before declaring it a Monumento Nacional in 1990 and converting it into a memorial of her life. The garden has been renovated with the help of the Jardín Botánico Cupaynicú to contain her favourite flowers, and there's a newly built garage housing the jeep she drove after the Revolution.

★ Granma landing site

Another 23 km brings you to **Niquero** where there is accommodation in a nice hotel with great views of the sea in one direction and a sugar mill in the other from its rooftop bar. Niquero bus station is full of horses and carts and *bicitaxis*; there are very few private cars in town. From Niquero a dirt road leads to the mangrove swamp where Castro's 82 revolutionaries disembarked from the yacht *Granma*, on 2 December 1956. By the dirt road is a small park containing a replica of *Granma* (the real one is in Havana) and the house of Angel Pérez Rosabal, the first person to help Castro after the landing. A guide is obligatory. A 2-km concrete path through the swamp takes you to a rather ugly concrete jetty and a plaque marking the occasion of the landing. It is a hot, desolate walk there and back, but hugely atmospheric when you imagine the men wearing heavy fatigues and carrying enormous packs with guns and ammunition struggling through the mud, mosquitoes, mangroves and razor grass. Every year on 2 December, hundreds of youths re-enact the whole journey from Mexico, disembarking here and heading off into the Sierra Maestra; it's worth visiting at that time.

Close to the site is **Playa Las Coloradas**, a reasonable beach with a *campismo* resort of cabins and entertainment for Cuban holidaymakers.

El Guafe

A few kilometres further on, just before you reach Cabo Cruz, is **El Guafe**, where there is a 2-km, two-hour circular path, **Sendero Ecológico** ① *CUC$5 including guide*, through the dry tropical forest. Along the path you can see evidence of Amerindian habitation, caves, burial sites and their ceremonial areas. Wildlife is also abundant, with butterflies along the path, birds in the forest and a wide variety of plants, including the tallest cactus in the country, called 'el Viejo Testigo', which was damaged by the 2008 hurricanes, but still lives to tell the tale.

Cabo Cruz

The dirt road ends at **Cabo Cruz** at the tip of the peninsula. There is a beach here, a mixture of stones and sand, with thatched parasols for shade, but it is not ideal for swimming because of the coral terraces just underwater. It is nice for a paddle after a hot walk at El Guafe, though. A ramshackle fishing fleet is parked under the eye of the 1871 lighthouse and there are a couple of kiosks selling fried fish if the restaurant is not open. A delicious fillet of freshly fried, piping-hot *minuto* in a bread roll will cost you about three pesos cubanos. Eat it sitting on the sea wall, then go back for another.

Ojo de Agua

Between Niquero and Media Luna there is a turning southeast across the peninsula, following the Río Sevilla for much of the way towards the south coast. Just before Ojo de Agua, three separate signs and plaques mark the spots where three groups of men who disembarked from *Granma* crossed the road in underground water conduits, before heading into the Sierra Maestra. The signs have the emblems of five palms in a heart, because the men arranged to reassemble at a place called **Cinco Palmas**. The spot nearest Ojo de Agua has the actual conduit through which Fidel and his group went, sitting at the side of the road.

South coast

Pilón (population 12,000) is a small town with a harbour on the south coast, where the road through Ojo de Agua joins up with the coast road from Santiago de Cuba. The best beaches in this area are around **Marea del Portillo** where there are a few hotels offering diving and other watersports. The sand is grey because of its volcanic origins and gets hot at midday, but the scenery is spectacular with palm-fringed bays at the foot of the mountains of the Sierra Maestra and the deep blue of the Caribbean Sea.

> **Tip...**
> Check road conditions before setting out as the area is liable to landslides after bad weather and the road is sometimes closed.

Listings Southwest Granma

Where to stay

Granma landing site

$$ Niquero
Martí 100 esq Céspedes, Niquero, T23-592368, www.islazul.cu.
2 star, 26 rooms overlooking the street, noisy a/c, restaurant, bar, parking.

Camping

$ Las Coloradas
Playa Las Coloradas, Ctra de Niquero Km 17, T23-578256, www.campismopopular.cu.
Reservations at **Campismo Popular** in Bayamo. International tourism is welcome here in the 28 1-star cabins that sleep 4-8, with fridge, fan and cold water. On the beach, very convenient for all the sights, with music and entertainment.

South coast

$$$-$$ Club Amigo Farallón del Caribe
Marea del Portillo, Ctra Granma Km 12.5/14 (15 km east of Pilón), T23-597081/597103, www.hotelescubanacan.com.
Popular with Canadian all-inclusive package tours. 283 rooms in 2 sections, Farallón del Caribe being the newer. Lovely views of mountains and sea with dark sand beach. Food and entertainment vary according to the season and numbers of guests, but bring items like syrup for your morning pancakes or ketchup for your hot dog if that is important to you as they often run out. There are few dining options outside the hotels and the buffet food is bland and boring; eat early for a good selection or book à la carte if it is

really busy. Tours of the local area are good, particularly to Cayo Blanco, when you get a decent lunch. Canadian guests usually fly in to Manzanillo, from where it is 1½ hrs' drive. Can be busy with Cubans on holiday in the summer months and at long weekends. There is actually a 3rd section to the resort, **Villa Punta Piedra**, 8 km east of Pilón, very small and run down, with shuttle buses 5 km to the other hotels and beach. Buffet restaurant, bars and pool, but all-inclusive means you can use the facilities of the sister hotels.

Where to eat

South coast

$ Ferlín
Ctra Granma, Marea del Portillo.
On the main road, an escape valve for guests at the all-inclusive resort wanting home-cooked, fresh food. Outdoor seating under thatched roof by a mango tree. Menu changes according to what's available, but it's all good and cheap, with lobster at only CUC$7 the most expensive item on the menu. Beer available but you can bring your own wine. Can accommodate groups but best to reserve.

What to do

South coast

Watersports, scuba-diving, snorkelling and sailing can be arranged at the resorts in **Marea del Portillo**. Scuba-diving is with **Centro de Buceo Albacora** (T23-597139), who take up to 8 divers to 17 sites at depths of 5-40 m.

Santiago & Guantánamo

hotbed of Revolution, wildlife and Caribbean culture

The mountains of the Sierra Maestra run along the foot of the island, with several protected areas and national parks providing a habitat for many rare plants and animals. The Sierra Maestra also provided shelter for guerrillas during the Revolution, with several sights (including Castro's command post) that can still be visited.

Santiago de Cuba, the second most important city in the country, is one of the oldest towns on the island, nestling in an attractive bay surrounded by mountains. It is a vibrant, cultured city with a very Caribbean feel, partly because of the influx of people from other islands over the centuries, who brought their music, coffee-making and culture to the region. It is the place to come for Carnival in July, a raw, ebullient celebration.

In contrast, sleepy Guantánamo came to the world's attention in 2002 when the US naval base on the coast nearby was chosen to incarcerate prisoners from the conflict in Afghanistan. The crowd-puller in this most easterly province is, in fact, Baracoa, a laid-back, friendly place, hemmed in by pine-clad mountains. It's one of the best places to visit for beaches, rivers, hiking, coconuts, cocoa and seafood, topped off by an active nightlife scene with lots of traditional and contemporary music.

Best for
Beaches ▪ Hiking ▪ Landscapes ▪ Music

Footprint picks

★ Cementerio Santa Ifigenia, page 341

Many notable figures who have shaped Cuba are buried in this grand cemetery.

★ Castillo del Morro, page 341

Take in the fabulous views from the clifftop fortress built to deter pirates.

★ Santiago carnival, page 350

Hot and steamy, ebullient and raucous, this is the best music and dance experience in the country.

★ El Saltón, page 359

Enjoy tranquility and relaxation with beautiful waterfalls and pools amid lush vegetation.

★ Museo Arqueológico La Cueva del Paraíso, page 370

This historic cave in the hills overlooking Baracoa has a wealth of Amerindian relics.

★ A boat trip up the Río Yumuri, page 375

Lie back and soak up the scenery as the boat glides through the canyon.

Essential Santiago and Guantánamo

Finding your feet

The **airport** at Santiago is served by regular domestic and international flights. The city is the end of the line for the main road and rail links from Havana and other major towns in the centre and west of the country. From Santiago transport fans out to other towns in the east. Train travel is not as reliable or comfortable as bus travel and many agencies have stopped selling rail tickets as a result of the irregular service. Some visitors to the eastern provinces fly into Holguín; there are good connections from here to Santiago, and public transport from Holguín to Guantánamo and Baracoa is improving but is not as regular. See also Essential Santiago page 331 and Essential Guantánamo page 361.

Getting around

There are good bus connections with **Viazul** from Santiago to Guantánamo, Baracoa and other towns in the region. For excursions there are buses on some routes out of the main towns, but it is usually easier to join an organized tour or to negotiate a day trip with a driver who can take you to your destination. Make sure everything is agreed and clear before you set off, as drivers have a reputation for changing the arrangement when you're a long way from base. Taxis can also be a convenient way of covering long distances if there is a group of you to share costs, but for individuals it is worth investigating official transfers to places off Viazul's routes. Tour operators in Santiago de Cuba, for example, can arrange door-to-door transfers direct to Holguín airport for flights. See also Transport, page 352.

Fact...

The song *Calor en Santiago* by Conjunto Rumba Habana perfectly sums up the city's climate in summer: "¡Candela, fuego, me quemo, el calor me está derritiendo!" – "Candle, fire, I'm burning, the heat is melting me!"

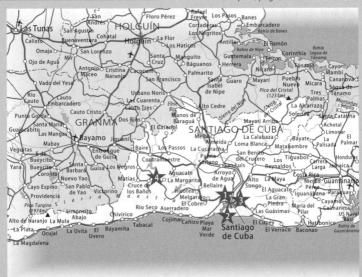

Driving

If you are driving yourself, it is possible to do a circular route from Santiago to Guantánamo, Baracoa, Holguín and back to Santiago (you could also start and finish in Holguín if your flight has arrived there). The trip from Santiago to Baracoa (five hours' drive) over the mountains is especially scenic and exciting (see page 367). The coastal road from Baracoa to Moa is also appealing.

When to go

Santiago's position at the foot of the mountains means that it is more protected from breezes than places along the north coast and is consequently several degrees hotter than Havana. This is not a problem in winter, but in the summer months of July and August it can be stifling. Unfortunately, this coincides with carnival in July, which is the most exciting time to visit the city; if you're in Santiago for the celebrations pace yourself and drink plenty of water. Although hurricane season officially starts in June, you are most likely to get storms from September to November, when you should be prepared for all your travel plans to be disrupted. The coolest time is from December to February, although if a cold front comes down from the eastern seaboard of the USA, anywhere on Cuba's north coast, such as Baracoa, can expect high seas and some rain. Baracoa is the wettest region in Cuba with annual rainfall of 2 m in the coastal zone rising to 3.6 m in the middle and upper valley of the Río Toa.

Time required

Two days are needed for the city of Santiago de Cuba and at least two nights for music and dance. Excursions from the city can occupy another two to three days. Baracoa is a long way off, so allow a day's journey getting there and away and at least two days in the region to make the visit worthwhile.

Tip...

If you are driving from Santiago to Baracoa via the *autopista*, there are several control points before and after Guantánamo city where security is tight. Sometimes you only have to show your passports, but you will be asked for your documents and licence at other military checkpoints, so keep them handy.

Santiago
de Cuba

Santiago de Cuba, 970 km from Havana, is Cuba's second city, with its own identity and charm. It is not a colonial gem along the lines of Havana or Trinidad – the centre is cluttered, with the feel of an overgrown country village, and there is heavy industry around its edge – but it does have an eclectic range of architectural styles from colonial to art deco. Its culture is richly interesting too, and different from Havana's: there's more emphasis on the city's Afro-Caribbean roots, and Santería plays a large part in people's lives. There are regional differences in the music, too, partly because of past immigration from the former French colony of Saint-Domingue, now Haiti. Carnival is an experience worth going out of your way for, with energetic dancing, parades, music and increasingly sophisticated costumes as the economy improves.

Weather Santiago de Cuba

January	February	March	April	May	June
27°C	27°C	27°C	28°C	28°C	30°C
21°C	21°C	21°C	22°C	23°C	24°C
70mm	40mm	50mm	50mm	130mm	100mm

July	August	September	October	November	December
30°C	30°C	30°C	30°C	29°C	28°C
25°C	25°C	24°C	23°C	22°C	21°C
60mm	90mm	100mm	190mm	90mm	80mm

Essential Santiago de Cuba

Finding your feet

International and domestic **Cubana** and **AeroCaribbean** flights arrive at the **Antonio Maceo airport**, 8 km south of the city on the coast. The railway station and long-distance bus terminal are next to each other, just north of the centre (opposite the rum factory on Avenida Jesús Menéndez). It takes about 30 minutes to walk from there to Parque Céspedes in the heart of the city, where there are many *casas particulares* and some hotels. Alternatively, you will find plenty of taxis to take you to your destination. (Arriving at night is not a problem as there are always taxis waiting for business.) The waterfront on the Bahía de Santiago de Cuba lies to the west of the centre, while Vista Alegre to the east of the centre is an attractive, spacious suburb, with appealing *casas particulares* and a lively cultural scene.

Best music venues
pages 348-349
El Patio de los dos Abuelos
Café Cantante
Casa de las Tradiciones
Casa de la Trova
Iris Jazz Club

Getting around

The city is easy to walk around with many of the sights congregated around Parque Céspedes. Urban buses cost 20 centavos. There are also horse-drawn *coches* and *bicitaxis* for short journeys around town. Plaza Marte is a central hub for lots of local transport; go there if you want to get a taxi late at night or to pick up the double-decker, hop-on, hop-off tour bus (CUC$5) for a trip around town, visiting the zoo, the cemetery and the Alameda.

City centre

feel the heat and the beat of this lively city

Spruced up in 2015 to celebrate its 500th anniversary, the city centre features beautiful pastel-coloured buildings in much better condition than many of those in the capital. The main squares have been repaired and repainted after hurricane damage, and a new *malecón* has been built by the Chinese.

Parque Céspedes and around

The small **Parque Céspedes** is at the centre of the town and everything revolves around it. Most of the main museums are within easy walking distance. The **Hotel Casa Granda** flanks the east side, while on the north side is the **Casa del Gobierno,** showing a strong Moorish influence, particularly in the patio. This building is not open to the public, but is used for government functions.

Santa Iglesia Basílica Metropolitana ① *Heredia entre Félix Pena y Gen Lacret (entrance on Félix Pena), daily 0800-1200, services: Mon, Wed 1830, Sat 1700, Sun 0900, 1830.* The white Cathedral occupies the south side of the square. The first building on the site was completed in 1524 but four subsequent disasters, including earthquakes and pirate attacks, meant that the cathedral was rebuilt four times. The building now standing was restored in 1818, with more new decoration added in the early 20th century. Further restoration was undertaken in 2015, with scaffolding in place for some time.

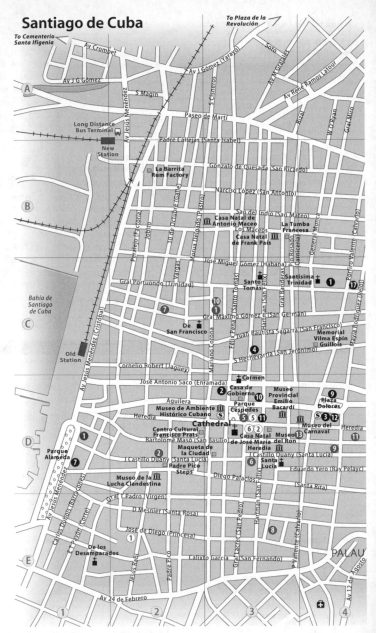

Santiago de Cuba

To Plaza de la Revolución

To Cementerio Santa Ifigenia

Av Crombet

Av J G Gómez

Av 1 Gómez (Yarayo)

Av M Grañales

Av René Ramos Latour

S Magín

S Cisneros

Soto

Rizal

W Bryan

Gral Miró

Paseo de Martí

Long Distance Bus Terminal

New Station

Padre Callejas (Santa Isabel)

Av Jesús Menéndez

La Barrita Rúm Factory

Gonzalo de Quesada (San Ricardo)

Narciso López (San Antonio)

Gral Banderas

General Moncada

Cuartel de Monada

Sao del Indio (San Mateo)

Casa Natal de Antonio Maceo

Los Maceos

La Tumba Francesa

Casa Natal de Frank País

Perfeto Fecoria

11 de Octubre (Galle)

Sorto

Joaquín Delgado (Trinidad)

Vargas

José Miguel Gómez (Habana)

P Rosado (Carnicería)

Bahía de Santiago de Cuba

Gral Portuondo (Trinidad)

Santo Tomás

Santísima Trinidad

Gral Maximo Gómez

De San Francisco

Hartman San (San Germán)

Félix Peña (Santo Tomás)

Juan Bautista Sagarra (San Francisco)

Memorial Vilma Espín Guillois

Old Station

S Hechevarría (San Jerónimo)

Mariano Corona

Porfirio Valiente (Trocha)

María Rodríguez (Rebol)

Cornelio Robert (Jaguey)

José Antonio Saco (Enramada)

Carmen

Casa de Gobierno

Museo Provincial Emilio Bacardí

Plaza Dolores

Aguilera

Museo de Ambiente Histórico Cubano

Parque Céspedes

Heredia

Cathedral

Heredia

Centro Cultural Francisco Prats

Casa Natal de José María de Heredia

Museo del Ron

Museo del Carnaval

Parque Alameda

Bartolomé Masó (San Basilio)

Maqueta de la Ciudad

I Castillo Duany (Santa Lucía)

Padre Pico Steps

Santa Lucía

I Castillo Duany (Santa Lucía)

Eduardo Yero (Ray Pelayo)

Museo de la Lucha Clandestina

Diego Palacios

Hartman San Pedro

(Santa Rita)

PALAU

Gral T Padró (Virgen)

D Mesnier (Santa Rosa)

José de Diego (Princesa)

Carlos Dubois (Barracones)

Padró (Corte)

De los Desamparados

Jesús Rabi

Padre Pico

Calixto García (San Fernando)

Gral Lacre (San Pedro)

P Valiente (Cathaño)

Av 12 de Agosto

Av 24 de Febrero

1   2   3   4

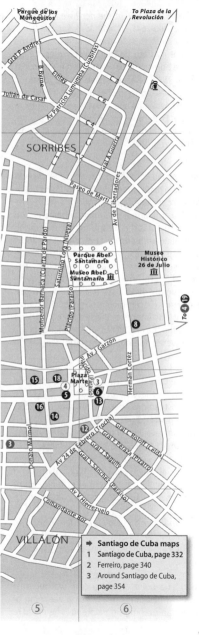

| 200 metres |
| 200 yards |

Where to stay

Casa Andrés y Ramona cp **1** *C3*
Casa Colonial Tania cp **2** *D2*
Casa Dulce cp **3** *D5*
Casa Flor María
    González cp **4** *C6*
Casa Granda **5** *D3*
Casa Irma Jordana Valls cp **6** *D3*
Casa Jardín cp **7** *C2*
Casa Manrique cp **8** *E3*
Casa Mayita cp **9** *D4*
Casa Migdalia Gámez Rodríguez cp **10** *C3*
Casa Yuliett cp **11** *D4*
Hostal Raúl y Kathy cp **12** *D6*
San Basilio **13** *D3*

Restaurants

Aurora **1** *C4*
Café Ajedrez **2** *D3*
Café Constantín **3** *D4*
Café Rumba **4** *C3*
Café Ven La Sofía **5** *D5*
Chocolatería Fraternidad **6** *D6*
Club Náutico **7** *D1*
Coppelia **8** *C6*
Don Antonio **9** *D4*
El Baturro **10** *D3*
El Holandés **11** *D3*
Isabelica **12** *D4*
Jardines **13** *D6*
La Bendita Farándula **14** *D4*
La Carreta **15** *D5*
La Terraza **16** *D5*
Primos Twice **17** *C4*
St Pauli **18** *D5*
Terrace Coffee Bar **19** *C6*

Bars

Cervecería Puerto del Rey **1** *D1*

Entertainment

Casa de las Tradiciones **1** *E2*
Casa de la Trova **2** *D3*
El Patio de los dos Abuelas **3** *D6*
Iris Jazz Club **4** *D5*
Salón del Son **5** *D3*
Terraza Matamoros **6** *D3*

➡ Santiago de Cuba maps
1 Santiago de Cuba, page 332
2 Ferreiro, page 340
3 Around Santiago de Cuba, page 354

Museo de Ambiente Histórico Cubano ① *Félix Pena 612, at the northwest corner of Parque Céspedes, T22-652652, Mon-Thu 0900-1300, 1400-1645, Fri 1400-1645, Sat, Sun 0900-2100, CUC$2, CUC$3 with guided tour in English or Spanish.* Next to a rather ugly bank on the west side of the square is the beautiful 16th-century **Casa de Diego Velázquez**, which houses one of the best museums in Santiago. The home of Diego Velázquez is the oldest house in Cuba, started in 1516 and completed in 1530. Velázquez lived on the top floor, while the ground floor was used as a contracting house and a smelter for gold. It has been restored after its use as offices following the 1959 Revolution and is in two parts, one from the 16th century, and one from the 18th century. Each room shows a particular period, demonstrating the development of Cuban material culture, featuring furniture, china, porcelain and crystal; there is also a 19th-century extension.

East of Parque Céspedes
Museo Provincial Emilio Bacardí ① *Entrance on Pío Rosado esq Aguilera, 2 blocks east of the Parque, opposite the Palacio Provincial, T22-628402, Mon-Thu 0900-1715, Fri 0800-1200, Sat 0900-1900, CUC$2, photos CUC$10, price includes guided tour in English.* The museum was named after industrialist Emilio Bacardí Moreau, its main benefactor and the collector of many of the museum's exhibits. This was the second museum founded in Cuba and has displays from prehistory to the Revolution downstairs, one of the most important collections of Cuban colonial paintings upstairs, while outside on one side there is a reconstruction of a typical colonial street front and a nice courtyard. The archaeology hall has mummies from Egypt and South America, including a Peruvian specimen over 1000 years old. The Egyptian mummy dates back to the 18th dynasty, 2000 years ago, and was personally acquired by Emilio Bacardí and brought back to Cuba. There are also exhibits of ancient art, ethnology, documents of the history of Santiago and a hand-made torpedo used by the rebels during the first War of Independence in the 19th century. Both the building and its exhibits were undergoing renovations in 2015 in honour of the city's 500th anniversary.

Calle Heredia and around On Heredia near the Casa de la Trova is the **Casa Natal de José María Heredia** ① *Heredia 260 entre Hartmann y Pío Rosado, Tue-Sun 0900-1700, CUC$1, guided visit CUC$2,* the birthplace of Santiago's most famous poet (see box, opposite). It is now a cultural centre and hosts a poetry workshop on Fridays from 1700.

If you are not going to be in town in July, you can get a flavour of the carnival by visiting the **Museo del Carnaval** ① *Calle Heredia esq a Carnicería, T22-626955, Tue-Sat 0900-1800, Sun 0900-1200, CUC$1.* The museum exhibits a dusty collection of instruments, drums and costumes from Santiago's famous July carnival. There are also lots of photos and newspaper cuttings but no explanation of their significance. Every afternoon except Saturday you can feel the beat of the *bata* drums when the folklore group, *19 de Diciembre*, perform in the courtyard, CUC$1.

To the south is a small **Museo del Ron** ① *San Basilio 358 esq Carnicería, T22-623737, Mon-Sat 0900-1700, CUC$2 including 2 cl of rum.* The single-storey colonial house built around a patio is very attractive, but the exhibits are limited and a shadow of the rum museum in Havana.

Plaza Dolores Plaza Dolores is worth noting as a point of reference if walking east from Parque Céspedes. It is known as 'Bulevar', although it is really just a widening of Aguilera. It's the most popular of the plazas for an evening's gossip and where you're

BACKGROUND
José María Heredia

José Martí said of Heredia: "The first poet in America is Heredia. Only he has captured in his poetry the sublimity, fire and ostentation of its nature. He is as volcanic as its entrails and as calm as its mountain peaks." In his short but eventful life Heredia created a poetic canon that transformed the form and content of Latin American poetry.

José María de Heredia y Campuzano was born on 31 December 1803 in Santiago de Cuba, the city his parents had fled to from Santo Domingo in 1801 from the invading Haitian troops. He had an itinerant childhood, the family being constantly uprooted by his father's work; they left their first house in Santiago de Cuba when Heredia was only three years old. He then spent time in the USA and Santo Domingo, as well as Havana and Matanzas. At the age of 20 he was exiled to the USA for his involvement in an independence conspiracy. There he wrote his ode 'Niagara', establishing him as a world-class poet. His death in Mexico aged 36 cut short a tragic life in exile for a man devoted to his country.

The house where Heredia was born still stands, at Heredia y San Félix, in spite of efforts by the colonial rulers of the 19th century to have it demolished. An association made up of influential people like Emilio Bacardí succeeded in buying the house, agreeing to hand over its restoration to the municipal government in 1902. Today, it has regained its original prestige as a national monument and is the most important of the numerous other cultural sites on Calle Heredia, the street formerly called Calle Catedral. The house is a now museum dedicated to the poet's life, as well as a cultural centre and meeting point for contemporary local poets.

most likely to be approached by Cubans. It's also popular with musicians and there are several restaurants.

Memorial Vilma Espín Guillois ⓘ *San Jerónimo 473 entre Calvario y Carnicería.* Just north of Plaza Dolores and opened in 2010, this museum is a tribute to one of the most influential women during and after the Cuban Revolution. Vilma Espín Guillois (1930-2007) was the daughter of an executive of the Bacardí company and the family lived here 1939-1959. Vilma studied Chemical Engineering in Boston, but after the failed Moncada attack, she became heavily involved with Frank País and the clandestine struggle in Santiago and the Sierra Maestra, and the house was frequently used as a meeting place and refuge. When things became too dangerous she moved to Fidel's base in the mountains where she fought with the other Revolutionaries. She also met Raúl Castro, who was to become her husband and the father of her four children: Deborah (1960), Mariela (1962), Alejandro (1966) and Nils (1976). In 1960, Espín founded the Federación de Mujeres Cubanas (FMC), which she chaired until her death. She created child care services and was instrumental in combating child malnutrition and illiteracy. She also fought against chauvinism and sexism, publicly denouncing the repression of homosexuals in 1992. Her daughter, Mariela, continues the fight for gay rights and is now President of the Cuban National Centre for Sex Education.

Plaza Marte A short walk east along Aguilera from Plaza Dolores, Plaza Marte is a pick-up and drop-off point for most urban transport. It's a quieter spot to sit than Parque

BACKGROUND
The Padre Pico steps in Santiago

The revolution in Haiti at the end of the 18th century brought a large influx of French immigrants to Cuba, many of whom settled in the southwest of Santiago de Cuba in an area known as Loma Hueca. They built a theatre there called El Tivoli, the name by which the neighbourhood came to be identified. The hill leading up to the Tivoli area was so steep that it had to be paved in staggered form, and these steps were named Loma de Corbacho, after the grocery store on one of the corners.

Decades later, in the Republic's first year, Emilio Bacardí, in his function as mayor, had the steps renovated. Locals wanted them to be named in his honour, but he proposed the name 'Padre Pico', in memory of Bernardo del Pico, a priest who had helped the poor in Santiago.

The Padre Pico steps gained further historical status when Castro chose their strategic location to fire the opening shots in his first offensive against Batista in 1956. As well as all that history, the steps give commanding views of the bay and mountains around Santiago, and now form an essential part of any walking tour of the city. See map page 332 (D2).

Céspedes; sometimes musicians play and there's a **Chocolatería** ① *open 1000-2200*, where you can see chocolates being made as well as buy them. Baseball fans come here to dissect the latest matches and loudly proclaim their points of view. Children under 10 will enjoy the plaza at weekends in the late afternoon when there are rides around the square on kids' bikes or in little goat carts, as well as other entertainment paid for in pesos.

Southwest of Parque Céspedes

To get a good idea of the layout of the city, visit the **Maqueta de la Ciudad** ① *Corona entre San Basilio y Santa Lucía, Tue-Sun 0900-2100, CUC$1, drink included, small bar*. This is a scale model similar to the one in Havana. Nearby is the **Centro Cultural Francisco Prats** ① *Corona entre Heredia y San Basilio, guided tour*, a remodelled colonial house exhibiting personal belongings of the brilliant investigator.

Museo de la Lucha Clandestina ① *At the top of Padre Pico steps, C Gen Rabí 1 entre Santa Rita y San Carlos, T22-624689, Tue-Sun 0900-1700, CUC$1*. The museum was founded to mark the 20th anniversary of the armed uprising in Santiago, Central Ermita and other parts of Oriente on 30 November 1956. The museum highlights the support given by the local urban population during the battle in the Sierra Maestra and has an exhibition of the citizens' underground struggle against the dictatorship. Housed on two floors, exhibits revolve around Frank País, from his early moves to foment a revolutionary consciousness to his integration into the Movimiento 26 de Julio under Fidel Castro. A guide speaking 'Spanglish' will take you round if you can't read Spanish. The building was originally the residence of the Intendente, then was a police HQ, a key target of the 26 July revolutionary movement. It is now completely restored after having been stormed and gutted during the Revolution. It is a beautiful mustard-yellow building with a marvellous courtyard and affords good views of the city. On Saturday afternoon the courtyard is the venue for conferences, performances and other cultural activities relating to the city's French roots. Many of the French staff of the Alliance Française attend.

Parque Alameda and waterfront Go down the hill to reach the Parque Alameda on the waterfront. The Chinese built a smart new *malecón* for the 500th anniversary of the founding of the city, and this is a pleasant area for a stroll or just to sit and watch the world go by. There is a micro-brewery, **Cervecería Puerto del Rey**, also inaugurated in 2015, if you're in need of a cold beer (or ice cream). You can take a **boat tour** ① *1000, 1300, 1600, CUC$2*, around the harbour, which gives you a different view of the city. A woman dressed in naval uniform sells tickets in the port area, principally in the Cervecería and in the Club Náutico.

City centre churches
There are several interesting churches in the centre. **Iglesia de la Santísima Trinidad (Carmen)**, on Félix Pena y San Jerónimo, was built in the late 18th century and has some neoclassical features. Two blocks west is **Iglesia San Francisco**, on Calle San Francisco, also 18th century. **Iglesia de Santa Lucía**, Santa Lucía esquina Pío Rosado, is a small church worth visiting in order to see the architecture in the surrounding streets. Three blocks south of the Museo de la Lucha Clandestina is **Iglesia de los Desamparados**, on General T Prado. **Iglesia Santo Tomás** is an 18th-century church on Habana y Félix Pena.

North of Parque Céspedes
Museo Casa Natal de Frank País ① *General Banderas 226 y Los Maceo, T22-652710, Mon-Sat 0900-1700, CUC$1*. Just north of the centre is the birthplace of the leader of the 26 July movement and of the armed uprising in Santiago on 30 November 1956, who was shot on 30 July 1957. He is considered a great hero of the Revolution and his face is often seen on posters and hoardings alongside that of Che, Fidel and other leaders. His tomb is in Santa Ifigenia cemetery.

Casa Natal de Antonio Maceo ① *Los Maceo 207 entre Corona y Rastro, T22-623750, Mon-Sat 0900-1700, CUC$1*. Another revolutionary hero, but this time from the 19th century, is celebrated nearby. Built between 1800 and 1830, this house was the birthplace, on 14 June 1845, of Antonio Maceo y Grajales, one of the greatest military commanders of the 1868 and 1895 wars of independence. The museum details his biography and his 32 years' devotion to the struggle for independence.

La Barrita Further to the northwest is the Bacardí rum factory, or La Barrita, where Ron Caney is made. The factory is closed to visitors since tourists 'stole' the technology by taking too many photos, but you can go into the shop and bar.

Parque Abel Santamaría and around
North of Plaza Marte, **Parque Abel Santamaría** commemorates one of Fidel's comrades who was captured by Batista's troops and had his eyes gouged out. Cuba's eye hospitals are now named after him. The park is on the site of the Hospital Saturnino Lora, which Santamaría was occupying at the time of his capture.

Museo Abel Santamaría ① *Gen Portuondo (Trinidad) esq Av de los Libertadores, T22-624119, Mon-Sat 0900-1700, CUC$1*. The remains of the hospital have been made into a museum, inaugurated on the symbolic date of 26 July 1973, the 20th anniversary of the attempted overthrow of the Batista regime. It has ten rooms exhibiting furniture from the old hospital, clothing and personal possessions of the revolutionaries and other things linked with the rebellion and the history of the place.

BACKGROUND
Santiago de Cuba

Santiago de Cuba was one of the seven towns (*villas*) founded by Diego Velázquez. It was first built in 1515 on the mouth of the Río Paradas but moved in 1516 to its present location in a horseshoe valley surrounded by mountains. It was Cuba's capital city until 1553 and capital of Oriente province until 1976. During the 17th-century Santiago was besieged by pirates from France and England, leading to the construction of the Castillo del Morro, just south of the city; it's still intact and now houses the piracy museum.

Because of its location, Santiago has been the scene of many migratory exchanges with other countries: it was the first city in Cuba to receive African slaves; many French fled here from the slaves' insurrection in Haiti in the 18th century, and Jamaicans have also migrated here from the neighbouring island. As a result, Santiago has a more varied and blended population than many other towns in Cuba.

Santiago is known as the 'heroic city' (*Ciudad Héroe*), the cradle of the Cuban Revolution, the Rebel City, or '*capital moral de la Revolución Cubana*'. Many of Cuba's heroes in both the 19th and 20th centuries were born here and started insurrections in the city and the surrounding mountains. The national hero, José Martí, is buried in Santa Ifigenia cemetery, just west of the city. The city played a major role in the early days of the Revolution in the 1950s and boasts two major landmarks of the clandestine struggle: the Moncada Garrison, now a school and museum, scene of Fidel Castro's first attack on the Batista regime in 1953, and La Granjita Siboney, the farmhouse where 129 revolutionaries gathered the night before the attack on the Garrison, which is also now a museum.

Museo Histórico 26 de Julio ⓘ *Av Moncada esq Gen Portuondo, T22-620157, Mon-Sat 0900-1700, Sun 0900-1300, CUC$2, guided tour in English, French, Italian, camera fee CUC$1, video camera fee CUC$5*. Two blocks east of Parque Abel Santamaría is the former Moncada Garrison, which was attacked (unsuccessfully) by Castro and his revolutionaries on 26 July 1953. Most of the men were captured, tortured and murdered. Fidel was caught later and imprisoned before being exiled. When the Revolution triumphed in 1959, the building was turned into a school. To mark the 14th anniversary of the attack, in 1967 one of the buildings was converted to a museum, featuring photos, plans and drawings of the battle. Exhibits include personal items of the revolutionaries, weapons used in the attack on the Moncada Garrison and during the battles in the Sierra Maestra. There is a homemade gun built by Che Guevara and a waistcoat that belonged to José Martí. Bullet holes, filled in by Batista, have been reconstructed on the outer walls. A guided visit is highly recommended to help you understand the brutality and carnage of the Batista regime.

Plaza de la Revolución

One of Cuba's foremost revolutionaries of the 19th century, General Antonio Maceo, is honoured in the **Plaza de la Revolución Mayor General Antonio Maceo**. The plaza, to the northeast of the centre, has a dramatic monument to the Revolution made of galvanized steel in searing, solid Soviet style, and a gargantuan bronze statue of the general on horseback surrounded by huge iron machetes rising from the ground at different angles. Fidel has made many stirring speeches from the platform; you can picture the plaza filled to capacity to hear him. It was also where the Pope said Mass during his 1998 visit; where rallies were held demanding the repatriation of both the Cuban boat boy Elián González in 2000 and the five Cuban heroes imprisoned in the USA in 2002-03, and where parades are held every 1 May on international Labour Day.

The **Museo de Holografía** ① *T22-643768, Mon-Sat, 0900-1700, Sun 0900-1300, CUC$1*, is housed below the monument in the Plaza de la Revolución. It features holograms, mostly of things associated with the Revolution and with General Maceo. A guided tour (in Spanish) shows you where the Pope rested after his speech in the plaza.

Avenida de las Américas

This major thoroughfare runs southeast from the plaza, passing the **Estadio Guillermo Moncada** (T22-641090/641078), where baseball is played from November to April.

Further along is the **Bosque de los Héroes** ① *Av de las Américas entre M y l, Ampliación de Terrazas, Mon-Sat 0900-1700*, the first monument in Latin America devoted to the memory of Che Guevara and his Cuban comrades who died in Bolivia. The architectural sculpture leaves shadows as the sun's rays change during the day, giving different images of the heroes. At night it is strikingly illuminated.

The junction of Victoriano Garzón and Avenida Las Américas in the eastern part of the city, where the hotels **Santiago** and **Las Américas** are situated, is known locally as **Ferreiro**, after the family that owned a large part of the surrounding area and emigrated to the USA after the Revolution.

Tip...

From Ferreiro, you can catch a bus or taxi to any part of town. Take care at night, as the three small squares at this junction are not lit.

Vista Alegre

To the east of Ferreiro off Avenida Manduley, the Vista Alegre district (or *reparto*) is an outstanding example of a leafy Cuban suburb, with grand art nouveau buildings that provide an early 20th-century contrast to the Mudejar style of the city centre. This is a vibrant cultural area, with several museums, cultural institutions and open-air music and dance events.

Casa del Caribe ① *Calle 13 154 esq Calle 8, T22-643609, www.casadelcaribe.cult.cu.* This world-renowned cultural centre specializes in popular art, music, dance and religion practised in the region. It has been organizing the annual Festival del Caribe, Fiesta del Fuego, since April 1981. If you are interested in *Santería*, there is a musical and religious ceremony at 0930 on Wednesdays. There are also rumba performances late Sunday afternoons. The museum also runs the **Casa de las Religiones Populares** ① *Calle 13 206, esq Calle 10, Mon-Sat 0830-1700, free, knowledgeable English-speaking* *guide, CUC$2,* one block away, which displays religious items particularly concerning *Santería*. There are no written explanations of the exhibits, not even in Spanish, so it is best to ask for a guide.

Other museums The **Centro Cultural Africano Fernando Ortíz** ① *Av Manduley 106 esq Calle 15, Mon-Fri 0900-1700,* displays items of African culture and organizes events. Although African themes dominate, the institute also includes Latin American and Caribbean culture. The **Museo de la Imagen** ① *Calle 8 106, esq 5, T22-642234, Mon-Sat 0900-1700, CUC$1,* displays cameras, photographs, film and television with pictures of the Revolution next to the cameras used to take them.

➡ **Santiago de Cuba maps**
1 Santiago de Cuba, page 332
2 Ferreiro, page 340
3 Around Santiago de Cuba, page 354

2 Ferreiro

Where to stay
Casa Gallart cp **1**
Casa Margarita
 Berrejo cp **2**
Las Américas **3**
Meliá Santiago de Cuba **4**

San Juan **5**

Restaurants
El Barracón **1**
El Zunzun **2**
Setos Cuba **3**

Entertainment
Casa del Caribe **1**

★ Cementerio Santa Ifigenia
Av Crombet, Rpto Juan G Gómez, T22-632723. Daily 0800-1730. CUC$1, CUC$5 for cameras, price includes guided tour in Spanish and English.

This grand and well-kept cemetery northwest of the city is well worth a visit. It features José Martí's mausoleum, a huge structure with a statue of Martí inside, designed to receive a shaft of sunlight all morning. Martí is surrounded by six statues of women, representing the six Cuban provinces of the 19th century. Along the path leading up to the mausoleum are signposts commemorating successful Independence battles, each decorated with a quote by Martí. There is an elegant changing of the guard ceremony every 30 minutes, free.

Also in the cemetery is the grave of Frank País, a prime mover in the revolutionary struggle, and other notable figures, such as Céspedes, the Bacardí family and the mother and widow of Maceo. There is a monument to the Moncada fallen and the tomb of Cuba's first president, Tomás Estrada Palma. More recently, the cemetery became the burial place of the musician, Compay Segundo, one of the stars of the *Buena Vista Social Club*, who was born in Santiago and died in Havana in 2003. It is said by some that Fidel Castro could be laid to rest here; a new access road was built in 2015, allegedly for his funeral cortège.

Bahía de Santiago
The Ruta Turística runs along the shore of the Bahía de Santiago to the **Castillo del Morro**. Transport along the road passes the marina at Punta Gorda (see page 184) and the port at Ciudadmar, where **ferries** ① *every 40 mins, CUC$2 per person, 10 mins*, depart to the resorts of **Cayo Granma** and **La Socapa** in the estuary. Cayo Granma was originally Cayo Smith, named after its wealthy owner, who turned the island into a resort for the rich. Now most of its 600 inhabitants travel to Santiago to work and it is just a fishing village. Hard hit by Hurricane Sandy in 2013, many buildings have still not been repaired. There are no vehicles. A *paladar*, El Marino, serves fresh seafood caught that morning in an idyllic setting looking across the bay towards Santiago.

★ Castillo de San Pedro de la Roca del Morro
T22-691569. Museum CUC$4, cameras CUC$1. Getting there: taxi from Santiago, CUC$15-25 round trip with wait; bus 212 from Plaza Marte or from opposite the cinema Rialto on Parque Céspedes stops in front of embarkation point for Cayo Granma.

First designed in the late 16th century but not completed until the early 18th century, this clifftop fort and World Heritage Site was intended to defend the bay and the city from attack from the sea but served as a prison for much of its history. It now houses the **Museo de la Piratería**, a museum of maritime history, charting (in Spanish) the pirate attacks made on Santiago during the 16th century. Pirates included the Frenchman Jacques de Sores and the Welshman Sir Henry Morgan. You can see many of the weapons used in both attack and defence of the city.

The fort has many levels and fascinating rooms whose purpose can be easily imagined, such as the prison cells, the chapel and the cannon-loading bay: a cannon is fired at sunset every evening. From the roof you can admire the thrilling views over the Bay of Santiago and Cayo Granma. You can also follow some 16th-century steps almost down to the waterline, where a narrow, grass-covered passage eventually leads down to a small beach, which you can also get to by road. There is a good restaurant on a terrace with a great view. Vendors line the access road selling crafts and cigars.

Tourist information

Tour agencies can give information on transport and offer organized tours as well as making reservations for transport and hotels. *Casas particulares* are a good source of information on cultural and entertainment matters and often offer their own unofficial transport; owners may recommend places to stay in other towns.

Where to stay

City centre
Hotels

$$$-$$ Casa Granda
Heredia 201 entre San Pedro y San Félix, on Parque Céspedes, T22-653021, www.hotelescubanacan.com.
Elegant building opened in 1914 and patronized by many famous movie stars and singers, as well as sports champions Joe Louis the boxer and Babe Ruth the baseball player. Faded grandeur, many rooms in need of renovation and can be noisy at night with competing music, but it is still a lovely place to stay if you want to be in the heart of the city. Excellent central location with terrace bar and café, overlooking park, great for people-watching, 5th-floor bar with even better panoramic views over city, great spot for breakfast (although food mediocre) and during carnival. Disco (karaoke) at the side of the hotel.

$$$-$$ Hotel E San Basilio
San Basilio 403 entre Calvario y Carnicería, T22-651702, www.hotelescubanacan.com.
A 2003 hotel in baby blue, close to the historical centre, nice decor with lots of plants and stylish pieces of furniture. 8 large and very comfortable rooms, all on the ground floor but the hotel entrance is up a flight of steep steps, high ceilings but no windows in most rooms, can be noisy.

Casas particulares

$$ Casa Mayita
San Basilio 472 Altos esq Reloj, T22-658973, kath_bateman@hotmail.com.
Newly renovated with colonial features preserved, 1st-floor corner apartment with floor to ceiling shuttered wooden doors throughout, opening onto a balcony running round the house, making it light, bright and airy. Roof terrace with views over the bay and the mountains. 2 bedrooms, 1 with 2 beds, the other with a double and single bed, new bathrooms. Run by Lirín, who speaks a little English. Breakfast available and supper on request, lots of *paladares* nearby.

$ Casa Andrés y Ramona
Corona 635 entre San Germán y Trinidad, T22-654349.
2 rooms, 1 larger than the other, roof terrace with amazing view of city and bay, covered table and chairs or sunny area. Meals are large and Andrés is a good cook. Friendly, hospitable, helpful, Andrés has a 1949 car and offers tours or taxi service, English spoken.

$ Casa Colonial Tania
Castillo Duany (Santa Rita) 101 entre Callejón Santiago y Teniente Rey, T22-624490, aquiles@cultstgo.cult.cu.
Tania García Terreno and family live in this huge old house, English, French and Italian spoken, 2 rooms, with windows, bedside lamps, desk, good bathrooms and furniture. Stairs up to roof terrace for sunbathing or great sunset watching with views over the bay and up to the cathedral.

$ Casa Dulce
Bartolomé Masó (San Basilio) 552 Altos esq Clarín, T22-625479, gdcastillo20@yahoo.es.
Delightful apartment, living room on corner has huge windows open to the breeze, 1 large bedroom, one of the best *casas*, run by Gladys Domenech Castillo, who is helpful, friendly, speaks some English and offers

really good food and internet access. The roof terrace has a table for meals, sunbed, amazing views of the city and harbour.

$ Casa Irma Jordana Valls
Santa Lucía (Castillo Duany) 303 entre San Pedro y San Félix, T22-622391, close to Parque Céspedes.
Huge colonial house, 1 room with double and single bed, access door to tiny patio, large bathroom with bathtub and bidet. 2nd L-shaped room with 2 double beds, smaller bathroom, high ceilings. Interior patio has flowering plants, the front room is cluttered with ornaments, dining room with TV opens onto patio. Meals and laundry service offered, only Spanish spoken.

$ Casa Jardín
Máximo Gómez (San Germán) 165 entre Rastro y Gallo, T22-653720.
Run by María Abono Segura, who can help with tours or travel problems. The house is a short walk from the centre and therefore quiet at night. Friendly and helpful, laundry services, parking outside with a guard overnight. Good meals, delicious food, rooms with a/c, fan and fridge, extra bed on request. The garden at the back is really special, covered in trailing flowering plants, pots everywhere, bananas, while up on the roof is a terrace with more pretty garden and vines, tables, benches, hammock.

$ Casa Manrique
Princesa (J de Diego) 565 entre Carnicería (Pio Rosado) y Calvario (Porfirio Valiente), T22-651909.
Run by Ivia Bello and Mario Nistal, 2 small rooms upstairs, simple but clean and good. Dining area outside rooms with fridge and all crockery so you can prepare your own cold meals, good food offered, laundry service, English and some Italian spoken. Small patio with view of cathedral and larger terrace upstairs for sunbathing and great view all around. Secure parking opposite for small fee.

$ Casa Migdalia Gámez Rodríguez
Corona 371 Altos entre San Germán y Trinidad, T22-627246, robert@cbcor.co.cu.
2 rooms in Migdalia's apartment, one of which is on the roof terrace for great views, and 2 rooms downstairs in her sister's apartment. The family is very helpful and friendly. Migdalia prepares fresh and delicious food; her daughter speaks English.

$ Casa Yuliett
Bartolomé Masó (San Basilio) 513 entre Clarín y Reloj, T22-620546.
This has 3 rooms of good standard, all with fridge, a/c, fan, 110v or 220v in bathroom, terraces for relaxing on. The family is on hand if you need help, but otherwise will leave you alone, friendly, central, good location. Onstreet parking can be arranged with a neighbour, CUC$3.

$ Hostal Raúl y Kathy
Heredia 610 ½ entre Marte y Paraíso, T22-624472.
Efficiently run, this is a hostal rather than a family homestay, but very comfortable, convenient and a lovely place to stay. The 4 rooms are bright and light, the beds comfortable with good linens, everything works. Best of all is the roof terrace with a glorious view over the city, where you eat a substantial breakfast and tasty evening meal, with several menu options. A lovely place to sit and relax. Parking arranged for a small fee. English spoken, Raúl Mora Herrero can help with transport, excursions and problems.

Beyond the centre
Hotels

$$$$-$$$ Meliá Santiago de Cuba
Av Las Américas entre 4 y M, Rpto Sueño, T22-687070, www.melia.com.
Built in 1991, the 15-floor hotel's modern design stands out like a beacon and is quite a landmark with its red, white and blue colour scheme. Supposedly 5-star, 302 rooms and suites now showing their age, some for non-smokers and the disabled but the smell of

smoke gets everywhere, 24-hr room service, lots of bars and restaurants, good view of city from roof top bar, swimming pools, tennis, sauna, car hire, business centre, overpriced WiFi access at CUC$12/2 hrs, post office, shops, will change most any currencies into dollars, staff helpful and friendly.

$$$-$$ Las Américas
Av de las Américas esq Gen Cebreco, T22-642011, www.islazul.cu.
70 spacious rooms, lively, popular with groups and can be noisy from other guests as well as traffic, pool on 2nd floor by restaurant, lots of evening entertainment. There is a restaurant but most guests go across the road to the Meliá for their meals other than breakfast. Nice reception staff, safety deposit, car hire, shop. Easy access to city centre, bus stop opposite hotel.

$$$-$$ San Juan
Km 4.5 Ctra a Siboney, T22-687156, www.islazul.cu.
On edge of town, but nice location, the former *Leningrado* is right beside the site of one of the last battles of the 1898 War of Independence. The remains of a huge ceiba tree are in the grounds, beneath which Spain and the USA signed the surrender of Santiago on 16 July 1898. It is also next to the zoo so be prepared for animal noises. Rooms are basic with noisy a/c but spacious, some in chalets, quieter than the rooms around the large pool, mostly Cuban guests, queues for restaurant and bar at weekends and during festivals, car hire, car park.

Casas particulares
Vista Alegre is more suburban, with wider streets, detached houses with gardens and lots of shady trees. It is quieter at night. Road signs are non-existent. Parking is much easier than in the centre. There are lots of places to stay on Calle 6.

$ Casa Flor María González
J 314 Altos entre Av Las Américas y 6, Rpto Sueño, upper floor, T22-645568.
1 large room, TV, desk, fridge. Not a fancy house, but homely. Flor María is a professor at the Oriente University and her husband speaks English and Russian. Entrance up steep stairs, a/c, fans, breakfast and dinner available and use of kitchen. Can arrange rooms in nearby *casas* if you are in a group.

$ Casa Gallart
6 302 esq 11, Rpto Vista Alegre, T22-643307, maydepedro@yahoo.es.
Glorious period house with a pretty fence topped with flowering hedge and steps up to a columned entrance, colonial style with all original floor tiles, shutters and fittings, high ceilings, antique furniture, spacious and airy. The owners, Pedro Luis Gallart and Maydeline Tauler, are a mechanical engineer and psychologist, respectively and are helpful and friendly. 2 a/c rooms, pretty courtyard garden to the rear, continental breakfast with fruit but no evening meal, although Pedro can give lots of recommendations for restaurants.

$ Casa Margarita Berrejo
6 406 entre 15 y 17, Rpto Vista Alegre, T22-642450.
One room in comfortable detached house crammed with antiques, ornaments and sculptures, but the real joy is the large garden, complete with hammock and swinging chair, very peaceful after a day's sightseeing. Breakfast and evening meal are offered.

Where to eat

City centre

$$$ Aurora
Gen Portuondo entre Gen Moncada y Calvario, T22-657386.
Walk through the family house to get to the tables in a lovely courtyard garden, under cover or under a tree. Fresh ingredients, nicely cooked, Cuban menu of soup, salad, main course with rice costs CUC$12-15. Family-run, friendly service, the chef can adapt dishes to your requirements if necessary. Popular so often busy.

$$$ La Bendita Farándula
Barnada 513 entre Aguilera y Heredia, T22-653739. Daily 1130-2330.
As you go in, there is a pizzería on the right but you need to turn left for the restaurant. Small, cosy *paladar* with 7 tables, run by Susana Carrasquedo. The house speciality is *Mar y Tierra* and you can have a wide variety of seafood, including lobster, crab, prawns and fish, or the more usual chicken and pork, even rabbit, all served with mashed potato, rice or seasonal vegetables. Good cocktails and the Mojito is not too sweet. Service is fine but nothing special. Reservations advised.

$$$-$$ Don Antonio
Aguilera entre Calvario y Reloj, Plaza Dolores, T22-652205. Daily 1200-2300.
Nice decor, bar inside serving all kinds of Cuban cocktails, tasty *criollo* food, reasonable prices, live music.

$$$-$$ Primos Twice
Calvario 262 entre Habana y Trinidad, T22-652278. Lunch and dinner.
A tiny restaurant in the front room of a house, friendly service, intimate atmosphere. The food is good and there is a wide variety of meats and seafood accompanied by salads, rice and vegetables, although some of the sauces can be a bit rich and heavy.

$$$-$$ St Pauli
Enramada 605 entre Barnada y Plácido, T22-652292. Lunch and dinner.
Close to Plaza de Marte, a popular place at night as it turns into a lounge bar after midnight. Before then, the food is good, prettily presented, extensive menu with vegetarian options.

$$$-$ Club Náutico
Av Jesús Menéndez, Malecón. Open 1200-1600, 1800-2355.
Fish and seafood specialities operating in both CUC$ and CUP$.

$$$-$ La Carreta
Saco 563 entre Barnada y San Agustín, T22-624570. Daily 1200-2400.
One of the larger restaurants with a/c. House speciality is *Carnes a la Carreta*, lamb, pork, lobster or fish accompanied by mixed vegetables. Good variety of drinks and a great Mojito. Traditional Cuban music and 2 screens show a mix of salsa.

$$$-$ La Terraza
Aguilera 602 esq Barnada. Lunch and dinner.
Upstairs on a covered terrace from where you get a lovely view of the city, good Cuban food, delicious seafood, great value. Sometimes live music.

$$ Jardines
Aguilera 762 entre Trocha y Pizarro, T22-652522, 0153-144780 (mob). Daily 1100-2300.
In what appears to be a residential house, go downstairs under the restaurant sign. Pleasant restaurant with lots of tropical plants, popular for celebrations and parties. There is the usual chicken, pork and seafood, but it is well-prepared, fresh and tasty, with plenty of side salads and vegetables and a good selection of bar drinks or teas. Good value.

$$-$ El Baturro
Aguilera esq San Félix, just off Parque Céspedes. Open 1200-2300.
Cuban food, cheap, convenient stop for sustenance, mostly Cuban clientele but hence popular with foreigners.

$$-$ El Holandés
Heredia entre San Félix y el Callejón,
T22-624878. Daily 1200-2300.
Colonial house 1 block from Plaza Céspedes,
very central and always busy, choice of
seating, on the balcony overlooking the street,
in the large dining room or patio with tropical
plants, the wooden tables are designed to
emulate an 18th century tavern. Among other
menu items are chicken or fish with fruit and
they offer a good stir fry or paella (if you are
prepared to wait). Opposite the Casa de la
Trova, so you get the benefit of the music.

Cafés and ice cream parlours

Café Ajedrez
Enramada y Santo Tomás. Tue-Sun 1000-1500.
Open-air café in cool architectural structure
designed by Cuban architect, Walter A
Betancourt Fernández, and chess board
tables. Coffee only.

Café Constantín
Plaza Dolores. Daily 0900-2100.
Coffee, ice cream, sweets and snacks,
sit in the patio or in an a/c room.

Café Rumba
San Félix 445A.
Great little spot with modern decor in a
colonial house with patio garden serving
drinks, snacks, sandwiches, pasta, tapas,
breakfast and fruit plates. Modern and
inviting, it also has a good cocktail bar with
a happy hour at 1700-1900. There is even
a beauty centre and you can get your nails
done here.

Café Ven La Sofía
Plácido entre Enramada y Bayamo,
Plaza de Marte. Daily 0900-2100.
Coffee, ice cream, sweets and snacks.

Chocolatería Fraternidad
Aguilera esq Pizarro, southeast corner of Plaza
Marte. Mon 0900-1700, Tue-Fri 0900-1230,
1300-2030, Sat, Sun 1000-1330, 1400-2130.
A welcome stop to cool off with a/c and ice
cream, hot or cold chocolate drink using local

cocoa, also coffees, all chocolate made on
site, you can watch the chocolate-making
process. Service can be cold too.

Coppelia
Av de los Libertadores y Victoriano Garzón.
Mon-Fri 1000-2100, Sat and Sun 1100-2200.
Known as La Arboleda. No queuing if you have
CUC$ but it is a bargain if you pay in CUP$.

Isabelica
Aguilera esq Porfirio Valente, Plaza Dolores.
Open 0900-2100.
Serves only coffee, several flavours. The
local speciality *Rocío del Gallo* is coffee and
rum, or there's the Café Isabelica, which is
coffee, rum and honey – ask for it here. You
will be charged in CUC$ unless you ask to
pay in CUP$.

Terrace Coffee Bar
Hotel Casa Granda. Open 24 hrs.
A pleasant place for a drink. Food is nothing
special but it is worth having a snack to
extend your stay as it is a prime site for
people-watching with a great view over
Parque Céspedes.

Beyond the centre

$$$ El Zunzun
Av Manduley 159, Rpto Vista Alegre,
T22-641528. Open 0900-0200.
In a pleasant old suburban house with
several rooms used for dining, resulting
in an intimate atmosphere and there is
live music. The food is Cuban and mostly
good, as is the service.

$$$ La Fontana
Hotel Meliá Santiago (see Where to stay),
T22-642634, outside by the shops.
Open 1100-2400.
Open-air but under cover, serving
surprisingly good pizzas and nothing like you
get on the streets. Large variety of sizes and
toppings from a small cheese and tomato
pizza to a large one with lobster, also pastas
chicken, meat or fish dishes if you are not
seeking a pizza fix.

$$$ Setos Cuba

Av Manduley 154 entre 9 y 11, Rpto Vista Alegre, T5355 2204. Lunch and dinner.
Elegant suburban mansion with columns at the front, separated from the road by a smart fence. Owned and run by Javier Toledo, a Spaniard (married to a Cuban) with a hotel and restaurant in Spain too. Generally considered to be the best restaurant in the city with a varied menu, delicious desserts, Spanish wines and olive oil. Cuban and Spanish dishes served in very pleasant surroundings with attentive service.

$$$-$$ Dolores

Terraza 209 entre 7 y 9, Rpto Sueño, T22-641791.
Nice garden, food can be excellent but service is variable.

$$$-$$ El Barracón

Av Garzón entre Paseo de Martí y Calle 1, opposite the 18-floor building, T22-661877/643242. Daily 1200-2300.
Very good *criollo* food, generous portions and popular with Cubans. From the standard chicken to smoked pork or even the tender lamb, all dishes are tasty and well-prepared with traditional sides. Decorated with exposed brickwork, stone and dark wooden furniture, the theme is slavery, with statues and pictures of plantation life.

$$$-$$ El Palenquito

Av del Río 28 entre Calle 6 y Carretera del Caney, Rpto Pastorita, T22-645220, see Facebook. Open 1200-2400.
A long way from anywhere but the No 24 bus stops outside or walk (90 mins from the centre) or take a taxi. Set in a large garden with rustic atmosphere, tables under a thatched roof and all the meat and lobster is cooked on the barbeque. Friendly service, tasty food and lots of it, good value. A lovely place to come for a relaxing lunch or dinner away from the city.

Bars and clubs

Bello Bar

Hotel Meliá Santiago de Cuba, Av las Américas, Rpto Sueno. Daily 1800-0200.
Up on the 15th floor with a panoramic view from the terrace. Dress smartly.

Cervecería Puerto del Rey

Av Jesús Menéndez entre Aduna y Duvergel, T22-669304. Mon 1600-2400, Tue-Sun 1200-2400.
On the Alameda, in a converted 1902 warehouse opposite the 1st shipping terminal built by the Spanish. This new micro-brewery, using Austrian technology, produces several types of beer (*clara, mulata, oscura* and *malta*), with 500 ml costing CUC$2. Malta is cheaper. You can sit upstairs on a mezzanine where ice cream and sweets are also sold or downstairs, where there is more substantial food and live music until midnight.

Terrace Bar

Hotel Casa Granda, Parque Céspedes.
Snacks, bar, nice atmosphere and good people-watching overlooking the square without any hassling.

Entertainment

Cabaret

Cabaret San Pedro del Mar, *Ctra del Morro Km 7.5, T22-691287, CUC$20 taxi there and back. CUC$5 entrance.* Reasonable food.
Club Tropicana Santiago, *Autopista Nacional Km 1.5, T22-642579. Closed Mon; restaurant 1200-2200, disco after the show 2000-0300. Arrange for a taxi to drop you off and collect you later.* Local show with emphasis on the Caribbean and Santiaguerans, it's different from Havana's version and considered one of the best shows in Cuba. Show and disco CUC$25-30, but hotels and tour companies offer a package including transport, snack and drink for groups.

ON THE ROAD

Daiquirí

The recipe for the daiquirí cocktail was first created by an engineer in the Daiquirí mines near Santiago de Cuba. Known as a Daiquirí Natural (1898), it includes the juice of half a lime, half a tablespoon of sugar, 1½ oz light dry rum and some pieces of ice, which you put in a shaker, shake and serve strained in a cocktail glass, with more ice if you want.

The idea of using shaved ice came later, added by Constante, the bartender at the Floridita in the 1920s. It was a favourite of Ernest Hemingway; he described it in his book, *Islands in the Stream*, and drank it in the company of Jean-Paul Sartre, Gary Cooper, Ava Gardner, Marlene Dietrich and Tennessee Williams, among others.

The recipe for this daiquirí includes 1½ tablespoons of sugar, the juice of half a lime, some drops of maraschino liqueur, 1½ oz light dry rum and a lot of shaved ice. Put it all in a blender and serve in a champagne glass.

Other refinements are the strawberry daiquirí, the banana, peach or pineapple daiquirí or even the orange daiquirí, made with the addition of fruit or fruit liqueur. The resulting mound of flavoured, alcoholic, crushed ice should be piled high in a wide, chilled champagne glass and served with a straw – aaah!

Clubs and music venues

Buró de Información Cultural/El Patio de los dos Abuelos, *Pérez Carbo 5 frente a Plaza de Marte, T22-623302*. EGREM agency, poetry, dance, live music in its open air patio bar. Rocks with live traditional son and boleros from 2130 until midnight and then recorded music until 0100 or so. Encourages visitors to join in. Small cover charge.

Café Cantante, Teatro Heredia, *Av de los Desfiles on the other side of Av de las Américas from the Plaza de la Revolución*. You can hear live boleros, son and other traditional music, Fri-Sun 2100, CUC$5. Can get crowded if a big name band is playing. Outside the theatre there is a large, open-air space, **Pista Pacho Alonso,** sometimes used as a disco, but also as a venue for big names playing salsa, rap, son, when the dancing can get frenetic.

Casa del Caribe, *Calle 13 154 esq 8, T22-642285*. Something going on most nights from 2000 with concerts outdoors in the courtyard. Boleros and traditional Cuban music during the week. Live Afro-Cuban, Haitian or Caribbean music and dance at weekends. See also Cultural centres, below.

Casa de las Tradiciones, *Rabí 154 entre José de Diego (Princesa) y García (San Fernando). Tue-Sun 2030-0100, CUC$2*. Also known as **La Casona**. Large colonial house with central patio, very cosy and local, rocking chairs and wooden stools around small tables made of barrels– like going dancing in someone's living room. Good music for listening and dancing 1500-2330 (good if you don't want a really late night), live *son, trova, boleros*, usually from 2000, small bar, CUC$2 entry. Not to be missed.

Casa de la Trova, *Heredia 208, around the corner from Casa Granda, T22-652689*. Traditional Santiagueran *trova, son* and *boleros*. Most of the big names in Santiago music play here at night, all live, CUC$3-10. Great upstairs dancefloor and seating area known as Salón de los Grandes, with tables and chairs on the wooden balcony overlooking the street below. Downstairs is also used, mainly for daytime concerts in the late morning and mid-afternoon, the room is open to the street and entry is only CUC$1. Tour operators offer night-time packages including transport, drinks and a CD.

El Patio de Artex, *Heredia 304 entre Carnicería y Calvario, T22-654814*. Former home of painters Félix and José Joaquín Tejada Revilla.Live music with fantastic local bands, lots of dancing, friendly, 2200–0200. Often also music and dancing in the morning at 1100. Free live son band at 1700 every day and live local bands at 2100, CUC$2.50. The programme changes daily. Friendly, good drinks, handicrafts for sale.

Hotel Casa Granda, *see Where to stay*. The roof terrace has wonderful views over the city and Santiago Bay and over to the Sierra Maestra mountains. Lots of space to dance. Saturday night live band, usually a main name such as the Septeto Santiaguero. CUC$5 cover, with CUC$4 against drinks. Bring a copy of your passport or else you will not get in.

Iris Jazz Club, *Paraíso y Aguilera, Plaza Marte*. The place to come to hear jazz in Santiago, with local and national musicians playing. Pleasant service, good drinks, low prices, a/c.

Salón del Son, *Enramada, just off Plaza de Marte*. Very popular, a/c, live bands, CUC$2 entry, drinks also reasonably priced. Live music every night. Service indifferent.

Santiago Café, *Hotel Meliá Santiago de Cuba, Av Las Américas. Open 2100-0300*. Smart night club with bar and cabaret, live music and disco. Separate entrance at lobby level, although hotel guests can enter via the 2nd floor. Get there early, otherwise there are often long queues, especially on Sat, with officious doormen slowing things down. Good drinks, great atmosphere.

Terraza Matamoros, *Heredia, opposite Casa de la Trova, 5th floor*. Live music every night, good atmosphere, small cover charge.

Cultural centres

Casa de África, *Av Manduley*. Has craftwork shop and Afro-Cuban music in the evenings.

Casa del Caribe, *13 154 esq 8, Vista Alegre, T22-643609, www.casadelcaribe.cult.cu*. Extensive library of Caribbean subjects, publishes magazine called *Caribe*, Afro-Cuban music and dance Sat nights, great authentic *folkórico*.

Centro de Estudios Africanos Fernando Ortiz, *Av Manduley y 5, Vista Alegre. CUC$1 entrance*. Artefacts and research centre.

El Tívoli, *Santa Rosa y Jesús Rabí*. Promotes influence of French culture. Named after neighbourhood where French settled in 18th century, fleeing from slave uprising in Haiti.

Hermanos Saiz, *Heredia*. Cultural centre that promotes poetry.

La Conga de los Hoyos, *Moncada y Av José Martí*. Specializes in conga music and promotes the festival of 24 Jun with conga drummers in the streets.

La Tumba Francesa, *Los Maceo 501 esq Gen Banderas. Mon-Sat 0800-1600, with dance displays Tue, and Thu 2030, CUC$2*. Like its counterpart in Guantánamo, it celebrates Haitian influence on Cuban culture, with traditional costumes, music, dancing and handicrafts.

UNEAC, *Bartolomé Masó y Pío Rosado*. National art and literature centre.

Festivals

Mar Festival Internacional de Trova 'Pepe Sánchez' Held over 2 weeks around Troubadour Day on 19 Mar. The composer, José (Pepe) Sánchez (1856-1918), is considered the father of trova and it is his birthday which is commemorated. There are formal and impromptu concerts all over the city, in theatres, streets and parks, with all types of *trova*, from traditional to '*filín*' to *nueva trova*.

Jul See box, page 350.

Aug Festival del Pregón Also known as *Frutas del Caney*, this is a festival of song when people dress up in traditional costumes and sell fruit in the street while singing. People converge on Parque Céspedes to recite or sing verses. *Pregón* is the name given to the musical refrain that peddlers used to call out to advertise their wares or skills, always in a minor key and somewhat melancholy, which have now passed into folklore.

ON THE ROAD
★ July in Santiago

Without doubt, July is the most exciting time of year to visit Santiago, as nearly the whole month is taken up with festivities. The **Festival del Caribe/Fiesta del Fuego** begins in the first week with theatre, dancing and conferences, and then continues through the month, running into **Carnival** (18-27 July) and Santiago's patron saint's day on 25 July. The partying stops briefly on 26 July for the rather more serious **Día de la Rebeldía Nacional**, which commemorates the unsuccessful attack on the Moncada Garrison on 26 Jul 1953. The rebels carefully chose the date to coincide with Carnival in order to catch Batista's militia drunk and off-guard and to use the noise of the celebrations to drown the sound of gunfire.

Santiago's carnival is a highlight of the city's calendar and well worth seeing. There are competitions and parades, with rivalry between the *comparsas* (congas) and *paseos* (*grupos de baile*). The whole city is covered in lights and all the doors are decorated. Other Cuban provinces are represented by stalls in Reparto Sueño, where they sell typical food and drink. The parades and floats are judged from 2100 and pass down Garzón where there are seats for viewing (CUC$2 for tourists). To get a seat go to the temporary Islazul office behind the seating area on the south side of the road between 1800 and 2000; good views are possible if you queue early. Wear no jewellery, and leave all valuables behind at your hotel.

New Year's Eve *Son* bands play in Plaza Marte and surrounding streets. Just before midnight everyone moves toward Parque Céspedes and sings the National Anthem. On the stroke of midnight the Cuban flag is raised on the Casa de Gobierno, commemorating the anniversary of the 1st time it was flown in 1902 when the Republic of Cuba was proclaimed. Afterwards, there's all-night drinking and dancing on the streets and in local bars.

Shopping

Art galleries and artesanía
Handicrafts and books are sold on the street on Heredia between Hartmann and Pío Rosado.
Casa de la Artesanía, *Lacret 724 entre San Basilio y Heredia*.
Fondo Cubano de Bienes Culturales, *Lacret 704 esq Heredia, T22-652358, fbcstgo@cult.stgo.cu*. Paintings, antiques and art works.
Galería 1927, *Ateneo Cultural, Santo Tomás 755 entre Santa Rita y Santa Lucía, T22-651969. Daily 0900-2000*.

Galería de Arte Universal, *Centre M y Terrazas, Vista Alegre. Tue-Sun 0900-1700*. Exhibition and sale of art work.
Galería la Confronta, *Heredia entre Carnicería y San Félix*. Contemporary art.
Galería Oriente, *underneath the Hotel Casa Granda on Parque Céspedes, San Pedro (Lacret) 653 entre Heredia y Aguilera. Daily 0900-1700*. Exhibition and sale of contemporary art.

Food
Several stores can be found in the Parque Céspedes area: ask for 'shopping', especially on Saco. There are shops on Plaza del Marte and on Garzón near **Helado Alondra**. There is a food market on Ferreiro opposite **Hotel Las Américas**. Herbs, spices and *Santería* items can be bought on Mon and Thu at Gen Lacret y Gómez. For honey, visit the **Casa de Miel**, Gen Lacret.

Music
Artex, *Heredia 304*. Music and videos as well as postcards and cultural items for dollars.

What to do

Sailing

Marina Marlin Santiago de Cuba, *Calle 1 A 4, Punta Gorda, T22-691446, mercado@marlin. scu.cyt.cu, VHF 16 and 72.* If you are arriving in Cuba by boat, officials will come on board. Customs and Immigration deal with all documentation, fees, taxes and charges promptly. The marina provides moorings (CUC$0.45 per ft including power and water), 24-hr duty manager (English spoken), boat repairs, commissary, fuel, water, cold showers, bar. Taxis and laundry can be arranged with residents outside the marina. Taxi drivers can take you to the market and help buy food for provisioning.

Tour operators

Cubatur, *Victoriano Garzón entre 3 y 4, T22-687010, www.cubatur.cu and on Facebook.*

Daily 0800-1200, 1300-2000. Helpful with knowledgeable guides and excellent value. Also offices at San Pedro 701 esq Heredia, in **Hotel Meliá Santiago de Cuba** and at the airport. Easy to book Viazul tickets, air tickets as well as tours, car hire, tourist cards and hotel reservations.

Ecotur, *San Pedro 701 entre Heredia y San Basilio, T22-687279, direccion@scu.ecotur.tur.cu.* Tours into the Sierra Maestra for hiking to Comandancia de la Plata or Pico Turquino. Also excursions to El Saltón and other sites of natural interest.

Havanatur, *main office is on Calle 8 56, entre 1 y 3, T22-643603, open 0800-1700, with other offices at Enramada esq San Pedro, the airport, in the hotels Meliá Santiago de Cuba, Casa Granda, Carisol-Los Corales, Sierra Mar Los Galeones.* They have very good guides who are fluent in most European languages.

Càlédöñiâ
languages culture adventure

Discover the real CUBA

Cuban specialists since 1999, we have travelled all over the island getting to know the country and its people… let us organise the trip of a lifetime for you!

- Tailormade itineraries
- Cultural and special interest tours
- Follow the Revolutionary Trail
- Trekking and cycling trips

- Dance and music holidays
- Spanish, salsa and percussion lessons
- Educational tours
- Flights and tourist cards

info@caledoniaworldwide.com   www.caledoniaworldwide.com   Tel:+44(0)1316217721

Transport

Air

Airport Antonio Maceo (SCU), is 8 km from town, T22-691014/691830. There is no bus service to/from the centre, but on arrival you will be greeted by numerous taxi drivers, some of whom may even manage to get into the Arrivals building. A taxi into town costs about CUC$10, 15 mins; agree the fare beforehand as meters are rarely used. There are flights most days to/from **Havana** with **Cubana** and **Aerocaribbean**, 1 hr 45 mins, 2-hr check-in. There are a few international flights, particularly from Canada in the high season, Dec-Apr, ferrying guests to the all-inclusive beach resorts. **Cubana** also has international flights from **Madrid**, **Montréal** and **Santo Domingo**. **Sunrise Airways** flies from **Port-au-Prince** (Haiti), and **Air Europa** from **Madrid**.

Bus

Local City bus journeys cost CUP$0.20. There is a regular bus service between Plaza Ferreiro (top of Av Victoriano Garzón) and Plaza Marte/Parque Céspedes. Bus No 214 goes to **Playa Siboney**; 207 to **Juraguá**.

Long distance Terminal moved in 2015 from the Plaza de la Revolución to the railway station on Av Jesús Menéndez. It is open 0700-2100, closed Sun afternoon, but if you turn up 30 mins before departure you can buy your ticket.

There are several daily Viazul (T22-628484) buses to/from **Havana**, with morning and afternoon departures, and one to/from **Trinidad**. To **Baracoa**, demand for buses can be great in high season. Get your ticket the day before (or Sat for a Mon journey). Once a busload of tickets has been sold no more will be sold that day, but if you turn up at

Tip...
For an overnight bus journey wear trousers and a fleece if you have one, as the a/c is very cold and not comfortable at night.

0500 the next morning they usually put on more buses depending on demand. On your return from Baracoa you will only be able to buy tickets on the day of travel because the number of seats depends on how many buses have come from Santiago: queue early. See page 462 for timetable.

Car hire

Cubacar, Rex, Havanautos and **Vía Rent-a-Car** are at the airport and in the main hotels. **Rex** is more expensive but has the best cars, 24-hr service (at the airport) and no extra charges.

Tip...
When parking in Santiago, make sure that there is always someone guarding your car, otherwise the police will consider it 'abandoned' and tow it away. Charges vary from CUC$1-3 per day/night.

Taxi

Local Cubataxi, T22-651038/9. You will be continually offered private taxis every time you go out, particularly near any of the hotels or plazas (lots hang around Parque Céspedes and Plaza Marte), but they will charge about the same as a **Cubataxi**. A *bicitaxi* can be arranged at Plaza Marte from about CUC$1. Horse-drawn *coches* are CUP$1.

Train

The station is opposite the rum factory on Av Jesús Menéndez. Book tickets in advance from basement office in new terminal. Relatively easy and quick, unlike the journey itself on which delays of 16 hrs or more are frequent. Do not enter the waiting room area but walk in from the left and there is a guard on the door. If there is a queue for tickets he will make you wait outside. To **Havana**, in theory, every 2 days, but very unreliable, departs 2000, 20 hrs; take a sweater to counteract the freezing a/c. See also Havana Transport, page 100, for fares and services.

Santiago de Cuba
Province

panoramic views over coffee country in the Sierra de la Gran Piedra

Excellent excursions can be made east through former coffee plantations to the monolith of La Gran Piedra. After the slave revolt in Haiti, large numbers of former slave owners were encouraged to settle in the Sierra de la Gran Piedra. Here they built 51 *cafetales*, using slave labour. During the Ten Years' War (1868-78) the revolutionaries called for the destruction of all the *cafetales*.

Tours of the area are organized by agencies in Santiago, often ending on the beach at Siboney (see below), but it is cheaper to hire a driver for the day for around CUC$35-60 (negotiable), including waiting time. Be sure to choose a good, modern car or jeep, as the roads are steep and tricky, with potholes.

Two kilometres before La Gran Piedra are the **Jardines de la Siberia**, an extensive botanical garden on the site of a former coffee plantation; turn right and follow the track for about 1 km to reach the gardens.

La Gran Piedra.
26 km east of Santiago de Cuba. CUC$2 to climb.

According to the Guinness Book of Records, this is the third largest solid rock in the world at 75,000 tonnes and 1234 m high. The summit, circled by buzzards, is reached by climbing 454 steps from the car park off the road (only for the fit). The view is tremendous. It is said you can see Haiti and Jamaica on a clear day (or, more likely, their lights on a clear night). Certainly you can see along the mountain range and down to the Caribbean Sea and Guantánamo, although you may also find yourself enveloped in cloud. Go in the morning for the best weather.

Hand-carved wooden curios, chocolate bars and coffee beans are sold by artisans on the steps, and there's a restaurant for more substantial fare.

Museo Cafetal La Isabelica
Ctra de la Gran Piedra, Km 14, CUC$2.

This ruined coffee plantation was originally owned by a French emigré from Haiti, Victor Constantin Cuzeau, who named it after his lover and house slave. When Céspedes freed the slaves, Cuzeau fled and Isabelica was thrown into a burning oven.

The site has been turned into a coffee museum and became a World Heritage Site in 2000. You can visit the former kitchen and other facilities on the ground floor, with farming tools and archaeological finds, as well as instruments of slave torture. Upstairs, the owner's house is done out in authentic 19th-century style. Take a tour to see how coffee is grown and made, ending with a cup of freshly roasted and brewed coffee, CUC$1.

Where to stay

$$ Gran Piedra
Ctra de la Gran Piedra, Km 14, T22-686147, www.islazul.cu.
Near the Gran Piedra, up in the hills, lovely setting, great views. 2 star, 22 simple rooms in stone bungalows with a bedroom, kitchen, sitting room, bathroom and balcony. You don't have to cook for yourself, though, as the restaurant and bar serve the usual Cuban fare. Worth staying here for a night if you want to climb up the Gran Piedra early the next morning.

Where to eat

There's a restaurant at La Gran Piedra and others in the villages around, where you can get a good, cheap meal for CUC$6; don't forget to follow it with local coffee.

③ Around Santiago de Cuba

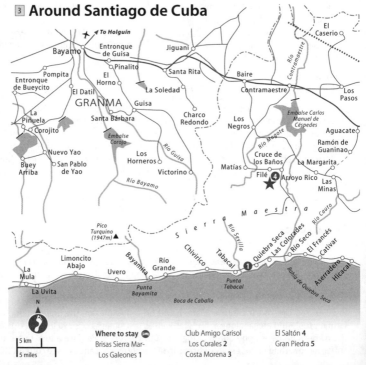

Where to stay 🛌
Brisas Sierra Mar-
Los Galeones 1

Club Amigo Carisol
Los Corales 2
Costa Morena 3

El Saltón 4
Gran Piedra 5

The Carretera de Siboney runs southeast from the city. Before it reaches the coast at Siboney, it becomes the Carretera Bacanao and heads east through the Parque Natural de Bacanao, a forested reserve with access to various beaches and other minor attractions. The latter might be worth visiting if you are in the area for some time, although they're not, perhaps, worth a special trip.

Siboney

Cubans take bus 214 from near bus terminal, or you can catch a colectivo/shared taxi from Parque Roosevelt, CUC$1, which leave when full.

On the coast southeast of Santiago, this is the nearest beach to the city. There's a reef just offshore, which is great for snorkelling, although the beach itself is stony and not particularly good, having suffered storm damage when the hurricanes ripped through in 2008. It gets very crowded and noisy at weekends when trucks disgorge passengers every 45 minutes. There are a few beach chairs and umbrellas to rent and toilets are available. You may be subjected to a certain amount of hassling on the beach. You will certainly be

→ **Santiago de Cuba maps**
1 Santiago de Cuba, page 332
2 Ferreiro, page 340
3 Around Santiago de Cuba, page 354

approached with offers of private rooms to rent (basic, better to stay in Santiago and do a day trip) and there are numerous street food stalls and *paladares*, mostly frequented by Cubans, although you will be charged in CUC$.

Two kilometres inland, is **La Granjita Siboney** ⓘ *Ctra Siboney, Km 13.5, T22-639168, Tue-Sun 0900-1700, CUC$1,* the farmhouse used as the headquarters for the revolutionaries' attack on the Moncada barracks on 26 July 1953. It now has a museum of uniforms, weapons and artefacts used by the 129 men who gathered here the night before, as well as extensive newspaper accounts of the attack. The road is lined with stone tributes commemorating the spots where revolutionaries were killed.

Siboney to Juraguá

About 20 km from Santiago, or half way between Siboney and Juraguá, look for a sign on the left to **Finca El Porvenir** ⓘ *Ctra de Baconao Km 18, daily 0900-1900, food served 1200-1700, CUC$2 includes a drink,* a nice freshwater swimming pool by the Río Firmeza with a bar and restaurant serving *comida criolla*, such as *asados* and barbecued meats, sometimes even suckling pig. The pool looks a bit green at first, but is actually clean and a wonderful place to stop off and cool down after sweating along the dusty highway, although there can be loud music at weekends. You can also go horse riding here.

Juraguá is a nicer beach than Siboney in a pretty horseshoe-shaped bay where the Río Juraguá flows out to the sea. It is a bit rundown and not really geared towards foreign tourism although further development is projected in this area.

Gran Parque Natural Baconao

At Km 6.5 on the Carretera Baconao is the **Valle de la Prehistoria** ⓘ *T22-639239, CUC$1, extra CUC$1 to take photos,* a huge park filled with life-size stone dinosaurs and Stone Age people. It's great for the kids but, due to the total absence of shade, it is like walking around a desert; take huge supplies of water and try to go early or late. Alternatively, you can get quite a good view of the monsters from the main road as you pass by. Nearby is **Mundo de Fantasía**, a small amusement park also good for kids. Admission appears to be free; ask the stone clown at the entrance!

Also in the area is the old car and trailer museum, **Museo Nacional de Transporte Terrestre** ⓘ *Ctra Baconao Km 8.5, Daiquirí (turn left at the junction for Playa Daiquirí), T22-639197, CUC$1, plus CUC$1 for a camera and CUC$3 for video.* The old classic American cars are not particularly well kept – you can see better examples on the streets of Santiago, many of them used as taxis – but they are interesting because of their history and former owners.

Continuing east at Km 35 is **Comunidad Artística Verraco**, a small artists' community, where you can buy original pieces of artwork, prices negotiable.

Further along this stretch of the coast is the **Acuario de Baconao**, which has many species of fish as well as turtles and sharks. It also puts on a dolphin show, using wild dolphins that have been captured for tourist entertainment and for export. You are strongly advised to avoid these highly controversial shows (see page 449 for further information).

Also of concern are the dolphin-breeding programme and crocodile sanctuary at **Laguna Baconao** ⓘ *CUC$1 including a boat trip to a floating bar,* a large murky lake (5 km round) in a beautiful setting. The crocodiles are kept in small enclosures with barely enough water to drink.

> **Tip...**
> **Daiquirí** beach is reserved for the military, while **Colibrí** beach has been developed as a drug rehabilitation centre and is also closed to foreign tourists.

ON THE ROAD

Diving on the south coast

The Sierra Maestra mountains all along this south-facing Caribbean coast offer a foretaste of what is to be found underwater, where the island platform gently shelves to a depth of 35 m and then the ocean wall drops straight down to a depth of over 1000 m in the channel between Cuba and Haiti.

Popular wreck sites off Playa Sigua, east of Siboney, include the 30-m passenger ship, *Guarico*, lying in 15 m. She lies on her port side with the mast covered in soft sponges. A ferry/tug wreck lies upside down in 35 m of water and the two vessels together span around 150 m. The metal structure is covered with large yellow and purple tube sponges. The 35-m *Spring Coral* lies in 24 m. Most of the structure is still intact with a great deal of marine growth offering many photo opportunities. An unusual site is the *Bridge*, dating from 1895 when a large railbridge broke and fell into the sea in 12 m, along with a train. Later a ship sank and was blown into the bridge underwater, adding to the mass of structures.

In the west of the province, the **Sierra Mar Hotel**'s dive shop offers a special wreck dive on the *Cristóbal Colón*, a Spanish ship lying on a slope in 9-27 m. She was badly damaged in 1898 by the US Navy during the Battle of Santiago in the Spanish American War. Although initially beached, attempts to refloat her were abandoned. This is an excellent shore dive with hardly any current, although in the wet season visibility is affected by run-off from the Sierra Maestra. There are 4 other wrecks in shallow water and they are ideal for a snorkel.

Diving is available at the Marlin centres at the **Carisol-Los Corales** and at the **Sierra Mar Hotels** (see page 360).

Playa Cazonal, next to **Hotel Corales**, is pleasant, but animals on the beach can be messy, and you should wear water shoes when swimming to protect both your feet and the coral reef.

Listings Southeast coast *map p354*

Where to stay

$$$$-$$$ Club Amigo Carisol Los Corales
Playa Cazonal, T22-356113-5,
www.hotelescubanacan.com.
Two 3-star hotels now run as one, although Los Caroles is older and run down, while Carisol is newer and better equipped; there is a 5-min walk between them. 310 rooms in total, mostly booked by Canadian agencies, a/c, all-inclusive, mediocre food, pool, lots of activities, including tennis, disco and other night time entertainment, car and bicycle hire, childcare and watersports but diving costs extra. The beach was badly hit by Hurricane Sandy in 2012. Tours include trips to Santiago or horse riding to a waterfall. Usually closed out of season.

$$ Costa Morena
Ctra Baconao, Km 38.5, Sigua, T22-356126,
www.islazul.cu.
A 2- to 3-star resort with simple, functional rooms all ocean front; block 5 and 6 have

been renovated. The beach is poor but there is a nice natural pool, good snorkelling and rock pools to explore. Short walk to Cactus Garden. Food monotonous, disco and entertainment. Most things improve if you tip well.

What to do

Diving

Diving (see box, page 357) is available at the Marlin centre at the **Carisol-Los Corales** (see above). Also boat rental, fishing, windsurfing, catamarans, banana boat, waterbicycles. The hotel has a **Havanatur** office whose guides are fluent in most European languages.

West of Santiago

an iconic shrine, Cuba's highest peak and a rugged road at the foot of the Sierra Maestra

Basílica Menor Santuario de Nuestra Señora de la Caridad del Cobre

T22-346 118, www.virgendelacaridaddelcobre.org. Getting there: no bus; a taxi costs CUC$20-30; you can also cycle. At Melgarejo turn left just after the petrol station, then in the village turn right at the crossroads; follow this road round to the right at the fork, leading to the church.

Twenty-nine kilometres west of Santiago is 'El Cobre', where the shrine of Cuba's patron saint, the Virgen de la Caridad del Cobre, is built over a working copper mine on top of the Cerro de Maboa.

The story goes that in the 17th century, three fishermen were about to capsize in Nipe Bay, when they found a wooden statue of the Virgin Mary floating in the sea. Their lives were saved and they brought the statue to its current resting place. There is a pilgrimage here on 7 September, the eve of the patron saint's day. Downstairs are many tokens of gratitude left by Cubans who have been helped by the Virgin in some way: a safe escape to Miami on a raft, a cure for a medical condition or success at some sporting event. It is quite common to see nuns dragging the infirm from a minivan into the church. Women with exposed shoulders are not admitted, so don't wear skimpy tops here, although they do hire rather attractive coveralls if you forget.

> **Tip...**
> Watch out for the touts swarming around you when you get arrive; they will try to sell you souvenirs and pieces of copper. It is probably best to take a bit of copper and offer some pesos cubanos, otherwise they will be waiting for you when you leave the church. Fortunately they are not allowed inside.

Southwest coast: Mar Verde to El Francés

There is a small, busy beach about 10 km west of Santiago called **Mar Verde**. Beyond is **Playa Bueycabón**, which is nothing special, and then **Caletón Blanco** (30 km west of Santiago), which is a nice beach, mostly frequented by Cubans. Like all the beaches in this area, it is quite narrow, with beige sand. A seawater swimming pool next to the sea has the remains of a diving board. Hold your breath as youths throw themselves 2 m or so into the air above the pool, getting the distance they need over the water to avoid being smashed on the pool's edge. When they are not doing that, the pool is a pleasant place to take a dip if you want the Caribbean without the waves. There is a café and restaurant and Campismo for Cubans. Further along is **El Francés**, said to be the best beach in the west but reserved for the military.

★ El Saltón

About 35 km inland from El Francés, near **Cruce de los Baños**, you will find El Saltón (see Where to stay, below), a mini-resort with a waterfall and several natural pools for bathing. It was originally designed as a health spa, but you don't have to be ill to stay there now. It is in a fantastic location in the Sierra Maestra, set into the side of a mountain some way down a track, a great place for a massage in a very relaxing environment. Day trips include a swim, lunch, hiking with a guide and horse riding, 0700-1700.

Southwest coast: Chivirico and beyond

Further west the wonderful coastal road runs along the base of the Sierra Maestra with beautiful bays and completely deserted beaches, some with black sand. The road is newly paved as far as the pleasant resorts at **Chivirico**, 1½ hours' drive, but thereafter it is still storm-damaged and 4WD is essential.

Many of the coastal villages have connections with historical revolutionary events. **El Uvero**, for example, has a monument marking the attack by Castro and his men on the Batista troop headquarters on 28 May 1957. The building that was attacked is now a small **museum** ⓘ *s/n entre Escuela Simbólica y Campo Deportivo*.

Pico Turquino

Access from Las Cuevas, 27 km west of El Uvero (before La Plata). Mandatory guide CUC$15 or go on a tour.

At 1974 m, Pico Turquino is the highest peak in the Sierra Maestra and in Cuba. There are only two legally established and maintained accesses to the mountain, from Las Cuevas and from Alto de Naranjo, see page 318. From Las Cuevas the guided hike sets out at 0630 and, depending on your level of fitness and speed, returns at 1730, just before dusk. It can often be difficult to get a guide without advanced booking, and it is quicker and easier to go on a tour. Day trips are offered for around CUC$90-100 per person, starting with jeep pick up in Santiago at 0500, a two-hour drive to Las Cuevas then the walk to Alto de Naranjo (four hours up, four hours down the other side), with lunch on Pico Cuba. You get back to the jeep at 1700 and return to Santiago at 1900. However, most tours usually go in the other direction, starting from the National Parks office at Santo Domingo and Alto de Naranjo, with overnight accommodation in the *refugios* in La Platica and/or Aguada de Joaquín, before descending to Las Cuevas.

Listings West of Santiago *map p354*

Where to stay

El Saltón

$$-$ El Saltón

Ctra a Filé, Puerto Rico, Tercer Frente, near Cruce de los Baños, about 35 km inland, T22-566495, www.hotelescubanacan.com.
In a beautiful valley surrounded by lush forests, with a waterfall and natural pools in the hotel grounds. Originally designed as a health spa and still great for a massage, the 24-room hotel is clean and pleasant with good service and an open air rustic restaurant. Sit and relax under the waterfall or go hiking, horse riding or birdwatching. If you are coming from Cruce de los Baños, there is a sign at the main junction to 'El Saltón y Filé'; it is 3 km from here to Filé. Cross the bridge in the village and at the crossroads turn left; it is a further 3 km to the hotel.

Southwest coast

$$$ Brisas Los Galeones
Ctra de Chivirico, Km 72, T22-29110,
www.cubanacan.cu.
All-inclusive, popular with elderly Canadians
in winter. Quiet, although there is plenty of
entertainment if you want it. 32 rooms, a/c
and fan, on a cliff overlooking the Caribbean,
lovely location, small and intimate, with
289 winding steps down to the sea, courtesy
bus to **Sierra Mar**. Snorkelling is good in this
area, but use water shoes in the water.

$$$ Brisas Sierra Mar
Playa Sevilla, Ctra de Chivirico, Km 60,
T22-29110, www.cubanacan.cu.
All-inclusive rooms on a decent beach.
Modern 200-room resort in terraced style,
with a/c, watersports, freeform pool on
terrace with bar and good sea view, shop,
many activities such as horse riding, bike
hire, tours and car hire.

Pico Turquino
The mountain *refugios* are basic wooden
lodges with bunk beds and mattresses; take
a sleeping bag and towel. It gets very cold
at night. If you need accommodation in the
area, ask around in Ocujal and Las Cuevas, or
there is a campsite at La Mula, east of Ocujal,
12 km from Las Cuevas.

What to do

Southwest coast
Diving (see box, page 357), boat rental,
fishing, windsurfing, catamarans, banana
boats and waterbicycles are available at the
Marlin centre at the **Sierra Mar Hotel**. There
is also a branch of **Havanatur** here.

Guantánamo

Guantánamo is the most easterly and most mountainous province in Cuba. The range of the Montañas de Nipe-Sagua-Baracoa runs through it, ending at the Atlantic Ocean on the northern coast and the Caribbean Sea to the south. The area around Baracoa is notable for its many endemic species of fauna and flora and is one of the most beautiful parts of the island.

Guantánamo city and around   *Colour map 4, C1.*

colonial town with a Caribbean flavour

The city of Guantánamo was founded in 1819 and was called Santa Catalina del Saltadero del Guaso until 1843. It lies north of the Bahía de Guantánamo, between the Jaibo, Bano and Guaso rivers which flow into the bay. The city is close to the infamous US naval base, but you will not come across it unless you make a specific trip to Mirador de Malones to view it through binoculars.

Guantánamo is a pleasant, fairly well-restored colonial town, but is noticeably different from other Cuban colonial towns in its architecture. The large influx of Haitian, French and Jamaican immigrants in the 19th century means that there is much less of a Spanish feel; the narrow, brightly coloured buildings with thin wooden balconies and wrought ironwork are more reminiscent of New Orleans than Madrid. This is also reflected in the

Essential Guantánamo city

Finding your feet

Guantánamo is some 80 km from Santiago on the Baracoa road. **Viazul** have buses from Santiago to Baracoa via Guantánamo. The **Viazul** bus is usually full at weekends and it can be difficult to get on another bus if you want to break your journey in Guantánamo, so seat reservation in advance is essential. Train services should be daily to and from Santiago, but you can't rely on them. There are flights from Havana six days a week, which then turn around and head straight back again.

Getting around

The town is small enough to walk around but there are horse-drawn *coches* for longer distances. A taxi or organized excursion is required if you want to go to one of the look-outs to see the American base. A number of streets have had their names changed, but locals often do not even know the official title. Avenida de los Estudiantes is known as Paseo, while Bartolomé Masó is known as Carretera.

local musical rhythms, notably the *changüí*, a colourful folk dance tradition originating in Haiti (see box, page 366).

Sights

The central square is the **Plaza Martí**, shaded by laburnum trees, with the **Santa Catalina de Ricci Cathedral** in the centre. This diminutive cathedral is believed to be the smallest in Latin America and was most recently restored in 2012. The two roads running north–south either side of the plaza, General Pérez and Calixto García, contain some of the most attractive colonial houses. The post office and the **Casa de la Cultura** are on the west side and the **Tumba Francesa** (see Entertainment) is on the east.

A block north is the magnificent **Palacio Salcines** ⓘ *General Pérez esq Prado,* an eclectic 1919 mansion topped by a cupola that was once the home of the architect, Leticio Salcines. Over the years it had many uses, including housing the main post office for the city on the ground floor until 1994. However, in 1999 restoration work began to rehabilitate the building and its internal decoration. After extensive work it was reopened with an art gallery, **Galería de Arte Salcines**, on the ground floor, the **Museo de Artes Decorativas** on the first floor and the **Centro Provincial de Patrimonio Cultural** offices on the top floor.

Two kilometres north, the **Plaza de la Revolución** has a modernist carved stone monument to the heroes of all the Wars of Independence. The **Museo Provincial**

Guantánamo

Where to stay
Casa Foster 1
Guantánamo 2
Manuel y Tatica cp 3
Martí 4

Osmaida Blanco
Castillo cp 5

Oro Azul 2
Taberna Las Ruinas 3
Vegetariano 4

Restaurants
1870 1

100 metres
100 yards

BACKGROUND

The US presence in Guantánamo

Situated in the area known as Caimanera at the mouth of the bay, the US naval base was established at the beginning of the 20th century, when Cuba became a protectorate of the USA following independence from Spain. Although the USA relinquished its right to intervene in Cuban affairs in 1934, it retained its naval base on a lease which expires in 2033. Cuba considers the occupation illegal but has taken no action to eject the American forces. In early 2002, the US base came to the world's attention when alleged al-Qaida and Taliban prisoners were transferred there to await military trial, following the war in Afghanistan. Huge metal cages were built to incarcerate the prisoners and security at the base was tighter than ever. There was international condemnation of the treatment of the captives, who were not awarded the status of prisoners of war and, as they were not on US territory, were being held outside the rule of law. In 2009 the incoming US President Barack Obama promised to close the prison camp by bringing to trial or repatriating the remaining prisoners, but progress has been painfully slow. There has been no mention of relinquishing the base to Cuba.

ⓘ *José Martí 802 entre Francisco Aguilera y Prudencio del Prado, T21-325872, Mon 1430-1800, Tue Sat 0830-1200, 1430-1800,* housing artefacts from the history of Guantánamo, is located in a former colonial prison built in 1861-1862. There is also a small museum near the Plaza de la Revolución which contains the space capsule in which the first Cuban went into space.

South of the centre is the **Casa Natal Regino Boti** ⓘ *Bernabé Varona 405, entre José Martí y Pedro Agustín Pérez.* Boti was a notable poet, essayist, historian and artist. He was born here on 18 February 1878 and lived and worked all his life in the same house.

Around Guantánamo

The **Buró de Turismo** at **Hotel Guantánamo** offers a **day tour** ⓘ *daily 0900 during high season, Tue and Sat only in low season,* departing from outside the hotel and taking in Guantánamo city (including la **Tumba Francesa**), Zoológico de Piedra and a farm a short distance from the city where visitors are treated to lunch and a performance by traditional *changüí* musicians. There is also a trip, with the same sights, going on to Baracoa on the same day.

The **Zoológico de Piedra** ⓘ *Ctra a Yateras Km 18, T21-865143. Mon-Sat 0900-1800, CUC$1, CUC$3 with camera, CUC$5 with video,* is an outdoor museum of 426 carved stone animals, set in a beautiful hillside location with tropical vegetation. Everything, from tiny lizards to huge bison, was carved directly from the rocks in their natural setting by the sculptor, Angel Iñigo Blanco (1935-2014).

A trip to the **Mirador de Malones** to view the Guantánamo Naval Base (see box, above) can only be done as part of an organized excursion, as the area is controlled by Gaviota. (Day trips from Santiago cost about CUC$20, depending on the size of the group.) The Cuban military has a command centre here and you will be shown round 'Castro's bunker'. You can see the extent of the US base through a telescope, with its golf course, cinema, McDonalds and other luxuries, and marvel at how the other half lives. There is a restaurant at the Mirador serving Cuban food.

Where to stay

Guantánamo city
Hotels

$$-$ Guantánamo
Calle 13 esq Ahogados, Plaza Mariana
Grajales, Reparto Caribe, T21-381015,
www.islazul.cu. 15 mins' walk from the centre.
Plaza Mariana Grajales, created in 1985, is
an important post-Revolutionary square,
a complex of artistic and architectural
monuments. Do not expect much from this
Soviet-style hotel, although the staff are
pleasant and helpful. There are 127 simple,
clean, a/c rooms, 8 suites, 12 cabañas, plus
pool, 2 bars, busy restaurant (food average),
nightclub, disco, mostly Cuban clientele.
Tours arranged to see the naval base.

$$-$ Martí
Calixto García esq Aguilera, T21-329500,
www.islazul.cu.
Part of the **Hoteles E** chain, rooms are of
a decent standard and the a/c works. It is
central and convenient, but it is also noisy
at night, particularly at weekends. Service
is poor; eat elsewhere.

Casas particulares

$ Casa Foster
Gen Pedro A Pérez 761 entre Jesús
del Sol y Prado, T21-325970.
Lissett Foster Lara runs this long-established
and comfortable *casa*. Central, close to
plaza, blue façade, spacious with
comfortable furnishings, 3 bedrooms
(2 double beds, 1 twin), a/c, balcony,
patio, roof terrace where you can have
your meals or eat indoors, secure.

$ Manuel y Tatica
Calixto García 718 entre Narciso López y
Jesús del Sol, T21-327720.
Room with double and single bed, a/c,
sitting room, old-style house with columns

to the front and steps up to large door
with grilled windows either side, in central
location. Good food available.

$ Osmaida Blanco Castillo
Gen Pedro A Perez 665 entre Paseo y
Narciso Lopez, T21-325193.
Bedrooms with a/c and private bathroom
but one has no windows, the other is nicer.
Outside seating on the rooftop.

Around Guantánamo
Hotels

$$$-$$ Caimanera
Loma del Norte, Caimanera, 21 km from
Guantánamo, T21-499414, www.islazul.cu.
Single, double and triple rooms, suites and
cabins in a pleasant location on a slight rise
overlooking the bay and the sea. A/c, TV, bar,
restaurant, pool. The closest you'll get to the
US base; you can only go here as part of a
tour group.

$$-$ Villa La Lupe
Ctra El Salvador Km 3.5, T21-382612,
www.islazul.cu.
2-star, just outside Guantánamo on the
Río Bano in a pleasant countryside location
with lots of trees, 50 functional rooms in
reasonably attractive modern blocks called
cabins, reached by concrete staircases, few
luxuries and food and service poor but there
is a decent pool and a squash court, peaceful
atmosphere.

Where to eat

Guantánamo city

$$-$ 1870
Flor Crombet, Parque Martí. Open 1200-2300.
Colonial style restaurant overlooking the
main square, good bar which is well-
frequented by locals. The restaurant is a/c
and rather austere but the food is all right,
despite the slow service.

$$-$ Girasoles
Calle 15 Norte.
Close to **Hotel Guantánamo**, in a detached house among the high-rise Soviet-style blocks. Quiet and pleasant, serving good creole food.

$ Sabor Melián
Camilo Cienfuegos 407 esq Donato Marmol, T21-324422. Open 1200-2400.
Cheap and popular among locals, serves typical local dishes, *comida criolla.*

$ Oro Azul
Aguilera entre Los Maceo y Calixto García, T21-323853/328351. Daily 1000-0300.
Light meals and snacks, cafeteria with nightclub in **El Patio**, live music, small groups, CUC$2 Mon-Fri, CUC$4 Sat-Sun.

$ Taberna La Ruina
Calixto García esq Emilio Giro. Daily 0900-2400.
Bar and restaurant run by a cooperative and very far from being a ruin, although the decor is unadulterated concrete. Typical *completas* of pork, fish, shrimp or chicken with rice, vegetables and salad, CUC$2.40-2.80. Live music at night with bands playing, recorded music at other times. CUC$, CUP$ and credit cards accepted.

$ Los Ensueños
Ahogados esq 16 Norte, T21-381601. Mon 1900-2200, Tue-Sun 1130-2330.
A la carte menu, international and Cuban with the inevitable pork and chicken, house special is the chicken 'Gordon Blue'.

$ Vegetariano
Pedro A Pérez esq Flor Crombet. Daily for lunch 1200-1430 and dinner 1700-2300.
A rare vegetarian restaurant but food is nothing special.

Entertainment

Guantánamo city
To see what's on, check www.gtmo.cult.cu/Cartelera.

Cinema
There is a cinema on Av de los Estudiantes, on the corner of the road to **Hotel Guantánamo**.

Live music and dancing
Casa de la Cultura, *Gen Pérez, southwest corner of Plaza Martí.* Has a varied programme of music and also holds exhibitions of photography and painting, usually run by **UNEAC**, José Martí near Plaza Martí.

Casa de la Trova Benito Odio, *Pedro Agustín Pérez esq Crombet, T21-355138. Tue-Sun 0900-1200, 1400-1800, 1900-2400.* Traditional music, guitar workshop.

Casa del Changüí Chito Latamblet Veranes, *Serafín Sánchez 706 entre Jesús del Sol y Narciso López, T21-324178. Tue-Fri 0700-2300, Sat-Sun 1000-0200.* This is the place to hear *changüí* bands playing. There are also other activities including children's entertainment.

Casa del Joven Creador, *Calixto García entre Prado y Aguilera, T21-327695. Open 0800-1800, plus 1900-2400 when there are performances.* The **Compañía Danza Fragmentada** (see Facebook) performs here as well as other regional companies. Weekly performance Thu 2030.

Casa de Promociones Musicales Guantanamera (Casa de la Música), *Calixto García 904 entre Crombet y Emilio Giro, T21-327266.* Various cultural activities day and night including children's entertainment, comedians, traditional music and dancing, rap and *trova* (Sun matinee).

Tumba Francesa, *Serafín Sánchez 715 entre Jesús del Sol y Narciso López.* Traditional folkloric music and dance. Shop sells good-quality Haitian-style handicrafts and souvenirs.

Theatre
Teatro Guaso, *Paseo esq Ahogados, T21-327240. Tue-Sun with performances at 1700 and 2030, also at 1000 on Sat-Sun.* Local and national dance and drama companies perform here.

Music in Guantánamo

The name of Guantánamo is known the world over, thanks to the song 'Guajira Guantanamera' which is the climax of the show for all but the most principled groups. (The way to look cool and Cuban is to cry "AE SALA", after the first 'Guantanamera' and "SONGOLOQUESONGO" after the second). The words to the verses are noble and mournful, based as they are on the poetry of José Martí. 'Guajira' is a rural style of *son* and is similar to the simple, improvizing 'Nengón', which developed in the mountains surrounding Guantánamo. The Valera Miranda family, still living in the hills, have kept this style alive. In Guantánamo itself, *Nengón* became the '*Son Changüí*' which, with its African thumb bass (*Marimbula*) and old style bongos, has stayed true to the roots of the original *son*. *Changüí* is tremendously complex, with backbeats, cross rhythms and constant bongo improvization but for many it is the most beautiful form of *son*. Catch it at the Casa de la Trova. Local grandad made good Elio Revé Matos (1930-1997), created a new *changüí* which brought him national fame (and a contract with Peter Gabriel) during the 1970s and 1980s. His background, like many Guantanamerans, is in the coffee plantations established in the sierra by French landowners following the Haitian Revolution in 1791. The *Tumba Francesa de Santa Catalina* was created during the 1890s by newly freed blacks in order to preserve the rich cultural heritage that had been developed on the plantations. One of only three such organizations still surviving (the other two being in Santiago and Sagua de Tánamo), the Tumba Francesa in Guantánamo still fulfils its original purpose. To the urgent rhythms of the Premier drums and the wooden percussion instrument the *Catá* (both of which originated in the Dahomeyan region of Africa), the elderly patrons recreate the dances of their great-great-grandparents. The singer (*Composé*) organizes the dance, calling the musicians to order and setting in train the ancient movements of the *Mason, Yuba* or *Frente*. Queen of *Composé* was Consuelo (Tecla) Benet Danger, the daughter of French-Haitian immigrant slaves and the only woman *Catá* player in Cuba, who sang and played until the age of 91.

What to do

Guantánamo city
Cycling
Contact **Josué Gaínza Matos** (Calle B 233 entre 7 y 8, Imías, Guantánamo), president of the local club, **Club de Cicloturismo La Farola** (www.clubcicloturismolafarola.com). He can also help with accommodation.

Tour operators
Havanatur, *on Calle Aguilera entre Calixto García y Los Maceo, T21-326365.*

Islazul, *commercial office is on Aguilera entre Calixto García y Los Maceo, T21-327197, Mon-Fri 0800-1200, 1400-1600.*

Transport

Guantánamo city
Air
Aeropuerto Mariana Grajales (GAO) is 16 km from Guantánamo, off the Baracoa road. Scheduled flight daily except Thu from **Havana**. **Cubana** office is at Calixto García 517 entre Prado y Aguilera, T21-355912.

Bus

The bus terminal, T21-326016, is 5 km southwest of the centre. Private cars and taxis run from the train and bus station to **Hotel Guantánamo**/town centre, CUC$1. **Viazul** stops here on its Santiago–Baracoa route, see page 374.

Car

There is a car hire bureau in the **Hotel Guantánamo**. **Servi Cupet** gas station at Prado esq 6 Este, the beginning of the Baracoa road. **Oro Negro** at Los Maceo y Jesús del Sol. There is also fuel in Songo on the way to Santiago and in San Antonio del Sur on the way to Baracoa.

Train

The station is in the centre on Calixto García, with unreliable trains to **Santiago** and **Caimanera**, but you will have to check whether they are running.

Baracoa *Colour map 4, B2.*

the tourist hot spot of the east

Small, low-key, attractive and surrounded by rich, tropical forests, Baracoa is the perfect place to come and spend a few relaxing days on the beach. Alternatively you can be more energetic and go hiking in the mountains or explore the many rivers that wind their way through canyons to the sea. The name Baracoa is an Amerindian word meaning 'existence of the sea' or 'land of water', a reference, perhaps, to the wet climate and the numerous rivers and waterfalls in the region.

Guantánamo to Baracoa via La Farola

From Guantánamo the road to Baracoa heads southeast to the coast. At **Playa Guamal**, just before Tortuguilla and two hours' car drive from Santiago, there is a rest stop with drinks and food. The road follows the coast with occasional detours inland around hills, through small towns and villages. At the entrance to **Imías** there is a right turn down a track to a stony beach, which makes another reasonable break in the journey if you have a picnic. There is a bar (with toilets) where evening gatherings and entertainment take place, but don't expect it to be open in the day.

At Cajobabo the road turns inland, north to Baracoa along a 48-km section known as **La Farola**, a viaduct that winds through lush, bright green pine forests in the mountains and then descends steeply to the coast. It can feel like a roller coaster as it bends and swoops down the mountains: motion sickness is common. This is the most spectacular part of the journey and requires intense concentration and care

Essential Baracoa

Getting around

The best way to get around Baracoa is on foot or by *bicitaxi*; these wait around the Parque Central close to the Cathedral, outside the Manuel Fuentes Borges tobacco factory and outside the Banco de Crédito y Comercio, with fares depending on how far you want to go. If you are staying at the Hotel Porto Santo you can get into town by *bicitaxi* or get reception to call you a cab. The bus station is within walking distance of the town centre.

Fact...

Some 80% of Cuba's coconut production comes from the Baracoa region.

by drivers. There are stopping places where you can take in the view, but expect to be approached by vendors at the best photo opportunities.

Sights

The **Parque Central**, or **Parque Independencia**, is halfway down Antonio Maceo, one of the main streets in town and partly pedestrianized as the Boulevard. The **Iglesia de la Asunción** ① *Tue-Sat 0800-1200, 1400-1600, Sat 1900-2100, Sun 0800-1200*, on the Parque was built in 1511, burned down by the French in 1652, and rebuilt in 1807. The church contains the cross, known as the **Cruz de la Parra**, said to have been planted there by Columbus. Catholics and restorers have carved off slices over the years, with the result that the cross has diminished to almost half its former size. Belgian historians confirmed in 1989 that the cross did indeed date from Columbus' time and was made from the native seagrape tree (*cocoloba diversifolia*).

The **Museo Municipal** ① *Fuerte Matachín, Av Martí, T21-642122, daily 0800-1200, 1400-1800, CUC$1*, is in the Matachín fort at the end of the Malecón to the east of the town (turn right as you come in from La Farola). It is a small museum with interesting but rather

Baracoa

Where to stay 🛏
Andrés Cruzata Rigores cp **1**
Casa Colonial Gustavo
 y Yalina cp **2**
Casa Colonial Lucy cp **3**
César Labori Balga cp **4**
El Castillo **5**
Hostal La Habanera **6**
La Colina cp **7**
La Rusa **8**
Porto Santo **9**
Yamilé Selva
 Bartelemy cp **10**

Restaurants 🍴
Al's **1**
Casa de Chocolate **2**
El Buen Sabor **3**
El Piropo **4**
Fuerte La Punta **5**
La Cacha Pizzería **6**
La Colonial **7**

Entertainment 🎭
Casa de la Cultura **2**
Casa de la Trova **1**
El Paraíso **3**
El Ranchón **4**

BACKGROUND
Baracoa

The Baracoa region has 56 archaeological sites, with traces of the three Amerindian groups who originally lived there: the Siboney, the Taíno and the Guanahatabey (see page 397). Christopher Columbus arrived in Baracoa on 27 November 1492. He planted a cross, now housed in the church, and described a mountain in the shape of an anvil (*yunque*), which was thereafter used as a point of reference for sailors. Copies of the first maps of Cuba drawn by an Englishman and showing the **Yunque de Baracoa** mountain can be seen in the museum. Baracoa was the first town founded by Diego Velázquez. On 15 August 1511, he bestowed the settlement with the name Nuestra Señora de la Asunción de Baracoa and, for four years, it was the capital of Cuba. Between 1739 and 1742, Baracoa's three forts were built. The oldest, **El Castillo**, also known as Seboruco, or Sanguily, is now the **Hotel Castillo**. The others were **Fuerte de la Punta**, now restaurant La Punta, and **Fuerte Matachín**, now the municipal museum. Baracoa became a refuge for French exiles after the revolution in Haiti and they brought with them coffee- and cacao-farming techniques, as well as their own style of architecture; as in Guantánamo, buildings here are much less Spanish than in other towns in Cuba. The French also created the first drinking-water plant. In 1852, Carlos Manuel de Céspedes spent five months in isolation in Baracoa as a punishment. The War of Independence of 1895 saw many revolutionaries disembarking at Baracoa. For centuries Baracoa was really only accessible by sea until the viaduct, **La Farola**, was built in the 1960s. This is one of the most spectacular roads in Cuba, joined to the mountain on one side and supported by columns on the other.

antiquated displays on the history of the town, ranging from prehistoric finds to memorabilia of La Rusa who died in 1978. Magdalena Rovieskuya was a Russian aristocrat, who left Russia in 1917 and settled in Baracoa, building a hotel (still called La Rusa) on the Malecón. She became very popular with the local people, and in the 1950s she gave her full support to the Revolution. Other items include a large cauldron for making sugar, the only armaments magazine of its type in Cuba, dating from 1739, and Baracoa's coat of arms presented to the town in 1838 by the Queen of Spain. The English-speaking conservation officer, Daniel Salomón Paján, is happy to give further information on local history and legends.

The **Casa del Cacao** ① *Maceo entre Maravi y Frank País, T21-642125, Mon-Fri 0700-2300, Sat-Sun 0700-0200, free*, is part museum, part restaurant, where you can discover the history of cacao and how chocolate is produced as well as partake of many different chocolate drinks, hot or cold. Snacks, cakes and sweets are available. The Baracoa chocolate factory was opened by Che in 1963 on the Moa road out of town.

Tip...
Baracoa chocolate is a bit dry and gritty but with good flavour.

Caves
The terraces of the Yara-Majayara geological area around Baracoa are perforated with many caves, which were used by generations of Amerindians before and after the arrival of Columbus and are now becoming tourist attractions. More than 500 petroglyphs have been found, along with evidence of irrigation canals and tools.

★ **Museo Arqueológico La Cueva del Paraíso** ① *Calle Moncada al final, 300 m uphill from the Hotel Castillo, Mon-Fri 0800-1700, Sat 0800-1200, CUC$3, tours CUC$15,* is located in a large and beautiful cave above the town. Its attractions include stalactites and stalagmites as well as petroglyphs and display cases containing archaeological finds from the area. There are ladders and a spiral staircase to climb to reach different levels; access is not easy for the less able. The mirador offers stunning views of the town and the bay.

In one chamber there are graves of Taínos lying in the traditional foetal position, with their funereal offerings still in situ. One skeleton, which is currently undergoing testing, could be that of the *cacique* Guamá, a rebel leader at the time of the Spanish invasion and the first known Cuban guerrilla, who fought against the Spanish for 10 years. It is believed that Guamá died from a blow to the head, possibly dealt by his brother after a dispute. Details of the burial suggest that the dead man was indeed a dignitary and that he died from a fractured skull.

Archaeological tours of other caves and petroglyphs in the area are available from the museum. They include a visit to the Cueva Perla de Agua, east of Baracoa, which contains rock drawings and has been made into the first Parque Arqueológico Turístico de Cuba.

Listings Baracoa *map p368*

Where to stay

Hotels

$$$-$$ Porto Santo
Ctra del Aeropuerto, T21-645106,
www.grupo-gaviota.com.
In need of some redecoration but the 83 rooms are fine for a short stay, with a/c, TV, safe box and Wi-Fi. Hotel has restaurant, bar, shop, beautiful swimming pool (CUC$10 for use by non-residents, of which CUC$9 is set against food purchase), car hire, night time entertainment with show. It's next to the airport and a small beach, peaceful atmosphere, friendly. Bicitaxis take you into town for CUC$3.

$$ El Castillo
Calixto García, Loma del Paraíso,
T21-645165, www.grupo-gaviota.com.
On the top of the hill, this hotel occupies a commanding position overlooking the town and the bay but you have to walk up hundreds of steps to get to reception and then your room. 62 a/c rooms, phone, TV and Wi-Fi in lobby lounge, pool (CUC$10 for use by non-residents, of which CUC$8 is for food) with great views, parking, friendly staff, food OK, excellent views, decent restaurant.

$$ Hostal La Habanera
Maceo esq Frank País, T21-645273,
www.grupo-gaviota.com.
Glorious pink colonial building converted to a hotel in 2003. If you want a central hotel this is the place, on a pedestrianized street close to restaurants, the Casa de la Trova and Casa de la Cultura, with a pleasant veranda where you can watch the world go by with a drink. Friendly staff, excellent service. 10 rooms, a/c, cable TV, Wi-Fi.

$$ La Rusa
Máximo Gómez 13, T21-643011,
www.grupo-gaviota.com.
Named after the Russian Magdalena Menasse (see page 369), who used to run the hotel and whose photos adorn the walls; famous guests have included Fidel Castro. Simple but updated rooms, average food, Wi-Fi. On the Malecón, this hotel has the benefit of sea views and breezes; work is being done to improve the area after severe hurricane damage, which is still evident in places.

Casas particulares

There are over 200 legal *casas particulares* in Baracoa now. Most charge CUC$15 in low season and CUC$25 in high season per room, before any commissions, but the better *casas* charge CUC$25. While most houses in Baracoa lack a view of the sea from the rooms, many *casas* have adapted roofs with terraces to catch the breeze and the view, where you can sit, sunbathe, eat and drink.

$ Andrés Cruzata Rigores
Wilder Galano Reyes 23 Alto entre Abel Díaz Delgado y Ramón López Peña, T21-642697, T015-246 5755 (mob), cruzata.bacoa2012@yahoo.es.
Apartment upstairs with own entrance, 2 comfortable a/c bedrooms, good showers, sitting room, kitchen, fully stocked fridge in each bedroom, roof terrace above with view over the town to the sea and awning for shade, nice place to eat or sit and enjoy a mojito or piña colada. Charming, experienced and helpful family offer lots of services such as laundry, good food and lots of it; their daughter speaks English, French and a little German.

$ Casa Colonial Gustavo y Yalina
Flor Crombet 125 entre Frank País y Pelayo Cuervo, T21-645809, 5281 3579 (mob), gustavoyyalina2013baracoa@gmail.com.
A lovely colonial home with several rooms sometimes used by groups. One room is on the roof terrace, catching the breeze and enjoying views over the town, the others are larger and more private, balcony, good bathrooms. Warm and friendly hosts, English spoken, tasty meals are served on the terrace and breakfast is good with hot chocolate and coffee, laundry service.

$ Casa Colonial Lucy
Céspedes 29 entre Rubert López y Maceo, T21-643548.
Lucy and her son Noel have a delightful colonial house decorated in typically Cuban style, with lovely views over the town and the sea from the roof terrace. 2 rooms with high ceilings, fridge, a/c, great food, organizes trips.

$ César Labori Balga
Martí 38 entre 24 de Febrero y Coliseo, T21-642507, 5291 1314 (mob).
A very welcoming and delightful family with several rooms to rent and expansion work in progress in 2015. There is a suite with 2 bedrooms and one bathroom, 2 further double bedrooms with bathrooms, a/c, small porch overlooking lush courtyard garden with aviary. Eldest son, César, runs this *casa* and mother Concepción cooks lovely local dishes; fresh fish in coconut milk, lamb and excellent coffee from her father's farm. English spoken.

$ La Colina – Alberto Matos
Calixto García 158 Altos entre Céspedes y Coroneles Galano, T21-642658, mob 5270 4365, inaudissd1969@gmail.com.
Elegant house 2 mins from the centre on hillside, lots of stairs, terrace with view over the town and the sea, 2 a/c rooms with up-to-date fittings, bicycle rental, English, French and Italian spoken, Al is helpful and friendly and can arrange trips for you. The property is now primarily a restaurant serving great food and drinks but service for guests has not suffered.

$ Yamilé Selva Bartelemy
Frank País 6 entre Máximo Gómez y Flor Crombet, T21-645357, 5271 8588 (mob).
Despite being a seaside town, this is one of the few houses to have a sea view from 2 light and bright rooms. The smaller room has the bigger bathroom, 2 beds, hot shower, sea breezes, a/c, fan, in hospitable household with charming couple, Ramón speaks some English, secure, comfortable, excellent food served on roof terrace.

Where to eat

The isolation of Baracoa has led to an individual local cuisine, mostly featuring coconut and fish. The best food can be had in *casas particulares*, which is where most people eat. Don't miss the *cucurucho*, also known as *dulce de coco* or *coco con chocolate (con frutas)*, a sweet coconut delicacy that is wrapped in dried palm leaves in a clever cone shape with a carrying handle. They are sold at the roadside up in the hills on La Farola for CUC$1 for 2. You can also buy cocoa balls the size of a tennis ball, 3 for CUC$1, which are delicious for making hot chocolate or using in cakes.

Restaurants

$$$-$$ Al's
Calixto García 158A entre Céspedes y Coroneles Galano, T21-642658. Open all day.
In the town centre, dining on the terrace with a fine view over all the town. *Criollo* food, specializing in seafood, cooked on the barbecue, great lobster and shrimp.

$$$-$$ El Buen Sabor
Calixto García 134 entre Céspedes y Coroneles Galano, 200 m from Parque Independencia, T21-641400. Daily 1200-2300.
Upstairs on the terrace with a good view over the town. Typical Baracoan dishes including seafood in coconut, seafood platter and meat cooked *a la parrilla*.

$$$-$$ La Cacha Pizzería
Martí 176 Altos entre Céspedes y Ciro Frías, T5339 5900 (mob).
Pizzas cooked in a wood-fired oven, so an improvement over the street pizzas, generous toppings. Lasagne also good. Friendly and good service, eat indoors or outside, Wi-Fi.

$$$-$$ La Colonial
José Martí 123, entre Maraví y Frank País, T21-645391.
Long-established, professional *paladar*, in a colonial house, subdued atmosphere, dining indoors or open air, extensive menu includes fish in coconut (*Pescado a la Santa Bárbara*) and other typical dishes of the region.

$$$-$ Fuerte La Punta
Av de los Mártires, T21-641480. Daily 1000-2200.
The fort at La Punta, which juts out into the bay west of the town, has been converted to a pleasant, breezy, open-air restaurant, with rustic tables and chairs inside the fort looking out through the cannon holes to the sea. Nice setting, reasonably priced food, fish in coconut milk, *pollo frito*, sandwiches, spaghetti.

Snack bars and cafés

Casa de Chocolate
Maceo esq Maraví. CUP$ only.
Serves a local version of hot chocolate with water, sugar and salt: not to everyone's taste but worth trying just in case, CUP$0.30 a cup. Ice cream CUP$1.60 a scoop. Snacks, cakes and sweets available.

El Piropo
Parque Independencia, T21-641206.
24-hr bar with outside seating. Fast food with occasional slow service, spaghetti, pizza, sandwiches, chicken. Also sells books, music, handicrafts, post cards and other miscellaneous items.

Entertainment

Cinema
Cineteatro El Encanto, *Maceo, next to Parque Central.* Shows movies and hosts cultural events.

Live music and dancing
Casa de la Cultura, *Maceo 124, T21-642364. Open 2000-2300, free.* Live music on its patio. Programme varies from day to day, with young local talent given the chance to shine. Nightly show of Afro-Cuban music by Bararrumba, which is highly recommended, very interesting to see all the costumes and instruments.
Casa de la Trova, *Maceo 149B esq Ciro Frías. Traditional music, Tue-Sun from 2100, CUC$1 entry.* CUC$2 for a mojito or Cuba libre, good *son* and friendly atmosphere. Seats around the edge but many people stand on the street and look through the windows (until it rains). Dancing in the centre. The local girls won't dance, so foreign women are approached to partner the men. Dancers always in demand.
El Paraíso, *Maceo 141 esq Frank País, T21-643446.* Karaoke and drinks bar, modern, entrance CUP$20 per couple.

El **Patio de Artex**, *in the Fondo de Bienes Culturales (see Cultural centres), Maceo 120, opposite the Casa de Chocolate. Open 1000-2400, entry free.* Bar with live traditional music and other cultural activities, outdoor seating.

El Ranchón, *up the hill above Calixto García on Loma Paraíso, T21-643268.* All the young people move up here after the **Casa de la Trova** and other places close. Open-air disco with live and recorded music, 2100-0130, although it doesn't really get going until after 2400. Great view over Baracoa and out to sea. Watch out for all the steps if you've been hitting the rum. Entrance CUC$1.

La Terraza de Cultura, *at Casa de la Cultura, Martí 124, opposite Casa del Chocolate, T21-645197.* Nightclub. Show starts at 2330, disco afterwards, CUC$1. Occasional comedy nights, good if your Spanish is up to it. A very popular venue.

Porto Santo and **El Castillo**. Nightly dancing and live music at these 2 hotels, the former is livelier, see Where to stay, above.

Festivals

Mar Semana de la Cultura in the last week promoting the cultural traditions of the area with lots of music and dancing going back to the roots of Cuban *son*. **Fiesta del Kiribá** is a farmers' fiesta, particularly for coffee farmers.

Apr Carnival takes place at the beginning of the month.

12-15 Aug Fiesta de las Aguas celebrates the foundation of Baracoa on 15 Aug 1511. There are conferences and courses about history and tradition, architecture, archaeology, traditional dancing, environmental events related to the Humboldt National Park, *Cayambada* (legend of the Rio de Miel), demonstrations by *treseros* (guitarists) and the **Feria de Arte Popular**.

Shopping

Fondo de Bienes Culturales, *Maceo 120, T21-643627. Mon-Fri 0830-1700, Sat, Sun 0830-1200.* Cultural centre promoting and selling art and handicrafts. As well as a tasteful souvenir shop

full of local artists' work, wooden carvings, paintings, etc, there is information about local artists; Baracoa has its own school of *artesanía*, where artists train in traditional methods using wood and coconut shell, producing the work on sale in the shop. The very friendly and helpful English-speaking Alberto Matos Llime is worth talking to if you have any questions about local history and culture.

Galería de Arte Eliseo Osorio, *Maceo 145, T21-641011. Mon-Thu 0900-2100, Fri 0900-2200, Sat 1600-2200.* Art for sale, art exhibitions and special events, such as the **Concurso Guayacán**, wood-carving demonstrations and exhibitions 6-8 Nov.

What to do

There are lots of guided tours on offer, taking you out into the countryside, up the mountains, into caves and to archaeological sites, with bathing in rivers, waterfalls and the sea (El Yunque, Playa Maguana, Rancho Toa, Finca Duaba, Yumurí, Cueva del Agua, Playa Blanca), with or without transport, food and other extras. Most official tours, however, depend on a minimum number of people. Note that any tours taking you into the Humboldt National Park incur an entry fee of CUC$10 and usually last all day.

Cubatur, *Maceo 149 esq Pelaya, T21-645306, cubaturbaracoa@enet.cu. Mon-Sat 0800-1200, 1400-1700, Sun 0830-1200.* Tickets and reservations, transfers and tours.

Ecotur, *Ciro Frías entre Maceo y Ruber López, inside Hostal 1511, T21-642478, ecoturbc@enet.cu. Mon-Sat 0800-1200, 1400-1700, Sun 0830-1200.* Contact Illiani Vera Londres for hiking and birdwatching, jeep excursions and other activities; extremely helpful.

Gaviotatours, *Cafetería El Parque, T21-645164, burobca@enet.cu. Mon-Sat 0800-1200, 1400-1800, Sun 0800-1200.* Their representative, Roger Quintero is very helpful.

Havanatur, *Martí 202 entre Céspedes y Coronel Galano, T21-645358, robertoc@havanatur.cu. Mon-Sat 0800-1200, 1400-1700, Sun 0800-1200.* The usual range of services, tickets and tours.

Norge Quintero Matos, *Bohórquez 47B, T21-643655, 5290 7568 (mob), www.baracoa.at.* A multilingual private guide who can arrange tailor-made tours to the local hotspots or off-the-beaten track hiking into the countryside, birdwatching and meeting farmers, with transport or using your hire car if you have one, friendly, entertaining and professional. A full day's excursion with transport costs around CUC$65, more if you want to go to the Parque Nacional Alexander Von Humboldt.

Transport

Air

Airport 100 m from **Hotel Porto Santo**. There are 3 scheduled **Cubana** flights a week from **Havana**, on Tue, Thu and Sun, 2 hrs, arrives 0800, returns to Havana 0900, CUC$135. There is also a **Gaviota** flight on Wed and Sat from Havana with a stop in Holguín, arriving in Baracoa at 1300. **Cubana**, José Martí 181, T21-645374, open for ticket sales Mon-Wed, Fri 0800-1200, 1400-1700. Note that it can be notoriously difficult to book flights to/from Baracoa in high season, even in Havana. It is usually easier to book a tour with an agency as they have greater access to seats, or you could fly to Holguín, and hire a car to drive from there.

Bus

Main bus terminal at the end of Martí near Av de los Mártires, T21-643880/641550, for buses to **Havana**, **Santiago**, **Camagüey** and **Guantánamo**. Make sure you reserve in advance at busy times and that your name is down on the list (*plano*), otherwise your reservation will not be valid. It has been known for travellers to get stranded in Baracoa due to high ticket demand.

Viazul departs from **Havana** at 1200 with a stop in Santiago at 0150 arriving in Baracoa at 0640, returning 0815 with a stop in Santiago at 1305, getting to Havana at 0355, CUC$66. There's also a twice-daily service from Baracoa to **Santiago** at 0815 and 1400, arriving at 1345 and 1900, CUC$15, departing Santiago at 0150 and 0800, via Guantánamo, see page 352 for details of tickets. In high season there is a Transtur bus, Tue, Thu, Sat from **Santiago** at 0700 arriving in Baracoa at 1200, returning at 1430. Transgaviota has a service from the Parque Central to **Holguín** on Sat at 0800, arriving 1430, minimum 7 passengers, returning according to reservation and demand. These **Transtur** and **Transgaviota** services are essentially charters and only run if there are enough passengers. Even so, they are more expensive than Viazul.

Car hire

Vía Car is at Hotel Porto Santo, T21-641665, and **Transtur** is in the Havanatur office, so if you are planning to end your self-drive journey here and fly back to Havana, make sure you hire a car with these companies (**Gaviota**). Scooters (*Motos*) can be hired at El Piropo on the Parque Independencia, T21-641671, 0800-1200, 1400-1700, CUC$30 for 24 hrs, CUC$25 per day for 2-4 days. There is a **Servi Cupet** station near the museum on Martí, closed Sun.

East of Baracoa

an atmospheric river trip and the lights of Haiti

Boca de Miel and around

The delightful tropical village of Boca de Miel is within walking distance of Baracoa. Head east past the stadium, along the beach, and then turn north and cross a large bridge. You can buy fruit here and watch the men fish. Around the bay is **Playa Blanca**, which is a bit rocky but is a pleasant local beach with trees for shade where vendors will try to sell you crafts and local specialities such as candied almonds.

★ Río Yumurí

The mouth of the Río Yumurí is 30 km east of Baracoa. There is a certain amount of hassling by ever-hopeful guides around the bridge at **Boca de Yumurí**, from where canoes take you upriver for CUC$2 per person. This is the most spectacular of Baracoa's rivers, running through a 180-m-deep canyon. Legend has it that the native Taínos threw themselves over the cliff rather than suffer slavery by the Spaniards. The boats pass through the canyon to a wider section of river and an island, where they drop you off for however long you want. You can continue walking upriver and swim. It's very quiet and peaceful, except at weekends or holidays when large parties come to relax. An organized trip to the canyon includes a visit to a farm where they cultivate cacao, but private guides and drivers will include such activities too, if requested.

Punta de Maisí

The most easterly point of Cuba is only 80 km from Haiti across the Windward Passage, and on a clear night it's possible to see the lights of the neighbouring island from the lighthouse here. There are caves on the point (La Patana, Los Bichos and Jaguey), which the Taínos decorated with drawings for ceremonial purposes. They were first explored in 1945 by Dr Antonio Núñez Jiménez, who discovered that the temperature inside is very high.

Northwest of Baracoa

a tropical paradise of rivers, mountains and beaches

From Baracoa to Moa is 74 km on an often rough road. The first part is very beautiful, with the road hugging the coast backed by the forested mountains of the Parque Nacional Alejandro von Humboldt, the greatest of Cuba's national parks.

Hiking tours of the park can be arranged from Baracoa; these are full day trips and involve walks in the forest, birdwatching and exploring the huge biological diversity, including many endemic species (see also page 446). The landscape is very beautiful, with the mountains of the Cuchillas de Moa and the Cuchillas de Toa coming down to the sea, indented by many rivers and bays. The highest peak in the Cuchillas de Moa is the Pico de Toldo, at 1175 m. Note that any tours into the Humboldt National Park incur an entry fee of CUC$10.

Playa Duaba and Río Duaba

Playa Duaba is 6 km northwest of Baracoa where the river meets the sea; you can swim in both. Historically, Duaba is notable for being the place where General Antonio Maceo landed on 1 April 1895 to start the second War of Independence. The **Duaba Recreational Complex** is signed to the right just after the chocolate factory and before the bridge over the Río Duaba. Here you can swim in the river and eat at **Finca Duaba**, where the food is good but the service not fantastic.

Head 4 km inland on a rocky road to **El Yunque** campsite (Santa Rosa de Duaba 456), where you will be met by people wanting to guide you either up El Yunque (see below) or on a 45-minute walk (take water) to waterfalls on the Río Duaba. The walk involves crossing the river at a certain point and scrambling up rocks. Depending on your haggling skills you will have to pay CUC$8. This is an excellent excursion, unspoilt and with no other tourists

El Yunque

A guided hike to the top of El Yunque, 575 m above sea level, provides a fantastic view over banana and coconut palms across the mountains and rivers to the bay of Porto Santo. There are lots of birds, butterflies and other wildlife too. Do not attempt the climb if you are unfit, as it is a long, hard slog (10 km, seven hours) in tremendous heat and you will need plenty of water and good boots. Tours start from **El Yunque Campismo** and can include lunch or a snack and a bathe in the Río Duaba (CUC$13 with an official agency, CUC$16 with transport to the Campismo, minimum eight people).

Río Toa

The Río Toa runs for over 120 km and has 72 tributaries. The valley through which it flows is part of the UNESCO Cuchillas del Toa Biosphere Reserve, which encompasses the Parque Nacional Alexander Von Humboldt.

Official tour agencies offer a long walk up the **Río Toa** through the biosphere forest, followed by a 45-minute return boat journey along Cuba's greatest river. Boat trips on the Río Toa cost CUC$5 per person, or CUC$18 with transport. Private guides also offer tours of the area, taking you through small farms, showing you the wildlife as well as the crops grown by local people, some of which you will be invited to try. Birdwatching is good in this area and there are lots of butterflies and lizards to look out for.

The road to Moa crosses the Río Toa northwest of Baracoa. Just before the bridge there is a sign to the right to **Rancho Toa** followed by another to **Finca La Esperanza**. These are both tourist facilities where you can get drinks, snacks or lunch, swim in the river or off the beach and take a boat between the two. Surrounded by cacao trees, they are good places to cool off after a nature walk in the area.

Playa Maguana

Playa Maguana, is a beautiful, curving white-sand beach 22 km northwest of Baracoa (CUC$5 by bus). The paved road ends just before the Río Toa bridge and parts of the route to Playa Maguana are very rough. The trees come right down to the sand, so there is shade under them or among the sea grapes growing further along the beach. The sand shelves quite steeply into the sea, which can

> **Tip...**
> Be very careful never to leave your things unattended and do not take valuables such as passports and tickets to the beach.

be rough at certain times of the year, particularly if there is a storm or a cold front coming down from the USA. This is the Atlantic, not the Caribbean, but the water is warm and inviting, and, once you're in, there is a tremendous view looking inland to the mountains. There are many families living near the beach who will cook lunch for you and a *paladar* serving seafood and fruit juices, although hygiene is not a top priority. You can hire beach chairs, CUC$0.50 per hour or CUC$2 for the day, pedalos and snorkelling equipment from the beach bar and restaurant. There is a 16-room hotel, **Villa Maguana**, a short walk away on its own private cove; the only place where you can stay on the beach although the rooms do not have sea views.

Nearby is a small public beach in a horseshoe-shaped bay with a rustic beach bar above it where you can get a lobster or fish lunch and drinks and enjoy the view from their breezy covered deck. Turn off the gravel road to the right by the sign for Villa Maguana, but carry straight on and bend to the right to park under the trees.

Towards Moa

After Maguana, the road continues to Moa and then to Holguín. The drive is beautiful as far as the **Bahía de Taco**, with luscious coconut palms, mountains, thatched houses and little coves with thin patches of white sand lapped by the aquamarine sea. Manatee have been seen in the Bahía de Taco. However, beyond the national park, the landscape changes and as you approach Moa you are confronted by the massive industrial complex based on nickel and cobalt mining and their export. It is a shock after the intense greens of the Baracoa region to see the bare red earth of the mines.

The **Pedro Soto Alba** mine was built in 1944 by the Americans to mine lateritic nickel and cobalt ore. The Moa Bay nickel plant was opened in 1959 to process these raw materials into mixed sulphides containing nickel and cobalt. The plant was nationalized in 1960 and is now run as a joint venture with the Canadian company Sherritt International, which ships the mixed sulphides to Canada for refining into finished nickel and cobalt.

On the plus side, the road improves around Moa and is more or less paved to Holguín, although don't be complacent as there are stretches of gravel or potholes to catch you unawares.

> ### Tip...
> If you are driving to Holguín, fill up before you leave Baracoa. The journey takes about five hourrs, and although there is fuel in Moa, you will use a lot getting to Moa along the rough, potholed, gravel and sand road, which can only be negotiated in a low gear.

Listings Northwest of Baracoa

Where to stay

Playa Maguana

$$$ Villa Maguana
Ctra a Moa Km 22.5, T 21-641204,
www.gaviota-grupo.com.
The only place to stay on the beach. 16 3-star rooms in 4 2-storey blocks, quiet, charming and simple but very remote, about 1 hr from Baracoa, taxi CUC$20. Restaurant for breakfast, lunch and dinner, and beach bar/*parrillada* with snacks and drinks 0700-2145, but you will get better food walking to the public beach and trying a private bar. Snorkelling gear available.

Towards Moa

$$ Miraflores
Av Calixto García, Rpto Miraflores, west of Moa on a hill, T24-606169, www.islazul.cu.

A modern block of 148 rooms in reasonable state of repair close to the smelter workers' apartment buildings, pool, gym, bar, restaurant. There's not much choice around here. Secure parking CUC$1.

Transport

Playa Maguana

A battered **Viazul** minibus leaves Parque Independencia daily at 1000, returning 1700, CUC$5 there and back. A taxi charges CUC$20-25, 1 hr on a terrible, unpaved road.

Towards Moa
Air

The **Orestes Acosta Airport** (MOA), 3 km from Moa, T24-607012, has 1 scheduled **Cubana** service a week from Havana.

The Islands

The Isla de la Juventud, or Isla, as it is known, looks as though it belongs on a scorched-edged pirates' map of old parchment bearing a single cross indicating buried gold. Tales of treasures still abound as it was once a lair for British and French *corsarios*.

Its history as a temporary home for Castro (in prison), for Martí (in exile), for the US Navy (another naval base) and for residents from other communist countries (as students) makes the island a curious destination for the traveller keen to get off the beaten track. Its modern-day appeal lies in exceptional diving off the west coast, ancient caves and its natural setting. Development is limited to Nueva Gerona, its main town, and the port area.

Cayo Largo, on the other hand, is a sun, sea and sand destination, where all-inclusive is the order of the day and you are totally isolated from the rest of Cuba. Visitors come for no other reason than to enjoy the idyllic beaches with pale golden sand and perfect conditions for swimming, sailing and other watersports.

Best for
Beaches ■ Diving ■ Relaxing

Footprint picks

★ Finca El Abra, page 388

The iconic political prisoner José Martí was held here under house arrest in the 19th century.

★ Presidio Modelo, page 388

An extraordinary architectural design for a prison where Fidel Castro and comrades were incarcerated in the 1950s.

★ Cueva de Punta del Este, page 389

This cave contains the most important aboriginal pictographs in the Caribbean.

★ Punta Francés, page 389

Dive in pristine waters teeming with fish and colourful corals.

★ Beaches on Cayo Largo, page 391

Sun, sea and sand.

Essential Islands

Finding your feet

Located 97 km off the southwest coast of the Cuban mainland in the Gulf of Batabanó, the Isla de la Juventud is the administrative centre for the 2398-sq-km 'Special Municipality', which includes Cayo Largo and the Archipiélago de los Canarreos. There are daily flights from Havana to both islands, plus international charter flights to Cayo Largo which is an all-inclusive holiday destination (for details, see Where to stay, page 393). There is a ferry from the south coast to Isla de la Juventud, but no sea transport to Cayo Largo.

Getting around

There is no inter-island transport, so to get from the Isla to Cayo Largo you need a private yacht. For transport on each island, see Essential Isla de la Juventud, page 383, and Essential Cayo Largo, page 392.

When to go

The driest time of year is between December and April. From June you can expect increased humidity and rain, with the risk of tropical storms or hurricanes from September until November. Isla de la Juventud and Cayo Largo have both been hard hit by hurricanes in the past. On Cayo Largo the beaches have changed considerably in recent years as a

result of storm action, but currently all are in good shape. There is usually a sea breeze at any time of year to cool things down and the islands are not as hot as the mother island of Cuba.

Time required

Two days each is enough for Isla de la Juventud and Cayo Largo, but you need to factor in travelling time. Getting to Isla de la Juventud by bus and ferry will take a day each way.

ON THE ROAD
Diving in the Archipiélago de los Canarreos

The area around **Punta Francés** in the west is probably the best diving spot on the Isla de la Juventud, with caves, tunnels, deep canals and valleys and all manner of sea creatures including turtles and manatee, which are protected. There are over 40 different corals and innumerable fish. The water is normally calm with temperatures ranging from 24°C in winter to 28°C in summer. The area is a marine reserve; you may only dive with an official operator.

There are many other exciting dive sites stretching east along the **Archipiélago de los Canarreos**, but these are really only possible on a liveaboard. The low-lying cays, with sandy beaches, mangroves, clear water and colourful reefs, have trapped many ships in the past and wrecked galleons add interest to modern-day diving. The biggest draw, however, is the superb coral reef and marine life, acclaimed by Jacques Cousteau and others. Green, hawksbill, leatherback and Ridley turtles are all present in these waters and are now protected.

There are two main diving areas around Cayo Largo. South of the island, the reefs **Los Ballenatos** and nearby **Cayo Rosario** are ideal for novice divers, with some pretty coral patches rising from a sandy bottom in shallow water. In the **Golfo de Cazones** north of the island there is a deep drop-off with steep walls, ridges and caves where you can find large pelagics and black coral. There is often a strong current here, so it is only really suitable for expert divers.

Isla de la
Juventud

Much of the island is flat, with a large area taken up with swamp in the Ciénaga de Lanier in the southern half of the island, a major draw for ornithologists. The northern half is more hospitable, with marble hills near the capital, Nueva Gerona, and the slate hills of Sierra del Cañada in the west. The area around the Presidio (Model Prison) is particularly beautiful, with its low green hills and citrus plantations. Mangroves line much of the coast, a haven for wildlife and migrating birds. Some of the south coast's white-sand beaches are inaccessible because of a military zone, but others may be reached with appropriate permits. There is, so far, no infrastructure in the area and roads are virtually non-existent. The beaches on the west coast have black sand.

Nueva Gerona *Colour map 1, C5.*

a low-rise, laid-back town where horses and bicycles are the main forms of transport

The capital, Nueva Gerona, dates from the 19th century and remains the only substantial settlement. Surrounded by small rounded hills, it is a pleasant country town with a slow pace.

The recent proliferation of private tourist-related businesses means that it is not as isolated as it used to be. Most development has taken place post-1959 (the island's entire population was just 10,000 in 1959), so there are few historically interesting buildings. The town centre is set out on the grid system where each block is about 100 m, with even-numbered streets running east–west and odd numbered ones north–south.

Tip...
To make the most of a day in town, you could ask the local **ICAP (Cuban Institute for Friendship with the Peoples)** office to arrange visits to places of social interest, where the rarity of visitors ensures a genuine welcome.

Essential Isla de la Juventud

Finding your feet

The **Rafael Cabrera Mustelier airport** (GER) is nearly 5 km from town and receives daily flights from Havana. A testing way of getting to the island is by the hydrofoil passenger ferry from Surgidero de Batabanó, 57 km south of Havana on the mainland south coast. There are daily crossings, but services and vessels are subject to change. It is usually crowded and the a/c is very cold.

Tip...

Do not even think about visiting the Isla without booking your return transport off the island. The plane and ferry are oversubscribed. See also Transport, page 387.

Getting around

There are several public buses on Isla de la Juventud, plus horse-drawn *coches*, which are recommended for short distances; the drivers are willing to show you the sights and give you an impromptu history lesson. If you want to explore more widely then you should book a tour with an agency (**Ecotur** is recommended; see page 387), or hire a car or taxi with driver/guide for about CUC$35-60 a day (nearly every car will turn into a taxi on request). Roads are generally in good condition and pass through some particularly beautiful areas of green rolling hills and citrus plantations. A good day's sightseeing will take in the **Model Prison**, the crocodile farm and the **Hotel El Colony**, where you can hire a kayak for an hour at the marina next door. Bear in mind that you cannot drive south of Cayo Piedra into the military exclusion zone without a permit; these can be obtained from **Ecotur**, the **Buró de Turismo** at **Hotel Villa Isla**, at car hire offices and at the **Ministry of the Interior**, Calle 16 at the harbour, see below.

Time required

If you hope to see the whole island, plan to spend more than a weekend, particularly if you want to see all the caves.

Sights

The **Río Las Casas** runs through the town heading northwards out to sea; this was traditionally the main route to the Cuban mainland. The boat that served as a ferry from the 1920s until 1974, *El Pinero*, has been preserved by the river at the end of Calle 28. It ferried Castro off the island when Batista's amnesty secured his release.

The **Parque Central** is two blocks west of the river, between Calles 28 and 30, and 37 and 39. The Parque attracts 'retired' men during the day and comes alive at night; it is also a good place to enquire about cars and guides: ask anyone, as everyone has a contact. The church of **Nuestra Señora de los Dolores** is on the north side of the square. A church was first built on this site in 1853 but was blown away by a hurricane in 1926. The present one, in colonial style, was built in 1929. Padre Guillermo Sardiñas, parish priest here in the 1950s, was the only priest to join Fidel Castro on his revolutionary campaign in the Sierra Maestra, leaving the Isla in 1957 to take up arms. The **Museo Municipal** ① *Calle 30 entre 37 y Martí (39), T46-323791, Mon-Sat 0800-1700, Sun 0800-1200, CUC$1*, on the south side of the Parque Central, is housed in the former Casa de Gobierno, built in 1853, one of the oldest buildings on the island. It has a small historical collection of items of local interest.

The **Museo Casa Natal Jesús Montané Oropesa (Museo de la Lucha Clandestina)** ① *Calle 24 entre 43 y 45, T46-324582, Tue-Sat 0830-1800, Sun 0830-1200, free*, has a collection of photos and other material relating to the Revolution and the uprising against Batista.

BACKGROUND
Isla de la Juventud

The Isla has been known by many names in its history. Early aboriginal inhabitants called it Camaraco, Ahao or Siguanea. Columbus named the island San Juan Evangelista (St John the Evangelist) when he arrived in June 1494. In the 16th and 17th centuries its use as a base by French and British pirates (including Welshman Henry Morgan who later gained respectability as governor of Jamaica) earned it another name, the Isla de Piratas (Isle of Pirates). Place names such as Estero de los Corsarios date from that era, as does Punta Francés, the lair of the French pirate Leclerc. The island's pirating past also earned it a place in world literature as the supposed model for Robert Louis Stevenson's *Treasure Island*.

Spain colonized the island in the 19th century, naming it Colonia Reina Amalia. From the 19th century until the Revolution its main function was as a prison where both José Martí and Fidel Castro served time. It became an enclave for US businessmen and communities of Japanese farmers in the first quarter of the 20th century, and it was officially known as the Isla de Pinos (Isle of Pines) in recognition of the abundant pine and casuarina (Australian pine) trees; local inhabitants (and their baseball team) are still called '*pineros*' by other Cubans. Yet another, unofficial, name, La Isla de las Cotorras (Island of the Parrots) is a reminder of just one of the feathered species that inhabit the island's pinewoods.

More recently, the island's population was swelled by tens of thousands of Cuban and international students, giving rise to its modern name, the Isle of Youth. After the Revolution, youth brigades were mobilized to plant citrus on the island and schools were set up for international students, mostly from Africa (Mozambique, Angola, South Africa, Ethiopia) and Vietnam. In return for help with citrus cultivation, the students received a totally free secondary education and returned to their countries at technical or postgraduate level.

All the schools are now closed. Now the major economic activities are citrus cultivation and processing (in conjunction with Chilean capital), marble quarrying (mainly for tourism and export), fishing and tourism. The Delita mine has estimated deposits of 1,750,000 oz of gold and close to 14,000,000 oz of silver.

The family home was used for meetings by conspirators before the Revolution and to support the relatives of those visiting political prisoners on the island. Jesús Montané Oropesa (1923-1999) took part in Moncada uprising, served time in El Presidio, sailed with Fidel Castro on *Granma* and, after the Revolution, served in government, both on the Isla and then as a Minister in Havana.

The **Planetario y Museo de Ciencias Naturales** ① *Calle 41 4625 y 46, T46-323143, Tue-Sat 0800-1700, Sun 0800-1200, CUC$2*, has exhibits relating to the natural history, geology and archaeology of the island, with a replica of the Punta del Este cave painting.

Tourist information

Ecotur agency is good for information and tours.

Where to stay

You are advised to stay in a *casa particular*. People will approach you at the ferry dock, or at the bus terminal in Havana (they will get a commission), so don't fret if you haven't reserved.

Casas particulares

$ Elda Cepero Herrera
Calle 43 2004 entre 20 y 22, T46-322774.
Self-contained apartment behind Sra Elda's house, with a/c bedroom and bathroom, kitchen, living room and terrace. A good option if you want privacy.

$ Tu Isla
Calle 24 entre 45 y 47, T5350 9128.
This is a hostal with lots of rooms to rent and a *paladar*, **El Galeón**, on the roof. It is spacious and the rooms are of good quality while outside there is a patio garden with jacuzzi. There is often live music and dancing on the roof, from where you get a lovely view of the green hills around the town and the sunset.

$ Villa Gerona
Calle 35 2410 entre 24 y 36, T5828 6809, vg@nauta.cu.
Close to the ferry and the town centre, Ramón López rents 3 a/c rooms, of which 2 have independent access. There's also a bar, a games room with billiard table, dominoes etc, while outside there's a large terrace with barbecue, plunge pool and loungers. Relaxed atmosphere, Ramón can give advice

Isla de la Juventud

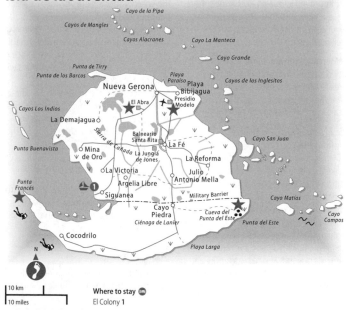

10 km
10 miles

Where to stay 🛏
El Colony **1**

on where to go and he and his staff are
friendly and helpful.

$ Villa Mas
Calle 41 4108 entre 8 y 10, T46-323544.
2 bedrooms, 1 with its own entrance and
bathroom, the other in owner's house
(Jorge Luis Mas Peña), a/c, fridge, good
meals served on the rooftop terrace.

$ Villa Peña
*Calle 10 3710 entre 37 y 39, T46-322345,
magui@ahao.ijv.sld.cu.*
2 ground-floor rooms in Sra Odalis Peña
Fernández' house (family lives upstairs),
with private bath, a/c, breakfast and dinner
available. Food is very good here and as
Odalis' husband Argelio works in the market,
they always have access to the freshest fruit
and vegetables. Good people-watching from
the veranda.

Where to eat

There are very few *paladares*, but these
have improved in quality and atmosphere
in recent years and they are inexpensive.
In your *casa particular* you can get an
excellent meal for CUC$6-8.

The **Mercado Agropecuario** (Calles 24 y 35),
is good for fresh fruit and vegetables and
there are a few basic places to eat in this area
where you can pay in CUP$.

$$ El Galeón
*Calle 24 entre 45 y 47, T5350 9128.
Daily from 1900.*
On the roof of Tu Isla *casa particular*, decked
out like a galleon but with the modern
addition of a screen showing music videos
when there isn't a live band playing. Meat
and fish cooked on the barbeque, very fresh
and tasty, the fish is whatever has just been
caught. Lovely place for a sunset mojito
or piña colada with a view over the town
to the hills beyond. Service is friendly and
good, making this the best option for an
evening meal.

$$ El Caney
Calle 3 401 entre 4 y 6.
A small *paladar* with a limited menu of meat
and fish but owner Toti makes sure everyone
is served and well fed.

Bars and clubs

Casa de los Vinos
*Calles 20 y 41. Mon-Thu 1300-2200,
Fri-Sun 1300-2400.*
Popular peso drinking spot with grapefruit,
melon, tomato and grape wines, last
orders 2300, so order early, wine served in
earthenware jugs, advisable to take glasses,
avoid the snacks.

Entertainment

Cabaret El Patio, *Calle 24 entre 37 y 39.*
Cabaret, 2 shows nightly at weekends, at
2300 and 0100, entry CUC$3 per couple,
Fri, Sat, Sun, lots of Cubans, popular.
Casa de la Cultura, *Calles 37 y 24.* Check
the schedule posted outside for music and
dance events.
El Pinero, *on the riverside by the old ferry boat.*
Young *pineros* meet up at weekends in this
al fresco venue for loud music and dancing
while stalls are set up to fuel customers with
drink and snacks.
Sucu Sucu, *Calle 39 entre 24 y 26.* See the
cartelera outside for what's on, sometimes
live music, sometimes theatre, or just go
in for a drink. *Sucu Sucu* is the name for the
local version of *son*.

Festivals

Mar Nueva Gerona has a **grapefruit festival**
and week-long **fiesta** around 13 Mar which
marks the end of the US hold on the island
(13 Mar 1926).

Shopping

For local artwork there is the **Centro de
Desarrollo de las Artes Visuales** (Calles 39

y 26). Handicrafts are sold at the **Mercado Artesanal**, Calles 24 y 35.

What to do

Tour operators

Ecotur, *C Martí entre 24 y 26, T46-327101, ecoturij@enet.cu. Mon-Sat 0800-1700.* Recommended trips to the south of the island include La Cañada, Los Indios, El Cocodrilo, Punta del Este, Rincón del Guanal, Jacksonville, with chances to see chocolate-scented wild orchids and the tocororo bird plus deer. Prices are CUC$12.50-15 per person if you have a car or they can hire you a car for CUC$90 per day. If more than 4 people a minibus needs to be hired. All trips must be booked at least 1 day in advance because permits must be secured for visits to the southern part of the island. Also sells tours for **Hotel Colony** at cheaper prices: seafari, snorkelling, diving and you can take advantage of the hotel's transport service, CUC$3. Guides speak English, Italian, French and German and are all naturalists.

Transport

Air

Rafael Cabrera Mustelier airport (GER), T46-322690, receives 2 scheduled flights a day from **Havana**, with **Cubana** (Nueva Gerona, T46-324259/322531, Mon-Fri 0800-1600, closed 1300-1400). Departures are 0550 and 1715, 35 mins; return flights are at 0705 and 1830, so you could do a day trip if you wanted. Fare CUC$82 return, 20 kg baggage allowance, book in advance. An unreliable bus marked 'Servicio Aéreo' runs between the airport and the cinema in Nueva Gerona.

Bus

Buses run from Nueva Gerona to **La Fé**, the **Hotel Colony** and **Playa Bibijagua**, but don't rely on any of these to run on a regular basis.

Car hire

Havanautos has an office in Nueva Gerona at Calles 32 y 39, T46-324432, but the hotels also have car hire desks (see Around the island). Local transport is often by horse and cart. There is a **Cupet-Cimex** fuel station at Calles 39 y 30.

Ferry

Tickets for the bus and *Kometa* hydrofoil ferry to Nueva Gerona via **Surgidero de Batabanó** are sold from the **Naviera Cubana Caribeña (NCC)** kiosk at the Astro bus terminal near Plaza de la Revolución in Havana. Call T7-878 1841 or T7-860 0330 to check times and to find out whether you need to go on the day of departure or several days beforehand because of availability problems. Theoretically the *Kometa* leaves Nueva Gerona at 0900, getting in to Batabanó at noon, returning at 1300, but like all Cuban transport you should check and then check again. You must have your passport to travel. The bus fare from Havana to Surgidero de Batabanó is CUC$5. At the port, there are some small buildings to the right of the waiting room area where you need to go to buy your passage, CUC$50, 1 way. From there you and everyone else will be checked, rechecked, checked and checked again. There is a 20-kg weight limit and they are fairly strict about it. You will also have to pass your stuff through an X-ray machine. If you have not organized your return trip, which is highly inadvisable, you need to go to the ferry port on Martí, Nueva Gerona, T46-324415.

> ### Tip...
> Bring all food and drink with you on the ferry. Delays due to mechanical problems are common, and the Cuban cafeteria will not sustain you (unless you only want cigarettes).

Around the island
political prisoners are no longer incarcerated here, but their memory lives on

★ Casa Museo Finca El Abra
3 km west of town, just off the road to La Demajagua, T46-396206. Tue-Sun 0900-1700, CUC$2, CUC$1 camera. Excellent guide, only Spanish spoken.

This is where José Martí came on 13 October 1870, after serving one year of a six-year sentence in prison in Havana. His father knew the finca owner, José María Sardá, and his wife, Trinidad Valdés Amador de Sardá, and Sardá knew people in government. Martí's transfer to the finca was arranged on condition he did not leave it. He returned to Havana on 18 December 1870. In 1926 a hurricane destroyed the finca, and so most of it is not original although it is old. However, the floor of Martí's bedroom is original. You can see the contents of the house and kitchen and some of Martí's belongings. Some of the 96 descendants of the Catalan military man-turned-finca owner still live in the finca. There are plenty of exhibits relating to the finca and the life of Martí, but it's much more interesting if you speak Spanish as the guide can bring the exhibits to life, especially the stories about the love triangle involving Martí, his wife-to-be and a Guatemalan lady. The finca is in a lovely setting with a backdrop of hills, approached along an avenue of oak trees. It is a pleasant walk from town or take a horse-drawn *coche*. There are two white posts at the entrance; otherwise it is not signed.

★ Presidio Modelo (Model Prison)
Reparto Chacón, about 4 km east of Nueva Gerona, T46-325112. Museum open Tue-Sat 0900-1630, Sun 0900-1300, CUC$1, CUC$3 camera, free admission.

The prison was built 1925-1932 by the dictator Gerardo Machado to a high-security 'panopticon' design first developed by Jeremy Bentham in 1791 to give total surveillance and control of the inmates. Although the building is now decaying, the huge circular blocks are a sinister and impressive sight, very atmospheric, especially towards dusk when it is easy to imagine the horrors of incarceration here. You can wander around the guard towers and circular cell blocks and see the numbered, tiered cells. The four circular blocks each had 465 cells with two men to a cell. On the sixth floor of each block were 15 punishment cells. Men would be placed naked in the cell for nine days without bread or water and then sent to work outside. The circular area in the centre was the dining room. All the wooden tables have been removed, but the metal supports remain; they randomly creak and moan, which is horribly eerie.

Inmates included many fighters in the independence struggle, 350 Japanese Cuban internees in the Second World War, and Fidel Castro and fellow Moncada rebels, who were held for 19 months in the medical wing, which is now the museum. Replacement beds have been installed and each bed is accompanied by a photograph and a potted history of all the Moncadistas, including details of whether they are still alive. Pictures and belongings have been carefully preserved. Fidel was removed from this wing to a separate room after singing to Batista through a window on one of his visits. Fidel's bed is not the original, but the bathroom with the chink of light by which Fidel read and wrote are authentic.

Castro returned to the island in 1959 to propose the development projects which were to transform it into the Isle of Youth. He closed the prison in 1967 and it became a school for a while before being turned into a museum.

North coast beaches

Playa Paraíso or Colombo is a small bay between Punta Bibijagua and Punta Colombo. There is a bar/restaurant here and the remains of an old railway line which was used to transport prisoners from a dock to the Presidio Modelo. **Playa Bibijagua**, 8 km from Nueva Gerona in the northeast, has very fine black sand, formed by waves eroding rocks of black marble. There is a *Campismo* here with a bar and restaurant as well as other services, lots of palm trees and 10 large marble sculptures by various artists.

La Jungla de Jones
Near Santa Fé in the centre of the island. Daily 0800-2000, CUC$3.

North Americans Harry and Helen Jones came to the island in 1902 to set up a botanical garden with a wide range of trees from around the world. Mr Jones died in 1938 in an accident and Mrs Jones was murdered in 1960 by escapees from the Presidio Modelo. The garden was neglected, and in its overgrown state, rumours soon emerged that it was haunted by Helen's ghost. In 1998 Tomás Betancourt López, a physicist, took on the project of restoration, becoming a forestry expert in the process. It is now called Finca Forestal La Jungla, although the original name still sticks. One of the most beautiful areas is a natural bamboo cathedral.

★ Cueva del Punta del Este
59 km southeast of Nueva Gerona, transport by rental car or by an organized excursion.

The caves (a National Monument) were discovered in 1910 by a shipwrecked French sailor and contain 235 pictures on the walls and ceilings, painted long before the arrival of the Spanish. The paintings have been attributed to the original Siboney inhabitants and are considered the most important pictographs in the Caribbean. It is believed that they might represent a solar calendar. There are seven caves in total.

Cocodrilo
Ctra Cayo Piedra, T46-327101, ecoturij@enet.cu. Daily 0700-1700, CUC$3.

It's well worth the one-hour drive (any car) from Nueva Gerona, including several kilometres of dirt road, to visit this crocodile farm on the southwestern tip of the island. You will be given a guided tour by the knowledgeable caretakers (in Spanish) of the hatchery and the breeding pens where the crocodiles stay for up to seven years until they are released. In the village of Cocodrilo there is a **turtle hatchery** ① *daily 0800-1800, CUC$1*, an experimental facility designed to conserve numbers of the four marine turtles found in Cuban waters.

★ Punta Francés

This beach and marine reserve is reached only by sea. It is the most beautiful beach on the island, with crystal clear water and soft pale sand backed by palm trees and forest. There is a ranger station with an information point and sun beds, but otherwise the sand is deserted and pristine. Visitors come on a day trip from the marina at **El Colony** hotel for snorkelling, diving (see page 390) or just to sit on the beach, but on Sundays cruise ships come by and then it is overrun with passengers and to be avoided.

Where to stay

There are 2 cheap and basic Gran Caribe hotels, Rancho el Tesoro and Villa Isla, in woods close to the river near La Fé. However, the facilities are little better than a *campismo* and you will be more comfortable in a *casa particular* in Nueva Gerona.

$$ El Colony
T46-398282, www.hotelelcolony.com (unofficial website).
40 mins by road from the airport, very isolated but in a lovely setting. Popular with divers, birdwatchers and fishermen. Not luxurious but clean and tidy. Staff are obliging. 77 a/c rooms with TV in main block plus refurbished cabañas, single and triple available, discounts for longer stays. Large pool and plenty of activities. Very peaceful during the week but can be noisy at weekends. Buffet is plentiful but boring. Packed lunches available. The beach is white sand with shallow water; look out for sea urchins and take loads of insect repellent.

What to do

Birdwatching
There are many endemic birds on the Isla de la Juventud and also many migrating waterfowl, particularly in the **Ciénaga de Lanier**, the 2nd largest swamp in the Cuban archipelago, where you can also find crocodiles.

Diving
See box, page 381. The **Centro Internacional de Buceo Colony**, part of Marlin Náutica y Marinas, T46-398181, has excellent facilities including underwater photography, and there is a recompression chamber. All dives are boat dives. A trip to Punta Francés costs CUC$33; a single dive is CUC$43. A non-diving partner can come along for snorkelling and the beach for CUC$42. Equipment hire for diving is CUC$10 per day, while snorkelling gear is CUC$6.

Fishing
Fishing is not allowed in the marine reserve, but the **Marina El Colony**, below, can arrange for a fishing trip to the south of the island.

Marina
Marina El Colony, has mooring for 15 boats, maximum draft 2.5m, VHF channels 16, 19, 68 and 72, a liveaboard, *Spondylus*, with a capacity for 10 divers and other facilities. Watersports are available, such as catamarans, CUC$10 per hr, max 4 people, a 2-person kayak, CUC$6 per hr and a single kayak, CUC$4 per hr.

Therapies
Aguas Medicinales La Cotorra (Balneario Santa Rita), *Calle 11, entre 16 y 18, near Santa Fé, T46-397961*. Has 3 thermal pools with, it is claimed, highly restorative qualities. Massage, acupuncture and other therapies are offered.

Transport

Bus
There are buses from Nueva Gerona to **La Fé**, the **Hotel Colony** and **Playa Bibijagua**, but don't rely on any of these to run on a regular basis. If you're staying at **Hotel El Colony** another option is to get on the staff bus, but times are not always convenient.

Car hire
The hotels have car hire desks, daily 0700-1900. About CUC$90 a day with insurance. Motorbike hire from the hotels is CUC$20-30 a day (**Transtur**, T46-326666). Local transport is often by horse and cart.

Taxi
A taxi from the airport to **Hotel El Colony** costs CUC$25, 40 mins.

Cayo
Largo

Cayo Largo is at the eastern end of the Archipiélago de los Canarreos, 114 km east of Isla de la Juventud and 80 km south of the Península de Zapata. It is a long, thin, coral island, 26 km long and no more than 2 km wide. There are beautiful white sandy beaches protected by a reef all along the southern coast, which, together with the crystal clear, warm waters of the Caribbean, make it ideal for tourism. A string of hotels lines the southern tip of the island and these are practically the only employers on the island. The northern coast is mostly mangrove and swamp, housing hungry mosquitoes as well as numerous birds (pelicans being the most visible) and iguanas. There are few Cubans on the island and the westernized, 'all-inclusive' nature of the place doesn't really recommend it to anyone wanting to see Cuba. On the other hand, if you want a few days on the beach with nothing but watersports to entertain you, then you should enjoy the resort. If you prefer your beach holiday with literally nothing, nudism is tolerated in certain spots.

Essential Cayo Largo

Finding your feet

Cayo Largo del Sur can only be reached by sea if you have your own boat. Charter flights come in from Milan, Frankfurt, Toronto and Montréal; there are also daily flights to and from Havana and weekly excursions from other tourist centres, such as Varadero. Day trips from Havana include transfers and lunch, but you have to pay extra for watersports and boat trips; two-day, one-night packages with meals, drinks, transfers and a half-day snorkelling excursion are also available.

Tip...
Scooters are notoriously dangerous because they slip on the sandy trails.

Getting around

You can hire a jeep, scooter or bicycle from your hotel to explore Cayo Largo. However, you should note that, other than the main road, the trails are soft sand and that you can only drive a short distance to the east before you will have to walk. Don't rely on your jeep having a functioning 4WD; lots of them are in poor condition. Organized tours explore the island and some of the smaller cays. There are also taxis and shuttle buses to take you to beaches or the marina. See also Transport, page 395.

★ Beaches and sights

The best beach on the island is **Playa Sirena**, which faces west and is spared the wind and currents that sometimes affect the southern beaches. It is also spared any hotels along its 2 km of white sand and so everyone comes on a day trip: a shuttle

Tip...
If there is a problem with the weather and the currents become dangerous, red flags will be flown to forbid swimming.

bus runs from the hotels (CUC$5 per person return from Olé Playa Blanca) or, if that isn't running, you may be taken by boat from the marina; you can also get a taxi or take a long walk. It has a restaurant, bar, shops and the watersports centre servicing all the hotels.

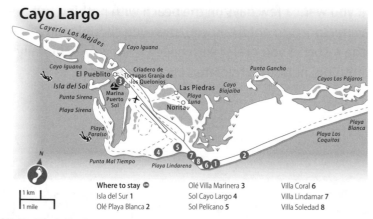

Cayo Largo

Where to stay 😊	Olé Villa Marinera 3	Villa Coral 6
Isla del Sur 1	Sol Cayo Largo 4	Villa Lindamar 7
Olé Playa Blanca 2	Sol Pelícano 5	Villa Soledad 8

South of Playa Sirena are **Playa Paraíso**, which has a bar and *palapas*, and **Punta Mal Tiempo**. Parts of these beaches are 'clothes optional'. The beach on which all the hotels are situated is **Playa Lindarena**.

Further east are the deserted beaches of **Playa Blanca**, **Playa Los Cocos**, and, in the northeast, **Playa Tortuga**, the main beaches where turtles lay their eggs. There are some 500 turtle nesting sites. There is a turtle farm, **Criadero de Tortugas Granja de los Quelonios** ① *El Pueblo Turístico (El Pueblito) northwest of the airstrip, open 0900-1800, CUC$1.* Ask here about helping to release baby turtles back into the wild; it is usually done twice a week at **Hotel Sol Cayo Largo**. The village of **El Pueblito**, together with the turtle farm and the little museum, can be toured as an excursion from your hotel on Monday, Wednesday and Friday for CUC$6 per person; register at the Club House at 1000.

Tame iguanas can be spotted at the nearby **Cayo Rico** (day trips available from Cayo Largo) and also on the appropriately named **Cayo Iguana** (closed to visitors at present). **Cayos Rosario** and **Avalos**, between Juventud and Largo, have not yet been developed. Catamarans make daily cruises to the neighbouring cays, CUC$70-80.

Listings Cayo Largo *map below*

Tourist information

There are tourist information bureaux in the hotels which will sell you excursions and tell you whatever you need to know. For online information, www.cayolargo.net.

Where to stay

All the hotels are all-inclusive and good-value package deals can be arranged from abroad as well as from Havana. Packages can be as low as CUC$400 per person for

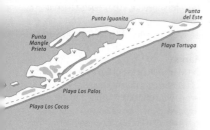

4 nights, including air and ground transport from Havana. You may have to wear a coloured plastic bracelet to indicate which package you are on. Prices include 3 meals and free use of all watersports and other activities such as tennis and volleyball. Always check what is included in your package. Medical facilities are available. There is no private accommodation on the island and you will not need any CUP$.

Sol Cayo Largo, soon to become **Meliá Cayo Largo**, is considered the best hotel on the island and more suitable for adults than some of the others, with a full range of facilities. The **Sol Pelícano** has more attractive architecture, a better bit of beach and is more family-oriented, but not quite so upmarket. **Olé Playa Blanca** is now part of the Iberostar group, with rooms and suites in the main hotel or in bungalows. The beach here is relatively unstable and tends to disappear in high winds. There was no beach at all at the end of 2015 and the walkways to the non-existent sand were closed. However, behind the dune, 90 m from the sea, is the hotel's new villa complex comprised of single-storey wooden cottages with verandas, built on a concrete base on stilts to avoid damaging the fragile environment. About 400 m away, east of the Isla del Sur, is another new 2-storey, wooden villa development. These villas have a sea view from upstairs and are a bit closer to the sea. The Italian tour operator, Gruppo Alpitour has exclusive use of the **Villa Coral** and **Villa Soledad** hotels, and Italians have all the rooms in the **Villa Lindamar** and the hotel **Isla del Sur**. These are all in a row along the beach and were under renovation at the end of 2015. Situated in the Pueblito, close to the marina, **Olé Villa Marinera** is a 22-room budget option used mainly by divers and deep-sea fishermen when on land. It's the sister hotel to the Olé Playa Blanca, and guests can use all the facilities at the larger hotel with a free shuttlebus that runs between the two.

Restaurants and bars

You will not find any *paladares* here, but there are several buffet restaurants and thatched snack bars (*ranchones*) attached to the hotels. You can dine around and try other hotel buffets on a package deal. The food is quite good and plentiful, including lots of lobster. A la carte restaurants have to be booked. Alcoholic drinks are included in all-inclusive packages. Most of the cocktails are rum-based and sweet. Frequently, essential ingredients are not available. Beer is often the best bet.

Entertainment

There is usually evening entertainment in the hotels. In El Pueblito **El Boulevar** is the main entertainment strip, with a couple of places to eat and drink, a **Plaza de la Artesanía** and

a **Casa del Habano** (cigar shop); there are street parties on Fri night, CUC$4.

La Movida, *El Pueblito, on your right as you come in to the village, T45-248305. Open 2300-0200.* Bar, disco, recorded and traditional music, lots of salsa, good meeting place between hotel staff and tourists, beer CUC$1.
Taberna El Pirata, *T45-248213*. Bar near the marina open 24 hrs, recorded and traditional music, pleasant open air veranda.

What to do

Diving
Hotels will arrange diving through the **International Scuba Diving Center** at the Marina. Rates in high/low season are CUC$39/31 for a single dive, CUC$76/60 for two dives on the same day, then CUC$117/92 for 3 dives, up to a package of 20 dives, CUC$508/499. Equipment rental is CUC$10 for a full set. A full range of courses is available. Snorkelling and glass-bottom boats are also available. For dive sites, see box, page 381.

Fishing
There is deep-sea fishing for marlin and other big fish, with international fishing tournaments held here. Contact **Avalon**, in El Pueblito at Villa Marinera, http://cubanfishingcenters.com. Boats take out no more than 4 clients, CUC$369 for 4 hrs, CUC$449 for 6 hrs, CUC$529 for 8 hrs.

Marina
The **Marina Puerto Sol Cayo Largo del Sur** at El Pueblito has 50 moorings for visiting yachts, who don't have to buy a tourist card to come here if they are not going on to anywhere else in Cuba, because the island is a free port. To clear customs, call the marina on VHF 6, or maritime security (*seguridad marítima*) on VHF 16. T45-248214. There are showers, laundry service, restaurant and bar for yachties.

Sailing and watersports

Sailing is popular, with a bareboat yacht charter fleet available by the day for longer rental. Other watersports include windsurfing, kayaking, jet skis, catamarans, and banana rides at Playa Sirena. Day trips on catamarans take you to see the iguanas, go snorkelling, visit a natural pool and spend time on a beach, CUC$69 on a boat taking up to 30 people, CUC$79 on the smaller, more exclusive boats taking no more than 10, which are sometimes clothes optional. You can also drive your own speedboat on a tour through the mangroves in the north of the island, 4 trips a day, max 10 people, CUC$29.

Tour operators

If you have booked from abroad, your holiday representative will try to sell you excursions at your initial briefing meeting. However, if you prefer, you can buy them independently from a Cuban tour operator such as **Cubatur**. Look through the books of excursions found somewhere around the lobby and see what takes your fancy. Book excursions early as spaces are limited.

Transport

Air

There are several charters and scheduled international flights to **Vilo Acuña International** airport (CYO), T45-248141. **Aerogaviota**, T45-248364, flies from **Aeropuerto Playa Baracoa**, 28 km west of Havana, T7-2098002, a former military air base. There are also daily flights from **Varadero**. On arrival a taxi will get you to the hotel quicker than the bus and will get you to the front of the check-in queue at reception.

Car hire

Any hotel can arrange jeep, scooter or bicycle hire. Scooters for hire by the hour (CUC$20 for 4 hrs) or by the day/week. Helmets are mandatory. Jeeps for CUC$11 for 1 hr or about CUC$50 for a day. Weekly rates available, including fuel and insurance. Credit cards are not accepted.

Taxi

Most taxi fares are around CUC$6-10 to anywhere from the hotels. However, there aren't enough taxis so you may have to wait. Some people prefer to get a taxi to the airport at the end of their stay rather than the shuttle bus, allowing them another couple of hours at leisure.

Background

History

Pre-Columbian society in Cuba

The recorded history of the Caribbean islands begins with the arrival of Christopher Columbus' fleet in 1492. Knowledge of the native peoples who inhabited Cuba before and at the time of his arrival is largely derived from the accounts of contemporary Spanish writers and from archaeological examinations as there is no evidence of indigenous written records.

The Amerindians encountered by Columbus in Cuba and the other Greater Antilles had no overall tribal name but organized themselves in a series of villages or local chiefdoms, each of which had its own tribal name. The name now used, 'Arawak', was not in use then. The term was used by the Amerindians of the Guianas, a group who had spread into Trinidad, but their territory was not explored until nearly another century later. The use of the generic term 'Arawak' to describe the Amerindians Columbus encountered arose because of linguistic similarities with the Arawaks of the mainland. It is therefore surmised that migration took place many centuries before Columbus' arrival, but that the two groups were not in contact at that time. The time of the latest migration from the mainland, and consequently, the existence of the island Arawaks, is in dispute, with some academics tracing it to about the time of Christ (the arrival of the Saladoids) and others to AD 1000 (the Ostionoids).

The inhabitants of Cuba and the other Greater Antilles were generally referred to as Taínos, but there were many sub-groupings. The earliest known inhabitants of the region, the Siboneys, migrated from Florida (some say Mexico) and spread throughout the Bahamas and the major islands. Most archaeological evidence of their settlements has been found near the shore, along bays or streams, where they lived in small groups. The largest discovered settlement has been one of 100 inhabitants in Cuba. They were hunters and gatherers, living on fish and other seafood, small rodents, iguanas, snakes and birds. They gathered roots and wild fruits, such as guava, guanabana and mamey, but did not cultivate plants. They worked with primitive tools made out of stone, shell, bone or wood, for hammering, chipping or scraping, but had no knowledge of pottery. The Siboneys were eventually absorbed by the advance of the Arawaks migrating from the south, who had made more technological advances in agriculture, arts and crafts.

The people now known as Arawaks migrated from the Guianas to Trinidad and on through the island arc to Cuba. Their population expanded because of the natural fertility of the islands and the abundance of fruit and seafood, helped by their agricultural skills in cultivating and improving wild plants and their excellent boat-building and fishing techniques. They were healthy, tall, good looking and lived to a ripe old age. It is estimated that up to eight million may have lived on the island of Hispaniola alone, but there was always plenty of food for all.

Their society was essentially communal and organized around families. The smaller islands were particularly egalitarian, but in the larger ones, where village communities of extended families numbered up to 500 people, there was an incipient class structure. Typically, each village had a headman, called a *cacique*, whose duty it was to represent the village when dealing with other tribes, to settle family disputes and organize defence.

However, he had no powers of coercion and was often little more than a nominal head. The position was largely hereditary, with the eldest son of the eldest sister having rights of succession, but women could and did become *caciques*. In the larger communities, there was some delegation of responsibility to the senior men, but economic activities were usually organized along family lines, and their power was limited.

The division of labour was usually based on age and sex. The men would clear and prepare the land for agriculture and be responsible for defence of the village, while women cultivated the crops and were the major food producers, also making items such as mats, baskets, bowls and fishing nets. Women were in charge of raising the children, especially the girls, while the men taught the boys traditional customs, skills and rites.

The Taínos hunted for some of their food, but fishing was more important and most of their settlements were close to the sea. Fish and shellfish were their main sources of protein and they had many different ways of catching them – from hands, baskets or nets to poisoning, shooting or line fishing. Cassava was a staple food, which they had successfully learned to leach of its poisonous juice. They also grew yams, maize, cotton, arrowroot, peanuts, beans, cacao and spices, rotating their crops to prevent soil erosion.

Cotton was used to make clothing and hammocks (never before seen by Europeans), while the calabash tree was used to make ropes and cords, baskets and roofing. Plants were used for medicinal and spiritual purposes, and cosmetics such as face and body paint. Also important, both to the Arawaks and later to the Europeans, was the cultivation of tobacco, as a drug and as a means of exchange. It is still of major economic importance in Cuba today.

They had no writing, no beasts of burden, no wheeled vehicles and no hard metals, although they did have some alluvial gold for personal ornament. The abundance of food allowed them time to develop their arts and crafts and they were skilled in woodwork and pottery. They had polished stone tools, but also carved shell implements for manioc preparation or as fish hooks. Coral manioc graters have also been found. Their boatbuilding techniques were noted by Columbus, who marvelled at their canoes of up to 75 ft in length, carrying up to 50 people, made of a single tree trunk in one piece. It took two months to fell a tree by gradually burning and chipping it down, and many more to make the canoe.

The Arawaks had three main deities, evidence of which have been found in stone and conch carvings in many of the Lesser Antilles as well as the well-populated Greater Antilles, although their relative importance varied according to the island. The principal male god was Yocahú, *yoca* being the word for cassava and *hú* meaning 'giver of'. It is believed that the Amerindians associated this deity's power to provide cassava with the mystery of the volcanoes, for all the carvings – the earliest out of shells and the later ones of stone – are conical. The Yocahú cult was wiped out by the Spaniards, but it is thought to have existed from about AD 200.

The main female deity was a fertility goddess, often referred to as Atabeyra, but she is thought to have had several names relating to her other roles as goddess of the moon, mother of the sea, the tides and the springs, and the goddess of childbirth. In carvings she is usually depicted as a squatting figure with her hands up to her chin, sometimes in the act of giving birth.

A third deity is a dog god, named Opiyel-Guaobiran, meaning 'the dog deity who takes care of the souls of the immediately deceased and is the son of the spirit of darkness'. Again, carvings of a dog's head or whole body have been found of shell or stone, which were often used to induce narcotic trances. Many of the carvings have holes and Y-shaped passages which would have been put to the nose to snuff narcotics and induce a religious trance in the shaman or priest, who could then ascertain the status of a departed soul for a recently bereaved relative.

One custom which aroused interest in the Spaniards was the ball game, not only for the sport and its ceremonial features, but because the ball was made of rubber and bounced, a phenomenon that had not previously been seen in Europe. Roman Catholicism soon eradicated the game, but archaeological remains have been found in several islands, notably in Puerto Rico, but also in Hispaniola. Excavations in the Greater Antilles have revealed earth embankments and rows of elongated upright stones surrounding plazas or courts, pavements and stone balls. These are called *bateyes*, *juegos de indios*, *juegos de bola*, *cercados* or *corrales de indios*. Batey was the aboriginal name for the ball game, the rubber ball itself and also the court where it was played. The word is still used to designate the cleared area in front of houses in the country.

The ball game had religious and ceremonial significance but it was a sport and bets and wagers were important. It was played by two teams of up to 20 or 30 players, who had to keep the ball in the air by means of their hips, shoulders, heads, elbows and other parts of their body, but never with their hands. The aim was to bounce the ball in this manner to the opposing team until it hit the ground. Men and women played, but not usually in mixed sex games. Great athleticism was required and it is clear that the players practised hard to perfect their skill, several, smaller practice courts having been built in larger settlements. The game was sometimes played before the village made an important decision, and the prize could be a sacrificial victim, usually a prisoner, granted to the victor.

The Amerindians in Cuba were unable to resist the Spanish invasion and were soon wiped out by disease, cruelty and murder, with only a few communities surviving in remote areas such as in the mountains behind Baracoa. The Spanish exacted tribute and forced labour while allowing their herds of cattle and pigs to destroy the Amerindians' unfenced fields and clearings. Transportation to the mines resulted in shifts in the native population which could not be fed from the surrounding areas and starvation became common. The 500 years since Columbus' arrival have served to obliterate practically all the evidence of the indigenous civilization in Cuba. Nevertheless, the legacy of the Taínos remains in names of places (Havana, Baracoa, Bayamo, Camagüey), rivers (Toa, Duaba, Yumurí, Caonao), domestic artefacts (*bohío* – farmer's cottage, *hamaca* – hammock, *cohiba* – tobacco) and in some areas farmers still use the same tools and plant the same crops (beans, yucca, maize) according to the four lunar phases as their forefathers did. Archaeologists and anthropologists have made significant discoveries around the country, but particularly around Baracoa, where a Taíno museum has recently been opened in a cave.

Spanish conquest

Cuba was visited by **Cristóbal Colón (Christopher Columbus)** during his first voyage to find a westerly route to the Orient on 27 October 1492, and he made another brief stop two years later on his way from Hispaniola to Jamaica. Columbus did not realize it was an island when he landed; he had heard from the inhabitants of the Bahamas, where he first made landfall, that there were larger islands to the south where there was gold, which he hoped was Japan. He arrived on the north coast of 'Colba', but found little gold. He did, however, note the Amerindians' practice of puffing at a large, burning roll of leaves, which they called *tobacos* or *cohiba*.

The Arawaks told Columbus of the more aggressive Carib tribe and he headed off towards the eastern islands to find them, discovering *La Isla Española*, or Hispaniola, which occupied the Spanish for the next few years with attempted settlements, feuds, rebellions and other troubles. On future expeditions, more settlers were brought from Spain to Hispaniola; adventurers who wanted to get rich quick and return to Spain. Although most died of tropical diseases, enough survived to impart their own European viruses on the Amerindians, decimating the local population. The Spaniards also demanded a constant supply of Amerindian labour which they were ill equipped to provide, having previously lived in a subsistence barter economy with no experience of regular work. The Spaniards' cruel treatment of the native inhabitants led to many of them losing the will to live. On the other hand, the need for a steady supply of labour pushed the Spanish into further exploration of the Indies. Slavers went from one island to another in search of manpower. Puerto Rico was conquered in 1508, Jamaica in 1509 and Cuba in 1511. From there they moved on to the mainland to trade in slaves, gold and other commodities.

Cuba was first circumnavigated by Sebastián de Ocampo in 1508, but it was **Diego Velázquez** who conquered it in 1511 and founded several towns, called *villas*, including Havana. From Cuba, Velázquez sent out two expeditions in 1517-1518 to investigate the Yucatán and the Gulf of Mexico. On the basis of their information he petitioned the Spanish Crown for permission to set up a base there prior to conquest and settlement. However, before the authorization came through from Spain, his commander, Hernán Cortés, set off without permission with 600 men, 16 horses, 14 cannon and 13 muskets to conquer Mexico, leaving Velázquez in the lurch.

The first African slaves were imported to Cuba in 1526. Sugar was introduced soon after but was not important until the last decade of the 16th century. When the British took Jamaica in 1655 a number of Spanish settlers fled to Cuba, already famous for its cigars. Tobacco was then made a strict monopoly of Spain in 1717 and a coffee plant was introduced in 1748. The British, under Lord Albemarle and Admiral Pocock, captured Havana and held the island from 1762-1763, but it was returned to Spain in exchange for Florida. Up until this point, the colony had been important largely as a refuelling depot for Spanish ships crossing the Atlantic, but the British occupation and the temporary lifting of Spanish restrictions showed the local landowning class the economic potential of trading their commodities with England and North America.

Independence movement

Towards the end of the 18th century, Cuba began its transformation into a slave plantation society. After the French Revolution, there were slave revolts in the French colony of Haiti, which became the first independent black republic. French sugar planters fled what had been the most profitable colony in the Caribbean and settled across the water in Cuba, bringing their expertise with them. Cuba soon became a major sugar exporter and, after 1793, slaves were imported in huge numbers to work the plantations. The island was under absolute military control with a colonial elite that made its money principally from sugar. The tobacco monopoly was abolished in 1816 and Cuba was given the right to trade with the world in 1818. Independence elsewhere in the Spanish Empire bred ambitions, however, and a strong movement for independence was quelled by Spain in 1823. By this time the blacks outnumbered the whites in the island; there were several slave rebellions and little by little the Creoles (or Spaniards born in Cuba) made common cause with them. On the other hand, there was also a movement for annexation by the USA, Cuba's major trading partner, supported by many slave owners who had a common interest with the southern states in the American Civil War. The defeat of the South and the abolition of slavery in the USA ended support for annexation.

By the 1860s Cuba was producing about a third of the world's sugar and was heavily dependent on African slaves to do so, supplemented by indentured Chinese labourers in the 1850s and 1860s. Although Spain signed treaties under British pressure to outlaw the Atlantic slave trade in 1817 and 1835, they were completely ignored by the colony and an estimated 600,000 African slaves were imported by 1867. Independence from Spain became a burning issue in Cuba as Spain remained intransigent and refused to consider political reforms which would give the colony more autonomy within the empire.

On 10 October 1868, a Creole landowner, **Carlos Manuel de Céspedes**, issued the *Grito de Yara*, a proclamation of independence and a call to arms, while simultaneously freeing his slaves. The first war of independence was a 10-year rebellion against Spain in the eastern part of the island between 1868 and 1878, but it gained little save a modest move towards the abolition of slavery. In 1870, the **Moret Law** freed all children of slaves born after 1868 and any slave over 60, but complete abolition was not achieved until 1886. In 1878, the **Convention of Zanjón** brought the civil war to an end. This enabled Cubans to elect representatives to the Spanish *cortes* (parliament) in 1879, but did not suppress the desire for independence. Many national heroes were created during this period who have become revolutionary icons in the struggle against domination by a foreign power. Men such as de Céspedes, Máximo Gómez and the mulatto General Antonio Maceo have inspired generations of Cuban patriots and are still revered with statues and street names in nearly every town and city on the island. One consequence of the war was the destruction of much agricultural land and the ruin of many sugar planters. US interests began to take over the sugar plantations and the sugar mills and, as sugar beet became more important in Europe, so Cuba became more dependent on the market for its main crop in the USA.

From 1895 to 1898, rebellion flared up again in the second war of independence under the young poet and revolutionary, **José Martí**, who had organized the movement from exile in the USA, together with the old guard of Antonio Maceo and Máximo Gómez. José Martí led the invasion but was killed in an ambush in May 1895 when the war had barely begun, and Maceo was killed in 1896. Despite fierce fighting throughout the island, neither the Nationalists nor the Spanish could gain the upper hand. However, the USA was now concerned for its investments in Cuba and was considering its strategic interests within the region. When the US battleship *Maine* exploded in Havana harbour on 15 February 1898, killing 260 crew, this was made a pretext for declaring war on Spain. Spain offered the independence fighters a truce but they chose instead to help the USA to defeat the colonial power. American forces (which included Colonel Theodore Roosevelt) were landed, a squadron blockaded Havana and defeated the Spanish fleet at Santiago de Cuba. In December 1898 peace was signed and US forces occupied the island. The Nationalists had gained independence from Spain but found themselves under **US military occupation** for four years and then with only limited independence granted to them by the USA.

During the occupation, the USA put the Cuban administration and economy back to rights. It eliminated a famine, introduced improved sanitation and helped to eradicate yellow fever with the scientific discoveries of a Cuban doctor, Carlos J Finlay. State education was introduced, the judiciary was reformed and an electoral system for local and national government was introduced. In 1901, an elected assembly approved a liberal constitution which separated Church and state and guaranteed universal adult male suffrage.

The **Republic of Cuba** was proclaimed in 1902 and the Government was handed over to its first president, **Tomás Estrada Palma**, the elected candidate of José Martí's Cuban Revolutionary Party, on 20 May. However, the new Republic was constrained by the **Platt Amendment** to the constitution, passed by the US Congress, which clearly made it a protectorate of the USA. The USA retained naval bases at Río Hondo and Guantánamo Bay and reserved the right of intervention in Cuban domestic affairs, but granted the island a handsome import preference for its sugar. The USA intervened several times to settle quarrels by rival political factions but, to quell growing unrest and a reassertion of pro-independence and revolutionary forces, repealed the Platt Amendment in 1934. The USA formally relinquished the right to intervene but retained its naval base at Guantánamo. (The lease on Guantánamo Bay expires in 2033.) Resentment against the USA for its political and economic dominance of the island lingered and was a powerful stimulus for the Nationalist Revolution of the 1950s.

Dictatorship

Even after the repeal of the Platt Amendment, the USA dominated the Cuban economy. Around two-thirds of sugar exports went to the USA under a quota system at prices set by Washington; two-thirds of Cuba's imports came from the USA; foreign capital investment was largely from the USA and Cuba was effectively a client state. Yet, despite the money being made out of Cuba, its people suffered from grinding rural poverty, high unemployment, illiteracy and inadequate healthcare. The good life, as enjoyed by the socialites in the casinos and bars of Havana, highlighted the social inequalities in the country and politics was a mixture of authoritarian rule and corrupt democracy.

From 1924 to 1933 the 'strong man' **Gerardo Machado** ruled Cuba. He was elected in 1924 on a wave of popularity and set about diversifying the economy and investing in public works projects. However, a drastic fall in sugar prices in the late 1920s led to strikes and protests which he forcefully repressed. In 1928 he 'persuaded' Congress to grant him a second term of office, which was greeted with protests and violence from students, the middle classes and labour unions. Widespread Nationalist popular rebellion throughout Machado's dictatorship was harshly repressed by the police force. The USA was reluctant to intervene again, but tried to negotiate a deal with its ambassador. The Nationalists called a general strike in protest at US interference and Machado finally went into exile. The violence did not abate, however, and there were more strikes, mob attacks and occupations of factories, which the new government was unable to quell. In September 1933, a revolt of non-commissioned officers including **Fulgencio Batista**, then a sergeant, deposed the government and installed a five-member committee chosen by the student movement, the *Directorio Estudiantil*. They chose as president a professor, **Dr Ramón Grau San Martín**, but he only lasted four months before Batista staged a coup. Batista then held power through presidential puppets until he was elected president himself in 1940.

Batista's first period in power, 1933-1944, was characterized by Nationalist and populist policies, set against corruption and political violence. Batista himself was a mulatto from a poor background who had pulled himself up through the ranks of the military and retained the support of the armed forces. He was also supported by US and Cuban business interests while gaining control of the trade unions by passing social welfare legislation, building low cost housing and creating jobs with public works projects. The students and radical Nationalists remained opposed to him, however, and terrorism continued. In 1940, a new Constitution was passed by a constituent assembly dominated

BACKGROUND

Our Man in Havana

Graham Greene's first visit to Cuba was in 1957 to research his book *Our Man in Havana*. He was originally going to set it in Lisbon, but decided on a more exotic location; he planned to sell the film rights to the novel before it was even written. He immediately took a liking to the unlimited decadence Havana had to offer, and spent much of his time at the Shanghai Theatre, a club which featured live sex shows. Greene's former connections with the British SIS (Secret Intelligence Service) gave him access to political society. He based some of the characters in 'Our Man' on Batista's soldiers: Captain Segura, with his cigarette case made of human skin, was based on the real-life Capitán Ventura. The plot of the novel involves a vacuum cleaner salesman being mistaken for a secret agent, who for fear of being discovered as a fraud, tries to carry out the orders given to him by providing diagrams of vacuum cleaner parts, pretending they are in fact the plans for an arsenal of nuclear weapons.

Greene's training as a secret agent allowed him to infiltrate all levels of political life: he made contact with Castro's rebel forces in the Sierra, offering them any help they needed. He was asked to smuggle a suitcase of warm clothes, to help them survive the freezing night-time temperatures of the Sierra Maestra, through customs on a Havana–Santiago flight.

In 1959, when Greene arrived for the second time in Havana to assist director Carol Reed in the filming of his novel, the Revolution had already triumphed. Greene's small act of support in 1957 had not been forgotten, and Castro gave his personal seal of approval to the film, although he felt it didn't capture the full extent of Batista's evil.

by Batista, which included universal suffrage and benefits for workers such as a minimum wage, pensions, social insurance and an eight-hour day.

In 1944, Batista lost the elections to the candidate of the radical Nationalists: Dr Ramón Grau San Martín, of the Partido Revolucionario Cubana-Auténtico, who held office from 1944-1948. His presidential term benefited from high sugar prices following the Second World War, which allowed corruption and political violence to continue unabated. Grau was followed into the presidency by his protégé, **Carlos Prío Socarrás**, 1948-1952, a term which was even more corrupt and depraved, until Batista, by then a self-promoted general, staged a military coup in 1952. Constitutional and democratic government was at an end. His harshly repressive dictatorship was brought to a close by **Fidel Castro** in January 1959, after an extraordinary and heroic three-year campaign, mostly in the Sierra Maestra, with a guerrilla force reduced at one point to 12 men.

Revolution

The dictator, Batista, was opposed by many, but none more effective than the young lawyer, Fidel Castro, the son of immigrants from Galicia and born in Cuba in 1926. He saw José Martí as his role model and aimed to continue the Revolution Martí had started in 1895, following his ideals. In 1953, the 100th anniversary of José Martí's birth, Castro and a committed band of about 160 revolutionaries attacked the Moncada barracks in Santiago de Cuba on 26 July. The attack failed and although Castro and his brother Raúl

BACKGROUND
Fidel Castro Ruz

Fidel Castro spent more than half his life as president, *jefe* (chief) and supreme *comandante* of Cuba. He passed from being the world's youngest ruler in 1959 to the longest serving head of state. He outstayed eight US presidents and survived hundreds of assassination attempts before handing power to his brother Raúl in 2006 at the age of 80. That year he had to undergo major abdominal surgery, the nature of which was kept a secret. The handover of power was originally temporary, but it became official and permanent in 2008. Although he no longer appears in public, he is actively involved in political life in Cuba, writing opinion pieces on world affairs for the *Granma* newspaper and meeting visiting dignitaries. His longest speech went on for seven hours, but Cubans were regularly called upon to listen to his rhetoric for four or five hours. Dramatic pauses gradually replaced the fire and arm waving of his youth and in many ways he mellowed with maturity. In 1996 he was received by the Pope in an historic photo opportunity which made him look almost sprightly in comparison with his host. He has always been instantly recognizable for his beard, now straggly and grey, and his military fatigues, although these were later occasionally replaced when abroad by a sober suit and, after his surgery, by a tracksuit.

escaped, they were later captured and put on trial. Fidel used the occasion to make an impassioned speech, denouncing corruption in the ruling class and the need for political freedom and economic independence. The speech has gone down in history for its final phrase, "History will absolve me", and a revised version, smuggled out of prison on the Isle of Pines, became the basis of a reform programme. In 1955, the Castros were given an amnesty and went to Mexico. There Fidel continued to work on his essentially Nationalist revolutionary programme, called the **26 July Movement**, which called for radical social and economic reforms and a return to the democracy of Cuba's 1940 constitution. He met another man of ideas, an Argentine doctor called Ernesto Guevara (see box, page 201), who sailed with him and his brother Raúl and a band of 82 like-minded revolutionaries, back to Cuba on 2 December 1956. Their campaign began in the Sierra Maestra in the east of Cuba and after years of fierce fighting Batista fled to the Dominican Republic on 1 January 1959. Fidel Castro, to universal popular acclaim, entered Havana and assumed control of the island.

Communism and the 1960s

From 1960 onwards, in the face of increasing hostility from the USA, Castro led Cuba into socialism and then Communism. Officials of the Batista regime were put on trial in 'people's courts' and executed. The promised new elections were not held. The judiciary lost its independence when Castro assumed the right to appoint judges. The free press was closed or taken over. Trade unions lost their independence and became part of government. The University of Havana, a former focus of dissent, and professional associations, all lost their autonomy. The democratic constitution of 1940 was never reinstated. In 1960, the sugar centrales, the oil refineries and the foreign banks were nationalized, all US property was expropriated and the Central Planning Board (*Juceplan*) was established. The professional and property-owning middle classes began a steady exodus which drained the country of much of its skilled workers.

CIA-backed mercenaries and Cuban émigrés kept up a relentless barrage of attacks, but failed to achieve their objective. In March a French ship carrying arms to Cuba was sabotaged. At the burial of the victims, Castro first used the slogan, 'Patria o Muerte'. Diplomatic relations were re-established with the USSR, North Korea and Vietnam, while China and Cuba signed mutual benefit treaties. Meanwhile, the USA cancelled Cuba's sugar quota and put an embargo on all imports to Cuba.

At the beginning of 1961, the USA severed diplomatic relations with Cuba and encouraged Latin American countries to do likewise. This was the year of the **Bay of Pigs** invasion, a fiasco which was to harden Castro's political persuasion. On 14 April 1961, some 1400 Cuban émigrés, trained by the CIA in Miami and Guatemala, set off from Nicaragua to invade Cuba with the US Navy as escort. On 15 April, planes from Nicaragua bombed several Cuban airfields in an attempt to wipe out the air force. Seven Cuban airmen were killed in the raid, and at their funeral the next day, Fidel Castro addressed a mass rally in Havana and declared Cuba to be socialist. On 17 April the invasion flotilla landed at Playa Girón and Playa Larga in the Bahía de Cochinos (Bay of Pigs), but the men were stranded on the beaches when the Cuban air force attacked their supply ships. Two hundred were killed and the rest surrendered within three days. The invaders' aircraft also took a beating when 11 were shot down, including all the B-26 bombers flown from Nicaragua. A total of 1197 men were captured and eventually returned to the USA in exchange for US$53 million in food and medicine. In his May Day speech, Fidel Castro, who had personally taken control of the defence of Cuba, confirmed that the Cuban Revolution was socialist.

The US reaction was to isolate Cuba, with a full trade embargo and heavy pressure on other American countries to sever diplomatic relations. Cuba was expelled from the Organization of American States (OAS) and the OAS imposed economic sanctions. Crucially, however, across the border in both Canada and Mexico, governments refused to toe the line and maintained relations (a policy which has now borne fruit for many Canadian and Mexican companies at the expense of US businesses). Nevertheless, in 1961-1962, the trade embargo hit hard, shortages soon appeared and by March 1962 rationing had to be imposed.

At this stage, Cuba became entangled in the rivalry between the two superpowers: the USA and the USSR. In April 1962, Russian President **Kruschev** decided to send medium-range missiles to Cuba, which would be capable of striking anywhere in the USA, even though all Castro wanted were short-range missiles he could point at Miami to deter invasion. In October, President JF Kennedy ordered Soviet ships heading for Cuba to be stopped and searched for missiles in international waters. This episode, which became known as the **Cuban Missile Crisis**, brought the world to the brink of nuclear war, defused only by secret negotiations between JFK and Kruschev. Kennedy demanded the withdrawal of Soviet troops and arms from Cuba and imposed a naval blockade. Without consulting Castro and without his knowledge, Kruschev eventually agreed to have the missiles dismantled and withdrawn on condition that the West would guarantee a policy of non-aggression towards Cuba. In November, Kennedy suspended the naval blockade but reiterated US support for political and economic aggression towards Cuba. In the following year he made a speech in Costa Rica, in which he stated, "We will build a wall around Cuba", and Central American countries agreed to isolate the island.

Castro's decision to adopt Marxism-Leninism as the official ideology of the Revolution was followed by the fusion of the 26 July Movement with the Communist Party, at that

BACKGROUND
An exploding cigar and other plots

The number of CIA-backed attempts on Castro's life is legendary, the most extraordinary stories so far published being about trying to kill him with an exploding cigar, or putting a special powder in his shoes to make his beard fall out. But, failing to assassinate or maim him, the US administration in the 1960s put an extraordinary amount of effort into trying to discredit him. Many covert plans were put forward to Operation Mongoose, an anti-Castro destabilization project at the Pentagon. One plan, codenamed Operation Dirty Trick, was to blame Castro if anything went wrong with US space flights, specifically John Glenn's flight into orbit in 1962. The Pentagon was to provide 'irrevocable proof' that if anything happened it was the fault of Cuban Communists and their electronic interference. Another idea was to sabotage a US plane and claim that a Cuban aircraft had shot down a civilian airliner. Yet another was to sink a US warship and blame that on Castro.

None of these came to anything, but sabotage did take place. Cuban émigré groups received help from a special CIA budget to destroy Castro's Cuba. In 1960, a French ship carrying a cargo of armaments from Belgium was blown up in Havana harbour, killing 81 people and wounding hundreds of others. Pressure was put on British companies by the USA to stop them trading with Cuba. Having 'discouraged' British ships from transporting a cargo of British Leyland buses and spare parts, but having failed to get the deal cancelled, it was therefore more than coincidental that an East German ship carrying the equipment was rammed in the Thames. Cuba has claimed other sabotage, such as supplying asymmetrical ball bearings to damage machinery, and chemical additives in lubricants for engines to make them wear out quickly. As classified documents of the Kennedy administration are released, more and more bugs keep crawling out of the woodwork.

time known as the Popular Socialist Party (PSP). The PSP had opposed the Revolution until the final stages of the overthrow of the Batista dictatorship and it took several years and two purges before the 'old' Communists were expunged and the new Communist Party was united behind the new official ideology. In October 1965, a restructured **Cuban Communist Party** (PCC) was founded and Cuba has been Communist ever since.

Economic policy during the 1960s was largely unsuccessful in achieving its aims. After a spell as head of the Central Bank, Che Guevara was appointed Minister of Industry, a key position given that the government wanted to industrialize rapidly to reduce dependence on sugar. However, the crash programme, with help from the USSR, was a failure and had to be abandoned. Sugar was king again but productivity plummeted and there were poor harvests in 1963-1964. The whole nation was called upon to achieve a target of 10 million tonnes of sugar by 1970 and everyone spent time in the fields helping towards this goal. It was never reached and never has been, but the effort revealed distortions in the Cuban economy which in effect increased the island's dependence on the Soviet Union. Castro jumped out of the frying pan into the fire: he escaped domination by the USA only to replace it with another superpower.

Social policy

Education, housing and health services were greatly improved and the social inequalities of the 1940s and 1950s were wiped out. Equality of the sexes and races was also promoted, a major change in what was a *machista*, racially prejudiced society. In 1961 300,000 Cubans volunteered to go out into the countryside, as part of a literacy campaign, to teach their comrades how to read and write. On 22 December of the same year, Cuba was declared free of illiteracy. Considerable emphasis was placed on combining productive agricultural work with study in rural areas. Education was made compulsory up to the age of 17, and free, while access to higher education was granted to all. It was the overall success of these social policies (see also box, page 416) that ensured the people's continued support for Castro in the coming decades, despite periods of severe economic difficulty, and kept him and latterly his brother Raúl in power.

1970s Soviet domination

During the second decade of the Revolution, Cuba became firmly entrenched as a member of the Soviet bloc, joining COMECON in 1972. Technicians came from Eastern Europe and Cubans were trained in the USSR. The Communist Party grew in strength and size and permeated all walks of life, influencing every aspect of Cubans' day to day living, while putting more central controls on education and culture. The Revolution was institutionalized along Soviet lines and the Party gained control of the bureaucracy, the judiciary and the local and national assemblies. Communist planners controlled the economy and workers were organized into government-controlled trade unions. A new socialist constitution was adopted in 1976. In 1971-1975 the economy grew by about 16% a year, but fell back after then and never recovered such spectacular growth rates again.

Cuba's foreign policy during this period changed from actively fomenting socialist revolutions abroad (such as Guevara's forays into the Congo and Bolivia in the 1960s) to supporting other left wing or third world countries with combat troops and technical advisers. Some 20,000 Cubans helped the Angolan Marxist government to defeat a South African backed guerrilla insurgency and 15,000 went to Ethiopia in the war against Somalia and then the separatist rebellion in Eritrea. Cuban advisers and medical workers went to Nicaragua after the Sandinista overthrow of the Somoza dictatorship in 1979; advisers and workers went to help the left wing Manley government in Jamaica and to the Marxist government in Grenada (until expelled by the US Marines in 1983). In September 1979, Castro hosted a summit conference of the non-aligned nations in Havana, a high point in his foreign policy initiatives.

The decade also marked a period of intellectual debate at home and abroad about the path the Revolution was taking. In 1971, the poet **Herberto Padilla** was arrested for cultural deviation and forced to confess his crimes against the Revolution. His treatment and cultural censorship brought accusations of Stalinization of cultural life. The Padilla affair split the Hispanic intellectual world, with writers such as Octavio Paz and Carlos Fuentes of Mexico, Mario Vargas Llosa of Peru and Juan Goytisolo of Spain renouncing their support for the Revolution, while Gabriel García Márquez of Colombia and Julio Cortázar of Argentina reaffirmed their support. Free expression was stifled and during this time the best Cuban art and literature was produced by émigrés. The debate widened to include civil liberties and political rights, and official secrecy made it difficult to gauge accurately the persecution of political prisoners, religious believers, intellectual opponents and homosexuals.

By the 1980s, the heavy dependence on sugar and the USSR, coupled with the trade embargo, meant that the expected improvements in living standards, 20 years after the Revolution, were not being delivered as fast as hoped and the people were tiring of being asked for ever more sacrifices for the good of the nation. In 1980, the compound of the Peruvian embassy was overrun by 11,000 people seeking political asylum. Castro's answer to the dissidents was to let them go and he opened the port of **Mariel** for a mass departure by sea. He also opened the prisons to allow prisoners, both political and criminal, to head for the USA in anything they could find that would float. It was estimated that some 125,000 embarked for Miami, amid publicity that it was the criminals, delinquents, homosexuals and mental patients who were fleeing Cuba. At the same time huge demonstrations were organized in Havana in support of the Revolution. Some relaxation in controls was allowed, however, with 'free markets' opening alongside the official ration system.

This was the decade of the Latin American debt crisis and Cuba was unable to escape the pressures brought to bear on its neighbours. Development projects in the 1970s had been financed with loans from western banks, in addition to the aid it was already receiving from the USSR. When interest rates went up in 1982, Cuba was forced to renegotiate its US$3.5 billion debt to commercial banks and, in 1986, its debt to the USSR. The need to restrain budget spending and keep a tight control over public finances brought more austerity. The private markets were stopped in 1986 and the people were once more asked for voluntary labour to raise productivity and achieve economic growth. Excess manpower, or unemployment, was eased by sending thousands of Cubans abroad as internationalists to help other developing countries, whether as combat troops or technicians.

The **collapse of the Communist system** in the Eastern European countries in the late 1980s, followed by the demise of the USSR, very nearly brought the end of Castro's Cuba as well. Emigrés in Miami started counting the days until they would re-enter the homeland and Castro's position looked extremely precarious. There were signs that a power struggle was taking place at the top of the Communist Party. In 1989, General Arnaldo Ochoa, a hero of the Angolan campaign, was charged with drug trafficking and corruption. He was publicly tried and executed along with several other military officers allegedly involved. Castro took the opportunity to pledge to fight against corruption and privilege and deepen the process of rectification begun in 1986.

The Soviet connection

Before the collapse of the Soviet system, aid to Cuba from the USSR was traditionally estimated at about 25% of GNP. Cuba's debt with the USSR was a secret: estimates ranged from US$8.5 billion to US$34 billion. Apart from military aid, economic assistance took two forms: balance of payments support (about 85%), under which sugar and nickel exports were priced in excess of world levels and oil imports were indexed against world prices for the previous five years, and assistance for development projects. About 13 million tonnes of oil were supplied a year by the USSR, allowing three million to be re-exported, providing a valuable source of foreign earnings. By the late 1980s up to 90% of Cuba's foreign trade was with centrally planned economies.

US relations

Before the Revolution of 1959, the USA had investments in Cuba worth about US$1 billion, covering nearly every activity from agriculture and mining to oil installations. After the Revolution all American businesses in Cuba, including banks, were nationalized; the

USA cut off all imports from Cuba, placed an embargo on exports to Cuba, and broke off diplomatic relations. Promising moves to improve relations with the USA were given impetus in 1988 by the termination of Cuban military activities in Angola under agreement with the USA and South Africa. However, developments in Eastern Europe and the former USSR in 1989-1990 revealed the vulnerability of the economy and provoked Castro to defend the Cuban system of government; the lack of political change delayed any further rapprochement with the USA. Prior to the 1992 US presidential elections, President Bush approved the Cuban Democracy Act (Torricelli Bill), which strengthened the trade embargo by forbidding US subsidiaries from trading with Cuba. Many countries, including EC members and Canada, said they would not allow the US bill to affect their trade with Cuba and the UN General Assembly voted in November in favour of a resolution calling for an end to the embargo. The defeat of George Bush by Bill Clinton did not, however, signal a change in US attitudes, in large part because of the support given to the Democrat's campaign by Cuban émigrés in Miami.

1990s crisis and change

In an effort to broaden the people's power system of government introduced in 1976, the central committee of the Cuban Communist Party adopted resolutions in 1990 designed to strengthen the municipal and provincial assemblies and transform the National Assembly into a genuine parliament. In February 1993, the first direct, secret elections for the National Assembly and for provincial assemblies were held. Despite calls from opponents abroad for voters to register a protest by spoiling their ballot or not voting, the official results showed that 99.6% of the electorate voted, with 92.6% of votes cast valid. All 589 official candidates were elected. Delegates to the municipal assemblies of people's power serve a two-year term. Delegates are directly nominated in neighbourhood meetings (the PCC does not put forward candidates), and ballot boxes are guarded by primary school children. Provincial delegates and national deputies are elected for a five-year term. The slate consists of up to 50% of the municipal delegates and the remainder selected by a national commission on the basis of proposals from the mass organizations. In the October 1997 elections, 97.6% of the electorate voted and 92.8% of the votes were valid (7.2% blank or spoiled).

Economic difficulties in the 1990s brought on by the loss of markets in the former USSR and Eastern Europe, together with higher oil prices because of the Gulf crisis, forced the government to impose emergency measures and declare a special period in peace time (1990-1994). Rationing was increased, petrol became scarce, the bureaucracy was slashed and several hundred arrests were made in a drive against corruption. In 1993, Cuba was hit on 13 March by a winter storm which caused an estimated US$1 bn in damage. Agricultural production, for both export and domestic consumption, was severely affected. In mid-1994, economic frustration and discontent boiled up and Cubans began to flee their country. Thousands left for Florida in a mass exodus similar to that of Mariel in 1980 on any craft they could invent. It was estimated that between mid-August and mid-September 30,000 Cubans had left the country, compared with 3656 in the whole of 1993. In contrast, the number of US visas issued from January to August was 2059 out of an agreed maximum annual quota of 20,000. Eventually the crisis forced President Clinton into an agreement whereby the USA was committed to accepting at least 20,000 Cubans a year, plus the next of kin of US citizens, while Cuba agreed to prevent further departures.

As the economic crisis persisted, the government adopted measures which opened up many sectors to private enterprise and recognized the dependence of much of the

BACKGROUND
Castro and the UN

In 1960, Fidel Castro visited the UN for the first time since becoming leader of Cuba. Relations with the USA were becoming sour and the hotels in New York were wary of giving lodging to the new government in case of reprisals from Cuban exiles and other potential violence. Hotels refused to accept his booking without a large deposit, which he refused to pay. Undeterred, Castro led his party to buy tents and headed for Central Park, where he intended to pitch camp, declaring he was still a *guerrilla* comandante. They never got there, however, for a young black leader called Malcolm X persuaded them to come with him to Harlem, where he found them rooms in the rundown Hotel Theresa in the heart of the black district. In addition he promised them security and protection from the émigrés provided by his black Muslims. It was a great occasion and Castro held court at the hotel, receiving eminent visitors such as Nehru and his daughter Indira Gandhi, Nasser, Kruschev and others, while also mingling with the public. His performance at the General Assembly was memorable: the audience was forced to listen to a speech lasting 4½ hours.

Thirty-five years later, he made another visit to the UN and went back to Harlem, although he lodged at the Cuban UN mission. Discarding the sober suit he wore to the UN General Assembly (where this time he was limited to a five-minute address but received a longer ovation than President Clinton for a speech which expressed the broad resentments of the Third World), he donned his military fatigues and cap and went to talk to an all-ticket audience at the Abyssinian Baptist Church about Cuba's educational and health achievements. Although he was again excluded by polite society (he was not invited to President Clinton's reception for 149 heads of state and left off the guest list for Mayor Giuliani's dinner party) he was courted by no less than 230 US business people and invited to lunch by the Rockefeller family.

economy on dollars. The partial reforms did not eradicate the imbalances between the peso and the dollar economies, and shortages remained for those without access to hard currency.

Cuba then intensified its economic liberalization programme, speeding up the opening of farmers' markets throughout the country and allowing farmers to sell at uncontrolled prices once their commitments to the state procurement system were fulfilled. Importantly, the reforms also allowed middlemen to operate. It had been the emergence of this profitable occupation which had provoked the government to close down the previous farmers' market system in 1986. Markets in manufactured goods and handicrafts also opened and efforts were made to increase the number of self-employed.

US pressure in the 1990s

In 1996, a US election year, Cuba faced another crackdown by the US administration. In February, Cuba shot down two light aircraft piloted by Miami émigrés, allegedly over Cuban air space and implicitly confirmed by the findings of the International Civil Aviation Organization (ICAO) report in June. The attack provoked President Clinton into reversing his previous opposition to key elements of the Helms-Burton bill to tighten and internationalize the US embargo on Cuba and on 12 March he signed into law the

Cuban Freedom and Democratic Solidarity Act. The new legislation allowed legal action against any company or individual benefiting from properties expropriated by the Cuban government after the Revolution. Claims on property nationalized by the Cuban state extended to persons who did not hold US citizenship at the time of the expropriation, thus including Batista supporters who fled at the start of the Revolution. It brought universal condemnation: Canada and Mexico (NAFTA partners), the EU, Russia, China, the Caribbean community and the Río Group of Latin American countries all protested that it was unacceptable to extend sanctions outside the USA to foreign companies and their employees who do business with Cuba. In 1997, the EU brought a formal complaint against the USA at the World Trade Organization (WTO), but suspended it when an EU/US agreement was reached under which Clinton was to ask the US Congress to amend Title IV of the law (concerning the denial of US entry visas to employees and shareholders of 'trafficking companies'). Clinton was also to carry on waiving Title III (authorizing court cases against 'trafficking' of expropriated assets).

In 1999, Human Rights Watch produced a report that strongly criticized the US embargo, arguing that it had helped Castro to develop and maintain his repressive regime, restricting freedom of speech, movement and association. It had also divided the international community, alienating Washington's potential allies who, it argued, should be working together to push for change in Cuba. The same year, the UN Human Rights Commission expressed concern about 'continued repression' in Cuba, following the trial and conviction of four Cubans for sedition. They were jailed for receiving funds and instructions from the USA aimed at obstructing foreign investment. A civil suit brought in Cuba claimed US$181 billion in damages from the US government for its aggressive policing over the previous 40 years, causing the deaths of 3478 Cubans. The case was seen partially as a retaliation for the Helms-Burton Law.

A spate of bombings at several Havana hotels caused alarm in 1997. After an Italian was killed by flying glass, the Interior Ministry announced it was holding a former paratrooper from El Salvador, Raúl Ernesto Cruz León, who confessed publicly on TV to working as a mercenary and planting six bombs. He did not say who he was working for, but it was assumed in Cuba that the Miami-based Cuban American National Foundation (CANF) was behind the bombings. Two Salvadorians were sentenced to death in 1999 for their part in the 1997 bombing campaign.

In January 1998, the Pope visited Cuba for the first time. During his four-day visit he held open-air masses around the country, attended by thousands of fascinated Cubans encouraged to attend by Castro. The world's press was represented in large numbers to record the Pope's preaching against Cuba's record on human rights and abortion while also condemning the US trade embargo preventing food and medicines reaching the needy. The visit was a public relations success for both Castro and the Pope. Shortly afterwards, 200 prisoners were pardoned and released.

In November 1999 a six-year-old boy, Elián González, was rescued from the sea off Florida, the only survivor from a boatload of illegal migrants which included his mother and her boyfriend. He was looked after by distant relatives in Miami and quickly became the centrepiece of a new row between Cuban émigrés, supported by right-wing Republicans, and Cuba. The US Attorney General, Janet Reno, supported the decision by the US Immigration and Naturalization Service (INS) on 5 January 2000 that the boy should be repatriated and reunited with his father in Cuba. Amid enormous controversy, the US authorities seized Elián on 22 April. The family finally took him home, amid celebrations in Cuba, where the boy had become a symbol of resistance to the USA.

The election of George W Bush to the US presidency was bad news for any prospects of a thaw in relations with the USA. A crackdown on spies was ordered and in June 2001, five Cubans (arrested in 1998) were convicted of conspiracy to commit espionage and murder in a US Federal Court in Miami. Castro referred to them as 'heroes', who he said had not been putting the USA in danger but had been infiltrating Cuban-American anti-Castro groups and defending Cuba. The prisoners known as the 'Miami Five' were held in separate prisons across the USA and were denied access to their families. In 2005 their convictions were overturned on appeal, but this was later reversed and the original convictions reinstated. Two prisoners returned to Cuba at the end of their sentences in 2013 and 2014, and the remaining three were released in a prisoner exchange in December 2014.

However, 2001 saw the first commercial export of food from the USA to Cuba, with a shipment of corn from Louisiana to Alimport, Cuba's food-buying agency. The debate on the lifting of sanctions was fuelled by the visit of former US President Jimmy Carter in 2002 and an ever-increasing number of Americans travelled to the island, legally or illegally. However, the thaw came to a grinding halt in 2003 when Castro had three ferry hijackers executed and imprisoned 75 journalists, rights activists and dissidents, many of whom had allegedly been encouraged by the head of the US Interests Section in Havana. Amid universal condemnation, the EU announced a review of its relations with Cuba and curtailed high-level governmental visits. In 2002, Osvaldo Payá, leader of the dissident Varela project (Félix Varela was an independence hero), delivered a petition with 11,020 signatures to the National Assembly demanding sweeping political reforms, but it was dismissed. Undeterred, Payá submitted a second petition in October 2003 with 14,384 signatures, calling for a referendum on freedom of speech and assembly and amnesty for political prisoners (Payá died in a mysterious car crash in 2012). At the same time, the US administration announced a clampdown on its citizens travelling to the island, with thousands of baggage searches and prosecutions. In January 2004, the USA cancelled semi-annual migration talks as relations deteriorated. With 2004 being another presidential election year in the USA, Cuba knew it was in for a rocky ride, but this time Bush hit out at ordinary Cubans as well as their government. Remittances were sharply curtailed and Cuban Americans were limited in their travel to the island, with only one trip permitted every three years to see a close relative, even if they were dying.

Recent events

In August 2006 Fidel Castro had his 80th birthday. The occasion was to have been marked by national celebrations, parades and speeches, but shortly beforehand Castro made the surprise announcement that he was about to undergo major abdominal surgery and that he was handing over the reins of power temporarily to his brother, Raúl. The nature of his illness, operation and subsequent condition was shrouded in secrecy, with rumours of terminal illness and even his death circulating in Cuba and in Miami. Coinciding with Fidel dropping out of the limelight, in the USA the Democrats won control of both houses of Congress and there were moves towards closer relations. Raúl made conciliatory noises to the USA, which the Bush administration rebuffed. By mid-2007, Fidel was well enough to receive foreign dignitaries and write articles on world issues. Nevertheless, he was still not seen in public and in 2008 the temporary handover of power became permanent. Raúl initially made attempts to liberalize the economy, allowing certain materialistic freedoms for Cubans with access to foreign exchange (permission to own laptops, stay in hotels.

etc) and introduced bonuses for workers who exceed their targets, but was stymied by the arrival of three devastating hurricanes, which between them caused US$10 bn in damage. This, together with the world financial crisis and a dramatic fall in the price of nickel, completely stalled the economy and seriously hampered the government's room for manoeuvre. The celebration of the 50th anniversary of the Cuban Revolution on 1 January 2009 was a low-key, no-frills, low-budget affair. Many factories had to close or cut output, energy was rationed, transport restricted and imports and budgets slashed as further austerity was required.

The succession to the Castro regime had long been thought to lie with the group of protegées groomed by Fidel, but in 2009 Raúl took Cuba and the world by surprise by replacing ten members of the Council of Ministers and other key personnel. Fidelista loyalists were removed while army and communist party officials were promoted to run the economy. Hopes were raised when US President Obama took office and lifted travel restrictions on Cuban Americans visiting the island. However, he kept the US trade embargo in place to press Cuba to improve human rights and political freedoms. Castro agreed to talks on migration and other issues, but refused to make concessions.

In February 2013, Raúl Castro announced that at the end of his five-year term of office, in February 2018, he would retire. That prospect, together with President Obama leaving office in January 2017, appears to have galvanized bilateral negotiations. In 2014, secret talks were held at the Vatican and in Canada, facilitated by Pope Francis, and in December the two presidents announced the beginning of a process of restoring normal relations between the two nations. This was to include the lifting of some travel restrictions for US citizens, giving US banks access to the Cuban banking system, fewer restrictions on remittances and, importantly, restoring diplomatic relations. In January 2015, Cuba released 53 political dissidents. In April, Presidents Obama and Castro met at the Summit of the Americas in Panama, and, following that, Cuba was taken off the US State Sponsors of Terrorism list. In July 2015 the Interests Section of both countries in Havana and Washington DC were upgraded to embassies. Charter flights from New York began, and four companies were approved to offer a chartered ferry service between Miami and Havana. However, the Cuban trade embargo remained in place, as it could only be lifted by a vote in the US Congress. Executive action could only lift some restrictions on travel and the import and export of goods between the two countries. In September, Pope Francis visited Cuba and the USA, saying Mass in Havana, Holguín and Santiago de Cuba.

Tourism to Cuba soared in 2015, not only from US citizens on approved cultural or educational tours, but also from Europe and elsewhere as travellers rushed to see the island 'before it changes'. At the same time, however, there was another exodus of Cubans fleeing the country for the USA, fearing that if the Cuban Adjustment Act were to be eliminated, the 'wet foot, dry foot' route into the 'land of opportunity' would be closed to them and the annual quota of migrants would be abandoned. Many took advantage of a visa-free agreement with Ecuador to fly to that country and travel overland from there through Central America, but their plans were stymied in November when Nicaragua closed its borders and some 8000 were stranded in Costa Rica. At an emergency meeting of the Central American Integration System (SICA) in December, it was agreed to start an airlift of Cubans in January 2016 from Costa Rica to El Salvador, from where they would be bussed to Mexico to make their own way to the US border. Nevertheless, Costa Rica closed its southern border to prevent more migrants becoming a burden on its resources, shifting the problem to Panama, while Ecuador re-imposed visa restrictions to stop the flow.

Economy

Following the 1959 Revolution, Cuba adopted a Marxist-Leninist system. Almost all sectors of the economy were state controlled and centrally planned, the only significant exception being agriculture, where some 12% of arable land was still privately owned. The country became heavily dependent on trade and aid from other Communist countries, principally the USSR (through its participation in the Council of Mutual Economic Aid), encouraged by the US trade embargo. It relied on sugar and, to a lesser extent, nickel for nearly all its exports. While times were good, Cuba used the Soviet protection to build up an impressive, but costly, social welfare system, with better housing, education and healthcare than anywhere else in Latin America and the Caribbean. The collapse of the Eastern European bloc, however, revealed the vulnerability of the island's economy and the desperate need for reform. A sharp fall in GDP of 35% in 1990-1993, accompanied by a decline in exports from US$8.1 billion (1989) to US$1.7 billion (1993), forced the government to take remedial action and the decision was made to start the complex process of transition to a mixed economy.

Transformation of the unwieldy and heavily centralized state apparatus progressed in fits and starts. The government initially encouraged self-employment to enable it to reduce the public sector workforce, but Cuban workers were cautious about relinquishing their job security. Some small businesses sprang up, particularly *casas particulares* and *paladares* in the tourism sector. Free farm produce markets were permitted in 1994 and these were followed by similar markets at deregulated prices for manufacturers, including goods produced by state enterprises and handicrafts. Cubans were allowed to hold US dollars and in 1995 a convertible peso at par with the US dollar was introduced, which is fully exchangeable for hard currencies. There was initial success in reducing the fiscal deficit, which was bloated by subsidies and inefficiencies.

Although commercial relations with market economies were poor in the late 1980s, because of lack of progress in debt rescheduling negotiations, Cuba made great efforts in the 1990s to improve its foreign relations. The US trade embargo and the associated inability to secure finance from multilateral sources led the government to encourage foreign investment, principally in joint ventures. All sectors of the economy, including sugar, tourism, oil, mining, telecommunications and real estate, were opened to foreign investment and in some areas majority foreign shareholdings allowed. The external accounts remained weak. Foreign debt was around US$11 billion (excluding debt to former members of COMECON – Russia claimed Cuba owed it US$20 billion), and Cuba's dependence on high-interest, short-term trade finance was a burden. Cuba was ineligible for long-term development finance from multilateral lending agencies because of the US veto. Low sugar and nickel prices, high oil prices, a decline in tourism after the 11 September 2001 terrorist attack and massive hurricane damage in 2002 and 2008 all hindered recovery from the economic crisis of the 1990s.

When Raúl Castro took over the presidency, he very gradually deepened the economic reforms, allowing more private enterprise and more foreign investment. A new foreign investment law was passed in 2014, which granted access to all economic sectors except public health, education and anything relating to the armed forces, and reduced taxes on profits, among other liberalizations. A list of 246 projects was published for which foreign investment of US$8.7 billion was sought. This was followed in 2015 by an announcement that Cuba was seeking US$8.2 billion of foreign investment in 326 projects, including opportunities in healthcare, tourism, transport, construction, agriculture, renewable energy and rum production. The aim was to get US$2 billion flowing into the economy each year, and it was clearly stated that the administration was actively avoiding dependence on any single market, having learned from its mistakes with the Soviet Union and then Venezuela. Cuba now trades with 75 countries and trade has tripled in the last decade, but it is still heavily reliant on oil imports from Venezuela, which is itself going through an economic crisis.

In conjunction with the drive to increase capital inflows, in 2015 Cuba reached agreement with the Paris Club of creditor nations, whereby US$8.5 billion of Cuba's total US$11.1 billion debt was forgiven and the rest restructured on easy terms. The deal was a big step towards restoring Cuba's international financial credibility, allowing potential investors to seek official credits. European companies had been putting pressure on their governments to come to an agreement before any lifting of the US embargo so they could get in before US companies.

Sugar was traditionally the leading foreign exchange earner. However, the industry consistently failed to reach the targets set, with output falling from eight million tonnes in 1990 to 1.8 million tonnes in 2015. Low world prices, poor weather and shortages of fertilizers, oil and spare parts limited any great improvement in income. Two thirds of the country's sugar mills have closed and the land under production has been cut by 60%, with consequent severe job losses. Sugar is now Cuba's seventh largest earner of foreign currency, behind services, remittances, tourism, nickel, pharmaceuticals and cigars. Cuban cigars are world famous, but **tobacco** farming has also suffered from lack of fuel, fertilizers and other inputs. Production is recovering with the help of Spanish credits and importers from France and Britain. A Spanish company has a shareholding in the cigar exporting company, Habanos SA, to boost sales abroad. The thaw in relations with the USA is expected to benefit cigar exports.

The opening of farmers' markets in 1994 helped to stimulate diversification of crops and greater availability of foodstuffs, but shortages still remained. Drought in the east, hurricanes and flooding have all in recent years affected crops of beans, grains, vegetables and fruit. The area of cultivated land fell 33% from 1997 to 2008, with Cuba producing only a third of the food it needed. Some 250,000 small family farms and 1100 cooperatives worked about 25% of the land but still produced nearly 60% of crops and livestock, far more than the state farms. In 2009 the government began distributing idle state land to private farmers in an effort to boost food production and cut the US$11 billion trade deficit caused by rising food imports and falling exports. In a marked shift away from inefficient state farms, Raúl Castro has made raising food production a national security priority. The supply of food for the capital has greatly improved, partly with the introduction of city vegetable gardens, *agropónicos*, or *orgánoponicos*, which now provide some 90% of the capital's fresh food, but the main staple, rice, is still imported to make up a shortfall in domestic production caused by inefficiencies and a lack of fertilizers.

The sudden withdrawal of **oil** supplies, when trade agreements with Russia had to be renegotiated and denominated in convertible currencies, was a crucial factor in the collapse of the Cuban economy. Although trade agreements involving oil and sugar remain, Cuba had to purchase oil from other suppliers with extremely limited foreign exchange. As a result, Cuba stepped up its own production: foreign companies explore for oil on and off-shore and investment has borne fruit, with over 90% of electricity generated by domestic oil and gas and half of all consumption met by domestic

BACKGROUND
Health

Free healthcare is provided to all Cubans by the state as their right. In the 1960s the state took on the task of curing the population of many infectious diseases, despite having lost half of its 6000 doctors, who left the country after the Revolution. Mortality rates were high and attention was focused on eradicating specific diseases, improving ante-natal and post-natal care and training large numbers of doctors and other health care workers. Health facilities in operation before the Revolution were consolidated into a single state health system. In the 1970s, there was more emphasis on community healthcare, and polyclinics were set up with specialist services around the country. Positive results were soon evident as mortality rates fell and life expectancy rose. By the 1980s, policy had shifted again, this time towards preventive medicine rather than curative care. Mass immunization programmes were carried out and screening became regular practice. In 1985 the Family Doctor programme was started to take pressure off the hospitals and clinics and provide continuity of care. Each doctor cares for 120 families as well as collecting health and social information on all patients, providing the state with a database on the health of the nation.

The results of this attention to healthcare are staggering. Cubans may be poor and live in inadequate housing but their health is equal to that of industrialized countries. 95% of the population has been vaccinated against 12 diseases and several (such as polio, diphtheria, measles and mumps) have been eliminated from the island completely. Between 1986 and 1993, the entire population was tested for HIV and the 'sexually active' population is still tested annually. No cases of HIV-positive new-born babies have been recorded since 1998 as a result of ante-natal screening. The UN Population Report puts Cuba's infant mortality rate at 4.5 deaths per 1000 live births

production. Agreements with Venezuela for preferential oil supplies eased the situation, but dependency on Venezuela has since become a concern, particularly after the death of President Jorge Chávez and political changes in that country.

Mining was expected to attract foreign interest, and in 1994 a new mining law was passed. Major foreign investors included Australian (nickel), Canadian (gold, silver and base metals) and South African (gold, copper and nickel) companies. Cuba's three nickel-processing plants make it one of the world's largest producers, and it produces 10% of the world's cobalt, but prices have been volatile, putting huge pressure on export earnings.

Tourism is now a major foreign exchange earner and has received massive investment from abroad. New hotel projects have come on stream and many more are planned. Most of the development has been along the Varadero coast, where large resort hotels attract package tourism, but the northern cays are undergoing major construction. Despite political crises, the numbers of visitors rose steadily from 546,000 in 1993 to over three million in 2014, and strong growth continued in 2015 with the arrival of greater numbers of European, Canadian and Chinese visitors as well as Americans. The sector was already benefiting from the relaxation of US restrictions on family visits for Cuban Americans and also from the lifting of the ban on Cubans visiting hotels, many paid for by relatives visiting from Miami. Travel and tourism now contributes 10% of GDP and provides jobs equivalent to 2.5% of total employment.

(UK 4.2 and Canada 4.4, USA 6.1). Life expectancy is 77 years for men and 81 years for women although spending on health per person is one of the lowest in the world. As a result of the intensive training of doctors, there is now a better doctor/patient ratio than anywhere in the world except Israel.

Healthcare is now also an export item. Cuba's expertise is sought by developing countries worldwide. Cuban doctors work abroad in teams to provide specific services and foreign medical students come to Cuba to receive training. The Carlos J Finlay Medical Detachment was set up in the 1980s to prepare community doctors and in the first graduation year it included 147 graduates (out of a total of 3440 that year) from 45 different countries. The Detachment was named after the 19th-century Cuban physician who discovered the mosquito as vector of yellow fever. In 1996, South Africa requested the services of 600 English-speaking Cuban doctors under a three-year contract to make up a shortfall caused by the emigration of South African doctors. Cuban emergency medical teams have helped overseas with hurricane relief and other natural disasters. In 2014-2015, 461 doctors were sent to fight the ebola outbreak in Sierra Leone long before teams arrived from wealthier, industrialized countries. Over 18,000 victims of the Chernobyl nuclear disaster, mostly children, have been treated at the Tarará medical facility outside Havana by Cuban medical staff since the programme was set up in 1990. Cuba has done more for the Chernobyl victims than all the rest of the world put together, paying for all accommodation and medical costs.

Exports of medicines and vaccines are also substantial, with sales now going to over 50 countries. In 1996 it was proposed that Cuba's debt to Venezuela, of around US$46 million, should be amortized with revenue earned from medicines exported to that country; for now the supply of oil is exchanged for medical staff and services. Brazil has bought the meningitis vaccine from Cuba, while Vietnam swaps rice for medical and pharmaceutical products.

A huge gap has emerged between those with access to CUC$ and those who live in the CUP$ economy. This has encouraged highly skilled professionals, such as doctors, particularly those with languages, to give up their training and become waiters or tourist guides. Many families try to ensure that at least one member has a job which brings in foreign exchange, while others depend on remittances from relatives abroad. Raúl Castro plans to unify the two currencies to eliminate distortions, but no timescale has been announced. Average monthly wages rose slowly from CUP$415 in 2008 to CUP$471 in 2013, but then jumped sharply to CUP$584 in 2014, although this was still equivalent to only US$24 a month.

Culture

Art

Until the 19th century Cuban artists were mainly concerned with emulating the styles fashionable in Spain at the time, to gain favour with their colonial rulers. But then painters began to develop styles that were endemic to the island. Even at the end of the 19th century, when Impressionism was revolutionizing painting in France, the Cuban style still retained its roots in the academic tradition of landscape and portrait painting. One of the artists known for his major contribution to the emerging Cuban style of painting was **Leopoldo Romañach**, born near Coralillo in Villa Clara in 1862, although he spent most of his life abroad.

It was the 1920s that saw Cuban artists finally developing their own avant-garde movement and the art magazine *Avance* made its appearance in 1927. **Víctor Manuel**'s (1897-1969) 1924 painting *Gitana Tropical*, with its echoes of Cézanne and Gaugin, caused a sensation when the public first saw it. Now it has become the painting that symbolizes the beginning of modernism in Cuban art. US encroachment on the failing Cuban sugar industry in the 1920s led to a new nationalism among artists and intellectuals, with painters looking to Afro-Cuban images for inspiration. The generation of painters of 1927-1950 are known as La Vanguardia. They combined the modernism of post-Impressionist European artists with the vibrant landscapes and people found in Cuba. Today, their paintings are worth a small fortune and there is a ready market in forgeries.

Wifredo Lam (1902-1982) is still Cuba's most famous painter. He spent many years in France and Spain, becoming friends with Picasso and André Bréton, who introduced him to primitive art. Lam blended synthetic cubism, African masks and surrealism to create an essentially Cuban vision. Although he did most of his major work in Cuba, he always intended to show those outside Latin America the reality there.

Amelia Peláez (1896-1968) looked west for her inspiration, to the mural painting of Mexico, although her early work was influenced by Matisse, Braque and Picasso. Her brightly coloured murals can be seen in the Tribunal de Cuentas building and the Office of the Comptroller in Havana. It was this divergence of influences that characterized Cuban art during the 1940s.

Carlos Enríquez (1900-1957) lived in Cuba, New York, Paris and Madrid, while his style evolved through surrealism to expressionism.

René Portocarrero (1912-1985) was one of the few painters not to be influenced by the movements in Europe. His big colourful paintings incorporate Afro-Cuban imagery. He travelled to Haiti, Europe and the USA and worked with ceramics and murals.

Mariano Rodríguez (1912-1990) studied under Mexican muralists. His most popular work is his series 'Gallos' (roosters) produced in the 1940s and he exhibited widely in the USA.

Mario Carreño (1913-1999) was a nomad for the first half of his life, working as a graphic artist in Spain, a muralist in Mexico, a painter in Paris before the war and an abstract painter in New York after the war, with only visits to his homeland. In 1957, he took up permanent residence in Chile and lived there until his death.

The 1950s and 1960s saw a big influence on painting of imagery from the cinema; a major group of artists around this time were known as the *Grupo de los Once*, and included **Luis Martínez Pedro** (1910-1990), originally an architect who exhibited his paintings worldwide and designed theatre sets and costumes for contemporary dance, and **Raúl Milián** (1914-1986), who didn't start painting until 1952 and never worked in oils, preferring water-based inks.

The Revolution had a strong influence on developments in the art world: the first national art school was founded in the early 1960s; and in 1976 the Escuela Superior de Arte was founded. These institutions gave more people access to the serious study of applied art. **Raúl Martínez** (1927-1995) was the most well known of the Cuban Pop Artists. Unlike their North American contemporaries, the imagery of Cuban Pop Art came from the ubiquitous faces of revolutionaries, seen on murals all over Cuba.

The 1970s was the most difficult era for artists in Cuba, with many political restrictions on their work; of the few that made it past the censors, **Flavio Garciandia** (born 1954) was the most notable, producing paintings which mixed abstract and figurative styles together.

The 1980s saw the emergence of conceptual art in Cuba, as elsewhere, and many alternative groups were formed, such as *Artecalle* – street art. There was also the *Puré* group, the most important member being **José Angel Toirac** (born 1966) who famously put Castro's image on Marlboro cigarette advertisements and Calvin Klein's Eternity. Though most of the better-known artists were now abroad, the art scene still flourished. Some, like the sculptor **Alejandro Aguilera** (born 1964), distorted patriotic symbols in a confrontational way. In Cuba, as in other parts of the world, the 1980s was a decade in which everything was questioned and deconstructed.

The 1990s saw the rise of performance art as a means of expression. **Carlos Garaicoa** is one of the bigger names in this field, already having taken part in the *1997 Havana Biennal* along with **Tania Bruguera**, who had also exhibited in the *1996 Sao Paulo Biennal*. Many alternative galleries have sprung up, the best being 'El Espacio Aglutinador', founded in 1994 by two well-known artists from the 1980s, **Sandra Ceballos** and **Esequiel Suárez**. The gallery, which gave an exhibition space to many up-and-coming artists ignored by state cultural institutions is in Sandra's home in the Vedado area of Havana, Calle 6, 602 entre 25 y 27. The 1990s also saw a return to painting, after the vogue for installation of the 1980s. This reflects the economic need, during the special period (see History, page 410), for artists to make saleable objects again, although it also has its conceptual roots in post-modernism.

The **Museo Nacional Palacio de Bellas Artes** reopened in 2001 and is essential viewing for anyone interested in colonial and modern Cuban art (see page 49). The national collection is divided between two buildings in Old Havana, one for Cuban art and the other for world art, with many pieces having been in private collections before the Revolution. Other state-run galleries in Havana are the **Centro de Desarrollo de las Artes Visuales** and the **Wifredo Lam Centre**, which has shows by contemporary artists. You can also see some small exhibitions of avant-garde work at the **Casa de Las Américas**. Look out for the many small private galleries around Old Havana and Central Havana as well. In the provinces there are several places where you can see local artists exhibit their work, either in galleries or in provincial museums. Online you can keep up with what's going on at www.cubarte.cult.cu.

ON THE ROAD

Korda and the making of an icon

Alberto Díaz Gutiérrez (1928-2001) was the son of a railway worker and tried a variety of jobs before turning to photography as a way of meeting beautiful women. The scheme worked; he established himself as a fashion photographer and married one of Cuba's most beautiful models. He took the name 'Korda' because he thought it sounded like Kodak and set up a studio in Havana where he lived the lifestyle of the successful and famous.

The 1959 Revolution changed his world completely and he became converted to the cause after a photographic expedition into the countryside that year. He saw at first hand the grinding poverty of the peasants and the inequality caused by the dictatorship. Instead of fashion pictures for *Vogue*, he took photos of the new leadership, which he sold to the newspaper, *Revolución*. He followed Castro, Che and their entourage around the country giving speeches and holding rallies or joining workers in the sugar harvest. On one of these occasions he took the photo of Che which was to make him world famous and convert the Argentine into an icon to inspire student revolutionaries for a generation. The occasion was the funeral in 1960 of 100 dock workers who were killed when a French freighter loaded with arms exploded in Havana harbour. Interpreted as a CIA-backed terrorist attack, the Cubans were furious and grief stricken at the funeral and Che's expression reflects the mix of emotions he felt as he surveyed the crowd before taking his leave. Korda's photo was rejected by *Revolución*, but it was precious enough to him to hang it on the wall of his studio for years.

Architecture

The oldest house in Cuba still standing today is Diego Velázquez's residence in Santiago, built in 1522. However, the most important architectural works of the 16th century were the forts of Havana and Santiago, built in response to the many pirate attacks Cuba suffered. The original fort on the site of the **Castillo de la Real Fuerza** in Havana was burnt to the ground in 1555 by the French pirate Jacques de Sores. Felipe II commissioned a new fortress but the work was delayed when the architect was replaced in 1562 by Francisco de Calona, who completed the reconstruction in 1582. The building is a technological marvel, considering the primitive resources available when it was built: the walls are 6 m thick and 10 m high, with huge triangular bulwarks at each corner; a drawbridge leads over the wide moat to the vaulted interior. The early 17th century saw the construction of two castles in Havana and Santiago, by the Italian architect Juan Bautista Antonelli. They are both known as **Castillo del Morro**, and both still stand. Also built in the 17th century were the Havana city walls. One and a half metres thick and 10 m high, they ran for nearly 5000 m around the edge of the bay. A few fragments remain at Calle Egido y Avenida del Puerto.

Baroque

The most notable Baroque building in Havana is the **cathedral**; completed in 1777, it features an eccentric, undulating façade, asymmetrical towers, and wooden-ribbed vaulting over its three naves. The increased power enjoyed by the church in the 17th and 18th centuries led to bishops such as Diego Evelino de Compostela having a big say in city

In 1967, Korda received a visit from the Italian publisher, Giangiacomo Feltrinelli, to whom he gave a print of the photo as a present. The matter might have rested there if Che had not been killed in Bolivia a few weeks later. A Ministry of the Interior official discovered the photo and hung a huge version of it on the building overlooking the Plaza de la Revolución where it served as a backdrop for Castro when he paid homage to his friend and colleague. Images of the event were screened on televisions all round the world and Feltrinelli realised what could be done with such a powerful picture. Without permission and without paying Korda a cent, Feltrinelli printed millions of posters of the photo which later adorned student rooms and were carried in demonstrations in Europe and Mexico in the late 1960s. This single image of Che has been used on posters, T-shirts, hats, books, cards and any number of other items to reinforce revolutionary thought or just to sell goods with the aid of a beautiful young man with a stern but wistful gaze. In December 1999 an exhibition in Paris called '*100 Photographs of the Century*' had Korda's photo of Che on the cover of the catalogue, in recognition of its impact.

For 20 years Korda did nothing about his copyright and received no royalties. It was only in 1998 when Smirnoff advertised a vodka with the picture of Che and the slogan 'Hot and Fiery' that he decided to take action. Incensed that Che should be used to advertise alcohol when he didn't even drink, Korda took the advertising and picture agencies to court and won. When damages were paid in 2000 he donated them to the Cuban health service to buy medicines for Cuban children, as he believed Che would have done. He died of a heart attack in Paris while attending an exhibition of his work and was buried in Havana. Despite a huge photographic legacy including an underwater record of Cuba as well as fashion and news photos, it is for the single photo of Che Guevara that he will always be known.

planning, with the result that many churches were built during this period. The gardens of Evelino's house in Calle Compostela, Havana, were the site of the first baroque church in Havana, **Iglesia de Nuestra Señora de Belén**, completed in 1718 and now a day-care centre for the elderly. The classic baroque façade features a nativity scene framed within a shell. Diego de Compostela also built the **Colegio de San Francisco de Sales** in Havana. A typical central patio, surrounded by thick columns and slatted doors, receives rainbows of light from the *mediopuntos* – semicircular windows with fan-shaped stained glass.

The **San Francisco de Asís** church in Old Havana was rebuilt in the baroque style in 1730. When a 40-m tower was added it became one of the highest religious buildings in Latin America. It is no longer a church and only the exterior, in particular the Escorial style of the façade, retains the baroque splendour of its day.

Colonial mansions

In a typical Spanish colonial house of some wealth, there was a series of large, airy rooms on the first floor surrounded the central patio, based on the Sevillian style; the ground floor was reserved for warehouses and shops, and the *entresol*, between the ground and first floors, was where the slaves lived. Ornate carved *rejas* adorned the windows, and half-doors set with coloured glass divided the rooms. A good example in Havana is **Casa de La Obra Pía**, on Obrapía and Mercaderes.

Neoclassical

The first neoclassical building in Havana was the **Templete**, a small doric temple on the Plaza de Armas. In the early 19th century, the cathedral in Havana had its baroque altars removed and replaced with neoclassical ones by Bishop Juan José de Espada. There are three fine neoclassical buildings in Matanzas: the cathedral, the **Iglesia de San Pedro Apóstol**, and the theatre. Many elaborate country houses were built around this time, for example **Quinta de Santovenia** near Havana, now an old people's home. Its inlaid marble floor, fountains and wrought-iron *rejas* are typical of the neoclassical period. The **Palacio de Aldama** (Amistad y Reina in central Havana) has a stunning neoclassical interior with fine decorated ceilings. It is now the **Instituto de Historia de Cuba**.

20th century development

One of the most notable art nouveau buildings is the **Palacio Velasco**, on Capdevila esquina Agramonte in Central Havana. Built in 1912, it is now the Spanish Embassy. There are also many good examples of art deco in Havana; the best is the **Edificio Bacardí** on Avenida de las Misiones, Old Havana (now renovated and looking fabulous), built in 1929 by the founder of Bacardi rum, and the neo-Renaissance **Casino Español**, now the Palacio de Los Matrimonios, on Paseo de Martí (Prado). The **Capitolio** was the brainwave of former dictator Machado, who sought to demonstrate his allegiance to the USA by erecting a copy of the Capitol building in Washington DC. Built in 1932, it has a 62-m dome and a 120-m very ornate entrance hall.

More examples of 1930s architecture can be seen in Santiago, where there are some attractive art deco buildings on the Malecón, as well as the **Palacio Nacionalista**. The **Vista Alegre** neighbourhood, begun in 1906, contains some outstanding examples of art nouveau, notably the Palacio de Pioneros. This pink building on Manduley entre 9 y 11 was one of the Bacardí family residences.

In Havana, the early part of the 20th century saw the development of Miramar, on the western outskirts of Havana, as a resort for the rich. By the 1950s, the development had reached as far west as the districts of Biltmore and the Country Club (now given the Amerindian names Siboney and Cubanacán), housing some 300 wealthy families. Booms in sugar and nickel sales saw major building operations take place after the two World Wars in Miramar and Nuevo Vedado and, after the Korean War, in the far western suburbs. The wealthy middle class also built property for rent (80% of Havana was rented to other nationals and foreigners). Landlords lived in houses built on the *manzana* (block) architectural style. Those that were built for rent were on a smaller scale, with fewer green areas and small apartments off passageways. Working-class areas within these suburbs or municipalities were also developed, such as Pogolotti (early 1900s in Marianao) and parts of San Miguel del Padrón, in 1948. Buena Vista, in Nuevo Vedado, was also a poorer area.

Aquiles Capablanca was the most popular architect of the 1950s. His **Tribunal de Cuentas** in Havana is one of the most admired 20th-century buildings in Latin America. He also built the **Office of the Comptroller**, in Plaza de la República. Both buildings feature murals by well-known artist Amelia Peláez. Capablanca employed many elements inspired by Le Corbusier, whose influence can also be seen in residential work of the 1950s; conical designs called paraboloids were incorporated in the roof, whose purpose was to allow fresh air to circulate in the building. These avant-garde designs were combined with a revival of the colonial construction around a central patio, which hadn't been used for 70 years. The **Tropicana** nightclub, built by Max Borges Jr in 1952, was another work of stunning originality: exotic, sinuous curves on the shell-like structure are combined with tropical vegetation and the architect's own sculptures.

Post-Revolution

The Revolution saw less construction of new buildings than the conversion of former emblems of the Batista dictatorship into more functional buildings for public benefit. This happened with the **Moncada Garrison** in Santiago, now a school and museum, and the **Capitolio** in Havana, first a library and museum and now under redevelopment. The focus for construction moved from the capital to the rest of the country, which had been largely forgotten. Exceptions were service buildings, such as the Almeijeras hospital on the Malecón, and educational institutions. A whole section of the bay was also developed for the fishing industry. The municipality of Havana del Este is post-Revolution. The Camilo Cienfuegos housing estate was built in 1959-1961 and Alamar in 1970. There is also the scientific complex near Siboney in the far west of Miramar, housing a state-of-the-art genetic biology centre and a neurological hospital, among other facilities. Some new structures of architectural merit did appear, such as the **School of Plastic Arts**: started in 1961 by Ricardo Porro, and completed after his defection by Vittorio Garatti in 1965, it has been described as resembling a stretched-out woman's body, with breast-like domes and curved walkways. Another good example of post-Revolution creativity is the **Coppelia** ice cream parlour, by Mario Girona, completed in 1966.

Soviet influence and materials after the Revolution saw the appearance of the grey monolithic buildings associated with the former USSR. However, the negative aura of such buildings in Eastern Europe has often much to do with the climate. Many similar buildings in Cuba, for example state-run hotels built during the 1960s and 1970s, have such wide, open-plan interiors and vast windows, often coloured with modernist stained glass, that the effect is entirely positive, allowing light and air to move freely through the building. The **Hotel Sierra Maestra** in Bayamo and the **Hotel Guacanayabo** in Manzanillo are good examples of this.

An excellent way to get an overall picture of the architecture of Havana is to visit the **Maqueta de La Habana**, on Calle 28 113 entre 1 y 3, Miramar. This is a detailed model of the city with a scale of 1 m:1 km, covering all its buildings dated by colour from the colonial period to the present.

Literature

The earliest known work of Cuban literature was a poem called *Espejos de paciencia*, published in 1605 by **Silvestre de Balboa**. An epic *canto* about the struggles between a Spanish bishop and a French pirate, it is an esteemed work for its time, though it now retains only historical value. Early schools of writers in Cuba were too influenced by Spanish literature to produce anything essentially Cuban and it was not until the first half of the 19th century that poets begin to formulate a voice of their own: the first collection of verse by a native Cuban was **Ignacio Valdés Machuca's** (1792-1851) *Ocios poéticos*, published in 1819.

José María Heredia y Heredia (1803-1839) is considered the turning point for Cuban letters. His *Meditación en el teocalli de Chobula* (1820) marked the beginning of Romanticism, not only in Cuba, but in the Spanish language. He was also the first of many Cuban writers to be involved in the struggle for independence. He was expelled from the country for his part in anti-colonial conspiracies, and wrote most of his work while in exile in Mexico and the USA.

Cuba's most prolific woman writer was **Gertrudis Gómez de Avellaneda** (1814-1873). Her anti-slavery novel *Sab* (1841) was the first of its kind to be published anywhere in Latin America, its theme predating *Uncle Tom's Cabin* by a decade. A glut of abolitionist novels followed, the most notable being *Cecilia Valdés* (1882) by **Cirilio Villaverde** (1812-1894). The poet **Domingo Delmonte** (1804-1853) led a protest against Cuba's continued acceptance of slavery after its official abolition in 1815, and many writers had to publish their anti-slavery novels in New York.

The most influential figure in Cuba's struggle for independence was **José Martí** (1853-1895). He was deported to Spain in 1880 for his part in the independence movement. He later died in battle during the second War of Independence in 1895. He wrote *Versos Sencillos* (1891), based on the drama of his own life, while in exile in the USA. Martí also wrote highly acclaimed prose, which appeared in political journals published in Argentina and Venezuela. Many of his prophesies about Cuba's political future have been fulfilled.

Two poets associated with the transition from romanticism to modernism are **Enrique Hernández Miyarés** (1859-1914) and **Julián del Casal** (1863-1893). The latter, influenced by Baudelaire, praised the value of art over nature in *Hojas al Viento* (Leaves in the Wind, 1890). His posthumous *Bustos y Rimas* (Busts and Rhymes, 1893) has been compared with the great Nicaraguan poet Rubén Darío. Another important modernist poet was **Regina Eladio Boti y Barreiro**. Although she only published three collections of verse, she was responsible for taking Cuban poetry from modernism to post-modernism.

In the 1920s, the *negrismo* movement began, which created non-intellectual poetry based on African dance rhythms. The poet **Lydia Cabrera** (1899-1999) dedicated her life to research of Afro-Cuban culture. As well as numerous stories, in which she created a prose based on the magical-mythical beliefs passed orally through black folklore, she published many books on the ethnography and linguistics of Afro-Cubans. The *negrismo* group consisted of poets both black and white, although its most famous member, **Nicolás Guillén Batista** (1902-1989), was mulatto. *Motivos de son* (1930), in which he incorporated African rhythms in his *son* poetry, is considered his best work. He joined the Communist party and after the Revolution, was made president of the Union of Cuban Writers, and declared the National Poet by Castro.

Two of Guillén's former colleagues on the Communist newspaper *Hoy* were the writers **Lino Novás Calvo** (1905-1983) and **Carlos Montenegro** (1900-1981). Novas Calvo is recognized as one of the finest short story writers in Latin America. He used the narrative techniques of Hemingway and Faulkner to capture the feel of Havana slang. He was the first of many writers to go into voluntary exile with the instalment of Castro's régime. *La Luna Nona y Otros Cuentos* (The Ninth Moon, 1942) is his best collection. Carlos Montenegro's *Hombres Sin Mujer* (Life Without Women) has been compared to Céline and Genet. He was jailed for life aged 18 for killing a sailor who sexually assaulted him. The novel is based on the sexual exploits of his 15 years in prison.

The major writers at the time of the 1959 Revolution were the novelists **Virgilio Piñera** (1914-1979) and **Alejo Carpentier** (1904-1980) and the poet **José Lezama Lima**. All publishers were merged into the National Printing Press, with Alejo Carpentier as manager. The founder of magical realism, Carpentier's early novels are among the most highly rated in Latin American literature. Many are available in English, including *Los Pasos Perdidos* (The Lost Steps), the most accessible of his richly baroque tales.

José Lezama Lima (1910-1976) scandalized post-Revolution Cuba with his novel *Paradiso* (Paradise, 1966), a thinly disguised account of his homosexual experiences. Primarily a poet, Lezama was one of the driving forces behind the *criollismo* movement of the 1940s and 1950s. His rebellious, apolitical stance is an inspiration to those young Cuban poets of today who seek to create a non-politicized poetry with a more spiritual dimension.

One of the most famous dissident novelists was **Reinaldo Arenas** (1943-1990). Dogged by state security for most of his youth, he was imprisoned several times as a dissident and a homosexual, and only managed to publish his novel *El Mundo Alucinado* (Hallucinations, 1971) by smuggling the manuscript out of the country through foreign friends. He finally escaped to Miami in the Mariel exodus, but, suffering from AIDS, he committed suicide in New York. His memoirs, *Antes Que Anochezca* (Before Night Falls) were published posthumously and have since been made into a film, see page 439. This and his other works are available in translation. Also available in English are the works of **Guillermo Cabrera Infante** (born 1929). In 1959 he became editor of the literary weekly, *Lunes de la Revolución*, but it was closed after two years when he got into trouble with the government. In 1962, he went to Brussels as cultural attaché, but resigned in 1965 and began exile in London in 1966. His witty novel about Havana nightlife during Batista's dictatorship, *Tres Tristes Tigres*, first version 1964, second version 1967 (Three Trapped Tigers, 1971), brought him literary fame. The book won him the Premio Biblioteca Breve in Barcelona in 1964, but led to him being expelled from the Cuban Union of Writers in 1968. Conflict between artistic creativity and the Revolution exploded in the 1970s with the Padilla affair. Herberto Padilla, a poet, won a literary prize in 1971, but instead of guaranteed publication, his book of satirical and questioning poems was blocked. He was imprisoned as a counter-revolutionary and forced to make a public confession of crimes he had not committed, a humiliating act which caused an outcry among the intellectuals of Europe.

As a reaction to the political restrictions placed on writers after the Revolution, a movement of experimental literature sprang up in the 1960s, influenced by the French avant-garde and North American pop culture. **Severo Sarduy** (1937-1993), who left Cuba for Paris immediately after the Revolution, was the leading member; his *¿De dónde son los cantantes?* (From Cuba with a Song, 1967), with its complex layering of cultural history and linguistic puzzles, is still regarded as a classic by Cuban intellectuals. Sarduy became a citizen of France in 1967 and lived there until his death.

Nowadays Cuban writers find it easier to express their ideas in public. Havana has its first legally recognized literary group. At the centre of the group is **Reina María Rodríguez** (born 1952), a poet who has gained admiration outside Cuba. Many young poets and writers see themselves as carrying on where literature left off after the 1960s, when the repressive measures of the Revolution induced a state of creative inertia and self-censorship. Writers such as **Pedro Juan Gutiérrez** and **Leonardo Padura Fuentes** (see page 453) openly discuss the difficulties of life in Havana and question the ethics of state-imposed hardship with the toll it takes on friendship, work and sex. There is also a new generation of Cuban American writers, whose parents fled in the 1960s, who are now discovering their roots.

Music and dance

There are few countries in the world with so rich a musical heritage as Cuba. No visitor can fail to be moved by the variety of sounds that surround them, whether it be a street corner rumba or a *septeto* in the Casa de la Trova. Music is everywhere – it seems that nothing can happen without it.

The origins of Cuban music lie in the movement of numerous, primarily European, and African cultures. Through the inauspicious conditions of migration, enslavement, war and colonization, elements of these disparate identities have fused into a Cuban identity,

BACKGROUND
José Martí (1853-1895)

Born into a poor family in Havana, José Martí dedicated his life from a young age to rebellion against the colonial Spanish rule. The head of his school, the poet and freedom fighter Rafael Mendive, was a strong influence on him, and it was his connection with Mendive that was used as evidence for Martí's sentence of forced labour for his part in the 1868 Independence Conspiracy while he was still a boy. The experience of gross injustice, slaving in the sun with old men and young boys chained at the ankles, implanted in the young Martí a lifelong commitment to the struggle for independence from Spanish rule.

Martí's sentence was commuted to exile. He was sent to Spain in 1871-1874, where aged 18 he wrote the first of many political essays, *El presidio político de Cuba*, in which he denounced the sufferings of his fellow Cubans at the hands of an authoritarian colonial rule. He completed his studies in Spain, and then went to Mexico to become editor of *Revista Universal*. From there he taught at the University of Guatemala in 1877. He then lived in Venezuela until 1881 and the last years of his exile were spent in the USA. He left in 1895 to join the liberation movement in Cuba, where he was welcomed as a political leader. Tragically, he was killed on 19 May that year while fighting in the War of Independence at Boca de Dos Ríos in the east, see also page 317.

José Martí's work was primarily concerned with the liberation of Cuba, but many of his poems focused on nature, with Man at the centre engaged in a continual process of betterment. He combined a love of poetry with a desire for his prose work to have some effect on the world; all his energies were directed towards securing a future in which justice and happiness could flourish. Although one of the greatest modernist poets, he did not share other modernists' views that the role of poetry was outside conventional society.

Martí also differed from his contemporaries in his rejection of contemporary European literature. He saw pre-Columbian culture as having far more importance to a Latin American poet. His views were expanded upon in his essay *Nuestra América*, in which he welcomed the contributing force of Amerindians and blacks in contemporary culture.

Martí set the tone for all his poetry with *Ismaelillo* (1882), demonstrating the simplicity and sincerity he felt was lacking in current Spanish poetry. He developed this style in 1878, with *Versos libres*, and later in his most admired collection *Versos sencillos* (1891), in which the upheavals of his own life were his biggest inspiration. Martí is perhaps best known in Europe by the song *Guantanamera* – an adaptation by Pete Seeger of Martí's verse, put to the melody of Joseíto Fernández. In Cuba, however, he is the figure head of Cuban liberation and has become an icon, deliberately exploited by Fidel Castro, of anti-colonialism, independence and freedom.

forged in the villages and on plantations, in tenements and dockyards. African music and dance forms whose paths might never have crossed on their own vast continent did so in Cuba, enriching each other, and drawing also upon European forms. The mirror image is equally true with European dances finding new, African interpretations, while musicians have absorbed African harmony and chorus styles as well as rhythm. Most of today's popular genres are neither Yoruba nor French, Ekiti, Ashanti, nor Spanish, but fusions from this vast cultural gene pool.

The Cuban music most universally accepted on the island is surely the **son**, which, in spite of its more urban variations and offspring, remains essentially rural. Played by Cuba's oldest and youngest musicians, it is a principal root of salsa, and, however unlikely it might at times seem, also *timba*. In its various forms *son* still thrives both in the countryside and cities throughout the island, pointing to the nascent character of urban culture. *Son* began its life in Oriente where old songs from Spain combined with African call-and-response choruses. The syncopated notes of the guitar and *tres* (a small guitar-like instrument) contributed to other genres such as *guaracha*, full of satire and humour, and soon evolved new ones such as the *guajira*, resulting in the famous '*guajira Guantanamera*', and *nengón*. With the addition of bongo, maracas and marimbula, *nengón* developed into the style known as **son changüí**. From Guantánamo (where *changüí* is still strong), the *son* reached Havana around 1909, along with elements of the new Permanent Army, and gained there the disdain of society, which disregarded and feared it as the music of the lower, particularly black, class. Persecuted by the authorities, *son* simmered in a few black neighbourhoods, existing there through illegal parties for some ten years. However, given Society's taste for expropriating the surplus value of the lower orders' uncouth labour, it was perhaps inevitable that they would eventually appropriate also their dynamic culture. By the early 1920s, and with tasteful modifications, small *son* combos were beginning to displace the cumbersome and expensive *danzón* orchestras from La Habana's exclusive dance salons. Capturing the most gifted writers and band leaders of the time this gentrification of *son* was not entirely without benefit to its continued evolution and precipitated its spread not just across social but also national boundaries. Although few if any recordings were made of *son* prior to this, a multitude followed, and whatever criticisms one might make, they remain a rich source of material for inspiration and re-interpretation.

As the 1930s approached, **Ignacio Piñero** formed his **Septeto Nacional**. (A *septeto* is a seven-piece band, including guitars, percussion, brass, vocals, playing traditional Cuban music.) Their *sones* not only featured his exceptional vocal improvisations (honed in the large choral societies called *Coros de Clave*), but added a hot trumpet to the central rhythm of the *clave*. **Nicolás Guillén** busied himself composing *sones* and *son* was now recognized as the sound of Cuba (to stand alonside such 'exotic' names as samba, conga and tango, in Europe and the USA it was marketed as the '*rhumba*'). The *septeto* style is still heard today in the popular music bars and Casas de la Trova. Piñero continued to innovate by mixing styles, creating *guajira son, bolero son* (also popularized by Santiago's *Miguel Matamoros*) and even *son pregón son* which used Havana street cries, including the famous *echalé salsita*.

A new development in the 1930s was **Arsenio Rodriguez' conjunto** style, which marked the beginning of modern **salsa**. To the traditional *septeto* came conga drums, *timbales* (or '*paila*' – optional), piano and more trumpets. This 'big band' *son* made much of the final, wild call-and-response or *montuno* section of the song. The later *Descargas* were improvised jam sessions over strong *paila*, conga and bongo rhythms, which had major influences on US jazz. The *tumbao* played by the *tumbadoras* is derived from rumba, so salsa combines elements of the three most prominent musical traditions: *son, danzón* and rumba.

During the 1950s, Beny Moré emerged as *Sonero Mayor* (meaning greatest singer and lyric improviser more than interpreter of *son*) and he remains one of the most revered figures in Cuban music history. Beny and his *Banda Gigante* were as adept with the newer

BACKGROUND
Alicia Alonso and the Ballet Nacional de Cuba

Although there was dancing in Cuba during the Spanish colonial period, with occasional visiting companies from Spain, ballet was not seen until 1842, when the great Romantic ballerina Fanny Elssler appeared at the Teatro Tacón. Performances by touring companies followed, including a visit by Anna Pavlova in 1917. Home-bred ballet started with the ballet evenings of the Sociedad Pro-Arte Música in 1931, whose conservatory produced Alicia Alonso and the two Alonso brothers, Alberto and Fernando, among other outstanding dancers and choreographers of their generation.

Alicia Alonso has been the most influential Cuban dancer and ballet director ever, having made her name on the world stage before returning to Cuba to direct the development of ballet. Born Alicia Ernestina de la Caridad del Cobre Martínez Hoyo in Havana on 21 December 1921, she studied in Havana and at the School of American Ballet in New York. After working on Broadway, in 1940 she became a member of the Ballet Theatre and temporarily joined the Sociedad Pro-Arte Música in Havana. She suffered periods off work because of a detached retina but returned to the Ballet Theatre in 1943 as ballerina. In 1948, she set up her own company in Havana, the Ballet Alicia Alonso, followed by a school in 1950, but continued to dance abroad, both with the American Ballet Theatre and as a guest of many other companies.

Alonso is known for her classical style and flawless technique, but she has also successfully interpreted modern roles. In New York she worked a lot with the choreographer Anthony Tudor, who once said of her during a rehearsal, "Oh, this excitable, temperamental Cuban, very savage, very primitive, you should try to be more educated!" Knowing that his remarks were hurtful, he asked when she would start crying. "Never!" came the reply, and she kept her promise. In fact, Tudor loved her superb technique, her spirit and her combination of vulnerability and defiance, but believed that her natural expressiveness and her tendency to show all her emotion in her face was vulgar and needed to be restrained. He held that the movement itself should show the expression. A compromise was reached. One of Alonso's most famous roles was, like Fanny Elssler, that of *Giselle*, but she has created roles in Tudor's *Undertow* (1945), Alberto Alonso's *Romeo and Juliet* (1946),

styles, mambo and cha cha cha, as with *son* and its variations. Of equal importance, the size of his orchestra allowed the introduction of American Big Band Jazz to the Cuban melting pot. The era also saw the arrival of such artists as La Sonora Matancera and Celia Cruz, both of whom found fame in exile. There, in the USA, Celia (died 2003) won world wide acclaim as the Queen of Salsa. Back in Cuba, Miguel Cuní, Félix Chapottín and Lilí forged a somewhat harder edged urban son to serenade the arrival of Castro's nationalist Revolution.

If Cuba of the sixties is remembered more in connection with Russian nuclear missiles than for earth-shattering music, the foundations were being laid for future musical revolutions. It's hard to find any virtue in the frankly awful experiments with pop music by Elio Revé and Juan Formell, but both talents went on to lead bands of enormous importance and popularity through the 1970s and 1980s. Formell's band, Los Van Van, have undergone a number of reinventions and remain very much at the cutting edge of today's music.

Balanchine's *Theme and Variations* (1947), de Mille's *Fall River Legend* (1948), and the title role in Alberto Alonso's *Carmen* (1967).

Alicia married Fernando Alonso, a dancer and ballet director, and brother of dancer and choreographer, Alberto Alonso. The three of them worked to establish the company, Ballet Alicia Alonso, which in 1961 became the Ballet Nacional de Cuba. The company became a showpiece for the Revolutionary government, even touring to the USA in 1978. The school's young dancers have a reputation for technique and artistic interpretation, winning many medals at international competitions. In Havana they perform a repertory of classical ballets, folklore-based works and modern dance at the Teatro García Lorca. Several important ballets have been especially created for the company. The grande dame of Cuban ballet is now blind, but continues to work and to oversee the company. Aficionados should visit the Museo de la Danza in Havana.

The world-famous ballet star, Carlos Acosta, is a product of Alonso's school and although for many years he danced as Principal Guest Artist with the Royal Ballet in London as well as other leading companies worldwide, he maintained close links with the Ballet Nacional de Cuba. In July 2009, he was instrumental in negotiating the visit by the Royal Ballet to Cuba, the first time for over 30 years that an international dance company had visited the island. The non-profit visit showcasing the company's classical and avant-garde repertoire was so popular that not only were all tickets for the performances sold out instantly, but thousands more watched on giant screens outside the Capitolio. The moment Acosta walked out on stage for the pas de deux of El Corsario, the knowledgeable audience rose to its feet with a standing ovation and cheers so rapturous that the dancers couldn't hear the music. Acosta grew up in a poor barrio, the youngest of 11 siblings and was in danger of going off the rails until his truck-driver father sent him to ballet classes to instil some discipline into him and ensure he was regularly fed. Frequently compared with Rudolf Nureyev and Mikhail Baryshnikov, he was known for his soaring leaps which earned him the nicknames of 'the flying Cuban,' or 'Air Acosta'. He has written his autobiography: No Way Home, A Cuban Dancer's Story (2007), and his ballet: Tocororo, A Cuban Tale was loosely based on his own life. In 2015, Acosta announced his retirement from the Royal Ballet and his plans to start a new contemporary dance company in Cuba, dividing his time between there and the UK with his British wife and family.

No less than the development of a popular education system on the island following the Revolution, US policy towards Cuba has had a powerful effect on the subsequent unfolding of popular Latin music in both countries, actually creating something of a schism. Cut off from its source, the music of Cuban exile and Puerto Rican communities has tended to become bogged in old musical language in the way of ex-pats, at the same time absorbing the economic ethos of the host nation. Polished and manicured and formularised, salsa has become a multi-million dollar industry in the USA and its southern sphere of influence, its product as personal as any other factory-produced commodity. Cubans on the other hand have never ceased to import, fuse and re-fuse ideas from their rich musical larder and from elsewhere and, less driven by market trends, their bands tend to develop distinctive sounds. Through the 1970s and 1980s the distinctions between genres such as *son* and charanga blurred somewhat, however, while economic pressure forced the replacement of acoustic with electric bass guitar. The Baby Bass (a substitute electric upright electric bass) which is de rigueur in salsa bands was almost unheard of in Cuba. This reality alone sent Cuban music off on its own path. Some bands began to borrow heavily from funk and other urban black American styles, but overall the feel of music from this era is quite rustic. As well as the bands mentioned above, Orquesta 440 (not to be confused with Juan Luis Guerra) stands out, as do Son 14, and Adalberto Alvarez y su Son, both the latter two being led by the same Adalberto.

Not for the first time, the new generation has continued the tradition of innovation to the point of creating a new music, timba. That a prominent pioneer such as Giraldo Piloto should protest his music to be merely *progressive son* alludes to the power of this revered tradition, the strength in Cuban culture of lineage principles as against individuation and, within this, the dependence of urban culture on its rural roots. Timba and Cuban rap were born not in the hills, but in the cities. They incorporate musical ideas from the outside urban world that resonate with city dwellers and certainly *timba* is the product of musicians who have enjoyed a technical training their predecessors could not have imagined. This is fundamentally urban music which perhaps has yet to become fully self aware, and you will hear little of it outside La Habana.

While *son* was appearing in Cuba's countryside, an African rhythm known as the yuka, which had survived on the sugar plantations, was joining forces with the Spanish *décima* and livening up the ports of Havana and Matanzas. This style soon came to be known as rumba. African rhythms were played on whatever came to hand: boxes used to pack fish or candles gave a good tone. Characters such as *Mama'buela* were created in mime and singers commented on current events or battled with each other for honours. This *rumba de cajón* also involved the stately *yambú* dance, where following the vocal section, a couple would mime courtship. Soon the rhythms passed onto drums, the large *tumba* providing a solid bass, the conga a repeated cross rhythm which was accompanied by brilliant improvisations on the small *quinto*. There are other terms like *llamador, trabajador, tres dos*, and *tres golpes* to describe the deeper-sounding drums, which seem to be named after their role in the rumba. To this was added a pair of *claves* and a struck length of bamboo known as the *guagua* or *cata*. The more sexual dance form known as *guaguancó* (still the main rumba style) demanded more rapid playing. Great rumberos emerged, such as Florencio Calle, Chano Pozo, Estéban Latrí and Celeste Mendoza, as well as groups who specialized in rumba, such as Los Papines, Conjunto de Clave y Guaguancó and the well-travelled Muñequitos de Matanzas, who used the rhythms of the Abakuá religion in their rumbas. The *Muñequitos* also play the Matanzas style known as *Columbia*. This rumba echoes African solo dancing, involving an element of danger such as the use of knives. Even faster playing underpins a singing style which makes use of Bantu phrases and ends in a call-and-response.

Rumba is a playfully competitive art form, although sometimes the competitiveness is not always so playful. The men, particularly the 'guapos', or 'hard guys', take it very seriously and people do get hurt, sometimes even killed. The rhythms have got faster, break dancing and karate moves have been incorporated into the dance, *rumberos* sing about the special period; in this way, rumba survives as a true reflection of Cuban street life.

Matanzas is also the birthplace of the danzón. The popular *Típica* orchestras, influenced by the great cornettist Miguel Faílde, added subtle African rhythms to the European Contradanza, along with a call-and-response *montuno* section, creating a balance between formal dance and syncopated rhythm, almost a Cuban ragtime. The Orquesta Típica slowly changed, adding piano and further percussion, while the 1920s saw a new arrival, the *charanga francesa*. Of French Haitian descent, this was another development of the *típica*, featuring wooden flute and strings as well as *pailas*. It is in this format, so different from its origins, that *danzón* is generally remembered and occasionally interpreted. It was the beginning of the **Charanga** style developed by contemporary Cuban groups such as **Orquesta Aragón** and **Los Van Van**.

During the 1940s and 1950s, **Orestes López** (*Cachao*) and the violinist **Enrique Jorrín** created the new **mambo** and **cha cha cha** styles directly from *danzón*. These driving rhythms are still popular all over Cuba, and were fundamental to the explosion of Latin music and dance worldwide.

The **canción habanera** is regarded as the first truly Cuban vocal style. Emerging in the 1830s as a mixture of the so-called *tongo congo* rhythm and Spanish melodies, it had its greatest exponent in **Eduardo Sánchez**. *Habaneras* were also composed by **Eduardo Lecuona**, a pianist who was internationally feted during the 1930s and 1940s.

Another *canción* style, involving simply a singer and a guitar, was developed during the 19th century in Oriente by **Pepe Sánchez**. His simple, beautiful songs, such as *Rosa No 1* and *Rosa No 2*, inspired others such as **María Teresa Vera** and the remarkable **Sindo Garay**, who claimed to be the only man who had shaken the hand of both Jose Martí and Fidel Castro! The romantic style known as bolero soon developed from *canción*.

Realizing the potential for expression offered by *canción*, young musicians like **Silvio Rodríguez** (1946-), **Sara González** (1951-2012) and **Pablo Milanés** (1943-) created the **nueva trova**. Their songs reflect the path of the Revolution, Silvio's '*Playa Girón*' telling its own story. '*Pablito*' is an exceptional composer and interpreter, especially of Guillén's poetry.

Cuban **jazz** is exceptionally healthy. **Orquesta Irakere** continue to renew themselves, inspired by the pianistic genius of Jesús 'Chucho' Valdéz (www.valdeschucho.com), while **Grupo Afro-Cuba** fuse jazz with traditional Cuban rhythms, including the *bata* drums of *Santería*. Among the generation of the 1980s and 1990s the incredible Grammy award-winning pianist **Gonzalo Rubalcaba** (www.g-rubalcaba.com) is supreme, composing pieces using *danzón* rhythms amongst others. The annual Jazz Festival in Havana was for years attended by **Dizzy Gillespie**, whose influence is evident in the playing of Cubans such as **Arturo Sandoval** (www.arturosandoval.com). Less well known but of no less virtue as the above are **Los Terry**, a family-based band from Camagüey, which plays an unusually rural form of Latin jazz. Lacking the polish of its New York equivalent that tends to struggle self-consciously to integrate Afro-Cuban elements, **Los Terry** have nothing to prove. If their jazz is elementally powerful, it is also totally absorbing in its complexity, dipping into Afro-Cuban folklore intuitively and naturally, rather than to make a point.

The rhythms and songs of **Santería** remain strong across the island. The three African *bata* drums are regarded as the most complex of all to master and the rhythms, each assigned to a particular deity, accompany the singing in old Yoruba. **Merceditas Valdés** (1922-1996) was loved throughout Cuba for her interpretation of these songs. Meanwhile, '*bembe*' parties on Saints' days are accompanied by singing and drumming. The singer **Lázaro Ros** (1925-2005) developed a band, **Síntesis**, who combine traditional *Santería* music effectively with jazz rock. Now led by Carlos Alfonso, ethno-fusion mixed with elements of Afro-Cuban roots defines its current style.

The music of the Cuban **carnival**, revived following the debilitating effects of the Special Period, is truly exhilarating. Both Havana and Santiago have their own styles of **conga**, the thunderous music which drives on the parade. In Havana, the conga drums, bells and bass drums of groups such as **Los Dandy La Jardinera**, support brass players as they belt out popular melodies, the lanterns spinning in the dancers' hands. In Santiago, each *barrio* is represented by massed ranks of *bocué* drums, bass drums and brake drums.

Ten classic timba/salsa nueva albums

1   **Azúcar Negra**, *Andar Andando* (Bis Music, 2000). After this first recording lead singer Haila from Bamboleo went her own way. Here you will find the most eloquent expression of *timba* at high tide.

2   **Bamboleo**, *Yo No Me Parezco a Nadie* (Ahí Na'Ma', 1998). Imagine two loud young women busting into a cabaret where a highly accomplished band is earning its daily bread. The girls bustle their way on stage, where, disarmed by decorum, nobody can prevent them from taking over the show. Undeniably lowering the tone, it nevertheless works out for the better as inspired by this raw energy, the band now realize their potential. Rough and smooth in perfect harmony, that was Bamboleo at their best.

3   **Conexión Salsera**, *Muy Caliente Para Ti* (EGREM, 1997). Featuring Danny Lozada en route for La Charanga Habanera, this is subtle in its use of contrasting chorus and lead vocal styles, beautifully focused percussion, and some of the greatest Cuban piano work on record. All quite understated, great for dancing Casino.

4   **Giraldo Piloto y Klimax**, *Oye Como Va* (Eurotropical, 2000). Piloto pilots his band through seamless changes of genre and style, a kind of aural painting. More a musician's than a popular band, the trajectory is towards jazz-rock-funk-*timba* fusion and in this field Piloto has no company let alone equals. Probably one of the greatest CDs released ever.

5   **Isaac Delgado**, *El Malecón (La Formula)* (Bis Music/Ahí Na'Ma', 2000). The king of salsa nueva when he pulls his finger out, you will find here a fistful of cracking dances, and a lot more besides. Songs tend to have long gentle intros, then the bass lets rip under a steaming rhythm section.

The cloaked and masked revellers of Los Hoyos and San Agustín sing in response to the wailing *corneta china*, a remnant of Cuba's Chinese communities. Other bands' *paseos* combine brass players with the usual barrage of percussion during the late July festivities. The carnival procession usually features the old *Cabildos*, whose drums keep alive the rhythms of Africa. In Oriente, the *Tumbas Francesas* parade the rhythms and dances developed by Africans in Haiti, before the 18th-century Revolution forced yet another move across the ocean.

All of this music can be heard in Cuba now: at the Casas de La Trova, at the Focos Culturales, in the theatres and the cafés, in the parks, the backyards and on the streets. From *changüí* to cha cha cha, from rumba to bolero, from *son* to *Santería*, the music of Cuba is gloriously, vibrantly alive.

The rise and decline of timba and salsa nueva

"*Que sabrosura viva, tremenda expresividad*," echoes the chorus, following an opening riff from '*los metales del terror*,' surely the scariest horn section ever. La Habana circa 1989 and like never before, a new band is rocking the city with a tribute to the neighbourhoods. This is not salsa as we've known it or might expect it. The structure and feel are fresh and innovative, actually disconcerting. Isn't it jazz or some weird form of rock? You have to pay attention though because this band overflows with virtuosity, breaking tradition consciously, rather than from incompetence. Not a slow number but it feels laid back, grounding you with

6   **David Calzado y La Charanga Habanera,** *Tremendo Delirio* (Universal 1997). For many, the definitive timba album, certainly none of the bands that formed from the CH's subsequent split have produced anything comparable. With the addition of Danny Calzado, it is phenomenal.

7   **Los Van Van,** *Te Pone La Cabeza Mala* (Caribe, 1997). Van Van's finest moment. Juan Formell and band had developed and ran parallel along with timba. They offer here the most complex crowd-pleasing music you could hope to find, music that seeks the highest common denominator while remaining truly popular. Singer Mayito shines through the frontline.

8   **Manolín (El Médico de la Salsa),** *De Buena Fe* (Caribe, 1997). Opportunist El Médico is a psychiatrist without a very good voice who turned to singing. Having attempted to straddle the Cuba/Miami divide, Manolín settled in the States after suffering power cuts during his gigs and other such 'accidents' on the island. Musically, this album has enormous depth in its arrangements, a master class in timba percussion, keyboard, chorus and bass, so who cares if he can't sing?

9   **NG La Banda,** *En La Calle* (Qbadisc, 1989). The one that started it all. Here you will find the young Issac Delgado, Giraldo Piloto, El Tosco, and the 'terror brass'. Such explosions are rare and this one hasn't dated a second. A million miles both from what preceded and what succeeded it.

10 **Paulo FG,** *Una Vez Más...Por Amor* (2000). Paulito runs the gamut between sublimely complex sophisticated timba, and slushy salsa romántica and ballads. This penultimate album contains a good handful of ultra smooth timba tracks that almost slide in one ear and out the other.

heavy *tumbadoras*, driving kit drums and bass, lifting you with blinding horn riffs, and there's a vocalist whose ease of delivery sends your head swimming. *"¿Quién se come el calamar? La gente de Miramar"* asks and answers the chorus. Then half the band cuts out leaving the bass booming and growling under syncopated thumps, to a rhythm section which has taken almost as much from jazz-rock and funk as its Afro-Cuban roots. Almost as much. The percussion breakdown or *'bomba'* in salsa makes its debut.

This was **NG La Banda**, as they said with characteristic modesty, *'la que manda,'* a talent concentrate from which some of Cuba's current leading artists emerged to form bands in their own right. The working title of *'bomba-son'* evolved through the 1990s and onwards with new bands and ideas taking shape from an unprecedented pool of talent. Each has added new ingredients to this urban fusion, lending diversity that defies homogenisation. Today the music has become known loosely as *timba*.

Not by chance, the pioneers of **NG** (new generation) **La Banda** were drawn largely from two other bands with histories in pushing forward the frontiers of traditional Cuban music. Though not necessarily for dance music, **Irakere** has been acclaimed internationally for its fusions of jazz with funk, disco, rock and Afro-Cuban rhythm. On the other hand **Los Van Van** had enjoyed 20 years or so as Cuba's number one dance band, combining elements of pop and pan-Caribbean rhythm within a modernized Charanga band. When some of these two bands' strongest elements got together, then the result was bound to be explosive. Principal among the founders was the multi-talented director **José Luis Cortés**

(El Tosco) (1951-) who lays claim with equally gifted **Giraldo Piloto** (now with his own band, Klimax, www.klimax.cult.cu) to be the inventor of this new music.

The emergence of *timba* rested upon the state education system and changing conditions of life no less than upon Cuba's traditions and gifted musicians. These days a musician or arranger's innate talent is complemented with the discipline of a comprehensive academy training. Through the early and mid 1990s the dissemination and development of technique and style among musicians continued, each innovation tested in the street practices and rehearsals that maintain contact between the public and even the most prestigious bands. A shouted joke or taunt from the crowd is transformed in a moment to a chorus line and improvised around. It becomes the line that hooks you when you hear the record; the symbiotic relationship between the bands and their audience gives inspiration to musicians while elevating to the stage the lives, dreams and preoccupations of Havana's youth. As such, and along with more familiar subjects, songs abounded about prostitution, the virtues of soya mince, girlfriends disappearing with rich foreign men and just the struggle to survive. Presented with irony, and the facility of street wit, *timba* constituted an antidote to the escapism of ubiquitous *telenovelas* (soap operas). It is pop music in the truest sense of the word and it has shaken salsa to its foundations.

Lagging a little behind *timba*, **salsa nueva** emerged as a music to bridge the gap between old and new. Integrating with salsa elements of *timba* such as syncopated bass lines and sparing use of a shouted chorus, it is more restrained and comprehensible to a traditional salsa ear. Eschewing the more nihilistic trends of incessant *bloques* (percussion breaks), structural shifts and breakdowns, it is also easier to dance to for anyone who needs something solid to hang on to. What culminated in a wave of inspired, original, infectious music around 1997, three years later had reached maturity, and was promising to extinguish in a final blast. Everything subsequently has been little more of an afterglow, although if you prefer sophistication and balance to youthful exuberance it is in this later period that you'll find a spattering of truly timeless gems. While bands of lesser originality begin to repeat themselves or go all out for the Latin pop market, some of the greatest band leaders are restrained by the confines of dance music, even for a musically sophisticated people like the Cubans. Each exploration by the likes of **Giraldo Piloto** might continue breaking musical boundaries, but ultimately estranges them from the mass audience upon which they once depended. Their music is just too complex and never settles into comforting recognizable formulas. In this context **Cuban rap** makes its appearance. First to make waves were **Orishas**. In spite of a hip hop parody stage act, their first CD fused rap to powerful effect with the morose nostalgia of the *guajira*. Another notable is **Clan 537** whose hit '¿Quién Tiró La Tisa?' is stunning more in its social than musical content. Officially, racism and class prejudices do not exist in Cuba, although they are deeply ingrained in Cuba's people and culture. However restrained by American standards, **Clan 537** show their resentment of this reality as frankly as *timba* artists in their day dealt with the problems they could. Like many bands, their style mutated into a fusion of Cuban and international styles, with some pure *reggaeton*.

Timba will never disappear though. Many bands whose reputations are built on other genres have nodded *timba*'s way and, in doing so, have incorporated its innovations into the mainstream. This is where *timba* now lies, so don't be surprised to hear syncopated electric bass lines and percussion breakdowns from the younger generation of *son* bands.

Cinema

One of the great success stories of the Cuban Revolution is the Cuban film industry. The Film Institute, known familiarly as **ICAIC** (Cuban Institute of Cinematographic Art and Industry), was set up by the new government in March 1959, only three months after the victory of the Revolution. Headed by **Alfredo Guevara**, it aimed to produce, distribute and show Cuban films to as wide a domestic audience as possible, to train film-makers and technicians, and to promote film culture generally. Open to anyone with an interest in film, excepting pro-Batista collaborationists, the institute built up an industry with an international reputation within 10 years, virtually from scratch.

Before the Revolution, films had been made in Cuba by foreign companies or amateurs. The staple diet of the Cuban filmgoer, even in 1959, was Hollywood movies. In the early 1960s, after the Bay of Pigs episode (1961) and the missile crisis (1962), several film directors (including **Néstor Almendros**), cinematographers and technicians, left the island, taking their precious equipment with them. Adequate government funding, which depended on the fluctuating Cuban economy, and state-of-the-art training and technology, became critical problems following the US trade embargo. The majority of the crew working on **Tomás Gutiérrez Alea**'s comedy *The Twelve Chairs*, for example (the assistant director, director of cinematography, camera operator, focus puller, camera assistant and continuity girls), were first-timers. Yet in learning to make the most of their scant resources, the Cuban film-makers introduced striking new techniques which, in addition to their youthful enthusiasm, improvisation and revolutionary focus, created a forceful impact on the world of film. Five Cuban films won international awards in 1960 alone. As Francis Ford Coppola remarked, "We don't have the advantage of their inconveniences". Measures such as the launch of the film journal *Cine cubano*, the inauguration of the Havana Cinemateca (1960), a national network of film clubs, and a travelling cinema (*cinemóvil*) showing films to peasants in remote rural districts, the nationalization of the film distribution companies, and the 1961 literacy campaign enabling 700,000 viewers to read the subtitles of undubbed foreign films for the first time, placed cinema at the forefront of revolutionary cultural innovation. Even the posters, designed under the auspices of ICAIC by individual artists, became world famous.

The types of films made during the 1960s were national, nonconformist and cheap. ICAIC aimed to keep as independent a criteria as possible over what constituted art, and encouraged imaginative, popular films, directly relevant to the Revolutionary process and challenging the mass culture of acquiescent consumption. The preferred format was the documentary shot on 8-mm or 16-mm film (40 were made in 1965), honed to perfection by **Santiago Alvarez**, but there were a good number of excellent features too: *Cuba Baila* (Cuba Dances), *Historias de la Revolución* (Stories of the Revolution), *El Joven Rebelde* (The Young Rebel, based on a script by Zavattini), *La Muerte de un Burócrata* (Death of a Bureaucrat) and *Aventuras de Juan Quinquin* (The Adventures of Juan Quinquin), the most popular feature in Cuba of all time, until the release of *Fresa y Chocolate* (Strawberry and Chocolate).

In 1967, the film director **Julio García Espinosa** published his seminal essay *For an Imperfect Cinema* which, with the work of **Octavio Getino** and **Fernando Solanas** in Argentina and **Glauber Rocha** in Brazil, laid the basis of the New Latin American cinema movement, also known as **Third Cinema**, a key concept in film culture today. Cuban cinema reached its high point in 1968, with groundbreaking films such as *Lucía* (Lucia) and *Memorias del Subdesarrollo* (Memories of Underdevelopment) and, in 1969, *La Primera*

Recommended Cuban comedies

If you know Spanish (and even if you don't) the following comedies are a must:
La Muerte de un Burócrata (Death of a Bureaucrat, Gutiérrez Alea, 1966), in which a worker is mistakenly buried with his identity card. His widow needs it to claim her pension but when the family try to exhume the body officially they are caught up in a Kafkian tangle of bureaucracy forcing them to dig up the body themselves. When the body starts to smell, they try to bury it again, with hilarious results. This is a side-splitting, but no less serious, criticism of state officialism.

The social satire *¡Plaff!* (Splat!, Juan Carlos Tabio, 1988) picks up on the same theme. A woman dies of a heart attack when an egg is thrown at her. Who threw the egg and why? This parody of a detective film delves deep into social issues, such as the Cuban housing crisis and the scarcity of resources, while lampooning 'imperfect cinema'. The preference for foreign imports is ridiculed when a home-made polymer made from pig shit at the Institute of Excrement is proved to be far superior to a Canadian brand. The highlight of the film, however, is when the director of the Institute asks for a new filing cabinet, to store the letters he has written asking for a new filing cabinet.

Adorables Mentiras (Adorable Lies, Gerardo Chijona, 1991) is a much more poignant comedy. An unsuccessful scriptwriter tries to impress a young streetwalker by pretending to be a film director, while she in turn deceives him by pretending to be a professional actress. The complex web of sex, lies and audiotape unravels when the writer's wife, who thinks he's gay, is delighted to find out he is having an affair with a woman. But the objective of this apparently farcical charade is deadly serious. Cuban society of the 1980s is shown to be rife with petty corruption, resulting from self-delusion and material constraints. Young people are urged to face reality and get on with their lives, even if it means painful compromise.

Carga al Machete (The First Charge of the Machete). Cuban film-makers, a number of whom had been trained in the **Centro Sperimentale** in Rome in the 1950s, were influenced predominantly by Italian Neorealism, French New Wave Cinema and *cinéma verité* – British Free Cinema (Tony Richardson and Lindsay Anderson), and the Soviet classics. Films shot on location, with hand-held cameras featuring ordinary people engaged in a revolutionary process, have remained the trademarks of classic Cuban cinema ever since.

By the 1970s, however, uncomfortable questions were being asked about the appropriateness of avant-garde art for the needs of the Cuban mass public. Tensions between creative artists and government bureaucrats exploded in the **Padilla affair** (1970), resulting in a five-year government clampdown. **ICAIC's** production programme was reduced to three features a year, while young, often amateur film-makers (average age 36), were favoured over the more experienced. Nevertheless, important films were produced, tending to focus on women's issues, historical and/or multiracial themes (particularly slavery and African-Cuban culture), with a view to consolidating a strong, cohesive sense of national identity. The black film director **Sergio Giral**'s *El Otro Francisco* (The Other Francisco) and Gutiérrez Alea's *La Ultima Cena* (The Last Supper), both depicting the courage and resistance of Cuban slaves, black director Sara Gómez's *De Cierta Manera* (One Way or Another), highlighting the problem of *machismo* among black men, and Pastor Vegas' *Retrato de Teresa* (Portrait of Teresa), denouncing sexist attitudes in post-revolutionary society, all date from this period.

In 1976, the **Ministry of Culture** was set up, ushering in yet another episode in Cuban film history. In 1982, **Julio García Espinosa** took over from Alfredo Guevara as the Head of **ICAIC**, and the organization was incorporated into the ministry. Until 1980 it had been self-financing. Nevertheless, despite the increasing influence of the Hollywood format (favouring sentimental melodrama and romance), perhaps indicative of a deeper crisis of belief, films still tended to be critical of Cuban social reality. Production figures increased to some six features a year during the 1980s, many of these co-productions with countries such as Mexico and Spain. By the end of the 1980s there were 60 million film goers, each Cuban visiting a cinema on average six times a year. The Cuban audiences, mostly young white-collar workers, technicians and specialists, tend to be educated and demanding. A network of video clubs and libraries were set up in the 1980s to meet their needs.

In the late 1980s, ICAIC recovered its independence and was restructured on the basis of three 'creation groups' each under an experienced film director in charge of encouraging and training young film makers. But, as Cuba moved into the special period (1990-1994) in response to the fall of the Eastern block and the intensified US trade embargo, ICAIC faced another crisis. After the release of a controversially critical film, *Alicia en el Pueblo de Maravillas* (Alice in Wonderworld), in a climate of political tension, moves were made to incorporate the Institute into Radio and Television, directly controlled by the **Central Committee of the Communist Party**. This strategy was actively resisted by leading filmmakers, such as Gutiérrez Alea, the plans were scrapped, and Alfredo Guevara was appointed director once more. Paradoxically, at a time when resources were scarcer than ever before, ICAIC produced its most successful film, *Fresa y Chocolate* (Strawberry and Chocolate, 1993), suggesting, perhaps, that the best Cuban films are made when circumstances are at their worst.

Daniel Díaz Torres followed his *Alicia* hit with *Kleines Tropikana* (Little Tropicana, Cuba/Germany/Spain, 1997), a hilarious pastiche of Gutiérrez Alea films and a fitting homage to the master. This satirical snapshot of Cuban xenophobia, played by the actors starring in *Alicia* and Vladimir Cruz *(Fresa y Chocolate)*, features a detective fiction writer, a dead German tourist and a British hippy girl, cleverly targetting European audiences. Music, laughter and social critique dominate the scene. Films of the late 1990s to watch out for are **Fernando Pérez**'s award-winning *La vida es silbar* (Life is to whistle, Cuba/Spain, 1998), **Manuel Herrera**'s *Zafiros locura azul* (Zafiros [Sapphires], Blue Madness, 1998) and **Juan Carlos Tabío**'s *El elefante y la bicicleta* (The Elephant and the Bicycle, 1998), all of which starred **Luis Alberto García** ('*Plaff!*' and '*Adorables mentiras*'). The first film is yet another sharp-edged comedy about life's illusions and disappointments, a bitter-sweet genre that the Cubans have made their own. As might be expected, the three protagonists (a dropout, a nurse and a ballet dancer) all have sexual hang-ups and are seen attempting to make sense of their chaotic lives in today's Havana. The second film is a musical biopic partly produced in the USA, again starring García. It tells the story of Miguel Cancio (the producer's father), founder of the 1960s quartet **Los Zafiros** who developed a unique blend of up-beat r&b and bolero music.

The international explosion of Cuban music, old and new, has led to a trend in Cuban musical documentaries. The film that has made the greatest impact in recent years is without doubt **Wim Wender**'s documentary *Buena Vista Social Club* (Cuba/Germany, 1998), a nostalgic reconstruction of the lives and times of the band of the same name. The late **Rubén González**'s piano playing, **Ibrahim Ferrer**'s crooning, accompanied by

BACKGROUND
Tomás Gutiérrez Alea (1928-1996)

The two most famous Cuban films, *Memorias del Subdesarrollo* (Memories of Underdevelopment, 1968), on the role of the intellectual in society, and *Fresa y Chocolate* (Strawberry and Chocolate, 1993), about gay issues in Cuba, were made by the director who has contributed more than any other to Cuban cinema.

Tomás Gutiérrez Alea made over 12 features and 13 documentaries/shorts. His films vary from the hilarious *La Muerte de un Burócrata* (Death of a Bureaucrat, 1966) to the sentimental romance *Hasta Cierto Punto* (Up to a Point, 1984). Except for *Cartas del Parque* (Letters from the Park, 1988), based on a screenplay by Gabriel García Márquez, they all have a sharp critical edge.

Gutiérrez Alea started filming in 1947, then studied at the *Centro Sperimentale* in Rome in 1953. His first serious work was a 1955 documentary on the charcoal workers, confiscated by the Batista police. During the Revolution he played a leading part organizing the cinema section of the Revolutionary army and made (with García Espinosa) the first post-victory documentary, *Esta Tierra Nuestra* (This Our Land). His first feature film, *Historias de la Revolución* (Stories of the Revolution) dates from 1960.

Since then, Gutiérrez Alea has won many international awards and retrospectives of his work have been shown across the world (including San Francisco, New York, Toronto and New Delhi).

Repeatedly, particularly in the late 1980s, he was refused entry into the USA. Yet in 1994, *Fresa y Chocolate* was nominated for an Oscar in the best foreign film category. Made primarily for a domestic market, it stages the dramatic encounter between a young Communist student and a gay intellectual. Both are patriotic Cubans but, while the student embraces the culture of Che and Fidel, the intellectual identifies with the refined artistic world of pre-Revolutionary Cuba. Each learns from the other, but the intellectual, hounded by the authorities, finally seeks political asylum in Europe. Gutiérrez Alea's last film, the road movie *Guantanamera* (1995), which returns to the macabre comedy format of *La Muerte de un Burócrata*, was completed shortly before his death. The leading actress in both films was his wife, Mirta Ibarra.

Ry Cooder on guitar (with his son, **Joaquín Cooder**, on drums) practising for two gigs in Amsterdam (April 1998) and New York (July 1998) and – above all – the stunning colour photography are quite unforgettable. Two Grammy Award-winning CDs are available: *Buena Vista Social Club* (WCD050) and *Buena Vista Social Club Presents Ibrahim Ferrer* (WCD055). The rhythmic soundtrack of *Tropicola* (Cuba 1998), directed by **Steve Fagin**, is exciting too, although this film is more concerned with contemporary problems in Cuba: the harmful effects of tourism and the dollar economy. Entirely different, but just as Cuban, is the wonderfully evocative short *Misa cubana* (Cuban Mass, Cuba, 1998), a collage of 16th- and 17th-century sacred music with a score written by maestro **José María Vitier**.

Cuba hit the headlines in several films made about the island in the USA and elsewhere. First there was *Cosas que dejé en la Habana* (Things I left in Havana, 1998) by Spanish film director **Manuel Gutiérrez Aragón** starring Jorge Perugorría (of *Fresa y Chocolate* fame). The film, funny yet critical, tells the story of three Cuban sisters who come to Madrid in search of a better world but are exploited by their aunt who, among other things, tries to marry the youngest girl to her gay son. Then **Roger Donaldson**'s political thriller *Thirteen Days* starring Kevin Costner, released in 2000, presented yet another version of the 1962 Cuban Missile Crisis, when the world was pushed to the brink of nuclear war. Despite its length (over two hours), the film received favourable reviews and was screened in Cuba. Costner and the producers were invited to dinner with Fidel and then collaborated with ICAIC to get the film put on in the island. Costner is still a frequent visitor to the island.

The most controversial film about Cuba in recent years (when aren't films about Cuba controversial?) is **Julian Schabel**'s *Before Night Falls* (2001), which is loosely based on the autobiography of gay Cuban writer **Reinaldo Arenas**' *Antes que anochezca* (Barcelona, 1992) (Before Night Falls, London, 1993). Arenas was born near Holguín in 1943 and was self-taught. After the Revolution he was given posts in the National Library and as editor of the famous *Gaceta de Cuba* (1968-1974). His first novel was published in Cuba in 1967, but in the early 1970s he ran into trouble with the authorities and was imprisoned for two years (1974-1976). He left Cuba in the Mariel exodus of 1980 and was employed in the USA as a literature professor. He contracted HIV and committed suicide in New York in 1990. His autobiography, although beautifully written, is hyperbolical (he boasts of having had 5000 gay sexual encounters before the age of 25) and especially hostile to Castro. It should not be read as documentary fact, as several of Arenas' Cuban friends and colleagues have since pointed out. The film represents events at an even further remove from historical reality, yet has been widely reviewed as an indictment of Castro's apparently brutal government. In other words, the film is deliberately politically biased. This is not to say it is not a good film; it is, but it is fiction and should be viewed as such. The Spanish actor Javier Bardem, playing Arenas, is powerful and convincing; the film also features famous Hollywood actors (Sean Penn, Johnny Depp) in cameo roles. Although the camera work is excellent, if you don't know Arenas's story you may be confused by the complex plot.

At the 2002 International Film Festival, the largest crowds queued to see *Balseros* (Rafters), a film documentary about seven Cubans who set sail for Miami in 1994, a time of economic crisis when Castro allowed thousands to flee on any home-made craft for Florida. Their stories show the pain of leaving families behind and the culture shock of living and working long hours in the USA. Directors **Carles Bosch** and **Josep Domenech** presented a frank account of the poverty driving Cubans to leave, but also the harsh reality of life elsewhere. In 2003, one of the most talked about films was a silent movie directed by **Fernando Pérez**, *Suite Habana*, a documentary of a day in the life of the city and its inhabitants, with a sound track limited to music and city noises. It can be interpreted as either a subversive criticism of Castro's system, or as a tribute to the courage and resilience of Habaneros, struggling against all odds to survive without losing their revolutionary dreams.

The big foreign film was the monumental *Che* (Steven Soderbergh, 2008), which was so long that it was divided into two films, *Che Part 1: The Argentine*, and *Che Part 2: The Guerrilla*. This blockbuster biopic of Che Guevara, starring Benicio del Toro, who won the Best Actor Award at the 2008 Cannes Film Festival, was filmed mostly in Spanish for veracity. The first part covers the Cuban Revolution, but was filmed in Mexico and Puerto Rico because of the US embargo. The second part is about Guevara's attempt to export revolution to Bolivia, with disastrous consequences. The film was shown to huge acclaim in Havana as part of the 2008 Latin American Film Festival, although Benicio del Toro was understandably anxious about such a knowledgeable audience. The state newspaper,

Granma, gave del Toro a glowing review, while the 2000-strong audience at the Yara cinema gave him a 10-minute standing ovation.

Meanwhile, Cuba mourned the death from cancer of film-maker **Humberto Solás** (1941-2008). He had a prolific output but first came to international attention with his 1968 film, *Lucía*, charting the lives and fortunes of three women called Lucía in different stages of Cuban history. It was filmed in Gibara, north of Holguín, a small town with which he maintained a long association. Solás was the first Cuban director to be nominated for an Oscar, with his film *Un Hombre de Exito* (1985). In 2001 he brought out *Miel para Oshún* (Honey for the Goddess Oshun, 2001), the story of a Cuban, Roberto (played by Jorge Perugorría, yet again), who was taken to the USA as a child after the Revolution and returns 30 years later to find his mother. Like Alea's *Guantanamera*, this is a road movie, more notable for its outstanding photography of the Cuban landscape than for its penetrating character analyses. Some of this film was again shot in Gibara and in 2003 Solás founded a festival for 'poor' cinema to be held annually in the town. The festival is dedicated to movies made against seemingly overwhelming odds and no film shown there has cost more than US$300,000 to make. After Solás' death the film festival was renamed in his honour as the Festival Internacional del Cine Pobre de Humberto Solás.

Lovers of wry humour at the expense of the Cuban predicament should seek out the films of **Juan Carlos Tabío**. His 2001 award-winning comedy, *Lista de Espera* (Waiting List) was scripted by Senel Paz and Arturo Arango and stars Vladimir Cruz (of *Fresa y Chocolate* fame) and Jorge Perugorría (now playing a blind man). The action takes place in a remote, dilapidated bus station. The passengers wait and wait for a bus but they are all full so they try and repair an old Soviet wreck in a collective effort to repair the broken dream. The bus is a metaphor for the better times that never materialize and the passengers' solidarity a comment on the resilience and blind optimism of those that try to make things work despite all odds. Tabío's more recent comedy, *El Cuerno de la Abundancia* (Horn of Plenty, Cuba/Spain 2008), again starring Jorge Perugorría, follows the hopes and aspirations of the extended Castiñeiras family from a small town in Cuba who hear they've inherited a fortune from the 17th century, left to them in a bank in London by three nuns. To escape the poverty and stagnation of their lives in Cuba they go through bureaucratic hoops to prove their parentage, squabbles between different factions of the family, love affairs driven by greed, but it all comes to nothing when they hear it has gone to a branch of the family in Miami. They are left with debts and broken marriages but at the end there is new hope of an inheritance and the cycle starts all over again.

A shortage of funds has led film makers to go into collaboration with foreign production companies, and many films are now made as joint ventures with Spain or Mexico. ICAIC is no longer capable of financing the entire industry. However, the Cuban film industry is progressing well in the 21st century and the International Film Festivals (Festival Internacional del Nuevo Cine Latinoamericano, www.habanafilmfestival.com, and Festival Internacional del Cine Pobre de Humberto Solás, www.festivalcinepobre.cult.cu) are major events that should not be missed. In 2015, of the nine Cuban feature films shown at the Havana Film Festival, five were independent and the rest produced by ICAIC.

Religion

The major characteristic of Cuban culture is its combination of the African and European. Because slavery was not abolished until 1886 in Cuba, black African traditions were kept intact much later than elsewhere in the Caribbean. They persist now, inevitably mingled with Hispanic influence, in religion: in *Santería*, for instance, a cult which blends popular Catholicism with the Yoruba belief in the spirits that inhabit all plant life. This now has a greater hold in Cuba than orthodox Catholicism, which has traditionally been seen as the religion of the white, upper class: opposing independence from Spain in the 19th century and the Revolution in the 1950s.

The Roman Catholic Church

Church and State were separated at the beginning of the 20th century when Spain was defeated by the USA and a constituent assembly approved a new constitution. The domination of the USA after that time encouraged the spread of Protestantism, although Catholicism remained the religion of the majority. Nevertheless, Catholicism was not as well supported as in some other Latin American countries. Few villages had churches and most Cubans rarely went to mass. Even before the Revolution, the Church was seen as right wing, as most of the priests were Spanish and many of them were supporters of General Franco and his fascist regime in Spain.

After the Revolution, relations between the Catholic Church and Castro were frosty. Most priests left the country and some joined the émigrés in Miami, where connections are still strong. By the late 1970s, the Vatican's condemnation of the US embargo helped towards a gradual reconciliation. In 1979, the Pope was invited to visit Cuba on his way back from a trip to Mexico, but he also received an invitation from the Cuban émigrés in Miami. Caught between a rock and a hard place, the Pope opted to go to the Bahamas instead. In the 1980s, Castro issued visas to foreign priests and missionaries and allowed the import of bibles, as well as giving permission for new churches to be built.

In 1994, Cardinal Jaime Ortega was appointed by the Vatican to fill the position left vacant in Cuba since the last cardinal died in 1963. A ban on religious believers joining the Communist Party has been lifted and Protestant, Catholic and other church leaders have reported rising congregations. In the archdiocese of Havana, there were 7500 baptisms in 1979 but this figure shot up to 34,800 in 1994.

In 1996, Fidel visited Pope John Paul II at the Vatican and the Pope visited Cuba in January 1998. Castro has stated in the past that there is no conflict between Marxism and Christianity and has been sympathetic towards supporters of liberation theology in their quest for equality and a just distribution of social wealth. During the Pope's visit to Brazil in October 1997, he criticized free market ideology which promotes excessive individualism and undermines the role of society, which he further emphasized in his visit to Cuba. The two septuagenarians clearly shared common ground on the need for social justice, although they were poles apart on the family, marriage, abortion and contraception, let alone totalitarianism and violent Revolution. At the Pope's request, Castro decreed 25 December 1997 a public holiday, initially for one year only, but it is now a regular event. Christmas Day was abolished in the 1960s because it interfered with the sugar harvest; a whole generation grew up without it and many people were unsure of its religious significance when it was reinstated. Nevertheless, artificial Christmas trees sold out and tinsel and religious imagery were to be found in many homes.

Pope Benedict XVI visited Cuba in 2012 to mark the 400th anniversary of the discovery of the Virgin of Charity statue now in El Cobre. President Raúl Castro attended

BACKGROUND
The Orishas

Every *toque de santo* begins and ends with the evocation of **Elegguá**, lord of the roads and crossroads and guardian of our destiny, dressed always in red and black. In the calendar of Christian saints he is equated with the Child of Prague. Most powerful *orisha* of all is red-clad **Changó**, lord of fire, thunder, war, drums and virility, who is syncretized with St Barbara. *Santeros* believe he was born of **Yemayá**, alter ego of the Virgin of Regla, Havana Bay's patron saint. Dressed in blue and white, she is mistress of the seas and goddess of motherhood.

Oggún (St Peter) is another war god and patron of blacksmiths. Brother to **Changó**, he is also his rival for the affection of **Yemayá**'s sensual dancing sister **Ochún**, the yellow-clad goddess of rivers and springs, beauty and sexual love. Christianized as the Virgin of Charity of El Cobre, she is Cuba's patron saint. Her shrine at the Basilica of El Cobre, outside Santiago de Cuba, is always filled with fragrant *mariposas*, the national flower, and the walls are hung with countless offerings from those whose prayers have been answered, including crutches, sachets of Angolan earth brought by returning veterans, a medallion left by Fidel Castro's mother after his safe return from the guerrilla struggle, and Hemingway's Nobel Prize.

Olofi or **Olorun**, syncretized as both the Eternal Father and the Holy Spirit, is the supreme creator of all things, but, say *santeros*, takes little interest in our world, and long ago handed over the care of it to **Obatalá** who, dressed all in white like his devotees or *hijos* (children), is god of peace, truth, wisdom and justice. In Christian guise he is Our Lady of Mercy. His son is **Orula** (colours: yellow and green), syncretized as St Francis of Assisi and others. Known also as **Ifá**, he is the ancient, implacable lord of divination. Unlike other *orishas*, who 'descend on' and possess their *hijos*, he communicates only with the *babalawo* or priest who interprets his predictions. Divination of what the future holds is a central feature of Regla de Ocha, and may be achieved through casting the *ékuele*, a set of eight pieces of turtle or coconut shell.

Other popular *orishas* include **Oyá** (St Teresa of Ávila), mistress of the winds and lightning, queen of the cemetery; and **Babalú Ayé**. Dressed in bishop's purple, covered in sores, limping along on crutches and followed by stray dogs, he is the deity of leprosy and venereal and skin diseases. Every 17 December thousands of his followers, make the pilgrimage to the chapel of St Lazarus, his Christian manifestation, at El Rincón on the southern outskirts of Havana.

Mass celebrated by the pontiff in the Plaza de la Revolución in Santiago and later they participated in talks in Havana. Relations were cordial, and the Pope declared he had no time in his busy schedule to meet with dissidents, although the government had taken the precaution of arresting dozens prior to his visit. Soon afterwards, in 2013, Pope Benedict retired and was replaced by the Argentine, Pope Francis, and it was under his stewardship that secret negotiations between Cuba and the USA were held in the Vatican and in Canada. The thaw in relations was announced at the end of 2014 (see page 413), and in 2015, Pope Francis visited Cuba and the USA. He did not criticize Cuba's human rights record, taking instead a more pragmatic approach and concentrating on religious matters. Raúl Castro met him at the airport and attended Mass; the Pope also met with Fidel Castro.

Afro-Cuban religion

From the mid-16th century to the late 19th century, countless hundreds of thousands of African slaves were brought to Cuba. Torn from dozens of peoples between the Gulf of Guinea and southern Angola, speaking hundreds of languages and dialects, they brought from home only a memory of their customs and beliefs as a shred of comfort in their traumatic new existence on the sugar plantations. The most numerous and culturally most influential group were the Yoruba-speaking agriculturalists from the forests of southeast Nigeria, Dahomey and Togo, who became known collectively in Cuba as *lucumí*. It is their pantheon of deities or *orishas*, and the legends (*pwatakis*) and customs surrounding these, which form the basis of the syncretic Regla de Ocha cult, better known as **Santería**.

Although slaves were ostensibly obliged to become Christians, their owners, anxious to prevent different ethnic groups from uniting, turned a blind eye to their traditional rituals. The Catholic saints thus spontaneously merged or syncretized in the *lucumí* mind with the *orishas*, whose imagined attributes they shared.

While the Yoruba recognize 400 or more regional or tribal *orishas*, their Cuban descendants have forgotten, discarded or fused together most of these, so that today barely two dozen regularly receive tribute at the rites known as *toques de santo* (see box, opposite).

Santería, which claims to have at least as many believers as the Roman Catholic Church in Cuba, in all walks of life including Communist Party members, enshrines a rich cultural heritage. For every *orisha* there is a complex code of conduct, dress (including colour-coded necklaces) and diet to which his or her *hijos* must conform, and a series of chants and rhythms played on the sacred *batá* drums.

Santería is non-sectarian and non-proselytizing, co-existing peacefully with both Christianity and the **Regla Conga** or **Palo Monte** cult brought to Cuba by *congos*, slaves from various Bantu-speaking regions of the Congo basin. Indeed many people are practising believers in both or all three. Found mainly in Havana and Matanzas provinces, **Palo Monte** is a much more fragmented and impoverished belief system than **Regla de Ocha**, and has borrowed aspects from it and other sources. Divided into several sects, the most important being the *mayomberos*, *kisimberos* and *briyumberos*, it is basically animist, using the forces of nature to perform good or evil magic and predict the future in ceremonies involving rum, tobacco and at times gunpowder. The focus of its liturgy is the *nganga*, both a supernatural spirit and the earthenware or iron container in which it dwells along with the *mpungus* or saints. **Regla Conga** boasts a wealth of complex magic symbols or *firmas*, and has retained some exciting drum rhythms.

The **Abakuá Secret Society** is, as its name suggests, not a religion but a closed sect. Open to men only, and upholding traditional *macho* virtues, it has been described as an Afro-Cuban freemasonry, although it claims many non-black devotees. Found almost exclusively in Havana (particularly in the Guanabacoa, Regla and Marianao districts), and in the cities of Matanzas, Cárdenas and Cienfuegos, it has a strong following among dock-workers; indeed, outsiders often claim its members have *de facto* control over those ports. Also known as **ñañiguismo**, the sect originated among slaves brought from the Calabar region of southern Nigeria and Cameroon, whose Cuban descendants are called *carabalí*. Some **ñáñigos** claim the society was formally founded in 1836 in Regla, across the bay from Havana, but there is evidence that it already existed at the time of the 1812

BACKGROUND
The Afro Trail

It is not so long since traditionalist believers were scandalized when the renowned jazz and salsa band **Irakere** started to use the sacred *cueros batá* (the three drums used in *Santería* rites) on stage. In these times, when all's fair in the scramble for tourist dollars, you may well find a more-or-less Disneyfied all-singing, all-dancing version of *lucumí* or congo ceremonies on offer as part of your hotel's entertainment. Enjoy the spectacle but season liberally with salt.

Alternatively you can witness expertly choreographed and largely genuine performances of Yoruba and Congo devotional and profane song and dance, as well as the intricacies of the *real rumba* in all its variants, at the Sábado de la Rumba sessions put on by the **Conjunto Folklórico Nacional** on Saturday afternoons at their Calle 4 headquarters in Vedado. Despite the colourful trappings, this is only incidentally a spectacle for tourists, who are regularly outnumbered by the Cubans fervidly chorusing the *santero* chants in Yoruba and swaying to the infectious *guaguancó*. The **Casa de Africa** (see page 52) is an untaxing and pleasant way to get a glimpse of the wealth of African cultures, in Cuba and in Africa itself. As well as small collections from various African countries, it houses the Afro-Cuban devotional artifacts collected by the late Don Fernando Ortiz, the founding father of Afro-Cuban ethnographic studies.

Also worth a visit is the **Museo Municipal de Regla** (see page 102). The most atmospheric way to reach Regla is by *lanchita* (ferry) across the bay from the terminal near the Plaza de Armas. The collection of history of African religions in Cuba, formerly in the **Museo Histórico de Guanabacoa** (see page 103) in the district popularly regarded as the Mecca of Afro-Cuban cults, is now in the Casa de Africa. Any *habanero* afflicted by aches and pains or generally down in the mouth will sooner or later be advised, "What you need is a trip to Guanabacoa."

anti-slavery conspiracy. **Abakuá** shares with freemasonry the fraternal aims of mutual assistance, as well as a series of seven secret commandments, secret signs and arcane ceremonies involving special vestments.

Land &
environment

Geology and landscape

Geologically at least, Cuba is part of North America; the boundary between the North American and Caribbean plates runs east–west under the Caribbean Sea to the south of the island. Along the plate margin is a deep underwater rift valley, which runs between Cuba and Jamaica. This feature is quite close to the Cuban coast to the south of the Sierra Maestra, with water plunging to 6000 m only a few miles offshore. Earth movements along the plate boundary make the eastern region of Cuba the most earthquake-prone part of the country, with earthquakes in Bayamo in 1551 and Santiago de Cuba in 1932.

Current plate movements are pushing Cuba to the west and the Caribbean plate to the east. What is now the Sierra Maestra in southern Cuba was probably joined 40 million years ago to geologically similar areas on the north coast of Haiti and the Dominican Republic. Plate movements since then have caused a displacement of around 400 km. Cuba is also being tilted gradually to the north. The northern coastline is gradually emerging from the sea. Old coral reefs have been brought to the surface, and now form much of the coastline, so that much of the northern coast consists of coral limestone cliffs and sandy beaches. A short way inland, old cliff lines marking stages of coastal emergence form a series of coral terraces, one of which runs just northeast of the **Hotel Nacional** in Havana. There are well-developed series of old cliff lines and coral terraces on the southeast tip of the island near Baracoa and to the west of Santiago near Cabo Cruz. By contrast the southern coastline is being gradually submerged, producing a series of wetlands and mangroves running from the Ensenada de Cortés in the west to the Gulf of Guacanayabo in the east, with fewer sandy beaches than the north of the island.

During the glacial periods of the last million years, sea levels worldwide fell by about 120 m; as much of the world's water was locked up in the northern ice sheets. The shallow seas which now form Cuba's continental shelf were dry land, and the coastline generally followed the line of Cuba's 4000-plus offshore islands: the Sabana island chain to the north and the Canarreos and Jardines de la Reina to the south. At this time, central Cuba was separated from the Bahamas by a narrow channel, about 32 km wide.

Cave systems which formed during glacial periods in what were then coastal limestone plains have since been flooded by the sea. In coastal areas such as the western Guanahacabibes peninsula and Playa Girón, there are small, deep lakes known to English-speaking geologists as Blue Holes where these submerged cave systems meet the surface.

There is no clear agreement about Cuba's more distant geological origins. The curve of the island follows the line of a collision in the Cretaceous period around 100 million years ago between an arc of volcanic islands and the stable Bahamas platform which then formed the southern edge of the North American plate. There is disagreement about whether this arc faced north or south, and about how the collision took place. But the powerful forces associated with the process produced a complex pattern of folding and faulting, while many rocks were greatly altered by heat and pressure. Many of Cuba's rocks predate this collision. These include the Caribbean's only pre-Cambrian rocks, metamorphics more than 900 million years old in the province of Santa Clara; and the Jurassic limestones, around 160 million years old, which form the Sierra de los Organos.

After the collision, what is now Cuba was submerged for long periods, and there were new deposits of limestone and other rocks. For most of the tertiary period, from 35 million years ago, Cuba was a series of large islands and shallow seas, emerging as a single land mass by the start of the Pliocene period five million years ago. Limestones of various types cover about two-thirds of the island. In most areas, there is a flat or gently rolling landscape. The most common soils, both formed on limestone, are terra rossa, stained bright red by iron oxides, and vertisols, black, fertile, and developing deep cracks during the dry season.

There are three main mountain areas in the island. In the west, the Cordillera de Guaniguanico is divided into the Sierra del los Organos in the west, with thick deposits of limestone which have developed a distinctive landscape of steep-sided flat-topped mountains; and the Sierra del Rosario in the east, made up partly of limestones and partly of lavas and other igneous rocks. Another mountainous area in central Cuba includes the Escambray mountains north of Trinidad, a double dome structure made up of igneous and metamorphic rocks, including marble.

The Sierra Maestra in the east has Cuba's highest mountains, rising to Pico Turquino (1974 m) and a different geological history, with some rocks formed in an arc of volcanic activity around 50 million years ago. Older rocks include marble, and other metamorphics. The country's most important mineral deposits are in this area; nickel mined near Moa is the third largest foreign currency earner, after tourism and sugar.

For those interested in further information on the physical and human geography of Cuba, the *Nuevo Atlas Nacional de Cuba* (Geocuba, Calle F y 13, Havana, T7-323494) provides a beautifully produced series of detailed thematic maps on every possible topic down to the distribution of ants and spiders, with informative commentaries.

Flora and fauna

When the Spanish arrived at the end of the 15th century, more than 90% of Cuba was covered with forest. When Fray Bartolomé de las Casas visited the island, he said *"La isla tiene de luengo cerca de 300 leguas y se puede andar toda por debajo de los árboles"* (the island is 300 leagues long and you can walk the length of it beneath the trees). However, clearance for cattle raising and sugar cane reduced this proportion to 54% by 1890 and 14% by 1959, although reafforestation since the Revolution has increased this figure. Some 75% of the land is now savannah or plains, 18% mountains and 4% swamps. The mesophytic semi-deciduous tropical woodland which covered most low-lying areas was hardest hit by forest clearance. Besides semi-deciduous woodland, vegetation types include rainforest, coastal and upland scrub, distinctive limestone vegetation found in the Sierra de los Organos and similar areas, savannah vegetation found on nutrient-deficient white silica sands, pine forests, xerophytic coastal limestone woodland, mangroves and other bird-rich coastal wetlands.

Cuba is characterized by extraordinarily high rates of biodiversity and endemism, particularly concentrated in four regions: the **Montañas de Moa-Nipe-Sagua-Baracoa**, which have the greatest diversity in all the Caribbean and are among the highest in the world, and 30% of the endemic species on the island; **Parque Nacional Sierra de los Organos** and the **Reserva de la Biósfera Sierra del Rosario** come a close second, with high rates of endemism, followed closely by the **Reserva Ecológica del Macizo de Guamuhaya**. There is a high proportion of endemic species, found only in Cuba, one region of Cuba, or in the extreme case of some snail species, only on one small mountain in the Sierra de los Organos. Around half the plant species, 90% of the insects and molluscs, 82% of the reptiles and 74 bird species are endemic.

Why the high proportion of endemics? Cuba has a five million-year history as an isolated land mass, with species following their own evolutionary path. There are also a number of specialized environments with geological or soil constraints such as chemical toxicity, poor water retention, low nutrient retention, on ultrabasic igneous rocks, silica sands and limestones. A catalogue is in preparation of all the flora and fauna found in Cuba's protected areas as well as a large percentage of those outside the reserves.

Flora

There are over 7000 plant species in Cuba, of which around 3000 are endemic, and 950 plant species that are endangered, rare, or have become extinct in the last 350 years. Oddities in the plant world include the **Pinguicola lignicola**, the world's only carniverous epiphytic plant; the **cork palm** (*Microcycas colocoma*), an endemic living fossil which is a threatened species; and the **Solandra grandiflora**, one of the world's largest flowers, 10 cm across at the calyx and 30 cm at the corolla.

There are around 100 different palm trees in Cuba, of which 90 are endemic. The Royal palm (*Roystonea regia*) is one of four species of *Roystonia*; it is the national tree and can be seen in the countryside throughout the island. Cubans use the small, purple fruits to feed pigs, as they are oily and nutritious. They develop in bunches below the crown shaft, which can weigh 20-25 kg. They would naturally drop one by one when ripe, but they are usually harvested before then by *trepadores*, men who skilfully climb the trunk of the palm by means of two slings, one supporting the thigh and another supporting a foot. You can also see many flowering trees: pines, oaks, cedars, etc, although original forest is confined to some of the highest points in the southeast mountains and the mangroves of the Zapata Peninsula.

There are a multitude of flowers and in the country even the smallest of houses has a flower garden at the front. The **orchid** family includes some 300 endemic species, but more are constantly being discovered. You can find orchids all over the island, especially in the mountainous regions, some of which live above 700 m. There is one tiny orchid, *Pleurothallis shaferi*, which is only 1 cm, with leaves measuring 5 mm and flowers of only 2 mm. The orchidarium at Soroa has over 700 examples of orchids and other flowers. To complement the wide variety of butterflies that can be found here, the butterfly flower, **mariposa**, a type of jasmine, has been named the national flower.

Fauna

Animal life is also varied, with nearly 14,000 species of fauna, of which 10% could be on the verge of extinction: 250 vertebrate species are endangered, rare or have become extinct in the last 350 years. The total number includes 54 mammals (40% endemic), 330 species of bird (8 genus, 22 species, 32 endemic sub-species), 106 reptile (81% endemic), 42 amphibian (93% endemic), over 1700 mollusc (87% endemic), 7000 insect and 1200 arachnid, as well as a variety of marine species.

There are no native large mammals but some genera and families have diversified into a large number of distinct island species. These include mammals such as the **hutia** (*Capromys*: 10 species, *jutía* in Spanish), a rodent, **bats** (26 species, Cuba has more species of bat per sq km than all North America) and the protected **manatee** with more than

20 breeding groups, mostly in the Ciénaga de Zapata and north of Villa Clara. Reptiles range from three types of crocodile including the **Cuban crocodile** (*Crocodylus rhombifer*) now found only in the Ciénaga de Zapata (there is a farm on the Zapata Peninsula) to iguanas to tiny salamanders. An **iguana**, *Cyclura nubila*, found only in Cuba and the Cayman Islands, is in danger of extinction. Cuba claims the smallest of a number of animals, for instance the **Cuban pygmy frog** (*Eleutherodactylus limbatus*, 12 mm long, one of some 30 small frogs), the **almiquí** (*Selenodon cubanus*, a shrew-like insectivore, the world's smallest mammal, found only in the Sierra de Nipe-Sagua-Baracoa), the **butterfly** or **moth bat** (*Natalus lepidus*, 186 mm, 2 g, often confused with moths at night, it eats mosquitoes) and the **bee hummingbird** (*mellisuga helenae*, 63 mm long, called locally the *zunzuncito*). The latter is an endangered species, like the **carpintero real woodpecker** (*Campephilus principalis*), the **cariara** or **caracara** (*Caracara plancus*, a hawk-like bird of the savannah), the **pygmy owl** (*Glaucidium siju*), the **Cuban green parrot** (*Amazona leucocephala*) and the **fermina**, or **Zapata wren** (*Ferminia cerverai*). Less attractively, there is also a **dwarf scorpion** (*Microtytus fundorai*, *alacrán* in Spanish, 10 mm long).

The best place for **birdwatching** on the island is the Zapata Peninsula, where 170 species of Cuban bird have been recorded, including the majority of endemic species. In winter the number increases as migratory waterbirds, swallows and others visit the marshes. The area around Santo Tomás contains rare birds such as the **Zapata rail**, the **Zapata wren** and the **Zapata sparrow** (*Torreornis inexpectata*, or *cabrerito de la Ciénaga*). The national bird is the forest-dwelling **Cuban trogon** (*Priotelus temnurus*, the *tocororo*), partly because of its blue head, white chest and red underbelly, the colours of the Cuban flag. Other good birdwatching places include La Güira and Soroa, west of Havana, Cayo Coco on the north coast and Najasa, southeast of Camagüey (contact local biologist Pedro Regalado), but there is no shortage of opportunities for spotting endemics anywhere on the island.

Protected areas

The first national park, the **Parque Nacional Pico Cristal**, was established in 1930, but with little regulation and less financing. Conservation only really got started in Cuba with the passing of Law 27 in 1980, which provided funds and legislation to set up more parks. They started in the **Sierra Maestra**, where there are now 13 parks, reserves and refuges. In 1985, UNESCO started working with Cuba in selecting first-class sites, collecting data on biodiversity and endemic species, highlighting the need to give priority to conservation and give total protection in some areas. Within a year a coordinating committee had set out financing needs and donations began to come in to develop the first international reserves in Cuba. Four biosphere reserves were established as pilot programmes and education programmes were offered to neighbouring communities on conservation and sustainable development. In 1991, a consultative group was formed which set up a new national system of protected areas: **Sistema Nacional de Areas Protegidas** (SNAP, www.snap.cu), and proposed 73 reserves. Overnight, 12% of Cuba's territory was protected, taking in 96% of vegetation and 321 species of vertebrate. Cuba also ratified the Cartagena Agreement for the protection of the marine environment and certain UNESCO conventions on World Heritage sites and Biosphere Reserves. In 1995, a new strategy was adopted, reorganizing the national environmental plan with the formation of 12 institutions. The key agency is the **Centro Nacional para las Areas Protegidas** (CNAP), which, together with the **Centro de Información, Gestión y Educación Ambiental** (CIGEA, www.cuba.cu/cigea/cigea.htm), now has responsibility for the protection of the natural environment.

A new environmental law passed in 1997 strengthened the legal framework for wildlife conservation. There is now a comprehensive system of protected areas covering 30% of Cuba, including its marine platform, and incorporating examples of more than 96% of Cuba's vegetation types, 95% of plant species and almost all terrestrial vertebrates. There are 11 categories of protection: *reserva natural, parque nacional, reserva ecológica, elemento natural destacado, reserva florística manejada, refugio de fauna, parque natural, área natural turística, área protegida recursos manejados, área protegida de uso múltiple* and *área protegida sin categoría*. These areas include 14 national parks and six UNESCO biosphere reserves: **Guanahacabibes** in the extreme western tip of the island; the **Sierra del Rosario**, 60 km west of Havana; Ciénaga de Zapata, an extensive ecosystem made up of mangrove forests, keys, seagrass beds, coral reef barriers and deep reefs; Buenavista on the north coast covering land and sea; **Baconao** in the east and **Cuchillas del Toa**. However, not all legally established conservation areas have any infrastructure, personnel or administration in place.

In practice, Cuba's record on preservation of species is not perfect. Crocodiles, highly endangered at the time of the Revolution were subsequently protected and breeding programmes were set up. Now that numbers have been brought to a healthy level in captivity, crocodiles are farmed, killed for their meat, skin and teeth, which are exported. Black coral, protected by CITES, is openly sold as jewellery. Despite the SPAW agreement, to which Cuba is a signatory, dolphins are caught in the wild and kept in dolphinariums for tourists' amusement or allegedly exported to other Caribbean islands for the same purpose. No zoo in the world now takes animals caught in the wild, relying instead on breeding in captivity, but Cuba does not apply this rule to dolphinariums.

National parks

Parque Nacional Alejandro von Humboldt 59,771 ha in the Montañas de Toa, near Moa, ranging in altitude from 20 m to 1168 m, and established with assistance from the German NGO, Green Gold. It is the nucleus of the **Cuchillas del Toa UNESCO Biosphere Reserve**, and basically the union of a group of reserves: Cupeyal del Norte, Ojito de Agua, Jaguaní, Alto de Iberia, Taco and Yamaniguey. This tropical woodland has examples of 16 of Cuba's 28 vegetation types and has the highest rate of endemism, with 150 species found only in this area. Of the 64 species of bird that have been recorded, 12 are endemic. Endangered species include the *Carpintero real*, the *almiquí*, the Cuban kite (*Chondrohierax wilsonii*, known in Spanish as the *gavilán caguarero*), the Cuban parakeet (*Aratinga euops*, or *catey* in Spanish), the Cuban parrot (*Amazona leucocephala*, or *cotorra* in Spanish) and the manatee.

Parque Nacional Turquino 17,450 ha national park in the Sierra Maestra, including Cuba's highest mountains: the Pico Turquino (1974 m), the Pico Suecia (1934 m) and the Pico Cuba (1872 m), it is managed in collaboration with WWF Canada. This park contains humid montane forest and has a high percentage of endemics, *Juniperus saxicola* trees, fruit-bearing *Rubus turquinensis*, and small frogs, *Eleutherodactylus albipes* and *Eleutherodactylus turquinensis*.

Parque Nacional Desembarco de Granma Includes the marine terraces of Cabo Cruz, 25,764 ha, which is managed in collaboration with WWF Canada. This is the world's second biggest series of marine coral terraces, a staircase-like formation of 22 old shorelines and sea cliffs formed on emerging coral coast, with dry tropical forest and mangrove. There have been 58 endemic plant species recorded here and the fauna includes species like the primitive lizard (*Cricosaura typica*) and a brightly coloured snail (*Ligus vittatus*), which only lives in a small area of the park. There is a network of interpretative paths, archaeological sites with petroglyphs and pictographs, manatees, and diving on the offshore reef.

BACKGROUND
Crocodiles

The endemic crocodile in Cuba, the *Rhombifer*, was facing extinction under the Batista dictatorship and it was only in 1959 after the Revolution that it gained a reprieve. A serious effort was made to set up farms and breed the species, with a programme to release some of the offspring into the wild.

There are now several crocodile farms around the island, but one of the most visited by tourists is at Guamá in the Zapata peninsula (see page 170). Here the animals are graded according to size and age and there are 25 sections containing a total of some 2000 crocodiles. A visitor will see only a small part of the farm, with a selection of crocs on display, from a group of 5-10 months old measuring less than a metre, to one of four years old with his mouth tied up so that he can be made to pose to be touched and photographed. The path circles some ponds in which you can see fully grown monsters which can live up to 100 years. They often lounge on the banks with their mouths open to regulate their temperature, giving you a good view of their teeth.

A crocodile reaches maturity at six years, laying eggs in the spring. It eats only once a week and its diet in Cuba is enlivened by dead or sick and dying domestic animals brought by their owners for disposal. As farmed creatures, the crocodiles' skin, meat and teeth are used and exported.

According to CITES they are endangered in the wild, but by farming them Cuba now has thousands of crocodiles in captivity. These farmed animals are used for meat and their skins are used in leather goods, but there is a CITES ban on the export of crocodile products. You will find farmed crocodile on menus in a few places in Cuba, which you can try if you wish. Wild crocodile is not permitted.

Parque Nacional La Bayamesa   21,100 ha in the Sierra Maestra around Pico Bayamesa (1730 m), north of Uvero.

Parque Nacional La Mensura Pilotos (Pinares de Mayarí)   5340 ha in the Altiplanicie de Nipe of pine forests with traditional coffee and livestock farming, while also home to 460 endemic species. There are interpretative paths, some ecotourism and you can see parrots.

Parque Nacional Pico Cristal   16,010 ha in the Sierra de Cristal of pine forest and broadleaved humid tropical forest, where you can find parrots and nightingales (*Myadestes elizebeth*) and possibly the *almiquí*. There is no administration yet in place. This was the first protected area in Cuba, dating from 1930, although it was never managed as such until recently.

Parque Nacional Caguanes   22,690 ha (5387 on land and 17,303 under water) in the Cayería Caibarién Caguanes, a group of small islands just offshore. Cayo Caguanes, which gives its name to the park, has 25 caves on only 1.1 sq km and is joined to the mainland by mangroves. Some caves have endemic invertebrates and a rare fresh water sponge has been found in flooded caves. They are also sites of prehistoric interest, with cave drawings and 40 archaeological sites. The park is also home to one of the 10 colonies in Cuba of sandhill cranes, known locally as *grulla* (*Grus canadensis nesiotes*), a tall, long-legged bird with a long neck which it stretches out in front of it when flying. In 2009 more caves were discovered on Cayo Fábrica, with a colony of butterfly bats.

Parque Nacional Viñales 21,600 ha in the Sierra de los Organos, with the distinctive mogotes. There is no administration in place for these limestone uplands with extensive cave systems (Santo Tomás and Palmarito are thought to be the largest in the Caribbean) and distinctive xerophytic vegetation, where you can find sierra palm (*Gausio princeps*), ceibón (*Bombracopsis cubensis*) and cork palm (*Mycrocicas calocoma*). Several types of snails have become so isolated that they live only on one part of a mogote.

Parque Nacional Marino Punta Francés, Punta Pedernales 17,924 ha of marine platform going down to 200 m, with untouched coral formations and abundant flora and fauna. There is no park management as such, but it is looked after by the International Diving Centre at Marina El Colony, Isla de la Juventud.

Reserva Ecológica Los Indios-San Felipe A 3050-ha reserve on the white-sand plains of Isla de la Juventud, administered in collaboration with WWF Canada. As well as exceptional bird life, there is pine-covered savannah with 24 endemics and the carniverous plants of the genera *drosera*, *pinguicola* and *utricularia*. Many plants and trees have adapted to become resistant to fire. As a result of management and protection of the area, it is now the site of one of the largest nesting groups of Cuban parrot, and is another of the sites for the sandhill crane.

Reserva Ecológica El Naranjal 3,068-ha reserve in the Guamuhaya mountains at an altitude of 70-870 m, where you can find the Cuban parrot, the Cuban parakeet and the *jutía conga (Capromys pilorides)*. Over 600 plant species have been recorded here, of which 22% are endemic and 12 are found nowhere else. An area of 12,494 ha in the Guamuhaya mountains (or Sierra del Escambray) is classified as **Paisaje Natural Protegido Topes de Collantes**, or protected natural landscape. Topes de Collantes is a popular hiking excursion from Trinidad. Abundant rainfall encourages mosses, lichens, ferns, orchids and other vegetation, home to many birds and invertebrates.

Reserva Ecológica Punta Negra-Punta de Quemados On the Maisí marine terraces are 3972 ha of the world's largest and best developed system of marine coral terraces, with 27 levels and the driest natural environment in Cuba, many endemic, and some unique plants. A substantial part of the first three levels is included in the reserve.

Refugio de Fauna Santo Tomás y Las Salinas These are two reserves which form the basis of the 70,277-ha **Parque Nacional Ciénaga de Zapata,** the main core area of the Biosphere Reserve and the Ramsar site that have the same name, and of the Gran Parque Natural Montemar. There is rich bird life here, in what is the largest wetland in the Caribbean. More than 170 species of bird have been recorded. At Las Salinas there are huge populations of waterbirds and at Santo Tomás there are two species found nowhere else in the world, the Zapata rail, known as the *gallinuela de Santo Tomás* (*Cyanolimnas cerverai*), and the Zapata wren, known as ferminia (*Ferminia cerverai*). The Zapata rail is dark, with a mixture of olive brown on top, slate grey underneath and on its forehead and cheeks, without any spots or streaks, except for white tips to its flank feathers and conspicuously white under its tail. Its bill is green, with red at its base, it has red feet and very short wings, so it does not fly very well. The Zapata wren measures 16 cm, it has short wings and a long tail, has a spotted head, greyish brown back with black bars and whitish underparts. It lives in the dense bushes and hardly ever flies but it has a loud voice, with a varied, musical warbling. There are also crocodiles (*Crocodylus rhombifer*), which are endemic, and the manatee, or sea cow.

Refugio de Fauna Silvestre Río Máximo 12,500 ha of mangroves on the north Camagüey coast, with saline and freshwater lakes and semi-deciduous coastal woodlands. It is a major site for flamingos with two colonies of some 4000 birds and the world's largest nesting population. There is also a large population of the American crocodile (*Crocodylus acutus*). Largest of all, however, is the number of water fowl which migrate here in season, when tens of thousands of duck (*Anas*, 11 species), glossy ibis (*Plegadis falcinellus*), white ibis (*Eudocimus albus*) (both known locally as *cocos*), roseate spoonbill (*Ajaia ajaia*) and other birds can be seen.

Refugio de Fauna Silvestre Río Cauto Delta Just north of Manzanillo, 60,000 ha of mangroves, hypersaline and freshwater lakes and wetlands, which are rich in bird life as well as home to flamingos and the American crocodile.

Refugio de Fauna Silvestre Hatibonica 5220 ha refuge overlooking the US naval base at Guantánamo Bay, with sparsely vegetated hill country and varied fauna including iguanas (*Cyclura nubila nubila*) and endemic cacti. Strange wind-blown, variegated rock formations, called *Monitongos*, characterize this arid landscape. There is an interpretative path: Los Monitongos.

Area Protegida de Recursos Manejados Cayos del Norte de Villa Clara 17,500-ha protected area above and below water down to 20 m in the Sabana de Camagüey archipelago, part of **Parque Nacional Cayo Guillermo Santa María**. Wildlife includes the second largest colony of manatees in the country around the Cayos del Pajonal, hutia or *jutía rata* (*Capromys auritus*) on Cayo Fragoso, flamingos on Las Picuas, iguanas on Cayo Cobo and endemic birds and reptiles on Cayo Francés and Cayo Santa María.

Reserva de la Biósfera Guanahacabibes On the extreme western tip of the island, covering 101,500 ha of 'dogstooth' landscape of bare limestone, with scattered pockets of soil and dry coastal evergreen and semi-deciduous woodland. Terraces and beaches are interspersed along the coast. There are two well-established nuclei of the biosphere reserve, **Reserva Natural El Veral** and **Reserva Natural Cabo Corrientes**, where an ecological station carries out research.

Reserva de la Biósfera Sierra del Rosario 25,000 ha of the Sierra del Rosario mountain range, with the best example of evergreen forest in western Cuba. There are three nuclei in the reserve, El Salón, Las Peladas and Las Terrazas, where there is an ecological station and the local community is directly involved with protecting the environment. Birdwatching is rewarding and you may see the bee hummingbird. There are nearly 800 plant species, of which 34% are endemic.

Reserva de la Biósfera Baconao 80,000 ha along the foothills of the Sierra Maestra, stretching east from Santiago de Cuba to Laguna Baconao. The reserve includes many tourist facilities such as hotels, a dolphinarium, the Valle de la Prehistoria and others, but the fauna and flora in the park are varied, with many endemic species.

Books

Architecture

Guía de Arquitectura La Habana Colonial *La Habana (1995)*, Sevilla. Useful guide to Old Havana, with maps, ground plans and photos.

Culture

Calder, Simon and Hatchwell, Emily *In Focus: Cuba, A Guide to the People, Politics and Culture (1999)*, Latin America Bureau (ISBN 0-906156 -95-5). One of an excellent series of books on Latin America and the Caribbean, covering history, economics, politics and culture.

Daniel, Yvonne *Rumba, Dance and Social Change in Contemporary Cuba (1995)*, Indiana University Press. Also in the series: *Blacks in the Diaspora* (ISBN 0-253-31605-7, paperback ISBN 0-253-20948-X). A good general book on Cuba as well as on music, portrait of life on the streets, the author is a professional dancer who completed her research in 1991.

Lumsden, Ian *Machos, Maricones and Gays, Cuba and Homosexuality (1996)*, Temple University Press, Philadelphia, also published in the UK by Latin American Bureau. Very readable account of the attitudes of Cubans towards gays since the days of slavery, with related treatment of blacks and women.

Pérez Sarduy, Pedro and Stubbs, Jean (Editors) *AfroCuba, an Anthology of Cuban Writing on Race, Politics and Culture (1993)*, Ocean Press, Melbourne, Australia, also by the Latin American Bureau (ISBN 0-906156-75-0). Collection of fiction, theatre, poetry, history and political commentary, dealing with the relationship between Africa and Cuba.

Literature and fiction

Arenas, Reinaldo *Antes que Anochezca (Before Night Falls, 1994, Viking)*. Autobiography of a homosexual growing up in Cuba after the Revolution, facing persecution, censorship and imprisonment. Arenas left Cuba in the Mariel boat lift but never settled in the USA, finally committing suicide in 1990 aged 47, when dying of AIDS.

Cabrera Infante, Guillermo *Tres Tristes Tigres (1967)* (Three Trapped Tigers, 1989, Faber & Faber). One of the funniest novels in Spanish, a tableau of Havana's nightlife in the time of Batista, written after the author emigrated.

Ferguson, James *The Traveller's Literary Companion, The Caribbean (1997)*, Windrush Press. A good introduction to Cuban literature and writings on Cuba, with chapters by Jason Wilson. Includes a good reading list.

García, Cristina *Dreaming in Cuban (1992)* Flamingo, London (1982) Knopf, New York. Cuba as seen by 3 generations of women, the grandmother who stayed behind, the daughter who emigrated to the USA and the granddaughter, who returns to visit.

Greene, Graham *Our Man in Havana: An Entertainment (1958)*, William Heinemann. Spy thriller set in Havana at the end of the Batista regime as the Revolutionaries close in.

Gutiérrez, Pedro Juan *Dirty Havana Trilogy, translated by Natasha Wimmer (2001)*, Faber and Faber. Pedro Juan gives up his job as a reporter to re-educate himself in his attitude to life and what makes him happy. This involves lots of sex, drugs, rum, music and other good things in life, highly explicit and with insights into what makes Havana tick. A prolific author, many of Gutiérrez' books are semi-autobiographical, told from the perspective of a disillusioned journalist. Not all of his works have been translated into

English yet. www.pedrojuangutierrez.com/biografia_ingles.htm

Padura Fuentes, Leonardo *Havana Quartet: Havana Red, Havana Black, Havana Blue, Havana Gold, translated by Peter Bush (2005, 2006, 2007, 2008)*, Bitter Lemon Press, and *Adiós Hemingway*, translated by John King (2005). Prize-winning detective fiction, all featuring Lieutenant Mario Conde of Havana, whose musings on life in the city, sex, friendship and drinking are as important as the plots, eminently readable, hugely atmospheric, take them with you. *The Man Who Loved Dogs* (2014), Bitter Lemon Press, starts with the premise that the man who murdered Trotsky in Mexico is living in secret exile in Havana. It is the story of revolutions, betrayal and the role of fear in consolidating power. Historical fiction, yet parts read like a thriller. http://leonardopadura.com.

History and society

Castro, Fidel *My Life (2008)*, Ignacio Ramonet (editor), Andrew Hurley (translator), Penguin. Castro's erudition, curiosity and astuteness are displayed here as he tells his story for the first time, from his parents and childhood influences to the US presidents he has known and outlasted.

Chomsky A, Carr B, Smorkaloff PM (editors) *The Cuba Reader: History, Culture, Politics (The Latin American Readers)* (2004) Duke University Press. An impressive and eclectic anthology of songs, paintings, photographs, short stories, essays, speeches, government reports, cartoons and newspaper articles that span Cuban history, written by and about Cubans of all political persuasions, living on and off the island.

Cooke, Julia *The Other Side of Paradise: Life in the New Cuba (2014)*, Avalon Publishing Group. Cooke is a journalist, but travelled in Cuba as a tourist. This book is the result of her encounters with Cubans and her insightful portrayal of the contradictions of Cuban society with the lost hopes and dreams of a generation.

Ferguson, James *A Traveller's History of the Caribbean (1998)*, Windrush Press. Concise and easy to dip into, from Columbus to Castro, with interesting asides on recent issues such as drugs trafficking, characters such as Fidel, and the US influence and intervention throughout the Caribbean.

Frank, Marc *Cuban Revelations: Behind the Scenes in Havana (Contemporary Cuba)* (2013), University Press of Florida. A journalist based in Havana, Frank unveils a portrait of contemporary Cuban politics and society with interviews and analyses of the impact US and Soviet policies have had on Cubans' life today.

Gott, Richard *Cuba: a New History (2004)* Yale University Press. Authoritative, concise and up to date history from pre-Columbian times to the 21st century giving a balanced perspective on the Castro era.

Symmes, Patrick *The Boys from Dolores: Fidel Castro and his Generation from Revolution to Exile (2007)* Robinson. A school photo from 1940 of 230 students at the elite Jesuit Dolores school in Santiago includes the 15-year-old Fidel Castro. This generation was educated to be Cuba's leaders and high-fliers and Symmes tracks them as they experience (or foment) revolution, regime change and, in many cases, exile, in a fascinating and gripping collective biography.

Thomas, Hugh *Cuba, or the Pursuit of Freedom (2002)*, Eyre and Spottiswoode, London. First published in 1971, this is the best history book specifically on Cuba.

Music and dance

Calvo Ospina, Hernando *Salsa! Havana Heat, Bronx Beat (1995)*, Latin American Bureau. An avid salsa dancer traces the development of modern salsa from the slave ships to New York commercial cut-throat business, via *son*, jazz and cha cha cha. Other Latin styles are covered, including Colombian *cumbia* and Dominican Republic *merengue*.

Roy, Maya *Cuban Music (2002)*, Latin American Bureau. Comprehensive and accessible, all you wanted to know about the historical and ethnic roots of Cuban music, the political dimension and the artists involved. Rumba, *danzón*, *son*, *guaracha*, are all explained. It includes the Buena Vista Social Club phenomenon.

Sublette, Ned *Cuba and its Music: From the First Drums to the Mambo (2004)*, Chicago Review Press. A comprehensive and entertaining history of Spain, Africa, the slave trade and Cuba, tracing the development of its music up to 1952 through sociological, political and historical influences and how it went on to influence Latin America and the world.

Travelogues

Miller, Tom *Trading with the Enemy: a Yankee travels through Castro's Cuba (1996)*, Basic Books. Set in the early 1990s this is a sharply observed travelogue. Detailing Miller's encounters with colourful Cubans from bartenders to baseball players, it steers away from political issues.

Smith, Stephen *Land of Miracles (1998)*, Abacus. A quirky travelogue set in the Special Period when times were hard and the Cubans had to be inventive to survive. Written by a British TV Channel 4 reporter, whose search for the real Cuba turns into a search for Castro.

Wildlife

Flieg and Sander *A Photographic Guide to the Birds of the West Indies (2000)*, New Holland Publishers Ltd. A useful pocket guide covering most of the endemics of the Caribbean islands.

Garrido and Kirkconnell *Birds of Cuba (2000)* Helm/Black, London, or Cornell University Press. Essential if you are visiting only Cuba. The best field guide.

Raffaele et al *A Guide to the Birds of the West Indies (1998)*, Princeton University Press. Birdwatching in the wider Caribbean, thorough and heavy.

Practicalities

Getting there

Air

The frequency of scheduled and charter flights depends on the season, with twice-weekly flights in the winter being reduced to once a week in the summer. Some of the longer haul flights, such as from Buenos Aires, are cut from once a week in winter to once a month in summer. Most international flights arrive at Havana's **José Martí** airport, but the international airports of Varadero, Holguín (for Guardalavaca beaches), Santiago de Cuba, Ciego de Avila, Cayo Coco, Cayo Largo, Santa Clara (for Cayo Santa María), Las Tunas, Manzanillo and Camagüey (for Santa Lucía beaches) also receive flights.

Buying a ticket
A **specialist travel agency**, such as **Journey Latin America** or **Cuba Direct**, will be able to get you better deals than anything you can find on the internet. The state airline, **Cubana de Aviación**, has flights from Europe (Madrid, Paris, Rome, Moscow), Canada (Toronto, Montréal), Central America (Managua, San José, Mexico City, Cancún), South America (Bogotá, Buenos Aires) and islands in the Caribbean (Santo Domingo, Fort-de-France). It is cheaper than its competitors but the service is worse, seats are cramped and some travel agents do not recommend it. Charter flights with accommodation packages can be good deals even if you ditch the hotel and tour Cuba independently. Early booking is essential as agents need at least 14 days' notice to get confirmations from Havana. **High seasons** cover the Easter period, the July to August European summer and the last three weeks of December.

Flights from the UK
Direct flights take about nine hours. **Virgin Atlantic** flies from London direct, while **Air France**, **Iberia** and **KLM** operate connecting services via Paris, Madrid and Amsterdam respectively. Indirect flights can be cheaper, but are more time consuming and less comfortable.

Flights from the rest of Europe
Direct flights are available from Amsterdam, Frankfurt, Madrid, Milan, Munich, Paris, Rome and Zurich depending on the season and the Cuban airport. Airlines offering scheduled flights to various Cuban cities include **Air Berlin**, **Condor**, **Swissair** and **Aeroflot**. All flights from Europe arrive in Havana around 2000-2130, returning overnight.

Flights from North America
Since 1962, US citizens have only been permitted to visit Cuba providing they can prove they are travelling for journalistic, cultural, sporting or scientific purposes, although many defied the ban and travelled via a gateway city, such as Nassau, Mexico City, Cancún, or Grand Cayman. However, in 2015 the rules were relaxed allowing 12 categories of travel, and more US citizens are now flying to Cuba on chartered flights from Los Angeles, Miami and Tampa, mostly either on people-to-people programmes or Cuban Americans visiting relatives. In December 2015, the governments of the USA and Cuba announced the resumption of direct commercial flights for the first time since the early 1960s and airlines such as **American Airlines** are expected to start flying in 2016. Up to 30 US flights a day will be allowed.

There are lots of charter and scheduled flights from Canada (Montréal and Toronto) to various airports in Cuba, particularly in winter.

Flights from the Caribbean and Latin America

There are flights from the Dominican Republic, Grand Cayman and Martinique and frequent flights to Havana from several Mexican cities. Avianca ⓘ *www.avianca.com*, flies to Cuba from most Central and South American countries. The Cuban charter airline Aerogaviota ⓘ *www.aerogaviota.com*, also connects Cuba with a growing list of other Caribbean and Central American countries.

Flights from Australia and New Zealand

There are no direct flights to Cuba from Australia or New Zealand; all flights connect in a European, Canadian or Latin American city. Even if you fly **Virgin** all the way, you will have to change airports in London (Heathrow–Gatwick). Round-the-world tickets offer the best deals, with Cuba added onto a South or Central American itinerary.

Airport information

Cuba has several airports classified as international, but Havana's José Martí airport is by far the largest. Terminal 1 is for domestic flights. Terminal 2 is for US charters. Terminal 3 is for international flights.

Arriving at José Martí International Airport Terminal 3 has exchange facilities open during normal banking hours, snack bars, shops and a 24-hour tourist information bureau (Infotur, limited information). Car hire desks are outside the door to your right. The airport is safe at night, which is when the European flights arrive. There is no airport hotel and you will need to take a taxi to any accommodation. See page 98 for transport from Havana airport into the city.

Immigration can be very slow with long queues. You should expect to take 1½ hours to clear Immigration, pass through security and collect your bags if arriving on a busy flight, eg **Virgin Atlantic** from London. Coming into one of the other airports (see page 457) is a more relaxed and speedy affair with less traffic.

Departures Allow plenty of time for check-in. The seating everywhere at Havana airport is uncomfortable. The restaurant upstairs, before you go through passport control, is OK for sandwiches or full meals and will be your last chance to hear a live Cuban band while eating. The food on offer in the departure lounge is awful, with a choice between a microwaved hot dog or a soggy pizza. As most European flights leave late at night this can be a problem if you have a long wait for a (delayed) **Air France** or **Iberia** flight, but you can savour your last mojito in this vast, uncomfortable shed. The selection of shops is limited but there is lots of rum, coffee and biscuits on sale. The selection of cigars is poor; if you know which brand you particularly want, get it in a specialist shop before you get to the airport. Rum costs much the same as elsewhere. The Cubita coffee, on the other hand, is marginally cheaper than in town.

Sea

There are no ferry services between Cuba and neighbouring islands, but a ferry to link Havana with Florida, USA, is in the planning stages. Havana, Cienfuegos and Santiago receive tourist cruise vessels.

Private boat

Before arriving in **Cuban territorial waters** (12 nautical miles from the island's platform) you should communicate with port authorities on channel HF (SSB) 2760 or VHF 68 and 16 (National Coastal Network) and 2790 or VHF 19A (Tourist Network). There are lots of rules and regulations and you must expect paperwork to take hours while the many bureaucrats board your boat and check you out. Not many 'yachties' visit the island because of the political difficulties between Cuba and the USA, although this is expected to change. For many years the US administration has forbidden any vessel, such as a cruise ship, cargo ship or humble yacht, from calling at a US port if it has stopped in Cuba. This effectively prohibits anyone who is sailing from the US eastern seaboard from calling in at a Cuban port on their way south through the Caribbean islands, or vice versa. However, it does not seem to prevent regattas being held between Florida and Cuban marinas.

There are now some 20 marinas and nautical centres around the island; the only prohibited area is the Bay of Pigs. The largest marina is the Hemingway in Havana, but there are three in Varadero and others in Cienfuegos, Cayo Largo, Santiago and several along the north coast. See the noticeboards for crewing opportunities on boats to Mexico, Florida, etc.

From Cienfuegos marina you can sail west to the Archipiélago de los Canarreos, visiting Cayo Largo, Isla de la Juventud and the many cays in between, or east to the Jardines de la Reina, stopping at Trinidad (Ancón) and the many cays south of Júcaro. There are several cruising guides to Cuba, all of which contain inaccuracies or out-of-date information. *A Cruising Guide to Cuba* by Amaia Agirre and Frank Virgintino can be downloaded from http://freecruisingguides.com.

Getting around

Shortages of fuel and spare parts in Cuba still cause difficulties in the supply of transport. The government has segregated tourists from Cubans and encourages them to hire cars or travel on dedicated buses to maximize foreign exchange income. Many cheap forms of transport are reserved for Cubans.

Internal flights are frequent and efficient but generally only link Havana with other towns, so you cannot criss-cross the island by air. **Roads** are in need of resurfacing, but there is little traffic, except in Havana, which is a bit of a nightmare if you have just arrived. Out of the city, roads are fairly empty and you can often travel for miles without seeing another vehicle. **Buses** operated by Viazul and paid for in CUC$ run on long-distance routes between cities commonly visited by foreigners, while the more extensive **Astro** bus network is reserved for Cubans. All long-distance travel by foreigners is paid for in CUC$. **Tour buses** are flexible, allowing you to stay a night or two in, say, Pinar del Río, before rejoining the tour for the return to Havana. **Transtur** now runs some of its tour buses as a scheduled service, for example between Havana and Trinidad. **Car hire** is available, although you may not get the car you want unless you arrange it in advance from abroad. The disadvantage of car hire is that it is expensive and petrol stations are not always conveniently located, but you will have the freedom of going where you want, when you want and you will have the roads almost to yourself. A good way of getting around and meeting the people is to hire a local taxi to take you out for a day. If there are two or three of you it can work out cheaper and more enjoyable than taking an organized excursion on a tour bus. Most **rail** journeys are fraught with difficulties and generally are subject to breakdowns and long delays. There have also been some fatal accidents. Repairs and new rolling stock are awaited.

Air

There are **Cubana de Aviación** or **AeroCaribbean** services between Havana and most of the main towns (see Transport sections in each chapter for details). Tourists must pay air fares in CUC$. It is advisable to pre-book flights at home as demand is very heavy, although you can get interprovincial flights from hotel tour desks if you are on a package deal. It is difficult to book flights from one city to another when you are not at the point of departure, except from Havana; the computers are not able to cope. It is often only possible for tourists to travel on packages that include flights, accommodation, meals and sightseeing.

Airports are usually a long way from the towns, so allow for extra transport costs. Delays are common. Internal flights are very cold; take warm clothes and possibly some food for a long flight.

Aerogaviota ⓘ *www.aerogaviota.com*, is a charter airline owned by the armed forces, with a growing list of national flights plus international flights to Central America and the Caribbean from Playa Baracoa airport outside Havana.

Rail

Train journeys are only recommended for the adventurous and patient traveller, as long delays and breakdowns must be expected. Arrive at the station at least one hour before the scheduled departure time. Fares are reasonable but have to be paid for in CUC$, which will usually entitle you to a waiting area, seat reservation and to board the train before the big rush starts. There is a CUC$ ticket office in every station. Tour agencies may sell train tickets, but many have ceased that service as trains are too unreliable. Long-distance trains allow only seated passengers. All carriages are smoking areas; they are extremely cold unless the air conditioning is broken, so take warm clothes, a torch (needed for the toilets) and toilet paper. Bicycles can be carried but often cost more than the fare for a person (see Cycling, page 19). The best source of information on trains, timetables and fares is **The Man in Seat 61**, http://www.seat61.com/Cuba.htm#Train%20times.

Tip...
Take your own food with you on train journeys. Cold fried meat with rice and black beans is sometimes sold in a cardboard box for CUP$15 – you have to tear off a piece of the box to use as an eating tool – but this is sold soon after leaving Havana and there will be nothing else available for the rest of the trip, however long that may be. You may be able to get something at intervening stations, but make sure you have pesos cubanos with you.

Road

Bus

Local The local word for a bus is *guagua*. Urban transport is varied: there are regular buses in Havana and other major centres, but you're likely to see horse-drawn *coches* in provincial towns. (Horses made a comeback during the crisis of the 1980s when fuel shortages limited motorized transport.) The huge double-jointed buses pulled by a truck, called *camellos* (camels) because of their shape, have been withdrawn from the streets of Havana and are now found only occasionally in the provinces. The urban bus fare throughout Cuba is 20 centavos for *camellos* and 40 centavos for all others. Urban tickets can only be bought in pesos cubanos and it helps to have the exact fare. The government prefers foreigners to use taxis rather than local buses.

Long distance For bus transport to other provinces from Havana there are two companies: **Viazul** and **Astro**, but foreigners can only travel on **Viazul (Viajes Azul)** ⓘ *Av 26 entre Av Zoológico y Ulloa, Nuevo Vedado, Havana, T7-881 1413, www.viazul.cu, ticket sales 0700-1700, 1900-2230*. The buses are reasonably comfortable and air conditioned; films are shown on longer journeys. Tickets can be bought online, but you pay 8% more than in the ticket offices. See box, page 462, for routes, schedules and fares. Children under 12 pay half price; those small enough not to need a seat travel free. It is essential to book in advance during peak season, especially in August, which can be very busy with an increased number of Cuban tourists. Even booking up to two or three days in advance may not be sufficient to guarantee a seat, especially if you are a family with children or travelling in a group. If you are picking up a **Viazul** bus en route between Havana and Santiago, for example, it's worth bearing in mind that a minimal number of seats will be allocated. There is a weight limit for luggage of 20 kg on all long-distance bus journeys and on the bus-ferry to Isla de la Juventud (see page 387).

Astro ⓘ *Terminal de Omnibus Nacional, Boyeros y 19 de Mayo, Havana, T7-870 3397/9401, daily 0700-2100*, is mainly used by Cubans who often have to book tickets

Tip...
Do not forget the etiquette for queues when buying tickets at **Viazul** head office and always ask who is last in line ('*El ultimo?*').

TIMETABLE

Viazul routes, fares and daily schedules www.viazul.com

Route	Fare	Departure times		
Havana to Santiago de Cuba	CUC$51	0030	0630	1500
Santa Clara	CUC$18	0425	1020	1930
Sancti Spíritus	CUC$23	0555	1150	2100
Ciego de Avila	CUC$27	0725	1355	2225
Camagüey	CUC$33	0925	1555	0025
Las Tunas	CUC$39	1130	1800	0230
Holguín	CUC$44	0350		
Bayamo	CUC$44	1340	2010	0515
Santiago de Cuba	Arrives	1555	2225	0730
Santiago de Cuba to Havana	CUC$51	0030	0630	1600
Bayamo	CUC$7	0250	0850	1820
Holguín	CUC$11	1010	2020	
Las Tunas	CUC$11	0425	1220	2140
Camagüey	CUC$18	0630	1425	2345
Ciego de Avila	CUC$24	0835	1625	0145
Sancti Spíritus	CUC$28	1000	1750	0310
Santa Clara	CUC$33	1130	1950	0440
Havana	Arrives	1605	2335	0825
Havana to Holguín	CUC$44	0930	1945	
Santa Clara	CUC$18	1355	2340	
Ciego de Avila	CUC$27	0225		
Camagüey	CUC$33	1835	0425	
Las Tunas	CUC$39	2040	0625	
Holguín	Arrives	2155	0740	
Holguín to Havana	CUC$44	0745	2115	
Las Tunas	CUC$6	0905	2235	
Camagüey	CUC$11	1105	0035	
Ciego de Avila	CUC$17	1340	0235	
Santa Clara	CUC$27	1625		
Havana	Arrives	2015	0920	
Havana to Trinidad	CUC$25	0700	1045	1415
Playa Girón	CUC$13	1030		
Cienfuegos	CUC$20	1210	1510	1755
Trinidad	Arrives	1350	1650	1935
Trinidad to Havana	CUC$25	0815	1600	
Cienfuegos	CUC$6	1000	1745	
Playa Girón	CUC$13	1925		
Havana	Arrives	1350	2320	

Route	Fare	Departure times				
Havana to Viñales	CUC$12	0840	1125	1400		
Pinar del Río	CUC$11	1155	1430	1620		
Viñales	Arrives	1245	1520	1710		
Viñales to Havana	CUC$12	0910	1400			
Pinar del Río	CUC$6	1000	1450			
Havana	Arrives	1235	1805			
Havana to Varadero	CUC$10	0600	0800	1300	1730	
Matanzas	CUC$7	0820	1010	1455	1940	
Varadero airport	CUC$10	0855	1045	1530		
Varadero	Arrives	0925	1115	1600	2025	
Varadero to Havana	CUC$10	0800	1200	1400	1600	1935
Varadero airport	CUC$6	0835	1235	1435	1635	2010
Matanzas	CUC$6	0910	1310	1510	1710	2045
Havana	Arrives	1120	1515	1715	1915	2250
Varadero to Trinidad	CUC$20	0730				
Santa Clara	CUC$11	1110				
Trinidad	Arrives	1405				
Trinidad to Varadero	CUC$20	1500				
Santa Clara	CUC$8	1805				
Varadero	Arrives	2125				
Trinidad to Santiago	CUC$33	0800				
Sancti Spíritus	CUC$6	0925				
Ciego de Avila	CUC$9	1050				
Camagüey	CUC$15	1315				
Las Tunas	CUC$22	1520				
Holguín	CUC$26	1640				
Bayamo	CUC$26	1815				
Santiago de Cuba	Arrives	2030				
Santiago to Trinidad	CUC$33	1930				
Bayamo	CUC$7	2150				
Holguín	CUC$11	2315				
Las Tunas	CUC$11	0040				
Camagüey	CUC$18	0245				
Ciego de Avila	CUC$24	0445				
Sancti Spíritus	CUC$28	0610				
Trinidad	Arrives	0730				

Route	Fare	Departure times	
Santiago de Cuba to Baracoa	CUC$15	0150	0800
Baracoa	Arrives	0640	1300
Baracoa to Santiago de Cuba	CUC$15	0815	1400
Santiago de Cuba	Arrives	1345	1900
Varadero to Santiago de Cuba	CUC$49	2145	
Santa Clara	CUC$11	0120	
Sancti Spíritus	CUC$17	0255	
Ciego de Avila	CUC$19	0420	
Camagüey	CUC$25	0620	
Las Tunas	CUC$33	0820	
Holguín	CUC$38	0945	
Bayamo	CUC$42	1110	
Santiago de Cuba	Arrives	1325	
Santiago de Cuba to Varadero	CUC$49	2000	
Bayamo	CUC$7	2220	
Holguín	CUC$11	2345	
Las Tunas	CUC$11	0105	
Camagüey	CUC$18	0310	
Ciego de Avila	CUC$24	0510	
Sancti Spíritus	CUC$28	0635	
Santa Clara	CUC$33	0815	
Varadero	Arrives	1135	
Viñales to Trinidad	CUC$37	0645	
Pinar del Río	CUC$6	0735	
Trinidad	Arrives	1615	

(in pesos) months in advance at busy times of the year. Away from the capital and off the beaten track, it is less controversial for tourists to travel on **Astro** to minor towns and pay in pesos; in fact you may have no other option. The **Viazul** terminal in Havana is a long way from the centre and you will have to get a taxi, but in other cities **Viazul** and **Astro** use the same bus terminal.

Tip...
Baggage handlers in Havana, Trinidad and some other tourist towns have an irritating habit of demanding a tip even though they hardly touch your bag. Any small coin will satisfy them.

Car

In view of the difficulties of getting public transport to out-of-the-way places, you can save a considerable amount of time and hassle by hiring a car. However, it is the most expensive form of travel. Breakdowns are not unknown and you may be stuck many kilometres from the nearest town. Be careful about picking up hitchhikers, although

Route	Fare	Departure times
Trinidad to Santa Lucía	CUC$23	1000
Camagüey	CUC$15	1440
Santa Lucía	Arrives	1630
Santa Lucía to Havana	CUC$41	1100
Camagüey	CUC$9	1250
Havana	Arrives	2220
Trinidad to Cayo Santa María	CUC$20	0730
Cienfuegos	CUC$6	0850
Santa Clara	CUC$8	1015
Camajuaní		1110
Remedios	CUC$14	1140
Caibarién	CUC$14	1150
Cayo Las Brujas	CUC$20	1230
Cayo Ensenachos	CUC$20	1240
Cayo Santa María	Arrives	1310
Cayo Santa María to Trinidad	CUC$20	1410
Cayo Ensenachos		1445
Cayo Las Brujas		1455
Caibarién	CUC$6	1520
Remedios	CUC$6	1530
Camajuaní		1610
Santa Clara	CUC$13	1705
Cienfuegos		1835
Trinidad	Arrives	1950

this can be an interesting way of meeting Cubans and of acquiring useful navigational information. Cubans drive on the right-hand side of the road.

Fuel Petrol stations are not self-service. Petrol and diesel are available in Servi Cupet stations and must be paid for in CUC$ at around CUC$1.10 per litre for Regular and diesel and CUC$1.30 for Especial. Car hire companies will fill the tank at the beginning of your rental period and you must return the car empty at the end. A number of hire cars use diesel, which can be more difficult to get hold of than petrol. Only the main fuel stations sell diesel.

Main roads *Autopistas* were incredibly empty of traffic during the 1980s and 1990s, but as the economy picked up, traffic increased. Cubans often use the hard surface for other purposes, such as drying rice on the roadside. Oxen, horses, donkeys, bicycles and tractors will be sharing the fast lane with you. The dogs on the side of the road are often not dead, just asleep. Watch out for low-flying vultures preying on any animals that really are dead. Cubans slow right down and give them a wide berth; they can do enormous damage to your car if you do hit one. Main roads can be good places to shop for fresh fruit and vegetables; vendors stand by the roadside (or in the road) or sell from broken down trucks.

Finding your way Most ordinary roads are in reasonable condition, but minor roads can be very badly maintained and signposting is uniformly atrocious or non-existent. Even where there are road signs, they are usually so bleached by the sun that they are illegible until you draw level with them. Finding your way across a large city like Havana can present problems, in spite of the courteous assistance of police and pedestrians. Your best bet is to get the *Guía de Carreteras* (Road Guide, published by Directorio Turístico de Cuba) and follow the distances marked between junctions. Getting into towns is usually easy; finding a road out again is more difficult. In Holguín, the metal street name plates have been removed and melted down to make cooking pots, so it is very difficult to find out where you are.

Safety There are numerous police checks on the roads. They will sometimes stop hired cars and try to impose a fine of CUC$30 for a traffic violation you may or may not have committed. If you can speak Spanish, try and discuss the matter with them and ask for evidence of the violation. They will usually not be able to produce any and will let you go.

Driving at night can be extremely hazardous and is not recommended. Even in major cities, you are likely to encounter horses, cattle, pigs, goats and sheep monopolizing the road without any semblance of lighting. In addition, cyclists, bullock carts and other vehicles without lights are common. It is best to travel early in the day and reach your destination before nightfall. During the winter months, November to March, sunrise is at 0700 and sunset at 1830 (2000 in summer months).

Car hire
There are state rental companies at international airports and most large hotels, or contact the companies direct. During July and August it is extremely difficult to hire a car without booking well in advance. It is advisable to arrange car hire from home before you travel. Drivers need to be minimum of 21 years of age, although for some vehicles the age limit goes up to 25 years. You must present your passport and home driving licence.

Costs All car rental agencies are state owned and operated, so there is no real competition on prices. **Cubacar** ⓘ *www.transtur.cu*, **Havanautos** ⓘ *www.havanautos.cu*, and **Rex** ⓘ *www.rex.cu*, all belong to **Transtur** ⓘ *www.transtur.cu*. **Vía Rent-a-Car** belongs to **Gaviota** ⓘ *www.gaviota-grupo.com*. **Rex** is the most expensive but also the best, with excellent customer service and good cars. Rental costs a minimum of CUC$40 a day (or CUC$50 for air conditioning) with limited mileage of 100 km a day plus CUC$10-20 a day for insurance, or CUC$50-88 per day with unlimited mileage. Weekly rental offers better rates. Most vehicles are Japanese or Korean makes; Suzuki jeeps can be hired for six to 12 hours in beach areas. Moped rental (*moto*) is around US$25 per day, cheaper for longer.

Non-US credit cards are accepted for the rental. If you pay cash it will have to be in advance and the company will still need a credit card for a deposit, which may be debited for the whole rental even if you have paid up front. Credit cards will be debited in CUC$, converted immediately to US$ plus tax (even if your bank is non-US) and then converted into your own currency, making it a more expensive way to pay. In practice, you may find car hire rates prohibitively expensive when small cars are 'unavailable' and a four-door sedan costing CUC$93 per day (unlimited kilometres, insurance included) is your only option. Staff have been reported to be 'unhelpful' in finding the car you want. However, it pays to shop around, even between offices of the same company.

Make sure the tank is really full when you start; you should leave it empty when you return the vehicle. If you hire a car in Havana but want to drop it off at the airport, companies will charge you an extra CUC$10 or so, although this is sometimes waived if you bargain hard.

Fly-and-drive If you want to drive from Havana to Santiago and return by air, try **Havanautos**. They will charge at least CUC$100 to return the car to Havana, but most companies will not even consider it. **Vía Rent-a-Car (Gaviota)** charges CUC$160, calculated at CUC$0.18 per km on a distance of 884 km from Santiago to Havana, but this is reduced to CUC$0.09 if the car is hired for more than 15 days. Fly-and-drive packages can also be booked from abroad.

Security Always take out full insurance and on return beware of extra charges for dirty exterior, dirty interior and scratches on the paintwork caused by flying stones. Watch out for theft of the windscreen wipers, licence plates, radio and spare tyre; you will have to pay about CUC$350 if stolen unless you take out the costly extra insurance. Always arrange secure parking overnight, usually by paying someone to watch your car for CUC$2. If you are stopped by the police, do not pay an on-the-spot fine. Instead, your misdemeanour should be noted on your car rental documents, and you pay the hire company at the end of your lease.

Cycling
For people who really want to explore the country in depth and independently, cycling is an excellent option. A good-quality bicycle is essential if you are going to spend many hours in the saddle, although that does not mean it has to be very sophisticated. We have heard from cyclists who have toured Cuba without gears, although they did have plenty of muscle. See also page 19.

Safety Look out for potholes. Cuba has an extensive network of tarmac and concrete roads, which are in good condition in areas of heaviest tourist use, but suffer from lack of maintenance and storm damage in rural areas. The old cars, buses and trucks on the roads may be fascinating to see, but they belch unpleasant fumes from their exhausts, which are difficult to avoid in towns. Watch out for railway crossings that have no barriers or warning lights. They often look unused, but it is absolutely essential that you stop and look for approaching trains, particularly in sugar-growing areas. Plan to finish each journey in daylight, as cycling in the dark is dangerous. Street lighting can be subject to power cuts. Other vehicles on the road often do not dip their headlights for bikes. Book your accommodation in advance to check they can safely store bikes.

Useful vocabulary A puncture is a *ponche*; to mend a puncture is *coger un ponche*; the man who mends your puncture is a *ponchero* and his workshop is a *ponchera*. Other useful words include: *la cadena* – chain; *el freno* – brake; *el cuadro* – frame; *los rayos* – spokes; *la goma* – tyre; *la cámara* – inner tube; and *el sillín* – seat.

Hitchhiking
With the shortage of fuel and decline in public transport after 1991, Cubans took to organized hitchhiking to get about. At every major junction outside towns throughout Cuba you will find the *Amarillos*: traffic wardens who organize a queue, stop traffic to find out where the trucks or vans are going, and then load them with passengers. Foreigners

are not allowed to use this service, nor to travel on trucks. Cubans also hitchhike (*a botella*) unofficially and get rides in ancient cars, trucks and other makeshift vehicles. Cubans are not allowed to carry paying foreigners in their vehicles unless they have a licence to operate a taxi, so be aware that if a Cuban agrees to give you a lift, he/she could get into trouble if the vehicle is stopped by the authorities.

Taxis

There are three types of taxi: **tourist taxis**, **Cuban taxis** (*colectivos*) and **private taxis** (*particulares*). **Tourist taxis**, paid for in CUC$, can be hired for driving around; you pay for the distance, not the waiting time. On short routes, fares are sometimes metered. **Cuban taxis**, or *colectivos*, also operate on fixed routes and pick you up only if you know where to stand for certain destinations. The flat rate fare is CUP$10. Travelling on them is an adventure and a complicated cultural experience. **Private taxis**, *particulares*, are cheaper than other taxis. A *particular* who pays his tax will usually display a 'taxi' sign, which can be a hand-written piece of board, but have a private registration plate. Some have meters; in others you have to negotiate a price in CUC$.

For long distances you can negotiate with official taxis as well as *particulares*, and the price should be around CUC$10 per hour. Taxis can work out cheaper than going on organized tours, if you are in a group and are prepared to bargain. As a general rule, the cost will depend on the quality of your Spanish and how well you know the area. One family paid CUC$80 to travel from Havana to Viñales by taxi, although someone else was quoted CUC$50 for the return journey.

Sea

There is currently only one journey you can do by public transport across the sea, and that is the ferry to the Isla de la Juventud (see page 387). It leaves from Surgidero de Batabanó on the coast due south of Havana, from where there are bus links.

Maps

Mapa Geográfico (Ediciones GEO) is one of the best, with a large map of Cuba, accompanied by several smaller maps of towns, regions and routes. It is one of the more accurate and up to date. The best map for drivers is the *Guía de Carreteras* (Road Guide, published by Directorio Turístico de Cuba), which has proved remarkably accurate. It grades all the roads, gives distances and marks fuel stations. *Cuba, Mapa de Carreteras* (Road Map), Ediciones GEO (1999), is a good general purpose map as well as being moderately useful for drivers. Its inset map of La Habana includes details of all the major road junctions around the capital. Ediciones GEO's *Mapa Turístico* of La Habana (with Cuba, Varadero, Trinidad, Santiago, Guardalavaca, Cayo Largo and Cayo Coco on the reverse) is good in that it includes a lot of the city. For individual states and areas there are very good provincial maps going under the name of *Mapa Turístico* (Ediciones GEO), usually including the provincial capital and sometimes other places of interest, but you will probably only find them in the relevant province. **Infotur** is worth trying, see page 481.

If you want to get hold of a map before leaving the UK, then visit **Stanfords** ① *12-14 Long Acre, London, WC2E 9LP, T020-7836 1321, www.stanfords.co.uk (also at 29 Corn St, Bristol, BS1)*. This is the world's largest map and travel bookshop, with more than 80 well-travelled staff and 40,000 titles in stock.

Essentials A-Z

Accident and emergency

Ambulance: T104. **Fire**: T105. **Police**: Policía Nacional Revolucionaria (PNR) T106.

Children

Cubans love children and the experience of travelling as a family in Cuba can be rewarding for both parents and offspring. The children will love the beaches and the sea, of course, but inland there are lots of opportunities for entertainment, with trips to amusement parks, caves, rivers, farms and plenty of animals. Cuba is also tremendously educational; how many children living in Europe or North America have seen sugar cane, tobacco or coffee growing? Who wouldn't enjoy seeing a *bicitaxi* or a horse-drawn *coche* and watching the oxen ploughing the fields?

Sightseeing can be a very hot activity for small children, but the promise of the beach in the afternoon can make it bearable. Many of Cuba's best beach resorts are remote from places of interest for sightseeing trips, which means several hours of sitting in a bus or car to get between the beach and the sights. Trinidad is recommended for families, as it combines sightseeing for the adults with the proximity of a beach for the kids and a relaxed atmosphere. For younger teenagers interested in music, many of the best venues in Havana offer afternoon *peñas* and discos popular with Cuban youth.

If travelling in high season (Dec-Feb) or the Cuban holiday season (Aug), hiring a car or buying **Viazul** bus tickets (see page 461) can be very difficult, so advance reservations are essential.

Health, food and facilities

Apart from the sun and the need to drink plenty of water, there are no particular health problems to watch out for. Diarrhoea and vomiting are the most common problems, so take the usual precautions, but more intensively (see Health, page 473, for further advice). Breastfeeding is best and most convenient for babies, but powdered milk is generally available and so are baby foods. Papaya, bananas and avocados are all nutritious and can be cleanly prepared. The treatment of diarrhoea is the same as for adults, except that it should start earlier and be continued with more persistence. Children get dehydrated very quickly and can become drowsy and uncooperative unless cajoled to drink water or juice plus salts. Upper respiratory infections, such as colds, catarrh and middle-ear infections are also common; if your child is prone to these ailments, then take some antibiotics against the possibility. Outer-ear infections after swimming are also common for which antibiotic eardrops will help. See also Health, page 473.

'Wet wipes' are always useful and sometimes difficult to find, as are disposable nappies. Restaurants have toilets for customers' use, but these may be very basic and unhygienic; public toilets can be found in the centre of some towns, but you cannot rely on it. There are unlikely to be any facilities for changing babies' nappies/diapers. Remember to take a good supply of toilet paper as it is not usually supplied.

Clothing

This is generally informal and summer calls for the very lightest clothing. Sunglasses, a high-factor sun lotion and some kind of head cover are recommended. A jersey and light raincoat or umbrella are needed in the cooler months; a jersey or fleece is also needed if you plan to travel on a/c internal flights, buses (particularly overnight on **Viazul** bus) or trains, which are very cold. You should be appropriately dressed to go into a church or temple. Cubans dress up to go out at night.

Customs and duty free

Duty-free allowances include personal baggage and articles for personal use, as well as 1 carton of cigarettes and 2 bottles of alcoholic drinks. You may take in up to 10 kg of medicine, so long as it is in its original packaging. It is prohibited to bring in fresh fruit and vegetables, which will be confiscated if found. On departure you may take out only 20 cigars without a receipt; 50 cigars in their original package, unopened, sealed with the official hologram, and up to an amount not exceeding CUC$5000 in the original packaging, unopened, sealed with the official hologram, with a formal sales invoice from the authorized store where they were bought. You can also export up to 6 bottles of rum and personal jewellery.

To take out works of art you must have permission from the **Registro Nacional de Bienes Culturales de la Dirección de Patrimonio del Ministerio de Cultura**. Books that are more than 50 years old may not be taken out of the country, nor those belonging to Ediciones R. For further details on customs regulations, see www.aduana.co.cu.

Disabled travellers

There are few facilities for disabled people. In the resort areas new hotels have been built with a few rooms adapted for people using wheelchairs, but the older, state-run, 3-star hotels usually have no facilities and neither do *casas particulares*. Cuba is not easy to get around in a wheelchair and a certain amount of determination is required. Pavements are usually built up much higher than the roads, because of rain and flash flooding, which makes crossing the road hazardous. Potholes and loose paving stones compound the difficulties. If you are travelling independently it is not impossible to get around and stay in private accommodation, but you will have to do plenty of research first to make sure you can have a ground-floor room and that passages and doorways are negotiable with wheels. You can use the bus company **Viazul** if you have someone to help you, or you can hire your own vehicle. Don't be discouraged, you will not be the first disabled person to travel around Cuba and Cubans are tremendously helpful and supportive.

Electricity

110 volts, 3 phase 60 cycles, AC. Plugs and sockets are usually of the American flat 2-pin type, so bring an adaptor from home if necessary. In some new tourist hotels however, European plugs are used, with 220 volts, check in advance if it is important to you. Some *casas particulares* now have both 110v and 220v, which is better for charging laptops, phones, etc. Do not be surprised if there are power cuts.

Embassies and consulates

A list of Cuban embassies can be found at http://embassy goabroad.com.

Festivals

January
New Year is celebrated around the country with great fanfare, largely because it coincides with **Liberation Day**, marking the end of the Batista dictatorship, on 1 Jan. There is lots of music and dancing, outdoor discos and general merriment, fattened pigs are roasted, washed down with copious quantities of rum.

Cubadanza is a twice-yearly dance festival with workshops and performances. Contact Danza Contemporánea de Cuba, www.dccuba.com.

Festival de la Trova 'Longina', in Santa Clara, celebrating the life of the great *trovador*,

Manuel Corona, with a pilgrimage to Caibarién, his birthplace on 9 Jan.

February
Havana International Book Fair is held at La Cabaña; a commercial fair in the castle, immensely popular with book-hungry families, who come for a day out. Look out for new book launches. Also held in many cities around the island, www.cubaliteraria.com.
Vuelta a Cuba is a cycle race from east to west of the island.
Cigar Festival, www.festivaldelhabano.com, is for true aficionados of Habanos. Held at the Palacio de las Convenciones, you can learn about the history of cigars and there are opportunities for visits to tobacco plantations and cigar factories.

March
Bienal de la Habana is held over a month and takes place every 2 years (next in 2017), gathering over 200 artists from 40 countries in the Centro de Arte Contemporáneo Wifredo Lam, Centro de Arte La Casona, Parque Morro-Cabaña, Pabellón Cuba and other venues, www.bienalhabana.cult.cu.
Spring in Havana: **International Festival of Electroacoustic Music in Havana**, with workshops and performances.
Festival Internacional de la Trova 'Pepe Sánchez' is held at the Casa de la Trova and the Sala de Concierto Dolores in Santiago with concerts, roving musicians, conferences and other events. www.cultstgo.cult.cu.

April
Festival Internacional de Cine Pobre de Humberto Solás, in Gibara, a film festival to showcase low-budget movies, www.festivalcinepobre.cult.cu.

May
Romerías de Mayo, Holguín. A cultural festival with young and old artists, musicians and intellectuals from Cuba and overseas, events take place all over the city.

Ernest Hemingway International Billfishing Tournament is one of the major events at the Marina Hemingway. www.internationalhemingwaytournament.com.
Festival Internacional de Poesía de La Habana, at Cuba Poesía, Hospital esq 25, http://www.cubapoesia.cult.cu.

June
Festival Danzón Habana, held at the Teatro América, Centro Hispanoamericano de Cultura y Unión Fraternal, at the end of the month, musicians and dancers celebrate *danzón* and each year it is dedicated to a different Latin American country; contact ireartes@hotmail.com.
Jornada Cuculambeana, Las Tunas. Celebration of traditional folk music of the area.

July
Cuballet de Verano is a summer dance festival with workshops and courses for dancers and dance teachers organized by Laura Alonso and ProDanza, www.prodanza.cult.cu.
Festival del Caribe 'Fiesta del Fuego' is held in the 1st week of Jul in Santiago, with theatre, dancing and conferences, continuing later in the month to coincide with the Moncada celebrations on 26 Jul. www.casadelcaribe.cult.cu.
18-27 Jul Carnival in Santiago, a week-long musical extravaganza taking in the city's patron saint's day, 25 Jul, but it traditionally stops on 26 Jul for a day of more serious political celebrations.

August
Cubadanza, the 2nd of the year, with workshops and courses, see Jan for details.

October
Festival Internacional del Son 'Matamoros Son', at Teatro Heredia, Santiago. Music and dancing to celebrate *son* and famous *soneros*.

Havana International Ballet Festival, held every other year in the 2nd half of the month at the Gran Teatro, Teatro Nacional and Teatro Mella. Run by Alicia Alonso, head of the Cuban National Ballet, www.festivalballethabana.cult.cu.

Fiesta de la Cubanía, Bayamo, with celebrations in the plazas of traditional folklore, music, dance and other cultural activities.

Fiesta de la Cultura Iberoamericana, in Holguín, celebrating all things Spanish and Latin American at the Casa de Iberoamérica.

Havana Theatre Festival, at theatres and plazas all over the city at the end of Oct and into Nov, contemporary international and Cuban drama, workshops and seminars, organized by **Cuba escena**, www.cubaescena.cult.cu.

November

Havana Contemporary Music Festival, held at UNEAC and theatres mid-month. www.musicacontemporanea.cult.cu.

Marabana, Havana's marathon, on the 3rd Sun of the month. www.inder.cu/marabana.

Festival Internacional de Coros, held at the Sala de Concierto Dolores in Santiago. www.santiagoencuba.com/festival_de_coros.htm.

December

International Festival of New Latin American Cinema, shows prize-winning films (no subtitles) at cinemas around Havana. This is the foremost film festival in Latin America with the best of Cuban and Latin American films along with documentaries and independent cinema from Europe and the USA. See the stars as well as the films, as the festival attracts big-name actors and directors, www.habanafilmfestival.com.

International Jazz Plaza Festival is held at theatres and the Casa de la Cultura de Plaza. It is one of the world's major jazz festivals with the best of Cuban and international jazz. There are masterclasses and workshops available and the event is organized by Grammy winner Jesús 'Chucho' Valdés. http://jazzcuba.com.

Gay and lesbian travellers

Cuba has in the past been notoriously homophobic and after the Revolution many homosexuals were sent to hard labour camps to be 'rehabilitated'. The Mariel exodus was characterized as being the flight of criminals and homosexuals, who could no longer stand their human rights being flouted. However, attitudes gradually changed, and although Cuba is still a macho society, there is an increasing tolerance of gays just as there is more religious freedom. The film, *Fresa y Chocolate* (see Cuban cinema, page 435), did much to stimulate debate and acceptance. For an excellent account of Cuban attitudes to homosexuals, before and after the Revolution and up to the present, read Ian Lumsden's *Machos, Maricones and Gays, Cuba and Homosexuality*, published by the Temple University Press, Philadelphia and Latin American Bureau, London. Gay travellers will not generally encounter any problems in Cuba: there are no laws against homosexuality and physical assaults are rare. However, in practice, there can be difficulties with accommodation if you want to stay in *casas particulares*, as some owners prefer not to rent rooms to same-sex partners, particularly if one of them is Cuban.

Gifts

Some items are in short supply in Cuba and will be much appreciated: T-shirts (preferably with something written on them), household medicines such as paracetamol or aspirin, cosmetics, cotton wool, tampons, soap, pens, pencils, notebooks and writing paper. Those with access to CUC$, such as *casa particular* owners, generally have access to imported goods, but schools, churches and other community organizations can distribute your gifts to those genuinely in need.

First aid

A well-stocked first-aid kit is recommended for your trip to Cuba; although the medical profession is well trained, supplies are limited. Things you might like to take for precautionary purposes include antibiotics for possible ear or sinus infections, nasal sprays, ear drops, antihistamine cream, diarrhoea remedies and seasickness pills. Be particularly careful to avoid infection from any lesions and make sure you are up to date with your anti-tetanus injections. If diving, you should avoid touching any coral (which will die if you do anyway) and not go poking about in holes and overhangs, where you might get stung or bitten by something you can't see.

Health

Cuba has a high-quality national health service and is one of the healthiest countries in Latin America. Travel in Cuba poses no health risk to the average visitor provided sensible precautions are taken. It is important to see your GP or specialist travel clinic at least 6 weeks before departure for general advice on any travel risks and necessary vaccinations. Check the details of your health insurance for Cuba and take a copy of your insurance policy with you. Also get a dental check, know your own blood group and if you suffer a long-term condition such as diabetes or epilepsy, obtain a Medic Alert bracelet/necklace (www.medicalert.co.uk). If you wear glasses, take a copy of your prescription.

Vaccinations

It is important to confirm your primary courses and boosters are up to date. There are no vaccinations demanded by immigration officials in Cuba, however it advisable to vaccinate against **tetanus**, **typhoid** and **hepatitis A**. Vaccines sometimes advised are **hepatitis B**, **rabies** and **diphtheria**. **Yellow fever** vaccination is not required unless you are coming directly from an infected country in Africa or South America. Although **cholera** vaccination is largely ineffective, immigration officers may ask for proof of such vaccination if coming

from a country where an epidemic has occurred. Check www.who.int for updates. **Malaria** is not normally a danger in Cuba.

Health risks

The most common affliction of travellers to any country is probably diarrhoea and the same is true of Cuba. Tap water is good in most areas of the country, but bottled water is widely available and recommended. Swimming in sea or river water that has been contaminated by sewage can be a cause of diarrhoea; ask locally if it is safe. Diarrhoea may also be caused by viruses, bacteria (such as E-coli), protozoal (such as giardia), salmonella and cholera. It may be accompanied by vomiting or by severe abdominal pain. Any kind of diarrhoea responds well to the replacement of water and salts. Sachets of rehydration salts can be bought in most pharmacies and can be dissolved in boiled water. If the symptoms persist, consult a doctor.

There is no malaria in Cuba but dengue fever has been reported and there are lots of mosquitoes in the wetlands, so take insect repellent and cover up to avoid being bitten. Sleep off the ground and use a mosquito net and some kind of insecticide. DEET (Di-ethyltoluamide) is the gold standard. Apply the repellent every 4-6 hrs but more often if you are sweating heavily. If a non-DEET product is used, check who tested it. Validated products (tested at the London

School of Hygiene and Tropical Medicine) include Mosiguard, Non-DEET Jungle formula and non-DEET Autan. If you want to use citronella remember that it must be applied very frequently (ie hourly) to be effective.

The climate is hot; Cuba is a tropical country and protection against the sun will be needed. To reduce the risk of sunburn and skin cancer, make sure you pack high-factor sun cream, light-coloured loose clothing and a hat.

Medical services

Medical services are no longer free for foreign visitors in areas where international clinics (Clínicas del Sol) and pharmacies (Farmacias Internacionales) exist (see www. healthservicecuba.com); these services are designed specifically for tourists and charge in CUC$ (credit cards accepted), although charges are generally lower than those in Western countries. Visitors requiring medical attention will be sent to these clinics wherever possible; emergencies are handled on an ad hoc basis. Away from Havana and tourist enclaves with on-site medical services, visitors are still treated free of charge. Make sure you have adequate insurance (see below). Remember you cannot dial any toll-free numbers abroad so make sure you have a contact number. The following are a list of medical services in Havana:

Clínica Central Cira García, 20 4101 esq 41, Playa, Havana, T7-204 2811, www.cirag.cu. Payment in CUC$, emergency health care, also the place to go for emergency dental treatment. There are other branches at the Hotel Comodoro, Sevilla, Habana Libre, Marina Hemingway, Terminal 3 at the airport and at Clínica Playas del Este, Villa Tarará, and Villa Panamericana to the east.

The **pharmacy** at the **Clínica Central Cira García** (open 24 hrs) T7-204 2880, sells prescription and patent drugs and medical supplies that are often unavailable in other pharmacies, as does the **Farmacia Internacional**, Av 41, esq 20, Playa, T7-204 4350, daily 0900-2100, and the **Habana Libre**, L y 23, Vedado, T7-838

4593. **Camilo Cienfuegos Pharmacy**, L y 13, Vedado, T7-8323507, ext 113, daily 24 hrs.

There are international clinics around the country in all tourist resort areas such as Varadero, Cayo Santa María and Guardalavaca. Medical procedures for foreigners, or health tourism, are run by **Servimed**, www.healthservicecuba.com.

Useful websites

www.bgtha.org British Global and Travel Health Association.
www.cdc.gov Centres for Disease Control and Prevention (USA).
www.fco.gov.uk British Foreign and Commonwealth Office travel site has useful information on each country, people, climate and a list of UK embassies/consulates.
www.fitfortravel.scot.nhs.uk A-Z of vaccine/health advice for each country.
www.itg.be Institute for Tropical Medicine, Antwerp.
www.nathnac.org National Travel Health Network and Centre (NaTHNaC).
www.nhs.uk/nhsengland/Healthcarea broad/pages/Healthcareabroad.aspx UK Department of Health advice for travellers.

Insurance

Travel health insurance is mandatory for entry into Cuba and must include sufficient cover for medical evacuation by air. We strongly recommend that you invest in a good insurance policy that covers you for theft or loss of possessions and money, the cost of medical and dental treatment, cancellation of flights, delays in travel arrangement, accidents, missed departures, lost baggage, lost passport and personal liability and legal expenses. Also check on inclusion of 'dangerous activities'. These generally include climbing, diving, horse riding, parachuting and even trekking. Always read the small print carefully. Not all policies cover ambulance, helicopter rescue or emergency flights home, and not all policies cover Cuba.

All loss must be reported to the police and/or hotel authorities within 24 hrs of discovery and a written report obtained. This is notoriously difficult to obtain in Cuba. **Asistur**, www.asistur.cu, is linked to overseas insurance companies and can help with emergency hospital treatment, repatriations, robbery, direct transfer of funds to Cuba, financial and legal problems, travel insurance claims, etc. For (24-hr) emergencies go to the main office: Prado 208, entre Colón y Trocadero, La Habana Vieja, T7-866 8339/866 8920, www.asistur.cu. There are also offices in Santiago de Cuba (Hotel Casa Granda, Heredia esq San Pedro, T22-686600), Varadero, Holguín and Cayo Coco.

Internet

Cubans' access to the internet is tightly controlled and limited to those who can afford to pay in CUC$. The only Cubans who are permitted to use the internet at home are civil servants, doctors and party representatives, on a regular phone line paid for in pesos; others have to pay in CUC$. However, restrictions on access to the internet are being relaxed as part of the negotiations with the USA. Wi-Fi hotspots have been introduced in most towns of any size and more are coming. These are usually in plazas, outside tourist hotels or outside the phone company's offices, and can be easily identified by groups of Cubans using their smart phones or tablets and chatting to friends and relatives abroad. Be careful of theft if you decide to do likewise. The telephone company, **Etecsa**, sells prepaid cards that give you an access code and a password code for when you log in; these cost CUC$2 per hr throughout the island.

Foreign tourists using the internet will invariably be asked to show their passport. If you need a computer terminal, the large, international hotels of 4 or 5 stars, such as the **Nacional**, **Habana Libre**, **Parque Central** and **Meliá Cohiba** in Havana and the **Meliá Santiago de Cuba** in Santiago,

have business centres with computers for internet access, but this is the most expensive way of checking emails. Nearly every hotel for foreigners now has internet access for its guests in some form or other and this is always worth trying even if you are not staying there. Most hotels now have 1 or 2 terminals in the lobby, which are not reserved for guests. The main telephone office in each town usually has internet access, but if not, look for **Telepunto** offices, or **Etecsa** cabins (large blue telephone boxes) with international and national phone services and a computer for internet access. The best place in La Habana Vieja is Etecsa's **Telepunto**, Habana 406 entre Obispo y Obrapía, T7-866 0547, daily 0830-1900, which has 12 terminals for internet access.

Language

Spanish is the official language, spoken fast with some consonants dropped. In the main tourist areas you will find staff often speak several languages, but off the beaten track you will need Spanish or very efficient sign language. **English** is becoming more commonly used; it is a university entrance requirement and encouraged by the influx of Canadian and now American tourists. **German**, **Italian** and **French** are spoken by many people working in the tourist industry and tour guides are usually multilingual. Many older people also speak **Russian**.

For a list of Spanish words and phrases, see Footnotes, pages 485-489. For details of Spanish language and other courses, see page 480.

Money

CUC$1=US$1 (before tax), CAN$1.38, €0.92, £0.68 (Jan 2016).

Cuba operates a dual currency system with a domestic peso and a convertible peso. There are plans to unify the 2, but no timetable has been announced.

The **peso cubano** (CP$ or CUP$), also referred to as *moneda nacional* (MN) has notes for 1, 3, 5, 10, 20, 50, 100, 200, 500 and 1000 pesos, and coins for 5, 20 and 40 centavos and 1 and 3 pesos. You must have a supply of coins if you want to use the local town buses (CUP$0.20 or 0.40). The 20 centavo coin is called a *peseta*. Cubans are paid in *pesos cubanos* and pay for most of their goods in the same currency.

The **peso convertible** (CUC$, pronounced 'cook') has a different set of notes and coins. It is fully exchangeable with authorized hard currencies such as euro, sterling and Canadian dollars. Foreigners are expected to pay for their accommodation, meals, transport and other items with the *peso convertible*. In some tourist enclaves, such as Varadero, Guadalavaca or the cays, the euro is accepted as well. Remember to spend or exchange any *pesos convertibles* before you leave as they are worthless outside Cuba. The exchange rate fluctuates around 24 *pesos cubanos* (CP$) to the *peso convertible* (CUC$).

There is no black market. Food in the *agromercados* (markets), at street stalls and on trains, as well as books and popular cigarettes (but not in every shop), can be bought in *pesos cubanos*. You will need *pesos cubanos* for the toilet, rural trains, food at roadside *cafeterías* during a journey and drinks and snacks for a bus or train journey. Away from tourist hotels, in smaller towns such as Manzanillo, you will need *pesos cubanos* for everything. Visitors on pre-paid package tours do not need *pesos cubanos*.

Exchange
In 2004 Cuba introduced a 10% tax on exchange transactions involving the US dollar so it is better to bring currencies such as euro, sterling, or Canadian dollars. It is best to bring lots of cash but take care not to bring any notes with writing or extraneous stamps on them as they will not be accepted. There are **banks** and **Cadecas** (*casas de cambio*) for changing money. The latter have longer opening hours and are usually open at weekends. If arriving at Havana airport, change what you need for a couple of days

at the exchange desk there, then go to a Cadeca in town for larger amounts. Wear a money belt to store your cash safely.

Plastic/Banks (ATMs)
Credit cards issued in the USA will not be accepted. A British credit card issued by a US bank (eg **MBNA**) is not valid. Visa or MasterCard **credit cards** are acceptable in most places. American Express, no matter where issued, is unacceptable.

You can obtain cash advances with a credit card at banks and Cadecas, but it is best to bring plenty of cash to avoid hefty fees and commissions. ATMs (dispensing CUC$ only) have been installed in most banks, but it is often quicker and easier to queue at the counter. All credit card transactions are converted from CUC$ into US dollars at point of use, and your bank or credit card company will then convert that into your own currency. This means that you pay the US dollar conversion tax as well as bank fees and commissions, making all credit card transactions very costly. There are no toll-free numbers for you to call if your credit card is lost or stolen. You will have to phone home to the financial institution that issued you the card in order to put a stop on its use. Make a note of this number before you leave home, together with your credit card account number and keep them separate from your card. If you get really stuck and need money sent urgently to Cuba, you can get money transferred from any major commercial bank abroad direct to a Cuban bank, to **Asistur** (see Insurance, page 475) immediately for a 10% commission, or to **Western Union** which is used largely by Cubans abroad to send money home to relatives.

Cost of living/travelling
Raúl Castro has increased wages and removed the cap on salaries to allow bonuses to be paid but still most state employees earn no more than CUP$300-500 a month, whatever their profession. Housing, education and medical care is provided

at no cost and some basic foodstuffs are still rationed and heavily subsidized (see Food and drink, page 30), but making ends meet is extremely hard. Most consumer goods are priced in *pesos convertibles*, and families have to have access to CUC$ to buy nice things for their home and family. It is therefore not surprising that Cubans will do almost anything to earn *divisa* (hard currency) and many families make sure that at least 1 member works in the dollar economy, eg tourism. The entire peso economy is subsidized, and although there are opportunities for travellers to use *pesos cubanos*, it is understandable that you will be expected to pay your way in CUC$. You earn hard currency, so you pay in hard currency.

It is important to remember that Cuba is competing in the Caribbean market, and its neighbours are selling themselves as luxury destinations. Compared with islands like the Bahamas or the Virgin Islands, it is cheap, but if you have just come from a backpacking trip through Central or South America and want a stop-off on an island before you go home, you will find your last few dollars don't go very far. However, by Caribbean standards, Cuba has it all. You can stay at luxury hotels (over CUC$100 a night for a double room), dine in elegant restaurants (up to CUC$50 per person) and frequent world-famous nightclubs, or for those on a mid-range budget you can stay in pleasant colonial hotels (CUC$60-80 for a double room), eat reasonably well (CUC$15-20 for a decent dinner) and find plenty to do in the evenings in the clubs, theatres and cinemas (CUC$2-10).

Anyone with a more restricted budget should consider staying with Cuban families in the *casa particular* system (CUC$20-35 per room), which is the equivalent of a bed and breakfast place in Europe. You can eat at private restaurants (CUC$7-15) or on the street, changing a few dollars into pesos to make resources stretch further, and head for a **Casa de la Trova** (CUC$1-5) for entertainment. At the bottom end of

the scale you could get by on CUC$40 a day, including transport, but few treats. It depends what you want to do, after all, sitting on the beach is free if you don't want a sunbed. A beer can cost CUC$1-3 depending on where you go and a mojito can vary from CUC$2 in a local bar to CUC$5 in the touristy **Bodeguita del Medio** in Havana, a Hemingway haunt. Based on 2 people sharing, this budget would include a simple *casa particular* of CUC$20 per room (CUC$10 each), CUC$3-5 for breakfast and CUC$7-10 for dinner in the *casa particular*, CUC$10 for transport or an excursion and CUC$10 for snacks, entry fees and entertainment, assuming you manage to buy some of your food with *pesos cubanos*. Increasing that budget by 50% would give you flexibility to take advantage of opportunities when they arise, stay in a more comfortable *casa* and have the freedom to explore a bit more.

Opening hours

Banks: Mon-Fri 0830-1530. **Cadecas/ Casas de cambio**: Mon-Sat 0800-1700, Sun 0800-1200 although these can vary. **Government offices**: Mon-Fri 0830-1230 and 1330-1730. Some offices open on Sat morning. **Hotel tourist shops**: generally open 1000-1800 or 1900. **Shops**: Mon-Sat 0900-1900, Sun 0900-1400, also variable.

Police

For emergencies dial T106. The main police station in Havana is at Dragones entre Lealtad y Escobar, Centro, T7-863 2441.

Post

When possible, correspondence to Cuba should be addressed to post office boxes (*apartados*), where delivery is more certain. Stamps can be bought in CUP$ at post offices, or at **Telecorreos** in certain hotels. Hotels will charge you in CUC$, making the stamps very expensive. Some postcards are now sold with postage included, look for the ones with the airmail stripe on the side. All postal services, national and international, have been described as appalling. Courier services are available, with **DHL Express**, www.dhl.com, in big hotels, *correos* or *telecorreos* in Havana and many other towns. They also provide a national service in Cuba.

Prohibitions

It is illegal to photograph military or police installations or personnel, port, rail or airport facilities. A fee is charged for photographs in some museums and national monuments. Cubans face more prohibitions than foreigners, particularly in the realm of politics and freedom of speech, but are usually happy to discuss their country, their government, their past and their future with you in private.

Public holidays

See also Festivals, page 470.
1 Jan New Year coincides with **Liberation Day**, marking the end of the Batista dictatorship. Liberation Day is celebrated around the country with great fanfare.
1 May Labour Day.
25, 26, 27 Jul Revolution Day.
10 Oct Beginning of War of Independence.
25 Dec Christmas Day.
    Other festive days which are not public holidays are **28 Jan** (birth of José Martí, 1853), **24 Feb** (anniversary of renewal of War of Independence, 1895), **8 Mar** (International Women's Day), **13 Mar** (anniversary of 1957 attack on presidential palace in Havana by a group of young revolutionaries), **19 Apr** (anniversary of defeat of mercenaries at Bay of Pigs, 1961), **30 Jul** (martyrs of the Revolution day), **8 Oct** (death of Che Guevara, 1967), **28 Oct** (death of Camilo Cienfuegos, 1959), **27 Nov** (death by firing squad of 8 medical students by Spanish colonial government, 1871), **7 Dec** (death of Antonio Maceo in battle in 1896). These dates are often marked by speeches and displays by school children.

Safety

The island is generally safer than many of its Caribbean and Latin neighbours and most Cubans are very hospitable. It is a serious crime to do anything to harm tourism and the penalties are extremely severe with long prison sentences. However, visitors should remember that some of the local population will do anything to get hard currency, from simply asking for money or foreign-bought goods, to mugging.
    Foreigners will be offered almost anything on the street – from cigars to cocaine to *chicas* (girls). Buying cigars on the street is not illegal, but they are often not genuine and may be confiscated at customs if you have more than 20 and cannot produce an official receipt of purchase.
    Visitors should never lose sight of their luggage or leave valuables in hotel rooms (most hotels and some *casas particulares* have safes). Do not leave your things on the beach when going swimming. Guard your camera closely. Pickpocketing and purse-snatching on buses is quite common in Havana and Santiago. Also beware of bag-snatching by passing cyclists. Street lighting is poor so care is needed when walking or cycling in any city at night. Some people recommend walking in the middle of the street. Dark and crowded bars can also be a haven for thieves.
    The police are usually (but not always) helpful and thorough when investigating theft. Ask for a stamped statement for insurance purposes, although this is reported to be like getting blood out of a stone from some police stations. In the event of a crime, make a note of where it happened.
    Take extra passport photos with you and keep them separate from your passport. If you have to get more photos while you are in Cuba, there is a place in Havana next to the **International Press Centre** at Calle 21

TRAVEL TIP

Sex tourism

Cuba had a reputation for prostitution before the Revolution and after a gap of some decades it has resurfaced. Despite government crackdowns and increased penalties, both male and female prostitutes are active, especially in the larger cities. If you are a man out alone at night in Havana, you will be approached frequently by both women and men. Be warned, foreigners on the lookout for a sexual partner are seen as fair game. The age of consent is 18 in Cuba, so if you are introduced to a young girl you are in danger of being led into a blackmail trap. Sexual encounters often take place in casas particulares, private homes where there is little security and lots of risk. A foreign man on his own will probably not be given the key to the house in case he brings a friend back in the early hours when the family is asleep. A Cuban must have his/her *carnet de identidad* in order to stay in a *casa*; the details are registered in the book alongside the foreigner's passport details to protect the owner and the tourist from robbery. However, if the Cuban 'visitor' is found to be staying in different places with different foreigners, she/he will be assumed to be a prostitute and will be re-educated or put in prison. If you go to an illegal *casa*, you have no protection and will probably be robbed. The *casa* owners face 15-year prison sentences for running brothels if too many *chicas* stay there.

esquina O, which produces them with a wait of about 1 hr.

Single travellers

Whether you are a man or a woman travelling on your own, and whatever your age and physique, you will be approached by hustlers, known as *jineteros/as* looking to make a quick buck out of you. Be careful who you allow to become attached to you, for obvious reasons, and if you choose to have a companion make sure that the terms and conditions are fully understood by both parties. Single men and women are targeted by Cubans of the opposite sex, not only for their dollars, but also as a way out of the country if they can find a marriage partner. Single women will encounter the usual macho attitudes found in all Latin American countries and can expect to receive stares, hissing and comments on their attributes. Rape is not common, but the usual precautions should be taken to avoid getting into a compromising situation, trust your intuition, as always. See also page 483 for Women travellers.

Smoking

Cubans are heavy smokers (48% of men and 26% of women, compared with about 25% of the population in the UK and USA) and every year about 6000 people die of smoking-related diseases. Fidel Castro gave up his trademark cigars in the 1980s and efforts are now being made to reduce smoking in the rest of the population. It is now banned in most workplaces including indoor restaurants and bars and it is illegal to sell cigarettes near schools. It is more common now to find 'no smoking' notices, although whether people take any notice is another matter. Cigarettes remain among the cheapest in the world.

Student travellers

Cuba is not geared up to offering student discounts unless you are part of a group that has been invited for a specific project. Foreign students enrolled on university courses in Cuba with the student *carnet* (student ID), are entitled to pay for goods and services (museums, nightclubs etc) in CUP$ like Cubans and to travel on the **Astra** bus network.

Studying in Cuba

There are no private schools but language courses are available at the universities of Havana and Santiago. In Havana, they generally start on the 1st Mon of the month and you study 20 sessions of 45 mins a week, Mon-Fri 0900-1320. There are different levels of study and Cuban cultural courses are also available, as are commercial Spanish and intensive courses. For details, see the **School of Foreign Languages**, University of Havana, http://web.flex.uh.cu/en. Spanish courses are also available at the **Universidad de Oriente** in Santiago de Cuba but are less structured and there are no books or other materials for students.

Taxes

Airport departure tax is now included in air fares. A tax of 10% is charged when you change US dollars but not on other currencies. Only the private sector (*casas particulares*, *paladares*) pays taxes. There is no sales tax.

Telephone *Country code +53.*

Empresa Telecomunicaciones de Cuba (**Etecsa**) is on Av 3 esq 76, Centro de Negocios Miramar, Edif Beijing, Miramar, in Havana, with offices elsewhere called **Telepunto**. There are also **Minipunto** cabins dotted around the city for phone services, internet and prepaid phone cards. There are phone boxes all over Havana, taking coins or phone cards; it is written on the side whether they are for local, national or international calls. **Cubacel**, which operates mobile phone service, is part of **Etecsa**.

To make a call to another province, dial 0 then the code and then the number. If you need the operator's help, dial 0, pause, then dial 0 again. Many public phones now take prepaid cards (*tarjetas*) which are easier to use than coins. If you do use a phone which takes coins, they only accept 20-centavo or 1-peso coins. For domestic, long-distance calls try and get hold of a peso phone card, eg 10 pesos, which works out much cheaper than the CUC$ cards, but which are not technically available to foreigners. There are 2 sorts of cards: '*chip*' and '*propria*', but only the latter has cheaper rates at night, otherwise they cost the same. The *propria* cards can be used to make calls from a private phone or from a cabin, dialling the personal code on the upper part of the card.

To phone abroad on a phone with **international dialling** facility, dial 119 followed by the country and regional codes and number. Many hotels and airports have offices where international calls can be made at high prices or you may be able to direct dial from your room. Look for the **Telecorreos**, **Telepunto** or **Etecsa** (www. etecsa.cu) signs. Collect (reverse charge) calls are possible to Argentina, Brazil, Canada, Colombia, Costa Rica, France, Italy, Mexico, Nicaragua, Panama, Puerto Rico, Spain, UK and USA. Dial 012, choose option 0 and follow instructions.

Phonecards (*tarjetas propias*) are green if used for international calls as well as domestic calls. They come in CUC$5, CUC$10, CUC$15, CUC$25 denominations and are valid for 6 months. CUC$1.95 per min (CUC$1.40 1800-0600) to USA and Canada, US$2.60 per min (US$2.20) to Mexico, Central America and the Caribbean, CUC$2.35 (CUC$1.65) to South America, CUC$3.05 (CUC$2.10) to the rest of the world CUC$3.65 (CUC$2.55).

Mobile/cell phones are commonly used in Cuba. If you want to rent a cell phone you can do so from **Cubacel**, at Telepunto, Habana 406 entre Obispo y Obrapía, Havana, or other **Telepunto** or **Etecsa** offices nationwide, T5264 2266, www.etecsa.cu. To call a Cuban cell phone from abroad, dial 53 + the phone number.

Time

Eastern Standard Time, 5 hrs behind GMT; Daylight Saving Time, 4 hrs behind GMT. However, Cuba does not always change its clocks the same day as the USA or the Bahamas. Best to check in the spring and autumn so that you are not caught out with missed flights and buses, etc.

Tipping

Rules regarding tipping have changed: it is now definitely recommended to tip a small amount (not a percentage) in hotels and restaurants. Some restaurants add a service charge; others leave it to your discretion. At times taxi drivers will expect (or demand) a tip. **Viazul** porters ask for tips in some bus stations (eg Trinidad) just for putting your luggage in the hold, but in others (eg Camagüey) they will do almost anything for you in return for a friendly chat. There is no service charge or tip for food or lodging at *casas particulares*. The attendants in toilets expect a tip in return for a sheet or 2 of toilet paper, *pesos cubanos* are useful for this. Musicians in bars and restaurants depend on your tips. Leaving basic items in your room, like toothpaste, deodorant, paper, pens, is recommended.

Tourist information

Various colourful, glossy brochures are produced by the tourist authorities, available in tourist offices worldwide, but for hard information you are better looking on the internet. Some of the best unofficial websites for travel information and news are **www.cubajunky.com**, **www.cubacasas.net**, **www.havanatimes.org** and **http://havanajournal.com**. Other useful sources include:
http://autenticacuba.com Has lots of information as well as details and addresses of hotels, tour operators, car hire companies, etc, but is not always up to date.

www.cubalinda.com Run by former CIA agent, Philip Agee, is particularly helpful for travellers from the USA. You can book tickets and excursions online.
www.gocuba.ca The Canadian tourist office site is better than most.
www.infotur.cu Background information and maps for sale as well as details of events and excursions.

Tour operators

UK and Ireland
Càlédòñiâ, 33 Sandport St, Edinburgh, EH6 6EP, T0131-621 7721, www.caledonia worldwide.com. Cuba specialists for tailor-made trips, dance and music holidays, hiking and Spanish language.
Captivating Cuba, T 01438-310099, www.captivatingcuba.com.
Cuba Direct, T020-3811 1889, www.cubadirect.co.uk.
Cubaism, Unit 30, DRCA Business Centre, Charlotte Despard Av, Battersea Park, London, W11 5HD, toll free T0800-298 9555, T044 20-7498 7671, www.cubasalsaholidays.com. Dance holidays in Cuba and one-to-one Spanish tuition.
Cuba Welcome, T020-7584 6092, www.cubawelcome.com.
Havanatour UK Ltd, T01707-537513, www.havanatour.co.uk.
Interchange, T020-8681 3612, www.interchangeworldwide.com.
Journey Latin America, T020-8622 8464, www.journeylatinamerica.co.uk.
Regent Holidays, T020-3553 0889, www.regent-holidays.co.uk.

Visas and immigration

Visitors from the majority of countries need only a passport, return ticket and **30-day tourist card** to enter Cuba, as long as they are going solely for tourist purposes. Tourist cards must be obtained in advance from Cuban embassies, consulates, airlines or approved travel agents, which is a hassle-free way of obtaining a card. UK residents and EU citizens can also get their tourist cards online at www.visacuba.co.uk. In the UK tourist cards cost £15 from the consulate or from travel agents (an administration fee may be charged). In other countries they cost US$15, Can$15, or up to AU$60-140 in Australia depending on how quickly you want it.

Nationals of countries without visa-free agreement with Cuba, journalists, students and those visiting on other business must check what visa requirements pertain and, if relevant, apply for an **official/business visa**.

Travelling from the USA

The US government does not normally permit its citizens to visit Cuba. US citizens should have a US licence to engage in any transactions related to travel to Cuba, but tourist or business travel is not licensable, even through a 3rd country such as Mexico or Canada. However, the Obama administration is relaxing restrictions where possible and visits to Cuba are now permitted by Cuban Americans to visit relatives and by any American for professional, religious or cultural programmes and humanitarian projects. In effect, it means that US travellers may visit on people-to-people programmes and organized tours with a specialist theme. Independent travel for recreation and general tourism is still not permitted. Any further relaxation of restrictions will depend on a vote in Congress. For further information on entry to Cuba from the US and customs requirements, US travellers should contact the **Cuban Embassy**, at 2630 16th St NW, Washington DC 20009, T202-797 8518. They could also contact the Friendship Associations listed below for the latest information on how to sidestep the regulations. US citizens on business in Cuba should contact **Foreign Assets Control**, Federal Reserve Bank of New York, 33 Liberty St, NY 10045.

Many US travellers conceal their tracks by going via Mexico, the Bahamas, or Canada,

where the tourist card is stamped, but not the passport. On your return, make sure that you have destroyed all tickets and other evidence of having been in Cuba. US travellers returning via Canada may be stopped at the border and threatened with massive fines. If you are stopped by an immigration official and asked whether you have been to Cuba, do not lie, as that is an offence. If they want to take it further, expect a letter from the **Office of Foreign Assets Control** (OFAC; Department of the Treasury). This will either ask for information on your suspected unlicensed travel, in which case you should refuse to incriminate yourself, or it will be a pre-penalty notice assessing a civil fine, often US$7500, based on the money OFAC believes you would have spent in Cuba without a licence. The latter gives you 30 days to pay the fine or request an official hearing. The **National Lawyers' Guild** has drafted specimen letters you can use to reply to OFAC in either case; for further information see www.cubalinda.com.

Visa extensions

Immigration in Havana airport will only give you 30 days on your tourist card, but for CUC$25 you can get it extended for a further 30 days at Immigration offices in Nuevo Vedado, Varadero or Santiago de Cuba (see below).

Havana

Inmigración, Factor esq Final, Nuevo Vedado, Mon-Fri 0830-1200. Go early, it gets busy and there are queues.

Santiago de Cuba

Inmigración y Extranjería, Calle 13 6 frente al despacho eléctrico, T22-641983, Mon and Fri 0900-1200, 1330-1630, Tue, Wed and Thu 0900-1200, in summer holiday mornings only. Go to **Bandec** on Parque Céspedes y Aguilera and buy special stamp (*sello*) for CUC$25, then return to Immigration for paperwork (15 mins).

Varadero
Inmigración, Calle 39 y Av 1, T45-613494, Mon-Fri 0900-1200, 1350-1630 for visa extensions.

Women travellers

Whether single or in pairs, all women will be hassled in the street by men offering places to stay, eat, party or their services as guides. They can be persistent and annoying, although rarely threatening or violent. You can try ignoring them, saying 'no', or politely chatting and declining their offer. It doesn't make much difference. Your size and age is no problem to potential *jineteros* and the sex tourism industry is as active for women as it is for men. Men report similar approaches from Cubanas when they are on their own. It is simply a method of relieving you of your dollars. If you wear clothes which are too revealing or provocative, you will be considered fair game. Going to a club on your own at night is also an open invitation to the very macho Cuban men. Do not go to remote beaches on your own, choose a well-populated beach instead where there are Cuban families or a hotel for foreigners.

Working in the country

Foreign workers are brought in to Cuba for specific skilled jobs, but you cannot just turn up and hope to find work. If you want to stay in Cuba for a few months on a temporary basis, it is best to contact one of the Friendship Associations listed below for volunteering opportunities. Work brigades go to Cuba for a couple of weeks or a few months, helping in farming, construction or other activities and can be a great way to get to know the country and its people at a grass roots level, while also being taken to sites of interest and being entertained with music and dance on the brigade. For details of business visas, see page 481.

Friendship associations

There are over 1600 solidarity organizations in some 120 countries. Many organize work brigades, charity tours and donations of medical supplies and equipment to beat the US trade embargo, and produce newsletters and magazines. Their support for the government is usually uncritical. The link organization in Cuba is the **Cuban Institute for Friendship with the Peoples (ICAP)**, in Havana, T7-838 2388.

Australia

Australia Cuba Friendship Society, in Brisbane, www.acfs-brisbane.org.au. It runs the Cuba Brigade, http://cubabrigade.org.au for volunteering trips to Cuba.

Canada

Canadian Cuban Friendship Association (CCFA), T416-410 8254, www.ccfatoronto.ca.

UK

Cuba Solidarity Campaign, T020-7490 5715, www.cuba-solidarity.org.uk.

USA

National Network on Cuba, www.nnoc.info; **Pastors for Peace**, T212-926 5757, www.ifconews.org; **Center for Cuban Studies**, T212-242 0559, www.cubanartspace.net; **Global Exchange, Cuba Project**, T415-255 7296, www.globalexchange.org.

Footnotes

Basic Spanish for travellers

Learning Spanish is a useful part of the preparation for a trip to Cuba; nothing will enhance your enjoyment of your visit more than being able to communicate directly with the Cubans themselves. It is a good idea to make an effort to grasp the basics before you go. As you travel you will pick up more of the language, and the more you know, the more you will benefit from your stay.

General pronunciation
Whether you have been taught the 'Castilian' pronounciation (*z* and *c* followed by *i* or *e* are pronounced as the *th* in think) or the 'American' pronounciation (they are pronounced as *s*), you will encounter little difficulty in understanding either. Regional accents and usages vary, but the basic language is essentially the same everywhere.

Vowels
a as in English *cat*
e as in English *best*
i as the *ee* in English *feet*
o as in English *shop*
u as the *oo* in English *food*
ai as the *i* in English *ride*
ei as *ey* in English *they*
oi as *oy* in English *toy*

Consonants
Most consonants can be pronounced more or less as they are in English. The exceptions are:
g before *e* or *i* is the same as *j*
h is always silent (except in *ch* as in *chair*)
j as the *ch* in Scottish *loch*
ll as the *y* in *yellow*
ñ as the *ni* in English *onion*
rr trilled much more than in English
x depending on its location, pronounced *x*, *s*, *sh* or *j*

Spanish words and phrases

Greetings, courtesies

hello	*hola*	I speak Spanish	*hablo español*
good morning	*buenos días*	I don't speak Spanish	*no hablo español*
good afternoon/	*buenas*	do you speak English?	*¿habla inglés?*
evening/night	*tardes/noches*	I don't understand	*no entiendo/*
goodbye	*adiós/chao*		*no comprendo*
pleased to meet you	*mucho gusto*	please speak slowly	*hable despacio*
see you later	*hasta luego*		*por favor*
how are you?	*¿cómo está?*	I am very sorry	*lo siento mucho/*
	¿cómo estás?		*disculpe*
I'm fine, thanks	*estoy muy bien,*	what do you want?	*¿qué quiere?*
	gracias		*¿qué quieres?*
I'm called...	*me llamo...*	I want	*quiero*
what is your name?	*¿cómo se llama?*	I don't want it	*no lo quiero*
	¿cómo te llamas?	leave me alone	*déjeme en paz/*
yes/no	*sí/no*		*no me moleste*
please	*por favor*	good/bad	*bueno/malo*
thank you (very much)	*(muchas) gracias*		

Questions and requests

Have you got a room for two people?	¿Tiene una habitación para dos personas?
How do I get to_?	¿Cómo llego a_?
How much does it cost?	¿Cuánto cuesta? ¿cuánto es?
I'd like to make a long-distance phone call	Quisiera hacer una llamada de larga distancia
Is service included?	¿Está incluido el servicio?
Is tax included?	¿Están incluidos los impuestos?
When does the bus leave (arrive)?	¿A qué hora sale (llega) el autobús?
When?	¿Cuándo?
Where is_?	¿Dónde está_?
Where can I buy tickets?	¿Dónde puedo comprar boletos?
Where is the nearest petrol station?	¿Dónde está la gasolinera más cercana?
Why?	¿Por qué?

Basics

bank	el banco	expensive	caro/a
bathroom/toilet	el baño	market	el mercado
bill	la factura/la cuenta	note/coin	le billete/la moneda
cash	el efectivo	police (policeman)	la policía (el policía)
cheap	barato/a	post office	el correo
credit card	la tarjeta de crédito	public telephone	el teléfono público
exchange house	la casa de cambio	supermarket	el supermercado
exchange rate	el tipo de cambio	ticket office	la taquilla

Getting around

aeroplane	el avión	insured person	el/la asegurado/a
airport	el aeropuerto	to insure yourself against	asegurarse contra
arrival/departure	la llegada/salida	luggage	el equipaje
avenue	la avenida	motorway, freeway	el autopista/la carretera
block	la cuadra		
border	la frontera	north, south, west, east	norte, sur, oeste (occidente), este (oriente)
bus station	la terminal de autobuses/camiones/guaguas		
		oil	el aceite
bus	el bus/el autobús/la guagua/el camión	to park	estacionarse
		passport	el pasaporte
collective/fixed-route taxi	el colectivo	petrol/gasoline	la gasolina
		puncture	el pinchazo/la ponchadura
corner	la esquina		
customs	la aduana	street	la calle
first/second class	primera/segunda clase	that way	por allí/por allá
left/right	izquierda/derecha	this way	por aquí/por acá
ticket	el boleto	tourist card/visa	la tarjeta de turista
empty/full	vacío/lleno	tyre	la llanta
highway, main road	la carretera	unleaded	sin plomo
immigration	la inmigración	to walk	caminar/andar
insurance	el seguro		

Accommodation

air conditioning	el aire acondicionado	pillows	las almohadas
all-inclusive	todo incluido	power cut	el apagón/corte
bathroom, private	el baño privado	restaurant	el restaurante/el paladar
bed, double/single	la cama matrimonial/ sencilla	room/bedroom	el cuarto/la habitación
		sheets	las sábanas
blankets	las cobijas/mantas	shower	la ducha
to clean	limpiar	soap	el jabón
dining room	el comedor	toilet	el sanitario
guesthouse	la casa particular (la casa de huéspedes)	toilet paper	el papel higiénico
		towels, clean/dirty	las toallas limpias/sucias
hotel	el hotel	water, hot/cold	el agua caliente/fría
noisy	ruidoso		

Health

aspirin	la aspirina	diarrhoea	la diarrea
blood	la sangre	doctor	el médico
chemist	la farmacia	fever/sweat	la fiebre/el sudor
condoms	los preservativos, los condones	pain	el dolor
		head	la cabeza
contact lenses	los lentes de contacto	period	la regla
contraceptives	los anticonceptivos	sanitary towels	las toallas femeninas
contraceptive pill	la píldora anti-conceptiva	stomach	el estómago

Family

family	la familia	boyfriend/girlfriend	el novio/la novia
brother/sister	el hermano/la hermana	friend	el amigo/la amiga
daughter/son	la hija/el hijo	married	casado/a
father/mother	el padre/la madre	single/unmarried	soltero/a
husband/wife	el esposo (marido)/ la esposa		

Months, days and time

January	enero	Friday	viernes
February	febrero	Saturday	sábado
March	marzo	Sunday	domingo
April	abril		
May	mayo	at one o'clock	a la una
June	junio	at half past two	a las dos y media
July	julio	at a quarter to three	a cuarto para las tres/ a las tres menos quince
August	agosto		
September	septiembre	it's one o'clock	es la una
October	octubre	it's seven o'clock	son las siete
November	noviembre	it's six twenty	son las seis y veinte
December	diciembre	it's five to nine	son las nueve menos
Monday	lunes		cinco
Tuesday	martes	in ten minutes	en diez minutos
Wednesday	miércoles	five hours	cinco horas
Thursday	jueves	does it take long?	¿tarda mucho?

Numbers

one	*uno/una*	sixteen	*dieciséis*
two	*dos*	seventeen	*diecisiete*
three	*tres*	eighteen	*dieciocho*
four	*cuatro*	nineteen	*diecinueve*
five	*cinco*	twenty	*veinte*
six	*seis*	twenty-one	*veintiuno*
seven	*siete*	thirty	*treinta*
eight	*ocho*	forty	*cuarenta*
nine	*nueve*	fifty	*cincuenta*
ten	*diez*	sixty	*sesenta*
eleven	*once*	seventy	*setenta*
twelve	*doce*	eighty	*ochenta*
thirteen	*trece*	ninety	*noventa*
fourteen	*catorce*	hundred	*cien/ciento*
fifteen	*quince*	thousand	*mil*

Food

avocado	*el aguacate/la palta*	hamburger	*la hamburguesa*
baked	*al horno*	hot, spicy	*picante*
bakery	*la panadería*	ice cream	*el helado*
banana	*el guineo*	jam	*la mermelada*
beans	*los frijoles/ las habichuelas*	knife	*el cuchillo*
		lime	*el limón*
beef	*la carne de res*	lobster	*la langosta*
beef steak or pork fillet	*el bistec*	lunch	*el almuerzo/la comida*
boiled rice	*el arroz blanco*	meal	*la comida*
bread	*el pan*	meat	*la carne*
breakfast	*el desayuno*	minced meat	*el picadillo*
butter	*la mantequilla*	onion	*la cebolla*
cake	*el pastel*	orange	*la naranja*
chewing gum	*el chicle*	pepper	*el pimiento*
chicken	*el pollo*	pasty, turnover	*la empanada/ el pastelito*
chilli or green pepper	*el ají/pimiento*		
clear soup, stock	*el caldo*	plantain	*el plátano*
cooked	*cocido*	pork	*el cerdo*
dining room	*el comedor*	potato	*la papa*
egg	*el huevo*	prawns	*los camarones*
fish	*el pescado*	raw	*crudo*
fork	*el tenedor*	restaurant	*el restaurante/el paladar*
fried	*frito*	salad	*la ensalada*
garlic	*el ajo*	salt	*la sal*
goat	*el chivo*	sandwich	*el bocadillo*
grapefruit	*la toronja/el pomelo*	sauce	*la salsa*
grill	*la parrilla*	sausage	*la longaniza/el chorizo*
grilled/griddled	*a la plancha*	scrambled eggs	*los huevos revueltos*
guava	*la guayaba*	seafood	*los mariscos*
ham	*el jamón*	soup	*la sopa*

spoon	*la cuchara*	to eat	*comer*
squash	*la calabaza*	toasted	*tostado*
squid	*los calamares*	turkey	*el pavo*
supper	*la cena*	vegetables	*los legumbres/vegetales*
sweet	*dulce*	without meat	*sin carne*

Drink

beer	*la cerveza*	ice/without ice	*el hielo/sin hielo*
boiled	*hervido/a*	juice	*el jugo*
bottled	*en botella*	lemonade	*la limonada*
camomile tea	*la manzanilla*	milk	*la leche*
canned	*en lata*	mint	*la menta*
coffee	*el café*	rum	*el ron*
coffee, white	*el café con leche*	soft drink	*el refresco*
cold	*frío*	sugar	*el azúcar*
cup	*la taza*	tea	*el té*
drink	*la bebida*	to drink	*beber/tomar*
drunk	*borracho/a*	water	*el agua*
firewater	*el aguardiente*	water, carbonated	*el agua mineral con gas*
fruit milkshake	*el batido/licuado*	water, still mineral	*el agua mineral sin gas*
glass	*el vaso*	wine, red	*el vino tinto*
hot	*caliente*	wine, white	*el vino blanco*

Key verbs

to go	**ir**		**to be**	**ser** **estar**
I go	*voy*		I am	*soy* *estoy*
you go (familiar)	*vas*		you are	*eres* *estás*
he, she, it goes,			he, she, it is,	
you (formal) go	*va*		you (formal) are	*es* *está*
we go	*vamos*		we are	*somos* *estamos*
they, you (plural) go	*van*		they, you (plural) are	*son* *están*

to have (possess)	**tener**	
I have	*tengo*	
you (familiar) have	*tienes*	
he, she, it,		
you (formal) have	*tiene*	
we have	*tenemos*	
they, you (plural) have	*tienen*	
there is/are	*hay*	
there isn't/aren't	*no hay*	

This section has been assembled on the basis of glossaries compiled by André de Mendonça and David Gilmour of South American Experience, London, and the Latin American Travel Advisor, No 9, March 1996.

Index

*Entries in **bold** refer to maps*

Acknowledgements

This sixth edition was revised and updated with the welcome help of a team of researchers in Cuba. Sarah Cameron travelled the length and breadth of the island by bus, car and plane, but much of the hard labour was carried out by Sarah's long-standing friends in Cuba: in Havana, Yamelis Elizalde painstakingly checked phone numbers, prices and opening hours, doing much of the essential updating work, while Federico Llanes was also of invaluable help, always on call to answer queries; Omelio Moreno in Santa Clara used an experienced eye to thoroughly update the text; multi-talented Julio Muñoz in Trinidad revised that section; the knowledgeable Santiago and Consuelo Andraca in Holguín checked details and updated; Deborah Susana Alfonso in Viñales gave advice on what was going on, as did Miriam Guerra de la Cruz in Camagüey and Gladys Domenech Castillo in Santiago de Cuba. In addition, Maite Valor Morales and Idolka María González Rizo provided a wealth of information on Morón, Cayo Coco and Cayo Guillermo; Arturo and Esmeralda Guerra in Bayamo were, as usual, a mine of information on that area; Andrés Cruzata Rigores helped tremendously in Baracoa and the invaluable Lester Mercedo elaborated on all the new developments in Remedios. Sarah is also grateful to the many *casa particular* owners who provided information on and insight into the current state of affairs in Cuba and developments in tourism there, particularly Rafael Requejo in Camagüey and Jorge Coalla Potts in Havana. The book has no doubt benefited from the knowledge and experience of so many Cubans, making it the most authoritative in its field.

Thanks are also due to Kath Bateman, who has danced her way round Cuba and is an expert on nightlife in Santiago de Cuba, to Journey Latin America for arranging flights and to Cuba Direct for car hire. Last, but definitely not least, thanks go to Jenny Box for driving the car in a circuitous route on all surfaces and in all weather conditions from Santa Clara to Baracoa, and for her cheerful company on the road trip.

Specialist contributors Art, architecture and literature by **Gavin Clark**; Music by **Dave Willetts**, with additional material by **Rufus Boulting-Vaughan**; Cinema by **Catherine Davies**, with assistance from **Steve Wilkinson** and updated by Sarah Cameron; Che Guevara by **Patrick Symmes**. Afro-Cuban religion by **Meic Haines**. Geology and climate by **Mark Wilson**.

About the author

After a degree in Latin American Studies, **Sarah Cameron** has been travelling and writing on the Americas ever since, both as an economist and as an author for Footprint Handbooks. Initially moonlighting for the *South American Handbook* while working for a British bank, in 1990 she parted company with the world of finance and has been contributing to the expansion of Footprint titles ever since. Sarah still dabbles in South America but concentrates on the Caribbean and is the author of all Footprint's Caribbean titles, covering all the islands. When she is not travelling around the Caribbean sampling beaches and rum cocktails, she retreats to her 17th-century farmhouse in rural Suffolk (England).

Credits

Footprint credits
Editor: Sophie Blacksell Jones
Production and layout: Emma Bryers
Maps: Kevin Feeney
Colour section: Angus Dawson

Publisher: Felicity Laughton
Patrick Dawson
Marketing: Kirsty Holmes
Sales: Diane McEntee
Advertising and content partnerships:
Debbie Wylde

Photography credits
Front cover: Kamira/Shutterstock.com
Back cover top: Frederic Soreau/
SuperStock.com
Back cover bottom: EJW/SuperStock.com
Inside front cover: Maurizio De Mattei/
Shutterstock, Ondrej Prosicky/Shutterstock,
lazyllama/Shutterstock.

Colour section
Page 1: Peter Schickert/Superstock. **Page 2**: Sergey
Uryadnikov/Shutterstock. **Page 4**: merc67/Shutterstock.
Page 5: Kamira/Shutterstock, Sergey Uryadnikov/
Shutterstock, BlueGreen Pictures/Superstock,
Eye Ubiquitous/Superstock, Attila JANDI/Shutterstock.
Page 6: Michael Runkel/Superstock, Alexey Goosev/
Shutterstock, Lee Frost/Superstock, Sergey Uryadnikov/
Shutterstock. **Page 7**: Dirk Renckhoff/Superstock,
Jan Sochor/Superstock, Fabian von Poser/Superstock,
Tupungato/Shutterstock. **Page 8**: claffra/Shutterstock.
Page 9: Sergey Uryadnikov/Shutterstock. **Page 10**:
Maurizio De Mattei/Shutterstock. **Page 11**: RiumaLab/
Shutterstock. **Page 12**: age fotostock/Superstock.
Page 13: Andrew McLachlan/Superstock, Leonardo
Gonzalez/Shutterstock. **Page 14**: The Visual Explorer/
Shutterstock, Michel Cramer/Shutterstock. **Page 15**:
Jekurantodistaja/Shutterstock. **Page 16**: Kamira/
Shutterstock.

Duotones
Page 36: mayakova/Shutterstock.com
Page 108: merc67/Shutterstock.com
Page 140: duchy/Shutterstock.com
Page 176: rmnoa357/Shutterstock.com
Page 244: Martchan/Shutterstock.com
Page 288: PHB.cz (Richard Semik)/Shutterstock.com
Page 326: Tupungato/Shutterstock.com
Page 378: yykkaa/Shutterstock.com

Publishing information
Footprint Cuba
6th edition
© Footprint Handbooks Ltd
February 2016

ISBN: 978 1 910120 63 7
CIP DATA: A catalogue record for this book
is available from the British Library

® Footprint Handbooks and the
Footprint mark are a registered
trademark of Footprint Handbooks Ltd

Published by Footprint
6 Riverside Court
Lower Bristol Road
Bath BA2 3DZ, UK
T +44 (0)1225 469141
F +44 (0)1225 469461
footprinttravelguides.com

Distributed in the USA by
National Book Network, Inc.

Printed in Spain by GraphyCems

Every effort has been made to ensure that
the facts in this guidebook are accurate.
However, travellers should still obtain advice
from consulates, airlines, etc about travel
and visa requirements before travelling.
The authors and publishers cannot
accept responsibility for any loss, injury
or inconvenience however caused.

All rights reserved. No part of this
publication may be reproduced, stored
in a retrieval system, or transmitted, in
any form or by any means, electronic,
mechanical, photocopying, recording,
or otherwise without the prior permission
of Footprint Handbooks Ltd.

Footprint Mini Atlas
Cuba

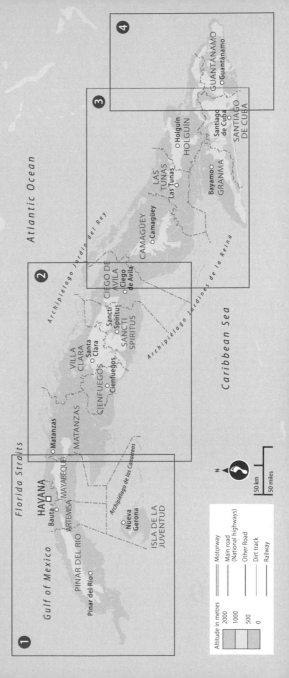

Gulf of Mexico

Florida Straits

Atlantic Ocean

Archipiélago Jardín del Rey

①

PINAR DEL RIO

o Pinar del Rio

ARTEMISA
HAVANA □
o Bauta
MAYABEQUE

Archipiélago de los Canarreos

o Nueva
Gerona

ISLA DE LA
JUVENTUD

MATANZAS
o Matanzas

②

VILLA
CLARA
o Santa
Clara

CIENFUEGOS
o Cienfuegos

SANCTI
SPÍRITUS
**Sancti
Spíritus**

CIEGO DE
ÁVILA
o Ciego
de Ávila

Archipiélago Jardines de la Reina

③

CAMAGÜEY
Camagüey

LAS
TUNAS
o Las Tunas

Bayamo
GRANMA

o Holguín
HOLGUÍN

**Santiago
de Cuba**
SANTIAGO
DE CUBA

④

GUANTÁNAMO
o Guantánamo

Caribbean Sea

N

50 km
50 miles

Altitude in metres
2000
1000
500
0

═══ Motorway
─── Main road
      (National highways)
─── Other Road
-·-· Dirt track
╫── Railway

Map 1

Gulf of Mexico

Archipiélago de los Colorados y de Santa Isabel

Cayo Arenas
Cayo Levisa
Palma Rubia
Cayo Inés de Soto
Manuel Sanguily
El Rosario
Parque Nacional La Güira
Cayo Jutías
Puerto Esperanza
La Palma
Pico Grande (521m)
San Cayetano
Parque Nacional Viñales
San Andrés
Santa Lucía
Pan de Azúcar (616m)
Ancón
Viñales
Punta Tabaco
Minas de Matahambre
El Moncada
Pilotos
Consolación del Sur
Pons
Santa Rita
Aguas Claras
Herradura
Cayo Rapado Grande
Dimas
Sierra de los Órganos
Sumidero
Cabeza
Puerta de Golpe
Cayo de Buenavista
Arroyos de Mantua
Pinar del Río
PINAR DEL RÍO
Mazón
Las Ovas
Alonso de Rojas
Mantua
Llanura del Norte
San Juan y Martínez
El Corojo
La Coloma
Playa el Guanal
Las Clavelinas
Guane
Las Canas
Golfo de Guanahacabibes
Isabel Rubio
Boca de Galafre
Punta de Cartas
Playa La Salina
Las Canas
Bolívar
Sandino
Las Coloradas
La Fé
Bailén
Cayos de San Felipe
Punta El Cajón
Cayos de la Leña
Reserva de la Biósfera Guanahacabibes
Manuel Lazo
Cayo Real
Cayo El Coco
Cabo de San Antonio
Las Tumbas
La Bajada
Vallecito
Las Martinas
Caleta Larga
Bahía de Corrientes
María La Gorda
Cabo Corrientes

Llanura del Sur
San Felipe
Alicanel
Rosario
Cordillera de

N

20 km
20 miles

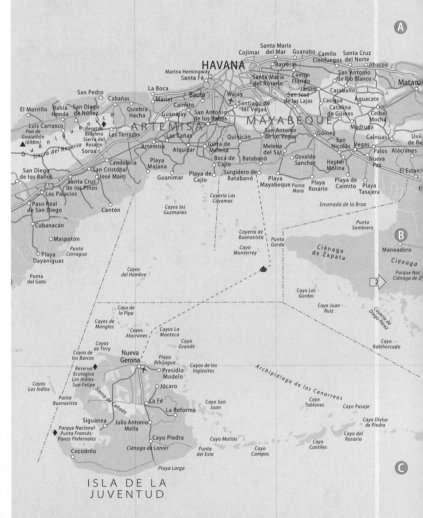

Map 2

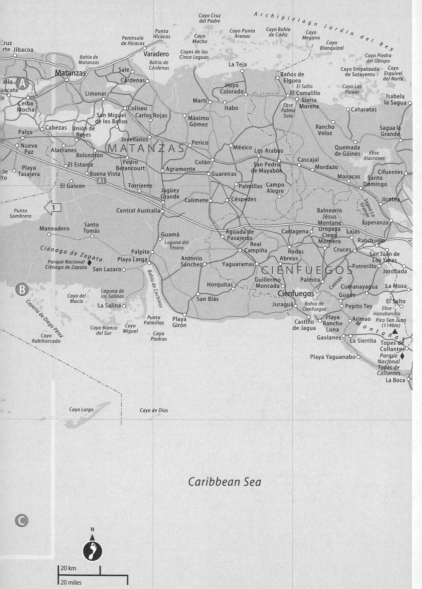

Caribbean Sea

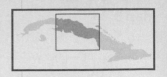
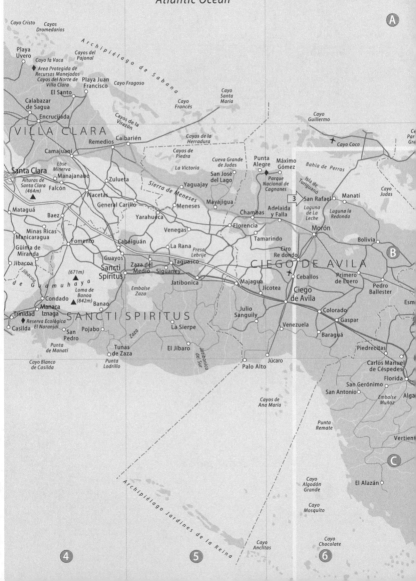

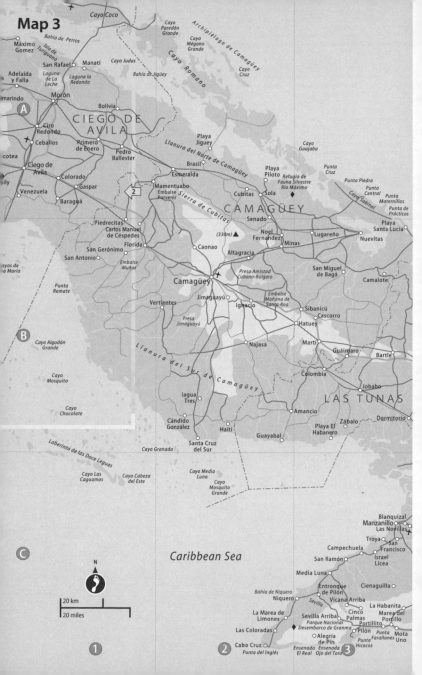

Map 3

Cayo Coco

Máximo Gomez

Bahía de Perros

Cayo Paredón Grande

Archipiélago de Camagüey

Cayo Mégano Grande

Cayo Judas

San Rafael   Manatí

Adelaida y Falla

Laguna de La Leche

Laguna la Redonda

Bahía de Jigüey

Cayo Romano

Cayo Cruz

amarindo

Morón

A

Bolivia

CIEGO DE AVILA

Ciro Redondo

Ceballos

Primero de Enero

Pedro Ballester

Llanura del Norte de Camagüey

Playa Jiguey

Cayo Guajaba

cotea

Ciego de Avila

Colorado

Gaspar

2

Brasil

Esmeralda

Mamentuabo Embalse Porvenir

Playa Piloto

Punta Cruz

Refugio de Fauna Silvestre Río Máximo

Punta Piedra

Punta Maternillos

Cayo Sabinal

Punta Central

Venezuela

Baraguá

Sierra de Cubitas

Cubitas

Sola

CAMAGÜEY

Punta de Prácticas

Piedrecitas

Carlos Manuel de Céspedes

(330m)▲

Senado

Noel Fernández

Minas

Lugareño

Playa Santa Lucía

ayos de a María

San Gerónimo

Florida

Caonao

Altagracia

Nuevitas

San Antonio

Embalse Muñoz

Presa Amistad Cubano-Búlgaro

San Miguel de Bagá

Camalote

Punta Remate

Camagüey

B   Cayo Algodón Grande

Vertientes

Jimaguayú

Ignacio

Embalse Mañana de Santa Ana

Sibanicú

Cascorro

Presa Jimaguayú

Hatuey

Cayo Mosquito

Najasa

Martí

Guáimaro

Bartle

Llanura del Sur de Camagüey

Colombia

Jobabo

Cayo Chocolate

Iagua Tres

LAS TUNAS

Dormitorio

Cándido González

Haití

Amancio

Zábalo

Playa El Habanero

Laberinto de las Doce Leguas

Santa Cruz del Sur

Cayo Granada

Cayo Media Luna

Cayo Mosquito Grande

Cayo Las Caguamas

Cayo Cabeza del Este

Blanquizal

Manzanillo

Las Novillas

Troya

San Francisco

C

Campechuela

Israel Licea

Caribbean Sea

San Ramón

Media Luna

Cienaguilla

N

Bahía de Niquero

Entronque de Pilón

Vicana

Arriba

La Habanita

20 km

Niquero

Sevilla

Cinco Palmas

Marea del Portillo

20 miles

La Marea de Limones

Sevilla Arriba

Portillito

Pilón

Mota Uno

Las Coloradas

Parque Nacional Desembarco de Granma

Punta Farallones

1

Cabo Cruz

Punta del Inglés

Alegría de Pío

Ensenada El Real

Ensenada Ojo del Toro

2

Punta Hicacos

3

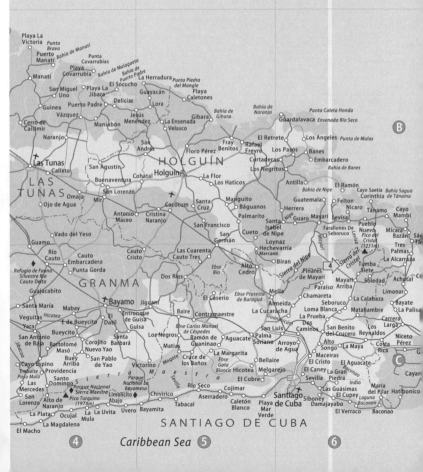

Atlantic Ocean

A

B

C

Playa La Victoria
Punta Brava
Puerto Manatí
Bahía de Manatí
Manatí
Punta Covarrubia
Playa Covarrubia
Bahía de Malagueta
San Miguel del Uno
Playa La Jibara
El Socucho
La Herradura
Bahía de Puerto Padre
Punta Piedra del Mangle
Playa Caletones
Guayacán
Guinea
Puerto Padre
Delicias
Lora
Gibara
Bahía de Gibara
Bahía de Naranjo
Punta Caleta Honda
Vázquez
Maniabón
Jesús Menéndez
La Ensenada
Velasco
Guardalavaca
Ensenada Río Seco
Cerro de Caisimir
San Andrés
Floro Pérez
Fray Benitos
Rafael Freyre
El Retrete
Los Pasos
Los Angeles
Punta de Mulas
Naranjo
HOLGUÍN
Holguín
Cortaderas
Banes
Embarcadero
Las Tunas
Calixto
San Agustín
Cohatal
La Flor
Los Haticos
Los Negritos
Antilla
Bahía de Banes
El Ramón
Cayo Saetía
Bahía Sagua de Tánamo
Corinthia
LAS TUNAS
Buenaventura
Santa Cruz
Manguito
Báguanos
Bahía de Nipe
Guatemala
Felton
Nicaro
Tánamo
Cayo Mambí
Omaja
San Lorenzo
Mir
Cacocum
Herrera
Guaro
Mayarí
Levisal
Micara
Bazán
Ojo de Agua
Antonio Maceo
Cristina Naranjo
San Francisco
Palmarito
Santa Isabel de Nipe
Cueto
Sierra Nipe
Loynaz
Pueblo Nuevo
Farallones De Seboruco
Pico del Cristal (1231m)
Tres Palmas
Sá Ts
Guamo
Vado del Yeso
San Germán
Hechevarría
Marcané
Mayarí
Tumba Siete
La Alcarraza
Achotal
Río Cauto
Cauto Embarcadero
Las Cuarenta Cauto Tres
Alto Cedro
Biran
Sierra del Nipe
Sierra del Cristal
Soledad
Cr
Refugio de Fauna Silvestre Río Cauto Delta
Punta Gorda
GRANMA
Dos Ríos
Ebse Bío
Piñares de Mayarí
Mayarí Arriba
Limonar
Guajacabito
Ebse Protesta de Baragud
Paraíso
Santa María
Mabay
Jiguaní
El Caserío
Mella
Chamareta
La Calabaza
Matabambre
La Palisa
Veguitas
Hicotea
Bayamo
Entronque de Guisa
Baire
Contramaestre
La Cucaracha
Almeida
Seboruco
Loma Blanca
Carrera Larga
Yara
E de Bueycito
El Datil
Guisa
Ebse Carlos Manuel de Céspedes
Ramón de Guaninao
La Prueba
San Benito del Crucero
Los Reynaldos
San Antonio de Baja
Bueycito
Corojito
Nuevo Yao
Santa Bárbara
Los Negros
Matías
Aguacate
Palma Soriano
Dos Caminos
Alto Songo
La Maya
Niceto Pérez
Cayo Espino
Bartolomé Masó
Buey Arriba
San Pablo de Yao
Victorino
Mogote
La Margarita
Ebse Gota Blanca
Arroyo de Agua
El Cristo
La Gran Piedra
Indio
Costa Rica
Embalse Paso Malo
Providencia
Santo Domingo
Sierra
Cruce de los Baños
Hicotea
Bellaire
Melgarejo
Sevilla
El Caney
El Cupey
Las Guásimas
Cayar
Las Mercedes
Alto de Naranjo
Pico Turquino (1974m)
Limoncito
Abajo
Parque Nacional Sierra Maestra
Parque Nacional La Bayamesa
Chivirico
El Cobre
Río Seco
Cojimar
Maestra
Sevilla
Santiago de Cuba
Siboney
Damajayabo
María del Pilar
Hatibonico
San Lorenzo
La Plata
Ocujal
La Uvita
Mula
Uvero
Bayamita
Tabacal
Aserradero
Caletón Blanco
Playa Mar Verde
El Verraco
Baconao
Laguna Baconao
La Magdalena
El Macho

SANTIAGO DE CUBA

Caribbean Sea

4

5

6

Map 4

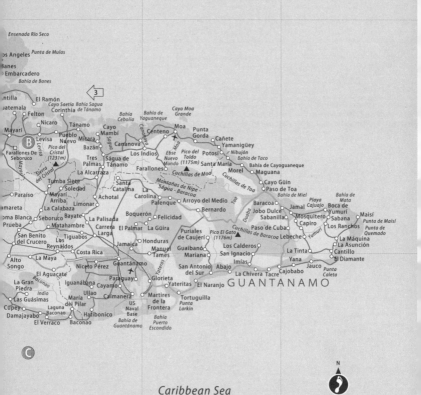

Atlantic Ocean

Ensenada Río Seco

os Angeles *Punta de Mulas*
anes
Embarcadero
Bahía de Banes

ntilla   El Ramón
uatemala   Corinthia   *Cayo Saetía Bahía Sagua*
   Felton   de Tánamo
Nicaro   Tánamo   *Bahía* *Bahía de*   *Cayo Moa*
Mayarí   Cayo   *Cebolla* *Yaguaneque*   *Grande*
Levisa   Pueblo   Mambí   Centeno   Moa   Punta
   Nuevo   Mícara   Cananova   Gorda   Cañete
Farallones De   *Pico del*   Bazán   Ságua de   Los Indios   *Ebse* Pico del   Yamanigüey
Seboruco   *Cristal*   Tres   Tánamo   *Nuevo* Toldo   Nibujón   *Bahía de Taco*
   (1231m)   Palmas   Farallones○   *Mundo* *(1175m)* Santa María   *Bahía de Cayoguaneque*
   La Alcarraza   Morel   Maguana
Paraíso   *Sierra*   Tumba Siete   Santa   *Cuchillas de Mod*   Cayo Güin
   del Cristal   Soledad   Catalina   *Montañas de Nipe*   *Bahía de Miel*   *Bahía de*
amareta   Mayarí   Achotal   Carolina   *Ságua - Baracoa*   Baracoa   *Playa* Boca de
oma Blanca   Arriba   Limonar   Palenque   Arroyo del Medio   Jobo Dulce   Jamal *Cajuajo* Yumurí   *Bahía de*
Prueba   La Calabaza   La Palisada   Boquerón   Bernardo   Sabanilla   Mosquitero   Sabana   *Mata*
   Seboruco   Matahambre   Felicidad   *Cuchillas de Baracoa*   Capiro   *Yumurí* Los Ranchos   Maisí
San Benito   Tiguabos   Carrera   El Palmar   Puriales   *Pico El Gato*   Lebeche   La Máquina   *Punta de*
del Crucero   Los   Larga   Honduras   de Caujerí   *(1176m)*   La Tinta   La Asunción   *Quemado*
   Reynaldos   Jamaica   Manuel   Guaibanó   Los Ignacio   Yana   Cantillo
Alto   La Maya   Costa Rica   Tames   Mariana   Imías   Cajobabo   El Diamante
Songo   Niceto Pérez   Guantánamo   San Antonio   La Chivera Tacre   *Punta*
El Aguacate   Iguanábona   del Sur   Abajo   *Caleta*
La Gran   Cayamo   Glorieta   El Naranjo   G U A N T A N A M O
Piedra   *Indio*   María   Ullao   Yateritas
Las Guásimas   del Pilar   Caimanera   Mártires   *Punta*
Cupey   *Baconao*   de la   *Larkin*
   Laguna   Habitonico   Frontera   Tortuguilla
Damajayabo   Baconao   US   Naval   Baconao   *Bahía*
El Verraco   Base   *Bahía de* *Puerto*
   Guantánamo *Escondido*

Caribbean Sea

20 km
20 miles